William John Charles Moens

The Marriage

Baptismal and Burial Registers

William John Charles Moens

The Marriage
Baptismal and Burial Registers

ISBN/EAN: 9783337297282

Printed in Europe, USA, Canada, Australia, Japan

Cover: Foto ©Suzi / pixelio.de

More available books at **www.hansebooks.com**

THE

MARRIAGE, BAPTISMAL, AND BURIAL REGISTERS,

1571 TO 1874,

AND

MONUMENTAL INSCRIPTIONS,

OF THE

DUTCH REFORMED CHURCH, AUSTIN FRIARS, LONDON.

WITH A SHORT ACCOUNT OF THE STRANGERS AND THEIR CHURCHES.

EDITED BY

WILLIAM JOHN CHARLES MOENS.

[*PRIVATELY PRINTED*]

LYMINGTON.

1884.

TO

His Majesty, William III,

KING OF THE NETHERLANDS,

AS THE PROTESTANT HEAD OF THE NATION

WHOSE PERSONAL HISTORY IT TENDS TO ILLUSTRATE,

THIS VOLUME,

BY HIS GRACIOUS PERMISSION, IS RESPECTFULLY

DEDICATED.

PREFACE.

Attention at last is being drawn to Parish Registers. Many are being copied and published; the atents of these are thus accessible to all, without loss of time and without expense being incurred by king long journeys to consult them, to say nothing of the difficulty found by many in reading the iting of olden times. Here in England, this work has been left to the Harleian Society and to a few uateurs, who, with an innate love of collecting and imparting genealogical lore, have devoted their time to ch work. With regard to this all-important source of family history, England, as a country, is far hind France and Belgium, where the old Registers of Baptisms, Marriages, and Burials have, for years st in all communes, been carefully transcribed and arranged in alphabetical order. These new Registers ? open, at the offices of the *Etat Civil*, for the free inspection of the public, and permission is generally corded to refer to the original Registers. Holland is slowly awaking to the consciousness of the desira.ity of a like state of things; the Town Councils of Amsterdam, Rotterdam, Haarlem, and other towns ve had, are having, or are about to have, their respective Parish Registers copied and arranged. The ciety formed to collect together all the matter connected with the history of the Walloon churches in olland, in the most spirited way possible, has had copied and arranged in one vast collection all the gisters of the numerous French or Walloon churches in the various towns of Holland, where the refugees m Belgium and France during the 16th, 17th and 18th centuries and their descendants assembled together r divine worship conducted in the French tongue, according to the tenets of the reformed religion. It is ach to be desired that the eighty-nine Registers of the French and Walloon Churches established at mdon, Canterbury, Norwich, Plymouth, Southampton, and Thorpe-le-Soken, dating from 1567 to the esent day, and now in the custody of the Registrar General at Somerset House. London, should be cated in a similar manner by some existing Society, or by one formed for the special purpose.

All, who have made research in the Low Countries for particulars of family history, have been nearly rtain to find, that as soon as they have traced back to the 16th century, there occurs a dark period of scurity, with but little sun to throw its light on the object of their search. The sought for name is und again abundantly in the earlier years of that century and those preceding it. Lucky, very lucky is e enquirer, if he can break through the darkness of the "times of the troubles," when the tyranny and il rule of King Philip II, carried into full effect by the agency of the cruel Duke of Alva, caused untold ousands of his subjects to fly for refuge to England, Germany, and Switzerland, in order to save their res and to worship their Creator openly and securely according to the tenets of the Reformed Church.

At first, and for some time after their coming to this country, the refugees married much amongst them-lves, but gradually as they became better known and appreciated many made alliances with English milies.[1]

The dark and difficult period, to the genealogist, of the times of the troubles in the Low Countries has en duly experienced by me in researches I have made in some sixty towns during the past eight years, r matter connected with my family history. I was aided in those researches with the most generous lp of very many friends residing in those towns, and I universally met with the greatest kindness from l the various officials, from whom I had to obtain leave to consult the Registers in the archives entrusted their care. I have felt that I, in my turn, could try to dispel some of the difficulties found in those rk times by editing the Registers of the Dutch (Nederduijtsche) Church at Austin Friars, London, which as the most important, in this country, of all the Churches of the Refugees from the Netherlands. Very many members of noble families were to be found amongst the strangers who sought refuge on our

---

[1] The entries of these marriages will be generally found in the Registers of the English parish churches, where the isbands so marrying went to worship with their wives and families.

shores ; many of their children and descendants were absorbed in this country by marriage, though many of them went to protestant Holland when the times became quieter.   England was thus, so to speak, a bridge, by means of which many Belgian families made their way to Holland, where they afterwards established themselves.

Nowhere can a reference be found to any earlier Registers than those now existing in the Archives of the Church.   From the following entry made in the minute book of the Consistory 13 May, 1571, it would appear that. prior to that date, no Marriage or Baptismal Registers had been kept.   " It is determined " that, for the future, all persons who marry in our Church, and the children who are baptized shall, with " the names of the fathers and witnesses, be entered in a separate Register."

From this date the Registers are complete.   The applications to marry, from 1569 to 1571, having previously been entered in the Minute Books.[1]

These Registers are in a good state of preservation, with the exception of a small portion of the marriages from 1612 for a certain number of years, where some of the days of the month have been cut off through carelessness when the volume was re-bound.

The celebration of Marriages having been discontinued in the Church for some years, they were again solemnized after the 20th December 1850, according to the following notice with the above date attached to it, which appeared in the London Gazette of the 2nd January 1857.—" The Dutch Church, Austin Friars " in the Parish of St. Peters-le-Poor, was duly registered for solemnizing Marriages therein, pursuant " to the Act of 6th and 7th William IV. Cap. 85."

From the commencement of the Registers the years were reckoned by New Style, beginning with 1s January.   Very many Baptismal entries were imperfectly made, the ceremony having often taken place a the homes of the parents and the details having apparently been forgotten by the Ministers officiating. These imperfect entries could not be arranged under family names, but are given as they appear afte letter Z.

Some Baptisms took place at Mortlake, in the Parish Church, and were entered in the Austin Friars Registers, many of the Dutch Colony having been engaged in the tapestry and carpet factory tha was established there shortly after the year 1619.   Some few entries of the tapestry weavers are to be found in the Parish Registers at Putney and Mortlake; the Low Country names soon being changed, such a Hullenberghe into Hulliberry, etc.

The Burial Register commenced only in 1675, though an order was made 26 April 1657, that such a book should be kept.   Stow, in his Survey of London, the first edition of which was published in 1598 stated that " Since this Church hath been appropriated to the use of the Dutch nation, few have been " buried here except the Ministers belonging to it, and the Elders or others of more eminent qualit " or wealth."   The various inscriptions given in the edition by Strype, 1720, are of a date later than 167ὄ A few stones, in which fine brasses were formerly inserted with armories quartered in the foreig. fashion, are still to be found in the South Aisle.   One in particular may be mentioned, with marks wher the brasses once were, with foreign quarterings of arms of a man with his three wives and numerous progeny but no record can be found of the names of the persons buried under it.   All the monuments and inscrip tions, noticed by Stow, of English families prior to 1550 have been removed.

From the Registers of the Austin Friars Church it appears that there were about 1000 Marriages and 4000 Baptisms between May 1571 and December 1601.   In the year 1591-2 there were more Baptism than in any other year; after 1593 they decreased greatly in number.   This points to the fact that many members of the church must have left London for Holland about that time.

In 1602 there were 107 Baptisms.   In 1691 there were 40 Baptisms.

1620	„	„	76	„	1700	„	„	24	„
1630	„	„	72	„	1766	„	„	1	„
1640	„	„	50	„	1800	„	„	3	„
1649	„	„	23	„	1811	„	„	10	„
1654	„	„	8	„	1820	„	„	1	„
1670	„	„	17	„	1839	„	„	0	„
1680	„	„	42	„	1844	„	„	5	„

These particulars taken every few years tend to shew the numbers frequenting the Dutch service.

[1] An earlier Minute or Act Book has recently been found from 1561 to 1563.   Not having yet examined thi small 4to. MS., I cannot say whether any applications to marry are there entered.

plain to English genealogists and others, that in the 15th and first half of the
hristian names appear, the second one almost invariably would be the baptis-
l that when two such names appear with "sen" added to the second with the
.s entered according to the then custom in Holland.   As an example may be
search that was made both abroad and in this country for Apollonia, daughter
: of Francis Tyssen, as given in the visitation of London, and whom he must
Hopeless seemed the search, when at last she was found under the guise of
tje (the diminutive of Apollonia).   Plooutje, Pleuntje, Leuntje, daughter of
rname of Ridley being omitted.   The proof was found in an original register
n the writing of the period.   In Friesland, so general was this omission of the
possible to make genealogical research with the aid of the Parish Registers,
ilone being of avail.   It is a curious fact that in Holland, these Notarial
l law of the country secret papers, not accessible to the public, who cannot,
to the family to which they refer, see deeds which affect him, unless he can
who drew them and their exact date.   This to a seeker after unknown particu-
while in the majority of cases the Notary under whose care the collection is
old writing of the period required.   This law holds good even for documents
ies. which can have no effect on property at the present day.   Research there-
only with family history but with the history of the nation and of painters and
; very difficult in that country, and why this law should not be altered or re-
ients before 1811, it is difficulty to say, seeing that the like documents are free
e and other archives in Belgium and other countries.   Even in the province of
·ere no Notaries in past times, and where all family and other documents were
es of the various towns, the Registers of the courts are always accessible and
igland all State and domestic papers up to a certain date, and all the records of
for research and inspection ; all Wills and Testaments previous to 1784, can be
erary inquirers without payment of fees, while all such documents to the present
encral public on the payment of a fee of one shilling, and copies are given at a
·stly to be hoped that the increasing interest in family and other research will
is law in Holland, which, alas, in times past, notoriously has not hindered but
iction of many all important family documents from these collections of deeds
altered, as wished for by many in that country, the law would be assimilated

he Marriage Register of the Dutch Church at Austin Friars is of a most im-
i places of both parties to the marriage being given in every case ; by means
:h can be pursued in those towns where the refugees came from.   The "Lidmaten
of the Church from 1584 are fortunately preserved, though an earlier one is
·st volume, arranged according to the baptismal name, only existing.   These give
y cases, and it is my intention to devote some spare hours to the copying and
f men who were admitted members of the Dutch Church.   Besides these, the
looks, where the banns were entered, also exist from 1615, these are also of great
anns were published at the church at Austin Friars of Marriages which were
h or perchance at English parish churches.   These Dutch churches established in
nber, viz., London, Norwich, Colchester. Maidston, Canvey Island, Yarmouth,
iapel Royal, St.James.   Unfortunately, with the exception of the Dutch Church,
ies, London, of Colchester and Norwich, all the Registers are missing.   Those
been stated, perfect from 1571, Burials having taken place only since 1675.
:h Chapel Royal, St.James, from the date of its establishment in 1689 to 1809,
he Registrar General at Somerset House, numbered 40 in the list of the Foreign
:ster, known to be in existence, consist only of the Baptisms from 1645 to 1728,
seems to have been discontinued ; this volume, the existence of which was un-
·ho had made every inquiry concerning these Registers, I found amongst some
incient box in the Austin Friars Church, where it had probably been reposing,
a hundred years.   Those of Norwich are imperfect, commencing only in 1676.

Burn, in his "History of the Foreign Refugees" (London, 1846), p. 202, stat "of this church was referred to in 1717, for the purpose of a grant of arms to Johi "contained the baptisms of several of his ancestors from 1593. It is now in po "or deacons of the church, etc." This is unfortunately not the case now, what 1816, for after careful inquiry made by the late Mr. J. R. Daniel Tyssen, the] and myself, no other Registers than those alluded to above can be found.

In the pedigree, given by Burke in his Landed Gentry, of De Horne, of Stan "Oliver de Horne, of Nova Kirk, near Ipres, Flanders, came over to Englan "1596 or 1597, and settled at Norwich." "But not well liking a strange cour "tion of the persecution in Flanders," says his great-grandson, "after his wife w "he named Abraham, *the first in the Register of that congregation there* (the Dutc "to God Almighty's protection, he shipt himself for Flanders to seek a settleme "return was taken sick of the plague, and dyed on ship board." If this stateme of Colchester (*b.* 1662, *d.* 1729), be correct, the lost Registers of the Dutch Chu in 1596 or 1597.

In speaking of the eight churches where Divine service was performed in numerous churches in this country of the refugees from Belgium, speaking the ; be forgotten. It is probable that many of the refugees frequented both the Du and no research can be complete without reference to the Registers of both Chu

The Registers still preserved of the French and Walloon Churches are as foll Canterbury from 1581, Norwich from 1595, Southampton from 1567, Thorney . 1654; these are, with the exception of the last which was in the possession of 1816, to be found, as before stated, deposited with the Registrar General at Soi

In course of time many curious alterations of the names of the strangers occu caused by the Registrars simply spelling them according to their pronunciation, Wilde," and "Field" for "Van de Velde," "Wood" for "du Bois," and so on

Many families are descended from those whose names are found in these De Horne, Vansittart, Corsellis, Boeve, Tyssen, Turck, Browne, De Bert, Van others. These families, as well as others without number descended from the r will find entries which they may have sought for in vain elsewhere.

With regard to the Burials, which, as has been stated, were only recorded fr which was £ 5 to £ 15, the entries are of importance, as they show in many ca: between various members of the church.

As a means of identifying the more important members, lists are given of deacons of the Austin Friars Church, with the dates of their appointment.

An account of the history of the Strangers from the Low Countries, and of will appear to many to be wanted as an introduction to the family particul: mother church of the refugees. This is given as an Historical Introduction. M "History of the Foreign Refugees," published in 1846, gave much gleaned froi and Stow's Works, and the Record Office. Since then the domestic series of St ged and calendars made. These and the MS. history of the Dutch Church by t which was published in 1873 by the Marnix Society of Utrecht, and the exhau Jan Utenhove," by the Dr. and Rev. F. Pyper, Leiden, 1883, together with Church, have enabled me to add to the knowledge imparted by the late Mr Cooper, F.S.A., who edited the Camden publication of 1862, gave lists of tl aliens resident in England, 1618-1688. We are also indebted to the Rev. D: "French Protestant Refugees," 1871, which includes many particulars of the now exist for an extended history of the Dutch strangers, which it is to be ho; up more seriously than has hitherto been the case.

My warm and hearty thanks are due, and are now given, to the worthy m Church, the Rev. A. D. Adama Van Scheltema, who has in every way given re: entrusted to his charge, and such facilities as were necessary to enable me to co The same acknowledgment and sincere thanks I also give to J. J. Howard Robert Hovenden, Esq., for so generously placing at my disposal the results of

inscriptions and armorial bearings on the monumental stones. It may here be stated that some sixteen to
eighteen stones with inscriptions are under the floors of the two vestries and the raised stone portion of the
chancel, these therefore could not be copied, though some portions of a few appear after the inscriptions
which are more or less perfect. This will account for the numbers of the inscriptions under nineteen being
missing.[1] Printers' difficulties in arranging the proof caused the numbers on the stones not to appear in
regular order. The information these inscriptions give, in addition to that found in the entries of the
Burial Register, is so important, that any publication of the Registers would be incomplete without their
addition, and I have most gladly availed myself of the kind offer to add these to the Registers. The time
taken to engrave the armories has caused much delay in bringing out the work, but the valuable addition
is been well worth waiting for. It is to be hoped that the result will prove useful to many both at home
and in the Netherlands, and also in America, where there are many families descended from the religious
refugees from the former country. Should this prove to be the case the labour of decyphering, copying,
and arranging the contents of the old Registers and Monumental Inscriptions, will not have been time
uselessly thrown away.

W. J. C. MOENS.

HISTORICAL INTRODUCTION.

Tnn earliest settlers from the Netherlands in this country, appear to have been William of Ypres and his followers, who were called over by King Stephen, to aid him against Maude the Empress, in the year 1138. William built a "great messuage, sometime called Ipres Inne," near the church of St.Thomas the Apostle, London, where he dwelt receiving great favour from the King.[1] It is stated that Flemish weavers came over to this country as early as 1253 and taught the art of making linen. King Edward I, at the request of the foreign merchants, gave them many privileges by the Carta Mercatoria,[2] which enabled the Strangers to reside and carry on trade in this country. This charter was confirmed 27 Richard III, 9 Henry VI, and 4 Edward IV. The Guildhall of London belonged in 1280 to German merchants,[3] who probably established themselves here to enjoy the privileges of this charter.

Several statutes were passed in the reign of Edward III[4] in favour of merchant Strangers, which gave them permission to bring their merchandize into this country and to sell it by wholesale or retail without let or hindrance, on paying the usual customs, subject, however, to the franchises and free customs granted by previous sovereigns to London and to other cities and boroughs. They had also protection and safe conduct to come and dwell in the realm, and "to return thither with their ships, wares, and all manner of merchandize."

About the year 1336, King Edward III, in order to draw to this country the profitable trade of manufacturing English wool, which had become almost a monopoly of the Netherlands' weavers, sent abroad 'Emissaries' to induce the journeymen or apprentices "to come over to England bringing their mystery, with them, which would provide their welcome in all places. Here they should feed on fatt beef and mutton till nothing but fulnesse should stint their stomachs; yea, they should feed on the labours of their own hands, enjoying a proportionable profit of their pains to themselves; their beds should be good, and their bed-fellows better, seeing the richest yeomen in England would not disdain to marry their daughters unto them, and such the English beauties, that the most envious forreigners could not but commend them."

"Persuaded with the promises, many Dutch servants leave their masters and make over for England." "The King having gotten this treasury of forreigners, thought not fit to continue them all in one place . . . . but bestowed them therow all the parts of the land that cloathing thereby might be the better dispersed."[5] A colony of "old Dutch, who left their country on account of an inundation, came to this country in the reign of Henry I, and settled in Pembrokeshire. "A prime Dutch cloth-maker in Gloucestershire had the surname of Web given him by King Edward there; a family still famous for their manufacture."[6] The abundance of Fuller's earth found in England seemed "to point out our land for the staple of drapery."

In 1356 these weavers of woollen cloth, brought in by Edward III from Flanders, lived in Candlewick-Ward, London; they were allowed to hold their meetings in the churchyard of St.Lawrence Poultney, while the weavers of Brabant met in that of St.Mary Somerset. "There were then, in this city, weavers of divers sorts: to wit, of drapery, of tapery and napery."[7] Another company of linen weavers from the Netherlands established themselves in London in 1368. "Saw one ever a stranger company than that band of a hundred and twenty Dutchmen, who came over to convert merry London to sadness," "marching bare backed, flogging each other as they went and chanting psalms through the streets of the city.,'

The Corporation of London obtained a charter in 1376, restraining foreigners from selling by retail, and in 1379, when Whittington was passing out of his apprenticeship, the city petitioned the King against certain rights of importation and sale which had been granted to them. The feeling against the Strangers was so

(1) Stow's London, Bk. III, 8.
(2) Burn's Refugees, p.1.
(3) Acta Regia, p. 93.
(4) 4th year, cap. 2; 37th year, cap. 2, 3, 11, 13, 17, 26, ; 38th year, cap 2.

(5) Fuller's Church Hist., IV, p. 110, 111.
(6) Fuller, IV, p. 112.
(7) Stow's London, Bk. II, 8.

ses of the foreign merchants were burnt.[1] " In the rebellion of Wat Tyler in
ad many Flemings as well as Englishmen ; they brought thirteen Flemings out
urch, in London, and seventeen out of another Church, and thirty two in the
places in the city, as also in Southwark, all which they beheaded." From this
istin Friars Church was used at an early day by the Strangers.[2]
ttington, Mayor, and in 1399, Drew Barringtine, Mayor, decreed that no foreigner
y woollen cloth except in Bakewell Hall, in Basinghall Ward, where a weekly
t.[3] In 1391, many noble Strangers attended the " royal Justs and Turnaments " at
Froisart, " namely Valerine, Earl of St. Pol, who had married the King's sister ;
Ostarvant, son to Albert of Baviere, Earl of Holland and Henault "[4]
y, after many misunderstandings with England, granted in 1446 numerous
English at Antwerp, which were confirmed at a meeting held specially for the
beginning of the reign of Edward IV, 1463, and in subsequent years, inquisitions
mes of the foreigners residing within the city of London, chargeable to the alien
lichard III, the Netherlanders resident in England, complained of the taxes
the terms of the intercourse, and in 1486 the foreign merchants appealed to the
mplain that they were charged so much a head passing from Calais to Dover and
een Jews or infidels ;" that besides this, a second toll was levied specially for
d Mayor levied " scavage " on them in London. Also that the custom dues on
cu raised from fourteen pence to five shillings and nine pence, and that the
earchers and packers, all levied black mail; that the English pirates so robbed
a shilling in the pound for insurance. The result was, after complaining for ten
ornary, 1495, a commercial treaty was made between Henry VII and Philip,
i accorded free trade to all towns and ports of each nation besides other mutual

eek, 1517, the citizens of London. incited by a sermon preached by Dr. Bell, a
ced and illtreated the Strangers, having been instructed to do so by one John
e 30th April their houses near Leadenhall and Blanchapelton were pillaged.
: 278 citizens and boys were arrested, and on the 7th day of May, John Lincolne,
named Betts, were condemned to death ; Lincolne was hanged, and the others
ed.[6]
nation of Luther and his adherents at the Diet of Worms in 1520, severe ordin-
d against the reformers and their followers, when many of them left the Nether-
le in England; some bringing large amounts of money with them.
nry VIII and the church, concerning the divorce of Catherine of Arragon, which
! Cardinal Fisher, Bishop of Rochester, and Sir Thomas More, brought easier
es from the Netherlands. The Pope, Paul III, resented this treatment of a high
and issued a sentence of excommunication against the King of England, which
September, 1535.[7] Speedy was the action and subtle was the response of King
es. Tyndale was at that date in prison at Vilvoorde, having been arrested in the
ie Procurator General of Brussels at the instance of Henry VIII, his council, and
l.[8]
new and entire translation of the Bible into English had been printed abroad.
lth, 1535, and was ready for issue in England when opportunity offered. That
the indignation of the English King at the action of the Pope. The printed
English Bible were soon imported as a trade article with the aid of the merchant
· refuge to this country from the severe laws enforced against all those who had
ured, the reformed religion. What better defiance to the Papal power could be
Bible in the vulgar tongue. That issue, ready printed, was permitted to be sold

openly, being provided in this country with a dedication to Henry VIII, signed by Myles Coverdale, in his own words "as I was required." Allegiance to the See of Rome was thrown off and very soon every encouragement was given to spread the truths of the Gospel.

While collecting materials for this short history of the Strangers from the Low Countries and of their churches in England, an important document came to light from the archives of the Dutch church at Austin Friars, which will go far to unravel "a tangle of misconception and conjecture" concerning the history of the first complete English Bible, of which Mr. H. Stevens, in his History of the Bible in the Caxton Celebration Exhibition of 1877, untied the first knots.

Before the newly discovered evidence is given at length, it would be well to consider the position of the controversy, both before and after Mr. Stevens' discovery of the reference made to the history of the Coverdale Bible by the Rev. Symeon Ruytinck in his Life of Emanuel Van Meteren, the author of the History of the Netherland wars, given at the end of the edition of 1614 and partially reprinted by Mr. Stevens in "The Bibles in the Caxton Exhibition," 1878. This rediscovery of details, apparently unknown to English students, was an important one and formed a fresh starting point for bibliographers. The passage in question was brought to the notice of Mr. Stevens at Geneva, and he relates that he nursed it with care for four years before he announced it to the English public at the time of the Caxton Celebration, 1877.

It will be granted that all the facts hitherto known of the history of this Bible of 1535 are comprised in the able and critical works on the subject by Mr. F. Fry, 1867; Dr. Eadie, 1876; and Mr. H. Stevens, 1877 and 1878. It will therefore be unnecessary to refer much, if at all, to the older writers, whose statements and opinions have been well sifted. The special thanks of all interested in the subject are due to these three authors for their able treatment of the matter, old and new, connected with the Coverdale Bible. Their critical writings contain all that can possibly be gleaned on the subject from internal and external evidence hitherto known.

In comparing the facts stated and the deductions made by these authors with the statements deposed to by Emanuel Van Meteren (for of these points alone is it necessary to treat in making remarks concerning the Dutch Church document) it has been considered prudent to keep as closely as possible to the very words used, giving references for the sake of satisfaction. The statement of Dr. Eadie,[1] that from 1528 till 1535 the places of Coverdale's residences were unknown, has been cleared up by Mr. Stevens' reference to Ruytinck's Life of Van Meteren, which also answered Mr. Fry, who writes[2] "we have not been informed where Coverdale resided whilst he was engaged in the work of translation."

Mr. Stevens however appears to hold that Coverdale only went abroad in 1534, and adduces this as an argument against the notion that he was the translator of the Bible that bears his name, the period elapsing from that date to the 4th of Oct., 1535, not giving sufficient time to get through his great task. Dr. Eadie relates that "Thomas Topley, an Augustine Friar of Stoke Clare, confessed, when examined in 1528, that having heard Sir Miles Coverdale preach, ' his mind was sore withdrawn from the blessed sacrament, insomuch that he took it but for a remembrance of Christ's Body.'"[3] All must agree with Dr. Eadie's conclusion that after such evidence it could have been no longer safe for Coverdale to remain in England. There is no reason to doubt Foxe's statement that he went to Hamburgh and was with Tyndale there in 1529. We know that Tyndale had been at Antwerp three years before this date, for the third edition of his translation into English of the New Testament was printed there at the end of 1526 by Christopher of Endhoven.[4] Mr. Stevens therefore may be mistaken when stating that Coverdale only left England to go abroad in 1534. There can be no reason to doubt that he was with the many other English refugees at Antwerp the greater part of the time he was absent from England until the date of the completion of the work of translating and printing the Bible of 1535. Mr. Fry writes[5] "it yet remains a mystery from what press it was issued;" on this point Dr. Eadie satisfies himself , stating[6] "from typographical evidence that his translation was completed and printed " in Zurich. It is difficult to imagine how Dr. Eadie gives Mr. Fry's " Bible by Coverdale " as an authority in this point.[7]

At all times and by all writers, except Mr Stevens, the great work of translating the first complete English Bible of 1535 has been attributed to Myles Coverdale, who was second alone to William Tyndale. In his name this Bible of Bibles was issued, and, as the sole translator, he signed the dedication to King Henry VIII, and wrote the prologue to the reader. Strong evidence was necessary to upset all the accumu-

---

[1] Vol. I, p. 257.
[2] The Bible by Coverdale, p. 4.
[3] Eadie, I, 256.
[4] Eadie, I, 174.

[5] Bible by Coverdale, p. 4.
[6] Vol. I, p. 271.
[7] Vol. I, p. 271.

ated evidence of ages, and to depose that self-depreciating, humble, and unambitious man from the position he has always held. To the place of honour that Coverdale occupied, the Antwerp merchant, Jacob
Van Meteren, was exalted, a position which the literary world was unwilling to accord to him, considering
that the text of Ruytinck did not justify Mr. Stevens' deduction.[1] The place of publication hitherto unknown was by Mr. Stevens' discovery announced to be Antwerp; the translating and printing of the work
being correctly stated to have been at the cost of the same Jacob van Meteren.

  "Though the study has been continued for seven years, after carefully considering the details of the
Ruytinck statement for four years, I find very little to modify or change," is Mr. Stevens' conviction even
now in 1884.[2] Nailing his colours, as he does, to the mast, it will be well to give in his own words the
history of his discovery and the deductions he draws. Some of these were correct, though his idea that the
Bible of 1535 was printed at Antwerp and "his conclusions that the translation itself was the work of
Van Meteren and only revised by Myles Coverdale, can hardly now be maintained."[3]

  It will no doubt be considered satisfactory by all interested in this subject, that the deductions so
authoritatively put forward in 1877 should be examined by the light of the new evidence so lately discovered.
It is certain that "any information in addition to that already reported cannot be devoid of interest to all
conversant with this branch of bibliography, and especially to those who are possessors of the first bible in
English."[4]

  Mr. Stevens writes as follows:[5] "As to Coverdale and our first complete English Bible, finished the
4th of October, 1535, THE MOST PRECIOUS VOLUME IN OUR LANGUAGE, what do we know? Absolutely
next to nothing. Where it was printed, or by whom, or under what circumstances, no historian or
bibliographer has as yet given us any trustworthy information." "No literary mystery for the past three
centuries has elicited so much inquiry, or so many investigators, especially of late and latest years; yet
up to the opening day of this Caxton Celebration, the 30th of June, 1877, all is but mere conjecture."
"The very variety of these conjectures proves their falsity, and shows that they are really and truly mere
conjectures, without the slightest base or foundation." He tells us[6] how the statement of Ruytinck, in the
life of Emanuel van Meteren, dropped into his mouth after "lying under our noses in most of our libraries
or two centuries and a half unnoticed." He "assigns the honour of producing our first English Bible to
Antwerp," "the home of JACOB VAN METEREN, the probable translator of our first Bible, who employed
Miles Coverdale "to set forth" and father "this speeyall translacyon".[7] "Coverdale's duties and re-
sponsibilities in revising and setting forth this special translation, at Antwerp, in 1534-35, at the cost and
charges of Jacob van Meteren, who was also, we believe, its original translator out of "Douche and Latyn"
into English were, we take it, precisely the same as when in 1537-38 he revised and set forth the Great
Bible in Paris at the cost and charges of Grafton and Whitchurch." "He was employed and required
not only to revise and see the Bible through the press, but to father the translation."

  We have in the above definite and positive statements of Mr. Stevens the following, viz:

  1.—That Jacob van Meteren was the original translator out of "Douche and Latyn."
  2.—That Coverdale was only the reviser and setter forth.
  3.—That the Bible of 1535 was so translated, revised, printed, and set forth at the cost and charges
      of Jacob van Meteren.
  4.—That it was printed at Antwerp.

  The statement of Mr. Stevens that the relation of Ruytinck concerning the history of the English Bible
of 1535 had been unnoticed for two centuries and a half can hardly be maintained. Jacobus Kok in 1790
wrote that Emanuel van Meteren was born in Antwerp in 1535, and that his father was a printer. That
when the wife of the latter was about to give birth to Emanuel, his father had printed a Bible in the
English language and had gone to England to arrange for the sale of his work.[8]

  Having shown the state of recorded knowledge on the especial points given in the document lately discovered, it will be well to give verbatim this all-important affidavit of the son of the man who, perhaps
more than any other, was connected with the whole business of the Bible of 1535.

  [9] "Emanuel Demetrius, marchant of Andwarp, aged about 74 yeares, doth witnes and can depose, That

(1) Vide Saturday Review, 18 Aug., 1877. Also Intro-
    duction to Caxton Celebration catalogue, by Geo.
    Bullen, p. 10.
(2) Athenæum, 12 July, 1884.
(3) Mr. Bullen's introduction to the Catalogue, p. 10.,
    Caxton Celebration, 1877.
(4) Fry's Bible by Coverdale, p. 5.

(5) Stevens, p. 36.
(6) Page 38.
(7) Page 39.
(8) Kok's Vaderlandsche Woordenboek, 1790, xxiii,
    p. 47. Vide also Van der Aa, 1852-1869—Woorden
    boek, under Van Meteren.
(9) Dutch Church Archives.

"he was brought in England Anno 1550, in King Edward's the 6 dayes, by his Father, a furtherer o
"reformed religion, and he that caused the first Bible at his costes to be Englissled by Mr. Myles Coverda
"in Andwarp, the w'h his father, with Mr. Edward Whytchurch, printed both in Paris and London, b;
"w'h meanes he, wel acquaynted, was one of the Suters for the erection of a Dutche Church at the Aug
"ustin Fryers and made this Deponent a member of the same Anno 1552.
    "And he doth wel remember, that the Churchyeard and houses on bothe sydes of the West dore of th
"Church were inhabited and possessed by the Members of the Church. And harde his sayd father an
"others of the Elders of the Church often tymes consel of buylding there, and making of an other dore fo
"the Church, at the Cestern to receyve the raynwater of the Church to the vse of washing or bleaching.
    "But the sayd Church, Anno 1553, in Queen Mary's tyme, was left and the Members dispersed, and fo
"a tyme was vsed for the Queen's storehous for provision of a navy that went to Conquet in Brittain an
"afterwards vsed by the Florentyn's marchants to say masse in. The Dutche pulpet always remayning in it
    "At the Queen Elizabeth's coming to the Crowne, the former gift of King Edward was fully confirme
"to the Strangers agayne, which bestowed great reparations, but the Churchyeard was then occupyed b
"the then Lord Tresuror, Marquis of Winchester, and his heyrs, who plucked down the lead of the Quyr
"and covered it with tyles that was in theyr possession, and the vse of the Churchyeard was differre
"and lost to offend neglected, yet often Interpellation made. Thus much I can depose, in London, 28 c
"May, 1609.
                                                    (Signed) EMANUEL DEMETRIUS."[1]
    This highly important and interesting document concerning Jacob van Meteren is an original copy mad
in 1610, which, with others of the same time concerning the Churchyard of the Austin Friars Church, wa
found by the Editor in an old box in that Church with a register of the privileges (vryheyden) of th
Dutch congregation. It is to be hoped that the discovery of this affidavit will bring about a new invest
gation and research into the history of the English Bible of 1535, and of its translator and printer.
    The following positive and definite facts connected with this Bible were thus deposed to by Emanu
van Meteren.
    1.—That Jacob van Meteren employed Myles Coverdale to translate the "first Bible" into Englis
at Antwerp.
    2.—That it was so translated at the cost of Jacob van Meteren.
    3.—That Jacob van Meteren and Edward Whitchurch printed the Bible of 1535 at Paris and Londor
    All these facts, with the exception of the place where the printing was done, and the addition of Whi
church's name, agree perfectly with the statement of Ruytinck.
    Mr. Stevens contends "that Coverdale was not himself the translator, but that Van Meteren wa
Coverdale simply aiding him, at his employer's cost, as a learned reviser, editor, proof reader, and gener
manager."[2] This does not bear the light of the very proof which Ruytinck had in his own possessio
or even of the statement made in the life of Emanuel van Meteren.
    Up to the time of finding this document, the only precise information, beyond that contained in the titl
pages of the Bible and the dedication and prologue by Coverdale, rested in the statement of Ruytinck, give
to English students by Mr. Stevens. This was written after the death of Emanuel van Meteren in Apri
1612. "Out of love which I had for him, I wrote his life and death, which can be read at the end of th
last edition of his book," published in 1614.[3]
    All the biographers of Jacob and Emanuel van Meteren took the particulars concerning that family an
the connection of the former with Coverdale from this life of Emanuel by Ruytinck, and they all refer t
it. The Rev. Symeon Ruytinck was the senior Minister of the Dutch Church, while Emanuel van Metere
was one of the oldest members of the congregation and the leading member of the merchant Strangers, a
the Netherland Consul; there must, therefore, have been constant communication between them. Th
whole history of the English Bible of 1535 must have been well known to both; to Van Meteren from hi
parents, and to Ruytinck as conservator of the archives of the Church. It is probable that the latte
knowing the story well, did not trouble himself to consult the deposition of the former, which was in h
keeping, but added carelessly, "and printing" when writing the life of his dear friend the historian, an
recording the fact that Jacob van Meteren paid the cost of translating the English Bible at Antwerp. Thu

(¹) Van Meteren or Demetrius; according to the custom
    of the day, learned and eminent men gave a latin
    rendering to their names.

(²) Stevens, page 7.
(³) Ruytinck's MS., Guildhall Library, Dutch Chur
    Collection, No. 7.

haking it to appear that the work was printed at Antwerp, when he should have put on record what was tated in the deposition, that it was printed "in Paris and London."

Mr. Stevens has a very high opinion of the son of Jacob van Meteren, who witnessed and deposed in 609 concerning the part his father had in the Bible of 1535. "This man, twin-brother of the Coverdale Bible, became a distinguished man, a scholar, and an historian. He passed most of his life in London as nerchant, and Belgian (Netherland) Consul. He died the 18th of April, 1612, in his 77th year. *He tever forgot the circumstances preceding his birth*, and frequently wrote his name "Emanuel Quis-Contra-Nos."[1]

It is true that Mr. Stevens was in 1878 inclined to doubt his own statements, for he then wrote "further and more careful investigation may compel us to somewhat modify some of these details, and to qualify thers; but, on the whole, we trust that our hurried account is substantially correct. We are indebted for he larger part of our statement to the Rev. Symeon Ruytinck, the bosom friend of our "Emanuel Quis-lontra-Nos," who was, we believe, for a time connected with the Dutch Church of Austin Friars in London." Doubtful as Mr. Stevens was in 1878, he, in 1884, "unquestionably" reaffirms his statements f 1877-8.[2] Again,[3] "Next came up the question of the translator into English, and I came to the conlusion that he certainly was not Coverdale, but might probably be Van Meteren himself."

All will, no doubt. after the publication of the deposition of Emanuel van Meteren, agree with the nference that Mr. William Aldis Wright draws[4] from the unfortunately expressed statement of Ruytinck, iz., "that Jacob van Meteren did not translate the Bible himself, but paid another for translating it." It rill be well to give the translation of Ruytinck's original statement, so correctly stated by Mr. Wright. acob van Meteren "displayed his especial zeal in defraying the cost of translating and printing the English Bible in Antwerp, employing for that purpose the services of a learned student, Miles Coverdale y name, to the great advancement of the kingdom of Jesus Christ in England." Ruytinck's statement an only be taken to mean :

1.—That Van Meteren paid "the cost of translating and printing."
2.—That Coverdale, as a learned student, was employed to translate.
3.—That the English Bible was printed at Antwerp.

This latter statement is corrected by the very document that Ruytinck had in his keeping. The deposition f Emanuel van Meteren concerning his father must be taken in preference to the printed statement of luytinck (perhaps altered by a reviser) concerning the father of his dear friend Emanuel. Both agree n what must have been considered, then as now, the more important portions of the statement, viz., at rhose cost, where and by whom the translation was made. In 1614, the question where it was printed, nd by whom, would have been considered of little moment.

The error of stating that it was printed at Antwerp must be laid on Ruytinck; the original Dutch clearly acans what Mr. Stevens maintained in this respect, but the place where the newly-discovered document ras found, and the relationship of the deposer to Jacob van Meteren, give a position, the strength of which an hardly be denied. That Jacob van Meteren is entitled to the honor of "having caused at his own osts" the Bible of 1535 to be translated into English may be considered as finally established. That it ras printed by Jacob van Meteren and Edward Whitchurch must be taken as the fact. unless the formal eposition made in due language be considered of no credit. Richard Grafton, when writing to Cromwell n 1537 for his interest to obtain the King's privilege to issue the edition of the Bible of that year, used the ollowing words: "Dutchmen, living in this realm, go about the printing of it: which can neither speak rood English, nor yet write none, and they wilbe both the printers and correctors thereof."[5]

The first edition was completed with a title page and introductory matter, which must have been supressed almost immediately; only one copy, belonging to the Earl of Leicester, has survived with this title iage and the one page of the introductory matter printed in the same type as the body of the work. The late of the final rupture of Henry VIII with the Pope causes it to be improbable that the printing was lone in London. Mr. Fry writes:[6] "It has been taken for granted by many, if not by all writers on this ubject, that the volume was printed on the continent." "I have a list of 14 writers who say that it is

(1) Stevens, p. 40.
(2) The Athenæum, 12 July, 1884.
(3) Ib. 26 July, 1884.
(4) Ib. 2 Aug., 1884.

(5) Strype's Cranmer, App. XX. — *Netherlanders* not *Germans*. as Dr. Eadie states.
(6) Bible by Coverdale, p. 27.

probable that this Bible was printed either in Zurich, Frankfort, Cologne, or Paris." "These opinions, however, are only suppositions on a subject where evidence should be adduced."

That prohibited Bibles were printed in Paris at an early date is proved by the catalogue attached to the Placard, published by the Emperor Charles V on the 31st July, 1546, concerning heretical books, which "had been declared to be evil or dangerous" by the Faculty of Divines of the University of Louvain. Among the forbidden books were the Latin Bibles printed at Paris by Robert Stevens in the years 1532 and 1540.[1]

The fact, stated by Mr. Stevens,[2] that "an exposcayo. vpo. the psalms of Miserere ...... made by Hierom Sauonarola" was printed at Paris in English by Francois Regnault without date, but probably before 1538, tends to show that English books on religious subjects were set up in type at Paris at about the date the Bible was printed. This, and the additional fact, also referred to by Mr. Stevens,[3] in the letter dated from Paris, 12th Sept., 1538, by Coverdale and Grafton to Cromwell, concerning Francis Regnault, the Paris printer, who "hath bene an occupier into England more than XL yere, he hath allwayes provyded soche bookes for England, as they moost occupied," may be taken as a clue to the name of the printer at Paris of the Bible of 1535. Regnault was also entrusted with putting into type the Great Bible of 1539. It will be of importance therefore that all the books printed by Regnault should be carefully examined, to see whether the paper he used had the same watermarks (crowns and bulls' heads) found in the paper of the Coverdale Bible and also whether any of the type used for this Bible is identical with that of other books printed by him.

There is no doubt but that the character of the initial letters (flowers and dotted ground) is very similar in the Coverdale Bible and the " Chroniques et Annals de Haynnau " by Jaques de Guyse, printed by him at Paris in 1532. The large Gothic type of the title pages of the latter book and of the Bible printed by Nycolson in Southwark in 1537 is also very similar in character. It will be required, however, and fairly so, that very direct evidence of identity of the type of the text of the Bible of 1535 with that of other books printed by Regnault or other printers will be required before the name of the printer of the Coverdale Bible will be considered to be revealed.

The statement made by Emanuel van Meteren that the Bible of 1535 was printed at Paris may be considered to hold good as regards the first edition of 1535, while London was undoubtedly the place where the later editions were printed by Nycolson. The fact that the Bible was translated by Myles Coverdale for and at the cost of Jacob van Meteren will be considered settled, confirmed as it is by Coverdale himself. His statements, in his dedication and prologue, with the light of the newly-discovered document stand out as clear as day. In the dedication in the first edition he writes, " as the Holy Ghost moved other men to do the cost hereof, so was I boldened in God to labour in the same." In the dedication of the edition of 1550, Coverdale mentioned his predecessors " whom I have been more glad to follow, according as I was required." Dr. Eadie says,[4] " the persons so referred to are unknown. For prudential reasons their names were not divulged, and probably they did not covet the perilous notoriety." It is evident that he who was at the cost of the work, whose name we now know, viz., Jacob van Meteren required Coverdale as translator, to follow the versions of certain predecessors, who, as he himself tells us, were the five interpreters, considered by Dr. Eadie[5] to be the Vulgate, Luther, Zurich or Swiss German Bible, the Latin version of Pagninus, and Tyndale's Pentateuch and New Testament.

It was openly confessed on the first title page that the Bible of 1535 was " translated out of Douche and Latin into English." Dr. Eadie draws attention[6] to the advice which Coverdale gave the reader in the prologue if he found an error even of one letter to " take thy pen and mend it, considering that thou art as much bound so to do as I am to correct all the rest." This clearly shows the use Coverdale made of the translations of those preceding him.

Dr. Eadie well has it,[7] " though Coverdale began and carried out the work without co-operation, he never exalts his version as one taken immediately from the Hebrew and Greek text." " The original title-page revealed the truth ' fayhfully and truly translated out of Douche and Latyn.' " This curt declaration expresses the simple fact which Dr. Eadie amply proves in Chapter XIX[8] from the 66 notes " loosely scattered throughout his (Coverdale) Bible. Also in summing up the various evidence known in 1875 he says,[9] " Coverdale, beyond all doubt, was the translator of the Old Testament after 2 Chronicles, and his translation was accepted by Rogers or Mathews in his Bible of 1537, which also contains all that Tyndale

(¹) Brandt's Hist. of the Reformation, Engl. Ed., Bk. III, p. 85.
(²) Page 16.   (³) Page 33.
(⁴) Vol. I, p. 274.
(⁵) Vol. I, p. 281.
(⁶) Vol. I, p. 255.
(⁷) Vol. I, p. 279.
(⁸) Vol. I, p. 286.
(⁹) Vol. I, p. 278.

ad completed. To Coverdale himself, therefore, and to no copartnery of any kind, is the Bible of 1535 to ? ascribed. He claims to be the one doer, and no one who knows his transparency of character can doubt is simple word."

Mr. Fry says, "We have no information that Coverdale was assisted by any scholars of the day," and Coverdale intended that he should be regarded as the sole translator."

Internal and external testimony prove the claim of Coverdale to be the translator into English of all that yndale left unfinished of the work he had commenced, and the reviser of what Tyndale had completed. ; is therefore much to be regretted that the mistaken sense of Ruytinck's statement should for a time are been put forward by one of our ablest Bibliographers.

We are told by Ruytinck not only that Jacob van Meteren knew the "noble art"[1] of printing, but that ? was learned in many languages. It may well be that he in some way assisted Coverdale when making ie of the "Douche" versions, which certainly would be the "Hoochduytsche"[2] not "Nederduytsche" or .e "Vlaamsche taal," as it was commonly called. The term Dutch being used only in England when eaking of the Netherlands. In the Netherlands "Deutsche" is used for German. There can be but little ubt that the original title page, etc., was suppressed because it was considered in England that the anslation should have been made from the original Hebrew and Greek. Coverdale, *in the foreign sense* pecially refers to these German translations. "To help me herein I have had sondrye translations, not ily in Latyn, but also of the Douche interpreters, whom, because of their singuler gyftes and special ligence in the Bible, I have been the more glad to follow for the most part."

Van Meteren, no doubt, looked upon the translation and printing of the English Bible as a trade transtion. It was necessary for the successful sale of the various editions in England that it should be issued an English name ; the difficulty must have been to find any one willing at that precise time, when all iew the fate of Tyndale, to father the work. Coverdale took the responsibility "to set forth this specyall inslacyon," which has been called and now will with perfect certainty continue to be called by his name. e took up the work of those who " wold also with al theyr hartes have perfournded that they beganne f they had not had impediment." Rogers' heart evidently failed him. He too was doubtless "desyred" place his name to his edition of 1537. revised from the translations of Tyndale and Coverdale, but it peared under his feigned name of Thomas Matthew. About this very time Rogers married Adriana att, alias Van Weyden, stated to have been a connection of Jacob van Meteren; what more probable an, as Mr. Stevens considers, "that the enterprising foreign citizen of Antwerp,"[3] namely, Van Meteren, got up and printed this Bible also, and sold the whole edition to Grafton and Whitchurch."[4]

It is evident that it was impossible for Jacob van Meteren to have brought out Coverdale's Bible in his rn name, for, had it become known in the Netherlands that it had been translated and printed at his st, he would certainly have shared the fate of Tyndale and probably would have been put on his trial at e same time. That he must have been in danger after the publication is shown by the fact that he found necessary to come to England for refuge with his children in 1550, returning for his wife, who with m was drowned by the sinking of the vessel in which they embarked two years later, it having been ruck by the cannon-shot of a French ship of war, by which it was attacked. Extraordinary precautions ust have been taken by him to conceal the fact that he was the responsible person in the risky business,) less than seventeen years having elapsed before he finally left Antwerp. It cannot be wondered at, .refore, that there has been to this time, when the facts are revealed by finding the affidavit of his son, much mystery around the matter.

Cranmer, Archbishop of Canterbury, and Cromwell, in order to promote the Reformation, which with e aid of the English Bible had spread so rapidly, sent to the Netherlands and Germany for learned prostant divines. Martinus Bucerus, Petrus Martyr, Paulus Fagius, Emanuel Tremellius, Joannes A Lasco, ce Baron of Lasco in Poland, with many others came over at the call.[5] The latter wrote to Cecil from mbden, in April, 1549, complaining of the troubles of the church there,[6] so that he must have come to ngland shortly after that date. Bucer was appointed Professor of Divinity and Fagius Professor of ebrew at Cambridge, the former being paid three times the usual stipend. The change of climate and

(¹) Van de Leene's Theatre de la Noblesse de Brabant, 1705, • 50, Article Moretus, "sans deroger audit annoblissement continuer l'exercise de Tipographie."

(²) Title page of Historie der Nederlandtscher oorlogen, Norwich, 1579. "Wt den Hoochduytchen in onse Nederlantsche sprake."

(³) Does Mr. Stevens mean a "buiten poorter," i.e., one living outside the town.

(⁴) Stevens' Bibles in the Caxton Exhibition, p. 75.

(⁵) Strype's Cranmer, p. 194.

(⁶) Ib. App. L.

diet soon caused both to fall ill. Fagius died not long after his coming to Cambridge, at the age of "sca:
forty-five," and was buried in the Church of St.Michael. Bucer died about 1551, and was buried :
St.Mary's Church. Emanuel Tremellius succeeded Fagius in his Professor's seat, but he soon returned
Heidelberg.[1] Peter Martyr was made Professor of Divinity at Oxford, but shortly after the death of Kii
Edward VI solicited leave to return to his country, exhibiting his letters of protection.[2]   It was record
by Simeon Ruytinck that the first recognized congregation of the religious refugees in England was esta
lished by some of the above divines in 1547.

It would appear by the testimony of Strype that in 1547 a congregation of foreign refugees met togeth
at Canterbury.[3] Jan Utenhove went to that town shortly after he came to England; he probably took
great part in founding the Walloon Church there,[4] which had, as its first minister, Francois du Rivier
who two years later occupied a similar position in the French and Walloon Church in London, which w
established in 1549. The refugees from France had greatly increased in numbers in consequence of tl
persecution of the Protestants by Henry II, and there were in 1548 over five thousand Netherlanders
London,[5] a large proportion being Walloons.

The refugees of this period soon found their way to Norwich; the benefits derived by that city fro
their residence there "for ten years past" being specially recorded in 1561.[6] This town and its neig
bourhood had been, since the time of Henry I, much frequented by traders and settlers from the Lo
Countries.   In 1336 there was a large increase in the Flemish stuffs or worsted manufacture at Norwic
which caused the city to grow greatly in size, the numbers of the Strangers being much augmented by t
intercourse between the two nations, occasioned by the marriage of Edward III with Philippa, daughter
William I, Count of Holland and Hainault.[7] A great trade in raw wool soon grew up between the t
countries, and "the king and state began now to grow very sensible of the great gain the Netherlands g
by our English wool, in memory whereof the Duke of Burgundy not long after instituted the Order of t
Golden Fleece, wherein, indeed, the Fleece was ours, the Golden theirs, so vast their emolument by t
trade of clothing. Our king therefore resolved, if possible, to reduce the trade to his own country."

"Happy the yeoman's house into which one of these Dutchmen did enter, bringing industry and weal
along with them. Such who came in strangers within the doors soon after went out bridegrooms, a
returned sons-in-law, having married the daughters of their landlords, who first entertained them, y
those yeomen in whose houses they harboured soon preceeded gentlemen, gaining great estates to the
selves, arms and worship to their estates."[8]

Returns were made for the Alien Subsidy of the City of Norwich in the reign of Henry VI a
Edward IV.[9] In the time of Henry VIII the prosperity caused by the foreign settlers declined, but t
new comers to Norwich in 1551 somewhat improved the trade of the place.

The Flemish-speaking refugees, finding the King Edward VI very favorably disposed towards the
appealed to the Duchess of Suffolk, "an enquiring and godly woman," to aid them in procuring a meeti
house for religious purposes. By her intervention, through Dr. Coke and Mr. Gecke, the king's scho
master, the matter was brought before the king. The Privy Council agreed to give part of the Church
the dissolved Monastery of the Augustine Friars, in London, to Martinus Micronius and Gualterus Delæni
ministers of God's word, for the use of themselves and their brethren. The arrangements were made
the Clerk of the Council, Mr. Armigall Wayd, and the Clerk of the Signet, Mr. Hannings, on a guaranı
being given by the Strangers.[10]

The grant, with other privileges, was confirmed by letters patent of the king, dated at Leigh, 24th Ju
1550, to Joannes A Lasco and Joannes Utenhove.[11] It was ordered that the Church should have a superi
tendent and four ministers, and that it should be a body corporate, according to the following extract fr
the patent. "Quod idem superintendens et ministri in re et nomine sint et erunt unum corpus corporatı
et politicum de se per nomen Superintendentis et Ministrorum Ecclesiae Germanorum et aliorum pereg
norum in fundatione Regis Edwardi Sexti in civitate Londinense."

(¹) Fuller's Hist. of Cambridge, pp. 128, 130.
(²) Fuller's Church Hist., viii, p, 8.
(³) Burn's Refugees, p. 2.
(⁴) Pyper's Life of Utenhove, p. 55.
(⁵) Ib. p. 53.
(⁶) State Papers, D. S. xx. 49.

(⁷) State Papers, D.S. xx. 49.
(⁸) Blomefield's Norfolk. Fuller's Church Hist. Bake
    Chron., f. 190
(⁹) Record Office, Subsidies, cxlix, 162 to 169.
(¹⁰) Ruytinck's MS., p. 12.
(¹¹) Dutch Church Archives. A copy given in Burne
    Reformation Records, Bk. 1, No 51.

The first superintendent, Joannes A Lasco, described as a Polish lord and a Professor of Divinity, had been made a Denison by letters patent of the king, dated June 27th, 1550. He acted likewise as a minister of the Church, with Micronius and Delœnus as his colleagues for the Netherland, and with Franciscus Rivius and Ricardus van Villers for the French and Walloon refugees, all the foreign churches in London being under his charge.

The king and Privy Council agreed to the articles of faith and the regulations for the services, drawn up by A Lasco in Latin, which were also adopted by the reformed churches in the Netherlands. King Edward "ordered also that hereafter it should be called by the new name of the Church of the Lord Jesus."[1]

On the 21st of September, 1550, divine service was first celebrated in the Austin Friars Church by the strangers, who soon found that the building was too small for their congregation. On the 5th of October four elders were appointed, one of these being Jan Utenhove who, as at Canterbury, was most zealous in the establishment of the Church at Austin Friars. The members of the church, who had settled chiefly in St. Katherine's parish and in Southwark, being troubled by demands that they should attend the services at their parish churches, A Lasco wrote to Cecil, the secretary of the Privy Council, asking that those of his church might have a warrant to the effect that they should not be disturbed in their religious services. About this time A Lasco translated the Psalms into Dutch verse and set them to music.

The church of the Strangers in London was progressing most favorably when King Edward VI died on the 6th July, 1553. Shortly before this date "the corporation of German merchants, who lived in the steel-yard (so called from the steel imported by them) was dissolved, because it had become detrimental to England by engrossing the whole woollen trade." This corporation of foreign merchants had great privileges granted to it by Henry III in consequence of the assistance he had received from them in his wars. Antwerp and Hamburgh had then the chief trade, and the foreign merchants there soon "had the markets of England in their hands, and set such prices, both on what they imported or exported, as they pleased, and broke all other merchants." On the complaint of the native merchant adventurers, it was adjudged that they had forfeited their charter.[3]

In the reign of Edward VI an act provided for the regulation of the cottons called Manchester, Lancashire and Cheshire cottons. These were not cotton, but "were really woollen fabrics sold originally under that curious name." The refugees from Ghent and Antwerp brought the true cotton manufacture to Bolton and Manchester. The merchants bought linen yarn in Ireland, which was woven "at Lyrpole," the finished article being sent for sale in the place where the flax was grown.[4]

On the accession of Queen Mary, the Strangers found another state of affairs. Soon after the contract marriage made with Phillip II, a proclamation was issued ordering all the Netherland and other Protestant refugees to leave the kingdom within twenty-four days. The congregation was soon dissolved as it did not wish to experience the treatment of which so many of the members had already had a taste in their own country. All who could do so immediately made arrangements to leave England. Joannes A Lasco, Martinus Micronius, and Joannes Utenhovius, with about 175 other persons, embarked in one of two Danish ships which were lying in the Thames; and 82 others, under the care of Walter and Petrus Delœnus, went on board the other Danish vessel. They sailed on the 17th September, 1553, from Gravesend together, the former vessel soon reached Denmark, and the latter arrived at Hamburg after many perils from storms, etc. Eventually all were reunited at Emden, where they soon re-established their church, meeting with much kindness from Anna, Countess of Oldenburg; the burgesses of the town being likewise well disposed towards them.[5]

The congregation of Walloon and French weavers established at Glastonbury also broke up on the accession of Queen Mary, and removed itself to Frankfort. It had been established in 1550 with the aid of Jan Utenhove, the Duke of Somerset and Sir William Cecil, who greatly favoured it. The Superintendent was Valerandus Pollanus who arranged with Somerset that five acres of pasture land, or sufficient for feeding two cows, should be allotted to each family. The Duke engaged to supply the Strangers with money to buy wool, and promised that they should be allowed to employ English men and women in spinning and other work.[6] The settlement, however, was not very prosperous; "the promises and articles"

(1) Fuller's Church Hist., VII, p. 407.
(2) Strype's Cranmer, App. LI.
(3) Rapin's Hist. of England, Vol. II, p. 249.
(4) St. James' Gazette. 11th May, 1882.

(5) Simplex et fidelis narratio etc. per Joannem Vtenhovium, s. l. 1560, p. 21.
(6) Strype's Cranmer, p, 242.

entered into by the Duke not having been kept, the community petitioned the Crown, 11th Decembe 1551, that they might be carried into effect.[1] An order was made by the Privy Council that this shou be done, and on the 22nd March following " void places and rooms about the monastery of Glastonbury were ordered to be handed over for the use of the Strangers. In December, 5 Edward VI, free denizatio was granted to Vallerandus Pollanus and 69 other persons.[2]

The archives of the church in London had been taken abroad with the refugees to Emden by Mart Micronius, but they appear to have been lost or left there.[3] The original letters patent of Edward alone have been preserved, and are still kept with great care in the archives at Austin Friars. Ne Minute or Act Books were commenced on the return of the religious refugees to London after the accessi of Queen Elizabeth, who "greatly favored the Reformation to the rejoicing of all true Christians."[4] Ha stedius, Utenhovius and Petrus Delænus, having been appointed ministers, at the instigation of Johann A Lasco, on the 10th December, 1559, with the elders and deacons, petitioned the Privy Council f the confirmation of the patent of Edward VI.[5] The answer given was, that it could not be done, but th the Strangers must have a superintendent under the Bishop of the Diocese, and that the church could n be permitted to be a " Corpus Corporatum politicum." All that could be obtained was a grant from tl Queen that use should be made of the Austin Friars Church under the supervision of the Justices, and th on those terms the Strangers should again have possession of their former place of worship. In Februar 1560, the Queen directed the Marquis of Winchester to deliver over the church of the late Augusti Friars to the Bishop of London for the celebration of divine service by the Strangers in that city.[6]

Finally the congregation had to submit to the supervision of the Bishop of London, who was to be, officio, their superintendent, and to whom in the future the ministers and elders had to refer in all matte and difficulties that might arise. Early in 1560 a meeting was called in order to arrange for the welfa of the church, two subsequent meetings being held for the purpose of making new rules and regulatior By consent it was settled " that the ministers, elders, and deacons shall not be appointed by all the mer bers of the church, but by the Church Council of the ministers, elders, and deacons." It was also agre that students should be admitted to learn God's word, and that a house should be provided and set apa for the poor of the congregation, and that necessary collections should be made.[7] Jealousy in trade matte was soon shown against the industrious Strangers, they and their church being troubled by the city co panies putting in force an old statute which prohibited aliens from holding houses or carrying on trad The ministers, elders, and deacons therefore petitioned the Queen on the 29th June, 1560, that the " po religious refugees might not be molested."[8] This was immediately granted.

In 1561 there was a serious quarrel in the church with Hamstedius, he being accused of a tendency anabaptism and certain other errors. He was brought before the Bishop and discharged from the ministr Easily accommodating himself to circumstances, he went to Oldersheym, near Emden, with his famil and engaged himself in the culture of the land.

In 1560, the two hundred alien families which had settled at Sandwich, with the approval of the Que and the mayor of that town, found it necessary to establish a church. Utenhove went to them on the 1 of October of that year to assist them in this matter, when he arranged for Jacolus Buccrus, who h studied God's word at London, to be their first minister.[9] By letters patent of 6th July, 1561, a gra was made to the mayor and others of Sandwich to permit the said two hundred alien householders to purs the trade of making says, bays, and other cloth. The number of persons was 406 in all, and the aisle St. Clements Church was granted to them for their religious services[10] upon payment of forty shillings a yea and afterwards, 25th of March, 1617, upon bearing the expense of a third part of all the repairs of tl church.[11] In 1562, Bishop Grindal required the French and Dutch ministers in his Diocese to give him " Catalogue " of their congregations.[12] This was duly sent in, the names of all strangers in Sandwich the 20th of January of the following year being included in the return.[13]

The records of the Austin Friars Church state that in 1563 there was a great plague in London, a that, within the year, 21,930 persons died of it, among them two of the ministers, Delænus and Carinæu

---

(1) State Papers, D. S. 36.71.
(2) Burn's Refugees, 92. (MSS. D. Hen. D. Epis. Lond.)
(3) Strype's Grindal, p. 108.
(4) The Minute Book 1560-3 has lately been found.
(5) State Papers, D, S, Vol. VII, Eliz. 62.
(6) Ib., Vol. XI, 24.
(7) Vide Subscription lists, D. Ch. Archives.

(8) Vol. I, p. 7, Letters etc. D. Ch. Archives, Guildha Library.
(9) F. Pyper's Life of Utenhove, p. 237.
(10) State Papers, D. S.
(11) Vestry Book of St. Clements, Sandwich.
(12) State Papers, D.S., No. 24.
(13) State Papers, D.S.

hd many members of the Dutch church; at that time nearly all the Strangers made their testaments. Godefridus Wingius, who had been schoolmaster to the children of Joannes A Lasco and who had been engaged in 1562 at Emden in superintending the printing of the Bible there,[1] was called from the ministry at Sandwich and appointed to fill the same office at Austin Friars. In his time, 1564, it was ordered by the consistory that no child should be presented for baptism unless there were godfathers and godmothers. Three years later there arose a great question and quarrel in the church concerning godfathers and godmothers. This was referred to Grindal, Bishop of London, who, with assisting commissioners, gave a decision in writing, dated 19th December, 1567, confirming the discipline hitherto used by the Dutch church, which was in conformity with the other reformed churches, and also with the rules of the elders and deacons who had been appointed to the Austin Friars church.

In 1564 the inhabitants of Norwich were in much distress on account of the decay of the worsted manufacture. The mayor, sheriffs, and others consulted the Duke of Norfolk, and it was decided to invite to their city "divers strangers of the Low Countries, which were now come to London and Sandwich for refuge" and "which strangers had obtained licenses from the Queen to exercise the making of Flanders commodities in Her Majesty's dominions."[2] On application being made, the Queen granted letters patent on the 5th November, 1564, for 30 master-workmen, each household to consist of 7 persons, and others not exceed 300 persons in all, being Dutch and Walloons, to settle in Norwich. This, though approved of by the mayor and aldermen, was objected to by the commonalty. The former, however, placed the mayor's seal to the admission of the strangers, and assigned to them, after spending £ 43 in fitting it up, the church of St.Mary at Tombland for their hall, with seals and all other utensils for searching and sealing their manufactures, at a rent of £ 13 per annum.[3] Rules and ordinances were made for their government, which were allowed and ordered by the Council on the 25th April, 1571.[4] Of the thirty masters admitted twenty-four were for the Dutch and six for the Walloons.[5]

It appears that the poorer Flemings who came over from Hammes and Guisnes had a burial place appropriated to them at Saint Katharine's, in Portsoken Ward, London; this was afterwards used for the refugees who came over in Queen Elizabeth's time. From Hammes and Guisnes, the name of this churchyard became corrupted into Hangman's Gains.[6]

In 1565 Francis Bertie, born at Antwerp, was granted by the queen the exclusive privilege of manufacturing white salt for the period of twenty years. In 1567 Anthony Beckx, alias Dolin, and John Carre, natives of the Low Countries, petitioned for permission to establish a manufactory for table glass, such as was used in France; this appears to have been granted.[7]

Though the refugees from the Low Countries were very numerous before 1567, yet in that year they increased very greatly in consequence of the arrival in the Netherlands of the Duke of Alva with an army of Spanish soldiers. The Duchess of Palma wrote to Philip II " that in a few days above 100,000 men had left the country with their money and goods, and that more were following them every day." "Those who still saw a possibility of effecting their escape from the fated land, swarmed across the frontier. All merchants deserted the great marts."[8]

In the next year, great numbers fled from France, the "edicts for the free exercise being broken, their ministers banished and much blood spilt."[9]

In June, 1567. the merchant strangers of the Low Countries, established in England, were discharged by royal warrant from the two payments of subsidies granted by Parliament.[10]

On the 21st July, 1567, Lord Cecil was informed that commissioners had granted a license, by letters patent, to establish " certain foreigners" in Maidstone, in nearly the same terms as the one granted for Sandwich, namely, that they should pay half strangers' subsidies; and on the 22nd July, Bishop Grindal backed up the petition of the strangers to the Queen to be allowed to settle at various towns, they representing that they were reduced to great extremities.

A renewed flight of refugees from the Low Countries was the result of the severity of the Duke of Alva in punishing the inhabitants of the various towns who had been engaged in the destruction of Images and in plundering churches.

(1) This Bible does not appear among those exhibited at the Caxton Celebration in 1877.
(2) Burn's Refugees, p. 61.
(3) Blomefield's Norwich, I, p. 282; II, 118.
(4) State Papers, D.S., LXXVII, 58.
(5) The names of these are given by Blomefield, p. 283.
(6) Stow's London.
(7) State Papers, D.S., Vol. XLIII, 45, 46.
(8) Burn's Refugees, p. 4. Motley's Dutch Republic, II, 114.
(9) Strype's Annals.
(10) State Papers, D. S., XLIII, 21.

In 1568, "the blood council, the inquisition, the new Bishops, the beheading of many noblemen, cause very many to fly from their country, and brought into England many trades, such as 'Bayen, Sayen, Try pen, Grosgreynen, Moccaden,' and many who worked on the land. These settled chiefly at Norwich Sandwich, Colchester, Southampton, and Maidston, where, by the favor of the Queen, they were able t serve God in their mother tongue."[1] Others found their way to various towns. License was granted b the Privy Council for the Strangers to settle at Great Yarmouth in 1568, and at Lynn, for thirty familie of ten numbers each, on the 8th June, 1570. Many went to Canterbury, where permission to settle ha previously been given by the Queen's letter in 1561, confirmed in 1567. The mayor of Southampto requested permission from the Privy Council on the 29th May, 1567, for 100 strangers or more to reside i that town to teach their arts of manufacture;[2] this was backed up by the Bishop of the Diocese on th 30th June of the same year. These petitions were the result of an application made by the refugees Leave was granted by the Council,[4] and according to the date of the registers of the Walloon Church c Southampton the Strangers must have been established there in the above year. The Chapel of St.Julia or God's House was given to them for religious purposes. At the end of the register of that church is a interesting list of the feasts and fasts observed by the various congregations of the refugees to this cour try.

At Dover there was a Dutch Church before 1576, and, from letters dated 1575, it would appear tha a settlement was made also at Thetford. The numbers of the refugees at these places soon increased, an restrictions were made by order of the Town Councils. At Lynn, on the 6th February, 1574, it was se forth that no more were to dwell in the town but such as were admitted into the congregation, which wa not to exceed the number stated in the Queen's grant; that vacancies by death or departure only were t be filled up; that none of their poor should be chargeable to the town; that they should have only te fishing boats, and that they should not buy victuals except for those of their own congregation.[5] Thes licenses enabled the Strangers to establish churches under their own ministers, and to hold the services i the Dutch and Walloon or French languages, the administration of which churches were kept quit distinct.

At a general congregation of Brethren, gathered together at Geneva 25th June, 1568, thirty-two article or propositions were agreed to, which had been framed for the use of the Dutch congregation in Londor These, through the ministers and elders, were published September 18th in the same year, with the per mission of their superintendent, Grindal, Bishop of London, in Dutch, English, and Latin, being printe by Jugg, the Queen's printer.[6]

From the year 1567, and at intervals afterwards, orders were sent by the Privy Council to the loc authorities to transmit complete and careful lists of the Strangers, giving their names and those of thei wives, children, and servants, with their residences, occupations, the length of time they had been in th country, and the places abroad where they had been born. In one of the early lists the number of Strar gers, registered in London alone, amounted to over 5300.

In 1568 there appears to have been some uneasiness on account of the increasing number of Strange coming to England, for, on the 15th September, Sir Francis Walsingham gave orders for all Strangers i London to be certified weekly.[7]

Returns were made of the Walloon and Flemish refugees residing in Rye on the 28th May, 1569.[8] I another return, made on 4th November, 1572, for the same town, the number was 641,[9] their chapel bein that of the Augustin Friars, in Conduit Street. By 1569 the Strangers at Norwich had much increase the Privy Council having authorised 1132 to reside there. The choir of the Friars Preachers' or Blac Friars Church was assigned to the Dutch congregation, and the Court, on 24th February, 1569, confirme certain articles, settled with the minister concerning the keeping of due order in the church.[10] In 1571 th Archbishop and other High Commissioners decreed that the Bishop of Norwich, and not the Mayor or cit zens, had jurisdiction over the Strangers in matters ecclesiastical.[11] The Dutch congregation continued t use the Black Friars Church by leave only, until 1619, when it was leased to them at 6s.8d. per annun In 1650 the Mayor and Council resumed possession of it for their own services, and the Dutch wei

---

(¹) Ruytinck's M.S.
(²) State Papers, D.S., XLII, 71.
(³) Burn, p. 80. B.M. Vesp., F. IX.
(⁴) State Papers, D.S., XLIII, 82.
(⁵) Burn's Refugees, p. 217.
(⁶) Strype's Life of Grindal, p. 131, and Appendix, No. XVIII.

(⁷) State Papers, XLVII.
(⁸) Cotten MS. Galba C. 110, fo. 267.
(⁹) Lansdown MS., XV. art. 70.
(¹⁰) Burn's Refugees, p. 197.
(¹¹) Idem, p. 198.

noved to the church of St.Peter's of Hungate. The latter, however, returned to their old church in 61, and on 15th June, 1713, a lease was granted for 200 years at the old rent of 6s.8d., and it has been lled, since 1619, the Dutch Church.[1]
The great number of Strangers much interfered with the interests and work of the natives of Norwich. ie result was that a strong party was made against them. In 1570 a conspiracy of certain gentlemen d others was discovered; these had intended to have raised a body of men, with sound of trumpet and it of drum, at Harleston Fair on Midsummer Day to drive the Strangers from the city and realm. The ult was that ten of the conspirators were indicted for high treason, three of whom were hanged, drawn, d quartered.[2]
In the same year the art of printing was introduced at Norwich by Anthony Solen, one of the Strangers. was made free of the city, the corporation being much pleased at a press being set up in their town.[3] is, no doubt, to Solen's press that we are indebted for those rare books in the Dutch language, printed Norwich, of which one of the scarcest is of the highest importance for the history of "the times of the ubles," namely, "Chronyc Historie der Nederlandischer Oorlogen, Troublen ende Oproeren, etc, tot desen e 1580, Gedruct tot Noortwitz;" the preface being dated 2nd December, 1579, and signed "Theophilus." highly was this work esteemed at the time of its publication that a French translation, s.l., appeared in 82, the preface being signed Theophile D.L.; an English edition, translated from the French by Thomas ocker, followed with the same subscription. Slightly altered in the text it appeared again, published at ons by Jean Stratius, as a new work in 1583, and another edition of the same in 1584.
This valuable history, (stated on the title page of the first edition in Dutch to have been written by lam Henricipetri, Doctor of Law at Basle, and to have been printed after the copy of Basle), is considered have been translated from the German by one of the ministers of the Dutch Church at Norwich, Theo-ilus Rickwaert, who was deposed, together with Isbrandus Balkius and Anthony Algoet, from that nistry by the decree of the Archbishop and other Commissioners in 1571, on account of the troubles and ferences concerning the government of the Church; all three being held incapable of being elected to e ministry again either at London or Norwich. Some professors of history in Holland consider that ckwaert was not the translator of this work, though it has been generally held that he was so. D.L. is ought to be the initial letters of dog Latin words meaning *rich way, Rickwaert.* The following entry m the Marriage Register of the Dutch Church at Austin Friars seems to settle this point against the ubting professors, reconciling, as it does, the two different names. "25 Mei, 1574, Karolus Rijckart, eseit Theophilus, van Nieukercke met Lowijseken Carboniers van Bevere."
In 1571 there were found to be 3993 Strangers, Dutch and Walloon, in Norwich, and by 1582 these had creased to 4679, although the plague had carried off no less than 2482 Strangers between 20th August, 78 and 19th February, 1579. It would appear that letters patent were granted for the hostage of the rangers, for in 1579 the city purchased for £70 13s. 4d. those granted to William Tipper for Norwich. License for Strangers to settle at Colchester was given on the 24th March, 1570. The congregation st formed there, consisting of eleven families, making fifty persons who came from Sandwich,[4] were scribed as "very honest, godly, civil, and well ordered people."[5] They had their church in Head Street,[6] r some time using St.Giles's, then All Saints' Church, and at last they had a church of their own in .Mary's Lane, in part of the late Mr. George Gray's house, and afterwards in that of Mr. Theophilus all.[7]
a agreement was made between the Strangers and the Bailiff and Commonalty of Colchester on the 25th pril, 1575, concerning their privilege to reside in the town, and to carry on their trades.[8] Before 1580 ey had formed themselves into a congregation, providing for their own poor, all their names being entered to a register. "Their numbers daily increased, and Colchester was upon the point of becoming a colony Flemings, the congregation being unable to restrain their increase; and the bailiffs were obliged to issue command that no Stranger should, for the future, be permitted to reside in the precincts of the town ithout their special consent."[9]
The customary complaints of the English weavers were made to the Privy Council in the reign of King

(1) Blomefield, II, 342, 343.
(2) Blomefield, p. 284, from "Dutch and Walloon Stran-gers," Norwich Archives, by N. Sotherton, fo. 16, 23.
(3) Idem, p. 295.
(4) Burn's Ref., p. 208.

(5) Wright's Essex, I, 335, letter from Bailiffs to Privy Council, Aug, 1st, 1570.
(6) Wright's Essex, I, 235. Burn, p. 214.
(7) Burn's Ref., p. 215.
(8) State Papers, D.S., LXXVIII, 9.
(9) Cromwell's Hist. of Colchester, Vol. I, p. 118.

James, but the Council ordered that the indictments and presentments should be no further proceede
with ; and that the said Strangers be not "from henceforth in any such sort molested."[1]   On the 17th
October, 1612, James I granted them letters patent to make Bays, Says, and other foreign draperies.[2]   Th
congregation was dissolved soon after 1728, the trade in Says and Bays having at that date decayed.

According to the order of Lord Cecil, returns were made in 1571 of the Strangers "residing and abiding'
in the town of London and its suburbs, Harwich, Colchester,[3] Great Yarmouth, Lynn, Dover, Sandwich
Ipswich, Norwich, Southampton, Boston, and the Cinque Ports.[4]   At this period many privileges wer
granted to the merchant Strangers; an important one being exemption from contributions to the subsid
within the city of London.[5]   It was soon found that the Strangers were most diligent in all busine
matters, and that they brought in new manufactures and were increasing the trade of the country.

In August, 1571, Sandys, Bishop of London, asserted his right to act as the superintendent of th
Church at Austin Friars, as his predecessor Grindal had done.   The Bishop of Norwich, however, dii
claimed all right over the Strangers' Church, established in this year at that town.

On 4th October, 1571, the first national Synod was held at Emden, where Petrus Dathenius represente
the Dutch Churches in England.   In 1572 many towns in Holland, having freed themselves from th
Spanish yoke by aid of the Water Geusen, the Prince of Orange wrote most gracious letters to the Chur
in London, requesting that faithful ministers might be sent to the mother-country.   Bartholdus an
Wingius immediately responded to the call, their places being filled by Joannes Cubus and Jacobus Regius
In the following year the Prince sent a special messenger entreating the Church in London to send hi
assistance in the way of provisions and military stores.[7]

The massacre of St. Bartholomew at Paris, on the 23rd August, 1572, caused many French protestan
to fly to England for refuge, and though these refugees increased so greatly in number they still receive
the monthly sacrament in the Dutch Church, which was called "Jesus Tempel."   At this time Chur
Reform was much desired by the English clergy, and great interest was taken in the rules and regul
tions of the Dutch Church.   The attention of the Privy Council was drawn to this, and instructions wer
given in writing that there should be no communication or encouragement given to the English Church b
that of the Strangers, and that the funeral sermons preached in Dutch at the parish Churches, on th
occasion of the burial of members of the Dutch Church, should be discontinued.   Orders were also give
that no parish clergyman should perform the ceremony of marriage for Strangers without the consent
the Consistory of the Strangers' Church.

At the latter end of 1572, Lord Burleigh induced many families of the refugees from the Low Countri
to settle at Stamford, which town chiefly belonged to him.   These settlers were mostly woollen weaver
but others worked in.steel, copper, and other trades.   Isbrandus Balkius, who had been deposed from th
ministry of the Dutch Church at Norwich by a decree of the Archbishop, with Casper Vosbergius, in th
name of the other settlers, petitioned Lord Burleigh to grant the Strangers' Church at Stamford certa
privileges set forth in ten articles.[8]   This congregation elected Balkius as the first minister, who furnishe
himself with testimonials from the Bishop of Norwich, dated 8th March, 1571, and continued "a gre
while" in Stamford.   This Church, however, was dissolved and dispersed sometime before 1711.[9]

In 1573, the London tradesmen, who found themselves powerless to restrain the refugees from selli
by retail, issued fly-sheets with the following : "Doth not the world see that you beastly brutes the Be
gians, or rather drunken drones and faint-hearted Flemings, and you fraudulent father-Frenchman, t
your cowardly flight from your own natural countries, have abandoned the same into the hands of yo
proud cowardly enemies ; and have, by a feigned hypocrisy and counterfeit show of religion, placed you
selves here in a most fertile soil, under a most gracious and merciful prince who hath been contented,
the great prejudice of her natural subjects, to suffer you to live here in better case and more freedom th
her own people.

"Be it known to all Flemings and Frenchmen that it is best for them to depart out of the realm
England between this and the 9th of July next; if not, then to take that which follows.   There shall
many a sore stripe ; apprentices will rise to the number of 2336, and all apprentices and journeymen wi
down with the Flemings and Strangers."[10]

(1) Wright's Essex, I, 335.
(2) Idem, p. 336.
(3) License to settle dated 24th March, 1570.
(4) State Papers, etc.
(5) Exemptions from Subsidies, Record Office.
(6) Coninck.

(7) Letters D. Church collection, Guildhall Library.
(8) Strype's Parker, App. LXXIII.
(9) Idem, p. 267.   Balkius appears to have gone
       Sandwich before 1578.
(10) Agnew's French Protestant Refugees, III, p. 12.

In 1575, the Burgesses appealed to the Bishop of London that the Church in Austin Friars should not be allowed to increase the number of its members, "and the Dutch Church claimed that none of its members should be married in the parish Churches. In this year the condition of the people of the Low Countries was so sad that great numbers of them had fled over hither and desired to join with the Dutch hurch in London, and to become members thereof. Yet so tender was the Queen of breaking with that roud and powerful prince, the King of Spain, that she would not admit of this, nor give countenance to ich as fled out of these countries under his subjection."[1]

By order of the Queen, the Lord Mayor was commanded to disperse these new-comers from London. he Bishop of of London was begged to represent their case to the Queen and Council, and the Council lvised that the new-comers should depart from London and should go to other parts of the country where hurches of their religion had been established. In this year the national Synod of the Netherland Reformed Churches in England met in London. The Austin Friars. Norwich, Colchester, Maidstone, and hetford Churches being represented by their ministers, and those of Sandwich and Yarmouth by their ders. For some time these Synods met yearly, then at intervals; but after 1609 it was arranged that iey should meet every third year.

The Anabaptists, against whom there was so much prejudice in Holland by those of the Reformed hurch, were found met together in London on Easter Day, 1575, and the whole congregation, consisting ! twenty-seven persons, was arrested by order of the Privy Council, and examined before the Bishop of ondon. They were afterwards brought to trial before the Council, when the ministers of the Dutch hurch appeared to give evidence against them, though they did all possible to avert the doom of Jan Tielmaker and Hendrik Terwoert, who were condemned to be burnt, the execution taking place on the 2nd July, 1575. The other prisoners were strictly admonished to amend their ways.[2]

In 1580, "the family of love" became numerous and troublesome. Henry Nicholas, of Amsterdam, ho had "first vented" this sect in Holland in 1550, came to England in the latter part of the reign of dward VI. and "joined himself to the Dutch congregation in London, where he seduced a number of tificers and silly women." Martin Micronius and Nicholaus Charineus opposed Nicholas and his followers, any of whom were English. The attention of the Privy Council was drawn to them, but with what fect does not appear.[3]

The "Pacification of Ghent" having been made in 1576, there was a great demand on the Church at ondon for ministers of God's Word to be sent to the fatherland. Few could be spared; though greatly ressed, Jacobus Regius refused to go to Ghent on the ground that "the harvest at London was so great id the labourers so few." Shortly afterwards he was persuaded to go there, but was recalled in 1584.

Isbrandus Balkius, the minister at Sandwich, and Jan van Roo, an Elder of London, represented the nglish Churches at the national Synod, held at Dordrecht in 1578.

On the 27th December, 1576, Sergeant Nicholas Burham wrote to Burghley concerning the condition of ie Strangers at Sandwich and Maidstone, to whom the Queen had granted letters patent for license to ttle.[4] Troubles arose between the refugees and the Mayor and Corporation of the former place; in 1582 iere was an enquiry made by the Privy Council to discover what authority such severe decrees were ade by the Corporation against the Strangers.[5] It would appear that there were large mercantile transtions between the Mayor, and others of the town, and the foreign merchants, for, in 1584, the Privy ouncil wrote, without avail, to the States of Zeeland and Holland to procure satisfaction for the losses istained by the merchants of Sandwich.[6]

In 1577, the Dutch Strangers inhabiting Halstead, in Essex, petitioned the Privy Council that forty milies might be permitted to inhabit that place, so that they might quietly follow their trades.[7]

In 1584, London again suffered severely from the Plague, when many of the Church, including one of ie ministers, Jan van Roo, who had taken orders in 1580, died from the effects of it.

In 1582, a certain German or Dutchman born, named Peter Moris, having made an "artificiall forcier," mveyed Thames water in pipes of lead over the steeple of St.Magnus Church at the north end of London ridge, and thus brought it to a water standard at the parting of the four ways at the east end of Cornhill.[8]

Sir Wolstane Dixie, Lord Mayor in 1586, gave £50 to the poor Strangers of the Dutch and French Church.[9]

The Prince of Palma subduing the rebellion in Flanders in 1584, after the arrangement with Ghent in this year, caused a renewed flight of Protestant Refugees to England, nearly all joining the foreign Churches in the various towns where they established themselves. Sir Francis Walsingham was a warm friend to them, and the position of the Strangers was again much improved when the Earl of Leicester took charge of the Netherlands, though they had to contribute their share towards the subsidies for maintaining the army and fleet. They urged that the cost of their poor and of the Church was very heavy and begged to be excused from paying, but the answer was that it was for the good of the Fatherland they were asked to contribute. The characteristic entry of £ 550 "for the *squeezed* Fatherland, by the Burdens of the High Council," appears in the lists of collections for charitable purposes.

When the Spanish Armada was fitting out for the purpose of conquering England, the Privy Council communicated with the Dutch and Walloon Churches of London, and, in 1588, the Strangers were required to find their proportion of soldiers. Ruytinck records that "the Armada was fought from the 25th to the 29th of October, and, by God's help, was destroyed by the English and Dutch vessels." The medals that were struck in commemoration of the great victory over the Spanish Fleet, were distributed to certain members of the Church through their minister, Jacobus Regius.[1]

"Many Strangers resided within the liberties of the Sanctuary, St. Martins le Grand, London. In 1588 a survey was taken of all the foreigners, French, Germans, Dutch, and Scots, also of their occupations. Many of these were cordwainers or shoemakers, tailors, button-makers, goldsmiths, pursemakers, linen drapers, stationers, merchants, silkweavers, and two silk-twisters, who were supposed to be the first silk throwers in London, and brought the trade into England. One of these latter was named John James, made denizen on the 19th December, 1567, and the other Anthony Emerick, made denizen the 1st January, 1574, both born under the dominion of Philip II. There were found, upon that survey, to be, of householders (denizens as well as others), their wives, children, and servants, one hundred and sixty-one in number, which, nevertheless, was less by half than it was some years before; for, in 1569, their number was 260."[2]

"In the year 1588, there being a loan charged by the Queen upon the city, the Companies of London subscribed separately. The Strangers also subscribed among them £ 4,900 " in sums from £ 300 to £ 100.

In 1589, soon after the death of the Duke of Leicester, heavy impositions were laid on the Strangers for the expenses of the seige of Bergen-op-Zoom. The Brethren in London, on paying, complained that they were under very heavy expenses to maintain five ministers and two ministers' widows, all their poor, and the expenses of the students, besides having to assist with money payments the Churches of Dover and Maidstone. These last payments do not appear in the list of collections for the poor of the various Churches, though, in 1588 and 1589, £ 56 were sent to the refugees of Ostende in Zeeland and £ 126 8s. 6d for the town of Geneva.

On the 18th April, 1590, Sir Francis Walsingham, "Secretary of Her Majesty," died, "to the great grief of the Strangers, to whom he had always been a firm and steady friend."

In 1593, London was again stricken with a very severe attack of the plague, 1,700 dying in one week. At this time there was a rising of the citizens against the Strangers, whose houses were pillaged on the 1st of May. On the 5th May, 1593, these verses were affixed to the wall of the Dutch Church at Austin Friars;

> "You Strangers that inhabit in this land !
> Note this same writing, do it understand ;
> Conceive it well, for safety of your lives,
> Your goods, your children, and your dearest wives."
>   etc.   etc.

By order of the Privy Council, the Lord Mayor and Aldermen gave orders for special constables to be sworn in from among the merchants and tradesmen. Some apprentices and servants who were found rioting "were put into the stocks, carted, and whipt."[4]

---

[1] Among the *Charities* of the Church, payments were entered in 1587 for Captain Suderman £60, Captain van der Cruyce £ 92, and Captain Hunibert £ 200. These amounts were probably for officers and men, provided by the Church, and considered as charity towards the Fatherland as suggested by the Privy Council.

[2] Stow's London, Bk. III, p. 111.

[3] Burn's Refugees, p. 11. Thirty eight subscribers names given. Stow's London, Bk. I, 283.

[4] Annals of Elizabeth, IV, pp. 167-8.

In 1596, the Strangers increased greatly in number at Southampton, and very many Strangers [...] the parish of St.Botolph, in Billingsgate Ward, London. In a presentment made, shortly before [...], the foreigners dwelling there it is stated as follows: " In Billingsgate Ward were one and fiftie hou[se]-lds of Strangers; whereof thirty of these households inhabited in the parish of Saint Butolph in [th]e iofe and principal houses, where they give 20 pounds a year for an house lately letten for [...]; [th]e neerer they dwell to the water-side, the more they give for houses; and within thirty ye[...] ere was not, in the whole Ward, above three Netherlanders, at which time there was within [...] rish levied for the helpe of the poore seven and twenty pounds by the yeere; but since the y[...] [...]ntifully thither, there cannot be gathered above eleven pounds: for the Strangers will not [...] at such charges as other citizens do."[1]
In 1599, the City companies again much troubled the tradesmen who were Strangers, as they [...] like manner some four years before. These immediately petitioned the Queen, who ordered her C[...] il write the following letter to the Lord Mayor:
"After our harty commendations to your Lordship, An humble peticion hath been exhibited [...] Majestie by divers poore Strangers and handicraft-men off the Dutch and French Congre[...] City off London, whereby they give her Majestie to understand that your Lordship will [...] zither to enter into bond, to forbeare to work at all within the citye, or ellse to commit th[...] Her Majestie understanding the course you mean to take with them, hath willed us to signif[...] [t]hat her pleasure is, you should forbeare to go forward in this your intention. And is't there [...] further matter, knowen to your Lordship, wherewith as yet wee are unacquainted, that doth make you [t]o take this strickt course, then wee praye you to certify the same hither unto us, that we may consider off the same. And in the meane season to suffer them to use that favorable libertye wich hitherto th[e]y have enjoyed, and so wee bidd your Lordship farewell. From the Court at Greenwich, the 29 of the Aprill, 1599.
Signed,

Lo. B. off Canterbury.	Mr. Chancellor of the Exchequer.
Lo. Keeper.	Lo. Admirall.
Lo. North.	Lo. Buckhurst.
Mr. Comptroller.	Mr. Secretarie.

Directed to Sir Stephenson,[2] Kt. Lo. Mayor off the Citye of London."
Notwithstanding the action taken by the Privy Council, the suits against the Strangers were [...] th in the City. These were, however, stayed by an order dated 31st October, 1601, sent by [...] easurer, T. Buckhurst, to the Attorney-General.
In this year, Queen Elizabeth visited His Excellency, Heer Noel Caron, the Ambassador from [...] [wh]o resided at Clapham, on which occasion a short oration was made to her by Mr. Geleyn van [...] der of the Church.
On the 1st September, 1601, Jacobus Regius died. He had been the faithful and beloved mini[...] [th]e Church for over twenty-five years. His son, Joannes Regius, alias Coninck, was received in Li[...] d shortly afterwards Simeon Ruytinck was nominated as the third minister. The latter wr[...] eat book " or history of the Netherlanders in England from 1301 to the year 1620, when it [...] [con]tinued by Cæsar Calandrinus to 1625 and afterwards to 1627 by Æmilius van Culenborgh. An [...] story also exists in MS., 4⁰, written by Ruytinck, which is dated " In London, 1 January, 1[...] In 1602, letters having been received from the Church at Geneva, appealing to the charit[y] London, a collection was made after an earnest sermon by Assuerus Regemorterus, the result [...] is that £ 310 19s. 3d. were sent to the brethren abroad who were in distress.
On the death of Queen Elizabeth, on the 23rd March, 1603, it was recorded by the Strangers th[...] is truly a mother in Israel, a refuge for the Strangers, a helper to her neighbours, and fam[...] [...] world."
About this time letters were received by the Church from a nobleman in Ireland request[...] [th]e Strangers should go to reside there, especially naming Crookhaven and Schoolhaven [...] [wh]ich offered many advantages.[4]

---

[1] Stow, Bk. II, p. 168.
[2] Sir Stephen Some.

[3] Many of the particulars here given are extracted from this MS.
[4] Ruytinck's MS.

d

The Prince of Palma subduing the rebellion in Flanders in 1584, after the arrangement with Ghent i this year, caused a renewed flight of Protestant Refugees to England, nearly all joining the foreig Churches in the various towns where they established themselves.   Sir Francis Walsingham was a wart friend to them, and the position of the Strangers was again much improved when the Earl of Leiceste took charge of the Netherlands, though they had to contribute their share towards the subsidies for mair taining the army and fleet.   They urged that the cost of their poor and of the Church was very heavy and begged to be excused from paying, but the answer was that it was for the good of the Fatherlan they were asked to contribute.   The characteristic entry of £ 550 "for the *squeezed* Fatherland, by th Burdens of the High Council," appears in the lists of collections for charitable purposes.

When the Spanish Armada was fitting out for the purpose of conquering England, the Privy Counc communicated with the Dutch and Walloon Churches of London, and, in 1588, the Strangers were require to find their proportion of soldiers.   Ruytinck records that "the Armada was fought from the 25th to th 29th of October, and, by God's help, was destroyed by the English and Dutch vessels."   The medal that were struck in commemoration of the great victory over the Spanish Fleet, were distributed to certai members of the Church through their minister, Jacobus Regius.[1]

"Many Strangers resided within the liberties of the Sanctuary, St. Martins le Grand, London.   In 158! a survey was taken of all the foreigners, French, Germans, Dutch, and Scots, also of their occupation Many of these were cordwainers or shoemakers, tailors, button-makers, goldsmiths, pursemakers, line drapers, stationers, merchants, silkweavers, and two silk-twisters, who were supposed to be the first sill throwers in London, and brought the trade into England.   One of these latter was named John Jame made denizen on the 19th December, 1567, and the other Anthony Emerick, made denizen the 1st Jar uary, 1574, both born under the dominion of Philip II.   There were found, upon that survey, to be, (householders (denizens as well as others), their wives, children, and servants, one hundred and sixty-on in number, which, nevertheless, was less by half than it was some years before; for, in 1569, their numbe was 269."[2]

"In the year 1588, there being a loan charged by the Queen upon the city, the Companies of Londo subscribed separately.   The Strangers also subscribed among them £ 4,900 " in sums from £ 300 to £ 100 In 1589, soon after the death of the Duke of Leicester, heavy impositions were laid on the Strangers fe the expenses of the seige of Bergen-op-Zoom.   The Brethren in London, on paying, complained that the were under very heavy expenses to maintain five ministers and two ministers' widows, all their poor, an the expenses of the students, besides having to assist with money payments the Churches of Dover an Maidstone.   These last payments do not appear in the list of collections for the poor of the various Chu ches, though, in 1588 and 1589, £ 56 were sent to the refugees of Ostende in Zeeland and £ 126 8s. 6(for the town of Geneva.

On the 18th April, 1590, Sir Francis Walsingham, "Secretary of Her Majesty," died, "to the gre grief of the Strangers, to whom he had always been a firm and steady friend."

In 1593, London was again stricken with a very severe attack of the plague, 1,700 dying in one weel At this time there was a rising of the citizens against the Strangers, whose houses were pillaged on th 1st of May.   On the 5th May, 1593, these verses were affixed to the wall of the Dutch Church at Austi Friars;

> "You Strangers that inhabit in this land !
> Note this same writing, do it understand ;
> Conceive it well, for safety of your lives,
> Your goods, your children, and your dearest wives."
>   etc.   etc.

By order of the Privy Council, the Lord Mayor and Aldermen gave orders for special constables to b sworn in from among the merchants and tradesmen.   Some apprentices and servants who were foun rioting "were put into the stocks, carted, and whipt."[4]

---

(1) Among the *Charities* of the Church, payments were entered in 1587 for Captain Suderman £60, Captain van der Cruyce £ 92, and Captain Humibert £ 200. These amounts were probably for officers and men, provided by the Church, and considered as charity towards the Fatherland as suggested by the Privy Council.

(2) Stow's London, Bk. III, p. 111.
(3) Burn's Refugees, p. 11.   Thirty eight subscriben names given.   Stow's London, Bk. I, 283.
(4) Annals of Elizabeth, IV, pp. 167-8.

In 1596, the Strangers increased greatly in number at Southampton, and very many Strangers s · ˙ l
n the parish of St.Botolph, in Billingsgate Ward, London. In a presentment made, shortly before 1598,
f the foreigners dwelling there it is stated as follows: " In Billingsgate Ward were one and fiftie how e-
holds of Strangers; whereof thirty of these households inhabited in the parish of Saint Butolph in the
hiofe and principal houses, where they give 20 pounds a year for an house lately letten for four a. d
The nearer they dwell to the water-side, the more they give for houses; and within thirty yeere her re
here was not, in the whole Ward, above three Netherlanders, at which time there was within the old
arish levied for the helpe of the poore seven and twenty pounds by the yeere; but since they can
dentifully thither, there cannot be gathered above eleven pounds: for the Strangers will not contribute
o such charges as other citizens do."¹

In 1599, the City companies again much troubled the tradesmen who were Strangers, as they had
n like manner some four years before. These immediately petitioned the Queen, who ordered her Counsel
p write the following letter to the Lord Mayor:
"After our harty commendations to your Lordship, An humble peticion hath been exhibited unto her
Majestie by divers poore Strangers and handicraft-men off the Dutch and French Congregation in
City off London, whereby they give her Majestie to understand that your Lordship will enforce the m
either to enter into bond, to forbeare to work at all within the citye, or ellse to commit them to prison.
Her Majestie understanding the course you mean to take with them, hath willed us to signifye unto you
that her pleasure is, you should forbeare to go forward in this your intention. And is't there be any
further matter, knowen to your Lordship, wherewith as yet wee are unacquainted, that doth make you
to take this strickt course, then wee praye you to certify the same hither unto us, that we may consider
off the same. And in the meane season to suffer them to use that favorable libertye wich hitherto they
have enjoyed, and so wee bidd your Lordship farewell. From the Court at Greenwich, the 29 of the
Aprill, 1599.
                                   Signed,

Lo. B. off CANTERBURY.	MR. CHANCELLOR OF THE EXCHEQUER.
Lo. KEEPER.	Lo. ADMIRALL.
Lo. NORTH.	Lo. BUCKHURST.
MR. COMPTROLLER.	MR. SECRETARIE.

Directed to Sir Stephenson,² Kt. Lo. Mayor off the Citye of London."
Notwithstanding the action taken by the Privy Council, the suits against the Strangers were con
ith in the City. These were, however, stayed by an order dated 31st October, 1601, sent by the Lord
reasurer, T. Buckhurst, to the Attorney-General.
In this year, Queen Elizabeth visited His Excellency. Heer Noel Caron, the Ambassador from the
ho resided at Clapham, on which occasion a short oration was made to her by Mr. Geleyn van Bee
lder of the Church.
On the 1st September, 1601, Jacobus Regius died. He had been the faithful and beloved minister
e Church for over twenty-five years. His son, Joannes Regius, alias Coninck, was received in his place
nd shortly afterwards Simeon Ruytinck was nominated as the third minister. The latter wrote the
eat book " or history of the Netherlanders in England from 1304 to the year 1620, when it was con-
inued by Cæsar Calandrinus to 1625 and afterwards to 1627 by Æmilius van Culenborgh. An abridged
story also exists in MS., 4º, written by Ruytinck, which is dated " In London, 1 January. 1618."
In 1602, letters having been received from the Church at Geneva, appealing to the charity of
London, a collection was made after an earnest sermon by Assuerus Regemorterus, the result of which
as that £ 310 19s. 3d. were sent to the brethren abroad who were in distress.
On the death of Queen Elizabeth, on the 23rd March, 1603, it was recorded by the Strangers that she
as truly a mother in Israel, a refuge for the Strangers, a helper to her neighbours, and famed through ut
e world."
About this time letters were received by the Church from a nobleman in Ireland requesting t
e Strangers should go to reside there, especially naming Crookhaven and Schoolhaven as sui
hich offered many advantages.⁴

(¹) Stow, Bk. II, p. 168.   (³) Many of the particulars here given are extracted
(²) Sir Stephen Some.   from this MS.
                                     (⁴) Ruytinck's MS.

James I, being proclaimed King on the 17th May, 1603, a deputation from the foreign Churches, viz., London, Canterbury, Norwich, Southampton, Colchester, Sandwich, and Maidstone, was presented to him on the 23rd of the same month, at the Court held at Greenwich, who congratulated His Majesty on his accession to the throne; Monsieur de la Fonteyne, minister of the French Church, making the address in French. The King answered shortly to the effect that he would act well to the Strangers, who on account of religion had taken refuge in England, and in the same way that the late Queen had done.

In this year London suffered much on account of the numerous deaths from the plague; no less than 3,385 persons died in one week from that cause. By this severe visitation 370 houses of the members of the Dutch Church were struck, 52 families being entirely destroyed; the loss by death to the members was no less than 670 persons, among them being their beloved minister, Assuerus Regemorterus.[1]

On the 14th January, 1604, a conference was held at Hampton Court, the King being present, concerning ceremonies and the government of the Church in England; the Archbishop and most of the Bishops assisted with many Doctors of Divinity. It is probable that some new light may be thrown on the discussions concerning this conference by the report given of the proceedings by Ruytinck in his MS.

In the following year the King came in state to London, passing from the Tower to Westminster, the route being adorned with triumphal arches. The members of the Church erected a very elaborate structure, 87 feet high and 37 wide, near the Exchange, designed by Christopher de Steur and Assuerus Regemorterus, the verses in Latin on each of the four sides being written by Monsieur Thorius, Jacob Cool, and Ruytinck. The architect was Coenraet Janszoon, and the chief decorators or painters were Daniel de Vos and Pauwel van Overbeke. It was draped with tapestry on satin, representing the King as risen like a phoenix from the ashes of the Queen; that the refugees from the seventeen provinces had taken refuge here, and that they had brought many new industries and trades to the country.

In this same year the foreign Churches formally congratulated Bancroft, Bishop of London, on his elevation to the See of Canterbury in the place of Archbishop Whitgift, who had died. In this year it was also arranged that the Dutch Church should yearly send a deputation to congratulate the newly-sworn Lord Mayor in a set speech, which, now that the corporation is so sorely threatened, may be appreciated if given at length:

"Right Honorable, Wee that compare here before your Honour are some of the Ministers and Elders of "the Dutch and French congregations in London. The end is, for to performe our duty off congratulation "in the name of our congregations (according to our yearly custome) unto your Honour whom itt hath "pleased God to call to that great dignitye, honour, and authoritye, to bee a chief magistrate off this "famous citye, under our most gratious King. Wee therefore pray the Almightye God in all humilitye "to make your Honour (by vertu off his holy Spiritt) fitt and sufficient for the full performance off all the "dutyes belonging to great a charge and calling, that so, by your faithfulness, the glory off God bee ad-"vanced and his Church edifyed. Besydes, wee beseech your Honour (according unto the exemple of "your predecessors) to bee favorable unto us Strangers, members off the sayd congregations, fled hether "for the truth of Godspell and charytably entertained hitherto in this honorable Citie. We shall be bound "to pray the Lord continually, as hitherto we have done, for your honour, happy, godly, and just govern-"ment, etc."

In 1605 it was found necessary to repair the Church of Austin Friars within and without, and a collection was made for this purpose. The members of the French Church now again sought to set up pretensions to a share in the Church, under power (as they alleged) of the patent of Edward VI. This was successfully resisted, and a long protest made against any such idea by the members of the Dutch Church.

The Papist plot to blow up the Houses of Parliament had its due effect upon the Strangers; Ruytinck filled several pages in giving a long account of the affair, and he wrote besides 176 lines of poetry in Dutch on the subject.

In the same year was founded the library of the Church, and their learned minister wrote a long article on the desirability of doing so, specially mentioning that two registers would be kept; one iu which to enter the books given to the library, with the names of their donors, and another with the books placed in alphabetical order, so that they might easily be found when required for use. This valuable library, which was greatly augmented by Marie Du Boijs[2] in 1650 and by later editions, together with the numerous auto-

---

[1] Buried at St. Helens, Bishopsgate, as Ahasuerus Roger Mortell, 11th Sept., 1603. Burn's Ref., p. 193.

[2] This lady, the widow of Pieter Du Boijs, of London, merchant, left in her will [P.C.C. Bruce 108] £300 as a fund to assist the service of the Church.

raph letters of the early reformers and others, was offered in 1862 by the Consistory of the Church, to be deposited in trust in the Guildhall library, so that the contents might more easily be accessible to the public. This offer was accepted by the Corporation of London on the 23rd July, 1863, the arrangement being finally settled by a deed signed on the 11th April, 1866. These books and manuscripts were most providentially saved from destruction during the fire that destroyed nearly all but the walls of the Church on the 22nd November, 1862, before the transfer of the library had taken place. An admirable catalogue of this collection has been made by Mr. Overall, the able librarian of the Corporation of the city of London, which was printed in 1879.

In 1606 the Common Council passed a resolution on the 15th April, founded on an old statute, that all foreign handycraftsmen, under a penalty of £5, should be prohibited from exercising their craft within the liberties of the city of London. The brethren petitioned the Crown, as they did formerly on a like occasion, finding that the Lord Mayor and Aldermen would pay no attention to their protests. Thanks to the assistance of the Earls of Salisbury and Dorset, to the great contentment of the Strangers, the Privy Council gave orders that the workmen should not be molested.

Certain persons were buried at an early date in the Church; it is recorded that Jacobus Gielis &c., one of the ministers, having died suddenly of the plague on the 19th September, 1607, was interred there.

In 1609 the lofty and beautiful spire, that was on a portion of the Church which had in 1550 been made over to the Strangers, fell down for want of the necessary repair which had been earnestly prayed for on the 4th August, 1600, by the Lord Mayor and Aldermen in a letter to the Marquis of Winchester, in which occurs the following extract : "That by disbursing of a small sum of money, of the value of £50 or £60, your Lordship shall do an excellent work, very helpfull to many, and most gratefull to all, and well English as Strangers." It is recorded, however, "but this took little effect."[1] The Privy Council wrote a letter to the members of the Church, ordering them to rebuild the spire, but an answer was returned that the spire did not belong to that portion of the Church which was given to them by King Edward VI, though they would willingly give a contribution towards doing so. Afterwards the Marquis of Winchester sold the materials of the spire, with the portion of the choir on which it had stood, to Henry Relfe an, an English merchant, who removed what remained of the spire and turned that portion of the choir into a dwelling house."[2]

In 1611 the consistory of the Church bought, after considerable trouble, from the Marquis of Winchester for the sum of £600, a house called the "Kerckof", standing against the Church, with the land adjoining : this property is still in the possession of the Church, and was some few years ago let on a building lease.[3]

"On the 27th November, 1610, a license was granted to the East India Company to admit merchant strangers into their society, to trade and have the same privileges as natives of England."[4]

On the 8th April, 1612, Emanuel van Meteren died, aged 77. He had lived in this country since 1550 and had been connected with all matters that concerned the Strangers, having acted to the greatest satisfaction of the merchants as Netherland Consul. A clever and well-read man, he wrote the history of the Netherland wars which gives one of the best accounts of the desperate resistance of the patriots against the oppressions of their Spanish rulers.

By an order of the Privy Council, dated 17th October, 1612, the Strangers of the Dutch congregation at Colchester were confirmed in "all privileges, liberties, and immunities, and shall be permitted to use their assemblies and congregations in as free, large, and ample manner as hath bene heretofore practised, etc." "Wherefore we will, charge, and command all our Justices of the Peace, Bailifs, and Aldermen of our said town of Colchester to permit and suffer the said Strangers of the Dutch congregation in our said town of Colchester peacefully to governe, use, and enjoy all such liberties, immunities, and freedoms as are intended unto them by this our ordinance and grant without any inditements, presentments, or other molestations to be done unto them or any of them in any wise, etc."[5]

In 1613 the Palsgrave, Frederick V, came to London to marry the King's daughter, the Princess Eliza-

---

(1) Stow's London, Ed. 1720, II, p. 114.
(2) About 12 years ago this house in Old Broad St. was demolished, when some of the columns of the old Church were found standing in their original position. Spacious modern offices now occupy the site.

(3) It was in a deposition, made in 1609 by Emanuel van Meteren concerning this property, that the interesting particulars concerning the Coverdale Bible were stated.
(4) Camden Pub., 1862, VII. State Papers, D.S., Vol. LVIII.

both, when Essex House was placed at his disposal and he was invested with the Order of the Garter. A deputation from the Dutch Church went immediately to congratulate him. It is related that the marriage took place in the Royal Chapel on the 14th February, 1613, with great state and rejoicings both on land and water.[1]

In 1614 a certain knight, Sir Walter Chute, petitioned his Majesty to appoint him to "an office to bee "erected for enregistring of Strangers, with a fee to belong to the same office of one shilling sterling, to "bee payed yearlye for every such Stranger, etc." This the Stranger Churches strongly objected to, and sent in a counter petition in which they stated that at all "our congregations both here in London and "elsewhere, as at Norwich, Cantelbury, Sandwich, Colchester, Southampton, and Yarmouth, there is a true "register kept already off the communicants, both men and women," so that lists could always be furnished "without any charge att all to be imposed upon these poor people." They further pleaded "that laudable "course alwayes observed in England aggreable to all other contries abroade, that Strangers live unter the "protection of the magistrates of the severall townes in wich they abide, and nott under the command of "any particular person, interessed only for his private profitt." The final result was that Sir Julius Cæsar and Sir Thomas Parry were appointed Commissioners of the said office.[2]

On the 9th August, 1615, the Bishop of London made a formal complaint against the Dutch Churches in London and Colchester because certain of their numbers went to English Churches and presented themselves at the communion table, and were therefore protected by the English clergy. He requested that they should continue in their own Churches. Many young people who had been born in this country thought fit, however, to go to worship where they pleased.

At this time there were renewed troubles about the Strangers exercising their trades in the various towns where they were established, neither they nor their children born in England being able to obtain the freedom of the towns for love or money. The Ambassador of the States, Sir Noel Caron, interceded for them with the King, who on the 30th June, 1616, issued an order that as "those Strangers are dayly "and grievously molested and debarred from their worke and labor by sundrye troublesome informers, be "cause the sayd Strangers are nott free off the city, nor have served seaven yeares prentiship," "These "are therefore to will and command all our Courts of Justice, etc., to permit and suffer the sayd Stran "gers, members of the outlandish Churches and their children, to enjoy the continuance of the said favors "etc." Great dissatisfaction arising in the various towns on the appearance of this order, the Strangers set forth a long relation shewing how they benefitted the country and the towns of their adoption, entitled "A shorte and true relation off the state off the Netherlanders in England against divers greevous accusations "off late, by misinformation, layd to their charge."[3]

In the beginning of 1617 the Austin Friars Church was repaired and put in order at a cost of £1,500 which amount was collected by subscription. The King desiring to go to Scotland in this year raised money on loan for that purpose, to which the Dutch merchants and other members of the Church placed their names for the amount of £20,000, security appearing to have been given by the members of the Privy Council.

Ruytinck gave particulars of the imprisonment and the execution of Sir Walter Raleigh on 28th October 1618; he also recorded the following verses written by one of his captains on his death:
"Cease bootlesse teares to weep for him, whose death
"Mayde way to haeven, for his that lent him breath.
"Long lidd hee captive, now at libertie,
"His world of woes turn'd to felicitie.
"What, is hee gone? No, wee enjoy him still,
"That learned worke, the laurell of his quill,
"Shall live and blaze his fame; those only die
"That leave no record to posteritie.
"The end the life, the evening crownes the day.
"For, Samson like his death doth vainquish more
"Than all his lifetyme hee had done before."

About this time a demand on the part of the Bishop of Norwich that the Members of the Stran

([1]) ...entable fact that the Registers of all the Royal prior to about 1700 are missing, one of them are stated by Mr. J. S. Burn, History of Parish Registers, published in 1862, to have been seen and consulted by him.

([2]) No trace of this office could be found at the Record Office on enquiry being made two years ago.

([3]) This is found at length in Ruytinck's MS.

ers' Church of that town should receive the Sacrament kneeling. This the Consistory objected to as the eformed Netherland Church had from the first been in the habit of taking it seated. Petty persecutions if this kind were continually offered, but the Strangers objected and with success to any innovations or hange of customs.

: On the 7th April, 1617, the Lord Mayor and Aldermen brought it about that Sir Ralph Winwood, Kt., ne of His Majesty's Chief Secretaries of State, Sir Fulk Greville, Kt., Chancellor of the Exchequer, and Sir Julius Cæsar, Kt., Master of the Rolls, should call before them four or five of the Aldermen and as aany of the Elders of the Strangers' Churches on the 16th of the same month to "informe themselves off the true state as well concerning the number of Strangers, handicraftsmen, as their continuance and aboad in and about the city." The respective parties having duly appeared and the old complaints of the Corporation heard as well as the justifications of the Strangers, the matter was dismissed, Sir Ralph Winwood having spoken in favor of the latter.

The Corporation however made fresh orders to enumerate the Strangers within the city, with the names f their wives, children, and servants, where they dwelt, what trade they used, and how long they had een resident in the country. This return, the order for which was given on the 1st July, 1617, was to e made separately for each Ward. The return as made by the Dutch congregation was:

HANDICRAFTSMEN.

Strangers, within the citye	181
Strangers, without the citye	260
Their children and servants borne here	432
Free denysens within the citye	36
Free denysens without the citye	41
Their children and servants borne here	96
Borne of parents Strangers within the citye	45
Borne of parents Strangers without the citye	60

MARCHANTS.

Strangers	100
Denysens	72
Borne here of Strangers or denysens	249

The total summe is	1572	persons.
Subduce the natifs	882	
Rest	690	
Subduce the denysens	77	
Rest	613	Strangers.

Both within and without the citye, old and younge, man and wyfe, riche and poore, child and servant, as neere as conveniently wee could gather."

It was deemd prudent by the Consistory to make a remonstrance upon certain of the vexed points, insisted on by the Corporation, and at the same time to give the return asked for. The Elders and Deacons said that this return was presented heretofore to the Privy Council, and that they could not give the names f those who belonged to their congregation, these names being easily ascertained by the officers of he several parishes wherein they dwelt. This answer had to satisfy their Worships for the time, but the Stran[gers] ... the Indies were much prejudiced by the serious disputes between the East India Companies of England and Holland.

In the Hillary Term, 1618, a serious and vexatious suit was commenced in the Star Chamber, in which it was alled that the presence of the Strangers was very prejudicial to the nation on account of their making lace ... y, which they sent out of the country against the statutes, whereby the bullion n the country was diminished. Sir Noel Caron, the Ambassador for the States, was instructed in the points necessary to lay the case for the Strangers before the King; he also laid before him their humble application. His Majesty who, as above related, had borrowed two years previously £20,000 from the Strangers, evidently thought them fair game for robbing and for extorting large sums of money from, as the following account will clearly show. The interest on the loan had only been paid for one year, and as the King's ministers had signed bonds of security they, as well as the lenders of the money, had become anxious about the repayment of principal and interest. The King sent the instruction of the Envoy and the supplication of the Strangers to the Solicitor-General, who immediately pushed on proceedings and issued a writ of *ne exeas regno*. The bail demanded for each defendant, 40 in number, was fixed at £2,000, which if not found, the prison of Newgate had to be taken as a residence. This sharp practice was strongly remonstrated against by Sir Noel Caron and the members of the Church. They represented that by the issue of the writ "your sayd suppliants are discredited, both at home and abroad, as if they were fugitifs and did intend upon malice to voyde the realme."

All was useless; the proceedings took their course and a number of disreputable witnesses, "bankrupts, beggars, thieves, rogues, and such like," swore that the merchant Strangers had sent no less than £2,740,000 in three years out of the country. The answer to this was, that no such sum had been coined in that period. It was also proved that one of the witnesses, by name Escaillet, a dissolute Walloon, had revealed how he had been released from jail by some of the agents concerned in the scheme, who paid his execution of £15 and who offered him rewards if he would give the evidence desired. It was demanded that these witnesses should all be cross-examined by counsel; this, however, was against the practice in the Star Chamber, where those accused were only allowed to give written answers on oath to the evidence against them, and that in due form by counsel.

On the 17th June, 1619, the King being informed that there was no great amount of evidence, wrote from Whitehall to the Judges that, understanding there were 160 persons charged by the Attorney General and that evidence was only produced against 18 or 19 of the delinquents, "wee have nott found it fitt to "proceed in a cause so exemplaric, and of so great importance by pesle mesle, or by fractions, butt rather "there by to require you to putt over the sentencing thereof, till all the defendants may receave their "judgement simul and semul, so as both the greatnes and the correction of the offence may bee more con-"spicuous, and our princely justice more publickly represented in the whole grosse and number of th'offen-"dors, being all associated in the censure as in the crime, and in our sayd Attorny's bill. And so, not "doubting of our discreet respect and care therein, wee bid you farewel."

The "princely justice" of the period by this time had become known to the Strangers, who moved heaven and earth to obtain real justice. The government in Holland, as well as the merchants there, took the matter up, for universal ruin impended over all the merchants trading between the two countries, letters being written to all persons of importance likely to help the Strangers. But all to no purpose, the Solicitor-General alleged that at least £7,000,000 of coin and bullion had been sent out of the country by the foreign merchants against the royal prerogative, statutes and proclamations. The evidence produced against some of the defendants was of a period before they had come to this country; they were in despair, the expenses for legal assistance and counsel being so very heavy that they found difficulty even in getting copies of the proceedings.

The Ambassador Caron laid before the King a carefully drawn up statement, shewing the impossibility of the truth of the evidence and also of the character of the witnesses. All to no effect; the judges, thir-teen in number, pronounced all guilty and condemned the following persons to pay fines, viz.

Courten	£20,000	J. Wolf	£5,000
Burlamachi	2,000	Zwester	4,000
Van de Putte	3,000	Rijckman	2,000
La Barre	20,000	Robert de Leau	20,000
Wybo	6,000	Stampeel	4,000
Trioen	15,000	Lievens	2,000
P. van Loor	8,000	Luls	8,000
Jacques de Beste	7,000	Clerck	2,000
Ph. Jacobs	5,000	Ant. Trioen	5,000

London was in an uproar; the victims, being sentenced, had to pay or after a short period to be sent to the Fleet prison. Their goods were seized, their bails were estreated, and everything was carried out with the greatest rigour. Petitions from all quarters came in to the King appealing to his clemency. Langele came over at the commencement of 1620 with letters from the States of Holland and from Carleton, the English Ambassador at Hague, who sent special letters on the subject. It was represented to the Privy Council that some of the merchant Strangers "are hardly able to pay their fines; many forswear the facts," and P. van Loro declared that he would leave England, " for those who on such evidence take away his oods, may take away his life if they chose, and that the whole affair would be injurious both in England and to the English abroad."[1]

Caron again interceded with the King at Easter time, when it was arranged that the fines should be reduced to £ 60,000. Those fined paid £ 34,000, with the exception of Van Lore, de Quester, Burlamachie, and Gillis van de Putte,[2] who were reserved to be dealt with according to the King's pleasure. The loan £ 20,000, with overdue interest amounting to £ 6,000, made up the required amount. On this settlement being made, Caron gave up the security that he had received from the King.

Fresh difficulties now arose as to the respective amounts due to the merchants on account of the loan, and as to the portions of fines remitted; the seizure of the goods of all those fined being still maintained, some of the witnesses confessed publicly on the Exchange that they had sworn falsely.

On the 3rd January, 1621, Simeon Ruytinck died, having only about a week before preached on Christmas Day. He was a great loss to the Church, being eager and active in all good works. Verses were written to his remembrance by many, in Latin and Dutch, which were collected and published by Izaak Elzevier, at Leyden.[3] Besides writing the history of the more remarkable events of the Dutch Strangers and Church in London, he left behind him seven works published during his lifetime.

On the 7th January, 1630, the Privy Council had before them a complaint from the Church at Norwich "which had continued a congregation in that citty by itselfe for the space of 60 yeares and more," to the "feet that many of their richer members wished to leave the congregation in order to be relieved from the burden of the subscriptions and the support of the Dutch poor, contrary to the order of Council of the 10th October, 1621, "for redresse of the like evil attempted by some of the Wallon congregation." The Privy Council ordered that the said decree should be enforced against all members of the Dutch Church, "although borne within this kingdom," "provided that nothing in this order contained have relation to Matthew de Boys, or doe any way binde him, he having formerly had sufficient license for his removall out of the Dutch congregation: onely he is to contribute to the poor of the Dutch congregation."[4]

A few months later the Star Chamber trouble recommenced. Sir Noel Caron, having disbursed £ 26,000 of his own money on account of the merchants in order to discharge their several fines, desired repayment. This was not forthcoming, and there was no other course for him but to appeal again to the King; this time, however, for himself. The Privy Council on the 5th July, 1621, wrote to their "verie loving friends," the ministers, elders, deacons, and the rest of the Dutch Church to arrange with those of the French Church that they might agree among themselves to do what in their "owne discretions shall be equal and reasonable for the levying and present satisfaction" of the amount due to the Ambassador. The natural answer of the Church, as a body, was to "informe their Lordships that the agreement of that great sum of £ 60,000 was never caused or procured by the meanes of persuasion of our Church." It begged, therefore, to be discharged "from the burden of such a business." The answer to this was that the excuse was not sufficient, and that the amount must be raised voluntarily or by a levy. Extraordinary Ambassadors having been sent by the States' General to London to arrange a payment of 800,000 guilders due by the Dutch East India Company to that of England, Caron referred to them the matter of the £ 26,000, of which he was out of pocket and responsible for in the State robbery of the Strangers. So the affair remained until 8th June, 1624, when the Ambassador induced the Privy Council to write again to the members of the Church, whose answer was to refer the Council to their former letter of 21st July, 1621, and to state also that Sir Noel Caron had employed one Mr. Henry Wood as his agent, therefore they begged to be excused from a business which would make "our persons very odious and our ministery unfruitfull." It is related in the manuscript history, continued by Calandrinus, that "the good Mr. Caron died at the end of this year (1624); he had done great good to the Fatherland," but no more is said of how he or his executors fared in the matter of the £ 26,000.

In March, 1622, a new Dutch congregation, under the rule of the Church in London, met together at Mortlake for the convenience of the Flemish tapestry weavers who had come from the tapestry works at Paris, established by Henry IV, and elsewhere in the previous year to the factory built about 1619 on the banks of the Thames by Sir Francis Crane, Kt. He had obtained a license dated 20th March, 1621, (O.S.) from the Archbishop of Canterbury, for this congregation to assemble in the parish Church of Mortlake,

(1) State Paper, D.S., James I, CXII, 1. Ruytinck's MS.
(2) Sir Peter van Lore had to pay £7,000 and Van de Putte £ 1,000, which sums were outside the accord. The two others were let off free.

(3) 1622 in 4to., and a second part in the same year.
(4) Kerckelyke Vryheden, D. Ch. Archives.

at Sir Francis Crane's house, or in any other suitable place. It was arranged that a minister and an Elder should be sent from London, when it was requisite, to perform the service. Many baptisms and some marriages of the Mortlake congregation were entered in the registers of Austin Friars and, at a later date, in the parish registers of Mortlake.

On 8th July, 1623, James I wrote to the King of Denmark to request that Francis Klein or Cleyne, a painter and a native of Rostock, might be allowed to come to England as soon as his services could be dispensed with. He arrived in London at the close of the year with his family and was given a gratuity of £100 a year by the King and his successor until the beginning of the civil wars. He was employed at the Mortlake tapestry works, "his designing being the soul, as the working is the body of that mystery."[1] Charles I granted an annuity of £2,000 for ten years, one moiety in payment of tapestry work and the other for the advancement and maintenance of the factory.[2] The five cartoons of Rafaele in tapestry work, now at Hampton Court, were copied from the original designs of that artist, which had been specially bought by the King as patterns. In a petition made about 1637 by the weavers who were nearly all from the Low Countries, it would appear that they were about one hundred and forty in number.[3]

In a survey made in September, 1651, by the Parliamentary Commissioners, the extent of these premises at Mortlake, situated in Queen's Head Court, is given, part of which still is standing, having been purchased and turned into small dwelling houses by Mr. Wigan of Cromwell House, Mortlake. The factory had been surrendered to the King by Sir Richard Crane, the brother of Sir Francis, then deceased, and was seized by the Commissioners as Crown property in the time of the Commonwealth. During that period the tapestry house remained in the occupation of John Holliburie (Hullenberge) who in the survey is mentioned as the master-workman.

The numbers of the Strangers in England had greatly increased by 1621, when those in London were stated to be ten thousand in number, carrying on 121 different trades.[4]

The industry of the refugees caused much interference with the trade of the citizens, who harassed them in every possible way by laying informations against them, so the Strangers wrote to the King in 1622, stating that they had paid contributions both to the parishes and to their own congregations, that they bore offices in both, that they paid duties to their halls and double ones to their Parish Churches, and that they kept their own poor, many in number, from begging in the streets. They therefore petitioned to be relieved from persecution by the Corporation of London according to the King's "whryting" dated June, 1616. The answer from the King, 8th June, 1622, informed them that "Commissioners in whome we put our "confidence" had been appointed, "to which wee wish the Petitioners to conforme themselves without "troubling us further in that whereof we are resolved." The result was that the poor Strangers had the following new taxes imposed on them, viz. "of handicraftsmen, for each master of a family, 40 sh. per "annum, and fore every servant, being a Stranger, 20 sh. per annum, and for every servant, being English "and not bound for seven years by Indenture, 10 sh. per annum, and of merchants using exportacion and "importation of goods, fore each master, 26 sh. 8d. per annum........and the value of half the customs "of the goods they buy and sell." On renewed petitions to the King, the above taxes were suspended until further orders, according to an order of Council, dated 7th March, 1622. In other towns the impositions on the Strangers had been heavy.

In March, 1620, the congregation at Norwich petitioned the Council that the English householders should pay twenty pence in the pound on their house rents for support of their ministers, as was paid by them.[5]

At this period there were Commissioners for the regulation of the Strangers, whose duty it was to enforce all the laws and orders concerning them and to see that the returns of their names, residences, and occupations were duly sent in.[6]

In June, 1621, it was proposed that the Strangers should pay twelve pence in the pound on their profits

(1) Manning's Surrey, III, 302. Rymer's Feed., XVIII, 112.
(2) Idem. and Brayley's Surrey, III, 469. The note of articles to be agreed upon between the King and "the workmen" touching a certain manufacture. £2,000 a year was to be assigned by His Majesty for its maintenance; the workmen were to make 600 ells yearly; some of the Hospital boys were to be trained up to it, and Mr. Cleyne the painter was to have £250 per annum and to choose an assistant. Endorsed Capt. Crane.

(3) State Papers, D.S., CCCXL, 51.
(4) Camden Soc., pub. 1862, IV. (State Papers, D.S. 1621, No. 146); Ib. XCVIII, 113.
(5) State Papers, D.S., James I, CXIX, 31 Jan., 1621.
(6) Idem, CXXXI, 12, 13, 14.

of trade;[1] that each householder should also pay annually twelve pence, and all others above seven years old six pence, as registration fees.[2]

In 1624, there was much trouble about the new tax, called Pirate Money, to be applied in suppressing the pirates of Algiers and Tunis, of one per cent. on all sales, which the English merchants did not collect until nine months after the King's order, though the Strangers had done so immediately. The latter considered that their collections, which had not been handed over, should go towards the Star Chamber business and that all should start fairly together. This arrangement was soon discovered, and, five or six years afterwards, the sum of £ 1,600 so applied was claimed by the Treasury.

It is put on record by Calandrinus that the "learned King James died in 1625"; no lamentations apparently being made by the Strangers who had been fleeced to the uttermost by His Majesty. Monsieur Gilbert Primerose, minister of the French Church, on behalf of the deputation of ministers and Elders of the foreign Churches, congratulated Charles I on his accession in a long and laudatory oration, in which the protection of the King was duly prayed for. This was granted in a few words.

On the occasion of the royal entry of the King and Queen into London in February, 1626, an elaborate triumphal arch was erected as before by the Dutch congregation in the centre of "Gracious Street," the designer of it being Bernard Jansen.[3] Then, as at the time of the accession of James I, the numerous deaths from the plague caused a diminution of the public rejoicings, the Dutch congregation suffering severely as at the last visitation.

About this time, by the consent of the Archbishop, the Churches of the Spaniards and Italians in London were united into one congregation.

Sir Henry Appleton, who had property in Canvey Island, in Essex, near to Southend, which had belonged to his grandfather Sir Roger Appleton in 1557, together with other proprietors "agreed to give one third of the island in fee simple to Joas Croppenburgh, a Dutchman, in consideration of his securing the island from the overflowing of the tides of the river Thames."[4]

On the 12th February, 1628, Croppenburgh and the two hundred poor Netherland Strangers, engaged for some few years previously in banking and cultivating this island, petitioned the King, praying for a reference to the Bishop of London, as they required permission to establish a small Church where service could be performed in their own language. The King granted the request, and Montaigne, Bishop of London, requested the Dutch congregation in London to appoint a minister. This was done, and a wooden chapel was erected. In 1712, it having become decayed, a new one was built by Mr. Edgar, an officer in the victualling office. In 1745 the present Church was erected, partly by a contribution of the inhabitants, but chiefly by a benefaction of Daniel Scratton, Esq., owner of property at Prittlewell. The latter endowed the Church with £ 20 a year to enable the vicar of Prittlewell and his curate to preach twenty sermons yearly in the chapel on the island.[5]

At the Synod held in London 1641, Cornelis Jacobsen, minister of the chapel, represented the congregation of Canvey Island. At those of 1644 and 1646 Abraham van der Bossche; and in 1647 Daniel Keteiar. In 1655 the chapel being without a minister, Joannes Beutacq was provisionally appointed; he, however, being accused of scandal, and the matter brought before the Synod held in London in 1655, was suspended and condemned. An extraordinary Synod was held in the following January to consider the cases of Beutacq and Joannes Aiton, the latter having caused trouble in the Church at Sandwich. The matter of Canvey Island was so far arranged that Beutacq was allowed to go in peace if he would cease annoying in any way the Church there.[6]

In 1622 an arrangement was made between the King, certain proprietors, and Cornelius Liens and Cornelius Vermuyden, the latter a Dutch engineer skilled in such works, to drain 360,000 acres of fen land in the counties of Northampton, Lincoln, Cambridge, and Essex. The owners of the fen land granted to the King 120,000 acres, reserving 50,000 acres for themselves and setting aside 20,000 acres to supply the funds necessary to keep the remainder perpetually dry.[7] In the following year the Commissioners of Sewers in Essex complained to the Council that Vermuyden had made the state of the land worse than before.[8] On the 16th July, 1625, Cornelius Vermuyden received a grant of land in Essex in recompense of

(1) State Papers, D.S., CXXI, 161.
(2) Idem, CXXII, 51.
(3) A long description of this arch is given by Calandrinus—vide Ruytinck's MS.
(4) Wright's Essex, Vol. II, p. 589.

(5) Wright's Essex, and Burn's Hist. Foreign Refugees, p. 220.
(6) Colloquium Book, Archives, Austin Friars.
(7) State Papers, D.S., CXXVII, 145.
(8) Idem, CXXXVIII, 2.

his charges for work done in the repair of Dagenham Breach.[1]   In 1626 he und
of fen land in the levels of Hatfield Chase, near to the river Humber.   The capi
Flemish and French refugees were engaged as labourers.   Troubles soon arose
the adjoining landowners, as well as the fishermen and the men who caug
broke the embankments and attacked the workmen, who killed an Englishman.
employed some native labourers and compensated those whose interests were affe
or Priem, who was born at Ypres (grandfather of the Rev. Abraham de la P.
interesting diary has been published by the Surtees Society) was associated w
work.   It is recorded that the latter " at the incredible labor and charges of J
" drain Hatfield Chase, whose name deserves a thousand times more to be hono
" in all our histories than Scaurus was in those of Rome, for draining a lake i
" as this."[2]   Matthew, Mark, and Luke Valkenburgh also had a large shar
3,204 acres of the reclaimed land.[3]

 In 1629 Cornelius Vermuyden was knighted, and a grant of the land recover
ment of a yearly rent and a fine of £ 10,000.[4]   In the grant that Sir Corne
manor and chase at Hatfield, he had the power to erect a building for religious
workmen might have service performed in their own language.   A chapel was c
a hamlet in the parish of Belton, in Lincolnshire, close to the borders of Yorks
Bedloe, a merchant, who lost much of the money expended, it not being repaid
was M. Berchett, who died 18th April, 1655 ; he was succeeded by Philippe
5th September, 1655; Jean Deckerhuel was minister in 1659; after him M.
in 1664 ; Jacques de la Porte in 1676 ; and finally John Conrad de Werneley
which date the services appear to have been discontinued.[5]   It would appear t
by the foreign workmen, some two hundred families, who baptized their child
ment in it, but Archbishop Niele compelled them to discharge their ministe
Churches.[6]   The Register of this chapel at Sandtoft, which was in existence v
1828, is not now to be found.[7]

 "About the year 1638-9 the Levels of Ancham (Ancholme) were drair
" Dutch, several of whom were overseers in the business."   " The great sluce
" cost above £ 3,000, and had twenty four doors."[8]

 Vermuyden then undertook the drainage of the Great Level, which spread :
36,000 acres being covered by the overflow of the water.   The Earl of Be
ousted from the work by Commissioners appointed, a grant of land being give
The King took the matter into his own hands, and Vermuyden was re-appoint
works.[9]

 About the year 1637, by arrangements made with the postmasters abroad, "
" ded beyond the Channel, and merchants were able to send a single letter to
" to Paris for ninepence."[10]

 In 1640 the Dutch and French merchants were asked to lend money to the
their late treatment refused to do so.   A new imposition of three pence in the
the goods of the Strangers in the port of London.   By a docquet, dated 28th I
the impositions for the years 1640 and 1641 was granted to the Earl of Ne
£ 10,000, that sum having been lent to His Majesty with interest at 8 per
made in favor of the Secretary Windebank for £ 3,000, also lent to His Majest

 Archbishop Laud attempted to annul the religious privileges of the Strang
on the 24th March, 1641-2, that there should be no more preaching or divine
at Great Yarmouth.   This did not suit the Bailiffs and Aldermen of that town,

(1) State Papers, D.S., IV, 67.
(2) Diary of Abraham de la Pryme. Surtees Society,
      pub. 1869, p. xv.
(3) Ib., Note p. 5.
(4) Gardiner's Fall of Monarchy of Charles I, Vol. I,
      p. 83.
(5) Pryme's Diary, Note p. 4, quoting from Hunter,
      S. Yorkshire, I, 165, 169, 170.

(6) State Papers, D.S.
(7) Pryme's Diary, Note
(8) Ib., p. 115.
(9) Gardiner, Fall of Mo
(10) Ib., Vol. I, p. 83.
(11) State Papers, D.S., C
      6.

the Dutchmen had brought would soon be lost by their departure, so they, on the 31st March, 1611, petitioned the King to annul the order, made a week before, to discontinue the service at the Dutch Church which was a house formerly belonging to Thomas de Drayton, temp. Edward III., and had been used for that purpose for forty years.[1] On behalf of all the Strangers' Churches, complaint was made to the Privy Council of the action of the Archbishop who, since 1633, had interfered with their charter of exemption from interference in their Church government, granted by Edward VI and renewed by his successor and the then King. The injunctions delivered April 13th, 1635, aimed at making the Strangers' Churches conform to the Church of England. These were, "1st, that all the natives of the Dutch and Walloon congregations in his Grace's diocese are to resort to their several parish Churches to hear divine service and sermons, and to perform all duties required of parishioners. 2nd, that the ministers and all others of the Dutch and Walloon congregations, who are not natives and born subjects to the King, or any other Strangers that shall come over, while they remain Strangers, may use their own discipline as formerly; yet it is thought fit the English liturgy should be translated into French and Dutch for the better fitting of their children to the English Church government."[2]

The members of the Dutch and Walloon or French Churches at Norwich petitioned Archbishop Laud on the 21st February, 1635, n.s., through Dr. Richard Montague, Bishop of Norwich, and again directly on the 26th June, that the injunctions lately issued by his Grace to the three congregations of Strangers at Canterbury, Sandwich, and Maidstone should be withdrawn.

The evil results, financially, both to the Strangers and to the towns where they dwelt were duly pointed out, as the charge of the poor would be thrown on the parishes, to say nothing of the horror felt at the idea of observing rites and ceremonies that they were not acquainted with, "yea, are offensive to some beyond the seas, from whence they shall be called." The answer given by Laud, on the 19th August of the same year, was that the children of the aliens might continue in the congregations, but that the second descent born in England should resort to their several parish Churches.[3]

These troubles somewhat ceased on the impeachment of Laud in December, 1640, but it was considered necessary to apply for an Act of Parliament to finally settle the position of the foreign Churches. In a draft of the Act presented to Parliament in 1642 the following Churches are named: London, Norwich, Canterbury, Colchester, Sandwich, Yarmouth, Southampton, Maidstone, and the Isle of Canvey, the Isle of Axolme in Lincolnshire, and (Hatfield Chase) in the County of York. In the same act there was a clause to the following effect: "Fore as much as in the said foraigne Churches there is noe use of licenses for marriage nor ought there any marriages to be there solempnized without publishing of bannes, whereby children and inferiors are kept in better awe of their parents and guardians, not doeinge to mary without their consents, and divers other abuses prevented. Bee it enacted by the authority aforesaid, that noe Bishop or other minister or officer of any ecclesiasticall court of this kingdom of England shall give or grant any license of marriage to or for any member of the same foraigne reformed Churches."

A request was also made to the House of Lords "in the behalfe of the reformed Forreine Churches in the realme" on the 21st January, 1842-3, "that there may be an ordinance of Parliament for setting of the liberty and exercise of their religion and discipline as they are used beyond the seas respectively in the reformed Churches of their severall nations, which they have hitherto enjoyed by the charter of King Edward VI (of ever blessed memory) autorized by his Parliament and the gracious favor of all our succeeding Princes of the reformed religion, Queen Elizabeth, King James, and His Majestie that now is, King Charles, whome God long preserve. In particular, 1.—That they may have free liberty to chose and ordaine their own ministers and all other officers belonging to their Churches according to their discipline. 2.—That no member of their congregations, being under the censure of their discipline by reason of some scandalous offence committed, be received in any member of any other Church with out a certificate from his own Church. 3.—That no Church or congregation of Forreiners be autorized in this realme who are not subject respectively to the Synods of their severall nations."

The following answer was returned by their Lordships: "Die Sabbathi, 21 January, 1642. O.S. The House being petitioned by two severall petitions, the one from the members of the French Church in London, subscribed to the said petition, and the other from the ministers and elders of the Dutch and Ffrench congregation within the city of London; both which petitions were referred to the consideration of the Lords' Committees perticularly appointed by the House, whose Lordships having mett and heard

---

[1] State Papers, D.S., CCCCLXXVIII, 80. Swinden's Yarmouth, p. 849.

[2] State Papers, D.S., CCCCLXXVIII, 80.
[3] Agnew's French Pr : Ref. Vol I, p. 13.

"the parties interressed therein, Report was made from the Committee from the Ffrench and Dutch
"Church, where upon it is ordered by the Lords in Parliament, that the Ffrench and Dutch congregacion
"shalle have the libertie and discipline as it is used beyond the seas in the reformed Churches in severall
"nations, and as by the charter of King Edward the Sixt, they have enjoyed it in his Raigne, and since in
"the severall Raignes of Queene Elizabeth and King James, as well as in the Raigne of His Majesty that
"now is; and lastly, that they may have free liberty to choose and ordaine their owne mynisters, and all
"other officers belonging to their Churches, according to their discipline, and as they have don heeretofore;
"and also that noe member of their said congregation being under the censure of their discipline, by reason
"of some scandalous offense committed by him, shall be receaved as a member of any other Church, with-
"out a certificate from his owne Church.

                                         "Signed, Jo: Browne, Cleric Parliamentore."

On the report of the Earl of Northumberland, a similar entry was made on the same day in the book of
the proceedings of the House of Lords.

In the beginning of October, 1645, the Parliament ordered a solemn thanksgiving-day for "the great
victories given by the Lord" at Bristol, Devizes, in Scotland, and near Chester; this was duly observed by
the Church at Austin Friars. On Thursday, 7th May, 1646, another thanksgiving-day was appointed to
be everywhere kept "for the victories that God lately has vouchsafed to our armies" at Exeter, Banbury,
Newark, and elsewhere. On November 28th, 1647, thanks were returned in the Dutch Church for the
victory in Ireland. In February, 1657, thanks were returned for the delivery of "his Highness the Lord
Protector" from great danger.[1]

On the death of Oliver Cromwell, the foreign Churches congratulated Richard Cromwell on his accession
as Lord Protector, who returned, 4th October, 1658, the following characteristic answer to the deputation:
"Gentlemen, Your expressions are of the best of Christians, concerning your losse and mine. It is indeed
"a great losse for you, for me, and for all the Protestant Churches. God alone is he that can make up
"that breach. Your expressions oblige me to be your friend. For your good wishes and prayers I owe you
"love. I look upon you as the heads and fathers of the severall forrein Churches which you represent.
"As Strangers you are to be pittied and as Christian Strangers you are to be valued. You are members of
"Christ and I hope so am I. I will love you as I love myselfe. Christ is the master, and the magistrate
"is but a servant. And shall a servant lift up himselfe against his master? Shall I hurt my hand? Much
"lesse suffer a member of Christ to be injured. I must confesse I am somewhat surprized to enlardge
"upon such a discourse as yours; but I shall wrap up all in this. You may be confident that I will
"maintaine you in your persons and in your liberties, religious and civill: and if any will hurt you I will
"defend you. And I will also procure the liberty of the afflicted Churches abroad. We are in the same
"bottom, and I shall bid defiance to all your and mine enemies."[2]

On the 6th November, 1659, a collection was made for the restoration of the Austin Friars Church.

The majority of the Dutch congregation in London sympathised with the Parliamentary side, though
there were some thirty Strangers who, in 1660, petitioned the King through Edward Love for denization,
on account of their loyalty in late times.[3]

On the accession of Charles II, the ministers of the Dutch Church were quite equal to the occasion, and
prayed with their congregation on the 28th June, 1660, more fervently than ever, and gave thanks to the
Lord for the blessed restoration.[4] All the Strangers who could prove their loyalty to the throne during the
Commonwealth came forward to ask for letters of denization, which were granted more freely than hitherto.

In the Act of Uniformity, made 13 and 14 Charles II, provision was made and a clause inserted in
favour of the Dutch and French protestant Churches in England. It was felt, however, that this did
not sufficiently make the foreign Churches secure from the penalties to which dissenters from the Church
of England were liable. A case for the foreign Churches was drawn up and printed for presentation to
Parliament, praying that "a proviso or clause may be added to a bill then depending for preventing the
growth of schism and for the further security of the Church of England," which would free those congregations from the penalties imposed on dissenters, and would enable them to continue their services in the
Dutch and French languages.

The destruction by the great fire of the greater part of London in 1666 brought serious trouble to the

(1) "Afkonding" book, Dutch Church Archives.
(2) Dutch Ch. Archives, Kerkelyke Vryheden, p. 27.
(3) State Papers, D.S., Vol. VII, 116.

(4) Memorandum or Afconding Book, Austin Friars
    Archives.

rangers resident there. They, in common with the citizens, found themselves homeless with the loss of
ir property, and besides they incurred the odium of all in consequence of a common belief that the dis-
er had been caused by some of their number. Cornelius Rietvelt, a Dutch baker, and others were com-
tted to the Gate House, Westminster, on a rumour that they had set their own houses on fire. They
titioned Lord Arlington for release, stating that such a charge was false, and complaining that the mob
d robbed them of all their goods.[1] One, Silas Taylor, wrote to Mr. Williamson, the Secretary of Lord
lington, from Harwich that there was a report that the great fire in London was believed to be the doing
the Dutch and French, and he hoped that they would be found out and made an example of.[2]
A broadsheet of " London's lamentation on its distruction by a consuming fire " dated 6th September,
66, described the progress of the fire, which broke out September 2nd in a French baker's house in Pud-
ng Lane, and named the French, Dutch, and Walloons as the originators of it.[3] A printed sheet in the
ndon Gazette, 10 September, 1666, gave " a true relation of that sad and deplorable fire " which broke
t 2nd September and was almost extinguished on the Thursday following. On the evening of that day
burst out again in the Temple, but was mastered by the Duke of York, who watched all night in person.
vers Dutch and French were arrested and severely examined by Lord Chief Justice Kelynge and others ; but
e manner of the burning, all in a train as it was blown forwards, proved it to be the heavy hand of God.[4]
is official notice did not allay the prejudice against the Strangers. Edward Taylor, a child 10 years of
e, the son of John Taylor, of York Street, Covent Garden, was examined by John, Lord Lovelace on the
h September, and he stated that he was with his father and his uncle, John Taylor, a Dutchman, and
t on the Saturday night they threw two fireballs in at an open window in Pudding Lane, and the same
Thomas Street, Fleet Street, and the Old Exchange : that they did the same for two or three days and
ghts afterwards ; also that some Frenchmen and Dutchmen, both men and women, went about the city
th fireballs. He also stated that his uncle gave his father seven pounds to undertake the business.[5]
Thomas Waade wrote from Whitby to Mr. Williamson that the destruction of London by fire was reported
be a hellish contrivance of the French, Hollanders, and fanatic party.[6] H. Muddiman wrote from
hitehall to Sir Edward Mansell on the 20th October, 1666, that the wretched Frenchman, who said he
ed London, had been executed at Tyburn, but that he denied the fact at the gallows.[7]
Though no accounts can be found of the direct effects of this disastrous fire on the Strangers connected
ith the Dutch Church, the result of the collections made in the Austin Friars Church shows the dimin-
hed resources of the congregations. In 1648, £520. 18s. 0d. were collected for the Church at Colches-
r ; in 1651, £111. 8s. 0d. for the Church at Sandwich ; in 1655, £261. 10s. 0d. for the Churches of
e Valleys of Piedmont. No other collection seems to have been made until 1675, when only £20 was
ntributed for a distressed Church in Cullickerland. After that date to 1687 the highest amount was
30, but generally only £10 was collected.[8] The French congregation was brought so low by the fire
at the members could not afford to pay their minister the small allowance which they had been accustomed
give him.[9]
Providentially the fire, though it nearly approached, did not reach the Austin Friars Church, so that the
rangers from the Low Countries had not the additional grief of seeing their "Jesus Tempel" consumed by
e flames as were nearly all the parish Churches of the City.
Before the revocation of the Edict of Nantes the Protestants in France were preparing to fly for refuge
om the persecution they clearly saw awaiting them, and in 1681 Henry Savile, the British Envoy in Paris,
ote to Mr. Jenkins, the Secretary of State, for facilities to be afforded to those who might take shelter in
ngland. King Charles II., by order in Council of the 21st July, of that year, promised to grant free
ters of denization under the great seal to all Protestants " who shall come hither for refuge and reside
re." The policy of the Government was most favorable for the religious refugees and little is to be
und of this period concerning the members of the Dutch congregation, who no doubt took advantage of all
ivileges granted to refugees on account of the troubles of their French brethren who came over in great
mbers on the revocation of the Edict of Nantes in 1685, which "drove into exile over 50,000 of the most
eful and industrious inhabitants of France.[11]
During the reign of Charles II and James II, the congregations of the Dutch Churches in England

[1] State Papers, D.S., CLXX, 62.
[2] Ib., CLXX, 93.
[3] Ib., CLXXX, 121.
[4] Ib., No. 150.
[5] Ib., CLXXI, 11.

[6] State Papers, D.S., Ib., 111.
[7] Ib., CLXXV, 111.
[8] Dutch Church Archives.
[9] State Papers, CLXXXIII, 85.
[10] Agnew's French Pr : Ref. Hist. Intr., p. 26.
[11] Burn's Ref., p. 17.

greatly decreased in number. The times had become quieter abroad so that many re
lands taking with them certificates of having been members of the foreign congregati
enabled them to join the Churches of the towns they settled in. Others went to
parish Churches.

On the 4th February, 1672-3, an Act for the naturalisation of "any person beir
born beyond the seas under foreign jurisdiction" was brought into the House of
result of the "great advantage found during the reign of some of your Majesty's roy
"manufactures which, having been taught by foreigners have since been practised
"improvement of the riches of this your Majesty's kingdom."

An amendment was made in Committee, 27th March, which limited the benefi
naturalized within five years from the 25th March, 1673-4. Another amendment re
the names of persons naturalized under the Act to be registered at the next Gen
When naturalized it was necessary for proof to be produced of their having receive
ding to the usage of the Church of England.

Many of the Strangers had become very wealthy by careful habits and successful
qualified by naturalization or by becoming English by birth, bought landed estates
country. The children of the more wealthy aliens generally allied themselves by
families, and soon their names alone betrayed their foreign descent, and these in s
English by altered spelling.

The coming to England of William, Prince of Orange,[2] the great grandson of W
successfully resisted the tyranny of Philip II, and freed the States of Holland from
hailed with joy by the descendants of the Netherland refugees. Their numbers w
by the host of Dutchmen of all conditions who came with him and followed his foo
to the throne. These were soon advanced to fame and fortune, obtaining high appe
and navy, and, in consequence, great odium and ill will was shewn to all the D:

In 1694 a Bill was brought into Parliament for naturalizing all Protestant alie
after being read a second time. Sir John Knight, M.P. for Bristol, represented hi
amendment "That the Sergeant be commanded to open the doors, and let us first l
House and then foreigners out of the kingdom.[3]

It was probably in opposition to this Bill that the Corporation drew up and prin
city of London in relation to the Bill for a general naturalization of all foreign Prote
minutely into the history of all the rights, liberties, and privileges claimed by th
and citizens of London, confirmed to them as asserted, not only by the Statute of :
the Statutes of 1 and 2 Edward III, 7 Richard II, 2 Edward IV, letters patent, 20t
Rot. Claus. 12 Hen. VI, M. 18 dorso., 4 Henry VIII, 22 Henry VIII, cap 8, 12
"officers of package, scavage, balliage, and portage of any goods or merchandizes c
born within this kingdom, or unfreemen, imported or exported into or out of the
liberties or ports thereof, unto or from the parts beyond the seas, etc." were "a1
and rightfully due to the Mayor and Commonalty and citizens of the city of London
general naturalization of all foreign Protestants now depending pass into law, the
tirely lost," etc., etc.

The King's partiality to his countrymen caused great jealousy, which was referre
True-born Englishman."

> "We blame the King that he relies too much
> On Strangers, Germans, Hugonots, and Dutch,
> And seldom does his just affairs of State
> To English Councillors communicate.
> The fact might well be answer'd thus :
> He has so often been betrayed by us.
> He must have been a madman to rely
> On English gentlemen's fidelity,
> For (laying other argument aside),
> This thought might mortify our English pride,
> That foreigners have faithfully obey'd him,
> And none but Englishmen have e'er betray'd him."[5]

(1) 9th Report, Commission on Historical MSS., Part II,   (3) Agnew, Hist. Intro., p. 51.
      p. 19.   (4) Printed Case, etc.
(2) Crowned with Queen Mary, 13 Feb., 1688-9.   (5) Agnew, Hist. Intro., p. 36.

King William III, wishing to establish the manufactory of linen in Ireland, invited Louis Crommelin rom Holland in 1698, who was then living at Amsterdam, the head quarters of the extensive linen trade hat had been carried on with so great success for very many years, cargoes being exported regularly to ingland, France, and other countries. Du Pin had started a corporation to carry on this manufacture 1 Ireland in 1692, by power of letters patent from the King and Queen, but there was so much discord etween the shareholders that it was soon discontinued.[1] By 17th and 18th Car. II, cap. 9, Irish acts, andlords and tenants were obliged under penalty to cultivate a certain porportion of the land with flax; he Sheriffs were empowered to levy for twenty years £20 in each county for prizes to those who produced he three best webs of cloth. This was extended for ten years more by a subsequent act.[2]

Crommelin with his family first settled at Lisnagarvey, and afterwards at Lisburn, co. Antrim, and btained a patent from the King which granted "£800 per annum for ten years as interest" on £10,000 dvanced by Crommelin and his friends for starting the venture. In addition to this sum "a pension of 200 a year to Crommelin, £40 to each of his three assistants, and £60 for a French minister." "Crom-lin brought from Holland 1000 looms and spinning wheels of an improved construction, and invited a umber of families (in general Huguenot refugees like himself), who complied and soon founded quite a lony among themselves."[3]

"Queen Anne's government issued a new patent which did indeed retain the same grand total of £1,180 er annum but re-distributed it." Crommelin was afterwards formally appointed as overseer of the Royal nen manufacture of Ireland, and devoted himself to "mind the public and continue his care in promoting 1e good of the kingdom."[4] The successful issue of the linen trade which brought such wealth to the orth of Ireland was thus due to the French refugees to Holland who there learnt that manufacture for hich Holland had been so long famed.

Soon after the arrival of King William III in London, a Dutch Chapel Royal was established at t.James' Palace in 1689 ; £160 being paid annually, and included in the King's Pension List, for each f the two Ministers appointed to do the duty, and about £20 for bread and wine for the Sacrament and her expenses. Service was there continued in Dutch until the year 1809, when it was discontinued.[5] . legacy was left by the late Sir Charles Barrow, Bart.,[6] the income of which was to be distributed) the poor of the Dutch Chapel Royal. This so-called Oliverian legacy was created by an assign-ient of Sir Charles Barrow to Messrs. Meier, Zornlin, and Waide for a term of ninety years. By an order o. N. 793, 24th September, 1708, it was levied at the receipt of His Majesty's Exchequer at Westmin-er.[7]

No record can be found of the address made to King William III by the Dutch congregation in London, hich, according to custom and especially on account of his nationality, must have been duly delivered. On the 14th February, 1709, a Bill for the naturalization of foreign Protestants was brought into the ouse of Commons, which received the royal assent on the 23rd March, 1709, there being a proviso "that no erson shall be naturalized, etc., unless he shall have received the sacrament in some Protestant or reformed ongregation within this kingdom." This act was repealed on the 9th February, 1712.[8]

When the Bill,[9] "for preventing the growth of Schism and for the further security of the Church of ngland, etc." was brought before Parliament in the reign of Queen Anne, the Dutch and French Protes-int Churches strongly opposed it. A case was carefully drawn up which represented "that they were first llowed and established in the reign of King Edward the VI, and afterwards in the reign of Queen Elizabeth, hd have now continued in this nation for above 160 years." "That they have introduced into this Realm iveral very great and profitable manufactures." "That they have always continued very dutiful and yal to the Crown and Government." "That in the act of uniformity, made in the 13th and 14th years King Charles II, there is provision made and a clause inserted in favour of the said Churches." "That y the Bill depending those that shall be present at the publick worship of the said Dutch and French hurches may be liable to the Incapacities in the said Bill mentioned, unless a clause be inserted for their emption." "Wherefore it is humbly hoped that a proviso or clause may be added for that purpose, they rforming their exercise in the Dutch and French languages."

(¹) Agnew, Vol. I, p. 169.
(²) Agnew, Ib.
(³) Agnew, Vol. II, p. 130.
(⁴) Agnew, Vol. II, p. 130-131.
(⁵) Dutch Chapel Royal Registers, Somerset House. Burn's Ref., p. 222.
(⁶) This creation does not appear in the Lists.
(⁷) Entry in Register of Dutch Chapel Royal.
(⁸) Agnew, Hist. Intro., p. 57-58.
(⁹) 12 Anne, Sess. 2, c. 7, repealed 5 Geo. I, c. 4.

On the coronation of King George I in 1714, the following address from
presented to His Majesty in the Dutch language by Mr. Theodore Bolton, (
Austin Friars Church, who was introduced by Viscount Townshend, one of His
taries of State.

" The most humble address of the Ministers and Elders of the French and L(
lished here by King Edward the 6th, and confirmed by Queen Elizabeth."
                    " MOST ILLUSTRIOUS GREAT AND MOST MIGHTY KING,
" Your sacred head being adorned with the royal crown of these powerful kin
" Protestants of Europe with such a joy, that the French and Dutch Churche
" with the greatest humility to cast themselves at your Majesty's feet, and amids
" of your faithful subjects, to testify the unexpressible joy of their souls, and to
" thanksgiving to the great God, who hath at so seasonable a time given the
" religion, justice, faithfulness, wisdom, and courage shine in their greatest glo
" the minds of all well-meaning persons are revived and delivered from their j
" threatned them : so that now we have a well-grounded hope that religion, li
" animated as with a new spirit, may again flourish and prosper.
    " We pray, Sire, the great King of all Kings, that he who hath brought you
" your reign so happily commenced with length of days, establish your throne
" make you a terrour to your enemies both at home and abroad, a refuge for the
" pillar of safety for all Protestants, and a refreshing shadow for fainting Christ
    " And with these wishes of all happiness and prosperity from the bottom of o
" beseech you for your royal favour, that it may please your Majesty to take
" wings of your protection, (which were established in the reign of King Edwi
" since continued through the benevolence of your Majesty's royal predecesso
" persevere to demonstrate our most dutiful obedience to your Majesty on all oc
" and pray to the Almighty God to bless your sacred person, His Royal Highne
" Royal House, both temporally and eternally."[1]

The condition of the Dutch Church in the year 1720 was assured and prospe
lowing extract.[2]

    " The present state of this Dutch Church in Augustin Friers, and the congr
" children of Strangers belonging to it, is thus.

    " They have two ministers. Mr. Biscop was lately one, and another who is 1
" twice every Lord's-Day, and once in the week besides; and they administer tl
" the last Sunday in the month, and lend their Church every first Sunday in t
" congregation, for their reception of the sacrament ; their own Church in Thr
" strait for them. The ministers have allowed them a good yearly salary, and :
" ently situate neer the said Church: and competent subsistance allowed also to
" MERSEN, a merchant and one of their Elders, at his own cost built a good hou
" which cost £400, and after, finished it within at a considerable further exper
" mendation, and the lasting memory of his charity and good will to this Chure
    " They maintain their poor at their own charge, which stands them in neer
" which they collect every Sunday, and week day customarily whensoever there
" door, by Deacons of the Church, who stand there with basins to receive wha
" throw in. They have a fair Almeshouse, built by themselves, standing in
" poor: together with a very handsome room for their Elders and Overseers to :
" for the good estate and ordering of these poor, as occasion may require."

Little of especial interest can be found concerning the foreign Churches in
The congregations gradually dwindled away, and one after another ceased to e:
Belgium merged with the French refugees, who came over in such great numl
weekly service in the Dutch language is conducted only at Austin Friars; the re
at Yarmouth, Colchester, Maidstone, Sandwich, Canvey Island, Dover,[3] etc., ha

(1) Newspaper cutting, Oct. 9th, 1714.
(2) Stow's London, Ed. 1720, Bk. II. p. 116 and 117.

(3) Many Dutch Refugees
    as shewn by the entr
    on many tombstones
    existing.—Standard :

to give particulars of the times when the services were discontinued. At Norwich alone is a small sum, &c., derived from the rents of small house property, which is distributed between a few poor descendants of the Dutch settlers. Once a year the minister of the Austin Friars Church goes there by appointment to hold a service and preach in the Dutch language. It is, however, with difficulty that these arrangements can be carried out, in consequence of the bad management and neglect in past years of the property belonging to that Church.

A report has not been found of the addresses made to the sovereigns succeeding George I, but the following answer given by Queen Victoria to the congratulations of the members of the Dutch Church, 31st July, 1837, on her accession, shows that the feeling expressed by Her Majesty is very gracious towards the Church founded by her predecessor, King Edward VI.

"I thank you for this loyal and dutiful address, for the sorrow which you express for the loss of His "late Majesty, and for your congratulations on my accession. I look back with great satisfaction to the "protection which you have found during so long a period in this country, and you may entirely rely upon "the continuance of that protection under my reign."

In 1862 a fire broke out on the night of the 21st November, entirely destroying the whole of the roof and interior fittings of the Church, which had just been thoroughly restored at a heavy cost. At first it was considered that the Church was not worth the cost of repairing, but much opposition was offered to the proposition of pulling down the walls which had been left standing. Mr. William Lightly and Mr. l'Anson, the architects consulted, advised a new building, which would save the heavier expense and greater trouble of the reconstruction of the old edifice. After considerable discussion it was thought advisable to repair the ruined Church; the total cost of doing so, including a new organ and the transfer of the library to Guildhall, being over £13,000, the fire insurance, etc. recovered being £12,000. The Church was re-opened again for divine service on October 1st, 1865, when a sermon was preached by Dr. Gehle, the text being 2 Chronicles VII, 15-16.

In 1866 the London and North Western Railway Company obtained power by act of Parliament to take the land in Sun Street, on which the Almshouses of the Austin Friars Church were built. The compensation was settled at £7000.[1] On the 18th December, 1867, the sanction of the Court of Chancery was obtained to rebuild the almshouses at Old Charlton, Kent; the foundation stone being laid by the wife of Mr. J. van Emschot Hollertt, a deacon of the Church.[2] At this present time ten poor members live there, there being two married couples and six women. It is just now proposed to enlarge the number of these alms-houses by building accommodation for eight more adults, and at the same time to be able to take in a certain number of convalescents and children, on the piece of ground purchased in 1867, which was left free for the purpose of building a residence for the minister; this arrangement, however, was not found convenient.

At the present time the number of the congregation varies from 50 to 80 persons, and double that number are present on festivals and the service on New Year's Eve, which was commenced by the present minister, the Rev. A. D. Adama van Scheltema. The annual amount of the Deacons' expenditure is about £800, £50 being distributed monthly to the poor of the Church, besides the cost of the almshouses. The Church and Deacon's funds are kept apart: these are derived to a great extent from the rent of the houses used as offices) built on the land on the south side of the Church, bought from the Marquis of Winchester in 1611 for £600, which the members of the Church had contended was their own, under the original grant of the Church by King Edward VI, and concerning which Emanuel van Meteren made the affidavit which gave the new particulars concerning the Coverdale Bible. There are also some other properties near London.

Een Register waerinne opgeteijckent werden die namen der gedoipen kinderen ende getuijghen onser Neederduijtscher Gemeinte tho Londen, beginnende vanden jare 1571.

---

1 Apl. 1583 Aalman, Henrick, f. Henricks.
27 Jun. 1596 Abeel, Elizabeth, f. Jan.
23 Mar. 1600 ,, Anna, f. ,,
6 Dec. 1601 ,, Maria, f. ,,
25 Oct. 1607 ,, Elias, f. ,,
31 Oct. 1574 Abeele, Van den, Jacob, f. Pieter.
17 Jan. 1591 ,, ,, Josias, f. Tobias.
23 Jul. 1592 ,, ,, Elsabet, f. ,,
24 Mar. 1594 ,, ,, Tobias, f. ,,
17 Feb. 1596 ,, ,, Nicolaus, f. ,,
14 Jan. 1599 ,, ,, Paulus, f. ,,
1 Nov. 1601 ,, ,, Carel, f. ,,
8 Jan. 1604 ,, ,, Jacob, f. ,,
14 Oct. 1606 ,, ,, Anna, f. ,,
14 May 1609 ,, ,, Carolus, f. ,,
,, ,, ,, ,, Joannes, f. ,,
14 Jun. 1612 ,, ,, Maria, f. Johan.
3 Jul. 1614 ,, ,, Joannes, f. Jan.
2 Sep. 1616 ,, ,, Abraham. f. ,,
11 Oct. 1618 ,, ,, Johannes, f. ,,
23 Jul. 1620 ,, ,, Daniel, f. ,,
10 Feb. 1622 ,, ,, Anna, f. ,,
26 Mar. 1598 Abeels, Nicolas, f. Willem.
4 Jan. 1601 ,, Willem, f. ,,
16 Feb. 1623 ,, Maria, f. Nicolaus.
25 Dec. 1627 ,, Maria, f. ,,
4 Jul. 1647 ,, Nicolas, f. Nicolas, junr.
16 Mar. 1656 ,, Nicholas, f. Lodewijck. Testes: William Abeels, etc.
5 Jul. 1657 ,, Helena, f. Lodewijck.
28 Nov. 1658 ,, Lodewyck, f. ,,
22 Apl. 1660 ,, Abram, f. ,,
12 May 1661 ,, Willem, f. ,,
6 Mar. 1664 ,, Abraham, f. ,,
29 Jan. 1665 ,, Willem, f. ,,
,, ,, ,, Lodewijck, f. ,,
6 Sep. 1612 Abels, Maria f. Elko.
30 Oct. 1597 Abiels, Johannes f. Jan.
18 Apl. 1813 d'Abo, Cornelie Marie Pauline f. Robert Christiaan Nicolai.
7 Mar. 1677 Abramse, Cornelia f. Pieter.
30 May 1587 Achtschelline, Sara f. Boudewijn.
6 Oct. 1588 Achtschellinck, David f. Jan.
11 May 1589 ,, Pieter f. Boudewijn.
4 Oct. 1593 ,, Daniel f. ,,
19 Dec. 1616 ,, Adriaen f. Abraham.
22 Jul. 1621 ,, Petrus f. Jeremias.
15 Aug. 1624 ,, Susanna f. ,,
23 Jul. 1626 ,, Jeremias f. ,,
26 Oct. 1628 ,, Samuel f. ,,
29 May 1631 ,, Elias f. ,,

17 Jul. 1636 Achtschellinck, Jeremias f. Jeremias.
18 Dec. 1575 Achter, Van, Daniel f. Daniel.
12 Aug. 1595 Acker, Van, Susanna f. Willem.
11 Nov. 1595 ,, ,, Abraham f. Abraham.
22 May 1599 ,, ,, Willem f. Willem.
14 Dec. 1606 ,, ,, Isaac f. Abraham.
6 Mar. 1608 ,, ,, Anna f. ,,
3 Nov. 1650 ,, ,, Jacobus f. Nicolaus.
21 Jan. 1610 Ackere, Van, Susanna f. Abraham.
1 Jul. 1649 ,, ,, Francois f. Nicolas.
21 Aug. 1597 Ackom, Van, Gielis f. Abraham.
15 Feb. 1579 Adams, Simon, van Harlingen.
10 Feb. 1583 ,, Susanna f. Simon.
4 Aug. 1588 ,, ... f. Willem.
18 Jun. 1592 ,, Abraham f. ,,
,, ,, ,, Sara f. ,,
9 Jan. 1597 ,, Hester f. ,,
11 Jan. 1601 ,, Maria f. ,,
24 Dec. 1693 Ademzen, Margaretha f. Saudert & Josyntje Thomassen.
27 Jan. 1650 Adriaen, Sara f. Johannes.
24 Aug. 1572 Adriaenssen, Sara f. Adriaen.
2 Ap. 1592 ,, Esther f. Gedeons.
22 Jun. 1670 ,, Heijndrick f. Jan & Anna.
4 Jun. 1690 ,, Gerrit f. Adriaen & Geertruijdt.
18 Mar. 1598 Adriaensz, Susanna f. Francois.
22 Jun. 1587 ,, Samuel f. Claes.
24 Ap. 1589 ,, Susanna f. Niclaes.
5 Sep. 1591 ,, Judith f. ,,
9 Jan. 1592 ,, Abraham f. Hans.
7 Ap. 1594 ,, Samuel f. Niclaes.
23 Nov. 1595 ,, Abigail f. ,,
17 Jul. 1597 ,, Abraham f. ,,
27 Dec. 1586 Aelbertinck, Sara f. Dierick.
7 Feb. 1576 Aelmans, Susanna f. Heindrick.
13 Dec. 1590 Aernouts, Arnoldus f. Cornelius.
14 Feb. 1703 Aertburgh, Van, Willemijntje f. Claes Jansen.

29 Jan. 1587 Aertsen, Sara f. Geeraert.
9 Nov. 1600 ,, Abraham f. Cornelis.
8 Jul. 1604 ,, Benjamin f. ,,
16 Dec. 1604 Aertsens, Susanna f. Arnout.
16 Nov. 1606 ,, Anna f. Wonter de Jonge.
14 Jul. 1607 ,, Daniel f. Arnout.
21 Meij 1598 Aertsz, Sara f. Cornelis.
26 Mar. 1600 ,, Sara f. Arnout.
22 Aug. 1602 ,, Elisabeth f. ,,
12 Sep. 1602 ,, Joh. f. Cornelis.
1 Mar. 1612 ,, (vide Artsz), Arnoldus f. Arnault.
29 Mar. 1614 ,, Philippus f. Mattheus.

19 Nov. 1615 Aertsz, Catharina f. Matthijs.
5 Mei 1616 „ Arnoldus f. Aernout.
6 Ap. 1617 „ Maria f. Matthijs.
23 Aug. 1618 Aertsen, Susanna f. Arnoudt.
6 Ap. 1690 Aeswielders, Maria f. Pieter.
7 Sep. 1606 Ageer, Sara f. Joos.
30 Apl. 1573 Aken, Van, Israel f. Jacob.
19 Feb. 1576 „ „ Elias f.
18 May 1578 „ „ Susanna f. „
9 Jan. 1575 Alart, Susanna f. Olivier.
10 Feb. 1577 Alaert, David f. „
20 Mei 1593 Alaerts, Isaac f. Gillis Baert.
28 Mei 1609 Albert, Elizabeth f. Willem.
30 Aug. 1612 Albertsen, Susanna f. „
1 Dec. 1605 Albertsz, Susanna f. „
15 Oct. 1690 Alckmaer, Van, Anna Geertruijt f. Jan.
30 Jul. 1679 „ „ Pieter f. Pieter Pieterson
20 Mar. 1608 Alekaes, Isaac f. Andries.
29 Aug. 1589 Alensone, Daniel f. Dierick.
2 Dec. 1604 Alewijn, (vide Allewijn), Sara f. Jaques.
19 Dec. 1613 „ „ Esar f. „
22 Aug. 1619 „ „ Sara f. Samuel.
11 Jan. 1601 Alewijns, Abraham f. Jaques.
16 Jun. 1689 Alexander, Adam f. Willem.
14 Oct. 1627 Alffen, Van der, Hendrick f. Severeijn.
28 Jun. 1629 „ „ Jacob f. Severein.
9 Oct. 1631 „ „ Ester f. Seberin.
18 Jul. 1598 Alget, Johannes f. Antony.
11 Oct. 1868 Alkemade, Van, Cornelis f. Leendert
Willem Van Ityn & Tonia
Van Ameyden Van Duyn.
26 Mar. 1870 „ Jacob f. „ „ & Tonia
Van Ameyden.
2 Aug. 1612 Alleman, Henricus f. Henric.
16 Ap. 1615 „ Joannes f. „
15 Feb. 1579 Allemans, Pieter f. Henricks.
14 Jul. 1650 Allen, Jan f. Henrick.
3 Oct. 1658 „ Catarina f. Henrij.
26 Nov. 1583 Allensson, Jonas f. Matthijs.
14 Aug. 1603 Allewijn, Anna f. Jacus.
20 Jul. 1626 Alleyn, Elisabeth f. Jan.
20 May 1652 Allin, Jacobus f. James.
27 Ap. 1589 Allnyt, Marie f. Anthoine.
6 Jun. 1813 Alphen, Van, Daniel Francois f. Daniel
Francois & Louise Rodol-
phine Julie Vignon.
29 Jul. 1855 „ „ Louiza Wilhelmina f.
Johannes & Geraldine
Allettho Van Pieterson,
weduwe Klaas de Leeuw.
26 Mei 1616 Aluwijn, Samuel f. Samuel.
16 Ap. 1690 Alvares, Bartholomeus f. Capt. Luijt Johan
& Elisabeth.
6 Aug. 1626 Alve, Van der, Elisabeth f. Scherijn.
9 Ap. 1690 Ameijde, Van der, Willem Eduard f. Jacob
& Eva Elizabeth Van
der Wijse.
20 Jun. 1690 Ampel, Van, Anna Maria f. Gillis & Marij.
16 Mar. 1692 Amijden, Van der, Jacoba f. Jacob.
2 Sep. 1655 Ancker, Anne-Caterine f. Pieter.
8 Ap. 1576 Angele, Susanna f. Jan.
23 Feb. 1574 Angelee, Moses f. „
15 Jul. 1571 Angeler, David f. „
24 Ap. 1678 Angell, Elisabeth f. Peter.
28 Ap. 1686 „ Petrus f. „
9 Sep. 1593 Anglois, l', Anna f. Pieter.

14 Sep. 1856 Anneveld, M
13 Dec. 1857 „ Jo
21 Ap. 1861 „ Jo
15 Mei 1572 Anwagem, V
8 Ap. 1591 Anycke, Abra
21 Mei 1594 „ Sara
27 Nov. 1572 Andries, Joan
29 Ap. 1632 „ Nath
1 Jun. 1679 Andriesen, J
29 Mei 1687 „
2 Feb. 1619 Andriessz, A
24 Aug. 1623 Anthoni, Fra
29 Oct. 1633 „ Joh
17 Nov. 1629 Antonij, Mar
24 Mei 1642 „ Elis
8 Jun. 1572 Anthonis, Al
1 Nov. 1590 Anthonissz, :
20 Mei 1638 Antonius, Ba
1 Jan. 1640 Anthonius, :
25 Ap. 1627 Appart, Jose
8 Jan. 1594 Arents, Joan
16 Sep. 1677 Arentsen, Al
15 Jun. 1589 Arentsz, Jan
22 Sep. 1583 Ariaanssen,
17 Jan. 1585 „
14 Dec. 1718 Armstrong, :
11 Mei 1679 Arnolt, Cath
23 „ 1588 Arnouts, Joa
12 Mar. 1592 „ Tau
2 Oct. 1681 Arns, Hendr
10 Sep. 1676 Arntsen, Al
21 Jun. 1616 Arschot, Va
7 Oct. 1571 Artis, alias d
31 Aug. 1572 Artis, Samue
Iom
25 Sep. 1575 „ Cathe
11 Dec. 1597 Artsen, Joan
19 Nov. 1609 Artsz, Maria
3 Oct. 1585 „
6 Aug. 1682 As, Van, Ar
12 Ap. 1607 Aschman, Su
1 Ap. 1619 „ Jo
31 Jan. 1574 Ashe, Elisab
24 Mar. 1616 Asenkerf, S:
23 Jul. 1571 Asse, Van,
17 Aug. 1572 „ „
24 Mei 1621 Assen, de, :
24 Jul. 1580 Assens, Elia
25 Feb. 1756 Assendelft,
10 Sep. 1615 Atendrix, J
21 Jan. 1599 Atkens, Abr
6 Nov. 1572 Audens, Al
30 Jul. 1629 Augustins,
9 Feb. 1632 Augustijns:
12 Aug. 1673 Augier, Dav
30 Mei 1680 Augiers, Jo
11 Jun. 1682 Ausier, Da

26 Apl.	1618	Bachaute, Van, Sara f. Lieven.
3 Dec.	1620	„ „ Johannes f. „
16 Nov.	1623	„ „ Maria f. „
14 Sep.	1572	Backelers, Daniel f. Jan.
25 Mar.	1582	Backens, Madeleene.
20 Feb.	1575	Backer, Susanna f. Jans. testes: Bartholomeus Moenen, Hans van Samsen, Seyken Geltsand, Elisabeth ux. Hans Moenen.
17 Jun.	1576	„ Joannes f. Jan.
16 Ap.	1581	„ Abraham f. „
13 Jun.	1585	„ Pieter f. Reymont.
11 Jan.	1586	Backer, de, Susanna f. Jan.
27 Nov.	1586	„ „ Samuel f. „
20 Feb.	1588	„ „ Jacob f. „
28 Ap.	1588	„ „ Elisabeth f. „
31 Mei	1590	Backere, de, Susanna f. „
19 Dec.	1591	Backer, Judith f. „
14 Jan.	1593	„ de, Jacobus f. „ test: Jacobus Regius, Pieter L'Hermite, etc.
28 Aug.	1595	„ „ Jacobus f. Robert.
18 Nov.	1599	„ „ Susanna f. Hans.
18 Mei	1600	„ „ Sara f. Tobias.
25 Jun.	1601	„ „ Sara f. Hans.
29 Mei	1603	„ „ Abraham f. Abraham.
28 Jun.	1603	„ „ Tobias f. Tobias.
11 Aug.	1605	„ „ Elisabeth f. Abraham.
7 Jun.	1607	„ „ Joannes f. „
6 Sep.	1607	„ „ Joannes f. Hans.
17 Ap.	1609	„ „ Tobias f. Abraham.
1 Nov.	1610	„ „ Jacob f. Hans.
5 Ap.	1612	„ „ Sara f. Abraham.
27 Oct.	1612	„ „ Abraham f. Hans.
30 Jan.	1614	„ „ Samuel f. Abraham.
21 Feb.	1615	„ „ Sara f. Hans.
23 Jul.	1615	„ „ Josias f. Abraham.
13 Mei	1617	„ „ Abraham f. „
14 Mar.	1619	„ „ Maria f. „
20 Ap.	1619	„ „ Sara f. Jan.
24 Aug.	1619	„ „ Willem f. Jacob.
5 Nov.	1620	„ „ Willem f. Jacob.
13 Sep.	1622	„ „ Daniel f. Abraham.
26 Dec.	1624	„ „ Sara f. Jacob.
29 Jan.	1626	„ „ Ester f. Abraham.
5 Aug.	1638	„ „ Sara f. Jacob.
14 Mei	1643	„ „ Maria f. „
30 Mar.	1645	„ „ Simeon f. „
27 Mar.	1678	„ „ Johannes f. Simon Jansen.
22 Nov.	1579	Backers, Esther f. Jan.
12 Ap.	1584	s'Backers, Salomon f. Wilhelmus.
12 Jul.	1590	Backers, de, Sara f. Jan.
2 Feb.	1575	Backereel, Maria f. Hermes.
7 Oct.	1576	„ Jonas f. „
13 Mei	1660	Bacque, Jan f. Nicolaes.
21 Feb.	1664	„ Ester f. Nocolas.
11 Feb.	1589	Bael, Mon f. Thomas.
3 Jul.	1589	Baele, Enock f. Anthony.
20 Jul.	1572	Baen, Moyses f. Mattheus.
18 Sep.	1593	Baerman, Marie f. Dierick.
18 Oct.	1585	Baert, Jacob f. Jacob.
27 Nov.	1586	„ Jannekin f. Cornelis.
26 Jan.	1589	„ Jacobus f. „
27 Dec.	1590	„ Sara f. Gillis.
11 Nov.	1591	„ Abraham f. Cornelis.

20 Aug.	1592	Baert, Maria f. Tobias.
1 Jan.	1594	„ Isaack f. Cornelis.
27 Ap.	1595	„ Salomon f. Tobias.
4 Jul.	1596	„ Daniel f. Cornelis.
30 Dec.	1604	„ Sara f. „
10 Oct.	1626	„ Joanna f. Abraham.
7 Oct.	1627	„ Joanna f. „
25 Jan.	1629	„ Cornelis f. „
17 Oct.	1630	„ „ f. „
11 Dec.	1632	„ Susanna f. „
2 Nov.	1634	„ Maria f. „
25 Feb.	1636	„ Abraham f. „
10 Dec.	1637	„ Elizabeth f. „
27 Nov.	1639	„ Susanna f. „
11 Ap.	1641	„ Joanna f. „
29 Ap.	1599	Baerts, Susanna f. Cornelis.
1 Ap.	1605	Baes, Judith f. Nathanael.
2 Oct.	1606	„ Nathanael f. „
5 Mar.	1609	„ Catharine f. „
14 Nov.	1594	Baesdorp, Van, Joannes f. Catherine. wed. van Jaens de Moor, het kint oudt weysende tusschen 2 ende 3 jaeren etc.
3 Nov.	1633	Baese, Van der, Tot Mortlake, Petrus f. Joris.
19 Dec.	1636	„ „ „ inde Engelsche Kercke, Elias f. Joris.
23 Ap.	1615	Bailliu, (vide Baliew), Joannes f. Jan.
19 Oct.	1617	„ Maria f. Jan.
28 Oct.	1621	„ Sara f. „
2 Jan.	1625	„ Abigail f. „
25 Jun.	1626	„ Elisabeth f. „
29 Aug.	1847	Bakker, Helena Maria f. Hendrik Jan & Maria Barneveld.
10 Aug.	1589	Balde, Jacob f. Niclaes.
2 Dec.	1604	„ Nicolas f. Nicolas.
30 Mei	1624	„ Joanna f. Jacob.
15 Feb.	1593	Balen, Maria f. Claes.
21 Dec.	1623	Baliew, (vide Bailliu), Rebecca f. Jan.
18 Mei	1851	Balman, Petrus Johannes f. Willem Frederik & Hendrika Herbus.
19 Jun.	1853	„ Jan Pieter f. Willem Frederik & Hendrika Herbus.
16 Sep.	1855	„ Willem Frederik f. Willem Frederik & Hendrika Herbus.
23 Sep.	1855	„ Helena Wilhelmina f. Jan Pieter & Harriet Plummer.
7 Jun.	1857	„ Anna Elisabeth f. Jan Pieter & Harriet Plummer.
22 Aug.	1858	„ Henriette Sophia f. Jan Pieter & Harriet Plummer.
13 Jan.	1861	„ Jan Eduard f. Jan Pieter & Harriet Plummer.
4 Oct.	1857	„ Hendrik f. Willem Frederik & Hendrika Herbus.
21 Aug.	1859	„ Anthony f. Willem Frederik & Hendrika Herbus.
16 Mar.	1862	„ Thomas James f. Willem Frederik & Hendrika Herbus.
28 Dec.	1808	Balmont, tot St. Mary le Bonne, Julien f. Julien, Baron de, & Sophia de Bellefort, dr. van Charles David, Baron de Beaufort.
17 Nov.	1631	Bamberge, Dierie f. Dierck.

25 Oct. 1610 Beijaert, Lucas f. Guiljam.
26 Ap. 1612 ,, Anna f. Guiliam.
12 Sep. 1613 ,, Nathanael f. Guiljame.
28 Mei 1615 Beijardt, Johannes f. Guiljam.
2 Mar. 1617 ,, Maria f. ,,
30 May 1619 ,, Susanna f. Guillame.
4 Jun. 1665 Beijaert, Maria f. Adrian.
7 Jul. 1588 Beijdaels, Sara f. Giclis.
10 Jul. 1586 Beijdail, Gillis f. Gillis.
21 Aug. 1586 Beijdaels, Laurens f. Laurens.
19 Jan. 1589 ,, Neelken f. ,,
2 Aug. 1590 ,, Peter f. ,,
2 Jul. 1592 ,, Janneken f. ,,
21 Feb. 1585 Beijdals, Joos f. Laurens.
27 Feb. 1701 Beijer, Johan f. William & Elisabeth.
31 Mar. 1667 ,, Elisabeth f. Adriaen.
22 Aug. 1669 ,, Willem f. ,, & Maria.
22 Oct. 1671 ,, Adriaen f. ,,
1 Jan. 1674 ,, Pieter f. ,, & Maria.
26 Ap. 1676 ,, Maria f. Frater Adrian & Maria.
31 Jul. 1678 ,, Adriaen f. ,, ,,
7 Jul. 1680 ,, Maria f. ,, & Maria.
11 Jun. 1632 ,, Cornelis f. ,, ,,
9 Ap. 1684 ,, Sarah f. ,, ,,
11 Jul. 1688 ,, Francoijs f. ,, ,,
21 Ap. 1704 ,, Elysabeth f. Wiljam & Elijsabeth.
... Jun. 1705 ,, Francois f. ,, ,,
7 Jul. 1706 ,, Sara f. ,, ,,
1 Mar. 1709 ,, Wiljam f. ,, ,,
23 Jan. 1711 ,, ... f. ,, & Elysabeth.
14 Jan. 1714 ,, Anna f. William & Elisabeth Wolff.
27 Jun. 1717 Beijerling, Wijnand f. Wijnand & Hanna Hall.
...... 1720 ,, Hanna f Wijnand & Hanna Hall.
2 Feb. 1595 Beijnaert, Hesther f. Josias.
5 Sep. 1619 Beijns, Nerias f. Jacob.
24 Nov. 1697 Beijrman, Maria Anna f. Arnold Boot, M.D. & Helena de Golls.
13 Mar. 1700 ,, Cornelia f. Arnold Boot, M.D. & Helena.
8 Nov. 1702 ,, Helena f. Arnold Boot, M.D.
14 Jan. 1582 Beijnens, Miriam f. Peeter.
30 Aug. 1614 Beijrens, Sara f. Eleazar.
6 Nov. 1597 Beijrents, Joannes f. Jacob.
12 Mar. 1588 Beijts, Jacob f. Adolf.
28 Aug. 1589 ,, Abraham f. ,,
18 Feb. 1616 Beget, Abraham f. Jacob.
23 Jan. 1586 Begnerts, Anna f. Alexander.
23 Feb. 1589 Begnorts, Samuel f. Xander.
20 Dec. 1607 Beillards, Barbara f. Abraham.
15 Mar. 1573 Beke, Van der, Susanna f. Adrinen.
10 Mar. 1588 ,, ,, ,, Jonas f. Jan.
27 Mei ,, ,, ,, Maria f. Mathys.
16 Dec. 1589 ,, ,, ,, Priscilla f. Jan.
27 Mar. 1592 ,, ,, ,, Elisabeth f. Goosen.
27 Oct. 1594 ,, ,, ,, Joannes f. Hans.
29 Jun. 1595 ,, ,, ,, Debora f. Mathijs.
16 Sep. 1606 ,, ,, ,, Isaac f. Abraham.
21 Oct. 1621 ,, ,, Abigail f. Frederick.
22 Feb. 1649 Beke, Op de, (v. Beek, Beeck) Maria f. D. Philippus.
1 Jan. 1651 ,, ,, ,, Philippus f. Frater
15 Jun. 1652 ,, ,, ,, Anna Caterina f. Frater Philippus.
6 Feb. 1651 ,, ,, Elizabeth f. Elias.
9 Jul. 1854 Bekker, Elizabeth Jacoba f. Gijsbertus & Kaatje Dekker.

24 Mar. 1622 Belchier, Joannes f. Jacob.
8 Jun. 1591 Beliwijs, Esther f. Pieter.
29 Jul. 1571 sBells, (deBell), Abigail f. Jan.
5 Jul. 1610 Bell, Paulus f. Pieter.
2 Jan. 1642 ,, Pieter f. ,,
8 Jan. 1643 ,, Jacobus f. Joannes.
20 Jul. 1645 Bel, Samuel f. ,,
19 Nov. 1648 Bell, Elisabet f. Pieter.
2 Aug. 1685 Bellaerdt, Johannes f. Johannes & Dorothea.
3 Jul. 1687 ,, Elizabeth f. ,, ,,
18 Jun. 1684 Bellard, Eleonara f. ,, ,,
26 Mei 1689 ,, Maria f. Johan & Dorothe.
7 Jan. 1683 Bellart, Elisabeth f. Johannes & Dorothea.
10 Mei 1579 Belle, Van, Susanna f. Hermans.
4 Aug. 1583 ,, ,, Anna f. ,,
1 Dec. 1611 Bellecher, Jacob f. Jacob.
28 Feb. 1612 Bellechier, ,, f. ,,
11 Jun. 1587 Bellovoijs, Van, (v. Belowijs), Daniel f. Pieter.
5 Sep. 1588 Belowijs, Catheline f. ,,
3 Aug. 1617 Belsier, Rachel f. Jacob.
3 Jul. 1614 Bembden, Van den, Petrus f. Hans.
24 Nov. 1611 Bemden, Van den, (v. Bende), Joannes f. Joannes.
3 Jan. 1574 Bemers, Jan f. Jan.
17 Jun. 1855 Ben, Van der, James f. Tobias & Ellen Morgan.
20 Jul. 1856 ,, ,, ,, John Morgan f. Tobias & Ellen Morgan.
21 Oct. 1610 Bende, Van den, (v. Bemden), Joannes f. Hans.
11 Jul. 1613 ,, ,, ,, Abraham f. Jan.
17 Aug. 1572 Bends, (v. Bent), Maria f. Klaas.
19 Oct. 1856 Benit, Jan Adriaan f. Jan Adriaan & Anna Elizabeth Frikke.
9 Mei 1858 ,, Jeannette Adriana f. Jan Adriaan & Anna Elizabeth Frikke.
17 Nov. 1746 Bennet, Johanna f. Sampson & Rachel Riethuizen.
10 Jan. 1686 Bennot, Elizabeth f. Nicolaes & Elizabeth.
13 Sep. 1631 Benoo, Catherina f. Jan.
17 Aug. 1628 Benoot, Johannes f. Jan, tot Mortlake.
7 Feb. 1636 ,, Franciscus f. ,,
30 Sep. 1634 Benou, Maria f. ,, ,,
15 Aug. 1686 Benson, Benjamin f. Benjamin.
13 Mei 1575 Eent, (v. Bends), Elizabeth f. Niclaes.
6 Jan. 1577 ,, Samuel f. ,,
4 ,, 1579 Bents, Elizabeth f. Nicolaus.
10 Ap. 1580 ,, Beata f. Klaas.
6 Oct. 1605 Benthem, Van, Maria f. Marten.
10 Aug. 1589 Bespiere, de, Catheline f. Guiliamo.
3 Mei 1627 Best, de, Elisabeth f. Jan.
23 Mar. 1572 Beste, de, Maria f. Gheleijn.
6 Jan. 1574 ,, ,, Susanna f. ,,
18 Mar. 1576 ,, ,, Sara f. ,,
11 Aug. 1607 ,, ,, Jacobus f. Jaques.
21 Jan. 1610 ,, ,, Anna f. ,,
29 Sep. 1611 ,, ,, Maria f. ,,
13 Dec. 1612 ,, ,, Lucretia f. ,,
26 Nov. 1615 ,, ,, Elisabet f. ,,
30 Mei 1618 ,, ,, Jaquemijnken f. Jacques.
20 Nov. 1571 Betber, David.
3 Oct. 1577 Betburch, Sara f. Gheraert.
2 Sep. 1593 Bethburrie, Maria f. Tobias.
27 Jul. 1595 ,, Tobias f. ,,
24 Jul. 1659 Betto, Anna f. Michiel.
28 Aug. 1660 ,, Anna f. ,, & Jannike.
4 Aug. 1663 ,, Barbara f. ,,

2 Ap.	1665	**Betto**, Rebbecca f. Michael.
30 Jan.	1592	**Berchtgrave**, de, Jacobus f. Pieter.
5 Oct.	1595	**Berck**, Van, Adriaen f. Jacob.
10 Dec.	1573	**Berdt**, (v. Bert, Berts), Susanna f. Nicolas.
11 Nov.	1674	**Berdt**, de, Johannes f. Jan.
23 Jul.	1679	,, ,, Maria f. Fr: Jan.
12 Oct.	1681	,, ,, Maria f. ,, ,,
2 Nov.	1684	,, ,, Guelaume f. ,,
14 Dec.	1572	**Berdts**, Jacob f. Gabriel.
26 Dec.	1578	**Berge**, Van den, (v. Bergh, etc.), Jois van Ghendt.
7 Mei	1588	,, ,, den, Maria f. Christoffels.
16 Jun.	1588	,, ,, ,, Petrus f. Petrus.
22 Nov.	1590	,, ,, ,, Margareta f. Niclaes.
19 Feb.	1604	,, ,, den, Samuel f. Tobias.
22 Feb.	1610	,, ,, den, Joas & Anna f. ,,
31 Jul.	1636	,, ,, Anna f. Jan.
14 Aug.	1853	**Bergendahl**, Bernard Adriaan f. Jens Christian & Francina Johanna Bernardina Cortmans.
12 Aug.	1855	,, Christine Kroppeline f. Jens Christian & Francina Johanna Bernardina Cortmans.
18 Sep.	1638	**Bergh**, Van den, (v. Berge), Elizabeth f. Abraham.
23 Jan.	1676	,, ,, ,, Deliana f. Jan Jansen.
28 Oct.	1677	,, ,, ,, Maria f. ,, ,,
20 Feb.	1681	,, ,, ,, Hester f. ,, & Mary Smit.
31 Dec.	1682	,, ,, ,, Johannes f. ,,
6 Jul.	1684	,, ,, ,, Ebenezer f. ,,
14 Sep.	1690	,, ,, ,, Isaac f. Isaac & Maria.
16 Oct.	1692	,, ,, ,, Maria f. ,, ,,
22 Mei	1707	,, ,, ,, Anna f. ,, ,,
16 Aug.	1752	,, ,, ,, Pieter f. Symen & Eunice Powell.
8 Mei	1586	**Berghe**, ,, ,, Joannes f. Jan.
26 Jan.	1587	,, ,, ,, Susanna f. Petrus.
11 Jan.	1590	,, ,, ,, Jacob f. Pieter.
18 Nov.	1591	,, ,, ,, Joannes f. Christophel.
21 Sep.	1592	,, ,, ,, Samuel f. Pieter.
25 Aug.	1594	,, ,, ,, Catherina f. Christoffel.
14 Jun.	1597	,, ,, ,, Maria f. Niclaes.
4 Feb.	1599	,, ,, ,, Catherine f. Nicolas.
25 Aug.	1605	,, ,, ,, Tobias f. Tobias.
4 Jan.	1607	,, ,, ,, Judith f. ,,
11 Mei	1701	**Bergsies**, Willem f. Kaas.
25 Dec.	1698	**Bergues**, Claes f. Claes.
9 Jul.	1725	**Berkenhout**, Anna Margaretha f Benjamin & Isabella.
21 Mei	1727	,, Cateleyne f. Benjamin & Isabella.
29 Sep.	1729	,, Benjamin f. ,, ,,
8 Feb.	1731	**Berkenhoudt**, Benjamin f. ,, ,,
31 Mei	1732	,, Lennarda f. ,, ,,
6 ,,	1734	,, Anna f. ,, ,,
30 Mar.	1736	,, Elizabeth f. ,, ,,
16 Apl.	1698	**Berlenbach**, Margariet f. Johannes Adam & Catharina.
18 Oct.	1614	**Bernaerds**, Bernardus f. Pieter.
19 Aug.	1617	**Bernards**, Bernard f. ,,
13 Jul.	1619	**Bernaerts**, Doricas f. ,,
20 Oct.	1583	**Berntz**, Benjamin f. ,,
30 Mei	1585	**Berntsz**, Eleazar f. ,,
16 Oct.	1586	**Berentsz**, Samuel f. ,,
17 Nov.	1588	,, Petrus f. ,,
28 Aug.	1589	**Berrewaerts**, Hendrick f. ,, Abraham.
28 Jun.	1747	**Berrij**, Kaatje f. Kobus & Judik Noewel.
29 Oct.	1749	,, Pieter f. Jacobus & Judith Novell.
3 Mar.	1751	**Berrij**, Vincent f. Jacobus & Judith Novell.
28 Mei	1581	**Bert**, Susanna f. Zingel.
19 Feb.	1615	,, , de, Joannes f. ....
24 Feb.	1622	,, ,, Elisabeth f. Jan.
16 Jul.	1629	,, ,, Johannes f. ,,
4 Oct.	1575	**Berts**, Tabitha f. Gabriel.
20 Ap.	1628	**Berten**, Cattcline f. Pieter.
12 Mei	1629	,, Alexander f. ,,
23 Dec.	1630	**Bertens**, Joos, Volwassen.
13 Feb.	1597	**Bertholemeus**, Sara f. Denijs.
9 Mar.	1716	**Berven**, Elisabet f. Jan & Aaltje.
11 Sep.	1593	**Berwart**, Elisabeth f. Abraham.
5 Mar.	1609	**Beucken**, Catarina f. Henric.
26 Sep.	1613	,, Pieter f. ,,
22 Aug.	1592	**Beughen**, Van, Anna f. Hans.
11 Dec.	1596	**Beughem**, Van, Anna f. ,,
1 Mei	1576	**Beun**, Jacob f. Matheus.
2 ,,	1591	,, Matthens f. Isaac.
27 Sep.	1612	,, Ester f. Tobias.
13 Aug.	1615	,, Tobias f. Abraham.
24 Jul.	1642	,, Niclaes f. Isaac.
6 Sep.	1608	**Beuns**, Mattheus, volwassen jonghman.
10 Sep.	1609	,, Anna f. Mattheus.
10 Mei	1612	,, Mattheus f. ,,
26 Sep.	1613	,, Abraham f. ,,
20 Jan.	1615	,, Joannes f. ,,
15 Mar.	1618	,, Mattheus f. ,,
24 Sep.	1620	,, Elisabet f. ,,
31 Mar.	1622	,, Rebecca f. ,,
25 Jan.	1624	,, Maria f. ,,
26 Jun.	1625	,, Wilhelmus f. ,,
5 Mar.	1615	,, Isaac f. Tobias.
25 Oct.	1627	,, Salomon, volwassen.
25 Oct.	1627	,, Geb. 12 Jan. 1618, Margarita f. Salomon.
25 ,,	,,	,, Geb. 27 Oct. 1621, Geertruyt f. ,,
25 ,,	,,	,, 12 Dec. 1623, Lauwrens f. ,,
29 Mar.	1629	,, Mattheus f. Salomon.
28 Sep.	1630	,, Christina f. ,,
16 Oct.	1632	,, Rebecca ,,
26 Feb.	1639	,, Salomon f. ,,
21 Aug.	1630	,, Susanna f. Mattheus.
8 Sep.	1639	,, Isaack f. Isaack.
28 Jan.	1644	,, Maria f. ,,
13 Dec.	1610	,, Johannes f. Salomon.
22 Feb.	1618	**Beus**, Arnoult, f. Jacob.
5 Nov.	1622	,, Maria f. ,,
30 Mei	1602	**Beusecom**, Adriaen f. Nicolas.
5 Sep.	1594	**Beusken**, (v. **Buskens**), Joannes f. Lion.
6 Mei	1599	,, f. Hans.
16 Dec.	1610	,, Jacomijnken f.
18 Jul.	1613	,, Isaac f. ,,
10 Mei	1606	,, Johannes f. Lijon.
6 Sep.	1635	**Beuterdroger**, de, (v. **Boterdroger**, etc), Andries f. Andries.
7 Mei	1609	**Beuthem**, Van, Mattheus Marten f. Marten.
28 Nov.	1630	**Bevoot**, Maria f. Jan.
7 Apl.	1614	**Bex**, der, Joanna f. Michiel.
1 Feb.	1573	**Bick**, de, Susanna f. Jan.
4 Oct.	1579	,, ,, Esther f. ,,
25 Sep.	1586	,, ,, Susanna f. ,,
14 Jul.	1588	,, ,, Elisabeth f. ,,
27 Jul.	1589	,, ,, Esther f. ,,
9 Ap.	1592	,, ,, Abigail f. ,,
20 Oct.	1592	,, ,, Johanna f. Hans.
22 Sep.	1594	,, ,, Abigail f. Jan de jonge.
25 Jul.	1596	,, ,, Esther f. Hans.

11 Aug. 1814 Bickerlaasten, John Marinus f. Adriaan
     Herman & Sarah Maria Van
     Yzendoorn.
16 Mar. 1572 Bie, de, (v. Bije), Abraham f. Tobias.
14 Mar. 1596 „ „ Johannes f. Jacus.
16 Mei 1597 „ „ Jacob f. Jaques.
9 Jul. 1598 „ „ Elisabeth f. „
21 Oct. 1599 „ „ Abraham f. „
23 Aug. 1601 „ „ Anna f. Jacus.
12 Dec. 1798 „ „ Johannes Pieter f. Gideon &
     Berdardina.
18 Dec. 1592 Biecke, Esther f. Jacus.
7 Oct. 1610 Biedenback, Van, Abraham f. Heijndrick.
21 Aug. 1595 Biele, Jacobus f. Jacob.
10 Sep. 1684 Eiemonte, Margariet f. Charles Louwis
     Massal.
16 Mar. 1634 Bierhuijs, (v. Birhous), Esdert f. Helmer.
25 Mei 1580 Bierman, Anna f. Dierick.
30 Aug. 1590 „ Sara f. Didier.
17 Mar. 1607 „ Catharina ⎰
     & Susanna ⎱ f. Pieter.
21 Mar. 1592 Biest, Van der, Elizabeth f. Jacus.
4 Apl. 1596 „ „ Anna f. Jaques.
28 Nov. 1624 „ „ de, Johannes f. Jacob.
28 Sep. 1595 Bieuc, de. Susanna f. Marten.
23 Oct. 1573 Bije, de, (v. Bie). Neesken f. Tobins.
12 Sep. 1602 „ „ Sara f. Jaques.
26 Feb. 1604 „ „ Anna f. Jacques.
21 Sep. 1600 Bijl, de, Jcennes f. Abraham.
5 Mar. 1587 Bijler, Van, Jonas f. Wolfaert.
16 Jun. 1588 „ „ „ f. „
20 Mei 1593 Bijlovoys, Aegidius f. Pieter.
18 Jul. 1602 Bijnck, Gabriel f. Gabriel.
25 Jul. 1696 „ .. f. „
18 Jul. 1596 Bil, de, Abraham f. Abraham.
28 Mei 1598 „ „ Maria f. „
12 Sep. 1602 „ „ Sara f. „
3 Feb. 1605 Bill, de, Salomon f. „
28 Jul. 1608 „ „ Anna f. „
6 Sep. 1610 Bil, „ Elisabeth f. „
16 Apl. 1620 Bilien, Susanna f. Jan.
29 Sep. 1586 Biliet, Maria f. Pieter.
2 Jan. 1576 Billen, Pieter f. „
16 Mar. 1578 „ Adam f. „
1 Mei 1580 „ Abraham f. „
21 Feb. 1583 „ Joannes f. „
3 Aug. 1572 Binnmos, Sara f. Michael.
10 Mar. 1605 Binck, Rebecca f. Gabriel.
5 Mar. 1609 Bincke, Catharine f. Hendrick.
27 Mei 1610 Binke, Mattheus f. „
12 Apl. 1631 Birhous, (v. Bierhuys), Anna f. Hellemer.
7 Jul. 1635 „ Hester f. Helmer.
31 Dec. 1637 „ Ottho f. Helmer.
8 Ap. 1632 Bisardt, Elisabet f. Lenard.
30 Jul. 1679 Biscop, Sara f. Samuel & Sara.
11 Sep. 1681 „ Catharina f. „ & Sara Ward.
24 Jan. 1683 „ Johanna f. „ „ „
17 Mei 1685 „ Maria f. „ „ „
12 Jan. 1690 „ Samuel f. „ „
8 Sep. 1577 Bits, Van, Abraham f. Niclaes.
1 Feb. 1590 Biurt, (v. Baert), Janneken f. Tobias.
13 Apl 1602 Bla, de, Johannes f. Daniel.
20 Jan. 1697 Black, Jannetje f. David & Elizabeth
     Van de Linde.
23 Jun. 1590 Blaeuvoet, (v. Blauvoet), Sara f. Mahieu.
1 Aug. 1592 „ Salome f. Marten.
15 Oct. 1636 Blake, Johannes f. Jan & Josina.
6 Feb. 1670 „ Samuel f. Johannes & Josina.
10 Dec. 1671 „ Sara f. Jan.

1 Dec. 1672 Blake, Gratie f. Jan.
4 Jul. 1675 „ Thomas f. „
31 Dec. 1676 „ Samuel f. „
11 Sep. 1580 Blanc, le, Pieter f. Pieter.
22 Sep. 1588 „ Elisabeth f. Dionisius.
20 Jan. 1699 „ de, Dionysius f. Daniel.
23 Mar. 1606 „ le, Elisabeth f. „
25 Aug. 1577 Blanck, de. Jacob f. Dionijs.
2 Oct. 1582 „ Dionysius ⎱ f. Dionijsius.
     „ & Cornelia ⎰
25 Mei 1607 „ . de. Daniel f. Daniel.
10 Aug. 1578 Blancke, le. Sara f. Dionijs.
3 Oct. 1574 Blanckesteijn, Jacob f. Jacob.
20 Jan. 1579 „ Jacobus f. „
31 Oct. 1585 Blancq, le, Joannes f. Denijs.
24 Mar. 1615 „ ., Ester f. Daniel.
20 Sep. 1590 Blauvoet. (v. Blaeuvoet), Guido f. Marten.
28 Jan. 1736 Blijdesteijn, Isaak f. Jan & Mary Pepper.
2 Mei 1757 „ Jan. f. „
23 Jul. 1758 „ Mariannef.,, „
30 Apr. 1761 „ Judith f. „ „
12 Jul. 1761 „ Abraham f.,, „
22 Jun. 1763 „ Mary f. „ „
6 Aug. 1764 „ Petronella f.,, „
31 Jul. 1765 Blijdestein, Anna f. „ „
17 Dec. 1766 „ John f. „ „
4 Feb. 1588 Block, Vander, Michiel f. Franchoijs.
28 Feb. 1813 Blom, Jan. f. Hendrik, van Amsterdam &
     Anna Philippina Willmans.
28 Sep. 1580 Blommaert, Samuel f. Hans.
23 Aug. 1621 „ Paulus f. Jan.
1 Aug. 1591 Blomme. David f. Vedast.
15 Jul. 1589 Blondeel, Elizabeth f. Jacob.
25 Oct. 1618 Bo. dela Maria, f. Raphael.
7 Jan. 1621 Bo, de le, Sijmeon, f. Raphel.
24 Dec. 1622 „ .. Judith f. „
8 Mei 1625 Bo. de la „ posthuma f. Raphael.
2 Feb. 1586 Bocholt, van „ f. Herman.
16 Mar. 1628 Bock, de, Gerard f. Hendric, tot Mortlake.
1 Mar. 1629 „ „ Elizabeth f. „ „
5 Dec. 1630 „ „ Salomon f. „ „
13 Apr. 1634 „ „ Timotheus f. „ „
28 Feb. 1576 Coddens, Adam f. Jaspar.
2 Mar. 1603 „ Elizabeth f. Adam.
25 Oct. 1607 „ Adam f. „
22 Ap. 1610 „ Sara f. „
29 Dec. 1610 „ .. f. „
20 Aug. 1615 „ Susanna f. „
15 Dec. 1616 „ Maria f. „
21 Dec. 1617 „ Rachel f.
11 Sep. 1625 „ Joannes f.
11 Sep. 1632 „ Anna f. „
19 Dec. 1633 „ Adam f. „
25 Mar. 1639 „ David f. „
12 Oct. 1602 „ Elisabeth f. „
22 Apl. 1572 Boddins, Catharina f. Adam.
13 Nov. 1575 Bode, de, Gideon f. Gillis.
1 Mar. 1579 „ David f. „
26 Oct. 1817 Bödeker, Catharina Louisa f. Frans Willem
     & Evar Catharina Moojen.
5 Mar. 1690 Bodvey, Pieter f. Luytenant Pieter.
1 Jan. 1653 Boecke, Johanna f. Elias.
2 Mar. 1600 Boecbinder, Petrus f. Thomas.
23 Mei 1605 Boeckbinder. Dionijs f. „
13 Jan. 1577 Boeije, Jacobus, f. Christiaan.
1578 „ Johannes f. Christiaans.
8 Jun. 1579 „ Christianus f. „
4 Aug. 1580 „ Elisabet f. „
8 Jan. 1576 Boels, Pieter f. Anthonij.

23 Mar.	1577	**Boel**, Benjamin f. Anthony.
22 Jul.	1587	**Boels**, Judith ont outrent, 8 maenden f. Anthony.
26 Jul.	1874	Boe-s. Goh. 27 Aug. 1873, Johanna Cornelia Adriana f. Adriaan & Sara Catharina Drugemans.
,, ,,	,,	,, Geb. 24 Mar. 1871, Jacoba Catharina Christina f. Adriaan & Sara Catharina Drugemans.
12 Mei	1601	**Boeve**, (v. **Bouve**), Hesther f. Andries.
15 ,,	1603	,, Guillame f. ,,
17 Mar.	1607	,, Maria f. ,,
11 Dec.	1608	,, Elisabeth f. ,,
1 Jul.	1610	,, Anna f. ,,
1 Mar.	1612	,, Andreas f. ,,
25 Sep.	1614	,, Petrus f. ,,
29 Oct.	1618	,, Abraham f. ,,
4 Apl.	1620	,, Abigaijl f. ,,
31 Mar.	1605	,, Petrus f. Lowijs.
7 Oct.	1606	,, Maria f. ,,
17 Apl.	1608	,, Esther f. Louijs.
28 Mei	1609	,, Abraham & Isaac } f. Lowijs.
8 Jul.	1610	,, Petrus f. ,,
20 Jul.	1611	,, Petrus f. ,,
4 Nov.	1612	,, Jacobus f. Louwijs.
22 Nov.	1615	,, Mattheus f. Louijs.
20 Feb.	1631	,, Andreas f. Willem.
8 Jul.	1632	,, Judith & Hester } f. Guiljam.
8 Ap.	1593	**Bogaert**, (v. **Bogard**), Elizabeth f. Alexander.
10 Jul.	1580	**Bogaerts**, Daneel f. Alexsander.
10 Sep.	1587	,, Isaak f. Sanders.
5 Jul.	1573	**Bogard**, Jacob f. ,,
16 Mar.	1576	,, Abraham f. Alexander.
17 Feb.	1579	**Bogards**, Sara f. Willem.
17 ,,	1572	**Bogarts**, Isaack f. Alexander.
30 Nov.	1578	**Bogardts**, Susanna f. Alexander.
8 Dec.	1583	**Bogardtz**, Abraham f. ,,
26 Oct.	1589	**Boije**, Jacolynkgen f. Pieter.
10 Mar.	1588	**Boyr**, Van, Elizabeth f. ,,
20 Sep.	1573	**Boijs**, du, Judith f. Laureyns.
13 Mei	1595	**Boijs**, de, Abraham f. Jan.
5 Jul.	1601	**Boijsse**, de, Abigail f. Maximiliaen.
7 Jul.	1577	**Bois**, de, Sara f. Laureijns.
26 Jul.	1579	**Bois**, du, Laurens f. Laurens.
12 Sep.	1585	,, ,, Thomas f. ,,
31 Oct.	1602	,, ,, Jacobmijntken f. ,,
24 Feb.	1684	**Boisaur**, he, (v. **Buisseur**), Maria f. Abraham & Maria Ricqut.
19 Mei	1678	**Boishant**, Francin f. Louis.
1 Mei	1642	**Boison**, Vanden, Jacques f. Joris, Tot Mortlake, in de Engelsche Kercke.
1 Dec.	1678	**Bokart**, Josua f. Jost Josua & Susanna Scholder.
12 Mei	1605	**Bol**, Leonora f. Pieter.
11 Dec.	1606	,, Thomas f. ,,
6 Jan.	1608	**Bolde**, Van der, Elisabeth & Judith } f. Artus.
15 Mar.	1618	**Boldewyn**, (v. **Bollewijn**), Sara f. Joos.
6 Feb.	1597	**Bollaert**, Pieter f. Pieter.
17 Dec.	1626	,, ,, f. ,,
13 Dec.	1629	**Bollart**, Joannes f. ,,
25 Mar.	1581	**Bolle**, Van, Gengomijn f. Herman.
28 Mei	1598	**Bolle**, Franciscus f. Jooris.
9 Dec.	1610	,, Charles f. Jacob.

9 Ap.	1620	**Bollewijn**, (v. **Boldewyn**), Jacobus f. Joos.
1 Mei	1621	,, Rogier f. ,,
12 Dec.	1705	**Bolmeijer**, Anna f. Jan & Anna.
13 Sep.	1702	**Bolmeir**, Maria f. Johannes & Johanna.
28 Jan.	1579	**Bolten**, Tobias f. Adam.
15 Jan.	1641	**Bolti**, Jacobus f. Adriaen.
19 Jan.	1643	**Boltie**, Daniel f. ,,
25 Apl.	1602	**Bombinder**, (v. **Boombinder**), Anna f. Thomas.
14 Oct.	1627	**Bommaert**, Geertruijt f. Goijvaert.
26 Ap.	1579	**Bon**, (v. **Bone**, **Bons**), Tobias f. Matheus.
18 Dec.	1580	**Bonchier**, le, Pieter f. Andries.
9 Feb.	1584	,, ,, Andries f. ,,
22 Jan.	1581	**Bone**, (v. **Bon**), Jonas f. Mattheus.
1 Mei	1582	,, Sara f. ,,
8 Feb.	1603	,, Johannes f. Pieter.
2 Mei	1591	**Boneval**, Joannes f. Marten.
15 Jul.	1593	,, Abigail f. ,,
6 Oct.	1689	**Bongaert**, Van der, Loisa Odilia Theodore f. Hermannus & Margriete Judith.
16 Nov.	1735	**Bongarde**, Leonard Daniel f. Frederik Daniel & Anna Van Koopstad.
2 Dec.	1606	**Bonharinck**, Johannes f. Christian.
26 Dec.	1605	**Bonneel**, Catharina f. David.
15 Feb.	1607	,, Susanna f. ,,
7 Aug.	1608	,, David f. ,,
26 Nov.	1609	,, Jacobus f. ,,
26 Mei	1611	,, Anna f. ,,
25 Oct.	1612	,, Samuel f. ,,
13 Mar.	1614	,, Ester f. ,,
8 Oct.	1615	,, Jeremias f. ,,
27 Jul.	1617	,, Nathaniel f. ,,
1 Nov.	1618	,, Sara f. ,,
9 Ap.	1620	,, Sijmeon f. ,,
11 Nov.	1621	,, Maria f. ,,
8 Feb.	1624	,, Paulus f. ,,
10 Jul.	1625	,, Elisabeth f. ,,
29 Jan.	1600	**Bonette**, Petrus f. Jan.
2 Jan.	1601	,, Johanne f. ,,
19 Ap.	1603	,, Jacobus f. ,,
6 Sep.	1604	,, Elias f. ,,
19 Nov.	1605	,, Maria f. ,,
26 Nov.	1607	,, Ester f. ,,
6 Mar.	1586	**Bonnette**, Elias f. Hendrick.
11 Jul.	1574	**Bonnijnck**, Maria f. Gheraert.
10 Jul.	1575	**Bons**, (v. **Bon**), Maria, f. Mathieuw.
9 Oct.	1572	**Bontenaken** Isaac f. Gillis.
24 Jan.	1574	,, Jacob f. ,,
25 Mei	1578	,, Susanna f. ,,
3 Jul.	1575	**Bonters**, Pieter f. Pieter.
27 Feb.	1575	**Bontevale**, Sara f. Gillis.
31 Jan.	1742	**Boods**, Anna Maria f. Johan & Johar Spillebout.
16 Oct.	1580	**Booij**, de, Johannes f. Gillis.
9 Nov.	1574	**Boom**, Vander, Pauwels f. Leenart.
24 Aug.	1623	,, ,, Petrus f. Lenard.
27 Ap.	1596	**Boombinder**, (v. **Bombinder**) Dionysius Thomas.
22 Jan.	1598	,, Susanna f. Thomas.
24 Oct.	1574	**Boone**, Abraham f. Marten.
23 Aug.	1581	,, Pieter f. ,,
1 Aug.	1583	,, Memorantia f. ,,
14 Feb.	1585	,, Marie f. ,,
6 Nov.	1586	,, Susanna f. ,,
21 Ap.	1589	,, Abigail f. ,,
31 Mar.	1590	,, Johannes f. ,,

1 Jul.	1677	Braem, Maria f. Caspar.
17 Dec.	1598	Braems, Pieter f. Geeraert.
39 Nov.	1600	„ Abraham f. „
31 Jan.	1608	„ Joannes f. Jan.
16 Mar.	1606	„ Daniel f. Daniel.
9 Feb.	1608	„ Susanna f. Daniel.
7 Jan.	1610	„ Maria f. „
27 Oct.	1611	„ Elisabeth f. „
4 Jul.	1613	„ Elisabet f. „
29 Aug.	1613	„ Daniel f. Jaques.
25 Mei	1607	Brand, Eliezer f. Geeraert.
16 Ap.	1609	„ Anna f. Geerard.
11 Jul.	1694	„ Vanden, Gerritje f. Roeland & Annetje Dothorst.
5 Sep.	1697	Brands „ Arent f. Roeland & Annetje Dothorst.
25 Mar.	1696	Brandt „ Maria f. Roelandt.
10 Dec.	1699	„ „ Elisabeth f. Roeland.
18 Mar.	1604	Brandts, Vanden, Judith f. Jan.
2 Jul.	1620	„ Johannes f. „
20 Feb.	1591	Brant, Vanden, Maria f. Benedictus.
1 Jan.	1593	„ „ Jacob f..
2 Jan.	1603	„ Sara f. Geeraert.
10 Feb.	1605	„ Daniel f. „
19 Mei	1611	„ Debora f. „
23 Oct.	1692	„ Vanden, Maria f. Roeland.
18 Oct.	1702	„ Catarina f. Roelant & Catarina.
9 Feb.	1707	„ Vanden, Anthoni f. Roelant & Catarina Vander Burgh.
24 Nov.	1594	Brants, Debora f. Gerart.
13 Jun.	1605	„ Martha f. Jan.
2 Sep.	1702	Erans, Bostiaen f. Bastiaen.
9 Aug.	1579	Brauwer, Joannes f. Willem.
11 Jun.	1583	Brauwers, Susanna f. „
18 Feb.	1584	Brauwier, Pieter f. Job.
21 Feb.	1580	Brauwiers, Esther f. Job.
17 Jan.	1574	Brawere, de, Abraham f. Vincent.
16 Aug.	1584	Brauwers, Isaac f. Simous, Trompettmaker.
8 Mei	1586	Brecston, Pieter f. Pieter.
2 Ap.	1579	Bree, Van, Samuel f. Hans.
24 Mei	1607	Bredenbach, Van, Hendrick f. ....
19 Jul.	1608	„ „ Elisabeth f. Heyndryck.
23 Aug.	1691	Bree, Van, Fop } f. Egbert & & Alida } Arentje.
4 Nov.	1688	Bree, de, Herman f. Dirck & Maria.
12 Mar.	1612	Breedenbach, Van, Sara } f. Hen- & Rebecca } dric.
27 Aug.	1576	Breen, Van, Johannes f. Hans.
3 Feb.	1583	„ „ Thomas f. „
18 Jul.	1585	„ „ Jonas f. „
8 Ap.	1588	„ „ Susanna f. Jan.
28 Sep.	1690	„ „ Abraham f. Jacob.
13 Aug.	1581	Brekmans, Maria f. Heijuderik.
21 Ap.	1618	Brent, Maria, f. Melof.
27 Jul.	1690	Brevinck, Janneken f. Jan & Saertje.
12 Dec.	1591	Bricstein, Abraham f. Pieter.
21 Jan.	1714	Barentz alias Bridley, Maria f. Albert & Maria.
29 Mei	1623	Briskin, Willem f. Willem.
20 Feb.	1625	„ Thomas f. „
14 Apl.	1622	Brocht, Abraham f. Abraham.
25 Dec.	1625	„ Abraham } f. & Sara }
27 Ap.	1690	Broeck, Vanden, Pieter f. Nicolas & Mettie.
13 Mei	1691	„ „ Jan. f. „ & Maria.
7 Oct.	1582	Broecke, Vanden, Susanna f. „
19 Sep.	1585	„ „ Joannes f. „
21 Ap.	1588	„ „ Elisabeth f. Niclaes.
18 Mar.	1593	Broecke, Vanden, Pieter f. Niclaes.
29 Ap.	1584	„ „ Joannes f. Jan.
10 Oct.	1585	„ Van, Abraham f. Jan.
13 Mar.	1614	„ Vanden, Elisabet f. Samuel.
20 Sep.	1618	„ „ Elisabet f. Pieter.
10 Sep.	1620	„ „ Michael f. „
16 Jun.	1622	„ „ Maria f. „
8 Feb.	1624	„ „ Petrus f. „
23 Sep.	1627	„ „ Abraham f. Adriaen.
13 Feb.	1603	„ „ Abraham f. Abraham.
9 Dec.	1604	„ Sara f. „
23 Nov.	1606	„ Van, Debora f. „
26 Nov.	1607	„ Vanden, Judith f. „
13 Nov.	1608	„ „ Isaac f. „
2 Feb.	1612	„ „ Maria f. „
3 Jul.	1614	„ „ Anna f. „
4 Aug.	1616	„ „ Anna f. „
11 Mar.	1617	„ „ Anna f. „
8 Nov.	1618	„ „ Joanna f. „
15 Nov.	1618	„ „ „ f. „
7 Oct.	1627	„ „ Anna f. „
2 Mei	1630	„ „ Abraham f. „
15 Ap.	1632	„ „ Isaac f. „
6 Aug.	1629	„ „ Salomon f. Salomon.
5 Mei	1622	„ „ Joannes f. „
15 Mar.	1628	„ „ Abigail f. „
18 Oct.	1629	„ „ Susanna f. „
27 Feb.	1631	„ „ Johanna f. „
11 Mar.	1632	„ „ Maria f. „
9 Feb.	1634	„ „ Eleazar f, „
6 Dec.	1636	„ „ Jacobus f. „
25 Mei	1640	„ „ Maria f. „
31 Jul.	1614	Broeckhoven, Van, Joannes f. Hans.
30 Aug.	1618	„ „ Maria f. Jan.
24 Oct.	1619	„ „ Abigail f. Hans.
17 Nov.	1622	„ „ Anna f. „
29 Aug.	1602	Eroedels, Joos f. Johannes.
10 Jan.	1601	Broeder, Maria f. Jacobus.
21 Dec.	1745	„ de, Anna f. Jacob & Jannetje Hoodo
1 Mar.	1629	Broederen, ... f. Joos.
29 Jul.	1571	s'Broeders, Rebecca f. Gilles.
3 Jul.	1631	Broeders, Susanna f. Joos.
22 Sep.	1633	„ Anna f. „
3 Apl.	1636	„ Elisabeth f. „
29 Mei	1586	Broeke, Van, Philips f. Fransois.
15 Dec.	1796	Broeke, Ten, Jane f. James & Rebec Waterhouse.
18 Mei	1807	„ „ Geb. 4 Jun., 1798, Rebecca James & Rebec Waterhouse.
„ „	„	„ „ Geb. 6 Feb. 1800, James James & Rebec Waterhouse.
„ „	„	„ „ Geb. 5 Oct. 1801, Susann Goodall f. James Rebecca Waterhou
„ „	„	„ „ Geb. 10 Mar. 1804, Ma Ann f. James & Rebe Waterhouse.
„ „	„	„ „ Geb. 13 Sep. 1805, Anth f. James & Rebe Waterhouse.
20 Dec.	1815	„ „ Amelius John f. Williar Amelia Arone Schnebbe
28 Jun.	1573	Bron, Joannes f. Jan.
30 Sep.	1575	Broon, Cornelis f. „
28 Jun.	1578	Brouijn, Daniel f. Pieter.
11 Sep.	1573	Broun, Osther f. Jan.

10 Mei	1593	Buren, Van, Abraham f. Jacques.
22 Nov.	1702	Burg, (v. Burij), Jacobus f. Engel & Jannetje Abrahams.
20 Mar.	1608	Burgaert, Barbara f. Herman.
27 Jan.	1731	Burgenkaten, Ten, Herman f. Herman & Mary.
5 Aug.	1694	Burghard, Anna f. Johannes & Maria.
15 Oct.	1587	Burgrave, de, Charle f. Pieter.
13 Oct.	1640	,, ,, William f. Philip.
19 Nov.	1704	Burij, Isaack f. Engel & Jannetje Abrahams.
29 Jul.	1707	,, Willem f. ,, ,, ,,
18 Mei	1709	,, Abigail f. ,, ,, ,,
6 Feb.	1712	,, Antony f. ,, ,, ,,
25 Jan.	1713	,, Susanna f. ,, ,, ,,
11 Feb.	1722	,, Elisabeth f. Abraham & Sara Willliams.
27 Oct.	1577	Burke, Susanna f. Jan.
17 Mar.	1650	Burkin, Anna f. Jacob.
27 Nov.	1651	,, James f. James & Jeane.
15 Oct.	1653	,, Johanna f. Jacob. Ged. in de Gabriel, Fan Church, Lowlen.
14 Oct.	1654	,, Johannes f. Jacob & Johanna le Tuillier.
13 Jun.	1596	Burlij, Samuel f. Humfrid.
10 Oct.	1591	Burman, Sara f. Dierick.
22 Mar.	1646	Burns, Abigail f. Isaac.
12 Jul.	1760	Burton, Philippus Albertus f. Hendrik & Maria Masse.
29 Mei	1696	Bursi, (v. Burci), Gabriel f. Marcus.
10 Aug.	1712	Busch, Daniel Lambert f. Hendrick & Anna Lambert.
6 Feb.	1715	,, Anna f. Hendrick & Anna Lambert.
17 Feb.	1717	,, Franciscus f. Hendrick & Anna Lambert.
2 Oct.	1720	,, Anna f. Hendrick & Anna Lambert.

22 Feb.	1635	Buser, Maria f. Lenard.
3 Ap.	1678	Bush, Johannes f. Johan & Maria.
4 Jun.	1598	Busicom, Van, (v. Buesecom), Joannes f. Nicolas.
5 Nov.	1590	Busken (v. Buesken & Buskens,) Jacob f. Lieven.
15 Jul.	1593	,, Leon f. Leon.
3 Oct.	1596	,, Jacob f. ,,
25 Nov.	1599	,, Anna f. Lion.
30 Mei	1602	,, Leo f. Leo.
30 Nov.	1600	,, Sara f. Hans.
30 Jan.	1603	,, Abraham f. ,,
5 Oct.	1606	,, Johannes f. ,,
30 Oct.	1608	,, Susanna f. Jan.
10 Nov.	1616	,, Lucas f. ,,
2 Jun.	1628	,, Anna f. ,,
22 Jul.	1638	,, Jacobus f. Lion.
21 Mei	1639	,, Elisabeth f. Lijon.
1 ,,	1642	,, Maria f. ,,
13 Aug.	1690	Bussche, Van den, Jasper f. Fr: Jasper & Anna.
11 Nov.	1691	,, ,, Anna f. Fr: Jasper & Anna.
21 Sep.	1578	Busschon, Susanna, komende vth Barberyen.
20 Ap.	1600	Busson, de, Jacobus f. Maximiliaen.
27 Mar.	1603	,, du, Marcus f. ,,
18 Dec.	1610	,, Susanna f. Maxiliaen.
3 Aug.	1628	Butler, Susanna f. Jacob.
20 Ap.	1643	Butterdroger, de, (v. Drogeboter, etc), Isaac f. Andries.
1 Aug.	1602	Buug, Jacobus f. John.
15 Dec.	1813	Buuren, Van, Hendrik Oostwald Eksteen f. Gerardus & Elisabeth Josina Eksteen.
27 Mar.	1580	Buven, ,, Joannes f. Jakes.
7 Oct.	1589	Buxstein, Elisabeth f. Pieter.

29 Jul.	1812	Caarten, Fredrik Herman Arnold f. Adriaan Herman Bicker & Sara Maria Van Ijzendoorn.
26 Dec.	1816	,, James Andrew f. Adriaan Herman Bicker & Sara Maria Van Ijzendoorn.
20 Jan.	1821	,, Herminah Hannah f. Adriaan Herman Bicker & Sara Maria Van Ijzendoorn.
22 Jan.	1828	,, Alfred Gerard } f. Adriaan Herman Bicker & Sara Maria Van & Isabel Frederica } Ijzendoorn.
20 Jan.	1740	Caddee, Susanne f. Bartholomeus & Martha Ludkins.
25 Dec.	1740	Cade, Jan f. Bart & Martha Loggin.
5 Dec.	1641	Caestarker, de, Johannes f. Jan.
4 Apl.	1589	Caf, (v. Calf), Isaac f. Hendrick.

15 Ap.	1750	Cahais, Susanna f. Jacobus & Susanna Beaufort.
21 Mar.	1756	,, Samuel f. ,, ,,
18 Nov.	1641	Calandrin, Isabella Maria f. Cesar.
19 Jul.	1646	Calandrinus, Jeane f. Cesar, tot Batterse
3 Jun.	1655	Calant, Jacobus f. Oliver.
17 Aug.	1656	,, Olievier f. Olivier.
9 Jan.	1814	Caleshoek, Martinus f. Gerrit & Maria Knos.
4 Mei	1698	Callenburgh, Matthys f. Matthys & Anna Hoedemaecker.
26 Sep.	1602	Calf, (v. Caf), Joos f. Joos.
21 Ap.	1605	,, Benjamin f. ,,
30 Aug.	1607	,, Joos f. ,,
1 Jul.	1610	,, Pieter f. ,,
22 Dec.	1586	Caliau, Elias f. Anthony.
8 Ap.	1589	,, Magdalena f. ,,
16 Aug.	1590	Caliou, Catherina f. ,,
20 Mar.	1692	Calowet, Sarah f. Pieter & Sara.

22 Jul. 1680	Citters, Van, Arnoudina f. van syne Excellentie de Heer Arnout, Ambassadeur, etc., & my vrou Johanna Parduin.	
9 Nov. 1681	„ „ Johannes f. Arnout & Josina Paraduijn.	
28 Feb. 1684	„ „ Maria f. Arnout & Josina Paraduijn.	
29 Sep. 1685	„ „ Wilhelmus f. Arnout & Josina Paraduijn.	
11 Nov. 1571	Claeszes, Kathelina f. Kristiaen.	
14 Dec. 1572	Claijs, Sara f. Christiaen.	
18 Mei 1589	Claesz, Salomon f. Evert.	
9 Jun. 1595	Claeijsz, Maria f. Everdt.	
2 Oct. 1597	Claeijssen, Elisabeth f. Evard.	
21 Dec. 1589	Claeijssen, Jacob f. Jan.	
21 Nov. 1591	Claesz, David f. „	
21 Oct. 1593	Claessen, David f. „	
23 Nov. 1595	Claisz, Marie f. „	
7 Ap. 1605	Claessz, Maria f. Hans.	
24 Oct. 1591	Claesz, Abraham f. Abraham.	
26 Feb. 1598	Claijsz, Anna f. Pieter.	
21 Mei 1620	Claeyssen, Albertus f. Aelbert.	
19 Dec. 1624	Claesz, Catharina f. Gillis.	
9 Mar. 1828	Claassen, Anna Catharina f. Georg. & Anna Catharina Korte.	
18 Ap. 1830	„ Carel f. George & Anna Catharine Korte.	
20 Mei 1832	„ Maria Elizabeth f. George & Anna Catharine Korte.	
16 Oct. 1835	„ Henriette f. George & Anna Catharine Korte.	
8 Oct. 1837	„ Louise f. George & Anna Catharine Korte.	
27 Mar. 1603	Claijens, Debora f. Pieter.	
9 Jul. 1612	Claijt, Robert f. Jan.	
27 Jul. 1613	Claij, Joannes f. „	
27 Mei 1655	Clarck, de, (v. Clerck), Anna f. Jacob.	
9 Feb. 1679	Clasen, Anna f.	
25 Oct. 1573	Cleijmans, (v. Cleijnman), Hester f. Pieter.	
14 Aug. 1575	„ Davie, f. Pieter.	
12 Ap. 1585	„ Johannes f. „	
8 Jan. 1587	„ Pieter f. „	
12 Mei 1588	„ Maria f. „	
8 Feb. 1590	„ Isaack f. „	
2 Dec. 1576	Cleijne, Elizabet f. Adolf.	
20 Mei 1582	Cleijnen, (v. Clienen), Sarra f. Olivijer.	
30 Mar. 1578	Cleijnmans, (v. Clienen), Daniel f. Pieter.	
9 Mar. 1623	Clemme, Van der, Kraft f. Alexander.	
20 Dec. 1797	Clenshaw, (v. Clinshaw), Elizabeth f. Jan & Elizabeth Gaul.	
12 Jul. 1576	Clerx, Isaack f. Jans.	
16 Oct. 1580	„ Samuel f. „	
13 Oct. 1577	„ Sara f. Hendrick.	
27 Mar. 1582	Clerckx, Jacob & Rachel } f. Hendrick.	
5 Sep. 1585	Clerck, de, Sara f. Robert.	
26 Jun. 1586	Clerck, Francoijs f. Simon.	
9 Jun. 1588	„ Elizabeth f. Sijmon.	
26 Ap. 1590	Clerx, Anna f. „	
9 Mei 1591	Clerck, Adriaen f. „	
1 Ap. 1593	„ Johannes f. „	
30 Mar. 1595	Clercx, Maria f. „	
31 Dec. 1598	Clerck, de, Susanna f. „	
14 Dec. 1589	„ „ Cathelina f. Anthonijs.	
24 Mei 1591	„ „ Elizabeth f. Anthenis.	
18 Feb. 1593	Clerc, Tobias, Illeg. f. Anthonis.	
6 Dec. 1601	Clerck, de, Abraham f. Jacob.	

24 Mar. 1601	Clerck, de, Abraham f. Pieter.	
15 Aug. 1602	„ „ Susanna f. „	
25 „ 1605	„ „ Ester f. „	
4 Dec. 1606	„ „ Maria f. „	
22 Mei 1608	„ „ Pieter f. „	
15 „ 1610	„ „ Anna f. „	
10 Nov. 1611	„ le Isaac & Jacob } f. „	
28 Oct. 1599	„ „ Joannes f. Isaac.	
1 Nov. 1601	„ „ Abraham f. „	
28 Oct. 1604	„ „ Joannes f. „	
25 Sep. 1608	„ „ Johanna f. „	
17 Dec. 1609	„ „ Jacobus f. „	
8 Oct. 1609	„ „ David f. David.	
14 Aug. 1614	„ „ Susanna f. „	
10 Aug. 1617	„ „ Sara f. „	
2 Jun. 1639	„ „ Sara f. Jacob.	
9 Sep. 1660	„ „ (v. Clark) Catarina f.,,	
27 Mar. 1575	Cleven, Van, Jeromias f. Alexander.	
17 Mar. 1588	Clienen, (v. Cleijnen) Maria f. Olivier.	
25 Sep. 1580	Clijnen, Johannes f. „	
11 Dec. 1586	Cliever, de, Jacobus f. Franchoijs."	
14 Nov. 1591	„ „ Samuel f. „	
20 Ap. 1593	„ „ David f. „	
18 Jan. 1586	Clincboom, Esther f. Willem.	
22 Oct. 1592	Clijnckboom, Elizabeth f. „	
3 Mar. 1601	Clinckart, David f. Abraham.	
15 Feb. 1747	Cainshan, Susanna f. Jan & Susanna de Haan.	
6 Nov. 1748	„ Maria f. „ „	
16 Sep. 1750	„ Elizabeth f. „ „	
19 Aug. 1753	„ Jan. f. „ „	
21 Ap. 1755	„ Sara f. „ „	
8 Aug. 1756	„ Anna f. „ „	
25 Jun. 1758	„ Elisabeth f. „ „	
18 Nov. 1759	„ Jacobus f. „ „	
8 Feb. 1761	„ Margaretaf. „ „	
10 Nov. 1791	Clinshaw, (v. Clenshaw), Pieter Jan & Elizabeth Cook.	
8 Jul. 1621	Cloij, Elizabeth f. Tobias.	
12 Aug. 1627	Clopper, de, Abigail f. Frederick.	
6 Mar. 1631	„ „ Frederijck f. „	
26 Jul. 1633	„ „ Andreas f. „	
24 Sep. 1587	Clopperijs, Hester f. Dierick.	
20 Sep. 1593	Clouens, Rebecca f. Pieter.	
21 Jul. 1605	Clouns, Jacobus f. „	
21 Mar. 1596	Clouwens, Sara f. „	
28 Mei 1598	Clouwijs, Susanna f. „	
21 Aug. 1631	Cnuijt, de, (v. Knuijt), Susanna f. Michiel.	
6 Oct. 1597	Cob, Henricus f. Henrick.	
22 Nov. 1601	„ Isaac f. „	
4 Aug. 1611	„ Anna f. „	
15 Nov. 1590	Cobbe, Henricus f. „	
20 Ap. 1595	„ Jacobus f. „	
10 Feb. 1600	„ Abraham f. „	
18 Mei 1679	Coci, (v. Cooci), Sara f. Pieter.	
18 Mar. 1683	„ Isaack f. „	
10 Jan. 1695	„ Maria f. Gabriel.	
5 Jul. 1696	„ Johannes f. „ & Maria.	
14 „ 1697	„ Susanna f. „ „	
15 Dec. 1700	„ Pieter f. „ „	
17 Mar. 1689	Cocie, Maria f. Pieter & Sara.	
9 Jan. 1681	Cocit, Abram f. ; test. William.	
28 Feb. 1608	Cock, de, (v. Cocq.), Jonas f. Jonas.	
11 Mei 1662	„ „ Dorothea f. Theodore.	
7 Jun. 1663	„ „ Theodorus f. „	
4 Sep. 1664	„ „ Maria f. „ & Christina Tierens	

13 Oct.	16 6	Cock, de,	Hannah f. John & Hannah.
3 Jul.	16 9	„ „	Johannes f. „ „
6 Mei	1691	„ „	Theodore f. ..
29 Feb.	1700	„ „	Agnieta Sarah f. Walter & Johanna.
18 Jul.	1705	„ „	Ida f. Walter & Johanna.
30 Jul.	1707	„ „	Walter f. „ „
6 Jan.	1710	„ „	Theodoricus f. „
24 Mar.	168.)	Cockraue,	„ Johannes f. Johannes & Hannah : test. Sir John Cockrane & Juffr. de Weduwe van Fr. Willem de Weert.
11 Oct.	1573	Cocq.	„ (v. Cock), Jacob f. Jacob.
12 Feb.	1576	„ de,	Elisabet f. Jacques.
21 Jun.	1607	„ „	Jacobus f. „
4 Jul.	1694	Cocquel (v. Cokel), Willem f. Willem & Maria Schaa.
13 Apl.	1589	Cockx, Anna f. Joris.
26 Feb	1633	„ William f. Makijs.
15 Oct.	1587	Cocz, Abraham f. Joris.
1 Oct.	1592	„ Jooris f. „
12 Oct.	1589	Coex, Jacobus f. Hendrick.
6 Nov.	1698	Cokel (v. Cocquel), Michiel f. Willem &
19 Nov.	1682	Ceket (v. Coci), Hendricus f. Peter.
5 Aug.	1683	Coeleman, Elizabeth f. Cornelis & Magdaleen Souwie.
15 Ap.	1688	Coelemeij (v. Koelemeij), Jannetje f. Cornelis.
21 Mar.	1680	Coelemij, Cornelis f. „
5 Jul.	1584	Coolen, ... f. Jan.
6 Feb.	1698	Coelom, Martha f. Ephraim & Maria Peters.
12 Ap.	1573	Coen, Zacharias f. Jan.
25 Sep.	1608	Coep, Johannes f. Henrick.
8 Oct.	1809	Coesvelt, William Henry f. Henry & Anna Christina Broekhuisen.
30 Dec.	1810	„ Johanna Christina f. Henry & Anna Christina Broekhuisen.
19 Jan.	1589	Coge, de, Elizabeth f. Franchoijs.
6 Ap.	1592	„ „ Jacobus f. „
9 Nov.	1595	„ „ Anna f. „
26 Dec.	1606	Cogge, de, Franciscus f. „
25 Aug.	1635	Cogghe, „ Jacobus f. „
17 Jan.	1608	„ „ Nicolaus f. Franchoys.
20 Feb.	1610	„ „ Matthews f. „
19 Dec.	1611	Coghe, „ Susanna f. „
9 Jun.	1614	„ „ Rebecca f. „
7 Nov.	1616	„ „ Catharina f. „
22 Nov.	1590	Cohorst, Joannes f. Jacus.
15 Jan.	1606	Coijgen, Van, Peeter f. Jacob.
5 Apl.	1692	Coijghen, Jacobus f. Jan.
14 Jul.	1633	Colduck, Nathanael f. Jan. Jansz.
16 Aug.	1674	Cole, Christianus f. Johannes & Catarina Dusart.
2 Feb.	1614	Colen, Bertholomeus f. Heijndrick.
6 Aug.	1592	Colgon, Petrus f. Jan.
29 Ap.	1606	„ Israel f. „
17 Mar.	1706	Colijn, (v. Colleins), Johannes f. Abraham & Anna Gerdon.
1 Mei	1597	Colijns, Clara f. Henric.
28 Feb.	1608	Colin, Joannes f. Geeraert.
12 Jan.	1701	Colleins, (v. Colijn), Peter f. Abraham & Anna Cordon.
6 Feb.	1726	Collignon, Charles f. Paulus & Anna.
6 Oct.	1594	Collij, Abraham f. Hendrick.
11 Jun.	1592	Collijns, Judith f. „
1 Mar.	1590	„ Susanna f. „

24 Aug.	1587	Colonels, Jacobus f. Pauwels.
11 Dec.	1586	Colve, Maria f. Anthonij.
14 Mar.	1596	Comer, Susanna f. Cornelis.
31 Jan.	1613	Conijn, Joannes f. Jan.
10 Jul.	1614	„ Anna f. „
4 Feb.	1685	„ Jacobus f. Jacobus & Susanna.
18 Mei	1577	Coninck, de, (v. Conijnck, Coninc, Connick), Pieter f. Jan.
24 Aug.	1607	„ „ Johannes f. Jaques.
14 Jan.	1610	„ „ Tobias f. „
25 Dec.	1611	„ „ Hendrick f. „
24 Oct.	1613	„ „ Theodorus f. „
6 Aug.	1620	„ „ Abraham f. Jacob.
2 Jun.	1622	„ „ Martinus f. Hendrie.
8 Sep.	1622	„ „ Jooris f. Passchier.
20 Feb.	1623	„ „ Samuel f. posthumus Samuel.
6 Mar.	1623	„ „ Anna f. Gabriel.
8 Mar.	1625	„ „ Anna f. „
25 Mei	1626	„ „ Samuel f. „
2 Feb.	1630	„ „ Elisabeth f. „
30 Jan.	1625	„ „ Jacobus f. Hendrick.
23 Jul.	1626	„ „ Maria f. „
19 Ap.	1629	„ „ Hendric f. „
27 Mar.	1631	„ „ Anna f. „
22 Dec.	1633	„ „ Sara f. „
1 Mei	1636	„ „ Johannes f. „
26 Nov.	1637	„ „ Maria f. „
10 Mei	1640	„ „ Johannes f. „
1 Jan.	1642	„ „ Johanna f. „
29 Feb.	1624	„ „ Andreas f. Andreas.
12 Mar.	1626	„ „ Anna f. Andries.
22 Dec.	1633	„ „ Gillis f. Antoni.
24 Aug.	1637	„ „ Johanna f. Pieter.
27 Feb.	16 6	„ „ Johannes f. Samuel.
29 Mar.	1657	„ „ Elisabet f. Do. Joannes.
10 Mei	1612	Conijnck, de, Martynken f. Anthony.
12 Jun.	1614	Coninc, „ Joannes f. „
27 Mar.	1626	„ „ Joannes f. posthumus Jan.
9 Ap.	1643	Conink, „ Hester f. Pieter.
1 Oct.	1648	„ „ Elisabet f. Samuel.
30 Mar.	1651	„ „ Lea f. „
5 „	1654	„ „ Maria f. „
15 „	1691	Coninckstijn, Van, Johannes f. Pieter & Susanna Maria.
13 Mei	1596	Conuick, de, Isaac f. Gulian.
31 „	1646	„ „ Hester f. Johannes.
14 Jun.	1646	„ „ Samuel f. Samuel.
19 Mei	1611	Conninck, „ (v. Cuenijnck), Elisabeth f. Paschier.
22 Aug.	1703	Cooci (v. Coci), Joseph f. Gabriel & Maria.
4 Sep.	1705	„ Sara, f. Gabriel & Maria.
1 Jun.	1617	Cool, Nicolaus, f. Pieter.
12 Jul.	1618	„ Hester f. „
25 Dec.	1619	„ Elisabet f. „
4 Feb.	1621	„ Joannes f. „
27 Jan.	1622	„ Susanna f. „
23 Mar.	1623	„ Maria f. „
6 Jun.	1624	„ Anthonintgen f. „
6 Aug.	1676	Coolenkamp, Maria f. Willem.
17 Jun.	1684	Coop, (v. Cop), Joos f. Hendrick.
28 Aug.	1663	„ Anna f. „
30 Nov.	1646	„ Mayken f. „
28 Aug.	1586	Coopmans, Janneken f. Fransois.
21 Sep.	1592	Cooreus, (v. Coreus), Jaspar f. Jaspar.
13 Ap.	1595	„ Cornelis f. „
18 Nov.	1614	Cop, Margareta f. Henrick.
9 Jan.	1681	Coppelvelt, Elias f. Elias.

28 Jun. 1581 **Coppens,** Joannes f. Cornelis.
16 Ap. 1587 „ Susanna f. „
9 Mei 1591 „ Elias f. Audries.
11 Sep. 1593 „ Lidia, f. „
28 Jan. 1591 **Copperebolle,** Van, Daniel f. Pieter.
10 Nov. 1605 **Corcelis,** (v. **Corselis, Courcelis,** etc.), Maria f. Seger.
2 Feb. 1612 „ Lucas f. Lucas.
3 Jul. 1628 „ Jacobus f. Nicolais.
27 Mar. 1597 **Corens,** (v. **Coorens**), Anna f. Jaspar.
14 Sep. 1600 **Corijn,** Tobias f. Lucas.
19 Aug. 1571 **Cornelis,** Samuel f. Dierick.
2 Aug. 1573 **Cornelissen,** Abraham f. Pieter.
7 Feb. 1574 „ Jacob f. Jan.
23 Oct. 1576 „ Ludovicus f. Arent.
2 Aug. 1588 **Cornelisz,** Cornelis f. Wouter.
13 Ap. 1589 **Cornelissz,** Susanna f. Anthonius.
2 Jan. 1592 **Cornelis,** Cornelis f. Pauwels.
14 Jan. 1627 „ Cornelius f. .... & Neelken.
12 Oct. 1627 **Cornelissen,** Anna f. Adriaen.
28 Sep. 1637 **Cornelisz,** Petrus f. Rutger.
17 Jan. 1677 **Cornelisen,** Johannes f. Jan.
7 Nov. 1683 **Cornelis,** Catharina f. Arent.
21 Mar. 1686 „ Jacobus f. Ouda & Annotje.
23 Mar. 1690 **Cornelissen,** Cornelis f. Pieter & Elsjo.
9 Ap. 1690 „ Cornelis f. Jan & Lammetje. Oofs.
3 Jan. 1692 „ Margrieta f. Pieter & Elsje Oliviors.
22 Oct. 1693 „ Sarah f. Pieter & Sarah.
18 Mei 1696 „ Leonoora f. „ „
5 Dec. 1697 **Cornelis,** Johannes f. „ „
11 Ap. 1703 **Cornelissen,** Jacob f. Jacob & Geertruidt Jacobs.
13 Mar. 1597 **Cornet,** Jacolijnken & Anna } f. Cornelis.
8 Aug. 1598 „ Elizabeth f. „
12 Mei 1616 „ Susanna f. Jacques.
21 Dec. 1617 „ Erasmus f. Jacques.
21 Feb. 1619 „ Catharina f. „
21 Oct. 1621 „ Maria f. „
9 Feb. 1623 „ Hubertus f. „
27 Jan. 1624 „ Susanna f. „
22 Jun. 1626 „ Catharina f. „
22 Nov. 1627 „ Thomas f. „
17 Jan. 1630 **Cornette,** Sara f. „
30 Jun. 1594 **Cornu,** Joannes f. Walram.
24 Aug. 1578 **Corselis,** (v. **Corcelis**), Lucas f. Michiels.
5 Ap. 1594 „ Michiel f. Zegher.
22 Feb. 1596 „ Jossynken f. „
17 Feb. 1600 „ Nicolas f. „
14 Feb. 1602 „ Josyntken f. „
18 Aug. 1611 „ Seger f. Seger.
14 Mei 1609 „ Joannes f. Lucas.
12 Aug. 1610 „ Micael f. „
25 Jun. 1615 „ Jacobmyntken f. Lucas.
30 Jun. 1616 „ Maria f. „
9 Aug. 1618 „ Ester f. „
18 Feb. 1627 „ Petrus f. Abraham.
27 Mei 1632 „ Samuel f. Nicolaus.
9 Nov. 1589 **Corte,** Samuel f. Arnout.
11 Aug. 1590 **Cosijn,** (v. **Cousijn**), Abraham f. Geeraert.
4 Mei 1595 **Cosijns,** Abigail f. „
11 Jul. 1697 **Cosse,** Robbertus f. Koenraat & Johanna.
26 Oct. 1581 **Coster,** de, Abraham f. Martin.
2 Feb. 1589 „ „ Joannes f. Gielis.
20 Sep. 1590 „ „ Sara f. Gillis.
28 Mar. 1597 „ „ Maria f. „

19 Aug. 1593 **Coster,** de, Sara f. Charles.
5 Jan. 1585 „ „ Philips f. „
10 Mar. 1594 **Coster,** Paulus f. Dierick.
8 Aug. 1596 „ Abraham f. „
1 Sep. 1594 „ de, Anna f. Fransois.
4 „ 1599 „ „ Abraham f. „
7 Ap. 1616 **Coster,** Geeraert f. Jan. Gerritson.
22 Aug. 1574 **Costere,** de, Isaack f. Gillis.
29 Ap. 1593 „ „ Elisabeth f. „
25 Mei 1595 „ „ Abraham f. „
18 Jun. 1587 „ „ Susanna f. Jan.
24 Sep. 1592 „ „ Magdalena f. Charles.
11 Nov. 1595 **Costerman,** Joannes f. Leenaert.
17 Dec. 1598 „ Abraham f. Leonard.
24 Jan. 1608 „ Elisabeth f. „
14 Feb. 1630 „ Anna f. Jan.
29 Nov. 1640 „ Thomas f. ....
3 Nov. 1644 „ Abraham f. Jan.
1 Feb. 1590 **Coudron,** Aarnot f. Aarnot.
9 Dec 1596 „ Jeremias f. Arnout.
24 Mei 1599 „ Sara f. Aaron.
21 Jan. 1612 „ Abraham f. Aaron.
9 Feb. 1606 „ Sara f. „
1 Jan. 1610 „ Janneken f. Abraham.
7 Feb. 1611 „ Joannes f. „
13 Feb. 1631 „ Johanna f. Jeromias.
26 Ap. 1635 „ Jeremias f. ....
20 Aug. 1640 „ Susanna f. ....
24 Mar. 1594 **Coudrons,** Susanna f. Arnout.
30 Oct. 1603 **Couper,** Marie f. posthumus Herman.
22 Sep. 1588 **Couroelis,** (v. **Corcelis**), Anna f. Seger.
12 Jun. 1590 „ Susanna f. „
14 Mei 1592 „ Jossine f. „
12 Feb. 1598 „ Abraham f. „
17 Jan. 1574 **Courseles,** Maria f. Michiel.
6 Nov. 1575 **Courselis,** Rachel f. „
15 Feb. 1573 **Courte,** Elizabeth f. Rogier.
23 Oct. 1597 „ Maria f. Guliame de Jonge ; te Guliame Courte de oude, etc.
23 Jul. 1574 **Courten,** Debora f. Guillame.
20 Mei 1599 „ Pieter f. „
9 Ap. 1601 „ Joannes f. „ , de Jonge.
29 Dec. 1605 „ Esther f. Guillame.
29 Nov. 1607 „ Guillame f. „
30 Jul. 1609 „ Maria f. „
13 Feb. 1614 „ Anna f. „
3 Nov. 1616 „ Johannes f. „
2 Sep. 1610 **Courtens,** Joannes f. „
5 Ap. 1590 **Cousenaere,** Janneken f. Jaques.
1 Jul. 1591 „ Elizabeth f. Jacus de Jongh
25 Mei 1595 **Cousenare,** de, Abraham f. Jaques.
25 Ap. 1596 **Coussije,** Vander, Janneken f. Jacus.
8 Sep. 1588 **Cousijn,** (v. **Cosijn, Cousijns**), Petrus f. Pieter.
24 Feb. 1594 „ Pauwel f. Gheeraert.
16 Mei 1596 „ Elisabeth f. „
2 Oct. 1597 „ Jonathan f. „
9 Jan. 1599 **Cousijn,** Jonathan f. Geerart.
13 Mei 1599 **Cousijn,** Vander, Maria f. Jacus.
25 Jan. 1601 „ „ Elisabeth f. „
27 Feb. 1603 „ „ Petrus f. „
25 Ap. 1602 **Cousijns,** Jeremias f. Geerart.
11 Mei 1600 „ Nathanael f. „
15 Oct. 1570 **Cox,** (v. **Coex,** etc.), Daniel f. Willem.
29 Mei 1586 „ Jacob f. Jooris.
31 „ 1590 „ Maria f. „
25 Oct. 1572 **Crabbe,** Abraham f. Christiaen, Van Brug
11 Dec. 1575 „ Sara f. „

13 Feb.	1617	Dale, Van, Aeltken, oud ontrent 56 jaren.
10 Oct.	1578	Dalen ,, (v. Dale, etc.), Debora f. Marten.
30 Jan.	1689	,, ,, Maria f. Willem & Geertruijdt.
14 Dec.	1606	Dalu, Willem f. Richard.
30 Aug.	1648	Dam, Elisabet f. Obadia.
15 Oct.	1587	Daman, Elizabeth f. Willem.
18 Sep.	1603	Damans, Ras fa. ,,
10 Aug.	1617	Damar, (v. Dammer), Anna f. Samuel.
7 Mei	1592	Damart, Salomon f. Guliame.
10 Feb.	1601	,, Zacharias f. ,,
17 Ap.	1587	Damen, Maria f. Jan.
20 Mar.	1617	Damer (v. Damher & Damar), Daniel f. Pieter.
21 Jun.	1579	Damher, Catherine f. Jans.
20 Nov.	1586	Dammaert, Samuel f. Guliamme.
24 Nov.	1594	,, Sara f. ,,
9 Dec.	1615	,, (v. Dammer), Samuel f. Samuel.
21 Jan.	1627	,, Lucas f. ,,
1 Feb.	1590	Damman, Catelyn f. Willem.
21 Mar.	1596	,, Jacomynken f. Jeremias.
17 Aug.	1598	,, Susanna f. ,,
7 Jan.	1621	Dammart (v. Dammer), Samuel f. Samuel.
1 Jan.	1574	Damme, Van, David f. Lieven.
5 Mei	1577	,, ,, Susanna f. ,,
24 Jan.	1583	,, ,, Elisabeth f. Elisabeth.
8 Feb.	1590	,, ,, Debora f. Adrinen.
21 Mar.	1591	,, ,, Nathaniel & Daniel } f. ,,
12 Sep.	1589	,, ,, Lydia f. ,,
27 Jul.	1595	,, ,, Jacob f. ,,
18 Jul.	1596	,, ,, Joanna f. ,,
25 Jun.	1598	,, ,, Joannes f. ,,
10 Dec.	1592	,, ,, Sacharias & Joannes } f. Jan.
18 Ap.	1594	,, ,, Jacobus f. Gulian.
6 Ap.	1595	,, ,, Susanna f. ,,
24 Sep.	1597	,, ,, Abraham f. Laurens.
9 Sep.	1599	,, ,, f. ,,
19 Oct.	1600	,, ,, Susanna f. ,,
19 Dec.	1602	,, ,, Rachel f. ,,
21 Mar.	1596	,, ,, Sara f. Guiliame.
14 Mei	1598	,, ,, Samuel f. ,,
29 Jun.	1600	,, ,, Maria f. ,,
26 Mei	1605	,, ,, Petrus f. ,,
24 Aug.	1606	,, ,, Elizabeth f. ,,
8 Jan.	1609	,, ,, Maria f. ,,
27 Jul.	1611	,, ,, Abigail f. Guiljam.
21 Jul.	1611	,, ,, Lea & Rachel } f. Guilliame.
28 Feb.	1612	,, ,, Anna f. ,,
10 Mar.	1616	,, ,, Judith f. ,,
12 Jul.	1614	,, ,, Petrus f. Louijs.
7 Aug.	1616	,, ,, Maria f. Louwijs.
30 ,,	1618	,, ,, Justus f. Lowijs.
21 Ap.	1622	,, ,, Stephanus f. ,,
19 Mar.	1626	,, ,, Elisabeth f. Samuel.
20 Mar.	1628	,, ,, Samuel f. ,,
17 Jan.	1630	,, ,, Maria f. ,,
22 Jul.	1632	,, ,, Sara f. ,,
27 Dec.	1618	,, ,, Isaac f. ,,
9 Jan.	1625	Dammer (v. Dammaert, etc.), Willem f. Samuel.
8 Dec.	1622	Dammert, Abigail f. Samuel.
17 Sep.	1592	Dampier, Abigail f. Willem.
5 Ap.	1573	Daneels, Sara f. Adriaen.
15 Jul.	1576	,, Jacobus f. ,,
30 Mei	1596	,, Esther f. Jan.
1 Ap.	1599	Daniels, Susanna f. Hans.
22 Nov.	1601	Daniels, Joannes f. Jan.
5 Mei	1605	,, ,, f. Hans.
28 Jun.	1635	,, ,, f. Jan.
21 Sep.	1690	,, Pieter Johannes f. Carel & Anna.
17 Feb.	1633	Danis, Maria f. Pieter.
14 Feb.	1602	Dappaert, Johannes f. Cornelis Jansz.
11 Jan.	1685	Darlij, Isaac f. Pieter.
18 Mar.	1711	Darveau, (v. Dervean), Jacob f. Jacob & Susanna.
16 Jan.	1715	,, Jacobus f. Pieter & Catrina
6 Feb.	1687	Datselaer, Van, Elizabeth f. Jan & Maria.
18 Jul.	1688	,, ,, Daniel f. Jan & ,,
25 Feb.	1691	Datseler, Susanna Johanna f. ,, & Mary.
17 Ap.	1693	,, Maria f. John & Maria.
24 Sep.	1694	Datseler, Van, Christopher f. Jan & Maria
9 Aug.	1696	Datzeler, ,, Elisabeth f. Johan & Maria.
8 Sep.	1594	Dauwe, Joannes f. Hans.
2 Nov.	1595	,, Susanna f. Jan.
1 Jun.	1600	,, Elizabeth f. Hans.
27 Nov.	1695	Davall, Catharina f. John & Helena Waecker.
27 Feb.	1586	Davids, Maria f. Adriaen.
30 Mei	1609	,, Abraham f. Pieter.
9 Feb.	1690	,, Edward f. Siukin & Cornelia Lahey.
1 Nov.	1597	Davidts, Johannes f. Robert.
9 Feb.	1606	,, Dominicus f. Pieter.
2 Jun.	1607	,, Petrus f. ,,
21 Ap.	1605	Dechange, Petrus f. Pieter.
15 Mar.	1590	Deckere, de, Lucretia f. Roelant.
1 Feb.	1685	Deeward, Esther f. Gerrit & Susanna.
3 Mei	1747	Degenkark, Jeremia f. Henrik & Anna Picart.
4 Sep.	1603	Degheste, Tobias f. Hans.
18 Dec.	1576	Deick, Joannes f. Baltasar.
... Feb.	1573	Deijnoot, Sara f. Andries.
19 Aug.	1627	,, Jacob f. Hendrick.
24 ,,	1628	,, Hendric.
24 Jan.	1630	,, Henricus f. Hendrick.
26 Jul.	1676	Deijnout, Daniel f. Christopher.
29 Mei	1679	Deinaut, Johannes f. ,,
16 ,,	1591	Deken, de, Daniel f. Joos.
28 Jul.	1850	Dekker, John Albert f. Geert & Janna de Man.
31 Jul.	1681	Delfou, Isaac f. Isaac.
15 Nov.	1640	Dellens, Sara f. Alaert.
21 Oct.	1677	Delward, Gerard f. Gerard.
30 Nov.	1679	,, Susanna f. ,,
11 Dec.	1687	,, Steven f. ,, & Susannah.
4 Feb.	1683	Delwart, Elizabeth f. Gerrit & Susanna Rumbald.
22 Aug.	1574	Demetrij, Ottilia f. Jurmannelis.
3 Ap.	1664	Demetrius, Maria f. Fr. Daniel.
6 Mar.	1678	,, Sara, geb. 24 Feb. 1678 f. Fr. Daniel & Maria.
11 Jun.	1679	,, Daniel f. Fr. Daniel.
24 Nov.	1680	,, Abraham f. ,, & Maria.
5 Feb.	1682	,, Anna Maria f. ,, & Maria Fineman.
23 Ap.	1684	,, Francoys f. ,, & Maria.
1 Mei	1687	,, Abigail f. ,, & ,,
27 Ap.	1690	,, Jan f. Gerrit & Rachel Mercier.
7 Oct.	1717	,, Maria f. Abraham & Sara Beijer.
17 Dec.	1682	Denecamp, Rachel f. Gerrit & Rachel Mercie
5 Oct.	1684	,, Maria f. ,, & ,,
24 Jan.	1686	,, Gerrit f. ,, & Rachel.
13 Mei	1688	,, Jannetje f. ,, & ,, Mercier

27 Sep. 1635 Dolins, Isaack f. Abraham.
5 May 1672 ,, Maria f. Frater Abram & Rebecca.
14 Jan. 1674 ,, Abraham f. ,, Abrahamus & Rebecca Elizabetha Sachtius.
13 Mei 1675 ,, Rebecca Elizabeth f. Frater Abrahamus & Rebecca Elisabetha Sachtius.
5 Sep. 1677 ,, Abraham f. Frater Abrahamus & Rebecca Elisabetha Sachtius.
14 Nov. 1678 ,, Daniel f. Frater Abrahamus & Rebecca Elisabetha Sachtius.
11 Feb. 1649 ,, Maria f. Johan.
4 Dec. 1653 ,, Sara f. Jan.
12 Dec. 1600 Dolder, Van, Anna f. Jacob.
17 Dec. 1601 Doldor, ,, Catheryne f. ,,
4 Jul. 1683 Domburgh, Elizabeth f. Guillaem & Jean.
5 Ap. 1685 ,, Johannes f. ,, & Johanna.
18 Aug. 1686 ,, William f. Guiljame ,,
24 Jun. 1688 ,, Maria f. Guillaume ,,
29 Jun. 1690 ,, Johannes f. William ,,
4 Sep. 1692 ,, Pieter f. ,, ,,
22 Jan. 1604 Donckel, Joannes f. Hans.
20 Dec. 1601 ,, Anna f. ,,
9 Jun. 1605 ,, Lambert f. ,,
1 Feb. 1607 ,, Abraham f. ,,
11 Jun. 1609 ,, Catharijna f. ,,
16 Jan. 1574 Donghen, Van, Samuel f. Adrian.
21 Mar. 1585 Doopere, de, (v. Dorper), Susanna f. Jan.
25 Feb. 1579 Doornaet, Joannes f. Pieter.
18 Nov. 1593 Doornaert, Susanna f. ,,
9 Feb. 1595 ,, Pieter f. ,,
27 Feb. 1597 ,, Maria f. ,,
17 Jan. 1602 ,, Gabriel f. ,,
22 Jan. 1604 ,, Susanna f. ,,
23 Nov. 1606 ,, Pieter f. ,,
2 Aug. 1609 ,, Joannes f. ,,
20 Dec. 1612 ,, Catharijna f. ,,
6 Oct. 1616 ,, Bartholomeus f. ,,
10 Sep. 1620 ,, Elisabeth f. ,,
22 Nov. 1629 Doorner, Gabriel f. Gabriel.
13 Mei 1577 Doornhove, Salomon f. Gillis.
14 Jul. 1588 Doorper, de, (v. Dorper), Elisabeth f. Jan.
30 Dec. 1576 Dopperans, Susanna f. Daniel.
15 Mar. 1593 Dorein, Daniel f. ,,
1 Feb. 1573 Doreijn, Johannes f. Jan.
20 Jan. 1586 ,, Anna f. Danels.
10 Jul. 1589 ,, Elisabeth f. Daniel.
22 Oct. 1590 Dorijn, Marie f. ,,
22 Jun. 1598 ,, Elisabeth f. ,,
25 Oct. 1576 Dormal, Johannes f. Ghijsbrecht.
Dormaals, (v. Tutelaer),
29 Jan. 1590 Dormael, Van, Abraham f. Pieter.
30 Mei 1588 Dorner, ,, Lowijs f. Lowys.
17 Nov. 1583 Dorpers, (v. Doorper), Susanna f. Jan.
26 Oct. 1589 Dorper, de, Catherine f. Jan.
29 Nov. 1590 Dorpere, ,, Judith f. ,,
31 Aug. 1592 ,, ,, Cornelia f. ,,
26 Feb. 1587 ,, ,, Elizabeth f. ,,
21 Oct. 1593 ,, ,, Joannes f. ,,
13 Jun. 1596 ,, ,, ,, f. ,,
6 Nov. 1597 ,, ,, Pieter f. ,,
31 Mei 1576 Dortyn, Jeremias f. Hans.
4 Jul. 1641 Dorwerft, Van, Frederick f. Adrian.
9 Nov. 1689 Dothhorst, Catharina f. Anthony & Anna Vander Burgh.
10 Mei 1579 Dottegnie, Anna f. Ferdinandus.
4 Jul. 1581 Dottenij, Jacobus f. Fernandus.
7 Nov. 1574 Dotignij, Tabitha f. Ferdinandus.

3 Jul. 1575 Dotignij, Pieter f. Ferdinandus.
10 Nov. 1594 Douffaij, Anna f. Pieter.
6 Jun. 1619 Draec, Nathanael f. Cornelis.
Draeck, (v. Moesens).
15 Jun. 1621 ,, Anna f. Cornelis.
13 Jul. 1623 ,, ,, f. ,,
27 Nov. 1625 ,, Joannes f. ,,
10 Aug. 1628 ,, Maria f. ,,
24 Mei 1635 ,, Jacobus f. ,,
12 Mei 1588 Drael, (v. Drele), Susanna f. Reijnier.
12 Jul. 1590 ,, Anna f. Renier.
11 Mar. 1593 ,, Geraert f. ,,
10 Nov. 1594 ,, Susanna f. ,,
27 Feb. 1597 ,, Johanna f. ,,
7 Oct. 1694 Drapentier, Johannes f. Johannes & Dorothea Tucker.
14 Sep. 1578 Dregge, Tobias f. Cornelis.
22 Mar. 1584 ,, Anna f. Cornelis.
12 Mei 1588 ,, Jeremias f. ,,
10 Feb. 1596 Dregge, Cathelyne f. ,,
29 Nov. 1590 Dreghe, Sara f. ,,
11 Feb. 1593 ,, Cornelis f. ,,
29 Sep. 1695 Dreereu, Jan Dirck f. Gerrit & Margarietje Hendricx.
26 Dec. 1589 Drele, Van, (v. Drael), Elizabeth f. Jacop.
5 Ap. 1846 Dreun, Geertruida f. Dirk & Ann Scheffer.
29 Aug. 1847 ,, Klaas Jan f. Dirk & Ann Scheffer.
13 Jan. 1850 ,, Adrianus Gillis Johannes f. Dirk & Anna Scheffer.
12 Ap. 1590 Dries, Susanna f. Marten.
2 Jan. 1592 ,, Susanna f. ,,
26 Oct. 1596 ,, Sara f. Benjamin.
17 Aug. 1598 ,, Maria f. ,,
8 Jan. 1601 ,, Samuel & Benjamin f. ,,
19 Aug. 1602 ,, Benjamin f. ,,
1 Mei 1597 ,, Samuel f. Samuel.
17 Dec. 1598 ,, ,, f. ,,
19 Jul. 1601 ,, Jacobus f. ,,
5 Sep. 1602 ,, Samuel f. ,,
11 Nov. 1604 ,, Abraham f. ,,
6 Mar. 1606 ,, Benjamin f. ,,
14 Feb. 1608 ,, Isaac f. ,,
18 Feb. 1610 ,, Anna f. posthuma Samuel.
21 Jun. 1579 Driessche, Van den, Pieter f. Jois.
14 Ap. 1583 ,, ,, Eduwardt f. ,,
29 Aug. 1585 ,, ,, Elisabet f. Joos.
13 Aug. 1587 ,, ,, Anna f. ,,
7 Mar. 1589 ,, ,, Joannes f. ,,
6 Ap. 1595 ,, ,, Judith f. ,,
9 Oct. 1610 ,, ,, Joannes f. Sijmon.
3 Mar. 1636 ,, ,, Theodorus f. ,,
17 Sep. 1637 ,, ,, Johannes f. Johannes
18 Oct. 1639 ,, ,, Sara f. Jan.
17 Oct. 1641 ,, ,, Samuel f. ,,
9 Mei 1592 Drincs, Lydia f. Herman.
25 Feb. 1630 Drijver, de, Samuel f. Samuel.
26 Aug. 1632 ,, ,, Abraham & Matthias f. ,,
16 Mei 1596 Droeshout, (v. Drousaut, Droussaert) Joannes f. Michiel.
4 Mar. 1606 ,, Susanna f. ,,
29 Mei 1605 ,, Johaneken f. Martin.
22 Feb. 1607 ,, Marten f. Marten.
28 Mei 1600 ,, Maria f. ,,

9 Jul.	1611	Droeshout, David f. Marten.
10 Oct.	1613	„ Hester f. „
18 Feb.	1616	„ Anna f. „
29 Sep.	1622	„ Daniel f. „
12 Dec.	1647	Drogeboter, (v. Boterdroghe), Elisabeth f. Andries & Elisabeth.
2 Feb.	1589	Drolmaels, Daniels f. Pieter.
17 Feb.	1639	Drooghboter, (v. supra), Jacobus f. Andries.
15 Mar.	1640	„ Petrus f. Andries.
27 Ap.	1572	Drossaert, de, (v. Drossart, etc.), Anna f. Henriex.
26 Jul.	1573	„ „ Jacob f. Henriex.
31 Mei	1576	„ „ Susanna f. Pieter ; test. Lucas d'Heere, Loysken ux. Caroli Ryckewarts, etc.
9 Feb.	1578	„ Hesther f. Pieter.
25 Mar.	1582	„ Samuel f. „
4 Feb.	1610	„ „ f. Samuel.
20 Feb.	1613	Drossaerts, Susanne f. „
15 Jun.	1572	Drossardt, de, Johannes f. Johannes.
10 Ap.	1580	„ „ Petrus f. Petrus.
12 Jan.	1584	Drossardts, Susanna f. Pieter.
6 Oct.	1588	Drossart, de, Jossinken f. „
13 Mar.	1586	Drossate, de, Jeronimus f. „
3 Ap.	1603	„ „ Pieter f. Samuel.
7 Dec.	1606	„ „ Samuel f. „
24 Jan.	1608	„ „ Gulielmus f. „
28 Sep.	1617	Drossate, de, Franchoys f. Samuel.
31 Mar.	1575	Drossijt, de, (v. Drossaert), Joannes f. Heindrick.
13 Feb.	1589	Droussaert, (v. „), Maria f. Jan.
26 Ap.	1601	„ Marten f. Michiel.
20 Mei	1599	Droussaut, Johannes f. „
2 Aug.	1603	Drousshaut, Guillame f. „
7 Feb.	1605	Dru, Daniel & Rogier } f. Robert.

11 Jul.	1602	Drue, Gulian f. Robert.
12 Feb.	1626	Druijten, Maria f. Jacob.
21 Jul.	1622	Druijf, Van, Abraham f. Seberyn.
12 Nov.	1615	„ „ Susanna f.
9 Mei	1613	Druijven, Van, Maria f. Sebnerijn.
8 Jun.	1589	Duemen (v. Duijman, Dume), Susanna f. Jan.
13 Ap.	1600	Dufeij, Petrus f. Pieter.
15 Jun.	1596	Duijman, Rebecca f. Herman.
31 Oct.	1611	Duijts (v. Duits), Cornelius f. Cornelius.
10 Jun.	1849	Duinkerk, Jan Hendrik f. James Morris & Johanna Maria Van Kooten.
10 Nov.	1850	„ Johanna Magdalena f. James Morris & Johanna Maria Van Kooten.
17 Sep.	1643	Duits, (v. Duijts), Philippus f. Cornelis.
3 Oct.	1598	Duijman (v. Duinen), Clara f. Herman.
3 Jul.	1600	Duijme, Andreas f. „
28 Oct.	1578	Duijmen, Johanna f. Jan.
28 Feb.	1580	„ Petrus f. „
19 Aug.	1582	„ Elisabeth f. „
17 Feb.	1594	Duinen, (v. Duijman), Anna f. Herman.
14 Jan.	1589	Duket, Abraham f. Lieven.
6 Jun.	1591	Dume, „ f. Jau.
10 Nov.	1584	Dumen, Joannes f. „
9 Sep.	1739	Dumont, Willem f. Abraham & Jannetje Santman.
29 Mei	1743	„ Johanna f. Abraham & Jannetje Santman.
23 Sep.	1744	„ Esaias f. Abraham & Jannetje Santman.
21 Jun.	1580	Dungen, Van, Magdalena f. Adriaan.
22 Mei	1645	Durerus, Elisabeth f. Casparus.
2 Oct.	1606	Durof, Jacobmyntken f. Abraham
20 Dec.	1590	Duwarts, Anna f. Jan
11 Jan.	1680	Duwe, Abraham f. Jacob.
11 Sep.	1692	„ Jacob f. „ & Rachel.

1 Oct.	1710	E, de, Michiel f. Daniel & Janneke.
14 Jun.	1663	East, William f. Jan.
8 Jul.	1604	Ee, Van, Daniel f. Geeraert.
19 Nov.	1615	Ecberts, Susanna f. Steven.
12 Sep.	1592	Echholt, (v. Eecholt), Maria f. Maurus.
24 Ap.	1636	Ecke, Van, Abraham f. Abraham.
27 Mar.	1780	Eckhardt, Frederik George f. Frans Frederik & Adriana Elisabeth Westerhoff.
30 Oct.	1726	Eckhoff, Maria f. Barent & Sara.
2 Oct.	1678	Edelman, Sara f. Arij Cornelisen.
25 Feb.	1582	Eduwaerts, Judith f. Jan.
1 Aug.	1585	„ Catherine f. „
21 Oct.	1571	Eduwardts, Johannes f. „
11 Oct.	1579	„ Abigail f. „
9 Feb.	1584	„ Thomas f. „
18 Mar.	1576	Eduwarts, Nathanael f. „
8 Dec.	1577	„ Elisabet f. „

21 Mei	1588	Eduwarts, Jacob f. Jan.
18 Feb.	1593	„ Maria f. „
20 Jan.	1578	Eecholt (v. Echholt), Sara f. Maurus.
31 Jan.	1585	Eechout, Judith f. „
27 Mar.	1586	„ Maurus f. „
30 Jul.	1587	„ Gielis f. Maurus.
1 Sep.	1597	„ Rebecca f. „
25 Aug.	1583	Eeckoudt, Cathryne f. „
10 Oct.	1588	Eeckhoff, Abigail f. „
28 Feb.	1591	„ „ f. „
28 Ap.	1580	Eeckoutz, Judith f. „
16 Feb.	1729	Eekhoff (v. Eckhoff), Marij f. Barent & Marij.
31 Aug.	1578	Eesbeeck, Van, Sara f. Steven.
13 Mei	1697	Eferson, Elisabeth f. Jan. & Maria Klerek.
18 Feb.	1776	Effen, Van, Justus Melchior f. Melchior Justus & Sarah Cornelia Diemel.

27 Jul. 1777 **Effen,** Van, Reneria Christina ⎫ f Melchi-
& Elizabeth Sophia. | or Justus
}& Sarah
| Cornelia
⎭ Diemel.
27 Jun. 1779 ,, ,, Catharina f. Melchior Justus &
Sarah Cornelia Diemel.
6 Mei 1781 ,, ,, Charlotta Johauna f. Melchior
Justus & Sarah Cornelia
Diemel.
3 Sep. 1783 ,, ,, Pieter Fredrik Justus f. Melchior Justus & Sarah
Cornelia Diemel.
21 Jun. 1579 **Egericks,** Samuel f. Bernardt.
11 Jan. 1629 **Egert,** Marie f. Christiaen.
12 Oct. 1589 **Eggerits,** Jacobus f. Jacus.
8 ,, 1587 **Eggerix,** Sara f. Jacob.
31 Mar. 1577 **Eggherickx,** Sara f. Bernard.
15 Mar. 1802 **Ehrlij,** Henry Gerard f. John Henry &
Sarah King.
12 Ap. 1696 **Eick,** Vander, (v. Eijck), Karel f. Jan. &
Maria Coppin.
22 Oct. 1704 ,, ,, Isaac f. Nicolaes & Janneke
Vander Sieur.
27 Ap. 1856 **Eielts,** Karel f. Eielt & Maria. Antonetta
Jelkman.
4 Mar. 1694 **Eijck,** Van, Abraham f. Claes & Janneke
Vanden Steene.
12 Ap. 1696 ,, ,, Elizabeth f. Nicolaes & Janneke Vanden Steen.
2 Sep. ,, ,, ,, Willem f. Klaes & Maria.
6 Feb. 1698 ,, ,, Maria f. Nicolaes & Janneke
Vanden Steen.
28 Ap. 1700 ,, ,, Abraham f. Claes & Janneke
Vanden Steen.
6 Jun. 1708 ,, ,, Jacob f. Claes & Janneke
Vanden Steen.
19 Jul. 1575 **Eijcke,** ,, Marten f. Dierick.
25 Feb. 1593 ,, ,, Abraham f. Adriaen.
25 Nov. 1710 ,, ,, Bartholomeus f. Nikolaus &
Janneke.
21 Nov. 1619 **Eijdner,** Joannes f. Christofer.
22 Jan. 1615 **Eijgner,** Anna f. Christofel.
15 Nov. 1693 **Eijl,** Van, Maria f. ....& Elisabeth Van Erp.
21 Ap. 1605 **Eijnthoven,** Rudolp f. Tobias.
10 Sep. 1607 **Eijndhoven,** Van, Catharyne f. ,,
7 Nov. 1613 ,, ,, Petrus f. ,,
7 Jul. 1616 ,, ,, Catharina f. ,,
3 Sep. 1685 **Eijsenbort,** Annesse f. Pieter.
26 Jul. 1801 **Eilbracht,** Auginita Theodora f. Joan
Philip, van Chintsunah in
Bengalen, & Joanna Pieternella de Mauregnault.
19 Dec. 1802 ,, Daniel Joan f. Joan Philip,
van Chintsunah in Bengalen,
& Joanna de Mauregnault.
13 Nov. 1808 ,, Joanna Pieternella f. Joan
Philip, van Chintsunah in
Bengalen, & Joanna Pieternella de Mauregnault.
24 Jun. 1810 ,, Jan Philip f. Joan Philip, van
Chintsunah in Bengalen, &
Joanna Pieternella de
Mauregnault.
10 Nov. 1811 ,, Antonia Maria f. Joan Philip,
van Chintsunah in Bengalen,
& Joanna Pieternella de
Mauregnault.

17 Sep. 1815 **Eilbracht,** Hendrik f. Joan Philip, van
Chintsunah in Bengalen, &
Joanna Pieternella de
Mauregnault.
22 Dec. 1816 ,, Jan f. Joan Philip, van Chintsunah in Bengalen, & Joanna
Pieternella de Mauregnault.
12 Jul. 1818 ,, Maria f. Joan Philip, van
Chintsunah in Bengalen, &
Joanna Pieternella de
Mauregnault.
29 Ap. 1804 **Eilbrecht,** Jacob f. Joan Philip, van Chintsunah in Bengalen, & Joanna
de Mauregnault.
19 Nov. 1592 **Einserinck,** (v. Enserinck), Arnaut f.
Nicolas.
23 Nov. 1617 **Elias,** Joannes f. Jan.
25 Dec. 1619 ,, Elisabet f. ,,
25 Ap. 1622 ,, Zacharias f. ,,
17 Oct. 1624 ,, Elisabeth f. ,,
20 Mei 1627 ,, Catharina f. ,,
28 Feb. 1630 ,, Abraham f. ,,
19 Oct. 1617 **Elijnck,** Susanna f. Abraham.
5 Jan. 1630 **Elinc,** Elisabet f. ,,
27 Jun. 1619 **Elinck,** Abraham f. ,,
25 Mar. 1621 ,, Maria f. ,,
16 Nov. 1627 ,, Wenefrid f. ,,
18 Nov. 1632 ,, Sara f. ,,
23 Aug. 1615 **Ellinck,** Agneta f. ,,
24 Feb. 1583 **Elsen,** Jacob f. Jacob.
6 Oct. 1583 **Eissen,** Susanna f. Everdts.
31 Jan. 1585 ,, Petrus f. Evaert.
6 Jul. 1591 ,, Abigail f. Renier.
23 Ap. 1581 **Elssens,** Susanna f. Everardt.
26 Jan. 1578 **Elst,** Vander, Jacob f. Jan.
10 Jul. 1580 ,, ,, Anna f. ,,
4 Jun. 1582 ,, ,, Maria f. ,,
22 Jan. 1598 ,, ,, (v. Est.), Elisabeth f. Jeremias.
3 Nov. 1605 ,, ,, Apollo Anthonis f. Jeronij-
mus.
21 Sep. 1606 ,, ,, Samuel f. Jeremias.
30 Sep. 1610 **Emans,** Elisabeth f. Jan.
16 Mar. 1614 ,, ,, f. ,,
26 Nov. 1615 ,, Anna f. ,,
20 Sep. 1618 ,, Joannes f. ,,
5 Mar. 1620 ,, Abigail f. ,,
23 Dec. 1621 ,, Maria f. ,,
30 Nov. 1623 ,, Lucas f. ,,
2 Jul. 1588 **Embucht,** Van, Catherine f. Herman.
26 Mar. 1738 **Emmerin,** Simmij f. Barent & Anna Arre-
gelo.
12 Feb. 1576 **Ende,** Vanden, Maria f. Heindrix.
9 Jul. 1710 **Ende,** ,, Anna Esther f. Philip &
Willemina.
31 Mei 1711 ,, ,, ... f. Philip & Willemina.
17 Dec. 1712 ,, ,, Maria f. Philip & Willemina.
18 Sept. 1716 **Enden,** ,, Louis f. Philip & Willemina.
11 Nov. 1750 ,, ,, Esther f. Louis, Jr. &
Sarah Frost.
3 Ap. 1636 **Engel,** Margrita f. ....
6 Aug. 1679 ,, Esther f. Pieter.
14 Nov. 1680 ,, Susanna f. ,,
4 Oct. 1682 ,, Maria f. ,,
14 Mei 1684 ,, Anna f. ,,
12 Oct. 1687 ,, Michael f. ,, & Esther.

24 Nov.	1594	Fabri, Catheline f. Hans.
28 Mar.	1596	„ Elizabeth f. „
12 Feb.	1598	„ Maria f. „
1 Jun.	1600	„ Matheus f. „
30 Aug.	1601	„ Peeter f. Jan.
18 Apl.	......	„ (v. Faebrij), Johannes f. Johannes & Susanna.
17 Jul.	1678	Fabrij, Elizabeth f. Jan.
8 Feb.	1688	„ Maria f. Jan. & Susanna.
13 Oct.	1861	Fabritius, Catharina Cornelia Johanna f. Anthony Johannes Cannegieter & Catharina Maria Wilhelmina Van Heusde.
26 Jul.	1863	„ Anthony Johannes f. Anthony Johannes Cannegieter & Catharina Maria Wilhelmina Van Heusde.
23 Jun.	1686	Faebrij, (v. Fabri), Susanna f. Jan & Susanna.
2 Feb.	1617	Fakon, (v Faucon), Rebecca f. Gedeon.
23 Nov.	1603	Farcij, Joris f. Joris.
30 Oct.	1672	Farington, Samuel f. Richard.
7 Sep.	1641	Farrer, Anthony f. John.
27 Aug.	1676	Farrington, Anna f. Johannes.
27 Aug.	1615	Faucon, (v. Fakon, etc), Gedeon f. Gedeon.
15 Mei	1614	Faulcon, Ester f.
4 Feb.	1621	Faulkan, Johannes f. Gedeon. „
28 Oct.	1597	Fautil, Rachel f. Willem.
19 Feb.	1710	Feber, la, (v. Febure, Fever & Fevre), Pieter f. Huybreght & Saertje Adriaens.
18 Jun.	1749	„ le, Johannes f. Jacobus & Aaltje Davids.
28 Ap.	1751	„ „ Pieter f. Jacobus & Aaltje Davids.
20 Jun.	1753	„ „ Jacobus f. Jacobus & Aaltje Davids.
13 Dec.	1671	Febure, le, Martha f. Carel & Margarita.
7 Oct.	1610	Feij, de, Maria f. Jaques.
1 Sep.	1594	Feijfer, de, Daniel f. Cornelis.
5 Mar.	1592	Feijfere, de, Abraham f. „
21 Sep.	1578	Feijten. Johannes f. Henricks.
30 Jun.	1701	Felten, Thomas f. Jan. & Anna Houwert.
7 Jul.	1706	„ Joost f. Jan. & Anna Houwert.
13 Mar.	1709	„ Karel f. „ „ „
9 Jul.	1710	„ Elisabeth f. Jan & Anna Houwel.
11 Oct.	1696	Felton, Johannes f. Johannes.
18 Ap.	1705	„ Anna f. Jan & Anna.
13 Ap.	1726	Fermijn, Theodorus f. Fr. & Hester.
5 Nov.	1648	Ferrij, Nicolaes f. Nicolaes.
20 Feb.	1715	Fever, la, (v. Feber), Sarah f. Huijber & Sarah.
25 Feb.	1724	„ le, Daniel f. Jan & Maria.
18 Apl.	1731	„ „ Pieter f. Jan & Maria de Haan.
27 Aug.	1732	„ „ Johannes f. Jan & Maria de Haan.
24 Feb.	1734	„ „ Abraham f. Jan & Maria de Haan.
9 Apl.	1738	„ „ Elizabeth f. Jan & Maria de Haan.
16 Dec.	1739	„ „ Willem f. Jan. & Maria de Haan.
16 Feb.	1746	„ „ Pieter f. Jan & Maria de Haan.
14 Mei	1747	„ „ Sara f. Jan & Maria de Haan.
23 Jan.	1743	„ „ Abraham f. Pieter & Maria Perne.
25 Nov.	1753	Fever, le, Willem f. Jan Jr. & Elizabeth Moxam.
8 Feb.	1756	„ „ Joannes f. Jan. Jr. & Elizabeth Moxam.
11 Jun.	1758	„ „ Carel f. Jan. Jr. & Elizabeth Moxam.
17 Aug.	1760	„ „ Jacobus f. Jan Jr. & Elizabeth Moxam.
30 Mar.	1760	„ „ Catryntje, geb. 28 Mei, 1756, f. Jacobus & Aaltje Davids.
30 „	„	„ „ Pieter, geb. 22nd Feb, 1760, f. Jacobus & Aaltje Davids.
13 Jul.	1760	„ „ David f. Jacobus & Maria Elizabeth Milo.
31 Oct.	1762	„ „ Daniel f. Jacobus & Maria Elizabeth Milo.
30 Oct.	1764	„ „ Maria Elisabeth f. Jacobus & Maria Elizabeth Mils.
19 Jul.	1767	„ „ Carel, f. Jacobus & Maria Elizabeth Milo.
1 Mei	1769	„ „ Sara f. Jacobus & Maria Elizabeth Milo.
13 Oct.	1771	„ „ Thomas f. Jacobus & Maria Elizabeth Milo.
13 Mar.	1774	„ „ George f. Jacobus & Maria Elizabeth Milo.
16 Jul.	1776	„ „ Richard f. Jacobus & Maria Elizabeth Milo.
3 Jun.	1764	„ „ Abraham f. Abraham & Maria Quantelo.
15 Sep.	1765	„ „ Pieter f. Abraham & Maria Quantito.
4 Nov.	1767	„ „ Emanuel f. Abraham & Maria Contito.
24 Sep.	1769	„ „ Maria f. Abraham & Maria Quaorgertoge.
9 Ap.	1775	„ „ Abraham f. posthumus Abraham & Maria Quantito.
10 Dec.	1769	„ „ Joseph f. Abraham & Maria Magdalena Petit.
10 Mar.	1771	„ „ Karel f. Abraham & Maria Magdalena Petit.
17 Mei	1772	„ „ Jacobus f. Abraham & Maria Magdalena Petit.
17 Oct.	1773	„ „ Pieter f. Abraham & Maria Magdalena Petit.
28 Mei	1775	„ „ Jacobus f. Abraham & M. Petit.
20 Ap.	1777	„ „ Hester f. Abraham & M. Petit.
16 Mei	1779	„ „ Carel f. Abraham & M. Petit.
4 Feb.	1781	„ „ Willem f. Abraham & M. Petit.
2 Feb.	1783	„ „ Joris f. Abraham & M. Petit.
30 Jan.	1774	„ „ Sarah f. Jan & Sarah Jones.
22 Nov.	1772	„ „ Pieter f. Pieter & Maria White.
23 Oct.	1774	„ „ Joseph f. Pieter & Maria White.
11 Aug.	1782	„ „ Edward f. Pieter & Maria White.
27 Jun.	1784	„ „ Charles f. Pieter & Maria White.
11 Ap.	1773	„ „ Johannes f. Jan & Maria Qual.

12 Dec.	1591	Franssen, Clara f. Pieter.
26 Oct.	1690	,, Sara f. Maerten & Aplony Janssen.
25 Aug.	1577	Franssz, David f. Reynier.
14 Dec.	1589	,, Maria f. Pieter.
16 Jun.	1583	Frantz, Johanna f. ,,
22 Oct.	1684	Fraser, Maria f. Hugh & Maria.
9 Sept.	1683	Fraiser, Catharina f. ,, ,,
24 Jan.	1613	Frederic, Elisabet f. Zacharias.
7 Mei	1618	,, Abigaijl f. ,,
18 Dec.	1599	Frederick, Benjamin f. ,,
17 Mei	1579	Fredericks, Hesther f. Hans.
9 Ap.	1610	Frederickx, Sacharias f. Sacharias.
11 Feb.	1602	Frederix, Susanna f. ,,
14 Jul.	1588	Frederix, Jaspar f. Jaspar.
14 Aug.	1575	Fredrix, Abraham f. Jan.
7 Nov.	1585	,, Jaspar f. Jaspar.
7 Jan.	1593	,, Maria f. Jasp.
18 Jun.	1690	Freeman, Johannes f. Samuel & Mida.
30 Jan.	1583	Frenoij, de, Elizabeth f. Mahieu.
22 Nov.	1584	,, Van, Joannes f. ,,
18 Jan.	1601	Fresare, Elizabeth f. Salomon.
15 Ap.	1599	Freschier, Susanna f. ,,
26 Mei	1594	Freschnaer, Sara f. ,,
29 Mar.	1597	Freschner, Isaac f. ,,
11 Jan.	1857	Friederich, Carel Wilhelm f. Carel Wilhelm & Johanna Lugthart.
26 Dec.	1858	Friedrich, Johanna Catharina f. Carel Wilhelm & Johanna Lugthart.
24 Mar.	1861	,, Maria Geertruida f. Carel Wilhelm & Johanna Lugthart.
26 Ap.	1863	,, Henriette Elizabeth f. Carel Wilhelm & Johanna Lugthart.
10 Ap.	1608	Fries, de, (v. Vriese) Catharine f. Jan.
3 Aug.	1595	Frisne, Abraham f. Salomon.
7 Aug.	1575	Frilichoven, Sara f. David.
20 ,,	1598	Frombout, (v. Frambout), Susanna f. Noel.
23 Oct.	1608	,, Judith f. Noel.
3 Feb.	1611	Frombout, Maria f. Noel.
6 Jul.	1614	,, Judith f. ,,
9 Mar.	1617	,, Abigail f. ,,
20 Aug.	1620	,, Matthias f. ,,
4 Sep.	1621	,, Guillame f. ,,
27 Ap.	1623	,, Elisabeth f. ,,
21 Dec.	1624	,, Anthonesse f. ,,
29 Aug.	1626	,, Ester f. ,,
10 Mei	1629	,, Catharina f. ,,
18 Feb.	1638	Fromanteel, (v. Formenteel, Fromenteel, etc.), Johannes f. Assuerus.
16 Feb.	1640	,, Assuerus f. Assuerus & Maria.
7 Apl.	1644	,, Esther f. ,,
11 Dec.	1664	,, Esther f. Joannes.
9 Sep.	1619	Fromenteau, Ester f. Jan.
15 Aug.	1622	,, Johannes f. ,,
6 Jan.	1636	Fromenteel, Timotheus f. Assuerus.
3 Mar.	1641	,, Murdochaes f. Johannes.
25 Dec.	1646	,, Andreas f. ,,
8 Aug.	1644	Frommenteel, Samuel f. ,,
22 Jun.	1634	Froumentel, Maria f. Assuerus.
9 Sep.	1632	Frumen, Abraham f. Ahusuerus.
1 Mar.	1607	Frutier, Joanna f. Jaques.
19 Ap.	1612	,, Esther f. ,,
27 Oct.	1616	,, Abraham f. ,,
28 Feb.	1619	,, Jacobus f. Jacques.
17 Jul.	1621	,, Isaack f. Jacob.
14 Sep.	1623	,, Jacob f. Jacques.
22 Feb.	1596	Fudlix, Anna f. Sacharias.
18 Oct.	1610	Fulter, Abraham f. Abraham.
28 Sep.	1681	Fuller, Willem f. Willem & Mary Van Wyn.
25 Jun.	1684	,, Maria f. Willem & Maria.
28 Sep.	1687	,, Sara f. ,,
17 Dec.	1815	Funtman, Henriette Elisabeth f. Hermanus & Anna de Groot.
27 Ap.	1595	Fusijn, Rebecca f. Pieter.

14 Mei	1581	Gaber, Van, Sara f. Joos.
14 Mar.	1596	Gabri, Abraham f. Cijpriaen.
13 Aug.	1598	,, Anna f. ,,
19 Oct.	1600	,, Susanna f. ,,
5 Dec.	1602	,, Johanna f. Cijprem.
2 Dec.	1604	,, Elizabeth f. Cypriaen.
25 Ap.	1595	Gabrij, Cijprianus f. Cijpriaen.
19 Ap.	1607	,, Carolus f. Cypriaen.
11 Dec.	1608	,, Maria f. ,,
14 Ap.	1611	,, Sara f. ,,
30 Jul.	1581	Galmaer, Jeronimus f. Jan.
5 Ap.	1573	Galmaers, Esther f. Jeroon.
30 Jan.	1586	Galmaert, Daniel f. Jan.
28 Aug.	1580	Galmaerts, Susanna f. Jeronimus.
16 Nov.	1585	,, Dinac f. ,,
27 Dec.	1584	Galmaet, Petrus f. Jan.
20 Jan.	1583	Galmardts, Sara f. ,,
8 Mar.	1584	Galmarts, Joannes f. Hieronymus.
3 Aug.	1578	Galmartz, Jan f. Jan.
17 Jan.	1580	,, Susanna f. ,,
7 Oct.	1571	Galmoots, Susanna f. Jheronymus.
27 Nov.	1664	,, Maria f. Nicolaes.
20 Sep.	1630	Ganne, Johannes f. Paulus.
12 Sep.	1630	,, Maria f. ,,
23 Jan.	1741	Gans, Willem Jacobus f. Bastiaans & Cathrina.
18 Nov.	1742	,, Bastiaan f. Bastiaans & Cathrina.
17 Sep.	1594	Garaerts, Daniel f. Marcus.
....	1571	Garofe, Gedeon f. Philip.
25 Mar.	1572	,, Samuel f. ,,
17 Dec.	1587	Garet, Catharine f. Pieter.
2 Nov.	1589	,, Jacobus f. ,,
26 Sep.	1591	,, Abigail f. ,,
7 Feb.	1591	,, Marie f. Jacques.

16 Jan. 1597 Garnoot, (v. Gernoot), Maria f. Daniel.
19 Aug. 1599 ,, Abraham f. ,,
29 Mar. 1601 ,, Elizabeth f. Daniel.
10 Jul. 1603 ,, Daniel f. ,,
17 Feb. 1600 ,, Sara f. Zacharias,
5 Jul. 1601 ,, Neeltken f. Sacharias.
22 Jan. 1604 ,, Sacharias } f. ,,
             & Esther }
27 Jan. 1605 ,, Tobias f. Elias.
28 Oct. 1610 ,, Gabriel f. ,,
5 Nov. 1613 ,, Maria f. ,,
5 Oct. 1617 ,, Catharina f. ,,
21 Sep. 1626 ,, Gabriel f. ,,
30 Oct. 1608 ,, Maria f. Enoch.
10 Dec. 1609 ,, Maria f. ,,
21 Nov. 1613 ,, Daniel f. ,,
20 Oct. 1616 ,, Enoch f. ,,
4 Feb. 1621 ,, Samuel f. ,,
9 Mar. 1623 ,, Petrus f. ,,
10 Jun. 1627 ,, Jacobus f. ,,
6 Jul. 1628 ,, Levina f. Tobias,
15 Jul. 1576 Gast, Anna, f. Hans.
19 Oct. 1578 ,, Mattheus f. ,,
19 Jul. 1584 ,, Marie f. ,,
27 Aug. 1581 ,, Isaac f. Govert.
9 Sep. 1582 ,, Abraham f. Gottfre.
15 Mar. 1584 ,, Sara f. Govardt.
8 Aug. 1585 ,, Marie f. Godefroit.
22 Dec. 1588 ,, Jacob f. Godefroy.
20 Oct. 1590 ,, Elisabeth f. ,,
3 Jun. 1592 ,, Daniel f. Ad. ,,
25 Sep. 1594 ,, Rebecca f. ,,
22 Aug. 1619 Gaten, Joris f. Joris.
16 Jul. 1738 Gaulius, (v. Goulius), Willem f. Coenradt
             & Elisabeth Dickson.
19 Oct. 1740 ,, Johannes f. Coenradt
             & Elisabeth Dickson.
12 Ap. 1752 Geaussint, Petrus f. Jan & Alida Schouten.
1 Feb. 1579 Geenen, (v. Gheenen), Jacobus f.
             Antonius.
19 Nov. 1581 ,, Joannes f. Antonie.
24 Sept. 1587 ,, Jacob f. Anthonis.
29 Jun. 1589 Geenes, ,, f. Anthony.
20 Jun. 1591 Geene, Daniel f. ,,
3 Ap. 1595 Geeraerdt, (v. Gheeraerdt, etc.), Maria
             f. Jan.
13 Sep. 1573 Geeraerts, Rachel f. Marcus.
25 Dec. 1586 ,, Magdaleene f. Marij.
22 Nov. 1590 ,, Susanna f. Merten.
8 Aug. 1591 ,, Maria f. Marcus.
15 Mei 1592 ,, Petrus f. Marten.
18 Feb. 1599 ,, Elizabeth f. Marcus.
2 Jun. 1611 ,, Susanna f. ,,
25 Sep. 1601 ,, Jauneken f. Hans.
30 Mar. 1595 ,, Magdalena f. Cornelis.
27 Nov. 1603 ,, Arnoult f. ,,
24 Sep. 1609 ,, Joannes f. ,,
26 Jan. 1612 ,, Rachel f. ,,
28 Sep. 1578 Geerardesz, Eduwardt f. ,, Eduwardts.
5 Nov. 1581 Geerards, Joannes f. Marten.
6 Oct. 1583 ,, Nathanael f. ,,
5 Mar. 1615 ,, Jacob f. Cornelius.
14 Nov. 1619 Geerardsz, Jackemynken f. Cornelis.
22 Mei 1599 Geerart, Catheline f. Hans.
23 Dec. 1604 ,, Hendricus f. Marcus.
5 Aug. 1593 ,, Hesther f. Marten.
14 Jun. 1606 ,, Anna f. Cornelis.
11 Dec. 1614 Geeretsz, Ester f. Pieter.

5 Feb. 1582 Geerkens, Johannes Hendrikus f. Hen-
             drikus Wierik & Wilhelmina
             Hogenboom.
4 Mei 1834 ,, Hendrikus Wierik f. Hendri-
             kus Wierik & Wilhelmina
             Hogenboom.
7 Aug. 1836 ,, Cornelius Willem f. Hendri-
             kus Wierik & Wilhelmina
             Hogenboom.
18 Mar. 1838 ,, Willem f. Hendrikus Wierik
             & Wilhelmina Hogenboom.
20 Mar. 1842 ,, Francina f. Hendrikus Wierik
             & Wilhelmina Hogenboom.
21 Aug. 1842 ,, Frederik f. Hendrikus Wierik
             & Wilhelmina Hogenboom.
18 Mei 1845 ,, Wilhelmina Hendrika f. Hen-
             drikus Wierik & Wilhelmina
             Hogenboom.
12 Feb. 1860 ,, Alice Elizabeth f. Johannes
             Hendrikus & Wilhelmina
             Elizabeth Malefijt.
20 Jul. 1862 ,, Johannes Hendrikus f. Johannes
             Hendrikus & Wilhelmina
             Elizabeth Malefijt.
26 Nov. 1587 Geernets, Maria f. Marten.
2 Mei 1619 Geersen, Abraham f. Pieter.
2 Dec. 1621 Geersz, ,,
12 Mei 1605 Geest, de, Isaac f. Jau.
24 Aug. 1634 ,, ,, Maria f. ,,
19 Oct. 1600 Geeter, ,, (v. Gheetere), David f. Jan.
10 Oct. 1602 Geetere,,, Dirck ,,
13 Mei 1606 Geewerts, Sara f. Dierick.
1 Nov. 1840 Gehle, Henri Jan Wolsteyn f. Hendrik,
             Th. Dr. & Anne Minter.
12 Dec. 1841 ,, Charles John f. Hendrik, Th. Dr.
             & Anne Minter, Inde Nieuwe
             Kerk te Amsterdam.
8 Jun. 1845 ,, Antoinette Stratenus f. Hendrik,
             Th. Dr. & Anne Minter.
13 ,, 1847 ,, Agatha Johanna Maria f. Hendrik,
             Th. Dr. & Anne Minter.
30 Jul. 1848 ,, Anna Frederica f. Hendrik, Th.
             Dr. & Anne Minter.
23 Mei 1852 ,, Adolph Thomas f. Hendrik, Th.
             Dr. & Anne Minter.
1 Jan. 1593 Geij, de, Susanna f. Jan.
10 Oct. 1790 Geisler, Joost Wilhelm f. Johan Wilhelm
             & Sibilla Geertruij Vrydag.
9 Mar. 1794 ,, Johan Wilhelm f. Johan Wilhelm
             & Geertruij Vrydag.
27 Sep. 1863 Gekelder, Roelof, f. Willem Lubbert, &
             Trijntje Roelof Pik.
19 Oct. 1595 Gelarts, Sara f. Marcus.
12 Mar. 1676 Gelder, Van, Susanna f. Jasper.
23 Dec. 1677 ,, ,, Francois f. ,,
20 Mar. 1681 ,, ,, Annetje f. Jasper & Ca-
             tharina Dievore.
15 Sep. 1695 ,, ,, Jasper f. Jasper & Susannah
             Reijt.
13 Jun. 1596 Geldolf, Jacobus f. Pieter.
12 Dec. 1585 Gele, Van, (v. Ghele), Sara f. Gillis.
22 Mar. 1590 ,, ,, Gillis f. ,,
4 Nov. 1632 Gels, Rebecca f. Willem.
29 Ap. 1593 Gelners, Pieter f. Anthonis.
5 Mar. 1581 Gems, ,, fa. Jau.
30 ,, 1645 Genuee, Van, Wilhelmus f. Johan.
21 ,, 1647 ,, ,, Hendrik f. Jan & Elisa-
             beth.

<table>
<tr><td colspan="3">

19 Dec. 1596 **Geraerts, (v. Geeraerts Gheraerts, etc.),** Martinus f. Marten.
1 Nov. 1597 „ Marie f. Hans.
3 Jan. 1613 **Geretsz,** Petrus f. Pieter.
9 Dec. 1632 **Gernoot,** Abigail f. Tobias.
27 Jan. 1639 „ Samuel f. „
2 „ 1687 **Gerretsen,** Arij f. Pieter & Maritje.
16 Aug. 1747 **Gerrie,** Maria f. Abraham & Margareta Hox.
5 Dec. 1697 **Gerrits,** Willem f. Willem & Anna.
22 Sep. 1614 **Gerritsz,** Gerardus f. Gerrit.
8 Ap. 1617 „ Rebecca f. Pieter.
18 Nov. 1632 **Gerritsen,** Judith f. Hendric.
28 Feb. 1692 „ Anna f. Dirck & Catharina.
12 Feb. 1693 „ Christiaentje f. Dirck & Catharina Rijders.
24 Feb. 1695 „ Catharina f. Dirck & Catharina.
13 Dec. 1696 „ Maria f. „ „
2 Jan. 1698 „ Gerrit f. „ „
27 Feb. 1704 „ Annetje f. Dirck & Katarina Rider.
2 Jun. 1706 „ Rebecca f. Dirck & Catarina Rijders.
22 Jun. 1707 „ Anna f. Dirck & Catarina Rijders.
18 Sep. 1709 „ Janneke f. Dirck & Catarina.
23 Sep. 1593 **Gertere, de,** Anna f. Hans.
21 Jun. 1607 **Gessel,** Daniel f. Kraft.
26 Dec. 1608 „ Abraham f. „
8 Sep. 1594 **Gheeldolf,** „ f. Pieter.
6 Jan. 1576 **Gheenen, (v. Geenen),** Sara f. Anthonis.
28 Jul. 1583 „ Pieter f. Anthony.
8 Nov. 1576 **Gheeraerts, (v. Geeraerts, etc.),** Tobias f. Marcus.
22 Aug. 1602 „ Marcus f. Marcus.
20 Ap. 1595 „ Susanna f. Marten.
23 Oct. 1596 „ Elisabeth f. Jan.
14 Aug. 1597 „ Cornelis f. Cornelis.
12 Mei 1575 **Gheerarts,** Sara f. Marcus.
7 Oct. 1589 „ Sara f. Marten.
15 Dec. 1584 **Gheerartsz,** Elisabet & Maria } f. Sanders.
13 Mei 1577 **Gheertsz,** Anna f. Ghijsbrecht.
14 Aug. 1575 **Gheesbeke, Van,** Susanna f. Steven.
2 Nov. 1598 **Gheesere, de,** Jonathan f. Jan.
6 Ap. 1595 **Gheest,** Lidia f. Hans.
30 Mei 1596 „ de, Janneken f. „
1 Jul. 1599 „ „ Jacob f. Jan.
17 Jan. 1602 „ „ Maria f. „
5 Mei 1590 **Gheetere, de, (v. Geeter),** Jan. f. Hans.
20 „ 1591 „ „ Elisabeth f. Jan.
25 „ 1596 „ „ Joannes f. „
7 Dec. 1578 **Gheldaff,** „ f. Jois.
24 Feb. 1583 **Ghele, Van, (v. Gele),** Joannes f. Gillis.
14 Nov. 1596 **Gherarts, (v. Gheeraerts),** Marcus f. Marcus.
3 Mei 1576 **Ghijsberts,** Marie f. Albert.
6 Mar. 1578 **Ghijsberts,** David f. „
8 Jun. 1690 **Gijsbrechtse,** Lijdia f. Klaes & Katrijn Claessen.
13 Oct. 1586 **Ghijselinc,** Johannes f. Daniel.
7 Nov. 1587 **Ghijselinck,** Sara f. „
28 Feb. 1590 „ Absolou f. „
25 Mei 1592 **Ghijselinx,** Sara f. „
2 Jun. 1586 **Ghijsels, (v. Gisels, etc.),** Gielis f. Jan.
16 Mei 1588 „ Maria f. „
16 Jul. 1577 **Ghilberts, (v. Gilberts),** Elisabet f. Matheus.

</td><td colspan="3">

3 Jul. 1608 **Ghistel, Van, (v. Gistel),** Anna f. Pieter.
30 Ap. 1587 **Ghix,** Joannes f. Godefroij.
29 Ap. 1576 **Ghuijssen,** Esther f. Fransois.
16 Ap. 1690 **Gibbens,** Jacob f. Jacob & Elizabeth Van Santen.
10 Dec. 1587 **Giele, Van, (v. Gele),** Helena f. Gielis.
17 Jun. 1688 **Gijsberts, (v. Ghijsberts),** Anna f. Matthys & Christiaentje.
27 Jul. 1690 „ Johannes f. Johannes & Catharina.
2 Mei 1692 **Gijsbertz,** Mattheus f. Johannes & Catharina.
13 Oct. 1695 **Gijsbert,** Ester f. Johannes & Ester.
13 Jun. 1697 **Gijsberts,** Elisabeth f. Johannes.
8 Dec. 1700 „ Phebon f. Jan.
10 Oct. 1588 **Gijselinck, (v. Ghijselinc),** Daniel f. Daniel.
19 Jun. 1593 „ Sara f. „
26 Oct. 1606 **Gijsels,** Daniel f. Jan.
14 Mar. 1721 **Gijsen, Van,** Margareta f. Elisabeth.
12 Sep. 1722 „ „ Jacob f. Francoijs & Elisabeth.
4 Jan. 1857 **Gijselman,** Hendrik Christiaan f. Warnar & Bartha Maria Haye.
17 Oct. 1858 „ Catharine Elizabeth f. Warnar & Bartha Maria Haye.
15 Oct. 1598 **Gilbert,** Pieter f. Ambrosius.
17 Jul. 1580 **Gilbertz, (v. Ghilberts),** Matthias f. Matthis.
1 Dec. 1583 „ Elsbeth f. Matthis.
4 Jun. 1587 „ Geertruijt f. „
10 Nov. 1588 „ Maria f. „
16 Aug. 1590 „ Mattheeus f. „
20 Dec. 1593 „ Anna f. „
24 Mar. 1574 **Gilbode,** Susanna f. „
18 Aug. 1605 **Gillis,** Magdalena f. Goosen.
27 Mar. 1626 „ Joannes f. Robert.
21 Jan. 1702 **Gilpen,** Eduard f. Ephraim & Christina.
6 Jul. 1851 **Giltjes,** Francois Leopold f. Jacob & Johanna Jacoba Jonker.
9 Apl. 1854 „ Fokke Jan f. Jacob & Johanna Jacoba Jonker.
30 Dec. 1855 „ Pauline Adolphine Emma f. Jacob & Johanna Jacoba Jonker.
26 Dec. 1858 „ Jeannette Helene f. Jacob & Johanna Jacoba Jonker.
9 Sep. 1610 **Gisels, (v. Ghysels),** Elisabeth f. Jan.
8 Ap. 1606 **Gistel, Van, (v. Gistel),** Petrus f. Pieter.
16 Jul. 1607 **Glabbach, Van,** Susanna f. Christian.
1 Jan. 1628 **Glorij,** Sara f. Philips.
19 Sep. 1674 **Godens,** Abraham f. Joris.
2 Aug. 1571 **Godschalck,** Sara f. Jan.
3 Sep. 1573 „ Abraham f. Joos.
8 Jan. 1587 „ Janneken f. Jacobus.
8 Dec. 1588 „ Samuel f. „
23 Aug. 1590 „ Esther f. „
13 Feb. 1592 „ Daniel f. „
3 Nov. 1594 „ Isaac f. „
14 Mar. 1596 „ Judith f. „
5 Oct. 1600 „ Maria f. Joos.
30 Mei 1602 „ Johannes f. „
21 Ap. 1604 „ Anna f. „
3 Nov. 1605 „ Anna f. „
27 Dec. 1606 **Godschalck,** Abigail f. Joos.
2 Apl. 1609 „ Justus f. „
31 Mei 1612 „ Petrus f. „
4 Aug. 1603 „ Anna f. Daniel.

</td></tr>
</table>

15 Jul.	1604	Godschalck, Catharijna f. Jacob.
30 Aug.	1607	„ Elisabeth f. „
17 Aug.	1623	„ Petrus f. Jan.
13 Jul.	1625	„ Catharina f. „
23 Aug.	1627	„ Abigail f. „
27 Nov.	1634	„ Elisabeth f. Johannes.
7 Jan.	1616	Godschalx, Jacobus f. Joos.
20 Apl.	1572	Goe, de, (v. Goes), Abigail f. Pieter.
4 Aug.	1639	Goedtval, (v. Goetval), David f. David.
27 Jan.	1572	Goermans, Daniel f. Tielmans.
11 Oct.	1573	Goes, (v. Goe), Susanna f. Nielaeys.
4 Ap.	1574	„ de, Bathseba f. Pieter.
30 Jun.	1746	Goesijn, Jannetje f. Johannes & Alida Schouten.
31 Jan.	1641	Goetaers, Carel f. ......, tot Mortlake.
15 Mar.	1646	Goetval, (v. Goedtval), Joannes f. David.
11 Apl.	1647	„ Jacobus f. „
7 Mei	1590	Goije, de, Abraham f. Jan.
21 Apl.	1580	Goijots, Hester f. Gabriel.
25 Dec.	1588	Goijou, de, Joris f. Jacus.
29 Apl.	1685	Gols, de, Anna f. Philip & Maria Van Delft.
12 Dec.	1688	„ „ Wilhelmus & Anna } f. Mr. Philip Philipsz, advoenet & Notaris & Maria Van Delft.
25 Aug.	1616	Gomaersz, Tobias f. Hans.
13 „	1615	Gomassen, „ f. „
27 Jul.	1629	Gomassem, Johannes f. Johannes.
8 Jul.	1600	Goomuck, Hester f. Geerart.
16 Apl.	1626	Gooris, (v. Jooris), Hermannus f. Saloman.
3 Jul.	1599	Goosen, Sara f. Lennert.
17 Jun.	1599	„ Anna f. „
23 Nov.	1600	Goossen, Johannes f. „
2 Nov.	1598	Goosens, Susanna f. Lennert.
29 Jan.	1598	„ Abraham f. Giclis.
14 Mei	1626	Gootens, (v. Grotens, Gotens), Willem f. Carel, tot Mortlake.
23 Dec.	1627	„ Johanna f. Carel, tot Mortlake.
29 Mar.	1630	„ Maria f. „
24 Mar.	1633	„ Elisabeth f. „
1 Mei	1643	„ Jonatan f. „
19 Jan.	1673	„ Maria f. Jonathan.
27 Mei	1576	Gore, Catharina f. Fransois.
20 Feb.	1582	Gorgu, Catrina f. Christiaan.
11 Dec.	1589	„ Jacob f. „
28 Jan.	1593	„ Abraham f. „
19 Nov.	1594	„ Maria f. „
5 Dec.	1591	Gorgue, Catelyn f. „
15 Nov.	1635	Gotens, (v. Gootens), Anna f. Carel.
6 Jnu.	1677	„ Maria f. „
28 Sep.	1589	Gouce, le, Joannes f. Hans.
5 Jun.	1586	Gouch, Van, Isaak f. Herman.
29 Jul.	1613	Gouche, le, Henricus & Anna } f. Stephen.
17 Aug.	1617	„ Anna f. Steven.
14 Mar.	1736	Goulius, (v. Gaulius), Gerard Karel f. Coenraed & Elizabeth.
9 Jan.	1620	Gounel, Johannes f. Jan.
10 Jan.	1574	Govarts, Susanna f. Steven.
7 Oct.	1694	Graaf, de, Nicolaas f. Cornelis & Maria.
31 Aug.	1746	„ „ Joseph f. Baltus & Suzanne Sijks.
28 Feb.	1748	„ „ Johannes f. Baltus & Suzanne Sijks.
3 Mar.	1751	„ „ Anna f. Baltus & Suzanne Sijks.

15 Jul.	1590	Graimt, Petrus f. Jan.
12 Feb.	1587	Grand, le, Judith f. Raphael.
1 Jan.	1604	„ „ Anna f. Jan.
25 Apl.	1592	Grande, le, Barbara f. Rafel.
10 Oct.	1591	Grasbecke, Van, Jacus f. Jacus.
3 Nov.	1594	Grauwel, Maria f. Hans.
21 Feb.	1572	Grave, de, Moses f. Jan, van Kassel.
24 Jan.	1574	„ „ Aaron f. „
11 Mar.	1576	„ „ David f. „
21 Jun.	1584	„ „ Jan f. „
5 Dec.	1555	„ „ Nicolaes f. „
22 Oct.	1587	„ „ Moses f. „
26 Oct.	1589	„ „ Jacobus f. Hans.
12 Apl.	1590	„ „ Joannes f. Giclis.
20 Jun.	1591	„ „ Marie f. Jan.
21 Sep.	1595	„ „ Susanna f. Aernont.
10 Feb.	1600	„ „ Arnont f. Arnout.
28 Sep.	1600	„ „ Judith f. Aernont.
3 Oct.	1596	„ „ Catheline f. Guillame.
30 Ap.	1598	„ „ Joanna f. Willem.
15 Aug.	1602	„ „ Petrus f. Guillame.
17 Oct.	1596	„ „ Jussynken f. Jaques.
24 Mei	1601	„ „ Isaac & Jacob } f. Jaques.
13 Mar.	1597	„ „ Marie f. Aaron.
22 Oct.	1598	„ „ Judocus f. „
3 Jan.	1602	„ „ Joannes f. „
2 Feb.	1606	„ „ Aaron f. „
19 Jan.	1608	„ „ Joannes f. „
17 Feb.	1639	Grebinck-hof, (v. Grevinckhoff), Johannes f. Jan.
15 Jan.	1688	Greenboom, Carel f. Hendrick & Anna.
2 Mar.	1589	Grenoot, Elizabeth f. Franchoys.
10 „	1605	Grets, de, Maria f. Conraed.
20 Dec.	1640	Grevinckhoff, Elizabeth f. Jan.
31 Aug.	1572	Griete, Pauwels f. Jan.
12 Oct.	1715	Grijp, Johanna f. Gerrit & Marytje Lodewijks.
7 Jul.	1717	„ Johannes f. Gerrit & Marytje Lodewijks.
30 Nov.	1670	Groen, Willem f. Heindrick & Jacomina.
15 Jul.	1733	„ Sara f. Jan & Abigael.
11 Jan.	1736	„ Elizabeth f. Johannes & Abignel Teris.
1 Nov.	1682	Groene, de, Maria Martha f. Johannes, M.D.
14 Jan.	1680	Groenen, (v. Gronen), Catarina f. Frederick & Elisabeth.
29 Nov.	1682	„ Van, Johannes f. Adam.
27 Mei	1683	„ „ Herman f. Frederick & Elisabeth.
19 Nov.	1684	„ Elizabeth f. Frederick.
3 Jan.	1686	„ Adam f. Fr. „ & Elisabeth.
23 Mar.	1687	„ Anthony f. „
5 Mei	1675	Groenevelt, Franciscus f. Johannes & Christina de Ruyter.
5 „	„	„ Franciscus f. Joannes.
4 Nov.	1677	„ Elias f. Johannes.
2 Apl.	1679	„ Christina f. „ & Christina.
14 Apl.	1734	Groeningen, Van, (v. Groningen), Jan f. Reynier Jansz & Saartje de Haan.
16 Jul.	1738	„ „ Daniel f. Reynier Jansz & Sara de Haan.
9 Nov.	1740	„ „ Hermen f. Reynier Jansz & Sara de Haan.
16 Oct.	1743	„ „ Willem f. Reynier Jansz & Sara de Haan.

3 Nov. 1723 **Groensvelt,** ,, Johannes f. Jan & Hendrika Borkeloo.
24 Mar. 1616 **Grollen,** Timotheus f. Jacob.
28 Sep. 1873 **Groman,** Willem f. Hendrik Jacobus & Geertruida Wilhelmina Hamerslag.
8 Jul. 1688 **Gronen,** (v. **Groenen**), Elisabeth f. Fr. Frederick & Elisabeth.
31 Jul. 1689 ,, Hanah f. Fr. Frederick & Elisabeth Vingerhood.
5 Dec. 1690 ,, Frederick f. Fr. Frederick & Elisabeth.
11 Jun. 1693 **Groonen,** ,, f. Frederick & Elisabeth.
18 Apl. 1731 **Groninge,** Van, (v. **Groeningen**), Mensje f. Reynier Jansc& Sara de Haan.
23 Apl. 1732 **Groningen,** ,, Antje f. Reynier Jans & Sara de Haan.
14 Jul. 1745 ,, ,, Pieter f. Reynier Jansen & Sara de Haan.
5 Jan. 1725 **Gronsvelt,** ,, (v. **Groensvelt**), Johannes f. Jan & H. Van Berkeloo.
14 Nov. 1680 **Groot,** de, Johanna f. Casparis.
6 Apl. 1794 ,, ,, (v. **Groote**), Johan Robert f. Nicolaas & Margaret Burgoyne.
6 Sep. 1812 ,, ,, Cornelis f. Cornelis & Maria Boer.
12 Jun. 1814 ,, ,, Margaretha f. Cornelis & Maria Boer.
12 Apl. 1816 ,, ,, Hendrik f. Cornelis & Maria Boer.
21 Mar. 1813 ,, ,, Dionisia Elizabeth f. Wynand & Rosalia Carolina Louisa Vignon.
13 Mei 1596 **Groote,** de, Johannes f. Pieter.
23 Aug. 1597 ,, ,, Margaret f. ,,
7 Aug. 1678 **Grootens,** Carel f. Carel.
25 Sep. 1681 ,, Hannah f. ,,
15 Oct. 1693 **Grootert,** (v. **Grotert**), Maria f. Jacob & Catharina Le Baiseur.
12 Mei 1695 ,, Elisabeth f. Jacob & Catharina Le Baiseur.
30 Oct. 1698 ,, Jacob f. Jacob & Catharina Le Baiseur.
2 Jul. 1704 ,, Abraham f. Jacob & Catharina Le Baiseur.
23 Jun. 1706 ,, Roelof f. Jacob & Catharina Le Baiseur.

20 Nov. 1709 **Grootert,** Maria f. Jacob & Catharina Le Baiseur.
14 Mei 1676 **Groten,** Maria f. Jonathan.
14 Nov. 1680 ,, ,, f. Carel.
10 Sep. 1682 ,, Elisabeth f. ,,
8 Aug. 1638 **Grotens,** Rebecca f. Carel, tot Mortlake, in de Engelsche Kercke.
28 Feb. 1697 **Grotert,** (v. **Grootert**), Abraham f. Jacob & Catharina.
8 Sep. 1700 ,, Roelof f. Jacob & Catharina.
14 Jun. 1702 ,, Philippus f. ,, ,,
4 Aug. 1703 ,, Samuel f. ,, ,,
26 Sep. 1708 ,, Philippus f. ,, ,,
19 Aug. 1711 ,, Catharina f. ,, ,,
21 Jun. 1590 **Grouwel,** (v. **Gruwel**), Sara f. Hans.
7 Jul. 1588 **Grove,** Esdras f. Gielis.
12 Dec. 1591 ,, de, Moses f. ,,
23 ,, 1593 ,, ,, Gillis f. ,,
12 Apl. 1596 ,, ,, Sara f. ,,
26 Feb. 1598 ,, ,, Jeremias f. ,,
20 Jul. 1600 ,, ,, Margriete f. ,, Gielis.
16 Oct. 1603 ,, ,, Anna f. ,,
14 Nov. 1619 ,, ,, Catharina f. Moses.
2 Oct. 1620 ,, ,, Ester f. ,,
13 Oct. 1583 **Guiots,** Frantzois f. Gabriel.
9 Apl. 1587 ,, Janneken f. ,,
14 Aug. 1689 **Grunbaum,** Anna Maria f. Hendrick & Anna.
10 Jan. 1571 **Grunekees,** Jan f. Joachim.
17 Dec. 1643 **Grunt,** Elisabet f. Hans Pieters.
20 Apl. 1590 **Grurius,** Samuel f. Simon.
14 Jun. 1579 **Grutere,** de, Abraham f. Wilhelmus.
12 Dec. 1591 **Gruwel,** (v. **Grouvel**), Sara f. Hans.
5 Aug. 1593 ,, Joannes f. ,,
2 Sep. 1576 **Gughelrave,** .... fl Sanders.
28 Aug. 1799 **Guitard,** Isaac f. Arend Jacob & Henrietta de Beaune.
21 Mar. 1804 ,, Anna Maria f. Arend Jacob & Henrietta de Beaune.
4 Jun. 1812 ,, John William f. Arend Jacob & Henrietta de Beaune.
20 Nov. 1670 **Gulick,** Van, Jacob f. Jan.
3 ,, 1672 ,, Anna f. ,, & Margaretha.
1 Sep. 1734 **Gulleback,** Rebecca, }
,, Rachel, } f. Jean & Hillige.
,, & Len }
24 Dec. 1587 **Gullens,** Cornelis f. Joos.
13 Nov. 1632 **Gumper,** Bertholomeus f. Paulus.

19 Dec. 1707 **Haaen,** (v. **Haen**), Johanna f. Evert & Johanna Buiner.
19 Jan. 1696 **Haan,** Anna Catharina f. Evert.
9 Aug. 1724 ,, de, Susanna f. Abram & Grietje de Val.
27 Mar. 1726 ,, ,, Sara f. Jan & Maria La Fever.
4 Sep. 1681 **Habrij,** Anna f. Jacobus.
13 Feb. 1625 **Habroeck,** Susanna f. Gerard.
5 Aug. 1683 **Hacker,** Johannes f. Pieter & Constantia.
11 Feb. 1685 ,, Jacob f. Pieter & Constantia van Wachtendonck.

23 Nov. 1687 **Hacker,** Jacobus f. Pieter & Constantia.
11 Jan. 1607 **Haddock,** Dorothea f. Israel.
25 Aug. 1576 **Haeck,** Anna f. Philips.
10 Oct. 1624 ,, Susanna f. Daniel.
28 Mar. 1622 **Haecken,** Petrus f. Winant.
8 Dec. 1594 **Haegen,** Vander, (v. **Haghen**), Tobias. f. Arnout.
13 Jan. 1600 ,, ,, Christoffel f. Arnout.
15 Nov. 1601 **Haeghen,** ,, Samuel f. Arnout.
8 Dec. 1611 **Haem,** wten, Petrus f. Jan Jansz.
4 Apl. 1619 **Haems,** Paulus f. Jan.

11 Apl.	1677	**Haen,** de, Hermannus f. Hermannus.	
30 Aug.	1702	„ (v. Haaen), Elysabeth f. Everr & Johanna Buiner.	
10 Jan.	1703	„ de, Saraf. Hermannus & Margareta.	
15 Nov.	1704	„ „ Maria f. Hermannus & Margareta de Vael.	
13 Oct.	1706	„ „ Hermannus f. Hermannus & Margareta.	
13 Jul.	1709	„ „ Elisabeth f. Hermannus & Margareta.	
11 Dec.	1586	**Haerschens,** Joannes f. Coenraert.	
29 Sep.	1612	**Haes,** (v. Hase, Haze), Johannes f. Coenraert.	
21 Jan.	1616	„ Guiljelmus f. Coenraert.	
30 Nov.	1617	„ Maria f. „	
16 Apl.	1620	„ Moses f. „	
9 Jan.	1681	„ de, Johannes f. Cornelis.	
21 Jan.	1588	**Haese,** de, Abraham f. Lieven.	
31 Aug.	1591	„ Jossine f. „	
14 Dec.	1585	**Hage,** Vanden, Elisabet f. Gillis.	
17 Dec.	1587	„ „ Sara f. „	
14 Dec.	1600	„ de, Sara f. Romeijn.	
2 Mar.	1602	„ Vanden, Cornelis f. Cornelis & Grietje Cornelis.	
22 Aug.	1813	**Hagedoorn,** Koert. geb. 13 Maert te Husumin Holsteyn, f. Wietse Jans & Annegyne Coerts Dick, wonachtig in Groningerland.	
27 Mar.	1580	**s'Hagers,** Magdalena f. Steven.	
4 Apl.	1591	**Haghen,** Vander, (v. Haegen), Joannes f. Gillis.	
24 Sep.	1597	„ „ Jacobus f. Arnout.	
28 Nov.	1602	„ „ Johannes f. „	
25 Oct.	1660	**Haijer,** Simon, een bejard persohn.	
19 Nov.	1588	**Halars,** Sara f. Christiaen.	
7 Jun.	1607	**Halbijn,** Anna f. Anthonis.	
20 Jun.	1813	**Halfkens,** Johanna f. Jacobus & Johanna Wilhelmina Breunes.	
25 Jul.	1598	**Halle,** Van, Marie f. Hans.	
24 Aug.	1600	„ „ Joannes f. „	
8 Aug.	1602	„ „ Maria f. „	
29 Jul.	1571	**Halmaels,** Hester f. Henrick.	
17 Oct.	1577	**Halmbeen,** Judith f. Arnoult.	
16 Dec.	1688	**Halowet,** Maria f. Pieter & Maria de Coning.	
2 Feb.	1635	**Halve,** Van der, Magdalena f. Cevereijn.	
2 Feb.	1590	**Hambach,** Van, Joanna f. Herman.	
15 Nov.	1593	„ „ Abraham f. „	
18 Mar.	1573	**Hamels,** Catherine f. Govaert.	
20 Feb.	1808	**Hamerslag,** Alida f. Tieleman Adrianus & Maria vander Heyden.	
25 Jul.	1869	„ Johanna f. Adrianus & Maria vander Heyden.	
26 Jan.	1873	„ Gerrit f. Tielman Adrianus & Maria vander Heyden.	
26 Nov.	1871	„ Gerard William f. Gerrit & Anna Elisabeth Slater.	
11 Mei	1600	**Hameus,** (v. Hammeus), Balduinus f. Balduinus.	
28 Feb.	1602	„ Susanna f. Balduinus.	
26 Feb.	1609	„ Elisabeth f. „	
8 Mei	1614	„ Charles f. D. „	
13 Jul.	1656	**Hamilton,** Maria f. Chrysostomus.	
24 Jun.	1660	„ Johannes f. „	
22 Mei	1664	„ Elisabeth f. „	
5 Jan	1673	„ Carolina f. „	
26 Sep.	1683	„ Maria f. Charles. „	
30 Nov.	1684	„ Charles f. „	

14 Nov.	1703	**Haminel,** Johannes f. Jan & Elsje Ninueve.	
7 Nov.	1680	**Hammen,** Van, Maria f. Dyrick.	
12 Aug.	1604	**Hammeus,** (v. Hameus), Jeremias f. Balduinus.	
10 Dec.	1644	**Hammick.** Lambert f. Mattheus.	
30 Mar.	1707	**Hamoet,** Elijsabeth f. Anthoni & Maria.	
5 Jun.	1642	**Han,** de, (v. Hane), Baudewijn f. Jacob.	
29 Mar.	1707	**Hanckel,** Jacob f. Jacob & Anna.	
15 Sep.	1583	**Handt,** de, Richardt f. Albert.	
9 Sep.	1638	**Hane,** Vander, (v. Hann), Francoijs f. Franchoijs.	
26 „	1641	„ „ Maria f. Francois.	
26 Jan.	1634	„ „ Jakus Josephus f. Jacob.	
17 Sep.	1637	**Hane,** Vander, Anna f. Jacob.	
4 Aug.	1639	„ „ Jacob f. „	
12 Mei	1644	„ „ Elisabet f. „	
3 Aug.	1648	„ „ Maria f. „	
18 Sep.	1649	„ „ Francois f. „	
9 Jul.	1654	„ „ Johannes f. Jacob.	
6 Mar.	1608	**Hanens,** Elisabeth f. Johannes.	
1 Mar.	1612	„ Catharina f. Jan.	
1 Mei	1853	**Hangjas,** Louis Marinus Antonius f. Marcus Levi & Maria Helena Carolina Wantenaer.	
22 „	1670	**Hann,** de, (v. Hane), Francoijs & Elizabeth.	
5 Jan.	1673	„ „ Jacob f. Francoijs & Elizabeth.	
26 Jan.	1617	**Hannen,** Johannes f. Johannes.	
4 Feb.	1610	**Hannens,** Anna f. Jan.	
7 Feb.	1697	**Hanninck,** Anna f. Lambert.	
27 Sep.	1685	**Hauseier,** Agnieta f. Daniel & Gisberta Huejes.	
17 Dec.	1626	**Hansen,** Maria f. Jacob.	
12 Mar.	1627	„ „ Maria f. Coeraert.	
21 Sep.	1595	**Hantoij,** Abigail f. Pieter.	
29 Nov.	1589	**Hantois,** Petrus f. „	
29 Apl.	1593	„ Anna f. „	
9 Aug.	1601	„ Isaac f. Pieter.	
		„ & Jacob	
14 Oct.	1610	**Harijngkoeck,** Van, Judith f. Daniel.	
23 Jun.	1605	**Harinckhoeck,** Elisabeth f. „	
21 Dec.	1606	„ Maria f. „	
28 Aug.	1608	„ Daniel f. „	
7 Feb.	1602	**Harinckhouck,** Van, Janneken f. „	
7 Jan.	1627	**Harinckhoeck,** Josias f. Mattheus.	
27 Aug.	1629	„ „ Van, Anna f. „	
16 Apl.	1615	**Harinckoecke,** Van, Anna f. „	
12 Mar.	1620	**Haringhcouck,** Gratia f. „	
10 Nov.	1616	**Harinchouck,** „ Anna f. Daniel.	
5 Apl.	1618	**Haringhoeck,** Petrus f. „	
15 Feb.	1688	**Haringkouck,** Anthonius f. „	
29 Jun.	1690	**Harlah,** Maria f. Frederic & Maria.	
2 Mar.	1693	„ Elizabeth f. „ „	
2 Jul.	1718	„ Vasmar f. „	
		„ Frederijk f. William & Helia Hagedoorn.	
29 Nov.	1721	„ Debora Charlotta f. William & Helia Hagedoorn.	
12 Feb.	1725	„ Samuel f. William & Helia Hagedoorn.	
3 Apl.	1727	„ Marten f. William & Helia Hagedoorn.	
24 Jan.	1580	**Harlen,** Jakemyns f. Hans Charles, van Diest.	
21 Aug.	1634	**Harmans,** Maria f. Abraham.	
27 Feb.	1610	**Harpe,** Van, Maria f. Abraham.	
10 „	1605	**Harrebach,** .. Paulus f. Paulus.	
9 Mar.	1617	**Harrewyn,** Elisabet f. Jacob.	

17 Jun. 1739 Harrigh, Van, (v. Horrigh), Christiaan f.
Johan Christopher Maurits & Anna Biels.
29 Jan. 1687 Harrison, Catharina f. Anthony & Francis.
13 Mar. 1580 Hart, de, Richaert f. Aelbert.
19 Jan. 1589 „ „ Thomas f. „
3 Apl. 1628 „ „ Dorothea f. Frederick.
29 Oct. 1633 „ Govert f. „ Test de Heer Ambassa: Govert Brasser, etc.
27 Jan. 1717 „ Anna f. Cornelis & Annetje De Val.
15 Jan 1615 Hartman, Sara f. Heijndrick.
15 Dec. 1616 „ Susanna f. „
29 Jan. 1693 „ Dirricksen f. Rutger & Maria.
24 Dec. 1693 „ Annetje f. „ „
22 Jun. 1701 „ Rutgart f. Rutgart & Catharina.
28 Jun. 1702 „ Maria f. Richart & Catharina.
... Mar. 1706 „ Isaac } f. Rutgert & & Rebecca } Catharina.
5 Oct. 1707 „ Catarina f. Rutgert & Catharina Nersoike.
10 Nov. 1583 Hase, de, (v. Haes), Catherine f. Lieven.
17 Jan. 1585 „ „ Anna f. Lieven.
6 Mar. 1586 „ „ Sara f. „
23 Jun. 1590 „ „ Susanna f. „
24 Feb. 1594 d'Hase, Abraham f. „
28 Dec. 1595 Hase, de, Lievinns „
29 Aug. 1624 „ „ Josephus f. Conradus.
4 Apl. 1643 Haselborn, (v. Hasselborn), Joannes f. Joannes.
17 Aug. 1595 Hasevelde, Van, Anna f. Daniel.
13 Sep. 1607 Haseveldt, „ Daniel f. „
19 Aug. 1599 Hasevelt, Geeraert f. „
28 Sep. 1600 „ Maria f. „
24 Nov. 1605 „ Catharina f. „
5 Jun. 1609 „ Van, Maria f. „
14 Apl. 1611 „ Joanna f. „
18 Oct. 1618 „ Daniel f. „
20 Feb. 1620 „ Anna f. „
30 Dec. 1621 „ Adam f. „
10 Oct. 1613 Hassel, Van, David f. Geevaert.
23 Jun. 1616 „ „ Abraham f. „
3 Oct. 1619 „ „ Matthias f. „
8 Jan. 1633 Hasselborn (v. Haselborn), Maria f. Jan.
18 Mei. 1634 Hasselborne, Catharina f. Jan.
25 Mei 1617 Hathoen, Anna f. Joris.
11 Oct. 1574 Hatroen, Joannes f. Guillame.
2 „ 1577 „ f. Gilleken.
25 Jan. 1590 „ Anna f. „
9 Jun. 1592 „ Guiliame f. Guiliame.
10 Nov. 1588 Hauthuijs, Abraham f. Pieter.
4 Oct. 1586 Hantijf, Jacobus f. Jaques.
29 Jul. 1604 Hauwaert, Van, Susanna f. Pieter.
11 Jul. 1613 Hauward, Ester f. Jan.
26 Aug. 1593 Hauwert, Van, Petrus f. Pieter.
12 Oct. 1596 „ „ (v. Hawert), Jacomynken f. Pieter.
12 Sep. 1602 Haven, Abraham f. Andries.
28 Dec. 1690 Haverveldt, Susanna f. Albertus & Ida.
12 Mar. 1592 Hawaert, Joannes f. Hans.
14 Apl. 1580 Hawoens, Maria f. Guiliams.
19 Nov. 1598 Haze, de, (v. Haes), Sara f. Lieven.
31 Mei 1863 Hazelbach, Johannes f. Pieter Ludovicus Jan Smit & Maria Magdalena Kok.
15 Jul. 1674 Hearne, Philippus f. Thomas & Aletta op de Boeck.

11 Mar. 1595 Heck, Vander, Jacob f. Gautier.
19 Oct. 1645 „ Van, Sara f. Abraham.
5 Jan. 1589 Hecke, „ Abraham f. Goutier.
26 Jun. 1597 „ Vander, Elizabeth f. „
5 Dec. 1641 „ Van, Isaac f. Abraham.
29 Jun. 1644 „ „ Johanna f. „
19 Jun. 1659 „ „ Judith f. „
19 Mar. 1628 „ Vander, Martina f. Jan, tot Mortlake.
25 Mei 1629 „ Van, Johannes f. „
17 Jul. 1631 „ Vander, Abraham f. Jan, tot Mortlake.
6 Mar. 1642 „ „ Anna f. Jan, tot Mortlake.
25 Dec. 1664 „ Van, Jan f. Johannes.
4 „ 1636 Hecken, Vander, Sara f. Jan, tot Mortlake.
19 Jan. 1612 Hecker, Hermannus f. Haerman.
25 Apl. 1614 Heckers, Petrus f. Herman.
2 Mar. 1623 „ Johannes f. „
25 Sep. 1601 Heede, Vander, Andries f. Joos.
7 Oct. 1610 Heel, Van, Rhode fa. Cornelis.
12 Nov. 1615 „ „ Cornelius f. „
30 Mar. 1623 „ „ Salomon f. „
24 Dec. 1620 „ „ Jacobus f. „
18 Oct. 1585 Heenens, Sara f. Anthonis.
8 Sep. 1639 Heeren, Maria f. Pieter.
10 Dec. 1643 „ Susanna f. „
22 Oct. 1731 Heerenberg, Jan Hendrik f. Elso & Aletta Christina.
5 Feb. 1600 Heerewegen, Van, Rogier f. Rogier.
28 Feb. 1602 Heesch, „ Heijndrick f. Heyndrick.
20 Oct. 1590 Heijden, Vander, Sophonius f. Eliaert.
8 Mei 1631 „ „ Johanna f. Jan.
30 Jul. 1633 „ „ Johannes f. „
31 Jan. 1637 „ „ Margarita f. ......
24 Apl. 1870 Heijdenrijk, Willem Frederik f. Pieter & Willemina Scherpenzeel.
24 Sep. 1597 Heijen, Ter, Sara f. Jan.
16 Jan. 1588 Heijlger, (v. Heiliger), Laurens f. Laurens.
15 Mei 1784 Heijliger, Judith Aletta, geb. 25 Ap. 1784, f. Johannes & Elizabeth Salomons.
„ „ „ „ Augustus Henry, geb. 28 Apl. 1783, f. Johannes Abz & Elizabeth Salomons.
26 Jul. 1579 Heijligers, Jacob f. Laurens.
11 Nov. 1582 „ Susanna f. „
2 Dec. 1694 Heijmans, Van, (v. Emans), Elizabeth f. Johannes & Agatha Reyckers.
27 Jun. 1697 „ Antony f. Mr. Jan & Agatha.
7 Mei 1699 „ Anna f. Jacobus & Saartje Van Dijck.
3 Oct. 1591 Heijmbach, Van, Sara f. Herman.
18 Jan. 1573 Heijn, Maria f. Jacob.
23 Apl. 1577 „ Helena f. „
29 Aug. 1596 „ de, Niclaes f. Pieter.
9 Nov. 1600 „ „ Barbara f. „
13 Feb. 1603 „ „ Margrieto f. Pierre.
24 Jun. 1604 „ „ Helena f. Pieter.
27 Jul. 1606 „ „ Maria f. „
15 Nov. 1607 „ „ Petrus f. „
23 Feb. 1574 Heijns, Jacob f. Jacob.
19 Jun. 1578 „ Susanna f. „
28 Apl. 1611 „ Magdalena f. Aernout.
3 Jul. 1614 „ Joannes f. „
2 Aug. 1616 „ Anna f. „

5 Mei 1622 Heijns, Philippus f. Simon, tot Mortlake.
25 Jan. 1693 Heijthuijsen, Van, Gerard f. Gerard Jr. &
Elizabeth Delme.
22 Feb. 1694 ,, ,, Elizabeth f. Gerard Jr.
& Elizabeth Delme.
26 Aug. 1696 ,, ,, Johannes f. Gerard Jr.
& Elizabeth Delme.
... Jun. 1701 ,, ,, Delmée f. Gerard Jr.
& Elizabeth Delme.
25 Dec. 1647 Heijthuisen, ,, Judith f. Gerart.
26 Jan. 1668 Heiligendag, Cornelis f. Hendrijck.
29 Sep. 1669 ,, Margaretha f. ,,
8 Nov. 1580 Heiligers, (v. Heijliger), Daneel f.
Lauwereijns.
24 Mar. 1600 Hekelaers, Maria f. Israel.
7 Feb. 1602 ,, Sara f. Isaac.
29 Nov. 1607 ,, Maria f. Israel.
21 Jan. 1610 ,, Sara f. Israel.
8 Dec. 1612 ,, Rachel f. ,,
18 Mei 1615 ,, Jacobus f. ,,
1 Oct. 1618 ,, Rebecca f. ,,
25 Apl. 1603 Hekelers, Abraham f. ,,
27 Apl. 1578 Hekkelaerts, Rachel f. Maijken.
21 Nov. 1624 Helandt, Elisabet f. post: Jacques.
20 Jul. 1595 Helden, (v. Helen), Abraham f. Dierick.
31 Mei 1597 ,, Van, Joannes f. ,,
7 Oct. 1599 ,, Willem f. Juris.
4 Jan. 1644 ,, ,, f. Willem.
28 Aug. 1631 ,, Maria f. ,,
3 Oct. 1637 ,, Johanna f. ,,
23 Aug. 1640 Helder, Clara f. ,,
6 Jun. 1585 Heldersum, Van, Assuerus f. Pieter.
21 Oct. 1593 Helen, (v. Helden), Nathanael f. Dierick.
21 Dec. 1606 Hellecom, Rebecca f. Jaques.
16 ,, 1691 Hellen, Martha f. Joris.
30 Jan. 1687 Hellin, Isabel f. George.
19 Oct. 1690 Helin, Mara f. ,,
25 Aug. 1695 ,, Thomas f. Joris.
13 Jun. 1858 Helmig, Anna Georgia f. George Lodewijk & Jacoba de Bruyn.
19 Jun. 1859 ,, Anna Georgia f. George Lodewijk & Jacoba de Bruyn.
27 Apl. 1862 ,, Louiza Wilhelmina f. George
Lodewijk & Jacoba de Bruyn.
20 Dec. 1573 Helst, Vander, Pieter f. Jan.
30 Oct. 1614 Hem, de, Sara f. Tobias.
1 Sep. 1616 ,, ,, Jacobus f. ..
1 Nov. 1586 Hembach, Van, Magdalena f. Herman.
29 Jul. 1666 Hen, Joris f. Marten.
17 Mei 1668 ,, Maria f. ,,
19 Dec. 1669 ,, Marten f. ,,
19 Mei 1672 ,, Elizabet f. ,,
16 Jan. 1709 Henckel, Jacob f. Jacob & Anna.
16 Aug. 1584 Henicks, Susanna f. Jakes.
9 Mei 1813 Hennefreunt, Christine Maria f. Johannes
& Johanna Hanse.
27 Apl. 1690 Henst, Marij f. Willem & Marij.
6 Feb. 1606 Heijndric, Heijndrick f. Mattheus.
23 Mar. 1602 Heijndrick, Robert f. ,,
1 Nov. 1607 Heijndrickz, Anna f. Pieter.
1 Apl. 1604 Heijndricx, Hendrick f. Laurens.
13 Oct. 1622 ,, Judith f. Pieter.
2 Jun. 1603 Heijndrix, Maria f. Mattheus.
1 Mar. 1607 ,, Mattheus f. ,,
22 Nov. 1610 ,, Heijndrick f. Pieter.
2 Apl. 1621 Heyndrixsz, Nicolaus f. ,,
2 Feb. 1606 Hendricksz, Hendrick f. ,,

20 Sep. 1618 Hendricx, Daniel f. Pieter.
28 Mei 1620 ,, Johannes f. Jan.
18 Apl. 1619 ,, Anna f. Erasmus.
28 Sep. 1620 ,, Jacob f. ,,
6 Apl. 1613 ,, Erasmus f. ,,
25 Sep. 1614 ,, Abraham f. ,,
28 Feb. 1612 ,, Catharina f. Mattheus.
26 Dec. 1614 ,, Daniel f. ,,
25 Oct. 1612 ,, Sara f. Pieter.
1 Jan. 1617 ,, Johannes f. ,,
13 Feb. 1617 ,, Elizabeth f. ,,
14 Mar. 1624 ,, Jaquemynken f. Jacques, tot
Mortlake.
20 Mar. 1625 ,, Maria f. Abel.
4 Jul. 1631 ,, Hendrick f. Gillis.
1 Nov. 1649 Hendricksen, Maria f. Lenert.
24 Nov. 1661 ,, Cornelis f. Dirick.
30 Jan. 1610 Hendricxsen, Abraham f. Mattheus.
18 Oct. 1629 ,, Susanna f. Pieter.
29 Mar. 1632 ,, Elisabeth f. Herman.
14 Jan. 1664 Hendriksen, Elisabet f. Hendrik.
7 Nov. 1574 Hendrix, Cornelis f. Cornelis.
13 Apl. 1617 ,, Isaac f. Erasmus.
21 Dec. 1617 ,, Petrus f. Carel.
24 Apl. 1687 ,, Sara f. Matthys & Neeltje
Vander Cloots.
10 Mar. 1636 Hendrixsen, Aelken f. Jan.
2 Apl. 1699 Hendrixsz, Maria f. Pieter.
5 Jun. 1625 ,, Daniel f. ,,
19 Oct. 1572 ,, Susanna f. Govards.
26 Oct. 1578 ,, David f. Geerard van
Zutphen.
8 Apl. 1572 Henricx, Rachel f. Philips.
8 Jun. 1596 ,, Anna.
25 Jul. 1572 Henricxs, Richael f. Cornelis.
4 Jan. 1579 Hermans, Sara f. Henrick.
18 Nov. 1638 ,, Catharina f. Jan.
21 Jan. 1631 ,, Abraham f. Abraham.
25 Aug. 1633 ,, Samuel f. ,,
12 Feb. 1633 ,, Magdalena f. ,,
27 Jun. 1592 ,, Janneken f. Adriaen.
21 Oct. 1576 ,, Maria f. Heimdrick.
17 Apl. 1580 ,, Daniel f. ,,
16 Jan. 1582 ,, Petrus f. ,,
9 Dec. 1601 Hermansz, Johanna f. Jacob.
14 ,, 1606 ,, Abraham f. ,,
9 Dec. 1582 ,, Anna f. Adolph.
7 Feb. 1613 Herbach, Van, Franciscus f. Paulus.
27 Feb. 1617 ,, ,, Abigail f. Pauls.
12 Oct. 1589 l'Herberge, Daniel f. Rozier.
18 Nov. 1610 Herberch, Van, Petrus f. Paulus.
17 Nov. 1574 Hercules, Isaac f. Israel.
22 Apl. 1621 ,, Samuel f. ,,
2 Jun. 1588 Herden, Vanden, Joannes f. Sylard.
27 Mar. 1864 Herderschee, Anna Elizabeth f. Jacobus
Gerhardus & Sarah Lam-
bert.
3 Feb. 1867 ,, Jacobus Gerhardus f. Jacobus Gerhardus & Sarah
Maria.
25 Oct. 1868 ,, Dirk f. Jacobus Gerhardus
& Dina Maria.
24 Nov. 1872 ,, Anna f. Jacobus Gerhardus
& Dina Maria.
15 Aug. 1588 l'Heremit, Pieter f. Pieter.
1 Dec. 1805 Herklots, Louisa Constantia f. Gerard
Arnold & Geertruida
Nieuwveen.

8 Nov.	1807	Herklots, Gerard f. Gerard Arnold & Geertruida Nieuwveen.
22 Sep.	1802	Henklots, Anna Christina f. Gerhard Arnold & Geertruida Neeuwveen.
19 Aug.	1639	Herlien, Vander, Debora f. Jan, tot Mortlake.
25 Oct.	1629	Herreman, Anna f. Abraham.
10 Nov.	1605	Herrewege, (v. Herwege), Hesther f. Rogier.
25 Apl.	1622	,, Van, Tobias f. ,,
22 Nov.	1601	Herrewegen, Van, Lijnken f. ,,
22 Oct.	1609	Herrewijn, (v. Harewijn), Maria f. Jacob.
13 Oct.	1611	,, Anna f. ,,
7 Mar.	1613	,, Abraham f. Jaques.
7 Apl.	1616	,, Jacob f. Jacob.
2 Aug.	1618	,, ,, f. ,,
27 Jan.	1622	,, Elisabet f. ,,
18 Jan.	1618	,, Maria f. Abraham.
23 ,,	1620	,, Van, Jacobus f. ,,
11 Nov.	1621	,, Sara f. ,,
11 Mar.	1593	s'Hert, Elisabeth f. Albert.
29 Dec.	1629	,, (v. Hart), Francintijen f. Frederick.
27 Sep.	1631	,, Maria f. ,,
10 Aug.	1718	,, Boudewyn f. Cornelis & Annetje.
26 Feb.	1611	Hertman, Benjamin f. Hendric.
28 Jun.	1612	,, Maria f. ,,
20 Mar.	1608	Hertoeghe, Heyndrick f. Rogier.
25 Mei	1589	Hertoge, de, Joannes f. Jan.
21 Dec.	1600	,, ,, Anna f. Guliam.
12 Aug.	1585	d'Hertoghe, Anna f. Jan.
25 Jun.	1587	,, Susanna f. ,,
18 Oct.	1598	Hertoghe, de, Debora f. Guillaem.
7 Mar.	1609	Herve, Francynken & Magdalena } f. ......
10 Nov.	1612	,, Van, Jacobus f. Rogier.
10 Mei	1610	Herwege, ,, (v. Herrewege), Ester f. Rogier.
22 Nov.	1584	Herwegen, Van, Hendrick f. Jaques.
4 Mei	1615	Herwegge, Rogier f. Rogier.
23 Apl.	1646	Herweghe, Vanden, Jan f. Jan.
19 Sep.	1591	Herwijck, Van, Anna f. Abraham.
17 Nov.	1594	,, ,, Abraham f. ,,
4 Mei	1600	Herze, ,, Sara f. Henrick.
4 Mar.	1651	Hesel, (v. Hessall), Christina f. Jan.
14 Nov.	1847	Hess, Helena Petronelle Josephine f. Charles Jacob & Johanna Maria Klint.
12 Apl.	1653	Hessall, Lea f. Jan.
5 Nov.	1648	Hessel, Anna f. ,,
8 Jul.	1655	Hessell, Johannes f. Johan.
28 Jun.	1772	Hest, Van, Reinier f. Jan & Marija Van Dalen.
17 Dec.	1587	Hesterman, Petrus f. Jan.
11 Dec.	1630	Hesterson, Johannes f. Johannes.
22 Apl.	1645	Hesvelboren, Jacob f. Johan.
13 Mar.	1706	Heuckel, Tilman f. Jacob & Anna.
14 Sep.	1589	Heumerkens, Franchoijs f. Engelman.
9 Jan.	1592	Heumerkes, Susanna f. ,,
29 Aug.	1585	Heupens, Magdalena f. Lieven.
25 Dec.	1708	Heurnius, Van, Tietske f. ...... bejaerde persoon.
9 Jan.	1631	Heurt, Abigail f. Hendrick.
24 Nov.	1586	Heuvel, Vanden, Susanna f. Jan.
5 Nov.	1648	,, Van, Anna f. Hendrick
29 Jun.	1585	Heuvele, Vanden, Joannes f. Hans.
30 Sep.	1585	Heuvick, Jacobus f. Jacob.
22 Mar.	1612	Hiel, Van, (v. Heyl), Eduward f. Cornelis.

3 Oct.	1703	Hijbrijgh, Jeronijmus f. Jacobus.
2 Jan.	1610	Hijens, Arnoldus f. Aernout.
20 Ap.	1590	Hil, Susanna f. Lambert.
22 Mar.	1575	Hilghers, Sara f. Laurens.
19 Feb.	1576	,, Abraham f. ,,
21 Aug.	1586	Hilgoos, Sara f. ,,
1 Dec.	1639	Hilharst, Elizabeth f. Gerard.
14 Mar.	1652	,, te, Jacob f. Gerart.
5 Feb.	1654	Hilhorst, ,, Joseph & Benjamin } f. ,,
28 Aug.	1608	Hilken, Anna f. Jan.
26 Apl.	1612	Hilken, Willem f. Jan.
25 Oct.	1610	Hilkens, Joannes f. ,,
5 Jun.	1576	Hillebrants, Johannes f. ,,
25 Apl.	1869	Hirsch, Jacoba f. Johannes Albertus & Jacoba Bak.
28 Mei	1871	,, Willem f. Johannes Albertus & Jacoba Bak.
31 ,,	1874	,, Albertus f. Johannes Albertus & Jacoba Bak.
22 Jan.	1800	Hobus, Johanna Susanna Jacoba f. Gillis & Maria Burgers.
4 Dec.	1625	Hocket, Philippus f. Philip.
24 Apl.	1631	,, Maria f. ,,
16 Dec.	1632	,, Anna f. ,,
21 Sep.	1634	,, Esther f. ,,
30 Dec.	1644	Hockquet, Pieter f. ,,
21 Aug.	1709	Hoe, Anna & Elisabeth } f. Thomas & Elisabeth Koelamey.
10 Dec.	1609	Hoee, Franciscus f. Jan.
4 Mei	1595	Hoeck, de, Jacomynken f. Jacus.
15 Nov.	1600	,, ,, Anna f. ,,
12 Mei	1605	,, ,, Sara f. Jaques.
1 Sep.	1605	,, Tobias f. Daniel.
12 ,,	1606	,, Joris f. ,,
18 Mar.	1610	,, Van, Phineas f. ,,
8 Aug.	1613	,, ,, Anthonius f. ,,
9 Dec.	1621	,, Elisabet f. ,,
18 Oct.	1635	,, Cateline f. Christiaen.
19 Dec.	1574	Hoecke, Vanden, Pauwels f. Bartholomeus.
29 Apl.	1576	,, Van, Daniel f. Bartholomeus.
26 Feb.	1600	,, ,, Tanneken f. Hans.
15 Mei	1636	Hoel, Maria f. Johannes.
25 Apl.	1578	Hoer, de la, Elijzabeth f. Gheeraerts.
27 Oct.	1633	Hoet, Maria f. Pieter.
10 Dec.	1634	,, Johannes f. ,,
10 Jan.	1636	,, Petrus f. ,,
5 Mar.	1637	,, Symon f. ,,
11 Mar	1638	,, Stephanus f. ,,
14 Jun.	1640	,, Hester f. ,,
15 Mei	1642	,, Sara f. ,,
14 Sep.	1645	,, Jacobus f. ,,
8 Feb.	1648	,, Daniel f. ,,
30 Nov.	1606	Hoeve, Van, (v. Hove), Abraham f. Jan.
5 Mei	1618	Hoeven, Vander, (v. Hoeven), Ester f. Hendric.
18 Nov.	1611	,, ,, Sara f. Hendric.
5 Jun.	1586	,, ,, Jacomyne f. Aernoudt.
13 Dec.	1590	Hoevenaer, (v. Hovenaer, etc.), Elisabeth f. Heinrick.
10 Feb.	1594	,, Hester f. Heinrick.
5 ,,	1598	,, Hendrick f. Hendrick.
26 Jul.	1631	,, Daniel f. ,,
28 Apl.	1689	Hoflandt, Arnoldus f. Johannes.
27 Nov.	1586	Hofman, (v. Hoofman), Isaac f. Hans.

4 Dec.	1586	**Hofman,** Maria f. Jacob.
12 Nov.	1588	,, Petrus f. ,,
9 Nov.	1589	,, Pieter f. ,,
18 Mar.	1593	,, Jacob f. ,,
5 Oct.	1595	,, Judith f. Hans.
17 Dec.	1598	,, Sara f. Jaques.
1 Jan.	1604	,, Jacop f. Jacques.
1 Jan.	1608	,, Elisabeth f. Jacob.
12 Oct.	1630	,, Abraham f. ,,
23 Jun.	1805	,, Sarah Maria f. Pieter & Sara Vrijdag.
2 Mar.	1589	**Hoffman,** Sara f. Jan.
23 Apl.	1592	,, Jacob f. Hans.
24 Feb.	1591	,, Maria f. Jacop.
23 Mar.	1595	,, Hester f. Jacob.
9 Jan.	1597	,, Pieter f. ,,
30 Nov.	1600	,, Abraham f. ,,
26 Oct.	1617	**Hofmeijer,** Samuel f. Mattheus.
30 Apl.	1620	,, Maria f. ,,
26 Jan.	1623	,, Sara f. ,,
16 Feb.	1772	**Hogenbergh,** Elisabeth f. Pieter Hendrik & Maria Linde.
29 Sep.	1586	**Hoijau,** Jaques f. Jaques.
3 Dec.	1587	,, Joannes f. Jacus.
18 Oct.	1590	,, de, Abraham f. Jaques.
18 Jun.	1592	,, ,, Joannes f. Jacques.
31 Mar.	1594	,, ,, Jacob f. ,,
1 Feb.	1596	,, ,, Jacobus f. Jacus.
30 Jul.	1598	,, ,, Mattheus f. Jaques.
14 Feb.	1641	**Hoijel,** Anna f. Joshua.
12 Dec.	1598	**Hoijnen,** Maria f. Andries.
9 Dec.	1604	**Hokel,** Jacobus f. Jaques.
17 Jun.	1638	**Hoket, (v. Hocket),** Pieter f. Philippus.
3 Jan.	1602	**Holden,** Maria f. Dierick.
29 Jul.	1604	,, Esther f. ,,
22 Mar.	1671	**Holijday,** Robert f. Heindrick & Adriana.
8 Jun.	1579	**Hollander, de,** Joannes f. Geerardt.
24 Mar.	1861	**Hollertt,** Johanna Maria f. Jan Van Enschot & Dionisia Jeannette Wilhelmina Catharina Van Dort.
30 Jan.	1639	**Hollevoet, (v. Holvoet),** Maria f. Michiel.
9 Mar.	1806	**Hollingworth,** Anna Catharina f. Thomas, van Yorkshire & Anna Maria Van de Linden, van Leeuwarden.
14 Mei	1637	**Holt, Van,** Anna f. Abraham.
13 Apl.	1628	**Holvoet, (v. Hollevoet),** Anna f. Osias.
2 Apl.	1682	**Hommel,** Johanna f. Johannes.
22 Dec.	1700	,, Elisabeth f. Jan & Elisabeth.
24 Dec.	1704	,, Jacobus f. ,, & Els Niuive.
6 Mei	1705	**Homoet,** Maria f. Anthony & Maria.
6 Jul.	1595	**Hont, de,** Abigail f. Joos.
20 Dec.	1573	,, Pieter f. Hendrick.
20 Nov.	1580	,, Susanna f. ,,
31 Mar.	1594	**Hoofman, (v. Hofman),** Maria f. Isaack.
10 Oct.	1585	**Hoofmans,** Abraham f. Jan.
22 Mar.	1612	**Hooft,** Eleazar f. Jacob.
13 Jan.	1628	,, Erasmus f. Jan,
28 Aug.	1630	,, Petrus f. posthumus Jan.
9 Jun.	1697	**Hoogendijck,** Johannes f. Jan.
27 Dec.	1593	**Hooghe, de,** Susanna f. Romain.
28 Sep.	1606	**d'Hooghe,** Judith f. Romeijn.
3 Jul.	1608	**Hooghe, de,** Joannes f. ,,
21 Nov.	1596	**Hooge, de,** Joannes f. ,,
13 Mar.	1603	**d'Hooge,** Maria f. Romain.
28 Apl.	1633	**Hoopman, (v. Hopman),** Maria f. Jacob.
17 Feb.	1594	**Hoorebeke,** David f. Zacharias.
8 Feb.	1590	**Hoorne, Van,** Marie f. Jan.
28 Dec.	1585	**Hoorskens,** Anna f. Conract.
16 Jul.	1690	**Hopman, (v. Hoopman),** Magdalena f. Benjamin.
16 Mei	1624	**Hoppe,** Henricus f. Dilijnus.
24 Jul.	1597	**Hoprebeke, Van,** Joannes f. Zacharias.
15 Mar.	1629	**Hoquet,** Catalina f. Philippe.
23 Jun.	1686	**Horneck,** Anna f. Philip & Anna Van Noort.
9 Mar.	1688	,, Sarah f. Philip & Anna Van Noort.
14 Mei	1690	,, Maria f. Philip & Anna Van Noort.
29 Aug.	1692	,, Pieternelle f. Philip & Anna Van Noort.
9 Nov.	1587	**Horrewijck, Van,** Sara f. Abraham.
22 Aug.	1736	**Horrigh, Van, (v. Harrigh),** Johannes f. Johannes Christoffel Maurits Anna Biels.
22 Sep.	1636	**Hoset,** Johannes f. Philippus.
8 Mar.	1593	**Hoslaet,** Anna f. Isaac.
11 Dec.	1575	**Hoste, (v. Oste),** Abraham f. Jacques.
7 Jul.	1577	,, Jacob f. Jacques.
27 Sep.	1579	,, Maria f. Jacob.
15 Nov.	1579	,, Susanna f. Jakes, van Ghendt.
7 Mei	1581	,, ,, f. Jacus f. Paschiers.
1 Sep.	1583	,, Jacob f. Jacob.
15 Apl.	1585	,, Lucas f. Jacob.
10 Sep.	1587	,, Janneken f. ,,
15 Dec.	1588	,, ,, f. Jaques.
22 Jul.	1593	,, ,, f. Jacus.
17 Aug.	1606	,, Joanna f. Jacques.
16 Aug.	1607	,, Jacobus f. Jaques.
20 Aug.	1609	,, Joanna f. ,,
20 Oct.	1611	,, Jacobus f. ,,
14 Nov.	1613	,, Ester f. Jaques.
30 Mei	1618	,, Maria f. ,,
28 Jan.	1586	,, Susanna f. Joos.
27 Oct.	1583	,, Abraham f. Pieter.
26 Jul.	1607	,, Elisabeth f. Abraham.
3 Dec.	1609	,, Abraham f. ,,
19 Jul.	1612	,, Priscilla f. ,,
4 Feb.	1616	,, Jaquemynken f. ,,
14 Nov.	1619	,, Johanna f. ,,
8 Mar.	1590	,, Peeter f. Pieter.
16 Ap.	1592	,, David f. ,,
2 Jul.	1609	,, Jacobus f. Daniel.
23 Sep.	1610	,, Joanna f. ,,
1 Aug.	1613	,, Sara f. ,,
16 Oct.	1614	,, Maria f. Dierick.
16 Mei	1616	,, Susanna f. ,,
20 Jan.	1618	,, Joanna f. ,,
25 Jun.	1620	,, Joanna f. ,,
8 Dec.	1622	,, Judith f. ,,
9 Mei	1624	,, Jacobus f. ,,
16 Aug.	1627	,, Maria f. ,,
27 Sep.	1629	,, Maria f. ,,
11 Aug.	1633	,, Jacobus f. ,,
21 Jul.	1635	,, Theodorus f. ,,
27 Feb.	1638	,, Maria f. ,,
27 Mar.	1627	,, Esther f. Samuel.
9 Aug.	1629	,, Catelina f. ,,
19 Sep.	1630	,, Samuel f. ,,
5 Mei	1675	**Hostie,** Joris f. Joseph.
10 Oct.	1585	**Hotse, Van,** Abraham f. Willem.
12 Mar.	1809	**Hotton,** Aaiken f. Martinus Gerrits & Aatje Klaassen.
25 Dec.	1623	**Houbrouck,** Joanna f. Geerard.

28 Oct.	1591	**Houck,** Maerten f. Jaques.
28 Jan.	1588	**Houdt,** de, Elisabeth f. Joos.
11 Dec.	1575	**Hout,** de, Pauwels f. Heindrick.
18 Dec.	1589	**Hout,** ter, Rebecca f. Maurus.
14 Sep.	1589	**Hout,** de, Joannes f. Joos.
20 Jul.	1591	„ „ Susanna f. „
25 Oct.	1575	**Houte,** Vander, Jeremias f. Jacques.
1 Sep.	1577	„ Vander, Samuel f. Jacques.
8 Mar.	1579	„ Van, Samuel f. Jacob.
17 Jan.	1580	„ Vander, Abraham f. Jacob.
8 Oct.	1690	„ Van, Johanna f. Jan & Elizabeth.
6 Jan.	1583	„ Vander, Petrus f. Jakes.
22 Apl.	1688	**Houten,** Van, Johanna f. Arnout & Maria.
13 Jul.	1690	„ „ Cornelis f. Arnoldus & Maria.
17 Mei	1704	„ „ Phanna f. Pieter & Marijtie Kuijsers.
6 Jan.	1850	„ Vanden, Clement Bartrum f. Henricus Leonardus & Maria Robinson.
14 Mar.	1852	„ „ Charles Albert, geb. 29 Sep. 1850, f. Henricus Leonardus & Maria Robinson.
„ „ „		„ „ Maria Elizabeth, geb. 5 Feb. 1850, f. Henricus Leonardus & Maria Robinson.
27 Aug.	1598	**Houthuijs,** Abraham } f. Pieter. & Sara }
9 Oct.	1681	**Houtheusen,** Jan f. Jan & Isabel Cransele.
31 Mar.	1689	„ Carel f. Jan & Isabel Cransele.
30 Aug.	1691	„ Anna f. Jan & Isabel Cransele.
16 Dec.	1683	**Houthousen,** Jan f. Jan & Isabel Cransele.
13 Dec.	1685	**Houthuijsen,** Catarina f. Jan & Isabel Cransele.
14 Apl.	1661	**Houwagen,** Van, Johannes f. Henrick.
16 Mar.	1580	**Houwarts,** Sara f. Hans.
29 Sep.	1594	**Houwe,** Van, Jonas f. Pieter.
6 Jun.	1692	**Houwel,** Willem f. Jan & Debora Walters.
3 Sep.	1693	„ Geertruijdt f. Jan & Debora Walkers.
12 Apl.	1696	„ Johannes f. Jan.
26 Apl.	1702	„ Maria f. „
24 Aug.	1600	**Houwert,** Van, Joanna f. Pieter.
28 Oct.	1696	**Houwten,** „ Jacobus f. Johannes Coenraets & Elisabet Beckaer.
15 Jun.	1572	**Hove,** Vanden, (v. Hoeve, Hoven), Johannes f. Johannes.
13 Dec.	1573	„ „ .... fs. Jan.
22 Mei	1575	„ „ Pieter f. Jan.
23 Sep.	1576	„ „ Maria f. „
5 Aug.	1610	„ „ Sara f. „
19 Dec.	1613	„ „ Joannes f. „
28 Apl.	1616	„ „ Maria f. Joannes.
9 Aug.	1629	„ Van, Aaromi fa. Jan.
21 Feb.	1613	„ „ Maria f. Cornelis.
19 Jan.		**Hoven,** Vanden, Stephanus f. „
26 Jun.	1608	„ „ Pieter f. „
13 Sep.	1702	„ „ f. Nicolaes & Maria.
27 Jan.	1628	**Hovenaer,** Hendrick f. Hendrick de Jonge.
27 Nov.	1631	**Hovener,** Abraham f. „
6 Dec.	1580	**Hoveniers,** Sara f. Pieter.
3 Mei	1606	**Hovvel,** Pieter f. Jaques.
30 Dec.	1745	**Howius,** „ f. Pieter & Anna Dollij.
23 Mar.	1572	**Hubrechts,** (v. Huybrecht), Catarina f. Ambrose.
26 Jun.	1689	**Hubree,** Christina f. Nicolaes & Cornelia.
27 Oct.	1594	**Hucklijr,** Israel f. Israel.

18 Oct.	1601	**Hudgebaut,** (v. Hudgebout, Hughebout, Hugebout, Hughebout, Huggebout, Hutsebout), Anna f. Charles.
10 Oct.	1619	„ Jacobus f. „
3 Apl.	1625	„ Johannes f. „
6 Jan.	1633	„ Carolus f. Abraham.
13 Dec.	1640	„ Maria f. „
10 Mei	1635	**Hudgebauts,** Samuel f. „
13 Aug.	1643	**Hudgebout,** Lucas f. „
10 Feb.	1600	„ Elizabeth f. Charles.
11 Feb.	1574	**Huerblock,** Susanna f. Gillis.
23 Oct.	1580	**Hues,** de, Segher f. Segher.
26 Mar.	1598	**Hugebout,** (v. Hudgebaut), Abraham f. Charles.
5 Jul.	1612	„ Anna f. Carel.
30 Oct.	1614	„ Charles f. Charles.
29 Dec.	1616	„ Joannes f. „
26 Jul.	1750	**Hugens,** Diederik f. Jan & Anna Tomlin.
15 Oct.	1598	**Hugenson,** (v. Huijge), Josijna f. Jaques.
26 Mei	1594	**Hugesz,** Abraham f. Jaques.
6 Aug.	1577	**Hughe,** Sara f. Pieter.
21 Sep.	1604	**Hughebout,** (v. Hudgebaut), Charles f. Charles.
13 Oct.	1605	„ Maria f. Charles.
17 Jul.	1608	„ Anna f. „
12 Aug.	1610	„ Abigail f. „
21 Sep.	1623	„ Carolus f. „
5 Jul.	1748	**Hughen,** Thurstan f. Jan & Anna Tomlin.
11 Mar.	1593	**Hughesz,** Nicolais f. Jacus.
25 Jan.	1596	„ Joannes f. Jaques.
8 Aug.	1630	**Huggebout,** (v. Hudgebaut), Johannes f. Johannes.
20 Apl.	......	**Huigen,** Lambertus f. William & Elisabet Martes.
29 „	1683	**Huijboom,** (v. Heydeboom), Johannes f. Adriaen & Margareta Hendricks.
1 Jan.	1688	„ Johannes f. Jan Pieters.
27 Mei	1694	„ Thomas f. Johannes.
22 Mei	1692	„ Maria f. James.
11 Sep.	1603	**Huijbrecht,** (v. Hubrechts), Esther f. Willem.
14 Apl.	1689	**Huydeboom,** (v. Huijboom), Arent f. Jan Pietersen & Elizabeth.
28 Aug.	1720	**Huijge,** Cornelis f. Willem & Elisabeth.
8 Mar.	1597	**Huijgen,** (v. Hrugens), Isaac f. Jacus.
5 Jan.	1718	**Huijgen,** Catina f. Willem & Lysbet Maartense.
10 Feb.	1600	**Huijgesen,** Elizabeth f. Jacus.
24 Oct.	1630	**Huijllenbergh,** (v. Hulenbergh), Philippus f. Philippus.
16 Dec.	1573	**Huijs,** Samuel f. Jacob.
1 Dec.	1577	**Huijsekerke,** (v. Husekercke), Samuel f. Adolf.
30 Nov.	1587	„ Gaspar f. Adolf.
19 Jan.	1574	**Huijskerck,** Jan f. „
28 Oct.	1575	**Huijssenkerk,** Jonathan f. „
30 Jan.	1670	**Huijstermans,** Jaquemyntje f. Matthijs & Margriete.
4 Jul.	1585	**Husekercke,** Maria f. Adolf.
2 Oct.	1572	**Huijsmans,** Paulus f. Jacobus.
25 Oct.	1642	**Hukets,** Johanna f. Philip.
6 Apl.	1629	**Hulenbergh,** (v. Huijllenbergh), Maria f. Philip, tot Mortlake.
11 Feb.	1593	**Hulet,** Susanna f. Salomon.
19 Mei	1594	„ Salomon f. „
23 Aug.	1640	„ Sara f. Philip. „

21 Apl.	1811	**Hulet,** Hormke Turriaams f. Turriaam	
		Harms & Knelsje Swiercs.	
9 Apl.	1609	**Hull,** Van, Petrus f. Pieter.	
3 Jan.	1611	,, ,, Anna f. ,,	
22 Oct.	1615	**Hulle,** Van, Abraham f. ,,	
19 Aug.	1639	**Hulleberch,** (v. Hulenberghe), Debora f.	
		Jan.	
11 Sep.	1642	**Hulleberg,** Philippus f. Johan, tot Mort-	
		lake.	
7 ,,	1653	**Hullenberg,** Elizabeth f. Jan. Jr., tot	
		Mortlake.	
21 Dec.	1632	**Hullenberghe,** Benjamin f. Philip, tot	
		Mortlake.	
12 Jul.	1635	,, Nathanael f. Philip, tot	
		Mortlake.	
20 Feb.	1638	**Hullenburch,** Anna f. Philippus, tot Mort-	
		lake, volgens der Consitorie	
		bewillinge ind' Ingelsche	
		Kercke.	
16 Jul.	1809	**Hulli,** Sarah, geb. 20 Aug. 1807, f. Hen-	
		drik & Mary Burroughs.	
29 Apl.	1810	,, Hendrik f. Hendrik & Mary Bur-	
		roughs.	
19 Jan.	1812	,, Elizabeth f. Hendrik & Mary Bur-	
		roughs.	
20 Jun.	1813	,, Abraham f. Henry & Mary Bur-	
		roughs.	
19 Nov.	1618	**Hulsbus,** Christianus, Studiosus.	
2 Nov.	1572	**Hulst,** Van der, Samuel f. Lievens.	
18 Jun.	1598	,, Van, Petrus f. Pieter.	
14 Oct.	1599	,, ,, Abraham f. ,,	

20 Sep.	1601	**Hulst,** Van, Isaac f. Pieter.	
5 ,,	1602	,, ,, Lucas f. ,,	
17 Apl.	1608	,, Van der, Joanna f. ,,	
1 Jan.	1611	,, ,, Jacobmynken f. ,,	
12 Jan.	1612	,, ,, Magdalena f. ,,	
6 Mar.	1614	,, ,, Tobias f. ,,	
21 Aug.	1628	,, ,, Lowijs f. Abraham.	
7 Mar.	1630	,, ,, Jacobus f. ,,	
25 Mar	1632	,, ,, Abraham f. ,,	
17 Mar.	1635	,, ,, Martha f. ,,	
5 Oct.	1637	,, ,, Samuel f. ,,	
1 Nov.	1704	**Hulster,** Van der, Govert f. Johannes &	
		Alida Van Malsen.	
25 Nov.	1593	,, de, Abraham f. Marinus.	
16 Nov.	1595	,, ,, Isaac f. ,,	
11 Feb.	1599	,, ,, Janneken f. ,,	
12 Oct.	1600	,, ,, Jacob f. Marinus.	
22 Aug.	1602	,, ,, Elizabeth f. Marius.	
12 Aug.	1604	,, ,, Abraham f. Marijn.	
30 Jul.	1587	**Hulstere,** de, Susanna f. ,,	
24 Oct.	1588	,, ,, Sara f. ,,	
21 Nov.	1591	,, ,, Janneken f. Marius.	
6 Jan.	1590	,, ,, Susanna f. Marcus.	
18 Nov.	1599	**Hulters,** Benjamin f. Christian.	
31 Mei	1863	**Hümel,** Geertruida Johanna (Geb. 22 Dec.	
		1857) f. Jan & Geertruida Jo-	
		hanna Wilhelmina Bremerkamp.	
6 Nov.	1681	**Hursijer,** Susanna f. Baltaus & Maria.	
9 Sep.	1621	**Hutsebout,** (v. Hudgebaut), Benjamin f.	
		Charles.	
19 Nov.	1609	**Huwijn,** Elisabeth f. Anthony.	

11 Mei	1623	**Jacksen,** Sara f. Jan.	
1 Apl.	1804	**Jackson,** Jane f. John & Johanna Cornelia	
		Van Eck.	
9 Mar.	1806	,, Hendrik f. John & Cornelia	
		Van Eck.	
10 Sep.	1809	,, Jan f. John & Cornelia Van Eck.	
15 Jul.	1571	**Jacobs,** Sara f. Otthonis.	
22 Apl.	1572	,, Abigail f. Willem.	
31 Mei	1575	,, Abraham f. Gillis.	
11 Nov.	1576	,, Abigail f. ,,	
8 Sep.	1588	,, Jacobus f. Heindrick.	
7 Mar.	1591	,, Petrus f. ,,	
8 Jun.	1600	,, Henricus f. ,,	
29 Mei	1603	,, Sara f. Hendrick.	
25 Feb.	1588	,, Pieter f. Pieter.	
23 Nov.	1589	,, Marie f. ,,	
17 Jan.	1591	,, Abraham f. ,,	
19 Nov.	1609	,, Elizabeth f. ,,	
27 Mei	1602	,, Joseph f. Joos.	
21 Dec.	1603	,, Maria f. Willem.	
30 Aug.	1607	,, Susanna f. Adrian.	
20 Oct.	1607	,, Phillipus f. Philip.	
4 Sep.	1608	,, Elisabeth f. ,,	
18 Jan.	1610	,, Philippus f. ,,	
15 Dec.	1612	,, Anna f. ,,	

13 Dec.	1614	**Jacobs,** Joanna f. Philip.	
11 Oct.	1618	,, Maria f. ,,	
21 Dec.	1623	,, Paulus f. ,,	
12 Feb.	1626	,, Maria f. ,,	
17 Jul.	1608	,, Anna f. Nicolas.	
1 Nov.	1610	,, Abraham f. ,,	
18 Mei	1618	,, Sara f. Nicolaes.	
8 Nov.	1618	,, Maria f. ,,	
9 Mei	1619	,, Nicolaus f. Nicolas.	
27 ,,	1619	,, Elisabeth f. ,,	
7 Oct.	1620	,, Jacobus f. Nicolaus.	
19 Nov.	1620	,, f. ,,	
20 Mar.	1608	,, Anna f. Lucas.	
19 ,,	1609	,, Maria f. ,,	
9 Dec.	1610	,, Catharina f. ,,	
10 ,,	1612	,, Susanna f. ,,	
13 ,,	1612	,, Jacobus f. ,,	
18 Dec.	1616	,, Abraham f. ,,	
17 Mar.	1616	,, Lucas f. ,,	
20 Mar.	1625	,, Anna f. ,,	
16 Sep.	1641	,, Jacobus f. Rombout.	
2 Aug.	1663	,, Elisabet f. Herman.	
17 Apl.	1681	,, Jacob f. Dirck & Maria.	
21 Feb.	1576	**Jacobsen,** Jacob f. Cornelis.	
24 Feb.	1577	,, ,, f. Otto.	

16 Mei	1596	**Jacobsen,**	Susanna f. Henrick.
9 Oct.	1645	„	Martha f. Laurens.
9 Sep.	1683	„	Dorothea f. Dirk & Maria.
			& Anna
2 Nov.	1690	**Jacobsse,**	Sara f. Jan & Sara.
21 Dec.	1613	**Jacobssen,**	Elisabeth f. Philip.
31 Oct.	1619	„	Jacobus f. „
8 Sep.	1622	„	Joannes f. „
6 Oct.	1622	„	Susanna f. Lucas.
30 Aug.	1573	**Jacobsz,**	Jacobus f. Otto.
6 Jan.	1577	„	Bertelmeus f. Gheerard.
1 Apl.	1593	„	Isaac f. Pieter.
1 Jul.	1596	„	Pauwels f. „
16 „	1598	„	Maeyken f. „
8 Mar.	1601	„	Susanna f. „
3 Feb.	1605	„	Jacobus f. Jacob.
21 Sep.	1606	„	Joos f. „
1 Jan.	1607	„	Janneken f. Nicolas.
17 Sep.	1609	„	Elisabeth f. Adriaen.
19 Jan.	1612	„	Mattheus f. „
10 Mar.	1616	„	Joanna f. Philip.
12 Jan.	1623	„	Petrus f. Jacob.
8 Feb.	1618	**Jaegher,**	de, Joos f. Lieven.
15 Sep.	1605	**Jager,**	Josyntgen f. „
29 Oct.	1609	„	„ Anna f. „
8 Sep.	1616	„	„ Rachel f. „
29 Jan.	1865	„	Geertruida Helena f. Teddo &
			Cornelia Helena Jansc.
31 Mei	1868	„	Isabella f. Ferdinand & Cornelia
			Helena Jansen.
1 Jun.	1572	**Jagers,**	Sara f. Erasmus.
12 Apl.	1607	**Jagher,**	de, Jacobus f. Lieven.
14 Jul.	1612	**Jaghere,** „	Abraham f. „
			& Sara
6 Dec.	1584	**James,**	Jacob f. Jan.
9 Jun.	1594	„	Anthonis f. Pieter, de Jonghe.
16 Mei	1602	„	Elisabeth f. „ . „
16 Dec.	1606	„	Petrus f. „ de Jonge.
22 Jul.	1604	„	Anna f. Isaac.
26 Feb.	1576	**James,**	Jan f. Jans.
6 Apl.	1578	**Jams,**	Daniel f. Jans.
13 Jan.	1583	„	Susanna f. Jams Jans.
10 Jul.	1571	**Jans,**	Susanna f. Judith.
1 Apl.	1855	„	Henry f. Willem Regts & Cornelia
			Heurietta Ouboter.
7 Oct.	1593	**Jansz,**	Janneken f. Abraham.
29 Jun.	1592	„	Abrahaм f. Augustijn.
21 Apl.	1595	„	Anna f. „
22 Aug.	1609	„	Joannes f. „
2 Sep.	1604	„	Susanna f. Beernart.
26 Jan.	1606	„	Susanna f. Bernart.
23 Jun.	1588	„	Judith f. Bertholomeus.
29 Mar.	1590	„	Maria f. „
5 Apl.	1635	„	Johannes f. Christiaen.
12 Apl.	1614	„	Maria f. Christoffel.
21 Aug.	1616	„	Jacobus f. „
23 Sep.	1571	„	Israel f. Coenraet, van s'Hertogen-
			bosch.
19 Jul.	1573	„	„ f. Coenraet.
28 Aug.	1574	„	Helias f. Conrad.
14 Oct.	1593	„	Cornelis f. Cornelia.
18 Apl.	1596	„	Jacobus f. „
27 Sep.	1601	„	Marie f. „
28 Sep.	1620	„	Abraham f. Dieric.
8 Jan.	1639	„	Carolus f. „
24 Mar.	1586	„	Abraham f. Geeraert.
16 Dec.	1593	„	Sara f. „
9 Jan.	1603	„	Abraham f. „

18 Apl.	1619	**Jansz,**	Anna f. Gerardus.
4 Feb.	1621	„	Elisabet f. Goerard.
9 Mar.	1623	„	Maria f. „
28 Mar.	1624	„	Joost f. Geeraert.
13 Dec.	1629	„	Sara f. Gerard.
30 Apl.	1637	„	Matthias f. „
4 Aug.	1586	„	Elizabeth f. Hendrick.
29 Jun.	1589	„	Maria f. „
27 Apl.	1595	„	Joannes f. „
13 Mar.	1597	„	Abraham f. „
			& Isaac
27 Dec.	1614	„	Maria f. Hendric.
25 Aug.	1608	„	Johannes f. Herman.
23 Dec.	1610	„	Magdalena f. „
22 Mei	1575	„	Jacob f. Jacob.
9 Feb.	1577	„	Sara f. Wolfaert.
14 Dec.	1600	„	Isaac f. Jacus.
10 Apl.	1603	„	Francholjs f. „
23 Dec.	1606	„	Sara f. Jaques.
13 Mei	1638	„	Maria f. Jacques.
25 Nov.	1639	„	Clara f. „
15 Mar.	1586	„	Joannes f. Jan.
5 Feb.	1587	„	Lucas f. „
29 Nov.	1601	„	Susanna f. „
4 Dec.	1603	„	Sara f. Hans.
3 Sep.	1585	„	Lysbet f. Jan.
11 Jan.	1610	„	Benjamin f. Jonas.
19 Jan.	1589	„	Joannes f. Lambrecht.
27 Oct.	1594	„	„ f. „
11 Dec.	1596	„	Sara f. „
2 Jan.	1603	„	„ f. „
10 Jun.	1604	„	Samuel f. Lambert.
23 Mar.	1600	„	Magdalena f. Nathanael.
21 Aug.	1586	„	Pieter f. Pieter.
5 Oct.	1606	„	Sara f. „
5 Feb.	1608	„	Joannes f. „
26 Sep.	1611	„	Catharina f. „
27 Nov.	1614	„	Petrus f. Petrus.
12 Nov.	1615	„	Anna f. Pieter.
15 Jun.	1623	„	Elisabet f. „
1 Apl.	1604	„	Sara f. Thomas.
24 Feb.	1684	**Janse,**	Annetje f. Albert.
20 Jun.	1703	„	Barent f. Barent & Annetje Schrij-
			ver.
23 Jan.	1715	„	Gerrit f. posthumus Gerrit & Elisa-
			beth.
18 Nov.	1658	**Jansen (& Janssen),**	Maria f. Abraham &
			Catarina.
7 Nov.	1574	„	.... f. Adriaen.
25 Oct.	1576	„	Joannes f. „
18 Oct.	1593	„	„ Abigail f. Augustin.
15 Jan.	1607	„	Anna f. Augustijn.
5 Mei	1583	„	Elizabeth f. Bartholomeus.
25 Oct.	1584	„	Joannes f. „
6 Nov.	1586	„	Sara f. „
28 Mei	1592	„	Sara f. „
3 Sep.	1592	„	Lucas f. Bernaert.
16 Feb.	1595	„	Heurick f. Berrent.
4 Jul.	1598	„	Anna f. Bernaert.
18 Mei	1701	„	Johannes f. Barent & Jannetje
25 Nov.	1576	„	Abigail f. Conraerdt.
8 Nov.	1579	„	Lidia f. „
14 Sep.	1572	„	Cornelius f. Cornelis.
29 Aug.	1574	„	Sara f. „
23 Mar.	1589	„	Janneken f. „
5 Sep.	1591	„	Elisabet f. „
28 Mei	1599	„	Heuricus f. „
1 Mar.	1573	„	Jacob f. David.

1591	**Jansen,**	Margriete f. Dierick.
1634	,,	Geeraart f. ,,
1690	,,	Elizabeth f. Frans & Annetje Gerrits.
1699	,,	Sarah f. Frans & Annetje Gerrits.
1573	,,	Johannes f. Gheeraert.
1576	,,	Andreas f. ,,
1579	,,	Gerardus f. Jacob.
1596	,,	David f. Gheeraert.
1633	,,	Iaack f. Geeraert.
1635	,,	Jacobus f. ,,
1641	,,	Johannes f. Gerhart.
1593	,,	Marie f. Henrick.
1600	,,	Susanna f. Hendrick.
1603	,,	Elizabeth f. ,,
1629	,,	Isaack f. ,,
1663	,,	Jan Jansen f. ,,
1666	,,	Elisabeth f. posthuma Hendrick.
1609	,,	Joannes f. Herman.
1599	,,	Susanna f. Hans.
1603	,,	Elisabeth f. Jan.
1640	,,	Maria f. ,,
1693	,,	Martha f. ,, & Maria.
1694	,,	Johannes f. Jan & Maria.
1694	,,	Geertruijdt f. Jan & Esther Krijns.
1701	,,	Isaak f. Jan.
1704	,,	Marike f. Hans & Maryken.
1707	,,	Jacob f. Jan.
1709	,,	Sara f. ,, & Martha.
1711	,,	Joseph f. ,, ,,
1582	,,	Geraert f. Jaques.
1584	,,	Jacob f. Jacob.
1596	,,	Abraham f. Jaques.
1609	,,	Elisabeth f. ,,
1629	,,	Jacobus f. ,,
1631	,,	Theodorus f. ,,
1636	,,	Johanna f. ,,
1596	,,	Maria f. Jooris.
1581	,,	Daniel f. Junger.
1591	,,	Lambert f. Lambert.
1592	,,	Abraham f. ,,
1598	,,	Samuel f. ,,
1600	,,	Abraham f. ,,
1607	,,	Joanna f. Lambrecht.
1643	,,	Maria f. Laurens.
1651	,,	Dorothea f. ,,
1653	,,	Hester f. ,,
1655	,,	Sara f. ,,
1662	,,	Sara f. Laurence.
1628	,,	Jaques & Janneken { fi. posthumi, de moeder heet Magdalene van Vlissingen.
1591	,,	Elisabeth f. Marten.
1575	,,	Sara f. Matthijs.
1678	,,	Claesje f. ,,
1598	,,	Rebecca f. Nathanael.
1599	,,	Anna f. Niclaes.
1577	,,	Johannes f. Philips.
1587	,,	Johannes f. Pieter.
1591	,,	Willem f. Willem.
1693	,,	Helena Margrieta f. Willem & Engeltje.
1580	,,	Johannes f. Wolfaert.
1575	,,	Joannes f. Wolters.
1577	,,	Jonas f. ,,

29 Mei	1580	**Jansen,** Tobias f. Wouter.
5 Oct.	1670	,, Charles f. ....
23 Sep.	1660	**Janson,** Elizabeth f. Henrick.
8 Mar.	1795	**Jansson,** Henrij f. Gerard.
11 Jul.	1697	**Janssoon,** Abraham f. Jan.
31 Jul.	1692	**Janzoon,** Johannes { f. Jan & Hester & Giertjen { Krijnsen.
10 Mar.	1611	**Jaspers,** Abraham f. Jan.
11 Jun.	1609	**Jaspersen,** Joannes f. ,,
15 Sep.	1607	**Jaspersz,** Abigail f. ,,
23 Jan.	1620	**Jaspssz,** Susanna f. Herman.
26 Dec.	1622	,, Catharina f. ,,
18 Nov.	1627	**Jeems,** Elisabet f. Abraham.
2 Jul.	1587	**Jems,** Tobias f. Jan.
9 Sep.	1599	,, Sara f. ,, de Jonge.
23 Aug.	1601	,, Elizabeth f. ,, ,, ,,
16 Jan.	1603	,, Maria f. ,,
27 Dec.	1597	,, Abraham f. Pieter.
20 Jan.	1600	,, Eva f. ,,
22 Jan.	1583	**Jennens,** Richards f. Richardt.
20 Mei	1680	**Jeune, le,** Mattheus f. Abram.
5 Jul.	1601	**Ifelaers,** Cathelyne f. Jan.
17 Feb.	1592	**Ijde,** Marie f. ,,
10 Jun.	1599	,, Cornelis f. ,,
12 Apl.	1601	,, Asuerus f. ,,
5 Dec.	1591	**Ijsebijter,** Abraham f. Pieter.
6 Jan.	1577	**Ijsebrant,** Anna f. Niclaeijs.
16 Mar.	1578	**Ijsebrants,** Joannes f. Niclaes.
11 Oct.	1579	**Ijsebrantz,** Susanna f. Hans.
22 Mar.	1691	**Ijsendijck,** Jacobus f. Johannes.
9 Aug.	1696	,, Van, Johannes f. Johannes & Sarah.
28 Oct.	1576	**Imelsen,** Daniel f. Dierick.
15 Jun.	1595	**Iummers,** Abigail f. Jan.
20 Jul.	1678	**Ingellam,** Anna f. Gerhact.
15 Dec.	1575	**Ingelsman,** Thomas f. Albert.
8 Apl.	1595	**Jode, de,** Anna f. Michiel.
23 Aug.	1597	,, ,, Adriana f. ,,
10 Dec.	1598	,, ,, Peeter f. ,,
19 Apl.	1601	,, ,, Joannes f. ,,
3 Apl.	1636	**Joes,** Grietjen f. Merten.
10 Jul.	1632	**Joije,** Petrus f. Pieter.
26 Jun.	1634	,, Judith f. ,,
21 Aug.	1636	,, Petrus f. ,,
26 Mar.	1587	**Jonas,** Pieter f. Guliamme.
17 Aug.	1591	,, Elizabeth f. Guliam.
8 Aug.	1591	**Joncheer, de,** Maria f. Joos.
29 Jul.	1593	**Joncheere, de,** Janneken f. Joos.
8 Apl.	1582	,, ,, Pieter f. ,,
12 Jan.	1595	,, ,, Susanna f. ,,
31 Aug.	1606	**Jonge,** Philip f. Marten.
15 Jul.	1739	**Jongh, de,** Adriaan Jacob f. Marten Adriaan & Maria Van Linden.
28 Sep.	1740	,, ,, Maria Anna f. Marten Adriaan & Maria Van Linden.
15 Apl.	1744	,, ,, Gerard f. Doms. & Maria Van Linden.
30 Jun.	1745	,, ,, Johanna Catharina f. Doms. M. A. & Maria Van Linden.
22 Feb.	1747	,, ,, Gerard f. Domine & Maria Van Linden.
15 Jan.	1749	,, ,, Martinus Philippus f. Marten Adriaan & Maria Van Linden.
12 Aug.	1733	**Jonghma,** Cornelis f. Gerard & Katrina.
2 Aug.	1741	**Jongsma,** Catharina f. ,, & Catharina Withfield.
6 Jul.	1746	,, Elisabeth f. ,, & Catharina Whitfield.

30 Aug.	1747	Jongsma, Elizabeth f. Gerard & Catharina Whitfield.	24 Apl.	1625	Joris, Henricus f. Cornelis.
5 Mar.	1749	„ Anna Elisabeth f. Gerard & Catharina Withfield.	10 Feb.	1628	„ Cornelis f. Jacob.
22 Feb.	1818	Jonker, Aaltje f. Ede Geerts & Aaltje Andries, woonachtig te Sapmeer bij Groningen.	7 Oct.	1691	Ipere, Van, Johanna f. Hendrick & Susanna Bosch.
			7 Jan.	1604	Iseudijck, Adriaen f. Johannes.
			2 Aug.	1640	Israel, Sara f. Hendrick.
11 Mei	1595	Jordaen, Philippus f. Laurens.	12 Dec.	1641	„ Hendricus f. „
16 Sep.	1599	Jordaens, Catheline f. Herman.	5 Nov.	1643	„ Daniel f. „
19 Nov.	1615	Joris, Jacobus f. Cornelis.	21 Dec.	1645	„ Hendrik f. „
30 Mar.	1617	„ Joannes f. „	23 Mar.	1647	„ Johannes f. „
14 Jan.	1621	„ David f. „	27 Aug.	1650	„ Wilhelmina f. „
9 Feb.	1623	„ Jacobus f. „	30 Jan.	1653	„ Anna f. „
			16 Feb.	1609	Ixem, Van, Maria f. Abraham.

29 Mei	1743	Kade, (v. Cade), Jacobus f. Bartholomeus & Martha Locken.	9 Nov.	1597	Keijrle, de, Judith f. Philip.
7 Apl.	1745	„ Christiaan f. Bartholomeus & Martha Locken.	29 Jul.	1571	s'Keijsers, Martha f. Willem.
			25 Jul.	1572	Keijsers, de, Raphael f. Boudewyn.
7 Jun.	1747	Kadee, Maria f. Barkel Mauwas & Martha Lutkens.	16 Nov.	1572	„ Susanna f. Willelmus.
			5 Oct.	1574	Keijser, de, Abel f, Willem.
4 Jan.	1573	Kaert, Jacob f. Jacob.	21 Mei	1576	„ „ Hester f. „
22 Feb.	1586	Kaij, de, Abraham f. Michiel.	3 Sep.	1579	„ „ Eva f. „
6 Mar.	1586	„ „ Pieter f. Gulian.	9 Mar.	1578	Keijsere,„ Lea f. „
3 Dec.	1690	Kamerlin, Matthys f. Pieter & Elizabeth.	8 Jan.	1581	Keijser, Susanna f. Herman.
11 Aug.	1583	Kampen, Van, Abraham f. Artus.	10 Mar.	1583	„ Keijsers, Marie f. „
11 Mar.	1750	Kamperdijk, Thomas f. Hermannus & Sara Cop.	18 Sep.	1608	Keijser, Maria f. Jan.
			14 Apl.	1611	„ Elizabeth f. „
7 Sep.	1755	„ Joannes f. „ & Sara Cope.	24 Apl.	1614	„ de, Katharina f. „
22 Mei	1757	„ Elisabeth f. „ & Sara Cope.	3 Mar.	1616	„ Joannes f. „
			24 Jan.	1621	„ „ Anna f. „
30 Mar.	1684	Kaniga, Anna f. Andries & Rachel.	8 Mei	1580	Keller, Andreas f. D. D. Danielis.
14 Mar.	1630	Kanteijs, Petrus f. Pieter.	9 Oct.	1597	„ Raphael f. Daniel ; test. Mynheer Noel Caron, etc.
26 Jun.	1748	Kap, Franciscus f. Franciscus & Maria Pullemans.	28 Oct.	1688	Kellm, Johannes f. George.
17 Nov.	1584	Karts, Joannes f. Heindric.	13 Sep.	1629	Kels, (v. Kelsso), Maria f. William.
14 Mei	1699	Kasier, (v. Casier), Maria f. Denijs & Maria.	7 Nov.	1630	„ Arnout f. Willem.
			22 Sep.	1635	„ Elisabet f. „
12 „	1579	Kaussinck, Israel f. Geerardts.	12 Oct.	1634	Kelsso, ... f. Wiljam.
7 Sep.	1635	Keck, de, Jacob f. Jakus.	17 Jun.	1635	Kemele, Van, Jacobus f. Charles.
29 Dec.	1680	Keckerbert, Carolus & Sara } f. Ernest.	26 Feb.	1659	Kemels, Jacob, een Jongman was on trent 23 jaren.
5 Mei	1700	Keer, Joanna f. Nathanael.	23 Mar.	1707	Kemps, Adam f. Allardus & Catarina Morre.
7 Jan.	1705	„ Stephen f. „ & Elijsabeth.	16 Dec.	1571	Kempen, Susanna f. Engelberts.
17 Sep.	1707	Keer, Thomas f. Nathanael & Elysabeth.	17 Apl.	1575	Kempe, Samuel f. „
19 Mar.	1587	Keerel, de, Maria f. Phlips. Test. Jan Boeve, etc.	11 Dec.	1577	Kempen, Judith f. Ingelberts.
			27 Mar.	1580	„ Egidius f. Engelberts.
30 Mei	1615	Keerle, „ Philip f. Abraham.	29 Sep.	1583	„ Judith f. „
25 Sep.	1589	Keersboom, Anna f. Pieter.	20 Dec.	1584	„ Elisabeth f. Engelbert.
12 Mar.	1682	Keestelaer, Susanna f. Jacobus.	26 Mar.	1587	„ Hester f. „
10 Mei	1577	Keij, David f. Willem.	12 Apl.	1590	„ Abraham f. Pieter.
17 Dec.	1581	„ Sara f. „	10 Sep.	1592	„ Tanneken f. „
23 Feb.	1589	„ Gulian f. „	8 Jun.	1595	„ Magdaleene f. „
20 Dec.	1590	„ de, Isaac f. Lieven.	20 Mar.	1597	„ Petrus f. „
23 Aug.	1570	Keije, de Joannes f. Willem.	24 Feb.	1600	„ Sara f. „
„	1672	Keijell, Hendrick f. Berut.	6 Nov.	1603	„ Pieter f. „
			25 Apl.	1587	Kempenaer, de, Janneken f. Hendric.

19 Apl.	1657	**Knuit,** de, Michiel f. Michiel.
27 Jan.	1684	**Kollim,** Van, Gerebrandt f. Gerebrandt.
15 Jun.	1572	**Kone,** (v. Kounen), Daniel f. Christiaens.
13 Jul.	1578	„ Christiaan f. „
26 Nov.	1581	„ „ f. „
16 Dec.	1582	**Konen,** Daniel f. „
25 Dec.	1582	**Kobber,** de, Pieter f. Geerard.
6 Sep.	1584	„ „ Elizabeth f. „
17 Nov.	1708	**Kocij,** Neeltje, f. Nicolaes & Neeltje Pietersen.
27 Oct.	1701	**Kock,** (v. Cock), Peter f. Walter & Johanna.
13 Aug.	1703	„ Johanna f. Walter & Johanna.
23 Sep.	1582	**Kockmans,** Abraham f. Jooris.
9 Aug.	1584	„ Sara f. Frantz.
14 Feb.	1580	**s'Kocks,** Susanna f. Frantzois.
4 Jun.	1582	**Kocks,** Willem f. Joris.
24 Feb.	1572	**s'Kocks,** Maria f. Jacob.
15 Aug.	1613	**Koeljechem,** Van, Susanna f. Jacob.
18 Nov.	1610	**Koeijegem,** „ Petrus f. „
10 Aug.	1702	**Koelemaij,** Johannes f. Dirck & Katarina.
13 Nov.	1680	**Koelemeij,** (v. Coelemeij), Cornelis f. Cornelis & Magdalena Sonije.
4 Sep.	1681	**Koelemij,** Jacobus f. Cornelis.
4 Jun.	1693	„ Judick f. Cornelis & Magdalena Sonje.
7 Mar.	1641	**Koels,** Wilhelmus f. Wilhelmus.
3 Aug.	1690	**Koert,** Johanna f. Jan & Petronella.
16 Dec.	1571	**Koerten,** Wilhelmus f. Wilhelmus.
31 Mei	1863	**Koesters,** Gerritje Pieters, geb. 4 Oct. 1862, f. Gerrardus & Krijna Sara Meeteren.
27 Nov.	1864	„ Mattheus, geb. 15 Apl., l.l. f. Gerrardus & Krijna Sara van Meeteren.
3 Jun.	1866	„ Gerrit Pieter f. Gerrardus & Krijna Sara van Meeteren.
27 Nov.	1870	„ Arie Francois f. Gerrardus & Krijna Sara van Meeteren.
28 Jul.	1872	„ Krijna Sara f. Gerrit & Krijna Sara van Meeteren.
28 Jun.	1874	„ Barendina f. Gerardus & Krijna Sara van Meeteren.
17 Jul.	1575	**Koetman,** Hester f. Jacob.
1 Jun.	1707	**Koje,** Karel f. Nicolaes & Pieternella Pieters.
6 Jan.	1712	„ Peter f. „ & Neeltje Pieters.
27 Mei	1627	**Koijtman,** Steven f. Hendrick.
2 Mar.	1630	**Kokatel,** Samuel f. Jan Baptiste.
1 Jan.	1572	**s'Konings,** (v. Coning, etc.), Sara f. Joannes.
15 Nov.	1579	„ Susanna f. Vincent.
1 Jul.	1660	**Koning,** de, Maria f. Johannes.
5 Nov.	1709	„ Joseph f. Aarent & Anna.
16 Feb.	1772	„ Jacobus f. Arent & „
22 Jan.	1786	„ Elisabeth f. Jan & Katrina Dixon.
22 Jul.	1790	„ Sarah f. Jan & Kitty Dixon.
8 Nov.	1795	„ Samuel f. Jan & Catrina Dixon.
29 Apl.	1705	**Kooij,** Van, Anna f. Nicolaes & Helena Pieters.
27 Apl.	1777	**Kooijstra,** John Cornelius f. John & Wijnefrida Van der Plank.
31 Mei	1778	„ Justus Bartholomeus f. Dr. Johannes & Wijnefrida Van der Plank.
23 Apl.	1780	„ Mary f. Dr. John & Wijnefrida Van der Plank.
23 Dec.	1702	**Koock,** (v. Cock), Michiel f. Kaes.
4 Oct.	1584	**Koolhem,** Van, Philip f. Philip.
14 Apl.	1703	**Kooningh,** de, (v. Coningh), Jan & Francyntje Taion.
12 Nov.	1587	**Koorfe,** Joannes f. Aernout.
11 Feb.	1729	**Kops,** Agnieta f. William Isak.
11 Feb.	1735	„ Anna f. „ Isaak.
5 Apl.	1812	**Koppiers,** Anna Christina Cornelia, geb. 16 Dec., 1810, te Stonden Massey, in Essex, f. Henry & Catharina Cornelia Buse.
2 Jun.	1813	„ James Henry f. Henry & Catharina Cornelia Buse.
8 Mar.	1815	„ William Henry, geb. 12 Sep. 1814, bij Ongar, Essex, f. Henry & Catharina Cornelia Buse.
11 Feb.	1582	**Korten,** Petrus f. Willem.
19 Oct.	1721	„ Johan Abraham f. Johan Abraham & Anna Maria Subels.
8 Jul.	1725	„ Anna Maria f. Johan Abraham & Anna Maria Subels.
12 Dec.	1683	**Korthals,** Anthonye fs. Willem & Helena Teunis.
15 Aug.	1591	**Kostel,** Joannes f. Dieric.
28 Aug.	1575	**Kostere,** de, (v. Coster), Maria f. Gillis.
8 Apl.	1577	**Kostere,** de, David f. Marten.
1 Nov.	1577	**Kostere,** de, Susanna f. Gillis.
23 Feb.	1578	„ „ Salomon f. Marten.
17 Jan.	1580	„ „ Sara f. „
20 Apl.	1584	**Kosters,** .... f. „
14 Dec.	1578	**s'Kosters,** Helene f. Jakes.
3 Jul.	1575	**Kounen,** (v. Kone), Judith f. Christiaen.
3 Jan.	1637	**Kouter,** Van de, Susanna f. Pieter.
22 Apl.	1638	„ „ „ Sara f. „
1 Nov.	1639	„ „ „ Johannes f. „
30 Aug.	1584	**Kraneerl,** Sara f. Nicolas.
23 Aug.	1590	**Kreket,** Maria f. Pieter.
5 Apl.	1629	**Krickman,** (v. Krieckman), Pieter f. Hendrick.
3 Mei	1631	„ Hendrick f. Hendrick.
1 Dec.	1633	**Krieckman,** Susanna f. „
6 Mar.	1636	„ Elskou f. „
20 Mar.	1870	**Krijnen,** Aaltje f. „ & Engeltje Guik.
1 Jul.	1582	**Krijns,** Johannes f. Govacrat.
23 Jul.	1684	**Krijper,** Gosuin f. Herman.
25 Dec.	1727	**Krijt,** Abraham f. Christopher & Sara de Hahn.
6 Jan.	1754	„ Abraham f. Abraham.
18 Oct.	1638	**Krintsen,** Catelina f. Pieter.
4 Dec.	1692	**Kroon,** Johannes f. Jan & Sara Laers.
18 Mar.	1694	„ Anna Catharina f. Jan & Sara Leers.
16 Nov.	1641	**Kroondorp,** Joannes f. Bernard.
16 Feb.	1673	**Kruis,** de, Michael f. Johannes.
16 Apl.	1693	**Krul,** Joost f. Joost & Anna Togelbergh.
27 Oct.	1695	„ Josua f. „ & „
11 Dec.	1698	„ Anna f. „ & „
17 Aug.	1572	**Krusen,** Zacharias f. Eliardt.
19 Jun.	1603	**Kuel,** Joanna f. Henry.
22 Jan.	1573	**Kuffel,** Van, Hester f. Niclaijs.
11 Dec.	1575	**Kuijl,** (v. Kule), Henricus f. Henricus, test Doctor Pieter de Meter, etc.
17 Aug.	1600	**Kuijnen,** Joanna f. Andries.
1 Nov.	1574	**Kuijpers,** Abraham f. Marten.
20 Nov.	1575	„ Sara f. Marten.

9 Nov.	1732	Lang, Elisabeth f. Conraadt & Mary.
11 Sep.	1642	Lange, Johannes f. Steffen.
6 Dec.	1573	Langele, (v. Leyngele), Josue f. David.
7 Oct.	1602	Langhe, Van, Abraham f. Herman.
13 Oct.	1577	Langhele, Abigail f. David.
25 Oct.	1590	Langle, Guliebrinus f. ,,
13 Dec.	1640	,, Johannes f. Francois.
5 Mar.	1639	Langlee, Anna f. ,,
3 Apl.	1853	Langenscheid, Carl Gotfried Antonia f. Carl Wilhelm & Wilhelmina Bentfelsen.
11 Feb.	1855	,, Godfried Cornelis f. Carl Wilhelm & Wilhelmina Bentfelsen.
12 Oct.	1856	,, Petronella Antoinette Adriana f. Carl Wilhelm & Wilhelmina Bentfelsen.
30 Mei	1858	,, Petronella Antoinette Adriana f. Carl Wilhelm & Wilhelmina Beutfelsen.
24 Jul.	1859	,, William f. Carl Wilhelm & Wilhelmina Bentfelsen.
21 Jul.	1861	,, Godfried Wilhelm Christian f. Carl Wilhelm & Wilhelmina Bentfelsen.
29 Mar.	1863	,. Quirinus f. Carl Wilhelm & Wilhelmina Bentfelsen.
7 Sep.	1864	,, Julius William, geb. 17 Jul. 1863, f. Carl Wilhelm & Wilhelmina Bentfelsen.
29 Nov.	1868	,, Sarah f. Carl Wilhelm & Wilhelmina Bentfelsen.
22 Sep.	1588	Lap, Paulus f. Toussain.
22 Jun.	1595	,, Maria f. ,,
14 Nov.	1596	,, Johannes f. ,,
3 Sep.	1598	,, Maria f. ,,
18 Dec.	1603	,, Anna f. ,,
11 Feb.	1610	Lardanois, Elcana f. Elcana.
29 Mei	1614	,, Maria f. ,,
1 Dec.	1616	,, Samuel f. ,,
1 ,,	1611	Lardonois, Anna f. ,,
9 Nov.	1712	Larebert, Jacobus f. Huybert Huybertse & Sara Adriaanze.
30 Mar.	1635	Larenus, Jeremias f. Jeromias.
8 Aug.	1585	Late, Van der, Daniel f. Lambrecht.
17 Sep.	1581	Laten, Van, (v. Lathem), Johannes f. Lowijs.
20 Sep.	1695	Later, de, Margarieta f. Anthony.
31 Jan.	1697	,, ,, Paulus f. ,, & Maria.
19 Mei	1583	Lathem, Van, (v. Laten), Thomas f. Lowijs.
16 Feb.	1641	Latsma, Esther, die huisvrouwe van Gillis Volkerts.
25 Dec.	1602	Lawe, Susanna f. Fransis.
22 Apl.	1578	Laureija, Marcus f. Marcua.
23 Sep.	1619	Laureijns, Elisabeth f. Abraham.
27 Nov.	1586	Laurens, Joannes f. Marcus.
22 Nov.	1590	,, Abraham f. Pieter.
29 Oct.	1598	,, Johannes f. Bartholomeus.
10 Jul.	1603	,, Jonas f. ,,
22 Aug.	1613	,, Marcus f. Hans.
5 Feb.	1615	,, Leonard f. ,,
12 Jan.	1617	,, Judith f. ,,
21 Mar.	1619	,, Johannes f. Johannes.
15 Jul.	1630	,, Johanna f. Abraham.
15 Mei	1636	,, Jacob f. ,,
13 Jan.	1572	Laurent, Jan f. Christiaens.
8 Sep.	1584	Laurents, Adam f. Marcq.
25 Jan.	1621	Lauwens, Josynken f. Abraham.
9 Mar.	1623	,, Susanna f.
26 Mar.	1626	,, Joannes f. ,,
7 Jul.	1629	,, Sara f.
8 Dec.	1588	Lauwensz, Abigail f. Bartholomeus.
5 Oct.	1606	Lauwereyns, Abraham f. ....
25 Feb.	1582	Lauwereijs, Joannes f. Marcus.
22 Nov.	1584	Lauwereins, Joannes f. Pieter.
17 Oct.	1585	Lauwers, Samuel f. Bartholomeus.
18 Jul.	1587	,, Esther f. ,,
15 Nov.	1590	,, Bartholomeus f. ,,
10 Jul.	1593	,, Elizabeth f. ,,
28 Mar.	1596	,, Daniel f. ,,
23 Nov.	1600	,, Debora f. ,,
22 Feb.	1586	,, Jacobus f. Hans.
11 ,,	1593	,, Susanna f. ,,
26 Jul.	1767	Leader, Sara f. John & Sara Camperdijk.
11 Sep.	1768	,, Willem f. John & Sara Camperdijk.
31 Dec.	1769	,, Elisabeth f. Jan & Sara Camperdijk.
5 Apl.	1772	,, Maria f. Jan & Sara Camperdijk.
12 Sep.	1572	Lebbewerck, Samuel f. Jooris.
22 Dec.	1689	Leberechts, Maria f. Jacobus & Elisabeth.
31 Jul.	1608	Lebreghs, Christoffel f. ,, & ,,
10 Jul.	1576	Leck, (v. Leeck), Elisabeth f. Herman.
26 Feb.	1579	,, Jan f.
8 Mei	1580	,, Salomon f.
30 Jan.	1583	,, Henrick f. ,,
6 Jul.	1585	,, Raphel f.
26 Jul.	1719	Ledden, Van, Catharina f. Hermen Jan & Martha.
28 Dec.	1602	Lee, Rachel f. Willem.
14 Jan.	1677	Leeck, Van, (v. Leck), Joris f. Gerrit.
26 Oct.	1587	Legonce, (v. Gonce), Elizabeth f. Hans.
24 Sep.	1611	Legouche, Susanna f. Stephen.
24 Jul.	1605	Lej (Leigh, or Lea), Rebecca f. Fransois, Engelsman.
3 Oct.	1574	Leije, Van der, Sara f. Vincent.
8 Apl.	1576	Leijen, ,, Joannes f. ,,
27 ,,	1595	Leijs, Abraham f. Gulian.
1 Apl.	1677	Leijster, Salomon, een bejarde persohn van die Jodische natie geboren in Polen.
1 Jul.	1589	Leemans, Janneken f. Symon.
12 Jul.	1590	,, David f. Simon.
2 Aug.	1593	,, Sijmon f. Sijmon.
6 Jun.	1596	,, Sara f. ,,
27 Jan.	1600	,, Elizabeth f. ,,
6 Sep.	1590	Leeman, Michiel f. Michiel.
31 Mar.	1591	Leemans, Maria f. ,,
27 Aug.	1592	,, Samuel f. ,,
10 Mar.	1594	,, Abraham f. ,,
4 Apl.	1596	,, Jossine f. ,,
10 Jul.	1596	Leeman, Abraham f. ,,
18 Dec.	1597	Leemans, Michiel f. ,,
16 Mar.	1600	,, Lucas f. ,,
31 Jan.	1602	,, Petrus f. ,,
7 Mei	1604	,, David f. ,,
26 Sep.	1602	Leeman, Abigael f. Gillis.
14 Mar.	1624	Leemans, Abraham f. Samuel.
2 Apl.	1626	,, Maria f. Lucas.
30 Mar.	1628	,, Jacobus f. ,,
7 Jun.	1629	,, Lucas f. ,,
2 Oct.	1631	,, Anna f. ,,
7 Dec.	1636	,, Maria f. ,,

11 Nov.	1591	Leemput, Van, Sara f. Daniel.
8 Jan.	1594	,, ,, Rebecca f. ,,
27 Dec.	1597	,, ,, Pieter f. ,,
17 Aug.	1617	,, Joannes f. Jan.
12 Dec.	1619	,, Maria f. Joannes.
15 Dec.	1622	,, Daniel f. ,,
14 Oct.	1627	,, Sara f. Jan.
15 Jan.	1632	,, Anna f. Johannes.
26 Nov.	1581	Leemputt, Vanden, Maria f. Pieter.
11 Aug.	1678	Leenders, Janneken f. Dirc.
26 Dec.	1593	Leenput, Van, Daniel f. Daniel.
31 Jan.	1580	Leenputten, ,, Petrus f. Pieter.
28 Mar.	1607	Leeu, de, Esther f. Elias.
12 Feb.	1699	Leeuw, ,, Johannes f. ,,
2 Feb.	1701	,, ,, Abraham f. ,,
23 Dec.	1702	,, ,, Isaack f. ,, & Anna.
23 Nov.	1851	,, ,, Elizabeth Gerardina Aletta f. Klaas & Gerardina Aletta van Pieterson.
8 Mei	1853	,, ,, Nicolas David f. Klaas & Gerardina Alletta van Pieterson.
18 ,,	1684	Leeuwaerden, Van, Lea f. Jan & Lea.
22 Mar.	1603	Leewarden, Van, Anna f. Adriaen.
2 Mei	1813	Leewen, Van, Jean Elise fs. Jan Anthony & Elizabeth Johanna Buyn.
21 Jun.	1584	Leijngele, (v. Langele, etc.), Catherine f. David.
22 Apl.	1582	Leijngle, David f. ,,
6 Mei	1593	Lemde, Van der, Maria f. Hendrick.
5 Apl.	1584	Lems, Daniel f. Frantzois.
24 Mar.	1588	,, Susanna f. Fransois.
28 Dec.	1589	,, Nicolaus f. ,,
15 Dec.	1633	Lenaers, (v. Leonard), Elisabeth f. Lucas.
21 Feb.	1591	Leenarts, Judocus f. Joos.
3 Nov.	1583	Lenardts, Jacob f. Matthys.
4 Mei	1600	Lenaert, Jacomyntken f. Gielis.
19 Jul.	1612	Lenaerts, Maria f. ,,
12 Aug.	1604	Lenart, Jacobus f. ,,
27 Oct.	1605	,, Magdalena f. ,,
30 Mar.	1647	Lenarts, Salomon f. Cornelis.
11 Feb.	1588	Lengele, (v. Langele), Elisabeth f. David.
25 Oct.	1685	,, Cornelis f. Cornelis.
17 Dec.	1579	Lengelee, Maria f. David.
16 Aug.	1640	Lengels, Jacob f. Jan, tot Mortlake.
16 Jul.	1587	Lenre, Van der, Daniel f. Jan.
21 Jul.	1639	Lens, de, Jaques f. Allaert, Papist ; de kints moeder, Sara le Grand synde van onse Gemeynte.
13 Feb.	1581	Lensen, Hendrick f. Godfridus.
6 Jan.	1572	Lensses, Bara f. Jacob.
13 Aug.	1598	Leonard, (v. Lenaers, etc.), Tanneken f. Gillis.
17 Jul.	1608	,, Susanna f. Gillis.
17 Oct.	1630	Leonards, Caterina f. Jacob.
13 Sep.	1612	Lepper, Maria f. Pieter.
23 Jul.	1615	,, Catheryne f. ,,
22 Jun.	1587	Lerberge, Van, Tanneken f. Rogier.
15 Aug.	1591	,, Marie f. ,,
1 Aug.	1591	Lespere, de, Abraham f. Guliam.
31 Jul.	1586	Lespiere, ,, Marie f. ,,
7 Feb.	1692	Letoij, Maria f. Anna.
21 Sep.	1591	Lethburne, Anna f. Tobias.
2 ,,	1610	Lettepotter, Magdalena f. ....
8 Mar.	1590	Leu, de, Joannes f. Jaques.
21 Jun.	1605	Leunarts, Abraham f. Jan.
5 Aug.	1599	Leunes, Eva f. Jan.
28 Feb.	1602	Leunis, Pieter f. ,,

30 Jul.	1690	Leuntrick, Johanna Catharina f. Jan Hendrick & Catharina.
5 Oct.	1695	Leut, Van, Agatha f. Pieter & Agatha.
10 Oct.	1697	Leute, ,, Maria f. ,,
12 Mei	1695	Leuter, Neelje f. Pieter & Gerritje.
25 Nov.	1610	Libaert, (v. Liebaert), Jacob f. Hans.
9 Oct.	1617	,, Ester f. Jan.
8 Aug.	1596	Libert, (v. Lijbaert), Petrus f. Seghor.
9 Mei	1689	Lichtenbergh, Maria f. Jan & Tountje Willems.
6 Jan.	1625	Liebartius, Samuel f. D. Carolus.
24 Nov.	1611	Liebaert, (v. Libaert), Maria f. Joannes.
26 Dec.	1613	,, Joannes f. Hans.
19 Sep.	1619	,, Sara f. Joannes.
10 Jun.	1621	,, Anna f. Jan.
6 Jul.	1623	,, Joannes f. ,,
12 Mar.	1581	Liedtz, Elizabeth f. Adriaen & Leo.
19 Jun.	1651	Lier, Van der, Christina f. ... Backer, synde bejaert op bedde.
20 Nov.	1664	Liest, Van der, Elisabeth f. Cornelis.
15 Jul.	1634	Liesfelt, Van, Maria f. Jan.
25 Apl.	1633	Liesveldt, ,, Elisabeth f. ,,
20 Feb.	1640	,, ,, Johanna f. ,,
29 Mar.	1573	Liesvelt, ,, Judith f. Adrianeken uxor Anthonis.
18 Jun.	1573	Lievens, Abraham f. Jan.
18 Aug.	1575	,, ,, f. ,,
2 Mei	1637	,, Maria f. ,,
18 Mar.	1593	Lijbaert, Maria f. Seghor.
9 Jan.	1686	Lijbrechts, Elisabeth f. Jacob & Elisabeth.
10 Jan	1686	,, Symeon f. Jacobus & ,,
13 Nov.	1692	,, Margarieta f. Jacob.
25 Jan	1702	,, Jacobus f. Jacobus & Elisabeth.
20 Mei	1577	Lijen, Van der, Joannes f. Vincent.
28 Jun.	1600	Lijnsbergen, Van, Laurentius f. Hendrick & Katharina.
18 Sep.	1597	Lijoens, (v. Lioens), Petrus f. Gillis.
23 Nov.	1617	
15 Mei	1642	Lijsten, Susanna f. Pieter.
1 Nov.	1640	,, Jacob f. ,,
13 Mar.	1576	Lijts, (v. Lits), Sara f. Adriaan.
4 Feb.	1685	Lillo, Van, Pieter f. Jacobus & Elisabeth.
13 Mar.	1687	,, ,, Ruth f. Jacobus & Elisabeth.
27 Mar.	1689	,, ,, Johannes f. Jacobus & Elisabeth Whitehorne.
8 Feb.	1691	Lilloo, .. Joris f. Jacobus.
3 Jul.	1586	Linde, Van der, Sara f. Baltazar.
21 Mar.	1591	,, ,, Enoch f. Hendrick.
11 Jul.	1591	,, ,, Elisabet f. Pieter.
7 Jul.	1594	,, ,, f. Balthazar.
4 Jun.	1730	,, ,, Maria f. Frederik.
4 Jun.	1732	,, Van, Jan Frederik f. Frederik & Maria Van Beerenbroeck.
14 Mei	1738	,, Rebecca f. Frederik & Maria Van Beerenbroeck.
5 Mei	1734	Linden, Van der, Frederik f. Frederik & Maria van Berenbroeck.
9 Mar.	1740	,, Rebecca f. Frederik & Maria van Berenbroeck.
15 Jul.	1582	,, Van der, Judith f. Balthazar.
13 Oct.	1583	,, ,, Pauwels f. ,,
3 Mar.	1588	,, ,, Esther f. ,,
28 Jul.	1583	,, ,, Rogier f. Geerardt.
22 Jun.	1585	,, ,, Catheryne f. Gommar.
21 Feb.	1591	,, ,, Maria f. Gommart.
2 Sep.	1593	,, ,, Esther f. Gommer.
9 Oct.	1586	,, ., Joannes f. Govaert.

21 Mar. 1824	**Lindeboom**,	Sarah f. Pieter & Antje Mac-William.
13 Aug. 1826	„	Adriana f. Pieter & Nansje MacWilliam.
27 Jul. 1828	„	Pieter f. Pieter & Nansje Mack Willer.
31 Jan. 1830	„	Wilhelm f. Pieter & Nansje Macwiller.
24 Apl. 1831	„	Maria f. Pieter & Nansje Macwiller.
3 Jul. 1836	„	Pieter f. Pieter & Nansje Macwiller.
18 Jun. 1848	**Lingeman**,	Geertruida Elisabeth f. Ludovicus Franciscus & Elisabeth Adriana Koster.
12 Mei 1850	„	Pauline Louise f. Ludovicus Franciscus & Elisabeth Adriana Koster.
22 Feb. 1852	„	Louise Francisca f. Ludovicus Franciscus & Elisabeth Adriana Koster.
5 Mar. 1854	„	Marie Agnes f. Ludovicus Franciscus & Elisabeth Adriana Koster.
9 Dec. 1855	„	Henriette Adrienne f. Ludovicus Franciscus & Elisabeth Adriana Koster.
7 Dec. 1856	„	Pieter Maurits f. Ludovicus Franciscus & Elisabeth Adriana Koster.
26 Dec. 1858	„	Floris Albert f. Ludovicus Franciscus & Elisabeth Adriana Koster.
20 Oct. 1861	„	Alice Grace f. Ludovicus Franciscus & Elisabeth Adriana Koster.
14 Feb. 1864	„	Ida Consuelo f. Ludovicus Franciscus & Elisabeth Adriana Koster.
28 Sep. 1873	**Lingeman**,	Henry Floris f. Hendrik Floris & Johanna Margaretha Surie.
11 Oct. 1575	**Linghelé**,	Caleb f. David.
15 Mei 1586	**Lingle**,	Thomas f. „
16 Aug. 1807	**Linschoten**, Van,	Geertruijd Paulina f. Francois Albert Leonard Strick & Elisabeth Pool.
2 Jul. 1809	„ „	Albert Andries Jan f. Francois Albert Leonard Strick & Elisabeth Pool.
25 Nov. 1810	„ „	Gerardina Wilhelmina f. Francois Albert Leonard Strick & Elisabeth Pool.
13 Sep. 1812	„ „	Susanna Cornelia Francina f. Francois Albert Leonard Strick & Elisabeth Pool.
24 Sep. 1815	„ „	Marinus Catharinus f. Francois Albert Leonard Strick & Elisabeth Pool.
1 Feb. 1573	**Linsen**, Jacob f. Jan.	
29 Aug. 1574	**Linx**, Isaias f. Adriaen.	
23 Feb. 1595	**Lioens**, (v. Lijoens), Anna f. Gillis.	
29 Jul. 1599	„ Gielis f. Gillis.	
27 Apl. 1602	**Lions**, Heijudrick f. „	

18 „ 1613	**Lions**, Jacob f. Gillis.	
14 Aug. 1614	„ Judith f. „	
3 Dec. 1615	„ Joanna f. „	
31 Oct. 1622	„ Maria f. „	
28 Oct. 1600	**Lip**, Cathelyne f. Tousain.	
24 Jul. 1586	**Lippevelde**, Van, Abraham f. Hans.	
10 Jan. 1591	„ „ Janneken f. „	
24 Oct. 1596	**Lipsen**, Joannes f. Dierick.	
29 „ 1598	„ Abraham f. „	
17 Sep. 1592	**Liscornet**, Samuel f. Hans.	
14 Oct. 1630	**Lisveldt**, Van, (v. Liesveldt), Rebecca f. Jan.	
9 Sep. 1628	**Lisvelt**, Rebecca f. Hendrick.	
28 Jul. 1577	**Lits**, Anna f. Adriaen.	
12 Jul. 1590	„ Petrus f. Lowijs.	
16 Mar. 1623	**Lodewick**, Anna f. Walrave.	
11 Apl. 1630	„ Judith f. „	
14 Sep. 1634	„ Johannes f. „	
14 Apl. 1636	„ Esther } f. Franchois.	
	& Johanna }	
13 Jan. 1577	**Lodewyck**, Sara f. Heindrick.	
23 Sep. 1589	„ Catharina f. Anthonij.	
28 Mar. 1591	**Lodewijck**, Joannes f. Anthoni.	
22 Feb. 1601	„ Catharina f. „	
25 Jul. 1606	„ Abigail f. Jan.	
22 Apl. 1621	„ Maria f. Walrave.	
19 Dec. 1624	„ Maria f. „	
21 Jan. 1627	„ Walrave f. „	
17 Jan. 1628	„ Walrave „	
23 Sep. 1627	„ Francois f. Francois.	
7 Nov. 1630	„ Francoijs f. Franchois.	
7 Jul. 1633	„ Abraham f. „	
15 Mar. 1639	„ Elisabeth f. „	
25 Jul. 1641	„ Isaac f. „ & Rachel.	
8 Dec. 1644	„ Rachel f. „	
13 Dec. 1704	„ Rebecca f. Charles & Margareta.	
3 Sep. 1598	**Lodewijckx**, Anthonj f. Anthony.	
8 Mei 1597	**Lodewycx**, Henricus f. „	
6 Aug. 1643	**Lodewijk**, Anna f. Francois.	
8 Jul. 1702	„ Mary f. Charles & Margaretha.	
5 Mar. 1593	**Lodewijx**, Anna f. Anthoni.	
5 Jan. 1595	„ Joannes f. „	
15 Apl. 1649	**Lodewik**, Walrave f. Francois Jr.	
13 Jun. 1603	**Loduwijcx**, Henricus f. Anthoni.	
16 Mar. 1617	**Loduwyck**, Franciscus f. Walraev.	
8 Aug. 1619	„ Franciscus f. Walraev.	
16 Jan. 1710	**Lodwick**, Charles f. Charles & Margareta.	
27 Apl. 1690	**Loeff**, Anthonia f. Stephanus.	
2 Nov. 1662	**Loeffs**, Isaac f. Abraham & Sara.	
19 Apl. 1607	**Loefsen**, Abraham f. Loef.	
10 Dec. 1690	**Lofting**, Maria f. Jan & Esther.	
28 Jun. 1590	**Loijr**, Van, (v. Loor), Margareta f. Pieter.	
27 Feb. 1595	„ „ Maria f. Pieter.	
14 Dec. 1596	„ „ Catharine f. „	
31 Oct. 1598	„ „ Catharina f. „	
1 Nov. 1601	„ „ Joanna f. „	
21 Mei 1592	**Loijre**, Van, Anna f. Pieter.	
13 Apl. 1612	**Loir**, „ Jacomyna f. Petrus Jr.	
10 Nov. 1649	**Lombard**, Nicolaus f. Petrus.	
25 Feb. 1589	**Lommelin**, Sara f. Loduwijck.	
11 Oct. 1590	**Lomwers**, Isaac f. Hans.	
15 Feb. 1579	**Loven**, Van, Catharina f. Philips.	
4 Oct. 1601	**Loo**, Van, Immanuel f. Jan.	
16 Jun. 1603	„ „ Adolff f. „	
23 Feb. 1608	„ „ Johannes f. Hans.	
18 Dec. 1608	„ „ Johannes } f. Jan.	
	& Adolphus }	
11 Mar. 1610	„ „ Petrus f. „ „	

17 Apl. 1638 **Maacht**, de, Joseph f. Wilhelmus.
16 Aug. 1640 **Maecht**, ,, Philips f. Guilliam, tot Mortlake.
11 Sep. 1681 **Maegd**, ,, Sara f. David & Esther.
23 Mar. 1634 **Maeght**, ,, Maria f. ,, tot Mortlake.
27 Aug. 1636 ,, ,, Anna f. ,, tot Mortlake.
28 Apl. 1639 ,, ,, Johanna f. ,, tot Mortlake.
12 Nov. 1642 Maecht, ,, Rachel f. ,, tot Mortlake, in de Engelsche Kercke.
26 Dec. 1687 Maegd, ,, Rebecca f. David & Esther.
8 Apl. 1677 **Maegdt**, ,, Esther f. David & ,,
27 Apl. 1684 **Maeght**, ,, David f. ,,
11 Dec. 1678 **Magte**, ,, Samuel f. ,,
22 Jan. 1643 **Magtk**, ,, Theophilus f. Guillame, tot Mortlake.
20 Oct. 1652 **Magth**, ,, Thomas f. David. tot Mortlake.
23 Mei 1585 **Maeijer**, ,, (v. Meijer), Susanna f. Pieter.
30 Jun. 1608 **Maelbout**, Joanna f. Pieter.
11 Nov. 1610 ,, Petrus f. ,,
16 Mar. 1679 **Maertensen**, Sara f. Hendrick.
24 Aug. 1628 **Maertsz**, Geertruyt f. Pieter.
15 Oct. 1629 ,, ,, f. ,,
20 Dec. 1576 **Maes**, (v. Maas), Sara f. Willem.
25 Sep. 1586 ,, Catheline f. Jaques.
9 Oct. 1597 ,, Hester f. Hans.
11 Mar. 1599 ,, Jacobus f. ,,
14 Apl. 1601 ,, Joannes f. ,,
26 Nov. 1615 ,, Josine f. Joos.
15 Mar. 1618 ,, Lowijs f. Joos.
26 Mar. 1620 ,, Maria f. ,,
6 Nov. 1625 ,, Joannes f. posthumus Joos.
17 Mei 1646 ,, Petrus f. Jan.
26 Sep. 1647 ,, Abigail f. ,,
25 Mar. 1649 ,, Isac f. Johan.
26 Sep. 1652 ,, Abigail f. ,,
11 Mar. 1655 ,, Joannes f. Joannes.
12 Aug. 1655 ,, Maria f. Daniel.
13 Sep. 1657 ,, Josias f. ,,
21 Apl. 1650 **Maeterlinck**, Maria f. Jan.
2 Jan. 1631 **Maeterlinckx**, Johannes f. Johannes.
29 Jan. 1626 **Maignet**, (v. Maniet), Maria f. ......
17 Mei 1599 **Maigniet**, (v. Mainet), Josua f. Michiel.
3 Sep. 1671 **Maijer**, (v. Meijer), Johannes f. Johan.
28 Mar. 1585 **Mainet**, Michiel f. Michiel.
26 Nov. 1592 ,, Maria f. ,,
28 Feb. 1594 ,, Jacob f. ,,
9 Apl. 1598 ,, Susanna f. ,,
14 Aug. 1617 ,, Susanna f. Jacob.
1 Nov. 1618 ,, Anna f. Jaques.
23 Nov. 1636 ,, Maria f. Josua.
12 Jan. 1640 ,, Johanna f. ,,
28 Feb. 1641 ,, Johannes f. ,,
3 Jul. 1642 ,, Anna f. ,,
3 Sep. 1643 ,, Michiel f. ,,
26 Dec. 1644 ,, Abraham f. ,,
6 Sep. 1646 ,, Isaac f. ,,
1 Aug. 1647 ,, Elisabeth f. ,,
1 Sep. 1650 ,, Jacob f. ,,
12 Mar. 1600 **Mair**, de, Tobias f. Jan.
9 Feb. 1595 **Maire**, le, Maria f. David.
31 Dec. 1598 ,, ,, Anna f. ,,
29 Jan. 1656 ,, ,, Maria f. Noe.
2 Dec. 1660 ,, ,, Margerite f. ,,
30 Jul. 1598 **Maistre**, de, Susanna f. Jaques.

5 Sep. 1596 **Maistres**, des, Joanna f. Jaques.
14 Oct. 1599 ,, ,, Marie f. ,,
2 Jan. 1603 ,, de, Sara f. Jacques.
16 Jan. 1586 **Malapert**, Lucas f. Guij.
16 Mar. 1589 ,, Elizabeth f. Guido.
21 Sep. 1592 **Malepart**, Lowijs f. ,,
13 Jan. 1702 **Malbouer**, Jacobns f. Jacobns.
21 Jul. 1590 **Malines**, de, Petrus f. Geerardt.
14 Nov. 1591 ,, ,, Samuel f. Gheeraert.
29 Mar. 1593 ,, ,, Maria f. Geeraert.
18 Apl. 1680 **Mallebrand**, Margriet f. Salomon.
10 Jan. 1591 **Man**, de, Stephanus f. Kaerle.
3 Jun. 1593 ,, ,, Tobias f. Caerle.
8 Sep. 1594 ,, ,, Anna f. Carel.
5 Dec. 1596 ,, ,, Magdalena f. ,,
31 Dec. 1598 ,, ,, Susanna f. ,,
13 Sep. 1601 ,, ,, Abraham f. ,,
20 Jan. 1639 ,, ,, Sara f. Abraham.
22 Mar. 1640 ,, ,, Sara f. ,,
30 Jan. 1642 ,, ,, Wilhelmus f. ,,
20 Apl. 1645 ,, ,, Anna f. ,,
10 Nov. 1753 **Mangring**, Femmetje f. Johan & Sarah.
8 Apl. 1582 **Maniet**, (v. Mainet, etc.), Anna f. Michiel.
2 Jun. 1586 ,, Catharina f. Michiel.
23 Mei 1591 ,, Elizabeth f. ,,
6 Feb. 1597 ,, G..onel f. ,,
25 Oct. 1601 ,, Janneken f. ,,
21 Jan. 1672 **Mansfeldt**, Samuel f. Samuel & Maria Margaretha Dogers.
7 Mar. 1686 **Marcelis**, (v. Marselis), Maria f. Jan & Anna.
11 Aug. 1689 ,, Amy f. Johannes & Anna.
25 Dec. 1690 ,, Alexander f. ,, ,,
7 Feb. 1574 **Marcelles**, Isaack f. Jan.
12 Jun. 1597 **Marchant**, Judith f. ,,
16 Oct. 1597 ,, Mattheus f. Samuel.
22 Jan. 1600 **Marchant**, Sara f. Samuel.
25 ,, 1603 ,, Lucas f. ,,
21 Dec. 1571 **Marcheijs**, Gabriel f. Frantzois.
7 Mar. 1602 **Mariat**, Marian f. William.
17 Aug. 1600 **Mariatt**, Abigail f. Willem.
10 Nov. 1575 **Marien**, Drias f. David.
20 Jan. 1577 ,, Abraham f. ,,
23 Mar. 1578 ,, Anna f. ,,
3 Mei 1579 ,, Hesther f. ,,
24 Jul. 1580 ,, Hester f. ,,
23 Feb. 1584 ,, Anna f. ,,
29 Nov. 1584 ,, Sara f. Jois.
1 Jan. 1672 **Marienburg**, Johannes f. Theodorus.
2 Mar. 1673 ,, Gertruit f. ,,
3 Dec. 1676 ,, Otto f. ....
21 Jan. 1680 ,, Mechelt f. Theodorus.
5 Jun. 1580 **Marisson**, Maria f. Jois.
30 Dec. 1582 ,, Maria f. ,,
7 Mei 1643 **Marolois**, Elisabeth f. Peter.
27 Oct. 1644 ,, Petrus f. Pieter.
17 Dec. 1646 ,, Joanna f. ,,
28 Nov. 1652 ,, Sara f. ,,
25 Mar 1576 **Marquinas**, Petrus } f. Paulus.
,, ,, ,, & Paulus }
2 Apl. 1579 ,, Barbara f. Franciscus.
30 Jul. 1581 ,, Jacobus f. ,,
28 Nov. 1585 **Marre**, Maria f. Jan.
1 Jan. 1590 ,, (v. Merregaren), Hester f. Jan.
20 Sep. 1584 **Marregaren**, Jan f. ....
16 Jan. 1590 **Marregaren**, Judith f. Jooos.
2 Jun. 1594 **Marregaeren**, Tobias f. Joos.
18 Sep. 1572 **Marregaete**, Aaron f. Philip.

18 Dec. 1614 Meijtsner, Christophorus f. Christopher.
12 Oct. 1651 Meir, la, Anna f. Hendrick.
21 Nov. 1611 Melbin, Alexander f, David.
11 Dec. 1614 Melckebeke, (v. Meckebeke), Susanna f. Nicolas.
10 Feb. 1620 ,, Magdalena f. Nicolas.
26 Aug. 1621 ,, Martha f. ,,
19 Jun. 1670 Melder, Van, Leonora f. Daniel.
8 Mei 1631 Melgelkamp, (v. Mingelkamp, etc.), Carolus f. Jan.
30 Mar. 1656 Melis, Franciscus f. Sebastiaen.
19 Oct. 1606 Melkebeke, (v. Melckebeke), Sara f. Nicholaes.
3 Jul. 1625 Mels, Elisabet f. Henric.
19 Jan. 1617 Melsen, Abigail f. Cornelis.
16 Sep. 1739 Mengeris, Barent f. Barent & Anna Halgeroot.
20 Jul. 1582 Mengiens, Susanna f. Gillis.
10 Mar. 1605 Mennick, de, Sara f. Livinus.
25 Sep. 1726 Mens, David f. Lucas & Rachel Poorter.
5 Oct. 1729 ,, Joseph f. ,, & ,, Poorter.
30 Jan. 1732 ,, William Carel f. ,, & ,, Poorter.
22 Jul. 1735 ,, Elisabeth f. ,, & ,, Porter.
26 Mar. 1738 ,, Joseph f. ,, & ,, Portier.
30 Nov. 1740 ,, Anna f. ,, & ,, Portier.
24 Feb. 1689 Mentinck, Lambertus f. Jan & Sophia de Graaf.
23 Jan. 1684 Mercken, Jonas f. Jonas & Catharina.
24 Jun. 1593 Mere, de la, Petrus f. David.
2 Jul. 1652 ,, ,, Jost f. Mattheus.
25 Jul. 1603 Merebeke, Van, Abraham f. Abraham.
4 Sep. 1611 Mergaert, (v. Merregaert), Jaques f. Jaques.
3 Feb. 1686 ,, Johannes f. Pieter & Maria.
10 Ap. 1687 Mergaerts, Ephraim f. ,, ,,
1 Oct. 1695 ,, Jacobus f. ,, ,,
20 Oct. 1697 ,, Maria f. ,, ,,
19 Aug. 1692 Mergarts, Johannes f. ,,
19 Mar. 1637 Mergelcam, (v. Mingelcamp, etc.), Maria f. Jan.
11 Oct. 1601 Meris, Jan f. Jesebrant.
4 Jun. 1592 Merregaeren, (v. Mergaert), Philip f. Joos.
13 Sep. 1612 Merregaert, Elisabeth f. Jaques.
5 Feb. 1615 ,, Lijdia f. ,,
7 Jul. 1603 Merregaren, Lowijseken f. Joos.
17 Mar. 1588 ,, Samuel f. ,,
10 Apl. 1575 Merregarne, Benjamin f. Philps.
28 Apl. 1588 Merrijsone, Jacob f. Joos.
30 Oct. 1586 Merrisone, Joannes f. ,,
11 Jan. 1590 ,, Susanna f. ,,
21 Mar. 1591 ,, Joseph f. ,,
25 Jul. 1601 Mernier, Stephanus f. Pierre. (Test: Martin Crommelin, etc.)
20 Oct. 1680 Mersche, Vander, Rebecca, een bejaert persoon, f. Jan.
20 Jan. 1579 Mersse, ,, Johannes f. posthumus Conrardus.
23 Sep. 1599 Mesmaecker, Margriete f. Hans.
12 Mei 1605 Messmaker, Pieter f. ,,
23 Oct. 1617 Messels, Maria f. Abraham.
29 Sep. 1616 Messiaen, Catharyne f. Jacob.
10 Mei 1618 ,, Maria f. ,,

14 Mei 1620 Messiaen, Joannes f. Jacob.
5 Sep. 1624 ,, Anna f. ,,
24 Dec. 1626 ,, Jacob f. ,,
26 Apl. 1704 Messinck, Willemyna f. Bernard & Martyntje Kuijper.
18 Jul. 1705 ,, Johannes f. Bernard & Martyntje Kuijper.
29 Nov. 1706 ,, Geertruijd f. Bernard & Martyntje Kuijper.
12 Jul. 1710 ,, Herman f. Bernard & Martha.
8 Jun. 1572 Mete, Van der, (v. Mets), Elizabeth f. Passchiers.
10 Jun. 1610 ,, Elizabeth f. Abraham.
15 Apl. 1578 Meteren, Van, Paulus f. Emanuel.
27 Dec. 1579 ,, Abigail f. ,,
8 Jan. 1583 ,, Magdalena f. ,,
9 Mar. 1585 ,, Paulus f. Immanuel.
4 Aug. 1586 ,, de, Nathanial f. ,,
19 Feb. 1615 ,, Van, Abraham f. Paulus.
21 Aug. 1616 ,, Jacobus f. ,, Test: Esther, Vidua Emmanuel Van Meteren.
13 ,, 1618 ,, ,, Philippus } f. Paulus. & Anna }
4 Jul. 1581 Mets, (v. Mete), Abraham f. Jan.
25 Apl. 1585 ,, David f. ,,
24 Sep. 1587 ,, Isaac f. ,,
20 Feb. 1592 ,, Joannes f. ,,
3 ,, 1605 ,, Johannes f. ,,
23 Feb. 1606 ,, Anna f. Abraham.
11 Jun. 1609 ,, Joannes f. ,,
8 Nov. 1579 Metz, Joannes f. Jan.
29 Dec. 1583 ,, Joannes f. ,,
23 Apl. 1853 Metzger, Elizabeth Catharina f. William & Elizabeth Herbus.
12 Feb. 1707 Meugh, Maria f. Cornelis & Maria Anna Boucher.
1 Nov. 1574 Meulemeester, de, (v. Molemeester, Muelemeester, etc.), Jooris f. Jan.
9 Oct. 1575 ,, ,, Abraham f. Willem.
3 Mar. 1588 ,, ,, Salomon f. Guiliame.
31 Mei 1590 ,, ,, Susanna f. ,,
2 Sep. 1591 ,, ,, Anna f. Guliam.
14 Feb. 1591 ,, ,, Andreas f. Jan.
20 Feb. 1592 ,, ,, Maria f. Jan.
8 Jun. 1617 ,, ,, Jacobus f. Andries.
14 Nov. 1619 ,, ,, Andreas f. ,,
25 Nov. 1621 ,, ,, Joannes f. ,,
11 Jul. 1624 ,, ,, Maria f. Andreas.
22 Nov. 1629 ,, ,, Elisabet f. Andries.
24 Dec. 1626 ,, ,, Josyna } f. .... & Andries }
20 Feb. 1575 Meulen, Van der, (v. Muelen), Joannes f. Anthonis.
21 Mar. 1585 ,, ,, Abigail f. Anthonis.
24 Jan. 1591 ,, Van der, Jeremynken f. Anthonijs.
21 Mar. 1602 ,, ,, Abraham f. Franchoijs
28 Mei 1620 ,, ,, Maria f. ,,
29 Oct. 1752 ,, ,, Johanna f. Vincent.
11 Jan. 1618 Meulenaer, de, Abraham f. Abraham.
23 Apl. 1620 ,, Jacobus f. ,,
11 Aug. 1622 ,, Elisabeth f. Francoijs.
28 Aug. 1586 Meulenare, de, (v. Muelenare), Anna f. Guiliame.
23 Jul. 1615 ,, ,, Joannes f. Abraham.
25 Jan. 1629 ,, ,, Maria f. David.

<table>
<tr><td>20 Nov. 1586</td><td>Meulener, Jacobus f. Pieter.</td></tr>
</table>

20 Nov. 1586 Meulener, Jacobus f. Pieter.
30 Sep. 1571 Meulerie, de, Hester f. David.
19 Feb. 1598 Meunincx, Abraham f. Adam.
14 Oct. 1595 Meunix, Cornelia f. „
13 Jun. 1675 Meurer, Flisabeth f. Jacob.
12 Oct. 1595 Meurs, Van, Goorgius f. Marten.
1 Mei 1597 „ „ Judith f. Marten.
15 Jul. 1599 „ „ Anna f. „
16 Nov. 1572 Michiels, Jacob f. Abraham.
23 Mei 1576 „ „ f. „
14 Aug. 1580 „ Isaac f. „
25 Feb. 1582 „ Elizabeth f. „
28 Dec. 1585 „ Joannes f. „
13 Apl. 1604 „ Hendrick f. Herman.
14 Apl. 1605 Michielsz, „ f. „
7 Jun. 1614 Michiels, Gillis f. Nicolaus.
13 Apl. 1619 „ Joanna f. Franchoys.
9 Jen. 1648 Michielsen, Samuel f. David.
3 Feb. 1650 „ Joseph f. „
20 Jun. 1651 „ David f. „
„ Mar. 1675 „ Anthony f. Anthony & Josyntje Willems.
17 Mei 1713 „ Elisabeth f. Nicolaus & Neetje Pieters.
13 Jul. 1598 Michielson, Jacob, oudt synen tusschen de 20 ende 21 jaer.
25 Nov. 1610 Middelaer, de, Maria f. Adriaen.
16 Feb. 1612 „ „ Rachel f. „
25 Jan. 1618 „ „ Johannes f. „
19 Mar. 1620 „ „ Judith f. „
17 Oct. 1613 „ „ Jacobmyntken f. „
31 Dec. 1615 Middeler, „ Sara f. „
7 Mei 1588 Middere, „ Joannes f. Jan.
20 Jul. 1592 Mielkens, (v. Millekens), Joannes f. .....
8 Sep. 1594 „ Pieter f. Jacob.
16 Jan. 1599 „ „ f. „
31 Jan. 1723 Mierop, Cuijk, van, Anna Magdalena f. Isaack & Cornelia.
8 Jun. 1589 Mijl, Catherine f. Dierick.
11 Apl. 1585 Mil, Pieter f. „
21 Feb. 1591 „ Esther f. „
11 Sep. 1586 Mijlemans, Philippus f. Philips.
16 Jan. 1590 „ David f. ......
27 Sep. 1723 Mijn, Van der, William f. Herman & Susanna Bloemendaal.
1 Jul. 1629 Mijtens, Elisabet & Susanna } f. Daniel.
19 Oct. 1673 Mildert, Van, David f. „
26 Dec. 1678 „ „ Catarina f. „
1 Oct. 1682 „ „ Maria f. „
2 Sep. 1684 „ „ Anna f. & Eleonora.
25 Dec. 1686 „ „ Henrietta f. Fr., & Leonora Christina.
15 Dec. 1680 Mildren, „ Abram f. „
17 Jan. 1742 Miles, Samuel f. Samuel & Johanna Hart.
24 Jun. 1744 „ Francyntje f. Samuel & Hanna Hart.
15 Jun. 1591 Millekens, (v. Mielkens), Jacob f. Jacob.
3 Oct. 1574 Milnare, Elisabeth f. Pieters.
19 Mei 1850 Min, Van der, Maria f. Coenraad Pieter Elisa & Anna Damman.
24 Aug. 1851 „ „ Petrus f. Coenraad Pieter Elisa & Anna Damman.
10 Oct. 1648 Minet, Jonas f. Andries.
1 Nov. 1649 „ Susanna f. „
27 Feb. 1651 „ Sara f. „
20 Mar. 1681 „ Elizabeth f. Andreas & Sara.

17 Jun. 1683 Minet, Joseph f. Andries Zalr. & Sara Van de Velde.
18 Dec. 1642 Mingekamp, Johannes f. Johan.
5 Oct. 1662 Mingelcamp, Maria f. Mattheus.
30 Sep. 1632 Mingelkam, (v. Megelkamp), Mattheus f. Jan.
17 Jan. 1658 Mingelkamp, Pieter f. Mattheins.
7 Oct. 1660 Minglecamp, Margriete f. Matthews.
26 Feb. 1665 „ Johannes f. Mattheus.
19 „ 1605 Minjot, Michiel f. Michiel.
15 Mar. 1607 Mijnjet, ... fs „
23 Sep. 1589 Minnaert, Abraham f. Hans.
10 Oct. 1591 „ „ f. „
18 Nov. 1593 „ Jacob f. „
15 Jun. 1621 Minnich, Samuel f. Jan Joris.
25 Mar. 1582 Moel, (v. Mol), Margriete f. Hans.
3 Aug. 1572 Moenen, Maria f. Joris.
25 „ 1611 Moerman, Eleazar f. Joos.
17 Jan. 1613 „ Abraham f. Joos.
5 Mar. 1615 „ Theodorus f. „
26 Sep. 1619 „ Eleonora f. „
20 Apl. 1617 „ Leonora f. „
18 Jul. 1613 Moesen, alias Draeck, Elisabet f. Cornelius.
12 Sep. 1605 Mogartij, Maria f. D. Leonardus.
17 Mei 1646 Moigil-camp, (v. Mingelcamp), David f. Jan.
4 Jan. 1657 Moijell, Helena f. Thomas.
21 Nov. 1658 Moijle, Catarina f. „
5 Mar. 1612 Moijse, Elizabeth f. Moijses.
30 Aug. 1573 Mol, de, Rebecca f. Pieter.
21 Jul. 1577 „ „ Elisabet f. „
20 Apl. 1579 „ „ f. „
11 Mei 1572 Moll, „ (v. Moel), Pieter f. „
14 Mar. 1574 Mol, „ Susanna f. Jan.
2 Aug. 1575 „ „ Abraham f. „
12 Feb. 1577 „ „ Sara f. „
28 Apl. 1583 Moll, „ Nicolaus f. Hans.
22 Nov. 1584 Mol, „ Joannes f. Cornelis.
26 Feb. 1587 „ „ Daniel f. „
29 Sep. 1588 „ „ Abraham f. „
14 Mar. 1591 „ „ Adriana f. Hans.
7 Mei 1592 „ de, Abraham f. „
30 Jun. 1583 Moll, Sara f. Cornelis.
16 Sep. 1627 Mol, Maria f. Philips.
Molder, de (v. Smolders).
16 Jul. 1572 Molemeester, (v. Meulemeester), Philippus f. Wilhelmus.
13 Mei 1571 Molen, Van der, (v. Molyn), Jacob f. Anthonis.
11 Aug. 1583 „ „ Abigail f. Anthonis.
28 Oct. 1571 Molenaers, Kathryn f. Pieter.
21 Dec. 1572 Molenaer, de, Michiel f. „
26 Mei 1583 „ „ Judith f. „
9 Aug. 1584 „ „ Sara f. „
12 Dec. 1608 Molhuijsen, Van, Sara f. Anthony.
11 Dec. 1586 Molijn, de, (v. Molen), Joannes f. Jan.
8 Mar. 1590 Molijn, Abraham f. Jan.
12 Apl. 1596 „ de, „ f. „
6 Apl. 1595 „ „ Pieter f. Pieter.
4 Sep. 1597 „ „ Susanna f. „
19 Mar. 1615 Molijns, Petrus f. Hans.
28 Jun. 1590 Molineaux, de, Salomon f. Guliam.
4 Apl. 1624 Molkeleque, Petrus f. Nicholas.
2 Jan. 1631 Moller, (v. Muller), Jacobus f. Franchoija.
27 Oct. 1861 Molteno, Percy Alport f. John Charles & Elisabeth Maria Jarvis.
9 Oct. 1634 Moma, Abraham f. Gerlac.

14 Feb.		Nutten, Van, Thomas f. Pieter.
25 Mar.	1649	,, ,, Joseph f. Thomas.

18 Jan.	1651	Nutten, Van, Thomas f. Thomas.
15 Mei	1603	Nuwaert, Susanna f. Jan.

20 Sep. 1584 **Obrij,** Pieter f. Hieronijmus.
1 Mei 1586 ,, Joannes f. Jeronimus.
6 Oct. 1588 ,, Elisabet f. ,,
1 Nov. 1590 ,, Anna f. ,,
1 Oct. 1854 **Oever,** Van den, Nicolaes Adrianus f.
Klaas & Marie Wil-
helmina van Goud-
riaan.
28 Sep. 1856 **Oever,** Van den, Gertrudes Hendrik f.
Klaas & Maria Wil-
helmina van Goud-
riaan.
13 Dec. 1857 ,, ,, Geertruida Hendrica
f. Klaas & Maria
Wilhelmina van
Goudriaan.
18 Mar. 1860 ,, ,, Pieter Johannes f.
Klaas & Maria Wil-
helmina van Goudri-
aan.
12 Apl. 1806 **Ohrlij, Eliza** f. Jan Hendrick & Sarah
Bray.
5 Mei 1808 ,, William Joseph f. John Henry &
Sarah Bray.
11 Apl. 1605 **Oijen,** Susanna f. Hans.
20 Apl. 1590 **Oket,** Anna f. Jooris.
22 Sep. 1594 ,, Philippus f. Joris.
14 Apl. 1601 **Oler,** alias **Pieter,** Samuel f. Anthony.
28 Feb. 1869 **Olifiers,** Cornelius Johannes Franciscus f.
Leonardus Christiaan & Cor-
nelia Wilhelmina Johanna
Maas.
29 Mei 1870 ,, Cornelius f. Leonardus Christiaan
& C. W. Maas.
30 Nov. 1656 **d'Olijslager,** Maria f. Pieter.
29 Nov. 1657 ,, Pieter f. ,,
30 Jan. 1659 ,, Joannes f. ,,
26 Dec. 1596 **Oltens,** Hester f. Christiaen.
26 Sep. 1813 **Ommeren,** Van, Pieter Fredrik, geb. te
Surinamen, f. Pieter.
1 Dec. 1678 **Omverhagen,** Machtelt f. ,,
18 Jan. 1699 **Onklaer,** Johannes f. Frans & Cornelia
Van Rijn.
6 Aug. 1673 **Onne,** Abraham f. Albrecht.
11 Oct. 1674 ,, Abraham f. Albert.
15 Oct. 1676 ,, Johannes f. ,,
19 Jan. 1636 **Ontrijns,** Sara f. Guiljame.
18 Jul. 1680 **Onversaeght, (v. Oversaeght),** Janneke f.
Pieter & Barbara.
8 Feb. 1685 ,, Maria f. Pieter & Barbara.
11 Sep. 1681 ,, Pieter f. ,, & Barber
Busaer.
4 Jun. 1571 **Ooms,** Susanna f. Hans.

9 Jul. 1690 **Oorlandt,** Johanna f. Hendrick & Mar-
garieta.
18 Mar. 1860 **Oosterveen,** Wilhelmina Gerardina f. Jan
& Cornelia Wilhelmina van
Heyningen.
13 Mar. 1689 **Oostrum,** Van, Margrieta f. Adrianus &
Maria Brouwer.
8 Oct. 1690 ,, ,, Josina f. Fr. Adrianus &
Maria.
11 Sep. 1608 **Ootger, (v. Ootgher Ootghere, Otger,**
Otgier, etc.), Ester f. Joos.
21 Apl. 1605 ,, Abraham f. ,,
6 Sep. 1573 **Ootgheer,** ,, f. Carel.
2 Nov. 1589 ,, Janneken f. Joos.
26 Nov. 1592 ,, David f. Joos.
10 Dec. 1581 ,, Elisabet f. ,,
8 Feb. 1579 **Opeeckardt,** Abraham f. Jan.
13 Jan. 1628 **Ophalfens,** Margareta f. ,, , tot Mort
lake.
23 Mei 1630 ,, Johanna f. ,,
16 Apl. 1637 ,, Francois f. ,, , tot Mortlake, inde Engelsche Kercke.
21 Aug. 1642 ,, Jan f. Jan, tot Mortlake.
1 Mar. 1646 ,, Pieter f. Jan, tot Mortlake.
16 Mar. 1634 **Ophalfers,** Maria f. Jan, tot Mortlake.
26 Jun. 1670 **Ophalven,** Francis f. Jan.
28 Jul. 1672 **Ophalvens,** Johannes f. Johannes Jr.
3 Feb. 1674 ,, Francis f. ,,
25 Jul. 1675 ,, Pieter f. ,,
20 Mei 1678 ,, Anna f. Jan & Anneken.
14 Jun. 1699 ,, Johannes f. ,, & Jacomina.
27 Jun. 1596 **Ophoogen,** Van, Pieter f. Ghysbert.
25 Aug. 1686 **Opmeer,** Catharina f. Jan & Emma.
23 Feb. 1690 ,, Johannes f. Johannes & Eva.
16 Dec. 1691 **Opmer,** Johanna f. ,, & Amy.
20 Aug. 1854 **Oppen,** Van, William Gerard f. Jacobus
Fritz & Christina Elisa-
beth Jansz.
17 Feb. 1856 ,, ,, Gerrit Jansz f. Jacobus
Fritz & Christina Eliza-
beth Jansz.
4 Oct. 1857 ,, ,, Jacobus Fritz f. Jacobus
Fritz & Christina Elisa-
beth Jansz.
11 Mar. 1576 **Oppenacker,** Sara f. Heindrick.
13 Jul. 1578 ,, Esther f. ,,
2 Aug. 1571 **Orblock,** Abraham f. Gillis.
10 Mei 1573 **Orsselare,** Van, Susanna f. Margriete.
1 Aug. 1587 **Orsele,** ,, Daniel f. Joos.
6 Jul. 1591 **Orssele,** ,, Josephus f. ,,
17 Jun. 1593 ,, Willem f. ,,
5 Mei 1594 **Osborne,** Susanna f. Jan.

11 Jul.	1585	Oste, (v. Hoste), Sara f. Pieter.
14 Jan.	1588	„ Elizabet f. „
17 Feb.	1594	„ Maria f. Pieter.
29 Feb.	1596	„ Joannes f. „
23 Aug.	1590	„ Samuel f. Jaques.
3 Aug.	1628	„ Johannes f. Samuel.
21 Jun.	1587	Otgeer, (v. Ootgeer), Elizabeth f. Joos.
31 Mei	1629	„ Johanna f. David.
26 Sep.	1630	Otger, Daniel f. „
3 Jan.	1647	„ Justus f. „
31 Dec.	1648	„ Joanna f. „
27 Dec.	1646	„ Sara f. Abraham.
9 Jan.	1684	„ Sara f. „ & Elizabeth Smith.
12 Mar.	1626	Otgheer, Elisabeth f. David.
28 Oct.	1627	Otgher, David f. „
9 Mar.	1651	„ Abraham f. „
24 Feb.	1686	„ Daniel f. Abraham & Elizabeth.
28 Dec.	1687	„ Willem f. „ & „
29 Oct.	1587	Otgier, Sacharias f. Hugo.
10 Mei	1589	Otten, Van, Willem f. Herman.
4 Mar.	1591	„ „ Maximiliaen f. „
23 Feb.	1702	Ottense, Maria f. Tierck & Vrouwtje Zipkens.
31 Mei	1646	Oudelandt, Elizabeth f. Cornelis.
20 Feb.	1645	Oudelant, Cornelis f. „
22 Oct.	1647	Oudelants, Peter f. „
7 Sep.	1690	Ougers, Elisabeth f. Sacharias & Dina Kolekmans.
2 Oct.	1692	Oulden, Leena Jacoba f. Robert & Adriana.
11 Sep.	1695	Oulry, Maria f. Thomas.
30 „	1696	. „ Thomas f. „ Thomasz & Sarah Hamilton.
11 Jul.	1602	d'Ouwe, Abraham f. Hans.
5 Mei	1605	d'Oude, Joannes f. „
14 Dec.	1606	„ Petrus f. „
26 Jun.	1608	„ Anna f. „
25 Mar.	1611	„ Maria f. „
2 Mei	1613	„ Joannes f. „
5 Mar.	1615	„ Jacobus f. „
9 „	1617	„ Maria f. „
29 Aug.	1619	„ „ f. Jan.
4 Aug.	1621	„ Thomas f. „
7 Sep.	1623	„ Abraham f. Hans.
14 Nov.	1624	„ Rebecca f. „

30 Jun.	1695	Ouwens, Johanna f. Frederick & Johanna Dircksen.
19 Aug.	1683	Oversaeght, (v. Ouversaeght), Maria f. Peter & Barbara de Saer.
30 Mei	1591	Overstaet, Van den, Susanna f. Marten.
30 Mei	1680	Overste, Elizabeth f. Nicolaes.
20 Nov.	1681	„ Sarah f. „
30 Sep.	1685	„ Willem f. „
21 Nov.	1686	„ Nicolaes f. „
13 Dec.	1682	Overstee, Nicolaes f. „
10 Mar.	1689	„ Maria f. „
11 Jun.	1690	„ Johannes f. „
25 Sep.	1692	Oversteen, Jacob f. „
22 Nov.	1857	Overzee, Van, Henri Antoine f. Henri Antoine & Martina Margaretha Paulina S'Graeuwen.
2 Jan.	1859	„ „ Francine Pauline f. Henri Antoine & Martina Margaretha Paulina S'Graeuwen.
8 Jan.	1860	„ „ Anna Sophia f. Henri Antoine & Martina Margaretha Paulina S'Graeuwen.
3 Feb.	1861	„ „ Mary Adelaide f. Henri Antoine & Martina Margaretha Paulina S'Graeuwen.
2 Feb.	1862	„ „ James f. Henri Antoine & Martina Margaretha Paulina S'Graeuwen.
31 Mei	1863	„ „ Henriette f. Henri Antoine & Martina Margaretha Paulina S'Graeuwen.
25 Dec.	1864	„ „ Adrinan f. Henri Antoine & Martina Margaretha Paulina S'Graeuwen.
25 Mar.	1866	„ „ Anna Catharina f. Henri Antoine & Martina Margaretha Paulina S'Graeuwen.
12 Oct.	1684	Ovoutense, Francoijs f. Jacob.

19 Jul.	1621	Pachet, Susanna & Judith } f. Jacob.
24 Oct.	1630	Padtbrugge, Elisabet f. Willem, tot Mortlake.
14 Dec.	1634	Padtbrugh, Dorothea f. „ tot Mortlake.
6 Nov.	1636	Padtbrug, Anna f. Guilliam, tot Mortlake.
1 Nov.	1640	„ Catarina f. Willem, tot Mortlake.
8 Aug.	1638	Padtburch, Willem f. Willem, tot Mortlake.
3 Jun.	1632	Paelmans, Petrus f. Pieter, tot Mortlake.

5 Oct.	1634	Paelmans, Sara f. Pieter, tot Mortlake.
19 Jan.	1637	„ Magdalena f. Pieter, tot Mortlake.
17 Jan.	1664	Paels, Cunera f. Robert.
11 Oct.	1629	Paeremau, (v. Perreman), Stephanus f. Pieter.
2 Jun.	1678	Paerinne, Thomas f. Michiel & Anneke Machie.
5 Dec.	1686	Paets, Van, Maria f. Adam.
29 Jan.	1688	„ „ Cornelis f. „
22 Sep.	1689	„ „ Willemina f. „ & Maria.
24 Aug.	1690	„ „ Willem f. „ & „

7 Feb.	1692	Paets, Van, Thomas f. Adam & Maria.
6 Apl.	1693	,, ,, Hendrick f. ,, & ,,
30 Dec.	1694	,, ,, Johannes f. ,, & ,,
4 Oct.	1696	,, ,, Maria Magdalena f. Adam.
1 Jan.	1646	Paff, Pieter f. Pieter.
24 Apl.	1603	Paijn, (v. Peijn), Sara f. Wonter.
27 Nov.	1608	Paladeyn (?), Anna f. Jaques.
26 Sep.	1703	Palbrug, Willem f. Johannes & Maria Elkyn.
3 Nov.	1573	Palme, de la, Elizabeth f. Salvador.
8 Apl.	1662	Palrave, Johannes f. Pieter Jr.
2 Jun.	1588	Pamele, Van, Cathelene f. Cornelis.
16 Nov.	1589	,, ,, Cornelis f. ,,
9 Sep.	1576	Pancras, Abraham f. Jan.
28 Mar.	1598	Pannes, Marie f. Hans.
18 Oct.	1599	,, Catherine f. ,,
4 Jul.	1602	Pannie, Catryne f. ,,
9 ,,	1592	Papparts, Isaac f. Herman.
7 Sep.	1589	Pappel, Elisabeth f. Matthys.
		Pappet, (v. Verbek).
7 Feb.	1591	Parasien, Jacob f. Jan.
7 Oct.	1627	Paraijn, Hulda f. Jacques de Jonge f. Jacques.
24 Apl.	1631	Parrain, Hulda f. Jacob de Jonge.
25 Mei	1634	,, Darius f. ,,
10 Oct.	1641	,, Zacheus f. Jaques.
2 Mei	1637	Pareijne, Elisabeth f. Jacob.
4 Oct.	1601	Paren, Jacus f. Jacus.
17 Feb.	1607	,, Isaac f. Jaques.
27 Jun.	1629	Parijn, Johannes f. ,, den ouder.
4 ,,	1653	Parin, Paulus f. Michiel.
23 Dec.	1683	Parrjen, Jannetje f. Samuel & Margareta le Fevre.
5 Mar.	1639	Parrijn, Jacobus f. Jacob.
19 Apl.	1640	,, Abraham f. Jaques.
28 Feb.	1643	,, Isaac f. Jacob.
4 Jan.	1680	Parnelj, Maria f. Michael.
22 Mar.	1685	,, Maria Magdalena f. ,, & Anna.
6 Apl.	1624	Pas, Van de, Willem, out 26 jaeren.
8 ,,	1624	,, ,, ,, Crispin f. Willem.
25 Sep.	1625	,, ,, Elisabeth f. ,,
25 Oct.	1627	Passchiers, Pieter, volwassen.
2 Dec.	1627	,, David f. Pieter.
15 Jul.	1632	,, Jonathan f. Pieter.
21 Mei	1609	Passeman, Helena f. Daniel.
10 Feb.	1577	Pasteijns, Samuel f. Willem.
28 Mei	1588	Pasteina, Geerardus f. Guiliame.
26 Feb.	1587	Pau, de, (v. Pauw), Elizabeth f. Jacop.
17 Mei	1590	,, ,, Joanna f. Jacob.
31 Mar.	1594	,, ,, Jacob f. ,,
17 Feb.	1601	,, ,, Samuel f. Hans.
19 Jan.	1606	,, ,, Jacobus f. Nicolas.
9 Jan.	1631	,, ,, Paulus f. ,,
22 Dec.	1635	Pauls, Maria f. Bartolomeus.
27 Jan.	1605	Paus, de, Soloman f. David.
11 Feb.	1607	Paus, de, Balthasar f. David.
17 ,,	1609	,, ,, Walraven f. ,,
7 Oct.	1610	,, ,, Leonora f. ,,
13 Mei	1621	,, ,, Anna f. Pieter.
5 Oct.	1623	,, ,, Abraham f. ,,
9 Aug.	1632	,, ,, Maria f. Salomon.
10 Sep.	1598	Pauw, ,, (v. Pau), Esther f. Hans.
10 Mar.	1612	,, ,, Elizabeth f. Nicolaus.
9 Oct.	1575	Pauwels, Samuel f. Jan.
15 Mei	1581	,, Maria f. Bartholomeus.
6 Feb.	1586	,, Sara f. ,,
7 Jul.	1588	,, Joannes f. ,,
1 Aug.	1591	Pauwels, Abraham f. Bartholomeus.
15 ,,	1593	,, ,, f. ,,
25 Jul.	1596	,, Sara f. ,,
30 Sep.	1599	,, Esther f. ,,
15 Mar.	1638	,, Sara f. ,,
6 Mei	1634	Pauwelsz, Johannes f. ,,
17 Jul.	1614	Pauwels, Jacobus f. Hendrick.
25 Mar.	1621	,, Anna f. ,,
25 Mei	1623	,, Johannes f. ,,
29 ,,	1625	,, Magdalena f. ,,
22 Apl.	1627	,, Anna f. ,,
19 Mei	1588	Pe, Van, Elizabeth f. Daniel.
8 Sep.	1590	,, ,, Daniel f. ,,
7 Mar.	1593	,, ,, Abraham f. ,,
11 Jul.	1596	,, ,, Daniel f. ,,
11 Mar.	1599	,, ,, Willem f. ,,
21 Sep.	1603	,, ,, Petrus f. ,,
23 ,,	1645	,, ,, Willem f. Willem.
12 Dec.	1650	,, ,, Daniel f. ,,
5 Dec.	1642	Pee, Jacob f. ,,
31 Oct.	1692	Peau, der, Thomas f. Johannes & Maria.
12 Aug.	1677	Peckel, Janneken f. Rutger.
16 Mei	1620	Peelen, Johannes f. Jan.
28 Jul.	1577	Peene, & Peenen, Van, Susanna f. Kaerle.
9 Oct.	1580	,, ,, Judick f. Carrel.
15 Mar.	1579	,, ,, Daniel f. Karel.
10 Feb.	1583	,, ,, Johanna f. ,, Testes. Pater, Rogier van Peene de oude, etc.
14 ,,	1585	,, ,, Samuel f. Karel.
27 Jun.	1585	,, ,, Daniel f. ,,
1 Jul.	1586	,, ,, Maria f. ,,
27 Aug.	1587	,, ,, Jonas f. Carel fs. Rogiers.
28 Apl.	1588	,, ,, Carolus f. Carel.
17 Aug.	1589	,, ,, Elizabeth f. ,,
16 Nov.	1589	,, ,, Jeremias f. ,,
12 Mar.	1592	,, ,, Jacop f. Carel, Rogiers sone.
22 Nov.	1590	,, ,, Paulus f. Carel, fs. Lucas.
27 Jun.	1592	,, ,, Lucas f. ,,
15 Feb.	1607	,, ,, Deboraf.
9 Feb.	1589	,, ,, Susanna f. Jacob.
21 Jan.	1593	,, ,, Jacob f. ,,
27 Dec.	1579	,, ,, Susanna f. Jan.
12 Mei	1582	,, ,, Joannes f. ,,
13 Jul.	1589	,, ,, Tobias f. ,,
26 Aug.	1593	,, ,, Jacob f. ,,
28 Jul.	1611	,, ,, Catharina f. Hans.
17 Jun.	1613	,, ,, Elisabeth f. Hans.
20 Nov.	1614	,, ,, Ester f. ,,
28 Jul.	1616	,, ,, Catharina f. Jan.
26 Nov.	1620	,, ,, Susanna f. ,,
11 Apl.	1591	,, ,, Joannes f. ,,
9 Dec.	1621	,, ,, Maria f. Isaac.
6 Apl.	1623	,, ,, Rachel f. ,,
23 Jan.	1625	,, ,, Susanna f. ,,
24 Jun.	1627	,, ,, Petrus f. ,,
28 Dec.	1614	,, ,, Anna f. ,,
4 Aug.	1639	,, ,, Samuel f. ,,
3 Mar.	1588	,, ,, Lucas fs. defuncti D. Lucas.
6 Dec.	1590	,, ,, Tobias f. Michiel.
5 Oct.	1578	,, ,, Lucas f. Rogiers.
3 Dec.	1581	,, ,, Abraham f. Rogier, den Jungen.

23 Jun. 1583 Peene & Peenen, Vau, Isaac f. Rogier, den Jongen. Testes. Pater, Karel van Peene fs. Rogiers, etc.
25 Oct. 1584 ,, ,, Jaquemynken f. Rogier.
17 Nov. 1586 ,, ,, Jacob f. Rogier.
10 Mar. 1588 ,, ,, Elizabeth f. ,,
22 Jun. 1589 ,, ,, Susanna f. ,,
28 Oct. 1590 ,, ,, Daniel f. ,,
31 Mei 1730 Peereboom, Matthijs f. Cornelia Campserdijk.
27 Jan. 1740 ,, Neeltje f. Abraham & Cornelia Campeldijk.
12 Feb. 1605 Peijn, de, (v. Paijn), Susanna f. Wouter.
2 Nov. 1578 Peijnardts, (v. Pinaert), Abraham f. Hans.
13 ,, 1597 Peijs, Maria f. Wouter.
14 Mar. 1598 ,, Abraham f. Jacus.
9 Nov. 1578 Peijster, de, Elias f. Christoffels & Margareta Oesselaers.
20 Jul. 1595 ,, ,, Elisabeth f. Christoffels.
22 Jan. 1598 ,, ,, Christophels f. Christophels.
24 ,, 1602 ,, ,, Maria f. Christoffel.
11 Mei 1606 ,, ,, Abraham f. ,,
13 Mar. 1608 ,, ,, Christophorus f. ,,
29 Jul. 1610 ,, ,, Sara f. ,,
21 Mar. 1613 ,, ,, Susanne f. ,,
28 Jun. 1618 ,, ,, Maria f. ,,
21 Jan. 1621 ,, ,, Johanna f. ,,
24 Nov. 1633 ,, ,, Jonas f. ......
29 Apl. 1638 ,, ,, Anna f. Jonas.
10 Oct. 1581 Peijstere,,, Cornelis f. Christoffel.
11 Nov. 1590 ,, Daniel f. ,,
8 Feb. 1599 Pele, Daniel f. Jan.
30 Aug. 1590 Pelen, Paulus f. Adriaen.
18 Apl. 1624 ,, Abigaijl f. Jan.
5 Oct. 1617 Peltiers, David f. David.
24 Jan. 1619 ,, Catharina f. ,,
13 Feb. 1586 Pelsenare, Herman f. Jan.
5 Mar. 1592 ,, de, Moses f. ,,
7 Sep. 1595 Pellaert, Abigail f. Fransois.
4 Feb. 1691 Peltzer, Sarah f. Johan.
18 Apl. 1602 Peneltier, Franchoijs f. Francoijs.
4 Mar. 1604 Penentier, Anna f. ,,
4 Jun. 1612 Penetier, Anna f. ,,
9 Oct. 1608 Pennetier, Judith f. ,,
24 Apl. 1614 ,, Joanna f. ,,
11 Mei 1589 Pensenael, de, Abraham f. Jan.
30 Jan. 1586 Peperman, Joannes f. Andries.
25 Apl. 1587 ,, Joannes f. ,,
2 Feb. 1589 ,, Maria f. ,,
23 Mar. 1589 ,, Johannes f. Joannes.
10 Sep. 1590 ,, Elisabeth f. Jan.
15 Apl. 1593 ,, Catherine f. ,,
28 Jan. 1593 ,, Thomas f. Hans.
,, ,, Catharine f. Jacus.
22 Sep. 1583 Pepers, Judith f. posthuma Cornelis.
29 Sep. 1589 Perceval, (v. Perseval), Sara f. Jacus.
16 Mei 1591 Percheval, Susanna f. Jaques.
7 Jul. 1605 Peren, Pieter f. Jacus.
14 Jan. 1621 Pergens, Margarita f. Jacob.
22 Apl. 1694 Perlkamp, Willem Hendrick f. Hendrick & Anna Catharina.
23 Sep. 1571 Perremans, Dinghentghen f. Lansloot.
25 Sep. 1586 Perseval, (v. Perceval), Janneken f. Hans.
3 Jul. 1589 ,, Joannes f. ,,
3 Feb. 1586 Persoen, Catheline f. Cornelis.

3 Mei 1611 Pertingou, Robbert f. Hendrick.
17 Oct. 1593 Peteren, v. Petrens, Petrus f. Pieter.
8 Feb. 1627 Peterens, Joannes f. Pieter.
25 Dec. 1587 Peterins, Joannes f. ,,
16 Oct. 1623 Petrans, Petrus f. ,,
24 Mei 1622 Petrens, Petrus f. ,,
10 Apl. 1634 ,, Willem f. ,,
24 Aug. 1636 ,, Johannes f. ,,
1 Jun. 1628 Pietrens, Jacobus f. ,,
25 Mar. 1602 Petrus, Jacobus f. ,,
13 Sep. 1590 Phijpher, de, Cornelis f. Cornelis.
27 Dec. 1692 Philips, Paulus f. Paulus.
18 Apl. 1703 ,, Elisabeth f. Johannes & Maria Vander Trans.
16 Sep. 1705 ,, Maria f. Johannes & Maria van der Trans.
5 Mar. 1690 Philipse, Eva f. Johannes & Maria vander Trans.
18 Jun. 1710 ,, Jacob f. Johannes & Maria.
18 Mar. 1691 ,, Janneken f. Philippus & Susanna.
21 Jun. 1691 Philipsen, Maria f. Johannes & Maria.
16 Oct. 1692 ,, Johannes f. ,, & Maria vander Trans.
25 Mar. 1694 ,, Eva f. ,, & Maria.
9 Feb. 1696 ,, Maria f. ,, & Maria
23 Jan. 1698 ,, Jannetje f. ,, & Maria
25 Dec. 1687 ,, Philippus Paulus f. Paulus & Francintje.
14 Mei 1690 ,, Philippus f. Philippus & Susanna Leeman.
16 Nov. 1692 ,, Susanna f. Philippus & Susanna Leeman.
23 Feb. 1701 ,, Philippus f. Philippus & Sara.
31 Oct. 1591 Philper, Robertus f. Richaert.
10 Jun. 1593 Philpot, Johannes f. Richard.
26 Aug. 1682 Pillaer, Abraham f. Jan & Catharina Glascock.
28 Apl. 1636 Pilcom, Vau, Daniel f. Daniel.
15 Apl. 1582 Picot, Petrus f. ....
30 Jul. 1577 Pifroen, Elisabet f. Hans.
24 Apl. 1586 Pifferoen, Joanna f. Jan.
19 Jan. 1589 ,, Moijses f. ,,
12 Apl. 1584 Piefferoens, Lea & Rachel. } f. Jan.
30 Aug. 1579 Piefferon, Joannes f. Hans.
29 Jun. 1573 Pieters & Pietersz, Susanna f. Pieter.
3 Oct. 1574 ,, Susanna f. ,,
3 Mar. 1605 ,, Elizabeth f. ,,
11 Dec. 1606 ,, Petrus f. ,,
12 Jun. 1608 ,, Christina f. ,,
18 Oct. 1610 ,, Geerard f. ,,
3 Feb. 1611 ,, Maria f. ,,
17 Jul. 1614 ,, Catharina f. ,,
4 Aug. 1689 ,, Elisabeth f. Aaron & Bridget.
26 Mei 1678 ,, Paulus f. Andrian.
12 Apl. 1685 ,, Willem f. Arent & Bridget.
25 Jul. 1686 ,, Pieter f. ,,
15 Jul. 1688 ,, Mattheus f. ,, & Brigitta.
21 Apl. 1734 ,, Gerrit f. Barent & Eva Van Doorn.
31 Oct. 1571 ,, Anna f. Bartholomeus.
20 Jan. 1611 ,, Maria f. Cornelis.
11 Apl. 1613 ,, Susanna f. ,,
26 Nov. 1615 ,, Maria f. ,,
8 Mar. 1618 ,, Cornelis f. ,,

58 BAPTISMS

26 Nov.	1620	Pieters & Pietersz,	Petrus f. Cornelis.
11 Oct.	1635	„	Petrusf. Doewe.
31 Jan.	1574	„	Maria f. Lambert.
10 Apl.	1576	„	Anthonius f. „
28 Dec.	1583	„	Lambrecht f. Lambrecht.
9 Jan.	1586	„	Elisabet f. Lambert.
7 Sep.	1595	„	Petrus f. Anthone.
4 Dec.	1603	„	Janneken f. Matthys.
27 Mar.	1812	Peterze,	Romke, geb. 15 Feb., 1788, te Ameland.
14 Mar.	1680	Pietersen,	Marten f. Adrian.
1 Dec.	1678	„	Maria f. Cornelis & Sara Williams.
15 Apl.	1683	„	Anna f. „ & „
31 Oct.	1683	„	Anna f. „
20 Nov.	1670	„	Susanna f. Jan.
5 Apl.	1601	„	Jacoba f. „ & Cornelia.
11 Nov.	1571	„	Tobias f. Lambert.
11 Sep.	1580	„	Maerta f. Lambrecht.
20 Jul.	1634	„	Rebecca f. Mattheus.
20 Apl.	1572	„	Elisabeth f. Pieter.
1 Mar.	1663	„	Jacob f. „
23 Feb.	1578	„	Hesther f. Tabacht.
22 Oct.	1581	„	Maria f. Willem.
21 Jan.	1582	Pijferoen,	Natancel f. Jan.
25 Jul.	1591	Pijfroen,	Susanna f. „
16 Oct.	1586	Pilcken, Van,	Abrahamf. Jan.
8 Sep.	1588	„ „	Sara f. Joos.
6 Aug.	1592	„ „	Jacob f. „
21 „	1595	Piliken, „	Jacob f. „
9 „	1590	Pilken, „	Isaac f. „
13 Sep.	1571	Pilget,	Becsalbe f. Jan.
26 Dec.	1613	Pille,	Pieter f. Sebastian.
19 Mar.	1615	„	Sebastiaen f. Jan.
3 Jun.	1621	„	Johannes f. Jan.
2 Sep.	1702	Pillen,	Johannes f. Abraham & Anneke Japiske.
8 Jan.	1615	Pin,	Christophor f. Christoffel.
8 Nov.	1618	„	Lucas f. Gerrard.
12 Mar.	1620	„	Jaquemynken f. Bernard.
10 Aug.	1625	„	Elisabeth f. Wernard.
19 Sep.	1626	„	Rebecca f. Wernar.
8 Jan.	1628	„	Cornelis f. Werner.
2 Aug.	1635	„	Paulus f. „
8 Sep.	1639	„	Casparusf. „
10 Jul.	1628	Pijn,	Hermon f. Jan.
27 Aug.	1581	Pins,	Sara f. „
23 Jan.	1592	Pinaert, (v. Peijnaert),	Abraham f. Jeremias.
11 Oct.	1590	Pijnaert,	Sara f. Jeremias.
8 Jan.	1596	Pijnart,	Anna f. „
16 Dec.	1677	Pippingh,	Zara f. Johannes.
12 Jun.	1678	Plaets, (v. Platts),	Sarai f. Jonathan & Catarina Bonte.
2 Mei	1703	„	Anna f. Jonathan & Anna.
12 Jul.	1571	Plaetzen, Van der,	Judith f. Cornelius.
15 Jan.	1572	Plantsoens,	Sara f. Henrick.
18 Dec.	1592	Plassche, Van der,	Samuel f. Philip.
17 Mar.	1605	„ „ „	Maria f. „
1 „	1607	„ „ „	Samuel f. „
9 Nov.	1595	Plasse, Van der,	Cathelyne f. Philip.
23 Apl.	1598	„ „ „	Paulus f. „
25 Nov.	1599	„ „ „	Anna f. „
6 Dec.	1601	„ „ „	Jacobus f. „
27 Jul.	1609	„ „ „	Philippus f. „
13 Feb.	1592	Platse, „ „	Cathelyne f. „
14 Mei	1581	Plateel,	Johannes f. Everaert.

13 Feb.	1586	Plateel,	Jacobus f. Gheraert.
10 Dec.	1579	Platteel,	Abraham f. Geerard.
12 Apl.	1676	Plats, (v. Plaets),	Maria f. Jonathan & Catharina Bonte.
10 Sep.	1673	Platts,	Jonathan f. Jonathan & Catharina.
27 Jan.	1675	„	Thomas f. „ & Catharina.
10 Mar.	1680	„	Elizabeth f. „
14 Dec.	1673	Plett,	Isaac f. Jan Jansen.
16 „	1652	Plovier, (v. Pluvier),	Judit f. Isaac.
22 Feb.	1685	„	Laurens f. Pieter & Margrieta.
2 Apl.	1579	Plugh, alias Martijns,	Martinus f. Jan.
27 Feb.	1687	Pluijmer,	Johannes f. Abraham & Magdalena.
4 Jul.	1688	„	Jan f. „ & Magdalena Adriaens.
20 Oct.	1689	„	Abraham f. „ & „ Adriaens.
12 Jul.	1691	„	Pieter f. „ & „
31 Aug.	1600	Plums,	Pieter f. Pieter.
21 Mar.	1630	Pluvier, (v. Plovier),	Elisabet f. Isaac.
28 Sep.	1623	Poecke, Van,	Catharina f. Pieter.
22 Jun.	1626	„ „	Petrus f. „
27 Mei	1627	„ „	Abraham f. „
24 Feb.	1631	„ „	Petrus f. „
13 Aug.	1629	„ „	.... f. „
14 Jan.	1588	Poedt,	Joannes f. Jan.
3 Oct.	1581	Poele, Van der,	Elisabeth f. Jan.
6 Oct.	1573	Poest, „ der,	Abraham & Sara } f. Pauwel.
18 Jan.	1578	„ „ „	Susanna f. „
22 Aug.	1624	„ „ „	Joannes f. Jan.
30 Jul.	1626	„ „ „	Samuel f. Jan.
12 Nov.	1629	„ „ „	Elizabeth f. „
1 Apl.	1649	„ „ „	Adam f. Adriaen.
7 Oct.	1604	Poeter, de,	Petrus f. Pieter.
15 Dec.	1594	Poitou,	Tobias f. Jan.
16 Mei	1596	„	„ f. „
8 Mar.	1590	Polaert,	David f. Fransois.
20 Feb.	1592	Polaerts,	Sara f. „
10 Oct.	1588	Pollert,	Jonathan f. Franchoijs.
9 Apl.	1587	Poolnaert,	Anna f. „
15 Aug.	1622	Polc,	Abraham f. Jan.
14 Feb.	1619	Pollard,	Johanna f. Johannes.
18 Mei	1617	Pollart,	Anna f. Jan.
8 Oct.	1854	Pols,	Frederic William f. Johannes Anthonie & Alberdine Lamberdine Feldhus.
7 Jan.	1855	Pompe,	Charles f. Adriaan & Anna Catharina sGraeuwen.
17 Nov.	1861	„	Jacobus f. Adriaan & Anna Catharina sGraeuwen.
9 Mei	1591	Pont,	Sara f. Eleasar.
1 Oct.	1592	„	Maria f. „
17 Nov.	1594	„ de,	Eleazar f. Eleasar.
24 Apl.	1597	„	Moses f. „
2 Sep.	1599	„	Susanna f. „
2 Sep.	1604	„	Maria f. „
25 Mei	1606	„	Abraham f. „
8 Jan.	1609	„	Susanna f. „
29 Sep.	1633	Ponter, Van de,	Cornelius f. Pieter Maerson.
8 Mei	1586	Populaer,	Samuel f. Anthony.
19 Nov.	1588	Populaer,	Samuel f. „
20 Sep.	1614	„	„ f. Samuel.
13 Oct.	1616	„	Petrus f. „
27 Mar.	1634	„	Elizabeth f. „
19 Nov.	1587	Populaire,	Samuel f. Anthony.
1 Mar.	1590	Poorte, Van de,	Abraham f. Nicolaes.

28 Jan.	1593	Poorte, Van der, Elizabeth f. Nicolaes.
25 Mei	1589	Poorten, de, ,, f. Sylvester.
13 Feb.	1592	,, Van der, Maria f. Hans.
28 Nov.	1591	Poorter, de, Rogier f. Pieter.
24 Mar.	1594	,, ,, Joannes f. ,,
19 Dec.	1596	,, ,, ,, f. ,,
25 Feb.	1594	,, ,, Neelken f. Rogier.
3 ,,	1599	Poortere, de, Anna f. Pieter.
17 Jun.	1519	,, ,, Robert f. ,,
15 Jan.	1559	Poortmans, Elizabeth f. Rogier.
8 Jan.	1619	Pootman, Joannes f. Arnouldt.
12 Mar.	1504	Porgue, Debora f. Christiaen.
18 Mei	1598	Porte, de la, Abraham f. Gielis.
9 Jan.	1597	,, ,, Sara f. ,,
23 Mar.	1600	,, de, Rebecca f. ,,
26 Mei	1672	,, de la, Sara f. Gabriel & Sara.
14 Oct.	1674	,, ,, ,, Gabriel f. ,,
15 Mar.	1676	,, ,, ,, Pieter f. ,, & Sara Kersteman.
28 Jun.	1677	,, ,, ,, Pieter f. ,,
12 Dec.	1680	,, ,, ,, Gabriel f. Fr.,, & Sarah.
1 Oct.	1682	,, ,, ,, ,, f. & ,,
20 Feb.	1681	Port, Van der, Bartholomeus f. Fr. Gerard & Johanna Verpoorten.
6 Jan.	1684	Porte, ,, ,, Catharina f. Do. Gerard & Maria de Mouson.
1 Aug.	1585	Portier, Catherine f. Pieter.
16 Sep.	1599	Post, Joannes f. Jan.
17 Feb.	1601	,, de, David f. ,,
3 Apl.	1603	,, Maria f. Hans.
22 Apl.	1602	,, Beerentje f. D. Lambertus.
15 Jul.	1576	Pot, Marie f. Andries.
13 Apl.	1587	Pottelberge, Joos f. Jeronimus.
21 Oct.	1593	,, Van, Sara f. ,,
8 Jun.	1590	Pottelberghe, Joanna f. ,,
24 Feb.	1586	Pottelsberge, Van, Sara f. ,,
3 Apl.	1589	Pottelsberghe, ,, Josias f. ,,
14 Feb.	1591	Potter, de, Judith f. Guiliame.
21 Oct.	1593	,, ,, Samuel f. ,,
21 Dec.	1595	,, ,, Daniel f. Guliam.
17 Apl.	1598	,, ,, Ezechiel f. Guiliame.
15 Mar.	1601	Pottere, ,, Abraham f. ,,
10 Jul.	1831	Potterveld, Sarah f. Pieter & Mary Bry-son.
7 Apl.	1833	,, Willem f. ,, & Mary Bry-son.
4 Oct.	1835	,, Frederik f. ,, & Mary Bry-son.
8 Jul.	1838	,, Matilda f. ,, & Mary Bry-son.
16 Feb.	1840	,, Eliza f. ,, & Mary Bry-son.
20 Mar.	1842	,, Rebecca f. ,, & Mary Bry-son.
19 Mei	1844	,, Pieter f. ,, & Mary Bry-son.
4 Oct.	1846	,, Thomas f. ,, & Mary Bry-son.
8 Dec.	1850	,, Jan f. ,, & Mary Bry-son.
5 Jun.	1625	Poucke, Van, Magdalena f. Pieter.
14 Mei	1633	,, Paulus f. ,,
14 Jan.	1636	,, Van, Rogier f. ,,
11 Dec.	1639	,, ,, Maria f. James & Maria.
8 Feb.	1691	,, ,, Sarah f. Johannes & Sara.
30 Apl.	1690	Praet, ,, Maria f. Christiaen & Susanna Verheccke.
24 Jun.	1593	Prate, Van der, Johannes f. Hans.
6 Mar.	1614	Prath, Sara f. Eduward.
25 Jun.	1626	Pré, de, Susanna f. Carel.
9 Nov.	1715	,, du, Margareta f. Samuel & Anna.
25 Mar.	1717	,, ,, Catharina f. ,, ,,
19 Mar.	1718	,, ,, Johannes f. ,, ,,
12 Aug.	1599	Prentis, Elisabeth f. Thomas.
29 Nov.	1601	,, Joannes f. ,,
23 Sep.	1601	,, Maria f. ,,
6 Jan.	1607	,, Anna f. ,,
3 Aug.	1609	,, Thomas f. ,,
7 Jan.	1610	Pres, de, (v. Pré), Samuel f. Carel.
8 Nov.	1590	Preu, ,, Abraham f. Nicolaes.
14 Dec.	1593	,, ,, Pauwels f. ,,
17 Nov.	1594	,, ,, Maria f. ,,
22 Apl.	1621	,, ,, Paulus f. Carel.
27 Aug.	1626	,, du, Isaac f. Abraham.
1 Dec.	1583	Preuth, de, Susanna f. Adriaan.
1 Jun.	1692	Preevo, Jacobus f. Pieter.
24 Nov.	1672	Prie, de, Maria f. Jacobus.
21 Feb.	1647	Priem, Andries f. Andries.
15 Jun.	1656	,, Esther f. ,,
18 Feb.	1649	Prijem, Abraham f. ,,
18 Mar.	1832	Priemer, Cornelia Wilhelmina f. Heinrich Wilhelm & Elisabeth From-bach.
16 Jun.	1695	Prijss, Jacob f. Isaas.
28 Jun.	1696	,, Sarah f. ,,
28 Apl.	1700	,, Isaak f. ,,
12 Mar.	1704	Prijs, Jacobus f. ,,
6 Oct.	1588	Pril, de, Anna f. Pieter.
13 Jul.	1600	,, ,, Maria f. ,,
24 Oct.	1602	,, ,, Catharyne f. ,,
17 Mar.	1605	,, ,, Petrus f. ,,
13 Sep.	1607	,, ,, Sara f. ,,
22 Oct.	1609	,, ,, Josijna f. ,,
17 Mar.	1594	,, ,, Susanna f. Joos.
17 Aug.	1595	,, ,, Lievine f. ,,
7 Mar.	1598	,, ,, Sara f. ,,
17 Jan.	1600	,, ,, Gillis f. ,,
20 Nov.	1603	,, ,, Gillis f. ,,
12 Dec.	1683	Primme, Andries f. ......
9 Sep.	1660	Prior, Laurens f. Arthur.
12 Jul.	1584	Prooffsten, Assuerus f. Willem.
22 Jun.	1572	Proost, Jonus ,, ,,
19 Sep.	1574	,, Joannes f. ,,
11 Mar.	1576	,, Maria f. ,,
7 Sep.	1578	,, Esther f. ,,
28 Nov.	1581	,, Johannes f. ,,
24 Sep.	1587	,, Elisabeth f. ,,
11 Mei	1645	,, Elisabeth f. D. Jonas.
9 Oct.	1743	Pruijs, Van, Willem f. Abraham & Margarietje vander Kade.
25 Apl.	1591	Pruijssen, Van, Sara f. Hans.
30 Jul.	1594	,, ,, Marie f. Jans.
27 Mar.	1580	Pule, Van der, Jacob f. ,,
21 Nov.	1619	Puijs, Thomas f. Thomas.
29 Jul.	1574	Puijt, de, (v. Puth), Abraham f. Joos.
11 Apl.	1585	,, ,, Lijdia f. ,,
10 Sep.	1587	,, ,, Sara f. ,,
27 Sep.	1590	,, ,, Maria f. ,,
6 Feb.	1592	,, ,, Abraham f. Joos.
16 Mei	1594	,, ,, Judith f. Jaques.
11 Mar.	1601	,, ,, Johannes f. Abraham.
12 Jan.	1606	,, ,, Maria f. ,,
21 Feb.	1608	,, ,, Abraham f. ,,
26 Nov.	1609	,, ,, Anna f. ,,
14 Mar.	1613	,, ,, Carolus f. ,,
12 Apl.	1618	,, ,, Anna f. Cornelis.

14 Mar.	1619	Puijt, de, Guiljelmus f. Cornelis.
21 Jan.	1621	,, ,, Agneta f. ,,
18 Mar.	1582	Puth, ,, (v. Puijt), Abigail f. Jois.
5 Jan.	1584	,, ,, Joannes f. ,,
21 Jul.	1588	Putte, Van der, Lidia f. Berneert.
18 Jan.	1590	,, ,, ,, Janneken f. Bernaert.
4 Feb.	1640	Put, ,, ,, Anna f. Gillis.
25 Aug.	1611	Putte, Van de, Petrus f. ,, & Sara Jaupin.
11 Mar.	1613	,, Van der, Gillis f. ,, & ,, Jaupin.

17 Jul.	1614	Putte, Van der, Gillis f. Gillis & Sara Jaupin.
5 Mar.	1620	,, Van de, Sara f. ,,
7 Mar.	1619	,, ,, Isaac f. Pieter.
27 Jan.	1628	Putter, ,, Catharina f. Carel, tot Mortlake.
25 Sep.	1681	,, Van, Catarina f. Cornelis.
7 ,,	1719	,, de, Catharina Maria f. Henricus & Maria Johanna.
8 Mei	1722	,, ,, Maria f. Henricus & Maria Johanna van Beck.

9 Apl.	1599	Quaedacker, Petrus f. Cornelis.
28 Sep.	1600	Quaefacker, Maria f. ,,
8 Dec.	1616	Quatroos, Rachel f. Tobias.
27 Mei	1582	Quinckens, Isaac f. Henrick.
24 Feb.	1663	Quintin, Peter f. Richard & Maria.
4 Mei	1665	,, Maria f. ,, & ,,
12 Dec.	1666	,, Samuel f. ,, & ,,
14 Jul.	1669	Quintine, William f. Richard & Mary.
26 Dec.	1582	Quirijns, Bartholomeus f. Christiaan.
24 Mar.	1594	,, Anna f. Lucas. Testes. Dominicus Charles & Elizabeth Mocus, etc.

25 Jan.	1599	Quirijns, Abraham & Isaac } f. Lucas.
26 Oct.	1600	Quirijns, Susanna f. Sijmon.
3 Mar.	1594	Quisthout, Catherine f. Jan.
21 Mar.	1596	,, Joannes f. Hans.
1 Oct.	1598	,, Daniel f. ,,
17 Oct.	1602	,, Maria f. Jan.
29 Jul.	1604	,, Joannes f. Hans.
6 Mar.	1608	,, Maria f. ,,
2 Oct.	1614	,, Adam f. ,,
10 Jan.	1619	,, Ester f. ,,
9 Jan.	1625	,, Maria f. Jan.
23 Feb.	1606	,, Judith f. Abraham.

23 Jun.	1583	Raassens. (v. Raessens), Isaac f. Geerardt.
8 ,,	1578	Raassinck. Abraham f. Geerardt.
27 Jan.	1622	Radclijff, Debora f. Willem.
26 Nov.	1704	Radcraft, de, Sara f. Paulus & Rebecca Take.
25 Mei	1709	Rade, Van der, Philip f. Philip & Willemyntje.
22 Sep.	1588	,, ,, ,, Joannes f. Jacob.
15 Nov.	1573	Rademaker, Johannes f. Joannes.
24 Apl.	1575	Radermacher, Stephanus f. ,,
4 Aug.	1577	Radermaker, Anna f. ,,
14 Jun.	1579	,, Abraham f. Johannes.
30 Aug.	1500	,, Henrick f. Scipio.
3 Feb.	1594	Rae, Van, Maria f. Jaques.
31 Aug.	1617	,, de, Maria f. Sijmon.
30 Jan.	1592	Raede, Van der, Rachel f. Jacop.
11 Jul.	1591	Raedt, ,, ,, (v. Raet), Sara f. Pauwel.

26 Sep.	1591	Raedt, de, Joannes f. Seur Jaschus.
16 Jan.	1603	,, ,, Peeter f. Daniel.
21 Jan.	1627	,, ,, Jacob f. Jacob,
11 Nov.	1576	Raessen, (v. Raassens), Sara f. Gheeraert.
26 Jun.	1586	Raet, (v. Raedt), Van der, Johannes f. Lowys.
26 Jun.	1590	,, Van der, Abraham f. Lowys.
9 Oct.	1586	,, de, Giclis f. Giclis.
8 Mar.	1590	,, ,, Petrus f. Fransois.
25 Dec.	1592	,, ,, Abraham f. Fransois.
23 Feb.	1595	,, ,, Sara f. Fransois.
19 Jul.	1597	,, ,, Daniel f. Franchoys.
14 Apl.	1601	,, ,, Daniel f. Franchoys.
10 Jan.	1604	,, ,, Daniel & Pieter } fi. Daniel.
13 Feb.	1620	,, ,, Susanna f. Sijmon.
17 Nov.	1622	,, ,, Cornelius f. Simon.

13 Nov.	1636	Rijcke, de, (v. Ricke), Elisabeth f. Cornelis.
4 Aug.	1633	„ „ Jacolus f. Cornelis.
12 Jul.	1668	„ Pieter f. Christian.
2 Dec.	1576	„ Van der, Elisabeth f. Dierick.
9 Sep.	1593	Rijckewaert, Joannes f. Jan. Testes: Jan Godschalck & Sara du Bois.
10 Jul.	1597	„ Susanna f. Jan. Testes: .... Maeyken, uxor Joos Ootgher.
4 Mei	1600	Rijckewart, Elisabeth f. Jan. Testes: David Stamers, Maeyken Hems & Eliz: Godschalck.
28 Apl.	1588	Rijenroij, (v. Reijenroij), Margriete f. Dierick.
2 Feb.	1593	„ Anna f. Dierick.
17 Jan.	1703	Rijk, Van, Jacob f. Nicolaes.
27 Mar.	1687	Rijkersijes, Rebecca f. Carel.
5 Aug.	1649	Rijlers, Anna f. Christian.
14 Apl.	1577	Rijnicks, Susanna f. Heyndrick.
15 Mei	1586	Rijselinck, Sara f. Jan.
28 Nov.	1652	Rijsboeck, Van, Maria f. Philip.
17 Dec.	1654	„ Johanna f. „
30 Nov.	1656	„ Carolus f. „
29 Jul.	1660	Rishoeck, Petrus f. „
18 Jan.	1663	Rijshoek, Jacob f. „
13 Mar.	1664	Rijshooke, Anna f. „
25 Jun.	1665	Rijshoek, Elisabet f. „
6 Jan.	1667	„ .... f. „
7 Mei	1706	Rijssen, Van, Daniel f. Daniel & Maria.
6 Jul.	1709	„ „ Maria f. „ „
9 Jan.	1711	„ „ Jan f. „ „
3 Mar.	1697	Rijswijck, Jan f. Abraham & Geesje Lelivelt.
8 Jun.	1698	„ Jan f. Abraham & Josina Lelivelt.
10 Jun.	1623	Rijt, Van, Catharina f. Cornelis.
21 Mar.	1585	Rijx, Maria f. Jaques.
9 Feb.	1640	Rilles, Paulus f. Willem.
26 Aug.	1770	Ringelduif, Johanna Elisabeth f. Jan & Anna.
19 Dec.	1669	Ripke, Christian f. Christian.
31 Mar.	1672	„ Aaron f. „ & Anna.
7 Dec.	1673	„ Daniel f. „ .
12 Nov.	1676	„ William f. „ .
25 Aug.	1678	„ Helena f. Christiaen.
12 Mei	1661	Riseleberg, Van, Willem f. Hendrick Willemsen.
27 Mar.	1578	Riviere, Van der, Johannes f. Salomon.
16 Feb.	1595	„ „ Margriete f. Hans.
18 Apl.	1596	„ de la, Joannes f. „
12 Jun.	1597	„ Van der, Pieter f. Jan.
3 Dec.	1598	„ de, Margriete f. „
2 Mar.	1600	„ Van der, Samuel f. „
29 Nov.	1601	„ „ „ Susanna f. „
6 Mar.	1603	Rivieren, „ „ Johannes f. „
23 Jan.	1648	Rix, (v. Ricksen), Elisabet f. Wouter.
25 Dec.	1642	Rixe, Johannes f. Wouter.
20 Feb.	1653	Rixem, Isaac f. „
25 Jul.	1641	Rixen, Maria f. „
2 Feb.	1574	Ro, Van, (v. Roo), Abraham f. Jan.
8 Dec.	1575	„ „ Sara f. Jan.
3 Mar.	1577	„ „ Isaac f. „
11 Dec.	1580	„ Van, de, Jacob f. Jan.
16 Mar.	1862	Robbers, Carolina Wilhelmina f. Cornelis Eliza & Carolina Wilhelmina Bremer.
11 Oct.	1674	Robbert, Esther f. Willem,
20 Jul.	1726	Robberts, Helena f. „ & Anna.
30 Dec.	1730	Roberts, William f. William & Anna.
10 Jan.	1591	Robs, Daniel f. Guiliame
18 Dec.	1589	Robsen, Sara f. „ .
27 Jan.	1628	Roccataliata, Jan Stephen f. Jan.
12 Jun.	1580	Roche, de la, Samuel f. Geerardts.
8 Apl.	1600	Rochus, Cornelis, oudt 21 Jaeren.
2 Jan.	1642	Rode, de, (v. Rhode), David f. Christian.
14 Mar.	1643	„ „ Joannes f. Christian.
1 Mei	1588	Roehorst, Elizabeth f. Jacus.
12 Oct.	1690	Roeij, de, (v. Rooij), Johannes f. Daniel & Jannetje.
17 Mei	1590	Roelant, Elisabeth f. Jan.
7 Jul.	1594	„ Maria f. Hans.
13 Jul.	1595	„ Joannes f. „
18 Mar.	1599	„ Abraham f. „
28 Mei	1598	Roelants, Jacobus f. Petrus.
4 Nov.	1716	Roelantse, (v. Rowlandson), Catharina f. Jonas & Elisabet van Kesteren.
28 Feb.	1722	Roelantzen, Catrina f. Jonas & Elisabet van Kesteren.
27 Mar.	1726	Roelantz, George f. Jonas & Elisabet van Kesteren.
20 Mar.	1687	Roelansen, Elizabeth f. Roelandt & Catharina.
29 Apl.	1860	Roelink, Frederika Bertha Johanna f. Gerhardus & Johanna Josephina Veerman.
19 Jan.	1862	„ Geertruida Johanna f. Gerhardus & Johauna Josephina Veerman.
25 Feb.	1865	„ Bernard f. Gerhardus & Johanna Josephina Veerman.
25 Nov.	1866	„ Hendrik Willem f. Gerhardus & Johanna Josephina Veerman.
25 Sep.	1870	„ Willem Carel f. Gerhardus & Johanna Josephina Veerman.
20 Apl.	1606	Roij, Van, Johannes f. Jacques.
22 Nov.	1607	„ de, Daniel f. „
12 Aug.	1764	Rolland, Anna Maria f. Albert Friedrich & Anna Ratcliff.
21 Dec.	1765	„ Sophia Sara f. Albert Friedrich & Anna Rathcliff.
26 Nov.	1767	„ Sara f. Albert Friedrich & Anna Ratcliff.
27 Aug.	1769	„ Philip f. Albert Friedrich & Anna Ratcliff.
16 Sep.	1770	„ Albertus Fredrik f. Albert Friedrich & Anna Ratcliffe.
26 Jul.	1772	„ Hannah f. Albert Friedrich & Anna Ratcliff.
3 Apl.	1774	„ Charlotte f. Albert Friedrich & Anna Ratcliff.
17 Apl.	1775	„ Elisabeth f. Albert Friedrich & Anna Ratcliff.
30 Mar.	1776	„ Johan Wilhelm f. Albertus Frederick & Anna Ratcliffe.
3 Feb.	1779	„ Joshua f. Albertus Frederick & Anna Ratcliffe.
2 Aug.	1782	„ Sophia f. Albertus Frederick & Anna Ratcliffe.
24 Sep.	1588	Rombout, Peeter f. Jochim.
9 Aug.	1586	„ Martinken f. Joachim.
12 Aug.	1671	Roo, Van de, (v. Ro), Anthonius f. Hans.
7 Sep.	1572	„ „ „ Susanna f. Jan.
18 Feb.	1599	„ „ „ Johannes f. Abraham.

2 Nov. 1600 Roo, Van de, Abraham f. Abraham.
26 Sep. 1602 ,, ,, Nathanael f. ,,
28 Jul. 1605 ,, Van, Benjamin f. ,,
26 Apl. 1607 ,, ,, Helena f. ,,
1 Apl. 1610 ,, de, Elisabeth f. ,,
8 Oct. 1611 ,, Van, Susanna f. ,
8 Aug. 1613 ,, ,, Petrus f. ,,
7 Jan. 1705 ,, de, Dirick f. Daniel & Janneken.
29 Jun. 1707 ,, ,, Janneken f. Daniel & Janneken van Dussel.
9 Oct. 1709 ,, ,, Franeyntje f. Johannes & Rebecca.
22 Apl. 1711 ,, ,, John f. John & Rebecca.
4 Jan. 1646 Roode, de, (v. Rode), Marie f. Christiaen.
13 Jun. 1647 ,, ,, Jan f. Christiaen.
8 Jun. 1656 ,, ,, Esther f. ,,
1 Jan. 1660 ,, ,, Matthijs f. ,,
8 Dec. 1653 ,, ,, Jan f. Jan.
1 Jul. 1655 ,, ,, Wilhelm f. ,,
11 Sep. 1659 ,, ,, Susanna f. ,,
1 Sep. 1662 ,, ,, Johannes f. ,,
12 Mei 1695 Roolj, de, (v. Roeij), Cornelis f. Daniel Jansen & Janneken.
21 Feb. 1630 Rooman, Hendrick f. Elias.
18 Mei 1634 Rosebeeck, Maria f. ....
23 Aug. 1632 Roosebeeck, Van, Sara f. Jan.
26 Jul. 1638 ,, ,, Esther f. ,,
12 Feb. 1693 Rosendael, ,, Catharina f. Jacob.
16 Jul. 1394 Rosendal, Cornelis f. Cornelis.
6 Aug. 1596 Roosendal, Daniel f.
28 Aug. 1623 Roose, de, Joannes f. Lieven.
18 Aug. 1590 Roost, ,, Jossinken f. ,,
10 Jan. 1613 Rosman, Arnouldt f. Benedictus.
19 Oct. 1700 Ross, Conche Regina f. David, uit Ross in Schotland, & Elisabeth Weert.
26 Dec. 1629 Rossel, Maria f. Jan, tot Mortlake.
3 Jun. 1632 ,, Anna f. ,, ,, ,,
5 Jan. 1576 Rosseel, Susanna f. Anthony.
2 Nov. 1634 Roselle, ,, f. Jan.
23 Jul. 1639 ,, Debora f. Jan, tot Mortlake.
5 Feb. 1637 Rossel, Nelleken ofte Cornelia f. Jan, tot Mortlake, inde Engelsche Kercke.
15 Oct. 1643 Rossel, Jan, f. Jan, tot Mortlake.
16 Nov. 1645 ,, Joannes f. Jan, tot Mortlake.
3 Jul. 1814 Rossum, Van, Hermannus Everhardus f. Abraham Everhardus & Theodora Elizabeth Lobi.
21 Jan. 1816 ,, ,, Willem Jan f. Abraham Everhardus & Theodora Elizabeth Lobé.
3 Mei 1818 ,, ,, Everhardus Theodorus f. Abraham Everhardus & Theodora Elizabeth Lobé.
18 Apl. 1819 ,, ,, Louis Herman f. Abraham Everhardus & Theodora Elizabeth Lobé.
20 Aug. 1820 ,, ,, Christiaan Johannes f. Abraham Everhardus & Theodora Elizabeth Lobé.
18 Jul. 1808 Rose, Frederik Cornelis f. Heer Simon Hendrik, oud Raad van Hollandsch Indie etc., & Johanna Susanna Senn.
20 Apl. 1572 Rotarij, Maria f. Joannes.

2 Jul. 1695 Rottermont, Gysbertina f. Abraham & Johanna Elisabeth.
10 Mar. 1573 Rousseau, ... f. Anthonis.
14 Aug. 1586 ,, Sara f. Anthoine.
9 Oct. 1608 Roussel, Joannes f. Anthonius.
13 Ap. 1600 Rousseel, ,v. Russel, Abigail f. Nicasius.
5 Jun. 1603 ,, Joannes f. Nicasius.
27 Oct. 1605 Roussel, Johanna f. ,,
15 Feb. 1607 ,, Maria f. ,,
18 Sep. 1608 ,, Cornelis f. ,,
23 Sep. 1610 ,, Maria f. ,,
26 Jul. 1612 ,, Elizabeth f. ,,
9 Oct. 1614 ,, Theodorus f. ,,
19 Mei 1616 ,, Isaac f. ,,
17 Jan. 1619 ,, Nicasius f. ,,
6 Feb. 1620 ,, Abraham f. ,, Testes : Abraham Herrewyn & Johanna we. Cornelis Jansz, avia infantis.
23 Aug. 1579 Rovers, Israel f. Arnoldts.
16 Mei 1714 Rowlandson, (v. Roelantse), Jannetje f. Jonas & Elisabeth van Kesteren.
15 Jun. 1746 Rozlandt, Roeland f. Johannes Juriaan & Willelmina.
9 Jan. 1642 Ruben, Jacobus f. Johannes & Marie.
18 Mar. 1638 ,, Johannes f. Jan.
3 Apl. 1643 ,, Jacob f. ,,
18 Apl. 1647 ,, Hugo f. Johannes.
10 Mar. 1588 Ruet, de, Susanna f. Soariasus.
9 Apl. 1644 Ruishout, (v. Rushout), Jacobus f. Johannes.
18 Oct. 1683 Ruishuick, Maria f. Philip.
12 Nov. 1704 Ruist, Willem f. Willem & Margareta Fils.
18 Feb. 1683 Ruigendijck, Johannes f. Nicolaes.
5 Mei 1680 Ruijgendijck, Elizabeth f. ,,
4 Sep. 1681 ,, Nicolaes f. ,,
23 Jan. 1687 ,, Jacob f. ,,
1 Jul. 1688 ,, Ezechiel f. ,,
19 Jan. 1690 ,, Jacob f. ,,
17 Apl. 1692 ,, Maria f. ,,
5 ,, 1713 ,, Cornelis f. Jacobus & Wilemijna Paats.
26 Dec. 1714 ,, Maria f. Jacobus & Wilemijna.
30 Dec. 1716 ,, Jacob f. Jacobus & Wilemijna.
8 Mar. 1618 Ruijs, Maria f. Thomas.
26 Mar. 1622 ,, Judith f. ,,
29 Feb. 1624 ,, Anna f. ,,
28 Oct. 1589 Ruijster, de, Abraham } kinderen van eenen dracht, waraf Isaac, & Jacob. } vader is Hans.
9 Jan. 1803 Ruijter, de, Paulus f. Jacob & Sarah Wright.
22 Sep. 1804 ,, ,, Thomas f. ,, & Sarah Wright.
28 Sep. 1806 ,, ,, Jan f. ,, & Sarah Wright.
7 Jan. 1810 ,, ,, Sarah f. ,, & Sarah Wright.
8 Dec. 1811 ,, ,, Francina f. ,, & Sarah Wright.
11 Apl. 1589 Ruijters, Elizabeth f. Hendrick.
31 Mei 1590 ,, Maria f. ,,
29 Aug. 1591 ,, Abraham f. Henric.
7 Nov. 1557 Ruijtinck, Jacomyne f. Jan.

11 Oct.	1590	Ruijtinck, Peeter f. Peeter.
16 Nov.	1591	,, Joannes f. Pieter.
28 Jan.	1593	,, Tobias f. ,,
2 Mar.	1595	,, Abraham f. ,,
24 Apl.	1597	,, Anna f. ,,
23 Aug.	1603	,, Elisabeth f. Sijmeon.
16 Oct.	1608	,, Johannes f. ,,
2 Nov.	1606	Rutingius, Sijmeon f. ,,
28 Apl.	1611	,, Petrus f. D. ,,
5 Apl.	1613	,, Paulus f. D. ,,
26 Jul.	1615	,, Maria f. D. ,,
11 Jun.	1618	,, Ester f. D. ,,
2 Oct.	1620	,, Jacobus f. D. ,,
12 Apl.	1629	Ruijtinck, Zacharias f. Roelandt.
11 Sep.	1589	Rullers, Maria f. Niclaes.
20 Feb.	1627	Ruschout, Justus f. Jan.
10 Mei	1629	Rushout, (v. Ruishout), Johannes f. Jan.
6 Jul.	1634	,, Abigail f. Jan.
11 Jan.	1596	Russel, (v. Rousseel), Susanna f. Nicasius.
9 Apl.	1598	Russeel, Ester f. Nicasius.
10 Aug.	1600	Rust, Mary f. Willem & Margriet Syles.
30 Dec.	1604	Rutchers, Adam f. Godefroij.
22 Oct.	1592	Rutkers, Judith f. Hendrick.
23 Nov.	1595	Rutgers, Christoffel f. Godefroij.
5 Dec.	1596	,, Adam f. ,,
10 Jun.	1599	,, Abel f. ,,
20 Sep.	1601	,, Sara f. ,,
27 Apl.	1606	,, Samuel f. ,,
8 Nov.	1607	,, Benjamin f. ,,
10 Jan.	1609	,, Isaac f. ,,
29 Feb.	1610	,, Jacobus f. Godefroij.
13 Dec.	1612	,, Elisabet f. ,,
13 Mar.	1603	Ruthgeers, Sara f. ,,
8 Mei	1603	Rutho, Susanna f. Melchior.
28 Feb.	1591	Rutchaert, Elizabeth f. Willem.
14 Nov.	1613	Rute, (v. Rutte), Pieter f. Jan.
30 Nov.	1595	Ruters, (v. Rutter), Abraham f. Abraham.
4 Sep.	1597	,, David f. Abraham.
22 Aug.	1644	Rutspin, Arnout f. Arnout.
20 Aug.	1690	Rutte, (v Rute), Maria Magdalena f. Pieter & Maria Penniux.
5 Mar.	1612	Rutter, Abraham f. Abraham.
30 Jul.	1637	Ruuijt, de, Renier f. Paulus.
12 Jan.	1589	Ruvere, ,, Joannes f. Pieter.

17 Mei	1705	Saal, Van der, Abraham f. Barent & Jannetje Nagel.
6 Nov.	1709	Sael, ,, ,, Abraham f. Barent & Jannetje.
18 Apl.	1731	Saal, ,, ,, Barent f. Barent & Maria.
2 Dec.	1827	Sack, John Frederick f. Frederick William & Anna Margaretha Suwerkrop.
20 ,,	1829	,, Sarah Margaretha f. Frederick William & Anna Margaretha Suwerkrop.
24 Mei	1840	,, Minna Henriette f. Frederick William & Anna Margaretha Suwerkrop.
24 Mar.	1841	,, Anna Friederica Ottilie f. Frederick William & Anna Margaretha Suwerkrop.
1 Oct.	1843	,, Gertrude Maude f. Frederick William & Anna Margaretha Suwerkrop.
27 Apl.	1572	Sael, Anna f. Mr. Jacob.
24 Jan.	1619	Sadelaer, Jacobus f. Pieter.
2 Apl.	1626	Sadeler, Anthonius f. ,,
26 Feb.	1629	Sadlar, Gratia f. Benjamin.
3 Feb.	1632	,, Abraham f. ,,
20 Mei	1572	Sager, de, Lazarus f. Steven.
19 Apl.	1576	Saghere, de, Martha f. Steven.
21 Jan.	1578	,, ,, Stephanus f. ,,
24 Mar.	1583	Sagers, ,, Joannes f. ,,
1 Nov.	1589	Sagere, ,, Simoen f. ,,
4 Jun.	1620	Saijon, Sara f. Jan.
9 Feb.	1623	,, Abraham f. Franchoys.
8 Dec.	1625	,, Anna f. ,,
7 Sep.	1628	Saijon, Maria f. Fransois & Marie.
30 Mei	1647	,, Francois f. Abraham.
26 Aug.	1587	Salabeen, (v. Salmbeen), Paulus f. Daniel.
13 Feb.	1589	,, Daniel f. Daniel.
27 Jan.	1591	,, Susanna f. ,,
17 Mei	1593	,, Joannes f. ,,
18 Aug.	1616	Salaerdt, Petrus f. Petrus.
23 Jan.	1622	Sallardt, Daniel f. Pieter.
21 Dec.	1623	Saelart, Pieter f. ,,
9 Aug.	1626	Salart, Benjamin f. Benjamin.
4 Mei	1630	Saelaert, Paulus f. ,,
4 Mei	1595	Salé, (v. Salle, etc.), Susanna f. Jan.
1 Dec.	1599	,, Catherine f. Jan.
3 Feb.	1605	,, Anna f. Hans.
10 Jul.	1608	,, Petrus f. ,,
14 Feb.	1619	,, Adam f. Richard.
26 Sep.	1591	Salij, de, Anna f. Jan.
21 Nov.	1592	Salins, Anthonis f. Aernout.
3 Aug.	1600	,, Jacob f. Arent.
12 ,,	1593	Salé, (v. Salé), Joannes f. Hans.
24 Jul.	1597	,, Martinus f. Jan.
14 Dec.	1572	Sallembien, (v. Salabeen), Samuel f. Aernoudt.
19 Jun.	1575	Salmbeen, Pieter f. Arnout.
15 Jul.	1576	,, Anna f. ,,
1 Sep.	1594	,, Susanna f. Daniel.
14 Nov.	1596	,, Petrus f. ,,
31 Mei	1573	Salmerts, Johannes f. Jan.
4 Mei	1572	Salomons, Susanna f. Goevaerts.
18 Jul.	1686	Samber, de, Hendrick f. Abraham & Margarieta Pounie.
30 Aug.	1579	Sameijns, Nicolaus f. Pieter.
1 Dec.	1583	,, Esther f. ,,

1573 **Samijn**, Johannes f. Pieter.
1574 ,, Abraham f. ,,
1576 ,, Maria f. ,,
1601 ,, Maria f. Jacus.
1605 ,, Wanter f. Jaques.
1572 **Samijns**, Pieter f. Petrus.
1575 ,, Maria f. Pieter. Test. Clays
Thyssen.
1582 ,, Tobias f. Pieter.
1585 **Sampsons**, Maria f. Ferdinandus.
1576 **Sande**, Van der, Marten f. Marten.
1578 ,, ,, ,, Sara f. ,,
1589 ,, ,, ,, Elisabeth f. Gilles.
1591 ,, ,, ,, Joannes f. ,,
1593 ,, ,, ,, David f. ,,
1596 ,, ,, ,, Frederijck f. Frederick.
1598 ,, ,, ,, Johannes f. ,,
1601 ,, ,, ,, Frederick f. ,,
1859 **Sanden**, Van der, Hendrik Cornelis f. Anthony & Julia Elizabeth Carolina Bohn.
1573 **Sanegreijn**, Susanna f. Geeraert.
1574 **Sanegrin**, ,, f. ,,
1622 **Santen**, Isaac f. Joris.
1640 ,, Van, Margarita f. Christiaen.
1642 ,, ,, Margerite f. ,,
1647 ,, ,, Lucas f. ,, Pawels.
1649 ,, ,, Johannes f. ,, Pauwels.
1651 ,, ,, Christian f. ,, Paulus.
1617 **Santgen**, Maria f. Thomas.
1621 ,, Lucas f. ,,
1610 **Santgens**, Abraham f. ,,
1605 ,, Jeronymus f. ,,
1612 **Santkens**, Jacob f. ,,
1614 ,, Susanna f. Thomas.
1609 **Sainctkens**, Joannes f. ,,
1626 **Santkens**, Petrus f. ,,
1576 **Santvoort**, de, Susanna f. Roelandus.
1575 **Sass**, Van, Jan f. Jan.
1576 **Sassen**, ,, Thomas f. ,,
1695 ,, ,, Peter f. Lucas & Maria.
Sauvage, (v. de Wilde).
1708 **Savoij**, Cornelia f. Jacobus & Trintge Host van Kauwenhoven.
1572 **Schaap**, Daniel f. Dierick.
1574 **Schaep**, Amos f. ,,
1577 ,, Daniel f. ,,
1596 ,, Elizabeth f. Amos.
1597 ,, Susanna f. ,,
1619 **Schaephuijsen**, Lucas f. Leonard.
1685 **Schaffer**, Lucretia f. Caspar.
1659 **Schaft**, Maria f. Anthony.
1662 ,, Jacobus f. ,,
1858 **Schaick**, Van, Jacob Gijsbertus f. Jacob & Marta Schouten.
1629 **Schalbers**, Catharina f. Rutger.
1638 **Schalie**, Johannes f. Johannes.
1645 **Schanternel**, Helena f. ,,
1616 **Schats**, Samuel f. Jochim.
1685 **Schawel**, (v. Schowel), Andries f. Jan & Judith.
1690 ,, Maria f. Andries.
1574 **Schebens**, Van, Jeremias f. Seijgers.
1689 **Scheffers**, Anna f. Casper & Willemintje.
1661 **Scheltens**, Hanna f. Johannes.
1664 ,, Johannes f. ,,
1660 **Schelton**, Elisabeth f. Johan.
1686 **Schenckel**, Barbara f. Hendrick & Barbara.

10 Jun. 1688 **Schenckel**, Maria f. Hendrick.
27 Mar. 1692 ., Jacob f. ,, & Maria.
19 Nov. 1693 ,, Hendrickje f. ,,
27 Feb. 1687 ,, (v. Schijnakel), Johannes f. Hubert & Elizabeth.
1 Jun. 1690 **Schenkel**, Johannes f. Hendrick.
14 Oct. 1572 **Scherberch**, Van, Samuel f. Seger.
29 Jan. 1671 **Schernol**, Van der, Pieter f. Antony Matias & Elisabeth.
16 Jul. 1690 **Scherpin**, Josephus Bernardus f. Johannes & Elisabeth.
31 Aug. 1609 **Scheuninx**, Joannes f. Jan.
26 Aug. 1646 **Scheveruel**, Robert f. Jan.
26 Jan. 1649 **Scheveeruel**, Johannes f. Johannes.
2 Oct. 1653 **Schevenal**, Elisabet f. Jan.
13 Dec. 1655 ,, Anna f. ,,
5 Jan. 1645 **Schevirnst**, Jan f. Johannes.
26 Sep. 1683 **Schijnckel**, (v. Schinckel), Sara f. Hubrecht.
22 Mar. 1685 ,, Elizabeth f. Hubrecht.
24 Feb. 1695 ,, Hubert f. ,,
20 Dec. 1696 ,, Johannes f. ,,
24 Mei 1696 ,, Pieter f. Pieter.
20 ,, 1695 **Schijnens**, Magdalena f. Bartholomeus.
15 Feb. 1691 **Schijnkel**, (v. Schinckel), Esther f. Huybert & Elisabeth.
24 Mar. 1695 ,, Rachel f. Hendrick.
20 Feb. 1576 **Schijnx**, Pieter f. Pieter.
21 Mei 1610 **Schildt**, Samuel f. Samuel.
27 Oct. 1661 ,, Johanna f. ,,
14 Sep. 1641 **Schilt**, Maria f. ,,
21 Mar. 1644 ,, Sara f. ,,
5 Jul. 1696 **Schinckel**, (v. Schijnckel), Hendrick f. Hendrick.
26 Mar. 1693 ,, Huibert f. Huibert & Elisabeth.
27 Jan. 1689 **Schinkel**, Sara f. Huybert.
8 Feb. 1682 **Schmits**, Anna Catharina f. Goswinus.
30 Jul. 1871 **Schmitt**, Franziska Johanna f. Wilhelm Herbert Gottfried & Johanna Geertruida Meyer.
10 Aug. 1665 **Schoeft**, Cornelia f. Pieter.
18 Jan. 1603 **Schoemacker**, de, Sara f. Maximiliaen.
10 Nov. 1680 ,, Elisabeth f. Jasper.
6 Nov. 1681 ,, Altgen f. Caspar & Elisabeth.
10 Feb. 1684 **Schoemaecker**, Marija f. ,, & Elisabeth.
25 Sep. 1687 ,, Anna f. Casper & Elisabeth.
15 Feb. 1691 ,, Willem f. Jasper & ,,
1 Aug. 1591 **Schoemaeckers**, Hester f. Maximiliaen.
15 Oct. 1588 **Schoemaker**, (v. Schumacker), Abraham f. Gillis.
1 Jul. 1593 **Schoemakers**, Joannes f. Maximiliaen.
19 Jan. 1595 ,, Maximiliaen f. ,,
23 Oct. 1597 ,, Johannes f. Gillis.
30 Jul. 1601 ,, Isaac f. ,,
7 Sep. 1578 **Schoemans**, Catherina f. ....
1 Aug. 1596 **Schoenmaeckers**, Joannes f. Gillis.
13 Feb. 1597 ,, Judith f. Maximiliaen.
24 Dec. 1598 **Schoenmaker**, Jeremias f. ,,
17 Feb. 1601 ,, Lenora f. ,,
17 ,, 1689 **Schoenmaecker**, Willem f. Casper & Elizabeth.
16 Jun. 1612 **Schoesetters**, Elisabeth f. Hendric.
14 Sep. 1617 ,, Henricus f. ,,
8 Apl. 1621 ,, Abraham f. ,,
7 Jul. 1622 ,, Isaac f. ,,
19 Dec. 1624 ,, Sara f. ,,

29 Apl.	1627	Schoesetters, Rebecca f. Hendric.
9 Dec.	1615	Schoensetters, Elisabeth f. „
5 Oct.	1613	Schousettes, Joannes f. „
4 Jun.	1582	Scholens, Michil f. Jan.
22 Sep.	1583	Scholle, Joan f. „
30 Jun.	1601	Scholier, Cornelis f. Herman.
4 Jul.	1591	Schollier, Lidia f. „
25 Aug.	1594	„ „ f. „
5 Dec.	1596	„ Pieter f. „
1 Jan.	1677	Scholten, Elizabeth f. Egbert.
30 Jan.	1678	„ Herman f. „
7 Mar.	1683	„ Jacobus f. „
26 Mar.	1684	„ Martha f. „ & Elizabeth.
10 Feb.	1686	„ Catharina f. Jacob & Catharina.
30 Aug.	1696	„ Rutger f. „ & Agnieta.
27 Feb.	1677	Schonevelt, Susanna f. Lovijs.
18 Jun.	1573	Schoonhaghe, Van, ... f. Guillam.
24 Mei	1677	Schorrer, Catarina f. Anthoni.
2 Jan.	1651	Schorstig, Flora f. George.
17 Mar.	1653	Schortztuck, Georgius f. Jurgen.
30 Mei	1613	Schouhareng, Susanna f. Matthias.
21 Apl.	1617	Schouharinck, Lowijse f. „
9 Jun.	1595	Schouter, Joannes f. Jacus.
7 Apl.	1661	Schouteten, Maria f. Christian.
1 Feb.	1663	„ Lydia f. „
8 Apl.	1688	Schowel, Jacobus f. Johannes & Judith.
13 Jul.	1690	„ Johannes f. „ & Judith van Niele.
9 Mar.	1688	Schowell, Jacob f. Andries & Susanna Conijner.
6 Sep.	1612	Schraem, Pieter f. Jan.
17 Nov.	1607	Schram, Maria f. „
12 Feb.	1609	„ Elisabeth f. „
9 Nov.	1609	„ Sara f. Bartholomeus.
6 Jan.	1611	„ Maria f. Hans.
4 Oct.	1614	„ Jacob f. Jan.
19 Jan.	1617	„ Phineas f. „
20 Sep.	1618	„ Magdalena f. „
9 Sep.	1621	„ Anna f. „
25 Jan.	1624	„ Joannes f. „
2 Apl.	1629	„ Sara f. „
30 Jan.	1673	„ Van der, Elizabeth f. Anthoni Matheus.
26 Mei	1573	Schrevel, Peter f. Peter.
16 Jul.	1572	Schrevels, Susanna f. Pieter.
30 Jan.	1575	„ Sara f. „
27 Aug.	1576	„ Pieter f. „
2 Feb.	1577	„ Hester f. „
17 Jan.	1580	„ Gillis f. „
28 Sep.	1578	Schrey-water, Joannes & Oliverius } fi. Oliverius.
15 Feb.	1606	Schreu, Martha f. Pieter.
20 Dec.	1629	Schrijver, de, Abraham f. „ tot Mortlake.
10 Mar.	1633	„ „ Isaac f. „ tot Mortlake.
3 Jan.	1636	„ „ Anna f. „ tot Mortlake.
13 Oct.	1639	„ „ Francis fa. „ tot Mortlake.
8 Jan.	1699	„ Johannes f. Barent & Annetje.
31 Dec.	1704	Schrijvers, Maria f. „ „
1 Dec.	1706	„ Susanna f. „
3 Sep.	1573	Schuddemadde, Marie f. Jacob.
9 Jun.	1588	Schuere, Vau der, Abraham f. Peeter.
2 Jul.	1592	Schueren, „ „ Charles f. Charles.
23 Apl.	1676	Schuijlder, Van, Cornelis f. Anthony.
23 Dec.	1677	„ „ Anneken f. „
22 Oct.	1587	Schuijten, (v. Schutens), Isaac f. Willem.
31 Oct.	1591	„ Bartholomeus & Anna } fi. „
3 Jan.	1628	Schuller, Margareta f. Rutger.
29 Mar.	1586	Schullers, Nathanael f. Joos.
6 Dec.	1685	Schumacker, (v. Schoemaecker), Mary f. Caspar & Elizabeth,
14 Jan.	1649	Schurtstuck, Christina f. Georgius.
25 Aug.	1616	Schut, (v. Schuts), Joannes f. Joris.
25 Jan.	1618	„ Daniel f. Joris.
15 Apl.	1621	„ David f. „
2 Jan.	1625	„ Jacobus f. „
9 Nov.	1630	„ Rachel f. „
16 Aug.	1607	Schute, Maria f. Georgius.
29 Mei	1586	Schutens, (v. Schuyten), Abraham f. Willem.
2 Nov.	1645	Schuts, Sara f. Jockum.
14 Jan.	1599	Schutt, Christynken f. Joris.
16 Mei	1585	Schutten, Susanna f. Willem.
21 Aug.	1698	Scordin, Pieter f. Pieter.
6 Jan.	1609	Sebern, Anthoni f. Jan.
27 Aug.	1611	Sebren, Susanne f. Jan.
21 Nov.	1686	Seckle, Coenraed f. Coenraed & Janneken.
13 Mar.	1659	Seecraft, Katelyne f. Cornelis.
2 Mar.	1656	Seercraft, Lydia f. „
3 Mei	1614	Seetlock, Joannes f. Heijndrick.
20 Oct.	1577	Seghers, Isaack f. Laurens.
23 Jun.	1588	„ Janneken f. Peeter.
4 Dec.	1586	Seijs, Abraham f. Willem.
18 Apl.	1591	„ Abigail f. Jan.
9 Jun.	1616	Sele, Elisabeth f. Hendric.
1 Jul.	1589	Selen, Catharina f. Jan.
22 Jan.	1615	„ Jacob f. Jacob.
3 Jun.	1621	„ Jaquemynken f. „
16 Dec.	1621	„ Maria f. Hendrick.
1 Jul.	1599	Selijns, Isaac f. Arent.
22 Mei	1603	„ Bartholemeus f. Aert.
8 Nov.	1650	Sell, Maria f. Daniel, in St. Olaves kerck in Southvaerck.
18 Apl.	1652	„ Daniel f. Daniel.
23 Oct.	1580	Selot, Abigail f. Jan den Jonghen.
6 Feb.	1612	Seltyns, Aert f. Aert.
18 Nov.	1576	Senegreijn, Sara f. Gheerard.
9 Feb.	1617	Seneschal, Maria & Martha } fæ. Jacob.
27 Jul.	1684	Seneschall, Anna Mary f. Jan & Mary.
3 Feb.	1868	Senft, Antje f. Pieter & Grietje Boerma.
27 Aug.	1871	„ Margaretha Christina f. Pieter & Grietje Boerma.
26 Jul.	1874	„ Abelia f. Pieter & Grietje Boerma.
7 Dec.	1873	„ Elizabeth, geb. 28 Dec., 1867, f. Christoffel & Franciska Bentfort.
20 Dec.	1601	Seps, Anna f. Authonius.
19 Jan.	1612	Serf, de, (v. Cerf), Joannes f. Jan.
4 Jul.	1574	Sergant, Daniel f. Jan.
12 Jun.	1586	Sergeant, Anna f. Hubrecht.
1 Mar.	1579	Sergiant, Elizabet f. Hermes.
8 Dec.	1583	Sergiants, Elizabeth f. „
7 Oct.	1582	„ Sara f. Jacob.
12 Sep.	1585	Seroen, Joannes f. Jan.
23 Oct.	1586	„ Janneken f. „
2 Apl.	1601	„ Abraham f. „
31 Mar.	1806	Serres, Catharine Louisa f. Hendrik Johan George & Catharina Johanna van Bagelgem, in de stad Cork, in Ireland.
23 Aug.	1807	„ Henry John George f. Hendrik Johan George & Catharina Johanna van Bagelgem.

7 Dec.	1589	Seruijns, Maria f. Pieter.
14 Mar.	1830	Setzer, Rosina f. Carel & Maria Vergeeth.
5 Jun.	1836	„ Dorothea f. Johan Karl & Maria Vergils.
9 Sep.	1574	Severs, Agnees f. Jan.
26 Jul.	1590	Sheijten, (v. Suten), Jacob f. Willem.
25 Sep.	1692	Shorter, Elisabeth f. Jeronymus.
6 Jan.	1696	Shovell, Claudius f. Johannes.
8 Oct.	1690	Shutleworth, Catharina f. Thomas & Catharina.
1 Dec.	1633	Sichen, Van den, Isaack f. Jan.
26 Aug.	1688	Sickley, (v. Sierkelyck), Johanna f. Coenraet & Johanna.
11 Nov.	1613	Sickraet, Cornelius f. Cornelis.
21 Mei	1620	„ Jacobus f. „
15 Jun.	1623	Sickracht, Henricus f. „
11 Aug.	1639	Sickraet, Daniel f. ....
26 Sep.	1641	Sijckraet, Anna f. Cornelis.
1 Sep.	1644	Sickraet, Abigail f. „
19 Mei	1650	„ Cornelis f. „
6 Nov.	1653	„ Maria f. „
16 Mar.	1617	Sicrat, Susanna f. „
27 Mei	1694	Sierkelijck, Anna f. Coenract & Johanna.
27 Nov.	1870	Sieverdink, Johan Adam f. Hendrick Jan & Christina Geertruida Margaretha Best.
27 „	„	„ Anna Maria Frederika, geb. 3 Sep. ......, f. Hendrick Jan & Christina Geertruida Margaretha Best.
31 Aug.	1873	Silverdink, Gerrit Jan f. Hendrick Jan & Christina Geertruida Margaretha Best.
21 Mei	1609	Sieverlynx, David f. David.
5 Dec.	1596	Sijbbola, Laureus f. Mijnaert.
17 Dec.	1598	Sijders, Elizabeth f. Pieter.
29 Jun.	1595	Sijluart, Joannes f. Ambrosius.
25 Sep.	1575	Sijmons, (v. Simons), Isaac f. Michiel.
11 Aug.	1577	„ Rebecca f. Michiel.
13 Nov.	1597	„ Agneete f. Willem.
16 Nov.	1613	„ Abigail f. Hans.
25 Feb.	1621	Sijon, (v. Sions), Vincent f. Fransoija, Vincentsz.
24 Apl.	1808	Sikkes, Sikkes f. Jan & Gezina Jacobs.
23 Feb.	1612	Silberlinck, Anna f. David.
26 Dec.	1614	Silberlincx, Susanna f. „
5 Sep.	1596	Silvoort, Abraham f. Ambrosius.
14 Dec.	1600	„ Anna f. „
26 Aug.	1573	Simoens, (v. Symoens), Abraham f. Michiel.
2 Mar.	1572	Simons, Abraham f. Hans.
25 Apl.	1591	„ Joannes f. Willem.
17 Jun.	1593	„ Carolus f. Isaac.
11 Feb.	1694	„ Marcus, bejaart jonghman.
18 Apl.	1619	Simson, Johanna f. Tobias.
12 Dec.	1799	Simpson, Ann f. Thomas & Ann Becket.
25 Mar.	1801	„ Thomas f. „ & Ann Becket.
8 Sep.	1804	„ Joseph f. „ & Ann Becket Bray.
27 Mei	1809	„ Eliza Hullman f. „ & Ann Becket.
18 Apl.	1811	„ William Henry f. „ & Ann Becket Bray.
22 Apl.	1813	„ Maria Charlotte f. „ & Ann Becket Bray.
26 Mar.	1598	Sina, Van, Fredericus f. Hans.
20 Apl.	1599	„ „ Johannes f. „
7 Jun.	1747	Sinksen, Annaatje f. Jan & Gerretje Gerrets.
27 Apl.	1589	Sinnicke, Van, Sara f. Adam.
11 Apl.	1619	Sion, (v. Sijons), Sara f. Jan.
18 Mei	1623	„ Susanna f. Jan.
14 Aug.	1631	„ Isaack f. Anthony.
21 Jun.	1702	Sipper, Bastiaan Salomon f. Abraham & Maria.
10 Sep.	1704	Sippel, Abraham f. Abraham & Maria.
31 Dec.	1645	Sittard, Henricus f. Henric Pauwels.
7 Sep.	1617	Sitthart, Jacobus f. Hendric.
17 Mei	1619	„ Petrus f. „ Pauwels.
2 Dec.	1688	Skinner, Elizabeth f. Albertus.
30 Aug.	1691	„ Albertus f. „
8 Mar.	1702	„ Elizabeth f. „
31 Dec.	1693	„ Anna f. Alexander.
29 Nov.	1702	Skiner, Johannes f. Alexander.
24 Mar.	1700	Skinner, Alexander f. „
10 Oct.	1736	Slaar, Elisabeth f. Pieter & Susanna Dochsen.
16 Dec.	1599	Slachoteen, Abraham f. Bernaert.
26 Apl.	1702	Slauwen, Johannes f. David & Judick.
13 Jan.	1638	Slechtriem, (v. Sleijtreme), Maria f. Hendrick.
18 Feb.	1649	Sleehagen, Maria f. Johan.
30 Mei	1647	„ f. Hans.
21 Jun.	1579	Sleijpe, Abraham f. Marten.
23 Dec.	1576	Sleijpen, Johannes f. „
7 Jan.	1582	„ Jeremias f. „
26 „	1584	„ Jacob f. posthumus Marten.
20 Jun.	1633	Sleijtreme, (v. Slechtriem), Elisabeth f. Hendrick.
25 Oct.	1635	Sleijtriem, Margarita f. Hendrick.
27 Mar.	1631	„ Anna f. „
11 Jan.	1620	Sleijtrienne, Hendrick f. „
27 Jul.	1656	Slingelant, Van, Elisabeth f. Simeon.
11 Dec.	1659	„ „ Paulus f. Simon.
11 Mei	1662	„ „ Geertruit f. „
1 „	1664	„ „ Baerthout f. „ & Jacomina Vaens.
13 Jan.	1666	„ „ Sijmon f. Simon & Jacomina.
26 Sep.	1813	Slingerlandt, Jan, geb. in Essequibo indo West Indien.
13 Jun.	1714	Slotemaker, Abraham f. Louis & Maria.
20 Jan.	1716	„ Isak f. „ &
21 Jul.	1824	Sluijs, Van der, David f. Jasper & Maria Cornelia Roghé.
3 Jan.	1602	„ Maria f. Gheeraert.
8 Mar.	1607	Sluijsen, der, Heyndrick f. „
1 Mei	1610	„ „ Susanna f. Gheeraert.
7 Oct.	1604	„ „ Samuel f. „
2 Aug.	1601	Smaistres, de, Judith f. Jacus.
23 Jul.	1758	Smallaan, Cornelius Wilhelmus f. Cornelis & Anna Pastre.
17 Aug.	1760	„ Samuel f. Cornelis & Anna Pastre.
20 Mar.	1763	„ Sara f. „ & Anna Pastre.
12 Aug.	1764	„ Anna f. „ & Anna Pastre.
2 Nov.	1606	Smeedts. (v. Smit, etc.), Sara f. Cornelis.
29 Mar.	1619	Smeelck, Anna f. Hendrick.
5 Oct.	1628	Smeeleke, Anna f. ..
22 Aug.	1555	Smet, (v. Smit), de, Joannes f. Guiliaen.
19 Oct.	1589	„ Joannes f. Jan.
17 Mar.	1611	Smetpond, des, Jacobuyne f. Bartholomeus.

5 Sep. 1630   **Smielks**, Sara f. Hendrick.
12 Jan. 1623   **Smile**, Jacobus f. Hendric.
4 Mar. 1621   **Smilck**, Thomas f. „
6 Jun. 1591   **Smidt**, de, Maria f. Pieter.
11 Sep. 1627   **Smidts**, „ Stephanus f. Steven.
27 Sep. 1573   **Smit**, „ (**v. Smet**), Abraham f. Jan.
8 Mei 1608   „ Pieter f. Jan.
22 Mar. 1696   „ de, Maria f. „ & Maria.
24 Dec. 1587   „ Hendrick f. Hendrick.
16 Jul. 1592   „ Janneken f. „
12 Aug. 1593   „ Abraham f. Aernout.
30 Apl. 1626   „ Willem f. Abraham.
6 „ 1628   „ Abraham f. „
5 Jul. 1629   „ „ f. posthumus Abraham.
9 Aug. 1629   „ (**v. Smith**), Sara f. Steven.
22 Jul. 1632   „ de, Johannes f. „
2 Aug. 1635   „ „ Stephannsf. „
2 Mei 1638   „ „ Mattheus f. Anthonius.
29 Jun. 1764   „ Lodewijk f. Hendrik & Christina Olijf.
31 Mei 1696   **Smits**, Johannes f. Johannes.
22 Feb. 1680   **Smith**, Anna Catarina f. Goswinus.
15 Apl. 1683   „ Elizabeth f. „ & Elisabeth Sanders.
15 Nov. 1685   „ Goswinus f. „
12 Jul. 1640   „ de, David f. Steven.
30 Aug. 1668   „ Maria f. Abram.
18 Sep. 1670   „ „ Johanna f. Abraham.
6 Jul. 1679   „ Christina f. Willem.
27 Feb. 1681   „ Elizabeth f. „
22 Mar. 1682   „ Willem f. Willem & Elisabeth.
25 „ 1683   „ Thomas f. „
27 Dec. 1685   „ Daniel f. „ „
9 Jan. 1687   „ Pieter f. „ „
1 Aug. 1694   „ Johannes f. Johannes.
16 Sep. 1801   „ James Cahais f. Thomas Gregory & Mary Elizabeth Fowler.
25 Jan. 1807   „ Elizabeth f. Thomas Gregory & Mary Elizabeth Fowler.
4 Jul. 1852   „ Ormond Edmund f. Ormond Edmund & Jansje Jansz.
30 Apl. 1854   „ George Cotton f. Ormond Edmund & Jansje Jansz.
10 „ 1857   „ Jeannette Christina f. Ormond Edmund & Jansje Jansz.
6 Mar. 1859   „ Agatha Henriette f. Ormond Edmund & Jansje Jansz.
17 „ 1861   „ Laura Johanna f. Ormond Edmund & Jansje Jansz.
12 Jul. 1868   „ Elizabeth Cornelia Maria f. Adrianus Marianus & Caroline Jane White O'Donald.
27 Mar. 1580   **Smolders**, Daniel f. Cornelis.
19 Aug. 1571   **Smulders**, Abraham f. „
10 Nov. 1850   **Snel**, Henry Daniel Rickier f. Hendrik Daniel & Alice Price.
30 Jul. 1690   **Snellert**, Arnoldus f. Leendert & Jannetje van Leuwen.
8 Dec. 1577   **Snepgadt**, Joanna f. Gillis.
23 Apl. 1576   **Snepgat**, Abraham f. „
22 Mei 1586   **Sneps**, Sara f. Marten.
10 Oct. 1588   „ Maria f. „
10 Sep. 1587   „ Catheline f. „
21 Dec. 1589   „ David f. „
23 Mei 1591   „ Joannes f. „
10 Sep. 1592   „ Catharina f. „
16 Feb. 1595   **Snider**, Hester f. Pieter.
7 Jan. 1593   **Snijders**, Petrus f. „

19 Dec. 1596   **Snijders**, Moses f. Pieter.
19 Feb. 1601   „ Sara f. „
19 Sep. 1602   „ Jacobus f. „
12 Jan. 1612   **Snoeck**, Mechline f. Hans.
11 Jul. 1613   „ Susanna f. „
20 Apl. 1620   **Soburn**, Joannes f. Jan.
1 Jun. 1589   **Soeck**, de, Jacobus f. Jacques.
21 Jan. 1606   **Soen**, Maria f. Pieter.
10 Apl. 1608   „ Johannes f. „
17 Jun. 1610   „ Abraham f. „
21 Jul. 1616   „ Susanna f. „
23 Apl. 1629   „ Elisabeth f. „
25 Dec. 1630   „ Catharina f. „
16 „ 1632   „ Petrus f. „
19 Feb. 1635   „ Johannes f. „
26 Mar. 1637   „ Elizabeth f. „
18 Mar. 1627   **Soene**, Jacob f. „
21 Jun. 1612   **Soenen**, Catharina f. „
15 Mei 1614   „ Joanna f. „
10 Jan. 1608   **Soenwens**, Abraham f. Abraham.
23 Sep. 1578   **Soillot**, Joannes f. Jans des Jungoen.
10 Aug. 1589   **Solderbek**, Van, Abraham f. Lowys.
18 Apl. 1591   **Solderbeke**, „ Salomon f. „
28 Apl. 1608   **Soleijns**, „ f. Arent.
16 Mar. 1617   **Solen**, Elizabeth f. Jacob.
15 Nov. 1618   „ Hendrick f. Hendrick.
23 Jan. 1597   **Solens**, Abraham f. Arent.
27 Oct. 1594   **Solijns**, Sara f. „
8 Mei 1687   **Solingen**, Van, Dirck f. Josua & Aletla.
20 Mei 1586   **Solt**, Van, Susanna f. Hans.
25 Jun. 1587   „ „ Elizabeth f. Jan.
6 Oct. 1588   „ „ Maria f. Hans.
7 Jul. 1588   „ „ Elizabeth f. „
15 Mar. 1590   „ „ Anna f. „
12 Jul. 1590   „ „ Marie f. „
9 Jan. 1592   „ „ Abraham f. Jan.
10 Dec. „   „ „ Willem f. Hans.
14 Oct. 1593   „ „ Maria f. Jan.
12 Jan. 1595   „ „ Paulus f. Hans.
9 Mei 1596   „ „ David f. „
20 Jun. 1596   „ „ Isaack f. Jan.
20 Aug. 1598   „ „ Daniel f. Hans.
15 Aug. 1624   „ „ Elisabet f. Abraham.
12 Mar. 1626   „ „ Joannes f. „
28 Oct. 1627   „ „ Maria f. „
7 Feb. 1630   „ „ Abraham f. „
16 Jul. 1676   „ „ Isaac f. „
13 Jun. 1675   **Sondergelt**, Willem f. Jacob.
16 Jul. 1676   „ Jacobus f. „
30 Sep. 1677   „ Joannes f. Jacob.
19 Nov. 1679   „ Jacob f. „
12 Nov. 1680   „ Isaac f. „
3 Apl. 1682   „ Pieter f. „
5 Oct. 1684   „ Thomas f. „
6 Apl. 1681   „ Dirck f. Dirck.
30 Jul. 1682   „ Willem f. „
9 Oct. 1687   „ Wilhelmus f. „
17 Feb. 1605   **Sonnick**, de, Samuel f. Joris.
15 Oct. 1587   **Sorhier**, Abraham f. Charles.
13 Sep. 1579   **Sorock**, Albrecht f. Albrechts.
11 Oct. 1591   **Souwijn**, Jacop f. Denijs.
20 Nov. 1651   **Sowden**, Jacobus f. Jan & Maria.
25 Sep. 1689   **Sowell**, Maria f. Peter & Maria.
5 Jan. 1591   **Sowijn**, Jacob f. Denijs.
3 Mar. 1661   **Spauwen**, Van, Elisabet f. Pieter.
14 Feb. 1664   „ „ Hendrick f. Petrus Anetta.
5 Sep. 1585   **Spe**, Susanna f. Jacob.

22 Aug.	1596	Spee, Jonathan f. Jacob.
29 Dec.	1689	Speck, Johannes f. Albert & Sara Barbe.
30 Aug.	1691	„ Abraham f. „ & Sarah.
16 Feb.	1623	Speckmeijer, Lucas f. Jacob.
24 Aug.	1620	„ Daniel f. „
18 Oct.	1590	Speckaert, Maria f. Hans.
25 Sep.	1575	Speeckaert, Elisabeth f. Jan.
25 Jun.	1587	„ Johannes f. „
20 Jul.	1589	„ Maria f. Hans.
26 Dec.	1591	„ Esther f. Hans.
30 „	1593	„ Zacharias f. Hans.
24 Feb.	1577	„ Sara f. Jan.
23 Jan.	1582	Speeckardtz, Anna f. Joannes.
20 Sep.	1584	Speeckardt, Pieter f. Jan.
12 Jul.	1573	Speekaerts, Maijken f. „
16 Jan.	1584	Speelhovel, Pieter f. Pieter.
30 Nov.	1609	Speelhoven, Sara f. „
24 Nov.	1610	„ „ f. „
28 Apl.	1611	„ Robert f. „
22 Mar.	1601	Speijts, Joanna f. Jacob.
1 Mei	1634	Spetebroot, Jacobus f. Gillis.
14 Aug.	1636	„ Judith f. „
8 Jul.	1638	„ Elisabeth f. „
4 Sep.	1651	„ Maria f. „
7 Oct.	1649	Spettebrot, Cataleina f. „
27 „	1652	„ Maria f. „
8 Mar.	1579	Spier, Van, Susanna f. Lowys.
11 Apl.	1669	„ Daniel { fi. Daniel. & Paulus
7 Jul.	1672	Spiers, Elizabeth f. Daniell & Maria.
22 Apl.	1572	Spiere, Van, David f. Jan.
25 Mar.	1578	„ „ Abigail f. Lowijs.
15 Mei	1586	„ „ Sara f. Hans.
9 Jul.	1587	„ „ Jacob f. Pieter.
3 Mar.	1588	„ „ Abraham f. Hans.
12 Oct.	1589	„ Isaac f. „
11 Mar.	1593	„ Van der, Susanna f. „
9 Apl.	1598	„ „ Joannes f. „
16 Sep.	1599	„ „ Susanna f. „
19 Nov.	1590	„ „ f. Steven.
29 Mar.	1619	Spieren, Van, Jacob f. „
29 Oct.	1587	Spierinck, Catharina f. Cornelis.
24 Feb.	1622	Spies, Maria f. Wilbert.
27 Mar.	1625	„ Barbara f. Wilbert.
24 Jun.	1623	Spijs, Joanna f. Wilbord.
16 Nov.	1595	Spoltman, Judith f. Nicolas.
19 Sep.	1592	Spooltman, Thomas f. „
21 Mei	1598	Spoormaecker, Ghijsbrecht f. Reynier.
19 Apl.	1601	Spormaeker, Elizabeth f. „
18 Dec.	1603	Spormaker, Eve f. „
20 Oct.	1717	Spont, Maria f. Simon & Maria Terpijn.
31 Mei	1719	„ Rebecca f. „ & Mary Therpine.
17 Jan.	1647	Sporwerdt, Elisabeth f. Jan.
27 Feb.	1684	Spree, Rebecca f. Pieter.
15 Dec.	1697	Spreew, Ruth f. „
19 Sep.	1686	Spreeuw, Adriana f. „
2 Mei	1689	„ Pieter f. „ & Elisabeth.
24 Sep.	1690	„ Sara f. „
5 Dec.	1694	„ Peter f. „
5 Aug.	1677	Spreu, Elizabeth f. „
12 Nov.	1690	Spriet, Van der, Willem f. Johannes.
10 Aug.	1687	Spritt, „ „ Johannes f. „ & Anna.
8 Jan.	1576	Sprock, Anna f. Albrecht.
8 Apl.	1578	„ Johannes f. Albertus.
5 Mar.	1581	„ „ f. „
20 Oct.	1583	„ Henrick f. „
14 Aug.	1586	„ Anna f. „

27 Feb.	1677	Spron, Van der, Johannes f. Willem.
29 Nov.	1573	Spurckels, Topias { fi. Denijs. & Sara
4 Nov.	1574	„ Gedeon f. Denijs.
5 Nov.	1577	„ Petrus f. „
30 Jan.	1592	Staelens, (v. Stalens). Jonas f. Arent.
27 Mar.	1592	„ Helias f. Anthony.
23 Mei	1596	„ Susanna f. „
1 Nov.	1593	„ Jacomynteken f. Abraham.
11 Jan.	1596	„ Sara f. Arent.
6 Apl.	1600	„ Jacobus f. Arent.
28 Mar.	1591	Staelpaert, Elizabeth f. Arnout.
16 Aug.	1599	Staene, Van der, Maeyken f. ...., oudt synde outrent 21 jaer.
29 Mar.	1590	Staes, Sara f. Willem.
22 Aug.	1585	Staat, Abraham f. Adolphs.
24 Dec.	1587	Staet, Anna f. Adolf.
13 Mei	1583	„ Daniel f. „
28 Jul.	1594	„ Samuel f. „
14 Nov.	1591	Staffemij, Van. (v. Stafné), Janneken f. Lucas.
6 Jan.	1594	Staffenaij, „ Joannes f. Hans.
23 Nov.	1580	Staffenj, „ Janneken f. „
18 Jul.	1602	Staffert, Catharyne f. Denys.
24 Jul.	1592	Stafné, Van, Catharina f. Lucas.
28 Apl.	1647	Staigart, Johanna f. Jan.
29 Aug.	1602	Staimer. Robert f. David.
21 Jun.	1640	Stale, Willem f. Jan.
24 Aug.	1587	Stalens, (v. Staelens), Sara f. Arent.
2 Nov.	1589	„ Janneken f. Arent.
29 Jul.	1593	„ Daniel f. Arnout.
28 Mei	1598	„ Abraham f. Arent.
23 Jan.	1603	„ Joannes f. „
1 Oct.	1604	„ Sara f. Arnout.
9 Aug.	1590	„ Elisabeth f. Anthoni.
24 Feb.	1594	„ David f. „
7 Mei	1598	„ Sara f. Pieter.
26 Oct.	1600	„ Jacomynken f. „
4 Mei	1592	Stalpaert, Joannes f. Aernout.
28 Nov.	1596	„ Petrus f. Arnout.
16 Sep.	1593	„ Abraham f. „
23 Dec.	1599	„ Sara f. „
6 Apl.	1617	„ Petrus f. Thomas,
23 Mei	1619	„ Johannes f. „
30 Mar.	1575	Stalpart, Isaack f. Arnout.
7 Mei	1598	„ Joannes f. „
2 Sep.	1591	Stampere, de, David f. Anthonj.
2 Feb.	1604	Stampoet, Arnoult f. posthumus Arnouldt.
13 Jul.	1690	Stamproy, Hermannus f. Johannes & Helena.
14 Oct.	1699	Standaert, Anna f. Willem & Catharina Gronen.
31 Aug.	1698	Standert, Catharina f. Willem & Catharina Gronen.
18 Sep.	1700	„ William f. William & Catharina.
14 Oct.	1713	„ Adolphus f. „ & „
28 Feb.	1716	„ Thomas f. „ & „
29 Jun.	1604	Stanier, Johanna f. David.
27 Oct.	1605	„ Jaques f. „
29 Mar.	1573	Stapaert, Daneile f. Jan.
1 Dec.	1588	Stappaerts, Abraham f. Heynelrick.
1 Dec.	1588	„ Abraham f. Herman.
18 Apl.	1591	Stappaert, Joannes f. „
12 Oct.	1606	„ Isaac f. „
10 Mar.	1611	„ f. „
25 Apl.	1619	„ Herman f. Abraham.
2 „	1583	Stappardts, Susanna f. Jan.

14 Jan. 1588 **Stappen,** Jeremias f. Wouter.
12 Oct. 1589 ,, Abraham f. ,,
19 Mar. 1592 ,, Isaac f. ,,
27 Jan. 1594 ,, Wouter } fi. Wouter.
& Catelyne
13 Jul. 1673 **Stark,** (v. Stirke), Susanna f. Willem.
28 Jun. 1573 **Staumiers,** Susanna f. Adriaenken.
22 Feb. 1607 **Stavelen, Van,** ,, f. Carel.
9 Mei 1602 **Staveren, Van,** Emanuel f. ,,
25 Dec. 1764 **Steehouwer,** Jan Willem f. Jan & Elizabeth Verbeck.
19 Jan. 1634 **Steen, Van den,** (v. **Steene**), Maria f. Paulus, tot Mortlake.
21 Dec. 1635 ,, ,, ,, Debora f. Paulus, tot Mortlake.
1 Jul. 1638 ,, ,, ,, Jonathan f. Paulus, tot Mortlake.
11 Sep. 1642 ,, ,, ,, Daniel f. Paulus, tot Mortlake.
13 Mar. 1692 ,, ,, ,, Pieter f. Bartholomeus & Francyntje Marlo.
21 Mei 1693 ,, ,, ,, Petrus f. Bartholomeus & Francyntje Marlo.
4 Aug. 1695 ,, ,, ,, Philippus f. Bartholomeus & Francyntje Marlo.
7 Feb. 1697 ,, ,, ,, Elisabeth f. Bartholomeus & Francyntje Marlo.
7 Mei 1699 ,, ,, ,, Fransen f. Bartholomeus & Fransin Marlo.
2 Mar. 1701 ,, ,, ,, Philip f. Bartholomeus & Francyntje Marlo.
27 Jul. 1703 ,, ,, ,, Johannes f. Bartholomeus & Francyntje Marlo.
24 Jun. 1591 **Steenart,** Cornelis f. Cornelis.
11 Jul. 1611 **Steenbergen, Van,** Elizabeth f. Jan.
11 Feb. 1613 ,, ,, Joannes f. ,,
31 Oct. 1616 **Steenberghe,** Isaac f. ,,
17 Aug. 1628 **Steene, Van de,** (v. **Steen**), Abigail f. Paulus, tot Mortlake.
4 Apl. 1630 ,, ,, der, Paulus f. Paulus, tot Mortlake.
27 Feb. 1632 ,, ,, ,, Catherine f. Paulus, tot Mortlake.
6 Aug. 1701 **Steenhuisen,** Johannes f. Hubert & Johanna van der Stoof.
6 Jan. 1695 **Steenkolen, Van,** Olof f. Adrianus.
27 Sep. 1696 ,, ,, Cornelia f. ,, & Catharina.
30 Jan. 1698 ,, Isbrant f. ,, & Catharina.
10 Nov. 1588 **Steenput,** Elizabeth f. Pieter.
20 Apl. 1589 **Steenstrate, Van der,** Marie f. Guiliame.
5 Sep. 1591 **Steenstraten,** ,, ,, Tobias f. ,,
28 Nov. 1591 **Steenvaert,** Daniel f. Everaerdt.
12 Nov. 1587 **Steenvers,** Daniel f. ,,
4 Jan. 1590 ,, Jonas f. ,,
2 Feb. 1615 **Steenweigen,** Abraham f. Jan.
4 Jan. 1702 **Steinnaw,** Gabriel } fi. Gabriel & Maria.
& ....
4 Oct. 1590 **Stel,** Maria f. Hans.
18 Apl. 1609 **Stelde, Van der,** (v. **Stelt & Stilt**), Abraham f. Pauwels.
29 Aug. 1847 **Stelling,** Lucia Louisa f. Gustav Ludwig & Maria Regina Christina Hillen.
13 Jan. 1850 ,, Maria Regina Christina f. Gustav Ludwig & Maria Regina Christina Hillebrand.

17 Nov. 1850 **Stelling,** Gerhard Heinrick f. Gustav Ludwig & Maria Regina Christina Hillebrand.
2 Jan. 1853 ,, Marianna Christina f. Gustav Ludwig & Maria Regina Christina Hillebrand.
8 Apl. 1855 ,, Alma f. Gustav Ludwig & Maria Regina Christina Hillebrand.
7 Jun. 1857 ,, Froukje Elisabeth f. Gustav Ludwig & Maria Regina Christina Hillebrand.
10 Apl. 1859 ,, Mathilde Maria f. Gustav Ludwig & Maria Regina Christina Hillebrand.
29 Sep. 1861 ,, Johan Casper f. Gustav Ludwig & Maria Regina Christina Hillebrand.
28 Apl. 1872 ,, Ann Christina f. Gustav Ludwig & Maria Regina Christina Schulze.
25 Mei 1873 ,, Ludewig Ernst f. Ludewig Gustav Ernst & Maria Regina Christina Schulze.
1 Jan. 1587 **Stelt,** (v. **Stelde**, etc.), Hester f. Hans.
21 Nov. 1596 ,, Van der, Elizabeth f. Lieven.
25 Apl. 1593 **Stelte,** Susanna f. Hans.
22 Apl. 1593 ,, Van der, Abraham f. Lieven.
9 Apl. 1598 ,, ,, ,, Debora f. ,, f. Willems.
6 Apl. 1600 ,, ,, ,, Isaac f. ,,
14 Oct. 1596 ,, Janneken f. Matheus.
13 Nov. 1597 ,, Joannes f. ,,
26 Jan. 1612 ,, Andreas f. ,,
17 Nov. 1614 ,, Joannes f. posthumus Matheus.
10 Nov. 1611 **Sten, Van der,** Geertruyt f. Alexander.
15 Feb. 1624 **Stephens,** Joannes f. Jan.
14 Jan. 1691 ,, Stephon f. Pieter.
16 Jul. 1572 **Sterck, de,** (v. **Stirck**), ... f. Pieter.
26 Mar. 1611 **Stere, Van der,** Balthasar f. Jasper.
3 Jan. 1609 **Steren,** ,, Joris f. ,,
21 Dec. 1606 **Steeren, Van,** Maria f. Gaspar.
13 Mar. 1586 **Steevers,** Abraham f. Everaert.
20 Oct. 1605 **Sterlinck,** Clara f. Jasper.
16 Oct. 1645 **Sterpijn,** Francois f. Jan.
31 Oct. 1585 **Steuperaert,** Henricus f. Mr. Pieter.
7 Dec. 1572 **Stevens,** Anna f. Ritsaert.
21 Nov. 1574 ,, Daniel f. Rutgheer.
12 Jul. 1576 ,, Anna f. ,,
10 Aug. 1578 ,, David f. ,,
6 Mei 1581 ,, Abigail f. Rutger.
10 Mar. 1583 ,, Sara f. ,,
13 Mar. 1586 ,, Joannes f. ,,
3 Jul. 1588 ,, Anna f. Richaert.
14 Mar. 1591 ,, Susanna f. ,,
11 Jul. 1602 ,, Elizabeth f. Rutgaert.
10 Feb. 1605 ,, Stephanus f. ,,
4 Jun. 1605 ,, Stevens f. Jan.
6 Mar. 1608 ,, Sara f. Rutger.
14 Nov. 1619 ,, Johannes f. Jan.
9 Jul. 1621 ,, Enoch f. ,,
31 Oct. 1626 ,, Sarah f. ,,
25 Dec. 1629 ,, Judith f. ,,
13 Oct. 1642 ,, Maria f. Richaerd.
19 Mar. 1681 ,, Jannetje f. Jan & Jannetje.
2 Feb. 1645 **Stijjaert,** Joannes f. Jan & Susanna.
7 Jul. 1609 **Stiler,** Cecelia f. Joris & Maria Perpet.
18 Mei 1577 **Stillekens,** Sara f. Jans.
19 Jan. 1634 **Stilo,** Wilhelmus f. Gerard.

7 Mar.	1581	**Stilt**, Van der, (v. **Stelte**), Samuel f. Lieven.
13 Oct.	1594	„ „ „ Sara f. Lieven, fs. Willem.
10 Feb.	1572	**Stilte**, Esther f. Mattheus.
17 Aug.	1574	„ Mattheus f. „
13 Dec.	1575	„ „ f. „
3 Nov.	1594	„ „ f. „
25 Nov.	1599	„ Andries f. „
6 Jun.	1602	„ Abraham f. „
27 Sep.	1607	„ Mattheus f. „
10 Dec.	1608	„ Ester f. „
21 Jan.	1610	„ Guillelmusf. „
18 Jun.	1613	„ Joannes f. „
7 Dec.	1596	„ Sara f. Philip.
7 Sep.	1600	„ Hester f. Ezechiel.
26 Nov.	1592	**Stilter**, de, Abigail f. Philips.
3 Apl.	1599	„ „ Elizabeth f. Philleps.
29 Sep.	1587	**Stiltere**, „ Ezechiel f. Philip.
21 Apl.	1589	„ „ Sara f. „
20 Dec.	1590	„ „ Susanna f. „
7 Jul.	1594	„ „ Esther f. „
23 Jul.	1676	**Stirke**, (v. **Stark**), Catarina f. Willem & Isabella.
21 Dec.	1604	**Stocks**, Jacques f. Ritsaert.
23 Jul.	1592	**Stoffaet**, Sara f. Rogier.
28 Jan.	1599	**Stoffoerd**, Isaac f. „
31 Oct.	1585	**Stoffoet**, Abraham f. „
25 Dec.	1589	**Stoffoot**, „ f. „
6 Dec.	1601	**Stoffs**, Susanna f. Richard.
22 Jul.	1855	**Stohrer**, Elizabeth f. Johann Andreas & Christina Maria van der Post.
18 Jul.	1858	„ William f. Johann Andreas & Christina Maria van der Post.
9 Sep.	1860	„ Henry George f. Johann Andreas & Christina Maria van der Post.
29 Mar.	1863	„ Albert f. Johann Andreas & Christina Maria van der Post.
12 Apl.	1579	**Stoll**, Hester f. Hans.
25 Apl.	1602	**Stomphous**, Elizabeth f. Balthaser.
11 Mar.	1604	**Stomphoust**, Anna f. Balthazar.
29 Feb.	1624	**Stone**, Anthonius f. Marcus.
14 Oct.	1604	**Stoppaert**, Joannes f. Herman.
26 Aug.	1593	**Storm**, Sara f. Hans.
16 Mei	1821	**Straalman**, Johannes Jacob geb. 11 Oct., 1813; Thomas Richard, geb. 9 Dec., 1815; George Eduard, geb. 25 Jan., 1820. } fl. Dirk Joannes & Abigail Constantia Bakker Heshuizen.
17 Jun.	1593	**Strampro**, Petrus f. Jean.
8 Jan.	1599	„ Pieter f. Jan.
15 Feb.	1596	**Stramproe**, Daniel f. „
2 Jun.	1594	**Stramproo**, Jacobus f. „
30 Jun.	1586	**Straseele**, Van, Elias f. Christiaen.
28 Feb.	1585	**Strazoele**, „ Jonathan f. „
26 Mar.	1587	**Straeten**, Van der, Abraham f. Guliamme.
2 Jul.	1592	„ „ „ Susanna f. Philip.
15 Nov.	1593	„ „ „ Joannes f. Hans.
23 Mar.	1595	„ „ „ Susanna f. „
17 Dec.	1682	**Stratteen**, Elizabeth f. Hendrick.
16 Aug.	1685	**Strattoun**, Anna Chatarina f. Hendrick & Maria.
16 Nov.	1687	„ Johannes f. Hendrick & Maria.

12 Aug.	1804	**Strick**, van Linschoten, Andrea Henrietta Elizabeth f. François Albert Leonard & Elizabeth Pool.
23 Mar.	1806	„ „ „ Albert Andries f. F. A. L. & E. Pool.
23 Feb.	1595	**Striep**, Van, (v. **ver Strepen**), Abraham f. Wouter.
6 Nov.	1599	**Strijde**, Marie f. Jan.
24 Jun.	1601	„ Joannes f. „
22 Apl.	1621	**Strijp**, Maria & Ester } fac. Abraham.
21 Jul.	1633	„ Van, Johanna f. Jan.
1 Mei	1642	„ „ Samuel f. „
11 Feb.	1638	**Strijpe**, Rebecca f. „
28 Aug.	1631	**Strijpen**,, Esther f. „
12 Dec.	1661	**Stringer**, Caterina f. Frans & Margriete.
25 Apl.	1619	**Stripe**, Van, Maria f. Abraham & Maria.
30 Mar.	1606	**Stromphuys**, (v. **Stomphous**), Adam f. Barthasar.
23 Jun.	1811	**Stulen**, Louisa Charlotta f. Gerrit Nack & Louisa Catharina Veremet.
25 Apl.	1813	„ Gerard Louis f. Gerrit Nack & Louisa Catharina Veremet.
28 Feb.	1580	**Stuppers**, Elizabeth f. Jan.
10 Jan.	1697	**Stutser**, Petrus f. Peter.
9 Apl.	1699	**Stutzer**, Elizabeth f. Pieter.
15 Sep.	1700	**Stutser**, Albertus f. „
19 Jul.	1702	„ Thomas f. „
8 Dec.	1706	„ Elisabeth f. „
9 Jan.	1709	„ Johannes f. „
6 Feb.	1712	„ Rutger f. „ & Elisabeth.
25 Nov.	1716	„ Maria f. „
3 Aug.	1783	**Suck**, Anna f. Jacobus Ludovicus & Hester.
30 Mar.	1786	„ Hester f. „ & „ Wilkins.
31 Jan.	1374	**Sughere**, de, Elisabeth f. Steven.
17 Jul.	1571	**Suijs**, Susanna f. Michiel.
30 Nov.	1572	„ Sara f. „
2 Sep.	1576	„ Johannes f. „
12 Jun.	1580	„ Sara f. „
11 Mar.	1689	**Suljard**, Godart f. Thomas & Johanna, geboorne Baronesse van Leefdael, tot St. James.
21 Nov.	1596	**Sumijfers**, Joannes f. Willem.
23 Feb.	1589	**Suten**, (v. **Sheyten**), Jacobus f. Willem.
22 Mei	1722	**Sutton**, Sara f. Timothy & Mary.
3 Oct.	1722	„ Catharina f. „ & „
30 Aug.	1723	„ Mary f. „ & „
17 Sep.	1725	„ Philip de Werth f. „ & „
24 Aug.	1726	„ Ann f. „ & „
7 Aug.	1727	„ Catharina f. „ & „
3 Oct.	1728	„ Timothy f. „ & „
11 Jan.	1731	„ Hannah f. „ & „
28 Mar.	1805	**Suwerkrop**, Anna Margaretha f. Johann Brahn & Lamke Bauwerman.
28 Jan.	1807	„ John Hillery f. Johann Bruhn & Lamke Bauwerman.
24 Mei	1812	„ Sarah Elizabeth f. Johann Brahn & Lamke Bauwerman.
28 Aug.	1814	„ Eduard Albert f. John Bruhn & Lamke Bauwerman.
9 Oct.	1582	**Swaassel**, Van, Pieter f. Christiaan.
6 Nov.	1586	**Swalme**, Vander, Lodewyck f. Zacharias.
20 Mar.	1586	**Swart**, de, (v. **Swerte**), Willem f. Govards.
29 Nov.	1584	**Swarte**, „ Anna f. Govards.

31 Dec.	1587	Swarte, de, Joannes f. Govaert.
11 Mar.	1593	,, ,, Abraham f. Govaert.
19 Oct.	1589	,, ,, Catharina f. Bernaert.
23 Jul.	1592	,, ,, Sara f. Bernaerd.
12 Sep.	1591	,, ,, Abraham f. Ambrosius.
15 Aug.	1592	,, ,, Sara } fæ. Ambrosius. & Rebecca
20 Jun.	1813	Swaving, Christina Elisabeth f. Cornelis Christiaan & Johanna Jacoba Westrik, geb. 18 Mar., 1808, in de Kolonie van Berbice.
20 Jun.	1813	,, Anna Louisa f. Cornelis Christian & Johanna Jacoba Westrik, geb. 1 Sep. 1810, in de Kolonie van Berbice.
20 Jun.	1813	Swaving, Catharina Maria f. Cornelis Christiaan & Johanna Jacoba Westrik, geb. 12 Mei, 1813.
21 Jul.	1588	Sweer, Abraham f. Joris.
17 Dec.	1618	Sweerds, Leonora f. Leonardus. Test. Myn Heer Karon, Ambassadeur, etc., oude Leonora Vierendeels huysvrouw van Sir Jan Bennet.
8 Feb.	1620	,, Anna f. Leonard.
6 Jan.	1575	Sweertsen, Sara f. Heindrick.
31 Jul.	1589	Swerte, de, (v. Swart), Jacomyntken f. Govaert.
1 Aug.	1591	,, ,, Catelyn f. Govaert.
4 Jan.	1596	Swol, Van, Catherine f. Jan.

17 Aug.	1572	Tack, Thomas f. Thomas.
11 Dec.	1607	Tacken, Johannes f. Rock.
16 Oct.	1597	Taelman, Samuel f. Josias.
18 Nov.	1599	,, Sara f. ,,
10 Dec.	1598	,, Abraham f. David.
11 Jul.	1694	Taij, le, Hannah f. Francoijs & Hannah Bilje.
1 Jun.	1589	Taken, Van, Judith f. Hans.
4 Oct.	1590	,, ,, Margriete f. ,,
2 Mar.	1595	,, ,, Isaac f. ,,
15 Aug.	1642	Talman, Catalina f. Peter, tot Mortlake.
28 Nov.	1571	Tansses, Maria f. Cornelis.
15 Oct.	1598	Taraijen, Samuel f. Jan.
25 Sep.	1614	Tarhem, Joannes f. Andre.
18 Jan.	1854	Tarner, William Frederick f. Herman Frederick Wilhelm & Mietje Schults.
20 Mei	1855	,, William Frederick f. Herman Frederick Wilhelm & Mietje Schults.
11 Oct.	1857	,, Catharina Maria f. Herman Frederick Wilhelm & Mietje Schults.
13 Nov.	1859	,, Maria Elizabeth f. Herman Frederick Wilhelm & Mietje Schults.
16 Jun.	1681	Tarrent, (v. Terrent), Esther f. Joseph.
13 Mar.	1593	Teeler, (v. Telare), Maria f. Anthoni.
20 Mar.	1767	Teijlingen, Van, Cornelia Anna f. Christiaan & Magdalena Wilhelmina Hester Klybert. Test. Heer Mr. D. G. van Teylingen, ontvanger & Reg. Schoepen der Stad Hertogenbosch, etc.
9 Feb.	1769	,, ,, Peter Isaac f. Christiaan & M. W. Klybert. Test. Heer Pieter Theodorus van Teylingen woonigtig te Yssel steyn, Heer Mr. Isaac van Teylingen Sch : te Rotterdam, etc.
1 Aug.	1591	Telare, (v. Teeler), Salomon f. Anthony.
28 Jun.	1612	Teugnagel, Librecht f. Isbrand.
18 Jan.	1596	Terentijne, (v. Tierenteijns), Susanna f. Jan.
26 Aug.	1666	Terhurst, Catarina f. ....
11 Mei	1668	,, Antoni f. Jan.
13 Jun.	1669	Terhurst, Frederick f. Jan.
12 Feb.	1665	Terkeurst, Maria f. ,,
29 Oct.	1671	,, Martha f. ,,
22 Mar.	1674	,, Sara f. ,,
2 Dec.	1593	Ternijen, Henricus f. ,,
12 Oct.	1600	,, Joannes f. ,,
1 Sep.	1678	Terrent, (v. Tarrant), Hanna f. Joseph.
23 Aug.	1801	Teschemaker, Frederik Thomas Emanuel f. Joan, R.Z., & Alida Esther Thierens.
6 Jan.	1597	Tersluijsen, Henricus f. Geeraert.
2 Jul.	1599	,, Joannes f. ,,
2 Aug.	1597	Teunis, Joannes f. Dierick.
10 Jun.	1825	Teunisse, Sophia Margaretha f. Zweeris & Maria Rotman.
22 Jan.	1827	,, Johannes f. Zweers & Maria Rotman.
21 Sep.	1828	,, Daniel f. Zweeris & Maria Rotman.
21 Mei	1843	,, Zweeris f. ,, & Mary Ann Weyer.
14 Apl.	1616	Teunissen, Joannes f. Willem.
15 Aug.	1683	Tfalck, Sara f. Claes & Sara.
23 Jan.	1575	Theeus, Maria f. Lodewijck.
1 Sep.	1577	,, Susanna f. ,,
21 Jan.	1599	,, Loduwyck f. Jacob.
26 Sep.	1677	Theeuwsen, Elizabeth f. Teeus & Maria.
18 ,,	1582	Theeuwes, Anna f. Lodowijck.
7 Sep.	1572	Theeuwes, Isaac f. ,,
26 Feb.	1570	,, Antonius f. ,,
20 Oct.	1583	,, Daniel f. ,,
27 Apl.	1619	Theunissen, Willem f. Willem.
20 Mei	1621	,, Carolus f. ,,
9 Nov.	1623	Theunisz, Joannes f. ,,
22 Jan.	1604	Theus, Loduwyc f. Isaac.

		Left		Right		

<table>
<tr><td>6 Mar.</td><td>1606</td><td>Theus, Jacob f. Isaac.</td><td>17 Feb.</td><td>1572</td><td>Tieroteyns, (v. Terentijen), Sara f. Simon.</td></tr>
</table>

6 Mar. 1606 Theus, Jacob f. Isaac.
5 Mar. 1609 „ Daniel f. „
5 Aug. 1611 „ Maria f. „
9 Feb. 1615 Teewsz, Isaac } fi. „
    & Rachel }
2 Mar. 1595 Theuws, Lodewyck f. Jacob.
3 Nov. 1596 „ Marie f. Jaques.
6 Jul. 1601 Theeuws, Susanna f. „
4 Oct. 1829 Thielspeet, Van, Jacoba f. Jan & Catharina Anna Peters.
9 Mar. 1831 „ „ Johanna Elizabeth Catharina f. Jan & Catharina Anna Peters.
9 Mar. 1833 „ „ Josephine Louise f. Jan & Catharina Anna Peters.
3 Mei 1835 „ „ John Roselli f. Jan & Catharina Anna Peters.
7 Feb. 1600 Thijs, Sara f. Jan.
6 Feb. 1589 Thijsmans, Jacob f. Jacus.
1 Feb. 1573 Thijssen, (v. Tijssen), Abraham f. Reynier.
1 Aug. 1616 Thijssz, Jacobus f. Gillis.
4 Dec. 1617 Thijssen, Symeon f. „
6 Jun. 1619 „ Daniel f. „
4 Mat. 1677 „ Maria f. Erasmus.
9 Aug. 1626 Thilenus, Maria f. D. Wilhelmus.
3 Dec. 1627 „ Johannes f. Willem.
3 Jul. 1630 „ Sara f. D. Willelmus.
8 Apl. 1632 „ Josina f. „ „
0 Jul. 1634 „ Wilhelmus f. „ „
6 Aug. 1604 Thomaer, Abigail f. Paschier.
0 Jan. 1613 „ Ephraim f. „
6 Oct. 1594 Thomas, Thomas f. Niclaes.
1 Apl. 1688 Thomassen, Hendrick f. Robert & Maria.
1 Sep. 1700 Thomasz, Jannetje f. „ & „
4 Jan. 1613 Thomshout, Magdalena f. Balthasar.
4 Feb. 1692 Thornton, Francis f. Thomas.
.. Sep. 1681 Thorpe, Philippus f. Jan & Maria op de Beeck, indie prochie van een Engels Predicant.
9 „ 1571 Thues, Abdies f. Jan.
7 „ 1578 Thuijs, Abraham f. Michiels.
1 Oct. 1688 Thurston, Gideon f. Thomas & Anna.
6 Apl. 1693 „ Lionel f. „
2 Feb. 1696 „ Jonas f. „
9 Mei 1698 „ Richard f. „ & Anna.
0 Oct. 1700 „ Frances f. „
3 Aug. 1702 „ Gastrek f. „
2 Nov. 1645 Tickets, Anthony f. Anthony.
6 Apl. 1862 Tiddens, Roelof Hendrik f. Pieter & Jantiena Donkela.
6 Nov. 1871 „ Egbert Jakob f. „ Jantiena Dinkela.
6 Jun. 1578 Tieckemakers, Hester f. Magne. Tieckemakers, uxoris Arnoldi. Test: Pater & Mater.
1 Feb. 1573 Tienssen, Jaspar f. Jaspar.
1 „ 1579 Tieone, Jobius f. Coruclis.
9 Mei 1580 Tiereteins, Abigail f. Simon.
7 Jul. 1606 Tierens, Elisabeth f. Anthouy.
1 Jun. 1609 „ Susanna f. „
4 „ 1640 „ Maria f. Anthonius de Jonge.
8 „ 1645 „ Francois f. Anthouy.
5 Mar. 1648 „ Elizabeth f. „
9 Nov. 1607 „ Abraham f. Frauchoijs.
9 Oct. 1609 „ Maria f. „
7 Feb. 1611 „ Esther f. „
1 Mar. 1612 „ Anthonius f. „
3 Jul. 1614 „ Franciscus f. „

17 Feb. 1572 Tieroteyns, (v. Terentijen), Sara f. Simon.
23 Mei 1585 Tierenteins, Susanna f. Simon.
27 Mar. 1575 Tieriaseins, „ f. „
20 Jan. 1577 Tierinteijns, Samuel f. „
21 Jul. 1586 Tierinteijns, Judith f. „
22 Mei 1595 Tiers, Cornelis f. Cornelis.
30 Nov. 1596 „ Jacomyntken f. „
16 Jan. 1599 „ Maria f. „
17 Nov. 1611 Tiggorits, Jonathan f. Coenraerd.
25 Mei 1596 Tigrots, Anna f. Conrad.
2 Nov. 1649 Tijbaut, Joannes f. Franchoijs.
7 Jun. 1599 Tijbouts, Jacomijnken f. Francois.
16 Apl. 1682 Tijkenbeeck, Antony f. Ubberick & Sophia.
13 Dec. 1673 Tijneteyn, Abigail f. Pieter.
8 Mar. 1573 Tijrenteyns, (v. Tiereteyns), Isaac f. Isaac.
7 „ 1602 Tijs, Joannes f. Jan.
25 Mei 1651 Tijssen, (v. Thijssen), Joannes f. Francois.
15 Mei 1681 „ Dorothea f. Francois & Susanna.
5 Feb. 1688 „ Ridley f. „ Jr & Maria.
6 Jul. 1690 „ Francois f. „
11 Jun. 1691 „ Dorothea f. „ „ „
31 Mar. 1693 „ Elizabeth f. „ „ „
24 Jan. 1695 „ Johannes f. „ „ „ Western.
19 Feb. 1696 „ Martha f. „ „
26 Mei 1697 „ Wilhelmus f. „ „ „ Western.
27 Jun. 1698 „ Samuel f. „ „
15 Dec. 1699 „ Maria f. Fr. Francois & Maria Western.
20 Oct. 1701 „ Dorothea f. „ „ & Maria.
21 Sep. 1615 Tilhaust, Samuel f. Geraert.
29 Mei 1612 Tilhorst, Maria f. „
18 Aug. 1644 „ Joannes f. „
14 Apl. 1650 „ Sara f. Gerard.
16 Jan. 1663 „ Van, Joanna f. „
1 Mar. 1579 Timmermans, Petrus f. Lieven.
22 Jan. 1581 „ Sara f. „
7 Apl. 1616 „ Jooris f. Paulus.
22 Mei 1597 Timmers, Elizabeth f. Jan.
12 Sep. 1583 Toebast, Joannes f. Adam.
8 Aug. 1585 „ Judith f. Pauwels.
15 Oct. 1587 „ Pauwels f. „
20 Feb. 1589 „ Daniel f. „
18 Mar. 1591 „ Daniel f. „
4 Nov. 1599 „ Elizabeth f. David.
22 Dec. 1601 „ Catherine f. „
16 Aug. 1603 „ Esther f. „
2 Feb. 1605 „ Maria f. „
19 Feb. 1607 „ Susanna f. „
29 Nov. 1608 „ Anna f. „
14 Mar. 1611 „ Michael f. „
19 Mar. 1588 Tombe, de la, Maria f. Didier.
4 Jan. 1590 „ „ „ Anna f. „
7 Jan. 1593 „ „ Susanna f. „
22 „ 1703 „ des, Pieter f. Philip & Johanna.
13 Jun. 1697 Tomfere, Van, Sarah f. Dirck.
24 Oct. 1742 Toug, de, Johannes f. Doms. & Maria Van Linden.
24 Jan. 1703 Tonger, Van, Thomas f. Gerrijt & Maria de Kijnt.
18 Aug. 1695 Tongere, „ Maria f. Dirck.
27 Apl. 1701 Tongeren, ., Hendrickje f. Gerrit & Maria.
6 Aug. 1701 „ „ Anna f. Dirck.
30 Jun. 1639 Torus, Elizabeth f. Jacob.
16 Sep. 1628 Tousnin, Petrus f. Thomas.
21 Sep. 1629 „ Jacobus f. „

27 Oct.	1631	Tounsen, Johannes f. Thomas.
19 Jul.	1601	Trappaert, Peeter f. Niclaes.
27 Sep.	1607	„ Elias f. Nicolaes.
22 Jan.	1609	„ Magdalena f. Nicolas.
26 „	1612	„ Maria f. „
9 Jan.	1603	Trapper, Elizabeth f. „
11 Aug.	1605	Trappert, Nicolas f. „
19 Sep.	1703	Trebben, Maria f. Johannes & Rachel de Voogh.
12 „	1708	„ Elijsabeth f. Hendrick & Maria Hoo.
2 Aug.	1685	Tranelle, (v. Trenel), Pieter f. Pieter & Janetje Dailje.
23 Jan.	1687	Trenel, Pieter f. Pieter & Janneken.
10 Feb.	1689	„ Jacobus f. „ „ Carder.
25 Dec.	1689	„ Maria f. „ „ Carter.
16 Apl.	1693	„ Maria f. „ & Maria Carter.
1 Dec.	1695	„ Johannes f. „ & Maria.
24 Jul.	1698	„ Elisabeth f. „ & Maria.
22 Dec.	1700	„ Maria f. „ „
4 Aug.	1703	„ Janneken f. „ „
21 Jan.	1705	„ Stephanus f. „ „
12 Jan.	1707	„ Johannes. f. Moses & Jemima Koolman.
3 Mei	1710	„ Mary f. „ & Mary Mitten.
21 Dec.	1572	Trijon, Moijses, f. Pieter.
27 Mar.	1575	Trioen, Maria f. „
15 Sep.	1577	„ Joannes f. „
13 Dec.	1579	„ Esther f. „
25 Mar.	1582	„ Samuel f. „
10 Apl.	1584	„ Joannes f. „
28 Aug.	1586	„ Daniel f. „
8 Apl.	1588	„ „ f. „
10 Jan.	1602	Trioen, Maria f. Moses.
23 Jun.	1603	„ Sara f. „
16 Dec.	1604	„ Petrus f. „
19 Oct.	1606	„ Elizabeth f. „
22 Jan.	1607	„ Johannes f. „
11 Nov.	1610	„ Jacobus f. „
21 Jun.	1612	„ „ f. „
8 Mei	1614	„ Joanna f. „
3 „	1606	Trips, Judith f. Joos.
18 Oct.	1584	Troijer, de, Leonora f. Noe.
25 Feb.	1593	True, Moses f. Geraert.
8 Jul.	1604	Truerniet, Pieter f. Pieter & Geertruyd van Brulle.
22 Feb.	1590	Truyen, Joannes f. Geraert.
7 Jul.	1594	„ Samuel f. Gheeraert.
29 Aug.	1596	„ Daniel f. „
5 Jun.	1598	„ Aaron f. „
12 Mar.	1690	Truster, Anna f. Thomas.
24 Mar.	1577	Tubal, Elizabeth f. Jan, Engelsman.
10 Jul.	1625	Tucklinck, Clara f. Jan.
23 Sep.	1627	„ Anna f. „
7 Nov.	1622	Tuckingh, Laurentius f. Johannes.
15 Feb.	1624	„ Jacomynken f. Jan, van Wesel
13 Oct.	1583	Tucks, Lea f. Jois.
9 Feb.	1595	Tuerman, Paulus f. Joris.
28 Feb.	1574	Tuinus, Abigail f. Octamaen.
12 Jul.	1601	Turck, Abraham f Herman.
5 Jun.	1603	„ Isaac f. „
13 Dec.	1607	Turloot, Josynken f. Rogier.
8 Oct.	1607	„ Michiel f. „
3 Mei	1579	Tutelaers, alias Dormaals, Josina f. Gysbrecht.

30 Aug.	1612	Uijtman, Abraham f. Albert.
21 Nov.	1602	Uijtwijc, Van, (v. Wijtwijc), Gabriel f. Dominicus.
21 Oct.	1624	Ullenbergh, Philippus f. Jan, tot Mortlake.
19 Mar.	1854	Uphoff, Suzanna Helena f. Stephanus & Helena Hendrika van der Zee.
30 Mar.	1856	„ Stephanus f. Stephanus & Helena Hendrika van der Zee.
10 Jan.	1705	Uven, Van der, Gamaliel f. Dirck & Mari van Brully.

12 Mar.	1704	Va, Ester f. Pieter & Ester Kavroo.
8 Jun.	1712	„ Thomas f. Isak & Martha Short.
4 Apl.	1714	„ Petrus f. „ „ „
20 Dec.	1717	„ Thomas f. Isack & Martha.
24 Dec.	1607	Vademont, Elisabeth f. Pieter.
27 Oct.	1611	„ Bartholomeus f. „
21 Dec.	1707	Val, (v. Vall), Ester f. Pieter & Ester.
3 Mei	1691	Vale, Isaac f. Abraham & Rachel.
19 Mar,	1698	„ Dorothea f. „
6 Sep.	1573	Valckaert, Reynier f. Denis.
14 Aug.	1575	„ Philips f. Denijs.
5 „	1576	„ ...... f. „

1581	Valckaert, Cornelus f. Denijs.
1578	Valckardtz, Jan f. Dionijs.
1579	„ Susanna f. „
1571	Valkaerts, Abigail f. Denijs.
1611	Valck, Susanna f. Hans.
1594	„ Jacobus f. Isaac.
1595	„ Susanna f. „
1599	„ Elizabeth f. „
1589	Valcke, Sara f. „
1590	„ Geeraert f. „
1592	„ Rachel f. Anthoine.
1613	„ Isaac f. Geeraerd.
1615	„ Willem f. Geeraert.
1601	Valewaert, (v. Valuwaert), Jacobus f. Cornelis.
1607	Valk, Joannes f. Hans.
1608	„ Elizabeth f. „
1700	Vall, (v. Val), Carel f. John & Helena Walker.
1591	Vallijn, Margariete f. Nicolaes.
1595	„ Janneken f. Niclaes.
1593	„ Elisabeth f. „
1592	„ „ f. Anthony.
1628	Valma, Marten f. Melchoir.
1603	Valuwaert, Cornelis f. Cornelis.
1705	Varin, Susanna f. Carel & Antonia de Groot.
1600	Vart, Van, Affken f. Pelgrim.
1596	Vaus, de, (v. Voos & Vouce), Anna f. Jan.
1598	„ „ Joannes f. Hans.
1705	Veau, der, (v. Derveau), Sara f. Pieter & Catarina.
1613	Vechter, de, Catharina f. Pieter.
1614	Vecker, „ „ f. „
1617	Veckers, „ Susanna f. „
1621	Vecker, „ Maria f. „
1625	„ „ Samuel f. „
1671	Veerom, (v. Veroon), Fredrik } fi. Gerrit. & Antony }
1674	„ Susanna f. Gerrit.
1682	Veen, Van der, Elisabeth f. Elias.
1684	„ „ „ Elias f. „ & Elisabeth.
1686	„ „ „ Gerard f. „ „
1687	„ „ „ Johannes f. „ „
1690	„ „ „ Thomas f. „ „
1815	„ „ Wietzijna f. Harm Jan & Grietje Jans Kiers.
1848	Veenman, Maria Charlotte, geb. 26 Jul., 1843, f. Hendrick Jacob & Elizabeth Webb.
„	„ Hendrik Jacob, geb. 4 Mei, 1847, f. Hendrick Jacob & Elizabeth Webb.
1849	„ Ferdinand } fi. Hendrick Jacob & Albert. } & Ann Elizabeth Webb.
1851	„ Ferdinand f. Hendrick Jacob & Ann Elizabeth Webb.
1660	Veer, Herman f. Hendric & Hester.
1662	„ Hendrick f. Hendricus.
1663	„ Hester f. Hendrick & Hester.
1664	„ Anthoni f. „
1860	„ Van der, Jane Wilhelmina f. Pieter & Sarah Dominey Rogers.
1806	Vefer, le, (v. Lefever), Catharina f. John & Sarah Koning.
1622	Veggher, de, Petrus f. Pieter.

28 Apl.	1605	Veillards, (v. Viellards), Maria f. Abraham.
21 Jan.	1683	Velde, Van de, Johannes f. Albertus.
15 Mar.	1685	„ „ „ Maria f. „
16 Mei	1686	„ „ „ Johannes f. „
19 Oct.	1606	„ Van den, Maria f. Artus.
16 Jul.	1690	„ „ de, Anna f. David & Anna Staplij.
14 Dec.	1692	„ „ „ David f. David.
27 Jun.	1697	„ Van de, Sarah f. David.
6 Feb.	1625	„ „ Johannes f. Jacob.
15 Feb.	1596	„ Van de, Catharina f. Isaac.
28 Jul.	1678	„ „ „ David f. Laurens.
12 Dec.	1683	„ „ „ Susanna f. „
26 Mei	1686	„ „ „ Pieter f. „
22 Apl.	1688	„ „ „ Rachel f. „ & Sarah.
19 Nov.	1690	„ „ „ Willem f. „ „
11 Mar.	1691	„ „ „ Hanna f. „ „
21 Sep.	1672	„ „ „ Abigail f. Paulus,
11 Dec.	1575	„ „ „ Pauwels f. Pauwels.
5 Nov.	1581	„ „ „ Pauwels } fi. Pauwels. & Dina }
24 Sep.	1583	„ „ „ Sara f. Pauwels.
5 Sep.	1585	„ „ „ Sijbilla f. „
21 „	1587	„ „ „ Abigail f. „
3 Jun.	1589	„ „ „ Paulus f. „
25 Jan.	1596	„ „ „ Abraham f. „
11 Sep.	1597	„ „ „ Paulus f. „
28 Oct.	1599	„ „ „ Petrus f. „
27 Feb.	1603	„ „ „ Elizabeth f. „
18 Sep.	1605	„ „ „ Paulus f. „
28 Mar.	1608	„ „ „ Petrus f. Paulus.
9 Aug.	1610	„ „ „ Anna f. „
12 Apl.	1612	„ „ „ Jacobus f. „
20 Feb.	1614	„ „ „ Rebecca f. „
30 Jul.	1615	„ „ „ Paulus f. „
18 Mar.	1617	„ „ „ Tobias f. „
10 Aug.	1619	„ „ „ Joos f. „
10 Jul.	1586	„ „ „ Elisabeth f. Pieter.
23 Jan.	1590	„ „ „ Susanna f. „
18 Apl.	1624	„ „ „ Jacquemynken f. „
29 Jun.	1629	„ „ „ Abraham } fi. Petrus. & Isaac }
2 Apl.	1735	„ „ „ alias Field, William f. William & Maria.
23 Mar.	1740	Velden, Van de, Sara f. William & Maria.
22 Jul.	1627	Velle, Abigail f. Jacob,
21 Aug.	1631	„ Maria f. „
2 Sep.	1694	Velten, Johannes f, Johannes.
6 Jun.	1602	Velthuijs, den, Susanna f. Dierick.
7 Oct.	1604	„ Dirick f. Dirick.
7 „	1593	Velthuijse, Eva f. Dierick.
9 Feb.	1595	Velthuijsen, Van, Joannes f. „
27 Jun.	1596	„ „ Elisabeth f. „ Testes. Andries Boeve ende Claercken, uxor Pieter, ende Goolken, uxor Dierick Cloppens.
15 Apl.	1595	Veltman, Abraham f. Roclandt.
20 Mei	1596	„ Sara f. Roclant.
18 Sep.	1597	„ Janneken f. „
21 Apl.	1599	„ Joannes f. „
3 Aug.	1600	„ Susanna f. „
17 Mar.	1678	Verbeeck, Johannes f. Gerrit.
25 Mei	1592	Verbek, alias Pappet, Tobias f. Matthijs.
4 Aug.	1575	Verbeke, Susanna f. Willem.
19 Jul.	1575	„ Abraham f. „ & Jorijne Smeerts.

'9 Apl.	1590	**Verbeke**, Abraham f. Goossens.
,5 Aug.	1591	„ Judith f. Hans.
19 Jun.	1597	„ Maria f. Jan.
9 Dec.	1599	„ Daniel f. Mathijs.
3 Apl.	1603	„ Jacobus f. „
4 Aug.	1605	„ Abraham f. Abraham.
13 Feb.	1620	**Verbiest**, Jacobus f. Jacob.
31 Mei	1691	**Verboom**, Maria f. Hermannus.
5 Nov.	1603	„ Martinus f. „ Hugo.
6 Jan.	1712	„ Hugo f. Hugo & Elisabet van Coperen.
9 Apl.	1583	**Verbrugge**, Johanna f. Jan.
1 Aug.	1585	„ Abraham f. „
20 Mar.	1614	„ Jacob f. Daniel.
13 Aug.	1684	„ Johannes } fi. Gerrit & & Maria Magdalena } Judith.
24 Mar.	1588	**Verburcht**, Anna f. Philps.
27 Jan.	1639	**Verchilt**, Samuel f. Samuel.
1 Jan.	1615	**Verclemme**, Joannes f. Alexander.
27 Apl.	1628	„ Johannes f. „
14 Oct.	1632	„ Helena f. „
17 Apl.	1586	**Vercoilge**, Melchior f. Rogier.
10 Oct.	1591	**Vercoille**, Sara f. „
14 Apl.	1588	**Vercoillien**, Anna f. „
15 Jan.	1603	**Verdere**, del, Rebecca f. Jacob.
27 Jun.	1585	**Verdonc**, Anna f. Thomas.
1 Sep.	1590	**Vereijcke**, Anthonis f. Adraen.
13 Mei	1571	**Verelst**, Jan f. Johannes.
18 Apl.	1647	**Vergesele**, Johannes f. Jan.
13 Jan.	1628	**Verhaegen**, Maria f. Christoffel.
22 Jan.	1682	**Verhaest**, Jacob f. Nicolaus.
7 Mar.	1596	**Verhage**, Anna f. Arnout.
26 Nov.	1626	„ Christoffel f. Christoffel.
2 Apl.	1631	**Verhagen**, Anna f. „
14 Mei	1640	„ Abraham f. ...... bejaert person, geb. te Rotterdam.
5 Mar.	1632	**Verhaghen**, Hester f. Christoffel.
30 Aug.	1691	**Verhasselt**, Susanna f. Aaron & Bridget.
4 Dec.	1692	„ Alice f. „ „ Pieters.
22 Jun.	1600	**Verhelst**, Petrus f. Jeremias.
15 Nov.	1600	**Verhielt**, Abraham f. Jacus.
10 Jan.	1585	**Verhouve**, Hesther f. Arnout.
12 Jan.	1606	**Verhulst**, Catharine f. Pieter.
1 Mar.	1607	„ Pieter f. „
18 Jun.	1600	„ Maria f. „
19 Nov.	1612	„ Tobias f. „
18 Mei	1595	**Verhult**, Jacobus f. Jan.
17 Oct.	1596	„ Sara f. Jaques.
22 Oct.	1598	„ Susanna f. „
17 Oct.	1602	„ Isaac f. „
28 Mar.	1591	**Verle**, Van, Sara f. Michiel.
20 Sep.	1573	**Verleye**, Abraham f. Paessebier.
11 Sep.	1631	**Vermeulen**, Mattheus f. Jan.
23 Mar.	1634	„ Petrus f. „
16 Oct.	1636	„ Esther f. „
5 Mei	1639	„ Jacobus f. „
7 Jun.	1640	„ Rebecca f. „
9 Jan.	1644	„ Maria f. „
24 Aug.	1645	„ Susanna f. „
15 Oct.	1646	„ „ f. „ & Hester.
31 Mar.	1653	„ Jacobus f. „
1 Nov.	1579	**Vermolen**, Sara f. Antonis.
22 Jan.	1626	**Vermuijden**, Catharine f. Cornelis.
21 Aug.	1634	„ Bartholomeus f. Sir Cornelius.
16 Jul.	1635	„ Anna f. „ „
14 Feb.	1598	**Verninck**, Abraham f. Hans.
19 Apl.	1668	**Veroon**, (v. Veerom), Johannes f. Gerrit.
20 Apl.	1615	**Verpoort**, Barbara f. Abraham.
13 Dec.	1618	„ Pieter f. „
15 Jul.	1621	„ Jacob f. „
24 Dec.	1626	**Verpoorte**, Elisabeth f. „
25 Sep.	1580	**Verpoorten**, Anna f. Eduaerdt.
7 Oct.	1589	**Verscheure**, Janneken f. Pieter.
24 Mei	1608	**Verschoren**, Anna f. posthuma Jan.
28 Jun.	1730	**Verschoven**, Johannes f. Nicolas & Clara.
27 Apl.	1589	**Versoene**, Marie f. Arent.
27 Sep.		**Verspellen**, Maria f. Adolf.
13 Jun.	1585	**Verspiere**, Joannes f. Pieter.
4 Apl.	1596	„ Jacobus f. „
19 Sep.	1591	„ f. Hans.
16 Feb.	1595	„ Tobias f. Jan.
26 Dec.	1596	„ Maria f. Hans.
23 Aug.	1584	**Versplert**, Sara f. David.
8 Aug.	1602	**Verspire**, Petrus f. Hans.
22 Mar.	1685	**Verspriet**, Willemijntje f. Johannes.
5 Dec.	1642	**Verst**, Van der, Jacobus f. Hubert.
8 Jun.	1690	**Verstaeg**, Huijbertje f. Adolf & Maria.
14 Dec.	1600	**Verstamen**, Mordochens f. Carel.
9 Aug.	1840	**Versteegh**, Pieter f. Pieter & Elisabet Catharina Paling.
15 Jun.	1845	„ Hermanus f. Pieter & Elisabet Catharina Paling.
12 Jul.	1846	„ Anthony f. Pieter & Elisabet Catharina Paling.
17 Jun.	1849	„ Willem Johannes f. Pieter & Elisabet Catharina Paling.
4 Oct.	1682	**Verstelle**, William f. Pieter.
6 Jnl.	1684	„ Margriet f. „ & Judith.
14 Mar.	1686	„ Margariet f. „
1 Jul.	1688	„ Wilhelmus f. „ „
27 Apl.	1690	„ Elizabeth f. „ „
22 Mei	1692	„ Willem f. „ „
25 Jun.	1693	„ Elizabeth f. „ „
24 Jul.	1695	„ Samuel f. „
5 Dec.	1585	**Verstraeten**, Philips f. Philips.
10 Mar.	1594	„ Lieven f. Lieven.
18 Jun.	1587	**Verstraten**, Catherine f. Haus.
26 Oct.	1589	„ Joannes f. Philips.
13 Oct.	1575	**Verstriep**, Beatrix f. Gheeraert.
7 Feb.	1577	„ Maria f. „
30 Jan.	1578	„ Anna f. „
5 Feb.	1598	**Verstrijpe**, Maria f. Wouter.
9 Nov.	1643	**Verstripen**, Johannes f. Jan.
1 Nov.	1587	**Verstueren**, Caterina f. Philips.
15 Jul.	1591	**Vervloet**, Elizabeth f. Abraham.
28 Nov.	1591	**Verwers**, Esther f. Michiel.
21 Oct.	1593	„ Michiel f. „
26 Dec.	1595	„ Abigail f. „
29 Mar.	1663	**Vett**, de, Maria f. Pieter.
31 Jul.	1664	„ „ Elisabeth f. „
19 Nov.	1665	„ „ Susanna f. „
14 Jun.	1668	„ „ Johanna f. „
28 Nov.	1669	„ „ Anna f. „
21 Mei	1671	„ „ Samuel f. „
1 Dec.	1672	„ „ Pieter f. „
12 „	1675	„ „ Anna f. „
19 Aug.	1606	**Vette**, „ Susanna f. Goyvaert.
14 Mei	1627	„ „ Joannes f. Jan.
19 Jun.	1628	„ „ Sara f. „
23 Mar.	1630	„ „ Susanna f. Hans.
19 Mei	1631	„ „ Petrus f. Jan.
19 Sep.	1633	„ „ Johanna f. „
2 Mei	1592	**Veuren**, Hester f. Willem.
18 Jul.	1669	**Victorijn**, Michiel f. Pieter.
19 Aug.	1674	„ Margaretha f. „

20 Feb.	1603	Vidder, de, Susanna f. Hendrick.
17 Feb.	1622	Viellards, de. (v. Veillards, Villias, Villijads), Maria f. Abraham.
7 Jan.	1585	Viellardts, ,. Joannes f. Joannes.
2 Mei	1513	Vieman, Maria Johanna f. Jan & Sarah Wilson.
21 Jun.	1631	Vihose, Thomasine f. Abraham.
31 Aug.	1690	Vijcht, Van der, Waender f. Herman & Aegtie Westhoven.
27 Apl.	1619	Vijven, Van, Gillis f. Pieter.
4 Jan.	1573	Vijvere, Van de, (v. Vijvre), Rachel f. Gabriel.
10 Feb.	1578	Vijvre, Van, Jeremias f. Gabriel.
3 Apl.	1586	Vijver, Van de, Beniamin f. ,,
10 Nov.	1594	Villas, de, David f. Jan.
27 Dec.	1590	Villars, ,, Elisabeth f. ,,
2 Feb.	1582	Vilere, Elisabet) fæ. Willem. & Sara)
28 Jan.	1589	Viliaers, de, Samuel f. Jan.
30 ,,	1597	Villiaers, ,, Hester f. ,,
1 Mei	1628	Villias, de, (v. Viellards), Francois f. Abraham.
28 Mar.	1624	Villijads, (,,), Abraham f. Abraham.
28 Jan.	1582	Villzands, Maria f. Joannes.
11 Apl.	1742	Vincent, Elizabeth f. Jan & Gerritje Gerrits.
20 Jun.	1745	,, Jacoba f. ,, ,, Gerrits.
31 Jan.	1591	Vinck, Van der, Joannes f. Jan.
21 Aug.	1672	,, Isac f. D. Petrus & Maria.
18 Jul.	1591	,, Maria f. Gabriel.
13 Mei	1593	Vincke, Joseph f. ,,
16 Dec.	1599	,, Jacobus f. ,,
3 Mei	1601	,, Susanna f. ,,
16 Feb.	1589	Vinckt, Van der, Gabriel f. Jan.
29 Mei	1586	Vinct, ,, ,, Susanna f. ,,
16 Oct.	1586	Vinne, ,, ,, Sara f. Heindric.
15 Jul.	1596	Vinsoen, Maria f. Laurens.
21 Dec.	1589	Vinson, Elisabeth f. ,,
3 Aug.	1572	Visch, Tabitha f. Hans.
16 Jul.	1611	Vischer, de, Joannes f. Samuel.
3 Jan.	1613	,, Samuel f. ,,
29 Nov.	1607	Visschel, ,, Ester f. ,,
23 Jan.	1575	Visscher, Jeremias f. Olivier.
24 Jun.	1575	,, de, Abraham f. Marten. Test. Staijs Thijssen, etc.
15 ,,	1578	,, ,, Susanna f. Marten.
22 Juu.	1690	,, ,, Anna Mary f. Maerten & Passchintje.
10 Jul.	1625	,, ,, Abraham f. Willem.
31 Dec.	1626	,, ,, Wilhelmus f. ,,
17 Feb.	1628	,, ,, Samuel f. ,,
13 Feb.	1631	,, ,, Cornelia f. ,,
9 Mar.	1634	,, ,, Wilhelmus f. ,,
5 Feb.	1637	,, ,, Cornelia f. ,,
13 Oct.	1639	,, ,, Willem f. ,,
27 Feb.	1642	,, ,, Hieronimus f. Wilhelmus.
31 Aug.	1589	Visschere,,, Gillis f. Gillis.
5 Apl.	1573	,, ,, Cornelis f. Marten.
7 Nov.	1847	Vissen, Anna Cornelia f. Leendert & Wilhelmina Jongmans.
21 Aug.	1836	Visser, Ketley Willem f. Alert Andries & Sarah Ketley.
28 Jul.	1872	,, Wilhelmina Hendrika f. Dirk Gratus & Maria ElisabethGiltjes.
29 Mei	1870	,, Jan Anthon f. Dirk Gerardus & Elizabeth Giltje.
1 Mei	1550	Viver, Van der, (v. Vyvere). Salomon f. Gabriel.
17 Mar.	1583	,, ,, ,, Esther f. Gabriel.
24 Jul.	1575	Vivre, ,, ,, Susanna f. ,,
1 Nov.	1572	Vlamincks, Susanna f. Jacob. & Sara
13 Dec.	1573	,, Sara f. ,,
2 Sep.	1585	,, de, Susanna f. Pieter.
28 Dec.	1585	,, ,, ,, f. ,,
23 Jan.	1620	,, ,, Elisabeth f. Hieronymus.
14 Oct.	1621	,, Philippus f. ,,
21 ,,	1623	,, Maria f. Jeronymus.
22 Feb.	1586	Vlemijns, Maria f. Pauwel.
6 Sep.	1629	Vleteren, Van, Maria f. Timotheus.
17 Mar.	1631	,, ,, Timotheus f. D. Timotheus.
31 Mei	1636	,, ,, Maria f. ,, ,,
8 Aug.	1638	,, ,, Timotheus, j. g.
1 Jun.	1639	,, ,, Jacobus f. Timotheus.
14 Mei	1640	,, ,, ,, f. ,,
9 Sep.	1574	Vliet, Van der, Anna f. Jan.
22 Jul.	1576	,, ,, ,, Elisabeth f. ,,
17 Nov.	1577	,, ,, ,, Abigail f. ,,
29 Sep.	1711	,, Van, Wiljam f. Fermeyn & Hester Chogels.
30 Nov.	1713	,, ,, Judith f. Fermeyn.
13 Mar.	1717	,, ,, Maria f. ,, & Hester.
7 Mar.	1720	,, ,, William f. ,, & Hester.
2 Oct.	1721	,, ,, Elisabeth f. ,, & Hester.
21 Mar.	1725	,, ,, William f. Fr. ,, & Hester.
13 Dec.	1579	Vliete, Van der, Benjamin f. Jan.
31 Aug.	1578	Voet, Michiel f. Henrick.
6 Mei	1593	,, Thomas f. Hans.
18 Jan.	1601	,, Sara f. ,,
26 Jun.	1603	,, Tobias f. Jan.
31 Mar.	1605	,, Susanna f. ,,
25 Nov.	1576	Voets, Clara f. Henrick.
29 Mei	1580	,, Michael f. ,,
21 Aug.	1582	,, Henrick) fi ,, & Catherina)
17 Dec.	1598	,, Susanna f. Hans.
1 Nov.	1674	Voge, Catarina f. Jan Pietersen.
9 Oct.	1608	Voket, Jacob f. Joris.
22 Aug.	1703	Volder, de, Adriaen f. Johannes.
25 Apl.	1705	,, ,, Elisabeth f. Adriaen & Elisabeth.
28 Oct.	1712	,, ,, Rebecca f. ,, & Elisabeth.
18 Dec.	1715	,, ,, George f. ,, & Elisabeth.
25 Jun.	1717	,, ,, George f. ,, & Elisabeth.
12 Feb.	1587	Volosenaere, de, Sara f. Jan.
8 Jun.	1735	Vonk, Maria f. Willem & Hendrina Henning.
25 Nov.	1627	Vooman, Jakemynken f. Elias.
11 Jan.	1713	Voorhart, Cornelis f. Cornelis & Catrina.
4 Aug.	1592	Voos, de, (v. Vaus), Samuel f. Jan.
14 Jun.	1584	Vore, Susanna f. Willem.
11 Mei	1690	Vordery, Joseph f. Pieter & Maria.
1 Apl.	1572	Vos, de, Abraham f. Vijnken, ghescit Zwart Vijnken.
11 Oct.	1574	,, ,, Tobias f. Pieter.
6 Aug.	1577	,, ,, Sara f. ,,
29 Mei	1580	,, ,, Sara f. ,,

4 Jun. 1582	**Vos, de,** Dancel f. Pieter.
19 Apl. 1584	,, ,, Pieter f. ,,
19 Jan. 1612	,, ,, ,, f. ,,
29 Dec. 1583	,, ,, Petrus f. Frantzois.
27 Jun. 1585	,, ,, Abraham f. ,,
24 Sep. 1587	,, ,, Isaac f. ,,
8 Nov. 1618	,, ,, David f. David.
5 Dec. 1619	,, ,, Maria f. ,,
14 Jan. 1621	,, ,, Judith f. ,,
27 Jan. 1622	,, ,, Elisabet f. ,,
16 Mar. 1623	,, ,, ,, f. ,,
5 Sep. 1624	,, ,, Georgius f. ,,
24 Mar. 1622	,, ,, Andries f. Paul.
20 Jul. 1623	,, ,, Daniel f. Daniel.
22 Mar. 1629	,, ,, Maria f. Michiel.
11 Dec. 1630	,, ,, Johannes f. ,,
15 Nov. 1635	,, ,, Johanna f. ,,
28 Feb. 1637	,, ,, Michiel f. ,,
22 Sep. 1689	,, ,, Maria f. Philip.
6 Dec. 1691	,, ,, Anna f. ,,
30 Jan. 1690	,, ,, Johanna f. Barent & Sara Barthem.
23 Jun. 1805	,, Petronella Francina f. Hermanus & Anna Margaretha Steenbergen.
17 Mei 1807	,, Pieter Constantyn f. Hermanus & Anna Margaretha Steenbergen.
10 Sep. 1808	,, Edward f. Hermanus & Anna Margaretha Steenbergen.
16 Mei 1810	,, William Drummond f. Hermanus & Anna Margaretha Steenbergen.
14 Sep. 1811	,, Augustus Gerard f. Hermanus & Anna Margaretha Steenbergen.
20 Jan. 1573	**Vosberghe, Van,** Hester f. Mr. Jaspar.
8 Nov. 1608	**Votter, de,** Govaert & Daniel } fi Govaert.
19 Mei 1594	**Vouce, de, (v. Vaus),** David f. Jan.
24 Apl. 1653	**Voust,** Sara f. Johan.
11 Dec. 1596	**Vrbanus,** Adriaenken f. Adam.
10 Nov. 1717	**Vreugdebergh,** Jannetje f. Jacobus & Maria.
11 Dec. 1715	**Vreugdenberg,** Pieter f. Jacob.
13 Jan. 1577	**Vrients,** Eva f. Jan.
1 Jan. 1691	**Vrijbergen,** Maria f. Willem & Elizabeth.
8 Dec. 1667	**Vrijs,** Magdalena f. Huen.
8 Aug. 1577	**Vrijlichoven,** Abigail f. Jacob.
5 Jan. 1606	**Vries, de,** Anna f. Jan.
28 Jun. 1612	,, ,, Janneken f. ,,
15 Jun. 1621	,, ,, Joannes f. ,,
23 Sep. 1781	,, ,, Martinus Jacobus f. Martinus, Chirurgijn te Kingston aan de Theemes, & Sarah Longhurst.

18 Jun. 1854	**Vries, de,** Reynemtje f. Simon & Reynemtje Mantel.
27 Jul. 1856	,, ,, Johannes Simon f. Simon & Reynemtje Mantel.
25 Feb. 1588	**Vriese,,** Abraham f. Jan.
10 Jan. 1590	,, ,, Sara f. ,,
2 Jul. 1592	,, ,, Isaac f. ,,
1 Aug. 1596	,, ,, Sara f. Hans.
8 Jan. 1598	,, ,, Hester f. Jan.
11 Feb. 1599	,, ,, Anna f. Hans.
18 Jan. 1601	,, ,, Henricus f. Jan.
21 Jul. 1622	,, ,, Arnout f. ,,
4 Mei 1589	,, ,, Abraham f. Pieter.
21 Jul. 1594	**Vriest,,** ,, f. Jan.
3 Mei 1586	**Vroe, de,** Pauwels f. Pauwels.
21 Jul. 1588	,, ,, Janneken f. ,,
26 Jul. 1590	,, ,, Judith f. ,,
21 Sep. 1592	,, ,, Tobias f. ,,
3 Apl. 1572	**Vrolick, de,** Maria f. Marten.
9 Nov. 1574	**Vrolicke, de,** Abigail f. Philippus.
19 Apl. 1579	**Vrolickhoven,** David f. David.
2 Feb. 1632	**Vrombout,** Andries f. Manuel.
24 Jun. 1573	**Vroment,** Hester f. Jan.
25 Apl. 1594	,, Joannes f. Pieter.
8 Aug. 1596	,, Abraham f. ,,
10 Nov. 1631	**Vromout,** Anna f. Jan.
29 Sep. 1867	**Vroom,** Hendrina Willemina Agatha f. Anton & Willemina Johanna Mathilda van de Wall.
23 Mei 1869	,, Jelis Johannes f. Anton & Willemina Johanna Mathilda van de Wall.
30 Aug. 1573	**Vroolick,** Sara f. Marten.
5 Jun. 1580	**Vroommoudts,** Susanna f. Jan.
8 Aug. 1574	**Vroomont,** Susanna f. ,,
14 Aug. 1580	,, Susanna f. Adolfs.
24 Oct. 1588	**Vsenkeic, (sic),** Margabous f. Adolfs.
3 Sep. 1646	**Vuefon,** Johannes f. Laureins.
4 Oct. 1646	,, Joannes f. Jan.
10 Jul. 1698	,, Susannah f. Willem & Margariet Fils.
10 Nov. 1700	,, Peter f. ,, & ,, Fild.
13 Oct. 1706	**Vuijst,** Pieter f. ,, & ,,
9 Jan. 1709	,, Willem f. ,, & ,,

21 Aug. 1693	**Waal, de,** Gerrit f. Nicolaas & Geertruid van Duven.
17 Jan. 1585	**Waarde, Van der,** Joannes f. Karel.
16 Mei 1591	**Wachteneel,** Jacob f. Hans

14 Feb. 1585	**Wachter, de,** Barbara f. Hans.
4 Apl. 1586	,, ,, Joannes f. Jan.
26 Dec. 1588	,, ,, Lieven f. Hans.
9 Feb. 1591	,, ,, Tobias f. Jan.

12 Mar.	1592	Wachter, de, Hester f. Jan.
3 Jul.	1636	„ „ Caterina f. Jacob.
3 Nov.	1637	„ „ Susanna f. „
12 Jul.	1640	„ „ Jacob f. „
12 Dec.	1641	„ „ Maria f. „
26 Jul.	1646	„ „ Jacob f. „
29 Oct.	1618	„ de, Elisabet f. „
7 Apl.	1651	„ „ Isaac f. „
16 Feb.	1661	„ de, Benjamin f. „ & Susanna.
1 Jun.	1587	Wachtere, de, Gillis f. Jan.
25 Dec.	1589	„ „ Maria f. „
16 Mei	1616	Wademondt, Petrus f. Pieter.
16 Oct.	1586	Wademont, Henricus f. Philips.
2 Feb.	1589	„ Elizabeth f. Philip.
7 Feb.	1591	„ Jacob f. „
8 Oct.	1592	„ Philippus f. „
12 Sep.	1596	„ Bartholomeus f. Bartholomeus.
8 Jan.	1601	„ Susanna f. „
26 Jul.	1607	„ Maria f. Pieter.
25 Oct.	1618	„ Philippus f. „
16 Apl.	1592	Waegenare, de, Joannes f. Aernout.
8 Sep.	1594	Waeghenaere, „ (v. Wagenaer, etc.),
		Susanna f. Gulian.
22 Jul.	1610	Waeghe, „ (v. Waghe), Johannes f.
		Gilles.
6 Oct.	1605	Wage, „ Johannes f. Gillis.
1 Jan.	1609	„ „ Susanna f. „
23 Apl.	1612	„ „ Maria f. „
6 Mar.	1586	„ „ Elisabeth f. Marinus.
8 Sep.	1605	„ „ Abraham f. Pieter.
12 Nov.	1611	„ „ Isaac f. „
15 Sep.	1616	„ „ Rebecca f. „
13 Jul.	1620	„ „ Henricus f. „
28 Jul.	1605	Wagenaer, Elisabeth f. Jacques.
26 Jul.	1607	„ Jacobus f. „
26 Mar.	1618	„ Joannes f. „
28 Mei	1620	„ Guiljelmus f. „
19 Oct.	1623	„ Lucas f. „
7 Mei	1626	„ Anna f. „
23 Jul.	1615	Wagenaere, de, Gillis f. „
3 Aug.	1578	Wagenare, „ Daniel f. Willem.
6 Dec.	1590	„ „ Debora f. Aernout.
20 Oct.	1583	Wagener, Isaac f. Rutgger.
8 Jan.	1598	„ de, Lidia f. Guliam.
15 Nov.	1601	„ ˙ „ Esther f. Niclaes.
7 Mar.	1582	Wagere, Sara f. Joos.
23 Dec.	1603	Waghe, de, (v. Wage), Petrus f. Petrus.
29 Mar.	1607	„ „ Elisabeth f. Pieter.
22 Aug.	1613	„ „ Anna f. „
8 Oct.	1592	Wagheman, Johannes f. Nicolaes.
11 Sep.	1608	Waghenaer, Guillelmus f. Jaques.
27 Jan.	1577	Waghenaere, de, Anna f. Guillaume.
21 Mei	1574	Waghenare, de, Abraham f. Guillaume.
10 Apl.	1575	„ „ Jacob f. Guilame.
10 Jan.	1585	„ „ Sara f. Willem.
9 Sep.	1595	„ „ Marie f. Guiliaeme.
13 Feb.	1586	„ „ Magdalecne f. Joos.
27 Dec.	1580	Wagheneer, de, Anna f. Guillame.
11 Apl.	1591	Waghenen, Joannes f. Niclaes.
7 Nov.	1609	Wael, de, Petrus f. Pieter.
17 Mei	1590	Waele, „ Jacob f. Mathens.
22 Aug.	1680	Waelters, (v. Walters,) Wouter f. Jacob &
		Judith.
21 Sep.	1589	Waelwijns, Debora f. Adriaen de Jonge.
30 Nov.	1589	Waerde, Van der, Pierijne f. Kaerel.
22 Aug.	1703	Waerteloo, Johannes f. Isbrant.
25 Apl.	1714	Wal, Van de, Sophia f. Edward & Catha-
		rina Dirksen.

4 Aug.	1704	Waldring, Cornelis f. Cornelis & Isabella.
2 Apl.	1592	Wale, de, Lydia f. Mathens.
17 Feb.	1594	„ Joannes f. Matthijs.
23 Jul.	1593	„ „ (v. Wallens), Ezechiel f. Jeronij-
		mus.
16 Jul.	1587	Walewijn, François f. Adriaen.
15 Nov.	1598	„ Petrus f. „
5 „	1609	„ Francis f. Franchoijs.
16 Oct.	1606	„ Abraham f. „
21 Mei	1609	„ Francicus f. Fransoijs.
17 Jun.	1613	„ Franchoijs f. Franchoijs.
8 Oct.	1615	„ Catharijna f. Fransoijs.
16 Nov.	1617	„ Abraham f. Franchoijs.
21 Mar.	1619	„ Hendric f. „
7 Jan.	1621	„ Susanna f. „
6 „	1624	„ Petrus f. „
23 „	1603	Wallewijn, Joannes f. „
18 Dec.	1596	Walkenzel, Daniel f. Hans.
12 Oct.	1589	Walle, Van de, Pieter f. Pieter.
17 Sep.	1592	„ „ „ Charles f. „
19 Jan.	1595	„ „ „ Theophilus f. „
7 Dec.	1600	„ Van, Anna f. „
22 Dec.	1620	„ „ de, Willem, bejaert persoon,
		Jonckman, geboren te
		Haerlem, out 24 jaren.
31 Jul.	1631	Wallosen, Van, Rebecca f. Jan.
23 Mei	1596	Wallens, (v. Wale), Jac. myntken f. Jeroni-
		mus.
5 Feb.	1609	Walleraven, (v. Walraven), Sara f. Abra-
		ham.
19 Jul.	1603	Walpergen, Milda f. Esaias & Sara.
30 Jun.	1661	Walraev, Johannes f. Pieter Jr. Test:
		Pieter Walraev Sr. ende syne
		huysvrouw.
22 Jan.	1661	Walrave, Stephanus f. Johannes.
13 Mar.	1664	„ Johannes f. „ Test.......
		Walrave et Prudentia Heeran
		ux. Petri Walrave.
27 Oct.	1670	„ Mattheus f. Matthens.
14 Nov.	1613	„ „ f. Abraham.
1 Mar.	1607	Walraven, Van, Isaac f. „
11 Feb.	1610	„ Jacolus f. „
28 Jun.	1612	„ Susanna f. Pieter.
14 Jun.	1663	„ Joseph f. „
14 Jun.	1663	„ Elisabeth f. Matthias.
29 Mei	1679	„ Ales f. Matthens.
9 Oct.	1614	Walschaers, Maria f. Nicolaes.
23 Oct.	1625	Walschaert, Johannes f. Johannes, tot
		Mortlake.
11 Apl.	1631	„ Joanna f. Jan, tot Mortlake.
14 Jul.	1633	Walschuert, Johannes f. Jan.
3 Jan.	1580	Waische, de, Henricus f. Henrick.
17 Dec.	1584	„ „ Susanna f. „
27 Sep.	1584	„ „ Catharina f. „
12 Feb.	1587	„ „ Hester f. Hendrick.
22 Jun.	1589	„ „ Jaques f. „
10 Sep.	1592	„ „ Catharina f. „
25 Feb.	1770	Walter, Anna f. Jacob & Sara de Koning.
9 „	1772	„ Elisabeth f. Jacob & Sara de
		Koning.
29 Mei	1774	„ Jacob f. Jacob & Sara de Koning.
20 Sep.	1776	„ Pieter f. posthumus Jacob & Sara
		de Koning.
23 „	1576	Walters, Susanna f. Geeraert.
26 Mei	1678	Waltersen, Christina f. Jacob.
22 Aug.	1592	Waus, de, (v. Wons), Johannes f. Jan.
16 Nov.	1589	Wanteneel, Isaac f. Hans.
20 Aug.	1681	Warinken, Aeltje f. Arent.

1 Apl.	1677	Warthe, (v. Werth), Benjamin f. Jan & Maria Willems.
16 Feb.	1619	Waterhuijsen, Elisabet f. Matthias.
28 Feb.	1574	Waterman, Jacob f. Michiel.
13 Mar.	1572	Watermans, Samuel f. „
17 Mei	1675	Watermee, Maria f. Pieter.
19 Jan.	1673	Watermere, Janneken f. „
17 Feb.	1628	Waterval, Johannes f. Mattheus.
25 Mei	1634	„ Aelken f. „
... Aug.	1631	„ Lucas f. „
29 Mar.	1674	Watson, Lettes fn. Jan.
14 Mar.	1585	Wauters, (v. Wouters), Judith f. Geeraert, van Emblden.
5 Jan.	1612	„ Jacob f. Hertger.
2 Oct.	1642	„ Arnoldus f. Arnout.
6 Apl.	1687	Webster, Sara f. John & Maria.
7 Nov.	1688	„ Sara f. „ & „ Kersteman.
25 Jan.	1702	Weddis, Johanna f. Jan & Margaretha.
9 Mar.	1681	Wee, du, Dijna f. Jacob & Rachel.
3 Apl.	1682	„ „ Isaack f. „ „
2 Sep.	1683	„ „ Eva f. „ „
13 Nov.	1687	„ „ Dinah f. „ „
18 „	1688	„ „ Jacob f. „ „
14 Sep.	1690	„ „ Anna f. „ „
18 Apl.	1641	Weerf, Van der, Abigail f. Hubaert.
		Weert, de, (v. Sweerds).
11 Feb.	1599	Weesthoff, Anthonij f. Anthonij.
3 Oct.	1602	„ Daniel f. „
7 Nov.	1708	Weidius, Marten f. Martin & Sara Hamerton.
23 Sep.	1711	„ Maria f. „ & Sara.
1 Feb.	1646	Weigel, Samuel f. Joannes.
1 Oct.	1598	Weignaert, (v. Weijniaert), Anna f. Jan.
25 Mei	1702	Weijck, Van, Casper Pieter f. Willem & Pieternella van Beugem.
9 Dec.	1610	Weijde, Van der, Isaac f. Heindric
15 Nov.	1612	Weijden, „ „ Jacobus f. Henric.
7 Apl.	1616	„ „ „ Paulus f. Hendrick.
11 Mar.	1638	Weijer, Petrus f. Engel.
6 Oct.	1583	Weijlandts, Sara f. Jan.
18 Sep.	1661	Weijld, Maria f. Johannes.
22 Oct.	1679	Weijman, Margaretha f. Jacob.
24 Aug.	1576	Weijmans, Hester f. Bartholomeus.
12 Jan.	1680	„ Helena Maria f. Johannes, Ghedropt, int landt.
1 Mar.	1682	„ Maria f. Jacobus.
2 Aug.	1682	„ Cornelis f. Jan & Evan van Kouwenhaven.
5 Nov.	1587	Weijnaert, (v. Weignaert), Susanna f. Jan.
2 Jul.	1594	„ Joannes f. Jan.
3 Aug.	1589	Weijniaert, Susanna f. „
4 Mei	1591	„ Judith f. „
16 Jul.	1592	„ Elizabeth f. „
22 Oct.	1590	Weijrt, Van, Isaac f. Hubrecht.
22 Sep.	1588	Weijs, de, Abraham f. Guiliame.
20 Jul.	1606	Welhuijs, Van, Jason f. Anthony.
28 Sep.	1634	Wellekens, Abraham f. Abraham Laurens.
16 Oct.	1636	„ Maria f. Lauwerens.
2 Aug.	1638	„ Sara f. „
15 Jul.	1641	Welleken, Anna f. Laurens.
20 Nov.	1632	Wellesen, Johanna f. Jan.
4 Mar.	1634	„ Johannes f. „
8 Mar.	1607	Wels, Jacob f. Jorijs.
2 Mar.	1673	Wentelaer, Susanna f. Jan.
6 Jul.	1634	Wercke, Van der, Catharina f. Hubert.
20 Feb.	1811	Werninck, Henry Hope f. Jan & Lina van der Kaaij.
5 Jun.	1812	Werninck, Maria Lena f. Jan & Lina van der Kaaij.
29 Jun.	1814	„ Thomas James f. „ & Lina van der Kaaij. Test ; Thomas James Warren, Lord Viscount Bulkeley, etc.
16 Mar.	1816	„ Jan Spencer Wynn f. Jan & Lina van der Kaaij. Test : Thomas John, Lord Newborough, Spencer Wynn, etc.
3 Jul.	1632	Wert, Van der, Johannes f. Hubert.
3 Nov.	1667	Werth, de, Maria f. William & Elisabet.
11 Apl.	1669	„ „ Hanna f. Willem.
19 Jun.	1670	„ „ Elizabeth f. „
1 Dec.	1672	„ „ Sara f. „
27 Sep.	1675	„ „ Philip f. William.
15 Oct.	1618	Wespinck, Maria f. Pieter.
8 Jul.	1578	Wessels, Adam f. Jan.
25 Oct.	1582	„ Johannes f. „
11 Jul.	1587	„ Joannes & Adam } fi. „
2 Apl.	1605	„ Sara f. „
26 Dec.	1608	„ Maria f. „
3 Mar.	1611	„ Sara f. „
24 Jan.	1613	„ Debora f. „
7 Feb.	1613	„ Sara f. Abraham.
25 Jul.	1613	„ Susanna f. Dirick.
22 Jan.	1615	„ Abraham f. Dirick.
21 Jan.	1616	„ Susanna f. Dieric.
9 Jun.	1617	„ Agneta f. „
31 Jan.	1619	„ Daniel f. „
10 Sep.	1620	„ Elisabeth f. „
16 Sep.	1621	„ Joanna f. „
24 Aug.	1623	„ Catharina f. „
19 Jun.	1625	„ Nathanael f. „
30 Dec.	1627	„ Isaac f. „
7 Nov.	1613	„ Joannes f. Josias.
28 Sep.	1617	„ Joanna f. „
13 Dec.	1618	„ Catharina f. „
16 Jan.	1620	„ Jacobus f. „
22 Jul.	1621	„ Josias f. „
18 Oct.	1632	„ Abraham f. „
2 Mar.	1634	„ Isaac f. „
23 Aug.	1615	„ Cornelia f. Wessel.
1 Jun.	1617	„ Anna f. „
24 Jan.	1619	„ Johannes f. „
14 Oct.	1621	„ Catharina f. „
24 Mei	1629	„ „ f. „
25 Jun.	1619	„ Mirjam f. Jan.
6 Jan.	1628	„ Abraham f. John.
23 Jan.	1620	„ Lijdia f. Abraham.
5 Mei	1622	„ Abraham f. „
2 Aug.	1635	„ Wilhelmus f. Isias.
9 Nov.	1606	Westels, Abraham f. Jan.
17 Sep.	1610	Westen, Lambrecht f. Lambrecht.
16 Mar.	1610	Westerman, Jacob f. Jacob.
27 Sep.	1610	Westermannus, Adam f. Jacobus.
21 Jun.	1863	Westerveld, Edward f. Hendrik Christiaan, & Eliza Sharpe.
11 Jun.	1682	Westreicker, Abraham f. Ulrich.
27 Feb.	1676	Westricker, Valentin f. Johau Ulrich.
21 Mar.	1680	„ Abigail f. Ulrich.
20 Nov.	1681	„ Elizabeth f. Jacob & Frances.
21 Feb.	1686	„ Johannes f. Hans Ulrich.
11 Jul.	1633	Wets, Anna f. Pieter.
30 Dec.	1644	Weust, Cataryne f. Severijn.
25 Mei	1587	Wibo, (v. Wijbo), Maria f. Peeter.
18 Mar.	1610	„ Petrus f. Hans.

Oct. 1577 **Wichars**, Judith f. Willem.
Nov. 1601 **Wicke**, Abraham ⎱ fi. Abraham.
         & Catherijne ⎰
Mar. 1665 **Wickler**, Joannes f. Joannes.
Oct. 1618 **Widon**, Benjamin ⎱ fi. Jacob.
         & Joseph ⎰
Jun. 1628   ,, Margriete f. ,,
Apl. 1621 **Wiedon**, Isaac f. ,,
Mei 1579 **Wielardts**, Daniel f. Adam.
Jul. 1580 **Wielartz**, Jacob f. ,,
Jul. 1573 **Wiels**, ... f. Gillis.
Oct. 1603 **Wier**, Van de, Jeremias f. Pieter.
Oct. 1587 **Wierden**, ,, der, Abraham f. Carel.
Jan. 1634 **Wiers**, Sara f. Engels.
Feb. 1600 **Wies**, Joannes f. Pieter.
 ,, 1588 **Wiest**, de, Elizabeth f. Kaerle.
Sep. 1589   ,,   ,, Susanna f. Carel.
Jan. 1592   ,,   ,, Abigail f. ,,
Mar. 1593   ,,   ,, Jacob f. Kaerle.
Nov. 1607 **Wiestijnck**, Elisabeth f. Michiel.
Aug. 1606 **Wiesting**, Michiel f. ,,
Mei 1614 **Wiggers**, Guiljam f. Guiljam.
Aug. 1589 **Wighenen**, Elisabeth f. Niclaes.
Sep. 1585 **Wijbo**. (v. **Wibo**). Jooris f. Pieter.
Mar. 1590   ,, Susanna f. Pieter.
Dec. 1592   ,, Johanna f. Josias.
Jul. 1602   ,, Maria f. Hans.
Jul. 1604   ,, Joanna f. Jan.
Jul. 1607   ,, Petrus ⎱ fi. Hans.
          & Johannes ⎰
Apl. 1608 **Wijbrands**, Eduwaert f. Eduwaert.
Apl. 1601 **Wijchuijs**, Johanna f. Jan.
Sep. 1680 **Wijck**, Van, Anna f. Charles.
Feb. 1615 **Wijde**, Van der, Judith f. Hendric.
Aug. 1609 **Wijden**, ,, ,, Joanna f. ,,
Nov. 1604 **Wijeden**, ,, ,, Abraham f. ,,
Nov. 1594 **Wijer**, ,, ,, Susanna f. Pieter.
Jan. 1597   ,,   ,, ,, Anna f. ,,
Mar. 1601   ,,   ,, ,, Catheline f. ,,
 ,, 1866 **Wijk**, Van, Anthonie, geb. 31 Mar., 1861,
         f. Anthonie & Maria Hendrika Lindenhovius.
,,   ,,   ,,   ,, Willem Frederik, geb. 12 Nov., 1684, f. Anthonie & Maria Hendrika Lindenhovius.
,,   ,,   ,,   ,, Charles, geb. 2 Mar., 1866, f. Anthonie & Maria Hendrika Lindenhovius.
Mar. 1582 **Wijlandtz**, Joannes f. Jan.
Jul. 1580 **Wijlant**, Sara f. ,,
Dec. 1585   ,, Maria f. ,,
Sep. 1588   ,, Abraham f. ,,
Feb. 1593   ,, Hester f. ,,
Apl. 1612 .. Franciscus f. Daniel.
Dec. 1739 **Wijlick**, Jacob f. Abraham.
Mar. 1582 **Wijllars**, Daniel f. Adam.
Jan. 1607 **Wijmeersch**, Andrus f. Gheleys.
Feb. 1610   ,, Van, Catharina f. Geleyn.
Jan. 1593 **Wijnaert**, Joannes f. Dieric.
Jul. 1577 **Wijnckens**, Abraham f. Heindrick.
Mar. 1805 **Wijnen**, Gerard f. Wijnand Gerard & Mary Porter.
Jun. 1807   ,, James f. Wijnand Gerard & Mary Porter.
Dec. 1809   ,, Johanna f. Wijnand Gerard & Mary Porter.

17 Jun. 1832 **Wijnen**, Gerard Sylvanus f. Gerard & Gabrielle Silvanie.
23 Apl. 1837   ,, Altred Gabriel f. Gerard & Gabrielle Silvanie de Bray.
8 Jan. 1587 **Wijngene**, Van, Abraham f. Daniel.
18 Dec. 1586 **Wijnghe**, ,, Isaac f. Willem.
20 Aug. 1592 **Wijs**, de, Jacob f. Laurens.
3 Apl. 1603   ,, Cathelyne f. Pieter.
7 Mei 1604   ,, de, Esther f. Guillame.
6 Oct. 1611   ,, Ester f. Jan.
22 Nov. 1618   ,, ,, Elizabet f. ,,
12 Oct. 1628   ,, ,, Anna f. ,,
3 Apl. 1631 **Wis**, ,, Sara f. ,,
28 Jun. 1590 **Wijse**, ,, Susanna f. Guiliam.
15 Apl. 1593   ,, Sara f. Willem.
13 Oct. 1594   ,, Judith f. Guiliame.
17 Apl. 1597   ,, Abigail f. Guliam.
30 Sep. 1599   ,, Salomon f. Guiliaeme.
3 Jan. 1602   ,, Susanna f. Guliam.
5 Jul. 1607   ,, Assuerus f. Guilhame.
16 Mei 1591   ,, Jeremias f. Laurens.
6 Sep. 1593   ,, Joannes f. ,,
5 Mei 1622   ,, Pieter f. Conrad.
26 Sep. 1613   ,, Salomon f. Jan.
16 Jul. 1626   ,, Barbara f. ,,
29 Sep. 1622 **Wijtterspraet**, Jacobus f. Gregory.
1 Jul. 1705 **Wijttoos**, Baudewijn f. Philip & Anna.
12 Feb. 1626 **Wijtwijck**, Van, Dominicus f. posthumus
      ...... fs. Dominicus.
4 Jul. 1736 **Wilcke**, Elisabeth f. Augustinus & Francina.
28 Jul. 1751 **Wilde**, de, Samuel f. Samuel & Francijna.
9 Nov. 1651   ,,   ,, alias **Sauvage**, Maria f. Jan.
9 Feb. 1648   ,,   ,,   ,, Abraham f. ,,
9 Feb. 1654   ,,   ,,   ,, Magdalene f. ,,
16 Sep. 1655   ,,   ,,   ,, Johannes f. ,,
7 Jun. 1607 **Wilhelms**, Esaias ⎱ fi. Christiaen.
         & Susanna ⎰
21 Jul. 1507 **Willarts**, Adam f. Adam.
20 Jun. 1585   ,, Maria f. ,,
20 Oct. 1586 **Williarts**, de, Abraham f. Jan.
28 Jul. 1605 **Willeburt**, Elisabet f. Johan.
8 Jan. 1699 **Willecom**, Catharina f. Jacob.
17 Nov. 1611   ,, Jacob f. ,,
15 Mei 1514   ,, Lucretia f. ,,
4 Feb. 1614   ,, Maria f. ,,
21 Sep. 1623   ,, Richard f. ,,
24 Dec. 1581 **Willems**, Jeremias f. Adam.
8 Sep. 1583   ,, Anna f. ,,
31 Oct. 1573   ,, Michiel f. Gueernert.
13 Nov. 1575   ,, Paulus f. Hendrick.
24 Apl. 1581   ,, Magdalene f. ,,
5 Sep. 1585   ,, Joannes f. ,,
7 Oct. 1589   ,, Sara f. ,,
2 Jun. 1709   ,, Jan ⎱ fi. Jan & Anna van
       & Elisabeth ⎰ Gelder.
13 Oct. 1583   ,, Kunera f. Lambrecht.
5 Sep. 1605   ,, Maria f. Pauwels.
5 Oct. 1601   ,, Maria f. Pieter & Anneken.
20 Jan. 1572 **Willemsen**, Marcus f. Gerardus.
16 Mei 1630   ,, Henderickus f. Jan.
11 Jun. 1645   ,, Jacobus f. Jacobus.
23 Oct. 1667   ,, Anna f. Jacob.
8 Sep. 1684   ,, Anna Maria f. Jacob & Anna.
29 Mar. 1683   ,, Jacobus f. ,,
10 Oct. 1675   ,, Willem f. Leendert.
11 Nov. 1675   ,, Willem f. Thomas.

M

20 Jan.	1678	Willemsen, Barbara f. Joost.
22 Jan.	1688	„ Maritje f. Pieter & Janneden.
25 Jul.	1585	„ Jacob f. Lambert.
17 Dec.	1587	Willemsz, Maria f. Lambrecht.
1 Mar.	1590	„ Abraham f. „
16 Sep.	1593	„ David f. „
20 Mar.	1597	„ Salomon f. „
1 Jan.	1600	„ Maria f. „
8 Nov.	1584	„ Rebecca f. Joos.
29 Jan.	1587	„ Nathanael f. „
23 Nov.	1589	„ Gulielmus f. „
26 Feb.	1587	„ Joannes f. Hendrick.
19 Jul.	1590	„ Cornelis f. „
18 Jun.	1592	„ Catherine f. „
26 Dec.	1596	„ Thomas f. Thomas.
11 Mei	1606	„ Christiaen f. Christiaen.
18 Feb.	1610	„ Guillaume f. Jeronymus
21 Jul.	1611	„ Josina f. Hieronijmus.
8 Aug.	1613	„ Rachel f. „
20 Feb.	1616	„ Maria f. „
6 Mar.	1617	„ Johanna f. „
4 Mei	1620	„ Jacobus f. „
17 Aug.	1623	„ Maria f. Gomar.
31 Jul.	1825	„ Jeremias f. „
8 Jul.	1627	„ Johanna f. „
13 Sep.	1629	„ Bernardus f. „
29 Feb.	1624	„ Thomas f. Thomas.
8 Oct.	1693	„ Anna f. Pieter & S.
28 Mei	1871	Willigen, Van, Johanna Maria Catharina f. Gerrit & Guurtje Veen.
6 Sep.	1612	Willis, Daniel f. Humfry.
27 Mar.	1614	„ Catharina f. Hnafred.
20 Feb.	1616	Willes, Maria f. Umphrij.
5 Jun.	1586	Wilmets, Joannes f. Jan.
14 Oct.	1792	Wilmoe, Elizabeth f. Leendert & Elizabeth Hartman.
2 Dec.	1571	Wilmoet, Jacob f. Daniel.
19 Jul.	1607	Wils, Leonardus f. Lambrecht.
14 Jan.	1610	„ Rachel f. Georis.
6 Mei.	1614	„ Debora f. Joris.
13 Jul.	1617	„ Elisabet f. „
13 Jan.	1619	„ f. „
14 Nov.	1596	Wilsen, Abraham f. Lambrecht.
28 Jan.	1599	„ Elizabeth f. „ Testes, Bartholomeus Crombrugge ende Christina uxor Jaques van Hoorue.
21 Mar.	1591	Wijnants, Daniel f. Jan.
1 Jan.	1615	Winants, Joanna f. Hans.
27 Apl.	1692	Winckel, Maria f. Hendrick, matroos.
23 Jan.	1588	Wingene, Van, Elisabeth f. Daniel.
8 Apl.	1632	Winger, Johannes f. Engel.
4 Dec.	1580	Winghe, Samuel f. Lowijs.
2 Feb	1584	Winghem, Van, Sara f. Willem.
3 Apl.	1589	Winghene, Van, Esther f. Daniel.
13 Nov.	1586	Winne, de, Johannes f. „
5 Dec.	1588	„ „ Peter f. „
14 Oct.	1591	„ Jeremias f. „
21 Jul.	1594	„ de, Susanna f. „
19 Jul.	1618	„ „ Jacobus f. Pieter.
24 Aug.	1617	Winnen, Petrus f. Hans.
20 Oct.	1622	„ Jonathan f. „
9 Jan.	1625	„ Rebecca f. „
16 Feb.	1589	Winterbeke, Van, Joannes f. Jan.
18 Oct.	1590	„ „ Magdalena f. „
8 Jun.	1590	„ „ Joanna f. Niclaes.
22 Apl.	1593	„ „ Nicolaes f. Nicolaes.
26 Oct.	1578	Wintgens, Abraham f. Henrick.
25 Mei	1620	Wisbije, Elisabet f. Pieter.
9 Oct.	1589	Wisele, Van, Sara f. Joos.
26 Jan.	1585	Wissels, Sara f. Jan.
11 Apl.	1697	With, du, Johannes f. „
20 Jan.	1678	Witt, de, Daniel f. Martinus.
24 Sep.	1679	„ „ Martinus f. „
15 Jan.	1682	„ „ Maerten f. Maerten.
27 Apl.	1690	„ Mary f. Jan & Mary.
30 Jan.	1589	Witte, de, Pieter f. Gielis.
1 Jun.	1587	„ „ Margriete f. Gillis.
19 Mei	1583	„ „ Esther f. Nicolas.
29 Jan.	1596	„ „ Susanna f. Jaques.
5 Feb.	1611	„ de, Joannes f. Jan.
8 Jun.	1589	Wittewrongel, Jacob f. Jacus.
12 Dec.	1591	„ Jacobus f. Jaques.
4 Jul.	1598	„ Anna f. Jaques.
8 Dec.	1616	„ „ f. „
1 Nov.	1618	„ Joannes f. Jacob.
13 Jan.	1594	„ Maria f. Jan.
24 Aug.	1374	Wittewrongele, Daniel f. Jacques.
13 Jan.	1579	Witts, de, (v. Witt), Philippus f. Niclaes.
15 Jun.	1679	Woedert, (v. Woodward), Johannes f. Servaes & Annetgen Rybbels.'
31 Oct.	1683	„ Sara f. Servaes & Annetgen Tibbel.
18 Oct.	1642	Woeringen, (v. Worigaen), Abigail f. Johan.
10 Apl.	1597	Woesthof, Maria f. Anthonis.
16 Dec.	1604	„ Abraham f. Anthonie.
25 Jan.	1607	„ Isaac f. Anthonius.
15 Oct.	1609	„ Susanna f. Anthony.
24 Oct.	1603	Woesthof, Anthonius f. Isaack.
22 Jun.	1600	Wooesthof, Mathias f. Anthoni.
5 Jun.	1609	Woestinck, Johannes f. Michiel.
18 Dec.	1592	Wolbort, Lea f. Sampson.
23 Jan.	1651	Wolf, Theodorus f. Ernest.
19 Dec.	1652	„ Benjamin f. Ernst.
26 Jun.	1659	„ Anna f. „
19 Feb.	1661	„ Hendrick f. Eruest.
15 Jul.	1662	„ Caterina f. Joris.
5 Apl.	1664	„ Maria f. „
1 Jun.	1691	„ Sara f. Hendrick.
19 Oct.	1656	Wolff, Catarina f. Ernst.
28 Jan.	1683	Wolfrant, Maria f. Abraham & Magdalena Koninghs.
18 Mar.	1648	Wolft, Ernst f. Ernst.
18 Jul.	1649	„ Paulus f. „
9 Dec.	1654	„ Sara f. „
23 Jun.	1612	Wols, Jooris f. Jooris.
19 Jul.	1573	Wolters, Samuel f. Gheeraerts.
1 Nov.	1605	Wonder, Pieter f. Willem.
5 Jul.	1612	„ Willem f. „
11 Dec.	1614	„ Susanne f. „
28 Sep.	1591	Wons, Van der, (v. Wans), Geeraert f. Jar
31 Aug.	1617	Woodstock, Elisabeth f. Dionijs.
1 Apl.	1685	Woodward, (v. Woedert), Abraham f. Ser vaes.
23 Mar.	1687	„ Abraham f. Servaes
14 Nov.	1688	„ Sara f. „ & Anna.
20 Apl.	1692	„ Isaac f. Servaes.
9 Dec.	1694	„ Jacob f. „ & Anneken.
17 Jul.	1681	Woodworth, Elisabet f. ,.
21 Jun.	1633	Worigaen, (v. Woeringen), Joannes f. Jar
15 Dec.	1633	Worigen, Van, Johannes f. Jan.
9 Jan.	1631	Worigen, Susanna f. „
25 Sep.	1649	Worrigen, Sara f. „
12 Jul.	1629	Worringe, ... f. „
26 Nov.	1645	Worringen, Joannes f. „

4 Dec.	1572	Wortele, Van de, Judith f. Joos.
2 Jun.	1588	Woudneel, (v. Woutneel), Abraham f. Hans.
7 Jun.	1699	Woust, Martinus f. Augustin & Elizabeth.
3 Apl.	1601	Wouterghen, Abigail f. Joos.
3 Apl.	1603	„ Van, Jacobus f. „
5 Mar.	1572	Wouters, (v. Wauters), Susanna f. Medaert.
1 Mar.	1579	Wouters, Samuel f. Geerardts.
3 Feb.	1584	„ Pieter f. Gerardts.
4 Mei	1589	„ Geerardus f. „
0 Jul.	1605	„ Sara f. Hutgert.
5 Jan.	1607	„ Robert f. „
3 Feb.	1610	„ Joanna f. Hartgee.
6 Mar.	1615	„ Wonter f. Jan.
9 Mei	1641	„ Maria f. Arnout.
4 Aug.	1644	„ Maria f. „
5 Mar.	1646	., Lidia f. „
5 Mar.	1676	„ Cornelia f. Jacob.

25 Jan.	1596	Woutneel, (v. Woudneel), Sara f. Hans.
17 Jan.	1591	Wringen, Van, Sara f. Daniel.
24 Feb.	1611	Wtman, Elizabeth f. Albert.
29 Jun.	1595	Wtwijck, Van, (v. Wijtwyck), Dominicus f. Dominicus.
6 Jun.	1596	„ „ Rachel f. Dominicus.
11 Jun.	1598	„ „ Joannes f. „
24 Aug.	1600	„ „ Elizabeth f. „
10 Mar.	1586	Zagere, de, Tobias f. Stevens.
12 „	1587	„ „ Lucas f. „
27 Jun.	1602	Zaselvelt, Daniel f. Daniel.
1 Aug.	1688	Zee, Van der, Jacobus f. Cornelis & Cornelia.
12 Aug.	1827	Zeebroek, Elizabeth f. Cornelius & Barbara Snabel.
15 Jun.	1679	Zeeuw, de, Catarina f. Jan.
1 Jan.	1587	Zinnick, Van, Gertruyt f. Adam.

25 Sep.	1575	Abigail	f. Emseen.
29 Oct.	1581	„	f. ......
21 Dec.	1589	„	f. ......
10 Jan.	1591	„	f. ......
8 Jun.	1595	„	f. ......
18 Mar.	1596	„	f. ......
5 Feb.	1615	„	f. ......
7 Jan.	1621	„	f. ......
25 Aug.	1675	Abram	f. ......
4 Nov.	1571	Abraham	f. ......
21 Nov.	1571	„	f. ......
20 Jan.	1572	„	f. ......
1 Nov.	1590	„	f. ......
22 Nov.	1590	„	f. ......
21 Aug.	1593	„	f. Hans.
23 Jan.	1603	„	f. ......
8 Jan.	1615	„	f. ......
1 Feb.	1627	„	f. ......
9 Oct.	1631	Abraham	f. ......
22 Jan.	1633	„	f. ......
24 Jul.	1636	„	f. Abraham.
17 Dec.	1646	...ieren, Van, „	f. Gerhaert.
2 Aug.	1585	Adolf	f. ......
17 Apl.	1681	Aeltje	f. ......
12 Nov.	1592	Anna	f. ......
21 Jun.	1584	„	f. ......
17 Dec.	1589	„	f. ......
27 Oct.	1594	„	f. ......
27 Apl.	1595	„	f. ......
2 Oct.	1597	„	f. ......
5 Feb.	1600	„	f. ......
26 Apl.	1612	„	f. ......
6 Jun.	1616	„	f. ......
17 Nov.	1616	„	f. ......
24 Dec.	1620	„	f. ......
2 Dec.	1624	„	f. ......
24 Mei	1627	„	f. ......
29 Mar.	1631	„	f. ......

28 Jun.	1635	Anna	f. ......
1 Apl.	1677	„	f. ......
27 Feb.	1631	Arnoldus	f. ......
27 Mar.	1628	Augustinus	f. ......
9 Mei	1591	Barbara	f. ......
3 Aug.	1625	„	f. ......
30 Oct.	1631	„	f. ......
20 Apl.	1572	Bodewijn	f. ......
30 Nov.	1589	Kaerle	f. ......
28 Sep.	1617	Carolus	f. ......
29 Apl.	1627	Carel	f. ......
5 Sep.	1630	Carolus	f. ......
30 Jan.	1582	Caterina	f. ......
7 Jan.	1582	Catharina	f. ......
22 Mar.	1582	Catharina	f. ......
1 Jun.	1585	Catherine	f. ......
2 Nov.	1589	Catheline	f. ......
4 Feb.	1593	Catharina	f. ......
21 Nov.	1619	„	f. ......
2 Jun.	1622	„	f. ...... tot Mortlake.
30 Nov.	1623	„	f. ......
22 Feb.	1631	„	f. Jan.
1 Apl.	1621	Charlotte	f. ......
24 Mar.	1622	Christoffel	f. ......
26 Aug.	1638	Clemens	f. ......
5 Apl.	1590	Van der ...Daniel	f. Jacop.
8 Aug.	1592	(illegible) „	f. ......
7 Nov.	1585	„	f. Renier.
22 Jan.	1590	David	f. Philips.
4 Jul.	1592	„	f. ......
2 Apl.	1620	„	f. ......
3 Aug.	1628	„	f. ......
2 Mar.	1591	Debora	f. ......
22 Aug.	1596	Debora & Judith }	fw. ......

12 Jun. 1608	Debora	f. ......
25 Nov. 1599	Dorothea	f. ......
24 Aug. 1617	,,	f. ......
22 Jul. 1677	Eduard	f. ......
24 Aug. 1578	Elizabeth	f. ......
10 Mei 1584	Elisabeth	f. Heurick.
22 Aug. 1585	,,	f. ......
20 Aug. 1585	Elisabet	f. ......
4 Jun. 1588	Elisabeth	f. ......
16 Jun. 1588	,,	f. ......
1 Nov. 1590	,,	f. ......
2 Jan. 1592	,,	f. ......
20 Aug. 1592	,,	f. ....
15 Jul. 1593	,,	f. ......
2 Aug. 1603	,,	f. ......
2 Apl. 1615	,,	f. ......
6 ,, 1619	,,	f. ......
30 Nov. 1023	,,	f. ......
27 Jun. 1624	,,	f. ......
19 Jan. 1634	,,	f. ......
11 Mar. 1638	,,	f. ......
27 Aug. 1676	.... (Illegible). ,,	f. Jan.
28 Jul. 1583	Emerentiana	f. ......
30 Aug. 1640	Engel	f. Engel.
20 Sep. 1612	Ester	f. ......
18 Apl. 1613	,,	f. ......
21 Sep. 1582	Esther	f. ......
3 Mei 1620	,,	f. ......
6 Apl. 1600	Eva	f. Anthonis.
29 Dec. 1647	Ezechiel	f. ......
13 Feb. 1625	Francijnken	f. ......
2 Jul. 1581	Fransoija	f. ......
12 Apl. 1682	George	f. ......
11 Dec. 1580	Gijselbrecht	f. ......
12 Mei 1605	Gillis	f. ......
10 Sep. 1609	Goolken	fa. ......
27 Mar. 1586	Guilielmus	f. ......
5 Sep. 1619	Helena	f. ......
23 Jun. 1616	Hendric	f. ......
8 Aug. 1619	,,	f. ......
6 Mar. 1586	Hendrick	f. ......
26 Nov. 1587	,,	f. Hendrick.
24 Feb. 1631	,,	f. ......
4 Jun. 1583	Heurick	f. ......
7 Oct. 1585	,,	f. ......
21 Jan. 1627	Henricus	f. ......
3 Apl. 1681	Hermannus	f. ......
24 Mar. 1577	Hester	f. ......
31 Jan. 1591	,,	f. ......
5 Dec. 1591	,,	f. ......
26 Aug. 1599	,,	f. ... ..
16 Mei 1577	Hesther	f. Emsen.
24 Jan. 1591	,,	f. ......
Feb. 1582	Jacob	f. O. ...
28 Jul. 1583	Jacobus	f. ......
1 Jun. 1589	,,	f. ......
26 Oct. 1589	,,	f. ......
6 Jan. 1590	Jacob	f. ......
1 Aug. 1591	Jacobus	f. ......
28 Jan. 1593	,,	f. ......
20 Jan. 1594	,,	f. ... ...
7 Mar. 1596	,,	f. ......
26 Nov. 1598	Jacob	f. ......

23 Sep. 1604	Jacobus	f. Geole.
18 Jan. 1607	,,	f. ......
25 Mar. 1610	,,	f. ......
20 Jan. 1611	,,	f. ......
17 Mar. 1611	,,	f. ......
10 Oct. 1613	,,	f. ......
26 Aug. 1619	,,	f. ......
15 Apl. 1621	,,	f. Jacob.
22 Jun. 1628	,,	f. ......
3 Jan. 1630	,,	f. ......
17 Jul. 1631	,,	f. ......
18 Dec. 1631	,,	f. ......
28 Jun. 1635	,,	f. ......
15 Dec. 1635	,,	f. ......
11 Jun. 1637	,,	f. ......
24 Jan. 1675	,,	f. ......
8 Sep. 1680	,,	f. ......
2 Aug. 1584	Janneken	f. ......
16 Mei 1587	,,	f. ......
21 Sep. 1589	,,	f. ... ..
8 Aug. 1631	,,	f. ......
28 Dec. 1585	Jaquemynken	f. ......
25 Jul. 1586	Jeremias	f, ...
19 Jun. 1608	Jeronymus	f. ......
21 Apl. 1588	Joanna	f. ......
21 Jan. 1627	,,	f. ......
2 Jan. 1625	Johanna	f. ......
22 Jan. 1643	,,	f. ......
19 Oct. 1690	,, Cunera	f. ......
7 Jan. 1582	Joannes	f. ......
28 Jan. 1582	,,	f. ......
15 Jul. 1582	,,	f. ......
19 Mar. 1588	,,	f. Reniers.
4 Aug. 1588	Joannes	f. ......
27 Apl. 1589	,,	f. Laureys
29 Jun. 1595	,,	f. Leonard
15 Aug. 1596	de ...... (Ill:) ,,	f. Jan.
29 Jul. 1604	,,	f. ......
43 Feb. 1611	,,	f. ......
1 Mei 1614	,,	f. ......
2 Apl. 1615	Johannes	f. ......
9 Mar. 1630	,,	f. ......
... Feb. 1582	,,	f. ......
5 ... 1587	,,	f. ......
28 Apl. 1605	,,	f. ......
3 Aug. 1628	,,	f. ......
12 Apl. 1629	,,	f. ......
7 Sep. 1630	,,	f. ......
11 Nov. 1632	Joseph	f. ......
27 Aug. 1676	Jossynken	f. ......
7 Jan. 1683	Jossynken	f. ......
20 Jun. 1630	Joris	f. ......
18 Mar. 1593	Isaac	f. ......
13 Apl. 1600	,,	f. ......
21 Jan. 1627	,,	f. ......
20 Apl. 1579	Isaack	f. ......
10 Sep. 1587	Judith	f. ......
30 Aug. 1601	,,	f. ......
3 Sep. 1592	,,	f. ......
7 Mei 1598	Judith & Debora	fæ. ......
16 Feb. 1578	Judith	f. ......
21 Aug. 1586		
7 Jul. 1588		
21 Dec. 1595		
25 Jul. 1596		
22 Aug. 1596		
2 Sep. 1604		

Date	Year	Name	f.	Date	Year		f.	Name	f.
27 Jun.	1612	Judith	f.	21 Aug.	1580		f.	Petrus	f. ......
28 Jan.	1627	,,	f.	21 Jun.	1584		f.	,,	f. ......
27 Dec.	1579	Justina	f. Marcus.	2 Nov.	1587		f.	,,	f. Herman.
11 Sep.	1603	Leonard	f. van de we-duwe...	19 Apl.	1590		f.	,,	f. ......
28 Feb.	1585	Lijdia	f.	15 Aug.	1591		f.	,,	f. ......
11 Nov.	1604	,,	f.	16 Sep.	1604		f.	,,	f. ......
27 Jul.	1617	,,	f.	10 Dec.	1609		f.	,,	f. ......
30 Mei	1588	Lodowicus	f.	22 Mei	1614		f.	,,	f. ......
8 ,,	1625	Lonijs	f.	30 Nov.	1623		f.	Pieter	f. Dierick.
3 Mar.	1590	—cket (ill:) Lucretia	f. Robert.	22 Mei	1631		f.	,,	f. ......
16 Jan.	1614	Marcus	f.	16 Nov.	1582		f.	,,	f. ......
23 Jul.	1579	Maria	f.	29 Oct.	1598		f.	Rebecca	f. ......
15 Mei	1581	,,	f.	3 Apl.	1681		f.	,,	f. ......
2 Dec.	1582	,,	f.	4 Feb.	1593		f.	Rocland	f. ......
4 ,,	1586	,,	f.	24 Feb.	1633		f.		
26 Dec.	1586	,,	f.	18 Mar.	1634		f.		
25 Aug.	1588	,,	f.						
19 Dec.	1588	,,	f.	22 Mar.	1590		f.	Salomon	f. ......
23 Feb.	1589	,,	f.	16 Mar.	1589		f.	Samuel	f. Cornelis.
8 Jun.	1589	Marie	f.	1 Jun.	1589		f.	,,	f. ......
14 Feb.	1591	Maria	f. Hendrick	11 Jan.	1596		f.	Sara	f. ......
9 Apl.	1592	,,	f.	8 Jul.	1571		f.	,,	f. ......
18 Jun.	1592	Marie	f.	10 Feb.	1572		f.	,,	f. ......
10 Nov.	1594	Maria	f.	31 Aug.	1572		f.	,,	f. ......
5 Jan.	1595	,,	f.	30 Aug.	1579		f.	,,	f. ......
23 Mar.	1595	,,	f.	20 Oct.	1583		f.	,,	f. ......
6 Apl.	1598	,,	f.	6 Sep.	1584		f.	,,	f. ......
30 Dec.	1599	Marie	f.	27 Nov.	1586		f.	,,	f. ......
23 Nov.	1600	Maria	f.	5 Feb.	1587		f.	,,	f. ......
26 Aug.	1604	,,	f.	28 Feb.	1587		f.	,,	f. ......
4 Feb.	1606	,,	f. Antoni.	20 Oct.	1588		f.	,,	f. ......
9 Feb.	1610	,,	f.	30 Mei	1588		f.	,,	f. ......
8 Nov.	1610	,,	f.	27 Apl.	1589		f.	,,	f. ......
20 Jan.	1611	,,	f.	7 Sep.	1589		f.	,,	f. ......
15 Feb.	1614	,,	f.	2 Nov.	1589		f.	,,	f. ......
12 Jun.	1614	,,	f.	20 Apl.	1590		f.	,,	f. ......
28 Jun.	1618	,,	f.	25 Oct.	1590		f.	,,	f. ......
30 Dec.	1621	,,	f.	17 Feb.	1594		f.	,,	f. ......
11 Aug.	1622	,,	f.	6 Mar.	1597		f.	,,	f. ......
13 Sep.	1629	,,	f.	1 Mar.	1601		f.	,,	f. ......
25 Oct.	1629	,,	f.	5 Jul.	1601		f.	,,	f. ......
5 Sep.	1630	,,	f.	13 Aug.	1604		f.	,,	f. ......
3 Mei	1631	,,	f.	8 Dec.	1611		f.	,,	f. ......
11 Mar.	1632	,,	f.	2 Mei	1614		f.	,,	f. ......
13 Oct.	1633	,,	f.	21 Mar.	1624		f.	,,	f. ......
5 Oct.	1639	,,	f.	22 Dec.	1631		f.	,,	f. ......
13 Apl.	1681	,,	f.	15 Apl.	1638	B.........	f. Joodocus.	,,	f. Joodocus.
19 Oct.	1690	Mary	f.	30 Aug.	1621		f.	Sijmeon	f. ......
14 Aug.	1586	Martinus	f.	29 Jul.	1582		f.	Simon	f. ......
16 Nov.	1589	Mathys	f.	6 Apl.	1578		f.	Susanna	f. ......
4 Sep.	1625	Michael	f.	3 Jan.	1580		f.	,,	f. Jusparus.
19 Oct.	1603	Michiel	f. Michiel.	11 Nov.	1582		f.	,,	f. ......
6 Jan.	1572	Moyses	f.	11 Aug.	1583		f.	,,	f. ......
16 Jan.	1578	Moses	f. Guiliame.	27 Jun.	1585		f.	,,	f. ......
6 Jan.	1633	,,	f.	5 Aug.	1585		f.	,,	f. ......
				25 ,,	1588		f.	,,	f. ......
18 Dec.	1597	Nathaniel	f.	4 Feb.	1588		f.	,,	f. ......
8 Dec.	1588	Neelken	f.	20 Jun.	1589		f.	,,	f. ......
17 Nov.	1611	Nicolaus	f.	16 Nov.	1595		f.	,,	f. ......
				21 Dec.	1611		f.	,,	f. ......
17 Jul.	1631	Orangia	f.	22 Nov.	1618		f.	,,	f. ......
				1 Dec.	1622		f.	,,	f. ......
20 Jul.	1595	Paulus	f.	6 Mei	1632		f.	,,	f. ......
13 Aug.	1611	,,	f.	26 Oct.	1634		f.	,,	f. ......
4 Jul.	1585	Pauwelijnken	f.	27 Oct.	1678		f.	,,	f. ......
30 Aug.	1633	Philippus	f.	4 Apl.	1680		f.	,,	f. ......
13 Mar.	1586	Peeter	f.						

4 Jan.	1573	Tabijtha	f. Jan.	4 Nov.	1571	Wilhelmus	f. ......
26 Sep.	1585	Tabitha	f.	13 Nov.	1631	,,	f. ......
2 Dec.	1595	Thomas	f.	4 Jan.	1590	Willem	f. Hendrick.
4 Jan.	1601	,,	f.	14 Nov.	1626	,,	f. ......
27 Sep.	1618	,,	f.	6 Nov.	1634	,,	f. ......
27 Oct.	1622	,,	f.	18 Mei	1690	,,	f. ......
10 Dec.	1679	,,	f.				
24 Mar.	1577	Tobias	f.	28 Mei	1584	Zacharias	f. Gonofeva.
26 Sep.	1585	,,	f.	5 Apl.	1590	,,	f. ......
				30 Mei	1594	,,	f. ......
1 Dec.	1700	Valentijn	f.	11 Mar.	1610	Zels	fa. ......

(1) Hier achtervolgen die namen der gheener die onser Neederduijtscher gemeinte getrauwet zijne beginnende van den Jare 1571.

(2) Register der persoonen die Ghetrout sijn inde Nederduijtsche ghemeijnte binnen Londen, van den jaere 1602.

12 Aug.	1582	Baijken	**Aalmans** met Pieter Hoste.
11 Apl.	1581	Cateryne van der	**Aardt** ,, Daniel van Boshuijsen.
4 Sep.	1628	Johannes van	**Abeele**, van Norwich, wedr. v. Maria van Ixem met Johanna de Weelde we. v. Andries Boeve.
... Aug.	1620	Elizabet	**Abeels** met Daniel Stact.
10 Sep.	1594	Barbara	**Abels** ,, Abraham van Acker.
10 Dec.	1611	Elko	,, , van Emden, met Ester Mils v. Londen.
8 Jan.	1594	Baudewyn	**Achtschellinck** v. Brussel met Geertruyt le Petin v. Brussel, we. Adam van Sinnick.
... Oct.	1615	Jeremias	,, v. Brussel met Susanna Burgley v. Rotterdam.
10 Sep.	1594	Abraham van	**Acker** v. Aken met Barbara Abels v. Antwerpen, we. Renier Craije.
3 Mei	1614	Anna	,, met Jacques Wittewrongel.
21 Nov.	1581	Symon	**Adams** v. Harlinghen met Margriete Elsen v. Venloo.
25 Apl.	1622	Francynken	,, we. van Jan Brusloo met Gillis Coene.
27 ,,	1857	Eliz: Margaretha	**Admiraal** met Gerardus Dubois.
9 Feb.	1589	Hubrecht	**Adraenssen** v. Bergen op Zoom met Francynken van den Bossche, v. Brussel, we. Passchier de Wevre.
29 Jun.	1584	Melken	**Adriaens** met Dieryck Hermans.
22 Apl.	1623	Susanna	,, we. Jeffrey Rans met Willem de Grave.
18 ,,	1591	Gedeon	**Adriaensen**, v. Norwyts, met Barbara l'epernans v. Brussel.
20 Mei	1571	Adriaenken	**Adriaensz**, we. Cornelis Jacobsz, met Christiaen Quirintzen.
7 Apl.	1608	Willem	,, v. s'Hertoghen Bossche met Maria Samijn, we. Nicolaes de Deuxvilles.
15 Mei	1581	Claeys	**Adrijaenssen** v. Amsterdam met Janneken Macequies v. Steenvoort.
21 Feb.	1604	Paschynken van	**Aecken**, we. Hans Heijns, met Dirick Janssz.
24 Nov.	1577	Margriete	**Aelberts**, we. Hans Drossaert, met Joos Gheldolf.
12 ,,	1594	Hendrick	**Aelbertss**, wt sticht v. Bremen, met Maeyken Loijs, v. Venloo, we. Hans van der Beke.
28 Jan.	1578	Hendrick	**Aelmans** (v. Alman), v. Maseijck met Lyntken Jannesnv, Antwerpen, we. Christiaer Crabbe.
17 Dec.	1594	Anna	**Aelst** met Joris Bolle.
10 Sep.	1611		,, ,, , we. Joris Bolle, met Jaspar Tyan.
19 Apl.	1577	Susanne	**Aernoudts** met Franchoys Bols.
18 Jul.	1598	Sybrecht	,, , v. Solinghen, met Tannekin Mus, v. Antwerpen, we. Joos vanden Eynde.
12 Apl.	1575	Margriete	**Aernouts** met Pauwels Puts.
31 Mar.	1608	Maeyken	**Aertooen** met Jan Evans.
18 Jul.	1591	Lyntgen	**Aertsen** met Bernaert Janssen van Loou.
4 Jan.	1615	Aruout	,, v. Andwerpen met Janneken Clamp, we. Jeronymus van der Elst.
31 Mei	1596	Cornelis	**Aertsz** v. Amersfort met Judith Beeckman v. Londen.
12 Sep.	1598	Wouter	,, v. s'Hertogenbossche met Anna van Asse v. Londen, we. Rogier Vercoolgen.
... Jul.	1613	Matthys	,, v. Gorchum met Catharina Mijleman v. Andwerpen.
28 Feb.	1572	Kaerken van	**Aken**, we. Jan Janssen ,met Nicolaus van der Luffel.
8 Oct.	1579	Kaarken	,, ,, , we. Niclaus van Luffel, met Franchois Janssens Diericksen.
25 Fel.	1595	Passschynken	,, ,, , we. Guilieme Ketele, met Jan Heijns.
12 Jan.	1608	Paschyne	,, ,, , we. Derick Jansz, met Jan Sonnevil.
14 Jul.	1573	Olivier	**Alard** v. Ghendt met Helena Heymdricks v. Oudenarde.
17 Jan.	1604	Willem	**Alberts**, uijt het sticht v. Munster, met Heylken Heijndrix, we. Herman Couper.
29 Nov.	1608	Isaac	**Albertssz**, v. Londen, met Susanne de Brune v. Lin (Lynn).
5 Feb.	1600	Jans	**Alewyns**, v. Antwerpen, met Ottilia van Metren v. Londen.
5 Jul.	1614	Samuel	**Alewyn**, v. Antwerpen, met Ester Garnoot v. Maidston.
1 Feb.	1574	Maijken	**Almans** (v. Aelmans) met Laurens Hughers.
5 Oct.	1692	Helena Exalto D'	**Almeras** met Hendrick l'atroon.
3 Feb.	1692	Margarita	,, ,, (v. Exalto) met Bastiaen Gommersbagh.
22 Jan.	1679	Petronella van	**Alten** met Benjamin de Bruijn.
5 Jul.	1603	Paulynken	**Anderlicht** met Charles Hutzebout.
29 Jan.	1594	Magdaleene	**Andries** met Aernout de Grave.
23 Sep.	1691	David	**Andrissen**, j. m. v. Delft, met Cornelia Mente, we. v. Joris Wintervoet, me attestatie v. St. James.
7 Mei	1611	Engel	**Annesen**, v. Vincke in Vlaenderen, met Agnete van der Stelte v. Gendt.

(1) Vol. I. (2) Vol. II.

1597	Barbel	**Anthoni** met Jan Nieuwiert.
1571	,,	**Anthonio**, we. Raas van Buere, met Marten Boven.
1573	Barbelken	**Anthonis**, we. Jaspar van Dale, ,, Jan Goolschalck.
1573	Tanneken	,, met Jan vander Vliet.
1613	Anna	,, met Abraham Elinck.
1594	Susanna	**Anthonisz** met Gillis de la Porte.
1575	Maijken	**Anthonissen** met L. Christiaens.
1580	Jan	**Antuenis**, v. Kouelens, met Cecilie Lambrechts, we. Adrians Goldtheen, v. Leyssen bij Treven.
1601	Hendrick	**Anthenius**, wt. d'lant v. Cleve, met Iken Mijsers v. Gelder, we. Dierick Nuaert.
1591	Maeyken	**Anxken**, met Adriaen Browers.
1573	Janneken	**Appels**, met Albrecht Sproek.
1607	Hendrick	**Archer** v. Huntingdoneshere met Esther Geerart, we. Jan Tijts.
1591	Jacomyne	**Ardewijns**, we. Geraert Janssen, met Geraert Pieters.
1577	Cathlyne	**Ardtssen**, we. Jakes Seeris, met Franchois Cousijn.
1604	Thomas	**Armedstede**, wt. Yorksheere, met Tanneken Libaert, we. Jaeus Nachtegael.
1604	Sibrand	**Aruol**, uijt t'landt vande Berge, met Elisabeth Molyn, we. Jan de Bick.
1603	Zibericht	**Arnold**, wt. lant van den Berghe, met Catharine Petit, we. Lambrecht Pieter z
1572	Arnoudt	**Arnoudtzn**, v. Amstelrdam, met Margriete Pieters, oiek v. Amstelredam.
1587	Jan	**Arnout**, v. Brouchorst in Ghelderlant, met Catelyne van Laeren v. Mechelen.
1598	Susanna	**Arnouts**, we. Franehoijs Bols, met Pieter Veghelman.
1609	Margareta	,, we. Paulus Rutts, ,, Robert Hendriex.
1599	Leonora	**Arondeaux (v. Arundeux)**, we. Tilman Brenij, met Huybrecht de Visscher.
1620	Isaac	van **Arschot**, v. Amsterdam, met Maria Pont v. Londen.
1598	Judith	**Artsen** met Jaques Samyn.
1595	Leonora	**Arundeux** met Tielman van Breen.
1575	Lysken	van **Ash**, met Gheerart Janssen.
1575	Melchior	van **Ashe**, v. Malssen, met Maijken Olrijs, we. v. Thomas Soen v. Brugghe.
1604	Samuel	,, v. Londen, met Geertruyt le Petit, we. Baudwyn Achtschellinck.
1583	Tanneken	van **Asse**, f. Molssens, met Rogier van Koodge.
1598	Anna	van ,, we. Rogier Vereoolgen, met Wouter Aertsz.
1699	Leonard	van **Asten**, wr. van Hester Harvey, met Geertruyd Weerels, we. v. Barent Koesvelt
1602	Martynken	**Auerhout** met Willem Hubrechts.
1604	Martynken	**Auechout**, we. Willem Hubrechts, met Tobias van Eyndhoven.
1609	Elisabeth	**Aurelis** met Jan Emans.
1574	Jossyne	van **Auweghem** met Niclaes Seghers.
1594	Elizabeth	van ,, we. v. Jaspar Boddens, met Franchoys Lamoot.
1604	Neesken	van ,, we. Francoys La Mote, met Francoys Cogghe.
1575	Janneken	**Auwers**, we. Joos Nauwes, met Phlips van Loeuen.
1587	Truijcken	van **Avesloot**, met Gielis de Grave.

1700	Barbara	**Ba - - ge** met Direk van Leuwen.
1574	Jan	**Baeck**, v. Emblem, met Elizabeth Redyuck v. Londen.
1595	Tobias	de **Backer**, v. Gent met Marie Proost v. Londen.
1602	Abraham	,, ,, v. ,, met Janneken de Molyn v. Gent.
1605	Sara	,, ,, met Adam Boddens.
1613	Susanna	,, ,, met Jan van den Brugghe.
1617	Jacob	,, ,, v. Londen met Sara van Damme mede v. Londen.
1571	Mayeken	**Backers**, we. Antony Warein, met Pieter Wellens.
1579	,,	,, we. Pieter Wellens, met Jan Gilhode.
1579	,,	,, we. Jans Gilhode, met Jan de Rijcker.
1581	,,	,, we. Jans de Rijker, met Cornelis Roisendaal.
1590	Tanneken	,, met Pieter Duffoy.
1599	Marie	,, met Willem Mariate.
1647	Sara	**Backlion** met Ernst Wolft.
1574	Hermes	**Bacquereel** v. Rousse met Agnees van Peene v. Resselare.
1579	,,	**Backereel** v. Roussen met Jakemyne van Peene v. Rysselar.
1626	Margarita	**Baeck**, we. Thomas Tobnam, met Dominicus van Wtwijck.

1 Nov.	1631	Jan	**Beertens** j.g. v. Haerlem met Dina Vermeulen, we. v. Gillis de Bois.
2 Dec.	1589	Hans	de **Behout**, v. Antwerpen, met Sara Goltschalcx v. Londen.
1 Jun.	1589	Macijken	**Beifkens** met Jan Wittewronghel.
18 Jun.	1611	Guiljam	**Beijaert** v. Ypere met Janneken van Gistele, we. Samuel Dries v. Antwerpen.
11 Jan.	1603	Guillame	**Eeijart**, v. Jperen met Janneken Droussaut v. Bruyssel.
3 Nov.	1590	Elizabeth	**Beijners** met A. Claessen.
14 Dec.	1591	Jacomyntken	**Beijnert** met Rene van den Coruput.
4 Sep.	1610	Ogken	de **Eaijr**, we. Fr. Michiels, met Paulus Tijpoots.
19 Oct.	1602	Miriam	**Beijrens** met Symeon Ruijtinck.
... Jun.	1621	Anna	,, Gomaer Willemsen.
25 Jul.	1571	Antonijne	s' **Beyrs**, we. Pauwel de Beijr, met Mrtthys Hoissts.
6 Feb.	1592	Cathelyne	**Beijtins** met Hans de Meij.
19 Jun.	1582	Elizabeth	van **Deke**, we. Jakes Palinck, met Bartholomeus Pieterssen.
3 Jan.	1585	Fransois	**Beke** v. Nieukercke met Debora Wallewijns van Sandwytz.
27 Jan.	1592	Hans	van den ,, v. Bremen met Maria Loijs v. Vendlo, we. Gheraert Coertes.
18 Jun.	1594	Clara	,, ,, met Pieter Clinckaert.
25 Jul.	1598	Sara	,, ,, met Jan James de Jonge.
1 Mei	1616	Maria	,, de ,, met Nicolas Jacobs.
15 Oct.	1616	Maria	,, met Pieter Winne.
... Apl.	1618	Susanna	,, met Jan van Ixem.
16 Jul.	1622	Elisabeth	,, met Cornelis Janssen.
16 Jun.	1640	Maria	,, met Carolus Liebaert.
6 Mei	1645	Susanna	,, met , we. William Shildrake, met D. Joannes de Molenaer.
17 Nov.	1646	Sara	van der ,, met Jan Dolens.
2 Apl.	1650	Elias	,, j.m. v. Vlijssingen met Anna Jacobs j.d. v. Londen.
9 Jul.	1644	Pieter	**Bell**, wr. v. Londen, met Lea Verras, j.d. v. Colchester.
30 Aug.	1691	Maria	**Bellamelis** met Jan Pietersen Lobbestall.
3 Jul.	1586	Fransois	van **Belle**, v. Dendermonde met Janneken Heuriblox v. Ghendt.
24 Jan.	1611	Jacob	**Bellecher** v. Colchester met Susanna Vervinck v. Londen.
9 Apl.	1594	Pieter	van **Belowijs**, v. Gent met Barbelken Sneckers v. Ghent, we. Fransois de Clievere.
3 Mei	1603	Elizabeth	van **Bembden**, we. Cornelis Lemmens, met Abraham van Dolden.
22 Feb.	1603	Cathelyne	van den ,, met Jacobus Goltschalck.
22 Sep.	1607	Hans	,, ,, **Bemden** v. Brussel met Elisabeth van Loer v. Londen.
12 Jul.	1590	Isaac	**Benij** v. Londen met Jossynken de Sterck v. Ipre.
12 Apl.	1604	Heylken	**Benniers**, we. Jan Pauwels, met Jan Michiels.
16 Aug.	1614	Jacob	**Bens** v. Leijden met Maria Cox v. Londen.
18 Nov.	1691	Frans	**Berckus**, wr. van Leentje Arentsen, met Mary der Kinderen, we. van Jan Claessen Dijckman, met attestatie van St. James.
13 Mei	1585	Jan	van den **Berge**, v. Campen met Lucretia Steenberchs van Oldenzeele.
27 Jan.	1594	Nicolas	,, ,, ,, v. Berghen op Zoom met Margriete van de Velde v. Ghent.
14 Sep.	1602	Pieter	,, ,, ,, v. Maleijn met Tanneken Gijtel v. Antwerpen.
21 Aug.	1616	Abraham	,, ,, ,, v. Maidston met Sara de Cerf v. Sandwich.
23 Jan.	1603	Elisabeth	,, ,, **Bergen**, met Hans Coenraet.
22 Nov.	1673	Ulrich	**Bergh**, j.m. v. Gottumberg, met Rebecca Elisabeth van Ruiller v. Amsterdam.
1 Oct.	1684	Johannes	,, j.m. v. Di ... met Anna Christina Cleijnetghens j.d. van den Haegh.
23 Nov.	1585	Pieter	van den **Berghe** v. Ghendt met Jacomynken Shouts v. Wackene.
27 Dec.	1585	Tanneken	,, ,, ,, met Wynant de Vriese.
1 Aug.	1587	Janneken	,, ,, ,, met Pieter van der Schuere.
31 Mar.	1589	Amplennis	,, ,, ,, v. Lanwe bij Cortrijcke met Elisabeth Baeten v. Tielen by Turnhout.
7 Mei	1592	Catheline	,, ,, ,, met Jacus Peperman.
10 Jan.	1594	Elisabeth	,, ,, ,, , we. Urbanus Junirot, met Joris Verbiet.
5 Feb.	1594	Pieter	,, ,, ,, v. Maseijck met Lynken Schouteten v. bij Maseijck, we. Godfridus Masius.
6 Jan.	1600	Celinken	,, ,, ,, met Jan Pieters.
20 Feb.	1603	Calleken	,, ,, ,, , we. Jan Pieters, met Pieter Tremont.
10 Apl.	1604	Elisabeth	,, ,, ,, we. Hans Coeract, met Adam Callerner.
17 Sep.	1611	Mayken	,, ,, ,, met Humfrey Willis.
3 Feb.	1582	Hans	,, **Berk**, v. Kleve met Colijutge Pannekoecke v. Brugge.
1 Sep.	1594	Janneken	,, ,, **Berken**, we. Moyses de Neckere, met David Cambier.
3 Sep.	1583	Jan	**Berlen** v. Hulstlue met Maijcken van de Velde we. Adriaan Huppardt v. Audenarde.
14 Sep.	1591	Macyken	**Bernaige**, we. Adriaen Ghyselinck, met Carle Brichnan.
19 Sep.	1583	Marten	**Bernts** v. Embden met Margriete Mordijns v. Audenarde, we. Jan van Sevenketen.
16 Oct.	1578	Pieter	**Berntsen** van der Elborch in Gelderlandt met Klaarken Kramers v. Antwerpen.
28 Oct.	1584	Eelken	**Berntssen** met Jacob Espee.
1 Mei	1582	Diericksken	**Berntz** met Lambrecht Willemssen.
1 Dec.	1584	Henrick	,, met v. Oldam in Gruningen landt met Janneken de Lande v. Kamrijeck.

3 Mei	1586	Judith	**Berrenoet** met Hendrick in de Smit.
27 Aug.	1629	Eliasar	**Berrens,** wedr. v. Londen, met Susanna van Crombrugge j.d. v. Londen.
1 Jun.	1585	Lambrecht	**Berrentsen** v. Noelen met Maeyken Fransten, we. Rijchaert Rijchaertsz v. Belle.
23 Oct.	1575	Tanneken	**Berrings,** we. Hendrick Martens, met Andries Coppens.
1 Jan.	1694	Clementia	**Bescers** met Hans Jurrigen Hefloe.
12 Jun.	1593	Susanna	de **Beste,** met Arnout Luls.
14 Dec.	1692	Anna	,, ,, met Joos Hauwe.
5 Feb.	1605	Catharina	,, ,, met David Bonncel.
1 Aug.	1613	Magdalena	,, ,, met Hendrick Pauls.
16 Sep.	1623	Anna	,, ,, we. Daniel Godfrey, met Jan Meijm.
2 Mei	1596	Denijs	**Bertholemeus** v. Maseijck met Margariete Jansz v. Heijmstede in Zeelant.
12 Apl.	1586	Geerbert	**Bertssen** v. Herentals met Lysken Dassen v. Steijn.
9 Mar.	1698	Christiaen	**Besemaecker,** j.m. v. Schiedam met Clara Langevelt j.d. v. Leyden.
4 Mei	1589	Tobias	van **Bethburin,** v. Londen met Maeyken de Cousenaere v. Engien.
12 Oct.	1596	Magdalena	**Beti,** we. Phlips de Brijer, met Goivaert van de Linde.
22 Aug.	1588	Jossijutken van der	**Betsele,** we. Christoffel Taclman, met Segher Pieters.
27 Dec.	1603	Truijken	van **Beuer,** met Noe Frombout.
29 Jun.	1591	Hans	van **Beughen,** v. Cleve met Tanneken Fordaens v. Antwerpen.
9 Jun.	1595	Maeyken	**Beun** met Jacus de Bie.
21 Oct.	1604	Tobias	**Beune** v. Londen met Maria Duymen v. Londen.
1 Nov.	1608	Matthens	**Beuns** v. Haerlem met Margareta Franckem v. Buckingainshere.
24 Jan.	1611	Matthens	,, v. Haerlem met Christyne Cuijpers v. Londen.
4 Oct.	1645	Margeriete	,, met Cornelis Leraroson.
18 Jun.	1627	Lion	**Beusken (v. Busken),** j.g. v. Londen, met Barbara Liefveldt j.d. v. Staeden.
17 Oct.	1591	Jan	**Beussinck** v. Munster met Susanna Clijpers v. Antwerpen.
13 Mei	1571	Margriete	van **Bevenkoter,** met Joris de Dobbelaer.
4 Jan.	1586	Jan	de **Bick,** v. Ghent met Betten Molijn, we. Marc Schockaert.
26 Oct.	1591	Hans	,, ,, v. Londen met Margriete Heurlinx v. Antwerpen.
18 Jan.	1597	John	**Bick** wt. Joreshere (Yorkshire) met Cathelīne Molijus v. Antwerpen.
9 Jun.	1595	Jacus	de **Bie,** v. Antwerpen met Maeyken Beun v. Londen.
22 Jun.	1600	Jans	de ,, v. Antwerpen met Heyltgen Clant v. Eusehede.
... Mei	1621	Abraham	de **Biellards,** v. Londen met Maeijken Snijders, we. van Eduward Simson.
30 Jul.	1588	Dierick	**Bierman** v. Sevender met Maria Werners uit d'lant v. Gulick.
5 Oct.	1574	Maiken	van der **Biese,** we. Hans Govaert, met Heindrick Hansen.
9 Mei	1591	Tanneken	,, ,, **Biest,** met Phlips van der Plaetse.
... Nov.	1617	Jacob	,, ,, v. Londen met Susanna Meersman v. Sandwich.
18 Dec.	1604	Marten	**Bigger** v. Leipsich met Rachel Heijndrix, we. Herman Jordaen.
16 Oct.	1689	Crijn Hendriex	**Bijl,** Van der, j.m. v. Vianen, met Amarentia van der Hair, j.d. v. 's Gravenhaegh.
4 Mar.	1592	Wolfaert	van **Bijlet,** v. Barucvelt met Clarcken Vrolijex v. Ghendt, we. Carel de Borcht-grave.
21 Apl.	1595	Abraham	de **Bil,** v. Maidston met Maeyken van Schoonderhase v. Londen.
10 Oct.	1633	Sara	de ,, met Abraham de Man.
1 Feb.	1573	Pieter	**Billen** v. Gravenbeegh met Margriete Heijndricks v. Antwerpen.
5 Aug.	1572	Nicolaes	**Billelijn** v. Breda met Janneken Laurens v. Antwerpen.
17 Mei	1608	Henric	**Bincke** bij Maseijck met Sara Janssz v. Londen.
16 Nov.	1648	Lenart	**Bisa,** wr. v. Roeremond, met Heilken Bastiaens, we. van Engelbrecht Bartels.
29 Mei	1604	Judith	**Bisschop** met Romeyn d'Hooghe.
1 Jul.	1599	Maximiliaen	de **Bisson,** v. Brugghe met Elizabeth Jansz v. Londen.
6 Dec.	1601	Daniel	de **Bla,** v. Bruijsel met Janneken Verckmen v. Hontschoten, we. Jan Wessels.
13 Aug.	1679	Catarina	**Blancart** met Frans Letoij.
7 Feb.	1660	Dierick	**Blancke,** j.m. v. Oldenburg met Maria Horn, j.d. v. Dunkerken.
5 Jul.	1573	Denis	le **Blancq,** v. Frelingien met Elizabeth Eijbens v. Hasselt.
22 Jan.	1577	Willem	**Blar,** v. Lanamo met Maijken Bocquet v. Eecloo.
9 Jan.	1592	Judith	de **Blau,** met Jan van der Elst.
15 Sep.	1578	Maijeken	a' **Blauwers,** we. Pieter Huygo, m. Jacob Sergiant.
29 Jul.	1572	Magdaleentgen	**Bilocxs** met Bartholomeus Corneliessen.
10 Aug.	1602	Jan	**Bloeme** v. (Groningh met Hermyntken Thyssen v. Arhnen.
5 Feb.	1605	Susanna	,, met Christophel de Peijster.
24 Mei	1858	Johanna Bernar- dina Immens	**Blom** met Johannes Jakobus Kotzé.
20 Jun.	1587	Lodwyc	**Blommaert** v. Antwerpen met Janneken van Hove v. Maseijck, we. Matheus Luls.
7 Mei	1577	Catherijne	**Blommarts** met Salomon v. der Riviere.
5 Feb.	1583	Hans	**Blummardt** v. Brugge met Marguerite Sbockbriedt v. Londen.
26 Dec.	1638	Anna	**Bochiljoen** met Gerard Tilhorst.
28 Mei	1594	Marie	van **Bocholt,** met Jan van Swol.
5 ,,	1594	Margriete	de **Bock,** met Abraham Nabuer.
24 Feb.	1596	Maria	le ,, met Charles Hudgebout.

Jan.	1577	Maijken	Bocquet met Willem Blar.
Sep.	1613	Baijken	Bocston, we. Aerts Solijns, met ..... Wigers.
Aug.	1619	Anna	Bodaen met Jacob Pergens.
Dec.	1586	Paschier	Boddens v. Thielt met Lievyne Maes v. Ghent.
Mei	1605	Adam	„ met Sara de Backer.
Feb.	1575	Gillis	de Bode, v. Mechelen met Sophie Verhouve, we. Hans Verscheijen v. Montfort.
Jun.	1675	Christiaen	Boeije v. Alverghem met Elisabet van Dinsburg, we. Jan Moenen v. Cuelen.
Mei	1584	Cornelis	de Boesijn, v. Antwerpen met Martijntge Rogiers v. Brugge.
Aug.	1583	Josijntgen	van Boetsele, we. Pauwels Buijs, met Christoffel Tielmans.
Nov.	1571	Giliaem	Bognaerdt v. Gendt met Goeltghen van Riemer v. Antwerpen.
Oct.	1574	Alexander	Bogardt v. Ghent met Lucia Cornelissen v. Antwerpen.
Mei	1578	Guilliaume	Bogarde met Susanna de Groote, attestatie v. Vlissingen.
Jul.	1592	Catherine	de Bohout, met Pieter le Gaij.
Jan.	1582	Pauline	du Boijs, v. Antwerpen, we. Mr. Jan Rickpottes, met Raphael van den Putte.
Aug.	1591	Wouter	de Bois, v. Meenene met Maeijken Boveval oock v. Meenene.
Jul.	1610	Judith	dn „ met Hans van Orsele.
Feb.	1639	Antonius	„ „ j.g. v. Haselbroeck in Vlaanderen met Catherina Hobbels, we. van Nicolaas Vereken v. Cammel in Vlaanderen.
Apl.	1857	Gerardus	„ „ omlt 27 jaar met Elizabeth Margaretha Admiraal j.d. omd 20 jaar.
Feb.	1599	Maeyken	Bolfermes, we. Hendrick Lamberts, met Geraert Luijten alias Graus.
Dec.	1593	Herman	van Bolle, v. Bruijssel, met Catelyne Getteels van Bruyssel, we. Huybrech Schaenaert.
Dec.	1594	Jooris	„ v. Meessene met Anna Aelst v. Sandwitche.
Feb.	1595	Jacob	„ v. Nienkerke met Cathelina Bolle v. Meessene.
„	1595	Catheline	„ met Jacob Bolle.
Apl.	1604	Susanna	„ met Marten Cromlinck.
Oct.	1616	Catharina	„ met Pieter Heeren.
Jan.	1612	Judith	„ met Gilis Lions.
Jul.	1630	Catharina	„ met Daniel van Pileom.
Oct.	1609	Maria	Bollen met Hans Liebaert.
Feb.	1630	Joos	Bollewijn, wr., met Maria Muninck, we. van Richard Pierson.
Mei	1638	Sara	„ met Jacob de Clerck.
Apl.	1577	Franchoijs	Bols v. Mechelen met Susanna Aernoudts v. Berghen op Zoom.
Aug.	1639	Adriaen	Boltie j.g. v. Solingen met Susanna Dunbar j.d. v. Rotterdam.
Apl.	1597	Ryntken	van der Bome, met Gielis de Caluwe de Morendorp.
Sep.	1605	Christiaen	Bonharinck v. Poperingh met Maeijken Hauwe v. Cassel.
Feb.	1605	David	Bonneel v. Norwich met Catharina de Beste v. Antwerpen.
Jan.	1618	Maria	„ met Abraham Verstripen.
Nov.	1623	Elisabeth	„ met „ van Solt.
Dec.	1574	Noel	Bonnesen v. Brugghe met Neelken van Osse v. Antwerpen.
Jun.	1595	Gheeraert	Bonninck v. Dousborg met Tanneken Cobbe wt t'lant v. Gulick.
Oct.	1571	Willem	Bonte met Janneke Verdonck.
Jul.	1596	Claerken	van der Boom, met Hubert Janssen.
Aug.	1626	Leonard	„ „ „ v. Amsterdam met Maria Lodewijck, we. Jan Galber.
Mar.	1593	Thomas	Boombender v. Rijsusberghe met Susanna Zaghers v. Antwerpen, we. Walranus Corne.
Mar.	1587	Jan	van den Boore, v. Oudenaarde met Pierrijne Deijmens v. Colseam, we. Pr. Hoste.
Oct.	1696	Arnoldus	Boot beijrman, M.D., j.m. v. Hoorne met Helena de Gols j.d. v. Amsterdam.
Feb.	1706	Hendrick	van Borchloon, j.m. v. Utrecht met Barbara Sophia Neernige.
Oct.	1574	Katherijne	Borluijt, we. Jan Pols, met Lievin van Wijnekele.
Jun.	1583	Sebastiaan	Borman v. Horne met Maijeken s'Visschers van Antwerpen we. Christoffel de Peijster.
Mei	1579	Loijseken	van der Borne, we. Dierick Melssen, met Arnoudt Elsson.
Jan.	1581	Anna	s'Borre met Jacob Bracht.
Feb.	1692	Josina Dammas	Borre, Van der, we. Pieter Keldermans, met Gerrit Pauwels Verstaegh.
Sep.	1632	Raphel	Borres j.g. met Thomasijntgen Duranel j.d., etc.
Jan.	1594	Neelken	Boschaert met Isaac van de Velde.
Apl.	1581	Daniel	van Boshuijsen, v. Schiedam met Caterijne van der Aerdt v. Turnhout.
Sep.	1607	Jacobmyntgen	van Bosijn, we. Daniel Blommaert, met Michiel Droessont.
Sep.	1587	Heindrick	Bosman v. Mechelen met Trynken Janssen v. Hemsberghe.
Mei	1612	Hendrick	„ v. Mechelen met Cresken Scheel, we. Pieter Snijders.
Mar.	1611	Jacobmyne	Bossar, we. Jonas de Coeq, met Robert Prat.
Jul.	1581	Beelken	Bossardt met Balthazar van de Linden.
Feb.	1583	Elizabeth	„ we. Jan van Achsepoel, met Rogier van Erwegen.
Dec.	1575	Betken	van den Bossche, met Gheeraert de la Hoir.
Feb.	1584	Jois	„ „ „ v. Nieuhoven met Maijeken Paret v. Antwerpen.
Nov.	1585	Tanneken	„ „ „ met Bartholomeus Mertens.

2 Feb.	1589	Lijsken	van den Bossche,	met Joos de Deken.	
9 Feb.	,,	Francijnken	,, ,, ,,	v. Bruyssel, we. Passchier de Wevre, met Huybrecht Adraensoen.	
16 Dec.	1589	Lijnken	,, ,, ,,	met Antheunis van der Meulen.	
25 Jul.	1590	Magdaleene	,, ,, ,,	we. Michiel Loose, met Marinus de Wage.	
1 Jun.	1591	Jacus	,, ,, ,,	v. d'Reijse met Catelijne Seraeckx v. Ghendt, we. Symon de Riddere.	
5 Mei	1594	Elisabeth	,, ,, ,,	, we. Joos de Deken, met Roelant Veltman.	
23 Juu.	1594	Lynken	,, ,, ,,	we. Anthonis van der Meulen, met Pieter de Molijn.	
13 Jun.	1598	Joos	,, ,, ,,	v. Deinse met Elisabeth Coels v. Antwerpen.	
4 Aug.	1612	Lijdia	,, ,, ,,	met Haus de Winne.	
8 Sep.	1612	Margareta	,, ,, ,,	, we. Willem Braeckbinck, met Pieter Priem.	
20 Apl.	1613	Abraham	,, ,, ,,	v. Maidston met Susanna le Sage v. Londen.	
11 Oct.	1575	Bartholomeus	van Bossu,	v. Gaesbeke met Peroneken Sprents v. Nipkerke.	
16 Oct.	1576	Pieter		Bouchler v. Pomier in Artoijs met Oijken Poppings, we. Mr. Jacob Soest, van Dockum in West Frieslandt.	
1 Nov.	1574	Mayken		Bouckelions, we. Jan Leeman, met Gheerardt Terhille.	
4 Oct.	1590	Lieven		Boudaert v. Deinse met Maelken Oons v. Antwerpen.	
15 Sep.	1607	Bernard		Boudewijn v. —otmarssen met Anna de Bruijne v. s'Hertogenbosch.	
30 Mar.	1600	Pieter		Boul v. Ceulen met Judith de Bruijne v. Louden.	
18 Feb.	1588	Laurens	de Boulougne,	v. Antwerpen met Tanneken van Hilegarde v. Brussel, we. Jeronymus Hermans.	
14 Aug.	1605	Geraert		Bouninck v. Doesburch met Tonyne van ...., we. Hans Lijscornet.	
18 Aug.	1577	Maijken		Bourgeois met Pieter Bronijns.	
1 Jan.	1585	,,		,, , we. Pieter Pronents, met Hans van den Heuvel.	
5 Mei	1607	Jacobmyne		Boussar met Jonas de Cocq.	
17 Jun.	1578	Adam		Boute v. Slijck int Sticht v. Kolen met Margariete s'Vos v. Audenarde.	
7 Mei	1592	Sara		Bouters met Lieven van der Stelt.	
14 Nov.	1602	Sara		,, , we. Lieven van Stolt, met Pieter Janssen.	
26 Jan.	1595	Jaspar		Bouts v. Emblen met Maeyken de Goij v. Brugghe.	
13 Mei	1571	Marten		Boven vit den Graefscap van Moerse met Barbel Anthonis, we. Raas van Buere.	
15 Dec.	1635	Christina	den	,, met Philips Olivier.	
3 Dec.	1611	Nise		Bovens met Roulant van Ecke.	
9 Aug.	1575	Jan		Boves v. Sonsbeke met Naentken Martens v. Lokere bij Belle.	
1 Nov.	1580	Marten		,, vt. grafschap van Mners met Trintgen Gilberts v. Geel int lant v. Gulick.	
31 Aug.	1591	Maeyken		Boveval met Wouter de Bois.	
19 Apl.	1597	Dominicus		Bowens v. Antwerpen met Susanna de Metue v. Londen.	
16 Jul.	1592	Claerken		Boxis met Peter Doornaert.	
... Jun.	1615	Itombout		Boxsteyns v. Mechelen met Catharina Haije v. Camfere. (Vere.)	
8 Aug.	1602	Maria		Brabant, we. Willem Page, met Pauwels Philips.	
6 Feb.	1593	Jean		Brabby v. London met Jacomynken Coets, we. Jan van der Broncke v. Ghendt.	
28 Jan.	1578	Jacob	van	Bracht, v. Venloo met Mechlyne Jacghers, we. Dierick van der Eycke.	
3 Jau.	1581	,,		,, v. Venlo met Anna s'Borre, Engelsche, v. Leijne in Middlesex.	
3 Mar.	1584	Pieter		,, v. Saligen bij Kolen met Josyntgen Speeckarts v. Brussel, we. Arnoudt Buys.	
1 Jun.	1619	Abraham		,, v. London met Susanna Salé, mede v. Louden.	
18 Jan.	1592	Willem		Braem v. Antwerpen met Debora Waelwijns v. Sandwijtss, we. Fransois Beke.	
1 Jul.	1595	Charles		Braems v. Sandwitch met Jossinken van der Spick v. Antwerpen.	
5 Jun.	1593	Tanneken		Braets met Pieter de Poortere.	
29 Mar.	1597	,,		,, , we. Pieter de Poortere, met P. Claessen.	
11 Dec.	1599	Jan		Braidense v. Utrecht met Mayken van Werwijck v. Ipren, we. Willem Pauwels.	
23 Sep.	1602	Franchoijs	van Brakel,	v. bij Oudenaerde met Maeyken Jacobs v. Gorcum, we. Thomas Louven.	
9 Aug.	1575	Tanneken		Brakelman, we. Jans van Auweghem, met Willem Brunijnck.	
6 Mei	1581	Susanna		Brakelers met Adriaen de Prust.	
3 Aug.	1574	Soetken		Brakelmans met Wolter Janssen.	
6 Oct.	1584	,,		,, , we. Wonter Janssens, met Willem de Kijje.	
9 Oct.	1586	Quintinken		,, met Hans Legonce.	
25 Feb.	1617	Jaques	van Braken,	v. Andwerpen met Susanna de Milan de Londres.	
28 Nov.	1585	Jaquemynken		Brakers, we. Renier Sergeants, met Hugo Wtghoers.	
... Feb.	1619	Gerard		Brand wt. Gelderland met Judith Stepen wt t'land v. Gulic.	
15 Apl.	1623	Sara		Brands met Samuel Leemans.	
26 Dec.	1593	Gheraert		Brans v. Eeppel met Lynken v. Taeken v. Antwerpen.	
10 Mei	1590	Benedictus	van den Brant,	v. Antwerpen met Barbelken Cueninx v. Cortrycke.	
27 Apl.	1585	Olievier		Brassens (alias Murkens), met Elizabeth Mostlers v. Londen.	
14 Oct.	1576	Jau		Brauwers v. Hoorne met Anna Sael, fa. Mr. Jacobs van Hoorne.	
9 Nov.	1578	Willem		Brauwer v. Hasselt met Pieryntge Cornelissen, we. Mr. Dierick de Voocht.	

1590	Elisabet	van **Brecht**, met Hans Perceval.
1606	Hendrick	,, **Bredenbach** v. bij Ceulen met Catharina de Waghe v. Gent.
1584	Pieter	**Breecksteen** v. Maastricht met Mechelt Mauritz van Rotten, we. Jan Martens.
1595	Tielman	van **Breen**, v. bij Ceulen met Leonora Arundeux v. Brussel.
1597	Jan	,, ,, v. Roosendaele met Elisabeth de Vrient v. Antwerpen, we. Franchois Nauwe.
1647	Arnout	**Breijdel** j.g. v. Brugghe met Maria Breijdel j.d. v. Brugghe.
1647	Maria	,, met Arnout Breijdel.
1612	Maria	**Breijnes** ,, Lucas Stendel.
1576	Evart	van **Bres**, v. Utrecht met Anna van Villes v. Loven.
1595	Marten	du **Breuck**, wt Cambersy met Pierijntken Cornelissen v. s'Hertogenbosch, we. Willem Brouwer.
1579	Jenne	**Brickée** met Frantz Kopmans.
1599	Josijnko	**Bricket** met Israel Hecklaers.
1591	Caerle	**Brielman** h. Thielt met Maeyken Bernaige v. Curtrick, we. Adriaen Ghijselinck.
1572	Tanneken	**Brijcken**, we. Hans Stapparts, met Pauwels Maas.
1599	Jau	**Brinsen** v. Goch met Agneta Pausmans oock v. Goch.
1617	Thonynken	**Brixe**, we. Pieter Consenaer, met Jacob de Hoeck.
1613	Tonyntken	**Brixes** met Pieter de Coussenaer.
1629	Anna	**Brochaert** met Jan Castens.
1618	Mechtel	**Brocht** met Daniel Looverbergh.
1601	Abraham	van den **Broeck**, v. Ghendt met Barbel van de Velde v. Bruijssel.
1612	Salomon	,, ,, ,, v. Norwich met Elisabeth Otgeer v. Londen.
1581	Klaes	,, ,, **Broecke**, v. Engen met ,, Edmwaerts v. Brussel.
1586	Joos	,, ,, ,, v. Lievolinge met Tanneken de Munck v. Gent.
1592	Janneken	,, ,, ,, met Lieven de Clerck.
1600	Franchoijs	,, ,, ,, v. Meesene met Lynken Partels v. Mechelen, we. Pieter Ruijtinck.
1617	Salomon	,, ,, ,, v. Norwich met Susanna Ryckwaerts v. Londen.
1619	Sara	,, ,, ,, met Jan Stevens.
1620	Abraham	,, ,, ,, v. Colchester met Sara, we. Josias Taelmans.
1626	,,	,, ,, ,, v. Londen met Sara van Liesveldt v. Staeslen.
1628	Sara	,, ,, ,, , we. Melchior Martin, met Jan van der Hecken.
1633	Anna	,, ,, ,, met Jacob de Hane.
1635	Johanna	,, ,, ,, met Franchoijs van de Hane.
1628	Joos	**Broeders** j.g. v. Londen met Rachel Verbrugge j.d. v. Maidston.
1575	Isabella	van **Broeke**, we. Pieter van Doorne, met Michiel Nauwe.
1605	Sara	**Bronchorst** met Jacques Hoste.
1577	Pieter	**Bronijns** (v. Pronents), v. Engen met Maijken Bourgeois v. Enghen.
1623	Margareta	**Broune**, we. Robert Broune, met Paulus van de Velde.
1613	Sara	**Broussart** met Isaac van der Brugge.
1715	Pieternella	**Brouwsens**, we. James Gout, met Christoffel Mes.
1591	Adriaen	**Browers** v. Antwerpen met Maeyken Anxen v. Naerden.
1690	Catharina	**Browne** met Thomas Dijke.
1613	Isaac	van den **Brugge**, met Sara Broussart, ondertrout te Maidston.
1610	Judith	,, ,, **Brugghe** met Adam Laureijns.
1613	Jan	,, ,, ,, met v. Maidston met Susanna de Backer v. Londen.
1616	Gillis	van den **Brugh**, v. Haerlem met Maria Jacobs v. Londen.
1580	Jan	**Brugman** v. Brussel met Grietgen Poels v. Turnout, we. Jacobs Vrolickhoven.
1607	Gabriel	,, v. Oudenaerde met Maria Steckman, we. Thomas Laurens.
1703	Jau	de **Bruijer**, j.m. v. Londen met Maria Steckman, we. Thomas Laurens.
1679	Benjamin	de **Bruijn**, j.m. v. Rotterdam met Petronella van Alten j.d. v. Amsterdam.
1590	Janneken	,, **Bruijne**, we. Jan Verbrugghe, met Jan van Pruijsschen.
1593	Tanneken	,, ,, , we. Jan Enghels, met Goos Hoornaert.
1596	Lijdia	,, ,, met Pieter Peterins.
1600	Judith	,, ,, met ,, Bout.
1604	Anna	,, ,, we. Zacharias van Horebeke, met Philip van der Plassche.
1607	Anna	,, ,, met Bernard Bowlewijn.
1631	Maria	,, ,, met Asuerus Frumenteel.
1607	Job	,, **Bruijr** v. Brugghe met Josyne Dubbeson, we. Jan Maet.
1619	Maria	de **Brul**, we. Jonas van Eijckenschot, met Pieter Waemaes.
1608	Susanne	,, **Brune**, met Isaac Albertssz.
1609	Jaques	,, ,, met v. Oudenaerde met Sara Foekeels, we. Herman Turck.
1612	Tanneken	,, ,, we. Bernard Bawdwijn, met Franchoijs Stampoen.
1575	Willem	**Brunijnck** v. Vreden met Tanneken Brakelman, we. Jans van Auweghem, v. Ghent.
1608	Anna	**Brunijax** met Daniel Hoste.
1628	Walter	**Brus**, geboren in Hantinghouscheere (Huntingdonshire), met Abigail Hooft v. Colchester.

12 Sep.	1585	Abigail	Bucerus met Pieter Garet.
13 Jun.	1614	Lieven	van Buchaute v. Gent met Susanne Douwe v. Londen.
15 Sep.	1612	Cornelia	de Buck met Josias Wessels.
. Mar.	1624	Guiljam	„ „ v. Londen Haerlem (sic) met Yken Beck v. Aken.
23 Oct.	1586	Susanna	Buens met Philip de Stiltere.
19 Apl.	1604	Pieter	Buerman v. Aecken met Susanna Muijart, we Pieter Hendricx.
1 Mei	1594	Nicolas	van Buesecom de Jonge v. Antwerpen met Cathelyne Roevers v. Brugghe.
2 Feb.	1579	Arnoudt	Buijs v. Salingen in laude van den Berge met Josijne Speeckardts v. Brussel we. Gillis s'Kosters.
25 Mei	1578	Jossintgen	de Buijsson met Joos van der Driessche.
26 Feb.	1679	Rachel	Buijston met Jacob Duwe.
25 Jan.	1592	Jans	van der Bulcke v. Antwerpen met Ester van Luffele v. London.
13 Apl.	1658	Catalyne	Bulst met Hendrick van Houvnagen.
13 Sep.	1590	Susanna	Bultinx met Jan Sijbrants.
21 Jun.	1575	Kaerle	de Burchgrave v. Roesselaere met Claerken Vrolix v. Ghent.
22 Jun.	1585	Cathelyne	„ , we. Jan van Dorne, met Cornelis Pieters.
30 Mei	1587	Phlips	van der Burcht met Lysken Cautsels, beijde v. Brussel.
18 Dec.	1593	Philips	„ „ „ v. Bruyssel met Janneken Overdaet, we. Jan de Ne.
28 Sep.	1585	Jan	Burdt met Elisabet van Oscelare, we. Joos van Wijusberghe, beijde van Gent.
12 Mei	1700	Jeronimina Adriana	Buren, Van, we. Jan Hatten, met Carel Magdou-les.
... Oct.	1615	Susanna	Burgley v. Rotterdam met Jeremias Achtschellinck.
31 Dec.	1605	Hans	de Burgrave v. Iper met Clarken Celot, we. Jasper Sterlincx.
27 Mei	1593	Lenard	Busch v. Oxfort met Sara Pieters v. Londen.
1 „	1582	Jaques	de Busijn v. Antwerpen met Catherine van Mets-hagen v. Antwerpen.
22 Jun.	1595	Hans	Busken v. Dovre met Maeyken Snicx v. Brugge, we. Jan van den Poorten.
10 Oct.	1637	Lijon	„ , wr. van Barbara Liesveldt, met Janneken Noodtstock j.d., beyde var Londen.
27 Dec.	1596	Pieter	de Busscher v. Meene met Sara van der Heijden v. Antwerpen, we Hans v. Hautloock
28 Jun.	1608	Pieter	„ „ v. Meenen met Catharine de Clerck, we. Pieter Clouns.
6 Sep.	1573	Beatrix	Busse met Jan van Wijck.
2 Jul.	1590	Joris	Buwaert v. Wijnoxberghe met Janneken s'Grooten v. Vloteren, we. Philips Regier

27 Oct.	1590	Ghijselbrecht	Caerluijn v. Ghendt met Barbara Simons v. Valenchine, we. Jaques van Navarre.
19 Jun.	1604	Jan	Calandt v. Enschede met Maijken de Martelare, we. Wouter Verstrepen.
9 Jul.	1594	Susanna	Calant, we. Jacus van den Raede, met Pieter Moriaen.
23 Dec.	1606	Moses	„ v. Maijdston met Sara Thomare v. Leijden.
25 Sep.	1649	Dorothe	„ met Francois Thijssen.
4 Dec.	1599	Joos	Calf v. St. Bress Vijne met Synken Wijbo v. Puthem.
5 Jun.	1604	Agneete	Callaerts, we. Geeraert van Basel, met Jan Sale.
11 Jun.	1592	Anna	van Callenberghe met Isaac Hoffler.
10 Apl.	1604	Adam	Callerner v. Andwerpen met Elisabeth van Berghe, we. Hans Coenraet.
17 Mar.	1613	Sara	de Calue met Engel Wier.
22 Oct.	1592	Pieter	de Caluwe v. Ghendt met Sara Verwilt v. Antwerpen.
24 Sep.	1594	Naenken	„ „ , we. Willem Prijs, met Abraham Coudron.
3 Apl.	1597	Gielis	„ „ , v. Monerdorp met Vijntken van den Bome v. Ghendt.
1 Sep.	1594	David	Cambier v. Sandwyts met Janneken van Berken v. Oudenaerde, we. Moyses de Neckere.
29 Dec.	1574	Catheryne	Cambiers met Jan Lievens.
19 Jan.	1591	Jaques	van der Camen v. Enghen met Anna van Duffele v. Bruyssel.
12 Mei	1680	Johaunes	van der Camer j.m. v. Harlem met Johanna Grondeijs j.d. v. Leyden.
3 Nov.	1590	Hans	van der Camer v. Engien met Clerken van Crombrugghe v. Ghendt.
12 Sep.	1587	Bierken	van der Cammen met Jacus de Caussenier.
25 „	1582	Artus	van Campen v. Antwerpen met Jacomyne van Peene v. Ronselaere, we. van Renier Backereel.
20 Aug.	1588	Belicken	van „ met Hans Faken.
19 Feb.	1661	Anna Diericx	van „ met Pieter Janson van Snigelbergh.
7 Aug.	1599	Metsken	Canes met Hans Mesmaker.
16 Apl.	1582	Hendrick	Cane v. Maestricht met Maeyken Ramers v. Maestricht.
16 Apl.	1582	Cathelyne	Canipets, we. Steven Resbecck, met Andries Koppiers.

28 Sep.	1572	Catherine	**Cannepens**, we. Abraham Kauweliers, met Steven van Eesbeke.
27 Nov.	1603	Maria	van der **Cappelle** met Eleazar Pont.
26 Dec.	1605	Pieter	,, ,, ,, v. Brugghe met Mayken Corijnssen v. Berghen-op-Zoom.
3 Mei	1608	Geeraert	,, ,, ,, v. Brugge met Catharina Jacobsz v. Antwerpen.
5 Feb.	1612	Gillis	,, ,, ,, v. Middelborch met Anna de Geijtere v. Londen.
25 Mei	1574	Lowijseken	**Carboniers** met Karolus Ryckart. gheseit Theophilus.
25 ,,	1607	Susanna	**Carnoit** met Herman Janssen.
15 Dec.	1593	Janneken	**Carpentier** met Pauwels de Vraeije.
9 Mei	1594	Gillett	**Carre**, we. Hector Potier, met Matthys Verbeke.
11 Feb.	1606	Mayken	**Carren** met Jeronymus Willemsz.
26 Aug.	1610	Pieter	**Carritse** v. Delft met Els Vaden uyt Devonshire.
31 Jan.	1659	Renert	**Carstens** j.m. met Anneken Janson j.d., beyde v. Thunderen in Holsteyn.
1 Nov.	1581	Christyne	**Casewel** met Jan Clerck.
7 Dec.	1602	Ananias	**Casier** v. Meenen met Elisabeth Saers uit Woesterscheere (Worcestershire), we. Eduwaert Juhal.
7 Apl.	1607	Maria	,, met Francheijs Pennetier.
21 Apl.	1679	Baltes	**Cassier** j.m. v. Amsterdam met Maria du Toij j.d. v. Leijden.
9 Feb.	1681	Baltics	**Casier**, wr. v. Amsterdam, met Maria Visais j.d. v. Canterbury.
2 Sep.	1662	Anna	van **Castart** met Melchior Moulart.
9 Apl.	1629	Jan	**Castens** j.g. v. Embden met Anna Brochaert, j.d., v. London.
23 Mar.	1652	Pierre	de **Caumont**, Marquis de Cugnac, met Elizabeth de Maijerne. Getrout inde Kerke van Kensington door Cesar Calandrin.
10 Sep.	1629	Maria	van de **Cause** met Abraham de Man.
31 Oct.	1592	Clarken	**Causemaker** met Isaac Simons.
12 Sep.	1587	Jacus	de **Caussenier** de Jonge met Bierken van der Cammen, beijde v. Engien.
7 Aug.	1593	Hendrick	de **Cautelen** v. Brussel met Catherina Mockaerts v. Brussel.
8 Nov.	1580	Melchior	**Cautereel** v. Antwerpen met Cathrijne Geeraedt v. Brugge.
30 Mei	1587	Lysken	**Cautsels** met Philps van der Burcht.
31 Jan.	1604	Elizabeth	**Cauwels** met Jan Ryewaerts.
28 Aug.	1599	Susanna	van **Cauwenberge** met Thomas Nederwaets.
29 Sep.	1631	Judith	**Cavecle** met Pieter de Somere.
31 Dec.	1605	Clarken	**Celot**, we, Jaspar Sterlincx, met Hans de Burgrave.
21 Aug.	1616	Sara	de **Cerf** met Abraham van den Berge.
. Jan.	1626	Anna	,, ,, met Christopher Verhaeghen.
3 Jun.	1630	Abraham	,, ,, , wr. van Maria Gijs, met Anna Janson j.d. v. Sandwich.
15 Oct.	1636	Abraham	van **Ceulen**, wr. met Susanne de Visscher, we. van Walrave Lodewyk.
.. Apl.	1615	Benjamin	**Champnes**, wt. Kent, met Rachel van Wtwyck v. Londen.
23 Oct.	1580	Maria	des **Champs** met Lowijs van Lathem.
28 Apl.	1607	Maria	**Charles** met Gabriel Brugman.
.9 Mar.	1624	Hester	**Chidly** met Lucas Loemans.
20 Aug.	1590	Gielis	int **Choor** v. Antwerpen met Lynken Stelfels v. Middelbourch.
11 Nov.	1593	Elizabeth	**Chosse** met Gulian de Coninck.
6 Jul.	1572	Jakes	de la **Choutiere** met Lyntgen Laurens oick van Antwerpen.
15 Mar.	1575	Laurens	**Christiaens** v. Utrecht met Maijken Antonissen v. Antwerpen.
22 Jun.	1578	Lyntgen	,, met Evert Steijnversen.
27 Feb.	1593	Ricornijnus	,, v. Londen met Abigail Thoris v. Sandwiche.
5 Dec.	1602	,,	,, v. ,, met Teuntken Clercx v. Weteren.
5 Aug.	1628	Maijken	,, , we. Frederic van der Sande, met Pieter le Clerck.
20 Jun.	1592	Bernaert	**Christiaenssen** v. bij Munster met Lynken Mocharts v. Brussel.
17 Oct.	1677	Elizabeth	**Christianors** met Pieter Pietersen.
8 Nov.	1571	Geertruijt	**Claes** met Jacob Huijsman.
3 Nov.	1590	Abraham	**Claessen** v. Noorwijts met Elizabeth Beyners v. Vtrecht.
29 Mar.	1597	Pieter	,, v. Steenvoorden met Tanneken Bracts v. Seghelsem, we. Pieter de Poorter.
20 Jul.	1619	Albert	,, v. Oldenborgh met Susanna van Coppurnolle, we. Willem Wouder.
14 Feb.	1574	Marens	**Claissen** v. Antwerpen met Tanneken Franses v. Antwerpen.
4 Jan.	1615	Janneken	**Clamp**, we. Jeronymus van der Elst, met Arnout Aertsen.
22 Jun.	1600	Heijltgen	**Clant** met Jan de Bie.
.8 Dec.	1611	Alita	,, , we. Jaques de Bije, met Herman Timmerman.
.6 Apl.	1612	Mechlijnken	,, met Erasmus Heijndrix.
3 Nov.	1640	Marcus	**Clarebout** j.g. v. Sandwich met Sara Cuijpers j.d. v. Sandwich.
3 Dec.	1611	Jan	**Clay**, wt Essex, met Lydian Craen v. Dordrecht.
5 Jun.	1604	Hans	**Clayssz** v. Ceulen met Catharijn Goemers, we. Hans Pannus.
17 Mei	1608	Evert	**Claeijssz** v. Leijden met Catharina, d'huijsvrouw Habrecht Reynols.
20 Oct.	1612	Alis	**Clarissz** met Dirick Wessels.
18 Apl.	1581	Digne	van der **Clasen**, we. Francheis Cordier, met Joris Wolff.
18 Jun.	1594	Tanneken	**Claude**, we. Pieter de Serpen, met Jacob Wolfaert.
11 Apl.	1577	Segher	**Cleijmans** v. Turnhout met Macyken Janssen v. Meerelen.

26 Mei	1594	Pieter	Cleijmans v. Turnhont met Maeyken van Tongeren v. Antwerpen, we. Evart Reijers.
19 Oct.	1602	Pieter	,, v. Turnhout met Maeyken van Staudonck v. Antwerpen.
28 Mei	1611	Hans	,, v. Londen met Janneken Baert, mede v. Londeu.
1 Jan.	1576	Adolf	Cleijn v. Keyserwert met Maijken Coningrave v. Bilsen.
1 Oct.	1684	Anna Christina	Cleijnetghens met Johannes van Bergh.
4 Mei	1630	Maria	Clement, we. Esaias Wattimus, met Abrahamus Dolens.
1 Nov.	1581	Jan	Clerck int Lincolschere (Lincolnshire) met Christyne Casewel uit Somersetshere.
5 Dec.	1588	Anthony	de ,, v. Lenele met Margriet le Fevre v. Comene.
11 Aug.	1590	Jan	,, v. Corksiele met Abigail Stel v. London.
25 Jul.	1591	Cathelyne	de ,, met Pieter T'loers.
30 Jan.	1592	Lieven	,, ,, v. Drongene met Janneken van den Broecke v. Ghendt.
17 Apl.	1597	Iscar	,, ,, v. Maydston met Lucynken van Mierbeke v. Vrselere.
28 Feb.	1598	Simon	,, v. St. Truijen met Maeyken Deckers v. Antwerpen, we. Niclaes de Gaen.
24 Jun.	1600	Pieter	,, ,, v. Geneva met Lynken Engelbusche v. Hasselt.
31 Jan.	1604	Isaac	,, ,, v. Maidston met Sara Conijncx, we. Jan Post.
27 Dec.	1604	Jan	,, ,, v. bij Sandwich met Baelken Heijlgers, we. Jan Evraerts.
15 Sep.	1607	Isaac	,, ,, v. Maidston met Anna Plateboot, we. Jan Broeder.
28 Jun.	1608	Catharine	,, ,, , we. Pieter Clouns, met Pieter de Busscher.
16 Aug.	1608	David	,, ,, met Susanna Michiels beyde v. Norwich.
5 Aug.	1628	Pieter	le ,, , wedr. van Catharina Engelbosch v. Geneven, met Maijken Christiaens, we Frederic van der Sande.
27 Aug.	1629	Maria	,, ,, met David Mienchol.
14 Mei	1638	Jacob	,, ,, j.g. v. London met Sara Bollewijn, j.d. mede v. London.
22 Jan.	1594	Maeyken	Clerckx, we. Jan Jacquaert, met David van Clinckenberch.
5 Dec.	1602	Teuntken	Clerex met Hieronijmus Christiaens.
26 Jun.	1576	Maijken	Clerx met Jan Jacquart.
17 Oct.	1591	Susanne	Clijpers met Jan Beussinck.
7 Mar.	1587	Margriete	van der Clijte, we. Claes Siers, met Jooris Lieven.
18 Jun.	1594	Pieter	Clinckaert v. Londen met Clara van der Beke v. Antwerpen.
3 Aug.	1602	Pieter	,, v. London met Martha Pieterssz ooe v. London.
26 Jun.	1604	Abraham	Clinckant v. Andwerpen met Maeyken Discans, we. Richard Park.
27 Dec.	1603	Jan	Clinckart v. Enghene met Clara Walbroek v. Andwerpen, we. Pieter Willemsz.
24 Feb.	1590	David	van Clinckerbergh v. bij Aken met Margriete van der Elst v. Muijsene, we Hendriel Beockman.
22 Jan.	1594	David	van Clinckenberch v. Aken met Macken Clerckx v. St. Truijen, we. Jan Jacquaert.
,, Mar.	1624	,,	Clinckenborgh v. Aken met Maijken Flinckenberge, we. Michiel de Hurter.
19 Aug.	1645	Elizabeth	Clobber met Samuel de Coninck.
22 Nov.	1614	Ester	Clockaert, we. Jan Abeels, met Samuel de Visscher.
29 Aug.	1626	Frederic	de Clopper v. Sandwich met Abigail Robberts v. Sandwich.
7 Apl.	1640	Anna	,, ,, met Adrian van der Werf.
11 Jun.	1587	Dierick	Clopperijs v. Essen met Martijuken Gieles v. Antwerpen, we. Mathijs Cokers.
27 Dec.	1593	,,	van ,, v. Essen met Ghoolken Stiers v. Antwerpen, we. Hendrick Jansson.
20 Jan.	1603	Grysollis	Cnappaert v. Iperen met Catelijne Vermeulen v. Iperen, we. van Carel Fustaen.
3 Nov.	1573	Jan	Cnudde v. Oudenarde met Maijken van Guiddeldonck v. Antwerpen.
3 Jun.	1595	Tanneken	Cobbe met Gheerraert Bonninck.
13 Jun.	1596	Elisabeth	de Cock, we. Adriaen Lammens, met Jan Post.
18 Apl.	1598	Joris	Cockx v. Eernot met Magdalena Creunelars v. Ipren, we. Jan van Vaelpoot.
5 Mei	1607	Jonas	de Cooq v. Norwich met Jacobmyue Bousgar v. Moesen.
9 Feb.	1589	Arent	Cedron v. Antwerpen met Josijnken de Beck v. Ghendt.
26 Jun.	1582	Pieter	Coelbier v. Cogge vt den lande v. Horne met Elizabet Ghiolen, we. Heynderickx Feyter
13 Jun.	1598	Elisabeth	Coels met Joos van den Bossche.
15 Sep.	1573	Jan	Coene v. Ghendt met Gheertruydt, we. Cooris de Meijere v. Ghendt.
22 Sep.	1605	Gillis	,, met Neelken Costerlinck, we David van Acker.
25 Apl.	1622	Gillis	,, v. Moosel met Francijnken Adams, we. Jan Brusloo.
23 Jan.	1603	Hans	Coenraet v. Aelst met Flisabeth van den Bergen v. Andwerpen.
28 Oct.	1588	Gheerrert	Coerdes v. Bremen met Marie Loij v. Vendloo, we. Pieter Janssen.
6 Feb.	1593	Jacomynken	Coets, we. Jan van den Broueke, met Jean Brabby.
14 Mar.	1588	Franchois	de Coge v. Yseghen met Janneken Doornaert v. Cortrijcke, we. Jan Seroen.
9 Apl.	1594	Fransois	de Cogghe v. Ysegem met Catheline de la Roche v. Oudenaerde, we. Jan van Peene.
6 Nov.	1604	Francoijs	Cogghe v. London met Neesken van Auweghem, we. Francoys Lamote.
11 Nov.	1606	Elisabeth	de ,, met Hans Valk.
22 Mei	1585	Francois	Cogo v. Ysegen met Catheline Verscheijden, we. Michiel de Munckere, van Eyndhoven
.. Aug.	1613	Jacob	Colo v. Colchester met Judith van Stavele v. Norwich.
25 Jun.	1675	Wilhelm	Colingcamp j.m. v. Amsterdam met Sara van Hereveen j.d. v. Harlem.
28 Apl.	1590	Lynken	Colia met Joos Leenaerts.
15 ,,	1725	Dominus Paulus	Collignon, Leeraar deser Gemeent, met Juffrouwe Anna Dupré, we. v. Mr. Samu Dupré, uyt kraght van een License.

11 Nov.	1593	Gulian	de Conick v. Brussel met Elizabeth Chosse uit Hartfortshier (Hertfordshire).
4 Sep.	1604	Jacques	de Conijnck v. Londen met Elisabeth Beemans v. Londen.
13 Feb.	1610	Antheunis	„ „ v. Gent met Maijken de Nets v. Ypere.
31 Jan.	1604	Sara	Conijnex, we. Jan Post, met Isaac de Clerck.
6 Mei	1589	Gulian	de Coninck v. Brussel met Maeijken van Schouhuijsen v. Antwerpen.
23 Jul.	1594	D. Jacobus	„ „ v. Cortrijck met Elizabeth Ruijtinck v. Noorwijts.
22 Oct.	1598	Sara	„ „ met Jan Post.
15 Feb.	1603	Jaques	„ „ v. Londen met Hester Lamote v. Colchester.
7 Feb.	1604	Joris	„ „ v. Ecloo met Susanna van Meulen, we. Jan Hartot.
4 Oct.	1614	Anna	„ „ met Gillis Thijssen.
. . Apl.	1616	Passchier	„ „ v. Eecloo met Adriana Rousseel v. Noremborgh.
. . Jul.	1621	Posschier	„ „ v. Eeckloo met Martynken Schoesettes v. Antwerpen.
8 Jul.	1628	Lea	„ „ met Samuel Populaer.
10 Aug.	1645	Samuel	„ „ j.g. v. London met Elizabeth Clobber j.d. v. Sandwich.
11 Sep.	1604	Elisabeth	Coninx met Jaques Waghenaer.
1 Jan.	1576	Maijken	Coningrave met Adolf Cleijn.
6 Apl.	1643	Joannes	de Coninck j.m. M.D. met Joanna Marolois, we. van Jacob de Backer.
5 Feb.	1661	Dorethe	Coninx, we. Gerret Engelaer, met Pieter van der Hagen.
20 Apl.	1602	Susanna	Connixs met Jeremias van Hulst.
4 Mei	1595	Jacus	van der Consie v. Engien met Maeijken Huijghens v. Antwerpen, we. Thomas Leewes.
14 Jul.	1594	Jacus	Cool v. Antwerpen met Maria Theeus v. Londen.
25 Sep.	1597	Margriete	de Coomen met Fransois Lampsens.
28 Dec.	1625	Jan	Coopland v. Sulfolke (Suffolk) met Abigail Lenards v. Londen.
7 Aug.	1605	Josyntken	van den Coornhuijse met Jacob de Cork.
24 Nov.	1607	Leonara	„ „ „ met Daniel de Croock.
18 Sep.	1610	Susanna	van Coppenolle met Willem Wonder.
20 Jul.	1619	„	„ „ we. Willem Wonder, met Albert Claessen.
25 Oct.	1575	Andries	Coppens v. Antwerpen met Tanneken Berrings, we. Hendrick Martens v. Antwerpen.
8 Nov.	1614	Lydia	Coppens met Hans Gomertsz.
29 Mar.	1597	Janneken	Corenbroeck met Conradt Digrets.
6 Mei	1593	Lucas	Corijn v. Waerden met Janneken Davids v. Maestricht.
7 Feb.	1585	Trijne	Corijns met Jan Maren.
26 Dec.	1605	Maijken	Corijnssen met Pieter van der Capelle.
7 Aug.	1605	Jacob	de Cork v. Londen met Josijntken van den Coornhuijse v. Meessene.
29 Jul.	1572	Bartholomeus	Cornelissen v. Vlissingen met Magdaleentgen Blloexs v. Nieupoorte.
28 Oct.	1574	Lucia	„ met Alexander Bogardt.
3 Jul.	1575	Arnout	„ v. Marcken met Lyneken de la Hoer v. Audenaerde.
18 Dec.	1576	Jacques	„ v. Biervliet met Lievyne Rotars v. Ghendt.
5 Sep.	1585	Claercken	„ , we. Pieter Cornelissen, met Dierick van Volthuijsen.
11 Jul.	1587	Priscilla	„ met Jan Verbeke.
11 Apl.	1591	Pauwels	„ v. Antwerpen met Maeyken van de Walle v. Yper.
9 Nov.	1578	Pierijntge	„ , we. Mr. Dierick de Voocht, met Willem Brauwer.
1 Jan.	1595	Pieryntken	„ , we. Willem Brouwer, met Martin du Brenck.
12 Feb.	1577	Arent	Corneliss v. Delft met Dierexken Pieters, we Herman Thijssen v. Vutrecht.
1 Aug.	1609	Aernout	„ v. Londen met Elisabeth Gast v. Londen.
. . Apl.	1615	Elisabeth	van den Corneput met Thomas Sarrel.
22 Apl.	1595	Cornelis	Cornet v. Bruggo met Susanna van der Vijvre v. Londen.
. 5 Jul.	1615	Jacob	„ v. Brugghe met Maria Truijens, we. Thomas Wilcoex v. Oest-Cappel.
5 Sep.	1586	Nicolas	van den Cornput v. Breda met Gheertruijt van Mechelen v. Rhetie, we. Andries van Londen.
14 Dec.	1591	Rene	„ „ v. Breda met Jacomyntken Beijnert v. Ipren.
3 Jul.	1599	Maria	Corselis met Pieter de Pril.
27 Jan.	1607	Rachel	„ met Rogier Turloot.
14 Nov.	1609	Anna	„ met Joannes Luce.
22 Oct.	1611	Susanna	„ met Tobias de Hem.
10 Mei	1601	Peroonken	Cortiels met Joris Schut.
3 Dec.	1588	Henrick	Cos v. Bruijnswijck met Margriet van der Putte v. Antwerpen.
21 Oct.	1589	Gerart	Cosijns v. Geertsberge met Lynken Vrient v. Breda.
14 Feb.	1598	Gomerijn	Costens, we. Gulian Verhoeve, met Gillis vander Haeghen.
6 Aug.	1594	Jacus	de Coster v. Brussel met Margriete Westhuijse v. Somerghen, we. Jan van Beveren.
14 Nov.	1598	Anna	„ „ met Franchoys Polaert.
8 Jan.	1604	Jan	„ „ v. Geosberghe met Maijken de Winne, we. Pieter Verspire.
25 Sep.	1610	Elisabeth	„ „ met Hans van Peene.
7 Jul.	1612	Esaias	„ „ v. Londen met Sara Damas v. Gent.
. . Mei	1621	Maria	„ „ met Daniel de Vos.
22 Sep.	1605	Neelken	Costerlinck, we. David van Acker, met Gillis Coene.
2 Feb.	1595	Lenaert	Costerman v. Loo bij Diest met Cathelyne Mennise v. Atrecht.
13 Apl.	1596	Tanneken	Costers met Cornelis Dregge.

6 Jul.	1600	Geertruyt	Costers, we. Mattheeus Scewes, met Antheunis Meijss.
30 Jan.	1601	Anthony	Cotron v. Brugge met Janneken Jacobs v. Naerden.
2 Aug.	1614	Anthoni	Cots v. Nordfolkshecre (Norfolkshire) met Catharina Gommaerts, we. Hans Claessz
15 Mei	1638	Catharina	van Cotten m. David Goetval.
20 Jan.	1692	Elizabeth	Coucke met Elias de Leeuw.
16 Jun.	1592	Jeremias	Coudron v. Antwerpen met Judith Haeutken.
24 Sep.	1594	Abraham	,, v. ,, met Naenken de Caluwe v. Antwerpen, we. Willem Prijs.
2 Apl.	1695	Margareta	,, met Jan van Gulick.
4 Jul.	1609	Abraham	,, v. Antwerpen met Margareta Willems, we. Denijs Bartholomeus.
15 Jun.	1626	Jeremias	,, v. Londen met Jacobmyne Rijckaerts v. Antwerpen.
26 Mar.	1638	Sara	Couper met Samuel Schilt.
17 Jul.	1604	Guillame	Courten v. Londen met Esther Trioen v. Londen.
20 Mei	1606	Margriete	,, , we. Matthijs Boudaen, met Jan de Money.
4 Aug.	1640	Pieter	Courts j.g. v. Vlm met Matgary Mills, j.d. v. Shatwell in Warwijkshire.
4 Mei	1589	Macyken	de Cousenaere met Tobias van Bethburin.
1 Sep.	1590	Jaques	,, ,, v. Engen met Catharine van Crombrugge v. Gent.
20 Apl.	1596	Maeijken	,, ,, , we. Tobias Bethurine, met Michiel Maniet.
9 Oct.	1613	Pieter	,, Coussenaer v. Engene met Tonijntken Brixes v. Ypere.
17 Mar.	1577	Franchois	Cousijn v. Yperen met Cathlyne Ardtssen v. Antwerpen, we. Jakes Sceris.
16 Feb.	1604	Geerart	,, v. Geesberghe met Elisabeth Rentmeesters, we. Nicolas de Valens.
21 Nov.	1626	Abraham	van de Couter v. Haerlem met Joanna Godtschalck, we. Jaques Verinn.
7 Mei	1662	Maria	Coutroix met Robbert Page.
17 Apl.	1645	Aletta	Cowper met Pieter Paff.
6 Dec.	1597	Trijsken	s' Cox, we. Pieter Akeloot, met Willem s'Muijsers.
11 Aug.	1614	Maria	Cox, met Jacob Bens.
.. Apl.	1626	Maijken	,, , we. Jacob Bens, met Enoch Garnoot.
26 Oct.	1574	Christiaen	Crabbe v. Brugghe met Lyneken Jeems v. Antwerpen.
3 Dec.	1611	Lydian	Craen met Jan Clay
3 Aug.	1602	Neesken	Craene met Melchior Rats.
31 Oct.	1577	Cornelis	Crebbondtsen v. Haerlem met Marie Janssen v. Amsterdam.
17 Sep.	1587	Dina	Creemers met Augustyn Janssens.
9 Jul.	1587	Marie	Cretone met Niclaes Enserinck.
9 Sep.	1571	Susanna	de Crets met Marcus Gemerts.
18 Apl.	1598	Magdalena	Creuwelars met Joris Cockx.
.. Jan.	1619	Anna	Crijnsen met Lenard Schaephuijsen.
20 Jul.	1581	Godefroy	Crijnts in lande v. Gulick met Marie Smedt v. Loeten int lande v. Luijck.
1 Mei	1597	Anna	Crimwaen met Reynier Spoormaecker.
19 Mei	1590	Magdalena	de Crits met Marcus Gemerts.
1 Sep.	1590	Catheline	van Crombrugge met Jaques de Cousenaere.
3 Nov.	1590	Clercken	,, ,, met Hans van der Camme.
9 Mei	1594	Bartholomeus	,, ,, v. Ghendt met Abigail van Iesen, we. Wonter Casier.
26 Mei	1607	Elisabeth	,, ,, met Abraham van Ixem.
27 Aug.	1629	Susauna	,, ,, met Eleasar Berrens
28 Jul.	1590	Carolije	,, Crombrugghen met Jacus de Puijt.
17 Apl.	1604	Marten	Cromlinck v. Ingelmunster met Susanna Bolle v. Zandwich.
24 Nov.	1607	Daniel	de Croock v. Andwerpen met Leonara van den Coornhuijse v. Meeseue.
6 Mei	1630	Adriaen	,, ,, , wedr. Van Esther van der Plaetse, met Johanna Oils, we. van Aernoud Eeckhoudt.
13 Sep.	1614	Joos	Croppenbergh, v. bij Gulick, met Catharina Hauwe, we. Hans Swart.
20 Dec.	1703	Jan Pieter	du Cros, j.m. v. Batie in Cuilel in Vivaiees, met Maria Sofia Gout, j.d. s'Gravenhage.
1 Feb.	1642	Joanna	ver Cruicen, we. Jonas de Peijster, met Jacob de la Forterie.
11 Jun.	1576	Sophie	van der Cruijce met Simon Remons.
25 Apl.	1581	Janneken	,, ,, met Rutger Wagonhorst.
5 Sep.	1596	Susannaken	,, ,, ,, met Noel Frambout.
25 Aug.	1629	Johanna	,, ,, ,, met Jonas de Peijster.
.. Sep.	1618	Timotheus	Cruso, v. Norwich met Catharina de Plantere v. Winoxberghe.
7 Jun.	1586	Jan	de Cueninck v. Curtryck met Adriane Heindrix v. Gent, we. Nicolas Fonteine.
10 Mei	1590	Barbelken	Cueninx met Benedictus van der Brant.
20 ,,	1600	Hendrick	Cuijl v. Londen met Maria Godtschalck v. Londen.
.. Feb.	1616	Elisabet	(Cuijper), we. Thomas Cuijper, met Cornelis Sickraed.
1 Aug.	1587	Catelyne	Cuijpers met Eliaert van der Heyde.
24 Jan.	1611	Christyne	,, met Mattheus Beuns.
3 Nov.	1640	Sara	,, met Marcus Clarebout.

4 Jun.	1611	Thomas	Dabbins v. London met Janneken Minnaert, we. Adrian van Damme.
3 Mar.	1655	Francois	Dacket, Jr., j.m. v. Norwich, met Maria Marolois, j.d. v. London.
1 Sep.	1589	Barken	van Daele met Anthony Staelens.
4 Sep.	1598	Janneken	Daijes met Thomas Prentis.
8 Jun.	1684	Janneken	Dailje met Pieter Trenel.
2 Oct.	1595	Magdaleene	van Dale met David Taelman.
8 Oct.	1595	Pieter	,, ,, v. Antwerpen met Elisabeth Moijus v. Antwerpen.
3 Mei	1609	Jan	,, ,, v. Cortrijcke met Elisabeth Dorpers v. London.
0 Nov.	1613	Pieter	,, ,, v. Sandwich met Clara Guadia v. London.
0 Mei	1576	Tanneken	,, Dalem met Conrad Reijnouts.
4 Dec.	1582	Janneken	,, ,, met Jan de Wachter.
7 Aug.	1596	Elizabeth	,, ,, met Hans van Leeuwerck.
7 Jul.	1612	Sara	Damas met Esaias de Coster.
9 Jul.	1584	Vijt	Damen uit dem Horssem broecke in dem lande v. Guylick met Susanna du Pon v. Antwerpen.
9 Nov.	1616	Sara	Damers met Abraham de Prent.
. Jul.	1613	Samuel	Damert v. London met Abigaijl de Puijt v. London.
9 Mei	1604	Anna	Damforts met Pieter Janssz.
3 Sep.	1586	Franchoijs	Damman v. Ypre met Sara de Hoeve v. Antwerpen.
9 Jul.	1604	Jeremias	,, v. Steenwerck met Catharyne s' Minders, we. Frederick van Dompsvilaers.
6 Dec.	1586	Adriaen	van Damme v. Ghendt met Catelyne van de Sande, we. Jan Janssen, v. Ghendt.
4 Apl.	1592	Willem	,, ,, v. Ghendt met Margareta Kes v. Amsterdam, we. Jeronimus Obrij.
8 Mei	1594	...... (Adrian)	,, ,, (v. Dabbins) v. Ghendt met Janneken Minnaert v. Brussel.
5 Jan.	1596	Laurens	,, ,, v. Peteghem met Jacomyntken Foits v. Ardoije.
4 Aug.	1604	Adrian	,, ,, v. Gent met Elisabeth Huijtinck v. Norwich.
8 Jan.	1584	Lowijs	,, ,, v. Cortrijcke met Susanna Stevens v. London.
1 Oct.	1617	Sara	,, ,, met Jacob de Backer.
. Jan.	1621	Philippote	Dammers, we. Richard Helston, met Jan Messinen.
8 Jan.	1635	Jan	Daniel j.g. v. Dantzick met Clara van der Kamme, we. Nicolaus Mattheus v. Em . .
8 Mei	1595	Hans	Daniels v. Caperijk met Neelken van Oije v. Erneghem.
4 Jan.	1586	Barbelken	Dannoots met Joos van Perken.
3 Oct.	1576	Jan	Dansé v. Fleuren met Margriete du Laijs v. Berghen In Henegouwe.
2 Apl.	1586	Lijsken	Dassen met Geerbert Bertssen.
6 Mei	1593	Janneken	Davids met Lucas Corijn.
8 Jan.	1594		Davids (sic) uit Welsh (Wales) met Lijnken Micharts v. Bruijssel, we. Hendrick de Cantele.
2 Jun.	1604	Jacobmijntken	,, , we. Abraham van Mierbeke, met Hubrecht Franckelem.
2 Apl.	1605	Pieter	,, v. Gent met Janneken Matthijs v. Andwerpen.
8 Oct.	1600	Jacomyneken	Davidts met Abraham van Mierbeke.
0 Jan.	1604	Nicolas	Dapperhans v. Wesel met Maeyken de Dorper, we. Cornelis Stiers.
5 Jun.	1604	Jan	Dawson v. Steijn bij t'lant v. Luijck met Maeijken Gillis, we. Hans Buijs.
8 Feb.	1598	Maeijken	Deckers, we. N. de Gaen, met Simon Clerck.
7 Nov.	1598	Lijntken	,, met Jan Ijselaer.
8 Oct.	1649	Janneken	Degels met Jonatan Hagedorn.
1 Mar.	1587	Pierijne	Deijmens, we. Pr. Hoste, met Jan van den Boore.
0 Oct.	1604	Elisabeth	Deijnkens, we. Willem Jong, met Jan Verspire.
2 Oct.	1571	Janneken	Deijnots met Rutger Stevens.
8 Jul.	1593	Tanneken	Deijnouts met Guiliacme de Waghenaere.
2 Feb.	1593	Joos	de Deken v. bij Bruijssel met Lijsken van den Bossche v. Bruijssel.
2 Jan.	1604	Jan	van Delft v. Colchester met Sara de Wiest v. Gent.
4 Sep.	1588	Reniers	Delinck v. Rouee met Lynken Bateman v. Antwerpen.
1 Mei	1576	Lijneken	Denijs, alias Ghijselars, met Jan Gheerartsen.
7 Dec.	1624	Mattheus	Denni v. Gloecestershire met Adriaenken Sneps v. Breda.
4 Mei	1626	Pieter	Dentier v. Cuelen met Judith de Vos v. Haerlem.
5 Nov.	1678	Pieter	Derveau, we. v. Amsterdam, met Janneken Sondergelt, j.d. v. Narden.
4 Mar.	1688	Maria	,, met Johannes van Poncke.
8 Sep.	1588	Nicolas	de Deuxvilles met Catelyne Theeus beijde v. Antwerpen.
8 Dec.	1590	Nicolas	,, ,, v. Antwerpen met Maeijken Samijn v. London.
5 Jan.	1595	Anthoni	,, Deuxvilles v. Antwerpen met Margarite Willemsz v. s'Hertogenbosch, we. Willem Flud.
5 Jul.	1602	Catharijne	,, Deux-villes met Jan van Puflleijn.
. Apl.	1621	Maria	,, Deuxvilles met Wilbord Spijs.
8 Nov.	1576	Gillis	van Diepenrijck v. Tongeren met Margriete Willemsz, we. Malachias van der Heijden v. Haerlem.
4 Jun.	1594	Gillis	,, ,, v. Tongheren met Gelijne van der Vijvre v. Oudenaerd, we. Noel van Boutcheler.
8 Oct.	1579	Franchois Janssens	Dierickssen met Klaerken van Aken, we. Niclaas van Luffel, beijde v. Antwerpen.

17 Jan.	1581	Lucie	**Dierickssen**, we. Geeradt Valck, met Willem Jacobs.
9 Sep.	1599	Gillis	**Dierix** v. Ghent met Sara van de Roo v. Londen.
10 Jun.	1622	Martin	**Dierixsen**, v. Dusseldorp met Anna Soen van Colchester.
29 Mar.	1597	Conradt	**Digrets** v. Noorenburg met Janneken Corenbroeck v. Oudenaerde.
30 Sep.	1691	Cornelia Catharina	**Dijck**, van, met Arent Schaasberg.
20 Sep.	1703	Hendrick	van ,, j.m. v. Leijden met Anna Maria Sax, j.d. v. Londen.
10 Dec.	1690	Thomas	**Dijke** j.m. v. Gillingham in Kent met Catharina Browne j.d. v. Amsterdam.
21 Jun.	1575	Elisabet	van **Dinsburg**, wo. Jan Moenen, met Christiaen Booije.
23 Oct.	1590	Maeijken	**Direx** met Gabriel Vinck.
6 Sep.	1590	Barbelken	van **Dirkele** met Pieter de Poortere.
26 Jan.	1604	Maeyken	**Discans**, we. Rd. Park, met Abraham Clinckant.
13 Mei	1571	Joris	de **Dobbelaer** v. Gent met Margriete van Bevenkoten v. Gent.
5 Oct.	1572	Joris	,, ,, v. Ghendt met Sara Henricksen, dochter v. Diericks Henricksen.
31 Jan.	1575	Jooris	,, **Dobbelare** v. Ghent met Maeyken van Rijme v. Antwerpen.
13 Mei	1572	Abraham	van **Dolden** v. Antwerpen met Elizabeth van den Korput v. Breda.
3 Mei	1603	,,	,, ,, v. Antwerpen met Elizabeth van Bembden v. Brussel, we. Cornelis Lemmens.
4 Mei	1630	Abrahamus	**Dolens** met Maria Clement, we. Esaias Wattinus.
10 ,,	1668	Pieter	**Dollart**, wr. v. London, met Janneke Michils, we. van der Briell.
24 Mei	1603	Frederick	van **Domsolaer** v. bij Amersffort met Catharijne S'Minders v. Engene.
11 Mei	1595	Abigail	van der **Donck** met Pauwels van de Velde.
17 Nov.	1607	Judith	,, ,, ,, met Nathaniel Baes.
10 Dec.	1611	,,	,, , we. Nathanael Baes, met Pieter Lepper.
18 Jan.	1601	Hans	**Donckel** v. Cortrijcke met Tanneken Switsers v. Ipren.
26 Nov.	1598	Tanneken	van der **Donct** met Eleazar Pondt.
27 Apl.	1596	Ghertruijt	**Dongherin**, we. Herman Leck, met Herman Kech.
14 Mar.	1588	Janneken	**Doornaert** met Franchois de Coge.
16 Jul.	1592	Pieter	,, v. Curtrick met Claerken Boxis v. Ypren.
.. Apl.	1626	Gabriel	,, v. Londen met Maria Jansz v. Gravesende.
8 Dec.	1577	Catherijne	van **Doorne** met Hans Ganst.
29 Apl.	1579	Margriete	,, **Doornijck** met Symoen Tirenteijns.
22 Sep.	1605	Tanneken	**Doreijn** met Heijndrick Wiro.
24 Feb.	1579	Wilhelmijne	van den **Dorpe**, we. Autonis Nant, met Pieter Persoons.
10 Jan.	1604	Maeyken	de **Dorpere**, we. Cornelis Stiers, met Nicolas Dapperhans.
1 Sep.	1594	,,	,, **Dorpere**, we. Dierick Rijenroij, met Cornelis Stiers.
23 Mei	1609	Elisabeth	**Dorpers** met Jan van Dale.
7 Sep.	1581	Josijntgen	**Dorpes** met Jan van Peene.
6 Dec.	1611	Maria	van **Dort** met Severijn van Druijf.
3 Jan.	1574	Ferdinandus	**Dotigny** v. Antwerpen met Maeijken van Walle v. Ypere.
28 Nov.	1596	Anna	,, met Willem Pill.
25 Nov.	1593	Pieter	**Douffay** v. Brugge met Anna Rockou v. Lnyck.
13 Jun.	1614	Susanna	**Douwe** met Lieven van Buchante.
6 ,,	1598	Reynier	**Drael** v. Brugghe met Susanna Vasseur v. Antwerpen.
. Oct.	1621	Maria	**Dragon** met Nicolaus Resever.
30 Apl.	1594	Cornelis	**Dregge** v. Mechelen met Judith Janss v. Lin.
13 Apl.	1596	,,	,, , de Jonge, v. Londen met Tanneken Costers v. Antwerpen.
20 Oct.	1594	Pieter	**Dreux** v. Londen met Adriaeneken Pepermans v. Bruyssel.
11 Jan.	1596	Benjamin	**Dries** v. Nootwijts met Sara Eeckholt v. Londen.
4 Mei	1596	Samuel	,, v. Middelborch met Susanna de Riviere v. Madtston.
30 Sep.	1600	Samuel	,, v. Middelburg met Susanna Hoste v. Londen.
10 Jan.	1604	Samuel	,, v. Middelborgh met Anna van Gistel, we. Pieter van den Berghe.
20 Nov.	1571	Janneken	van den **Driesche** met Sijbrecht van den Qoives.
17 Nov.	1634	Jan	,, ,, ,, j.g. v. Londen met Gerdtruij Rousel j.d. v. Norenburch.
14 Sep.	1572	Marie	,, ,, met Wilhelmus van der Scheinhagen.
25 Mei	1578	Joos	,, ,, **Driessche** v. Brugghe met Josintgen de Buijsson v. Brugghe.
.. Jul.	1621	Catharina	de **Drijver** met Jan Worringen.
9 Sep.	1645	Abigail	,, , we, met Pieter Wademont.
.. Apl.	1616	Maria	**Droeshoudt** met Dierick Wessels.
30 Oct.	1604	Marten	**Droeshout** v. Bruyssel met Jannekens Molijns v. Antwerpen.
15 Oct.	1611	Michiel	**Droeshout** v. Brussel met Martha Sleuwen, we. Jan Lambert.
30 Dec.	1628	Michiel	,, , wedr. van Martha Lambert, met Sara Wagenaer, we. Jaques Selam.
29 Sep.	1607	Michiel	**Droessont** v. Breussel met Jacobmijntgen van Bosijn, we Daniel Blommaert.
25 Jan.	1575	Pieter	de **Drossaert** v. Antwerpen met Lijneken van Rens v. Cortrijck.
2 Sep.	1628	Johanna	,, (v. Drossche), , we. Joos de Neve, met Daniel Mijtens.
24 Dec.	1587	Pieter	de **Drossaerts** met Catheline s'Vleeschouwers, beyde v. Ghendt.
3 Jan.	1604	Samuel	de **Drossate** met Ester Proost, we. Sijmon Guijrin.
10 Apl.	1604	Susanna	de **Drossche** (v. Drossaert) met Joos de Neve.
26 Oct.	1602	Marten	**Droushout** v. Bruijssel met Anna Winterbeke v. Bruijssel.

Aug.	1595	Michiel	Droussart v. Brussel met Susanneken van der Ersbek v. Ghendt.
Jan.	1603	Janneken	Droussant met Guillame Beijart.
Nov.	1607	Severijn	van Druf v. Aecken met Tanneken de Waghe v. Gent.
Dec.	1611	,,	,, Druijf v. Aecken met Maria van Dort v. Wolfenbuten.
Nov.	1607	Josljno	Dubbeson, we. Jan Maet, met Job Bruijr.
Apl.	1710	Philip	Duee v. Amsterdam met Anna Frans v. Amsterdam—Ondertrowt.
Apl.	1616	Sara	Duffardt met Jan Leemput.
Jan.	1591	Anna	van Duffele met Jaques van der Camen.
Mei	1590	Pieter	Duffoij v. Brugghe met Tanneken Backers v. v. Bruijssel.
Apl.	1579	Jan	Duijmen v. Lochem in Gelderlandt met Barbel Heekaren, we. Jans Peper.
Jul.	1604	Elisabeth	,, met Abraham Veillardts.
Oct.	1604	Maria	,, met Tobias Beune.
Mei	1602	Jaques	Duijs v. Andwerpen met Sara Verhaghen v. Maidstone.
Jan.	1658	Maria	Dumbelle met Christian Rolofsen.
Aug.	1630	Susanna	Dunbar met Adriaen Boltie.
Apl.	1725	Anna	Dupree, we. Mr. Samuel Dupree, met Dominus Paulus Collignon.
Sep.	1632	Thomasijntgen	Duranel met Raphael Borres.
Aug.	1588	Matthijs	Durmans uit lant van Gulick met Marie Schulder v. Londen, we. Willem Peters.
Aug.	1721	Cornelis	Dut.. v. Haeften met Geertruda Dutrij beijde van Amsteldam.
Aug.	1721	Geertruda	Dutrij met Cornelis Dut..
Feb.	1679	Jacob	Duwe j.m. v. Amsterdam met Rachel Buijsten j.d. v. Leijden.
Sep.	1590	Maecyken	Dux met Dierick Kuster.

Dec.	1611	Roulant	van Ecke v. Groeningen met Nise Bovens v. Dusseldorp.
Aug.	1584	Jacob	Ederick v. Brussel met Tointgen Verhille v. Antwerpen, we. Jan Penartz.
Jun.	1576	Anna	Eduwaerts met Jan Eijfelaers.
Nov.	1581	Elisabeth	,, ,, Klaes van den Broecke.
Nov.	1597	,,	,, ,, Abraham van de Roo.
Jun.	1603	Judith	,, ,, Daniel Passeman.
Sep.	1573	Maurus	Eeckholt v. Minden met Susanna Seghers v. Enghen.
Jan.	1596	Sara	,, met Benjamin Dries.
Aug.	1596	Daniel	Eelder v. Wilsborch met Lucretia van de Putte, v. Londen, we. Niclaes Vincent.
Sep.	1572	Steven	Eesbeke v. Dornick met Catherine Cannepen v. Audenarde, we. Abrahamus Kauweliers.
Jun.	1618	,,	Egberts v. Embden met Sara Visch v. Londen.
Jul.	1573	Elizabeth	Eijbens met Denis le Blancij.
Oct.	1589	Adrianenken van der Eijcke	,, Dierick Pigghe.
Jun.	1580	Susanna	van Eijcken ,, Joris Vrancken.
Jun.	1576	Jan	Eijfelaers v. Ankercke int lant Gulick met Anna Eduwaerts v. Beke int lant v. Cleven.
Sep.	1614	Christopher	Eijgenaer nijt der Slesen met Maria Quatroos v. Middelborgh.
Mei	1604	Tobias	van Eijndhoven v. Andwerpen met Martijnken Aucchout, we. Willem Hubrechts.
Jan.	1590	Elisabeth	Eldertoun met Gillis Baert.
Sep.	1576	Barbelken	Elijuck met Wolfaert Janssen.
Jun.	1613	Abraham	Elluck v. Gent met Anna Anthonis van der Tholen.
Jan.	1629	Abraham	,, , wedr. van Mary Waterthon, met Elisabeth Jonas, we. Robert Franckx.
Aug.	1629	Jan	Ellis, we. van Blandina Marsterson v. Sandwich, met Margarita Drosser, we. Richard Stokes.
Jan.	1585	Catherine	Els met Hans Honseer.
Nov.	1581	Margrieto	Elsen met Symon Adams.
Jan.	1581	Catheryne	van Elspel, v. Michel Aalst, met Marten Geerardts.
Dec.	1580	Jacob	Elssen v. Venlo met Catherine s'Portere v. Mechlin.
Mar.	1579	Arnoudt	Elsson v. Kleve met Loijseken van der Borne, we. Dierick Melssen.
Jul.	1571	Catherijne van der Elst	, we. Waalramus Lodowijcksen met Willem Jacobsz.
Oct.	1571	Grietgen ,, ,, ,,	met Hendrick Beeckmans.
Feb.	1500	Margriete ,, ,, ,,	, we. Hendrick Beeckman met David van Clinckerberghe.
Jan.	1592	Jan ,, ,, ,,	v. Londen met Judith de Blau v. Antwerpen.
Aug.	1605	Jeremias ,, ,, ,,	v. Londen met Lynken Santken, we. Dierick Jansz.
Dec.	1609	Neelken ,, ,, ,,	, we. Joris Farey, met Adriaen Middelaer.

12 Dec.	1600	Jan	Emans met Elizabeth Aurelis, beyde van Londen.
21 Jan.	1582	Helena	Emondts met Gielis van Ghele.
8 Nov.	1579	Govardt	Emplborch v. Keempt bij Hasselt met Christijne Pellinckton v. Peckum (Peckham) bij Londen.
5 Jun.	1707	Arnoldus	Emmori j.m. v. den Haegh met Helena Tammerus j.d. v. Heusden.
14 Jul.	1607	Jaspar	van Enden v. Andwerpen met Elisabet Rademaker, we. Jaspar Wauters.
22 Jan.	1596	Elisabeth	Endraerts, we. Hendrick d'Hertoge met James Ward.
24 Jun.	1600	Lijnken	Engelbusche met Pieter de Clerck.
17 Jul.	1695	Reynier Balthes	Engelhof j.m. met Trintje Antonissen van der Heijde, beyde v. Amsterdam.
30 Jul.	1622	Joos	Engels v. Oudenaerde met Jaquelyne Padtbrugge v. Bruyssel.
24 Jul.	1627	Jan	„ j.g. v. Oudenare met Maria Fourmenteau j.d. v. Colchester.
7 Jan.	1680	Elisabeth	„ met Jan Goslijn.
15 Dec.	1700	Marijtje	„ met Juriaen Wil.
26 Feb.	1579	Thomas	Engelsch v. Dorwijs int lande v. Gulick met Mattgen van der Lodwich v. Maasscijcke
17 Jun.	1582	Govardt	„ v. Kaster uth den lande v. Gulick met Thamar van der Mersse v. Brugge
26 Mei	1584	Maijcken	d' Engelsche, we. Jan Willems, met Pieter van de Linden.
6 Apl.	1589	Jan	Engelsfield v. Londen met Sara Janssen v. Harderwijck, we. Thomas Spiere.
2 Jul.	1635	Mary	English met Jan Hoijel.
9 Jul.	1587	Niclaes	Enserinck v. Suytphen met Marie Cretone v. Londen.
13 Mei	1651	Helena	Erfort met Stephen de Keijn.
17 Aug.	1595	Susanneken	Ersbek met Michiel Droussart.
5 Feb.	1583	Rogier	van Erwegen v. Brugge met Elizabeth Bossardt, we. Jan van Achsepoel, v. Rijsel.
28 Mei	1583	Pauwels	van Esbergen v. Antwerpen met Maijcken Janssens v. Brussel, we. Heurick Willemsz.
23 Sep.	1576	Gheetruijt	Escholt met Matheus Ghilbert.
28 Oct.	1584	Jacob	Espee v. Dixmuijde met Eelken Berntssen v. Vntrecht.
5 Sep.	1577	Cornelis	van Essen v. Antwerpen met Janneken Rosseau v. Mouceau, we. Pieter Douffaij.
28 Jun.	1580	Edewaert	Etssten v. Eswijler bij Gulick met Lijsben Permans v. Hantwerpen.
11 Oct.	1699	Alexander	Ettum j.m. v. Bommel met Clasina Exalto (d'Almeras) j.d. v. Leerdam.
31 Mar.	1608	Jan	Evans v. Glocester met Maeijken Aertooen v. Londen.
31 Mar.	1589	Lowijseken	van Evenacker met Jan Nachtegale.
5 Nov.	1698	Elisabeth	Eventscher met Epsie Focken.
11 Jul.	1587	Elisabet	Everaerts met Heindrick d'Hertoge.
13 Dec.	1608	Benjamin	„ v. Colchester met Josyntken de Hase v. Londen.
21 Feb.	1637	Pieter	Everard, wr. van Esther Hovaerts, v. Colchester met Sara de Marez, we. Pieter de Raedt.
6 Nov.	1578	Frantzijne	Everarden met Geerardt Trenijen.
19 Jul.	1689	Engeltje	Evers, met Pieter Scheffer.
8 Jun.	1592	Cornelis	Eversen v. Wagene in Ghelderlant met Catheline Ghilberts v. Thilkerck, we. Marten Boove.
.. Feb.	1618	Dierick	Everts v. Ceulen met Hester de Hoeck v. Cantelberge (Canterbury.)
2 Mei	1626	Dierie	Evertsz v. Ceulen met Elisabet Wicke v. Gelderlandt.
11 Oct.	1699	Clasina	Exalto (v. D'Almeras) met Alexander Ettum.

13 Apl.	1596	Willem	Faber v. Heijnsberch met Neeken Kerijns v. Wtrae.
6 Mar.	1700	Hermannus	Fabritius j.m. v. Leeuwarden met Geertruijdt van der Wolf, we. Joris Goudesael.
12 Oct.	1575	Claerken	Faes met Lucas Reijners.
3 Apl.	1576	Lijneken	„ met Sibert Rippen.
9 Feb.	1613	Tobias	Faillart v. Colchester met Ellsabeth Lions v. Brugghe.
14 Oct.	1571	Jan	Fait v. Utrecht met Neeltgen Willems v. Delft.
20 Aug.	1588	Hans	Faken v. Antwerpen met Belieken van Campen v. Vtrecht.
5 Apl.	1613	Godeon	Faulcon v. Londen met Sara Stelter v. Londen.
.. Nov.	1613	Jan	de Febbre v. Brugge met Tanneken, we. Michiel de Jode.
14 Aug.	1604	Heijndrixken	Feljt met Willem Wondec.
22 Feb.	1593	Susanna	Felix met Jan Teraijen.
10 Jul.	1593	Susanna	Felix met Renier de Hooghe.
7 Sep.	1630	Jan	Femeulen j.g. v. Sandwich met Esther Gerebardt j.d. v. Colchester. (v. Vermeulen.
15 Feb.	1603	Anna	Fenne met Esaias Nachtegnal.
18 Jul.	1688	Rachel	Ferré met Johannes Moone.
5 Dec.	1588	Margriet	le Fevre met Anthony de Clerck.

Jul.	1597	Jan	de **Fevre** v. Brugghe met Margriete Hasen v. Leeuwe, we. Jan van den Borsche.
Nov.	1689	Margaret	**Ffield** met Willem Vuijjet.
Nov.	1605	Susanna	de **Flandres** met David Silverlinck.
Jul.	1710	Philip	la **Fleur** j.m. v. Maestright met Anna Margerita Vout er. we. Willem Scot.
Mar.	1624	Maijken	**Flinckenberge.** we. Michiel de Hurter, met David Cliuckenburgh.
Jun.	1588	Margriete	**Flinckenborg** met Jan van Mernen.
Dec.	1578	Pieter	**Floerkin** v. Serehom met Janneken Nexsons v. Borbourg, we. Gillis Snepgatt.
Mei	1609	Sara	**Fockeels,** we. Herman Turck, met Jacques de Brune.
Sep.	1600	Sara	**Focktols** met Herman Turck.
Nov.	1698	Epsie	**Focken,** soldaet onder de Heer Ittersum, met Elisabeth Eventscher.
Feb.	1576	Aelbrecht	**Fockes** v. Anghen in West Vrieslant met Lijncken Molie sons v. Brenssel.
Feb.	1590	Abraham	**Focket** van bij Ghersberge met Tanneken Persoons v. Antwerpen.
Aug.	1573	Herman	**Foget** v. Westerholt met Anna Baes v. Kent.
Jan.	1573	Cecilia	**Fogghe** met Johannes Nicasius.
Feb.	1590	Willem	„ v. Londen met Piermiken de Vinl v. Poperinge.
Jan.	1596	Jacomyntken	**Foits** (v. Forts), met Laurens van Dan me.
Dec.	1601	Clerken van der	**Fonteijne,** we. Franchoijs Garret met Jan Troeman.
Jun.	1591	Tanneken	**Fordaens** met Hans van Benghen.
Jun.	1591	Margriete de la	**Forterie** met Sigismundus Minghen.
Feb.	1642	Jacob	„ „ „ , wr, met Joanna ver Cruioen, we. Jonas de Peijster.
Feb.	1604	Jacobmijntken	**Forts** (v. Foits), we. Laurens van Damme, met Hendrick Mensvelt.
Aug.	1594	Bernard de la	**Fosse** v. Brugghe met Abigail Vrombouts v. Sandwits.
Jul.	1627	Maria	**Fourmenteau** (v. Fromentee) met Jan Engels.
Mei	1609	Johanna de	**Fraij** met Ambrosius van Regemorter.
Sep.	1596	Noel	**Frambout** (v. Frombout) v. Sandwich met Susannaken van der Cruijce v. Antwerpen.
Mei	1594	Franchoijs	**Franck** v. Lessen met Gheetgin Jacobs wt d'lant v. Miers. we. Jan Povelicht.
Nov.	1609	Hans	„ uijt Franckenlandt met Jacobmijntge Sisaux v. Belle.
Jan.	1604	Hubrecht	**Franckelem** v. Maseijck met Jacobmijutge Davids, we. Abraham van Miorele.
Nov.	1608	Margareta	**Franckem** met Matthous Benns.
Jan.	1595	Hubrecht	**Francklijn** v. Maseyck met Susanna Vijsschers v. Antwerpen.
Apl.	1710	Anna	**Frans** met Philip Duec.
Feb.	1574	Tanneken	**Franses** met M. Claissen.
Mei	1592	Jaques	**Franssens** v. Antwerpen met Catheline d'Heer, noe v. Antwerpen.
Feb.	1604	Hubrecht	**Franssen** v. Iperen met Magdaleene Ramon, we. Louijs de d'Etenber.
Oct.	1586	Cateline	**Franssens** met Gillis de Crome.
Jun.	1585	Maeyken	**Fransten,** we. Rijclaert Rijckaert-z, met Lambrecht Perrentsen.
Jan.	1582	Nelleken	**Frantzen** met Henrick Gorltsen.
Sep.	1604	Maria	**Frederick,** we. Jan Luter, met Michiel Wietynek.
Sep.	1584	Jasper	**Fredericks** v. Amsterdam met Maijken Krijts v. Antwerpen, we. Gerradt Raassens.
Mar.	1592	Jasper	**Fredrix** v. Amsterdam met Sara van Pottelsberghe v. Noorden.
Feb.	1593	Pieter	**Fremant** v. Ipre met Lievine de Prnet v. Rouce.
Apl.	1582	Mahieu	de **Frenoij** v. Oostbrugge met Grietken van den Wille v. Ghendt.
Sep.	1609	Elizabeth	„ „ met Abraham Wege.
Mar.	1698	Sarah	**Frijars** met Hendrick van de Wall.
Feb.	1593	Prudence	**Friscobaldi** met Jacobus Wijbo.
Feb.	1591	Cornelia	**Frissard,** we. Willem Stanmelaer, met Hans Jacob Trettenbaeck.
Dec.	1603	Noe	**Frombout** (v. Frambout) v. Sandwich met Tmyeken van Bever v. bij Aelst.
Jul.	1619	Noe	„ v. Sandwich met Catharina Nison v. Hendbergh.
Dec.	1619	Abigail	„ , we. Bernard la Fosse, met Jan de Langle.
Apl.	1641	Johannes	**Fromenteel** (v. Fromenteau) j.g. met Susanna Lukens j.d. v. Stelen.
Apl.	1646	Elisabet	„ met Andries Priem.
Aug.	1621	Catharina	**Fromenteen** met Jan Thomar.
Jan.	1625	Jacob	**Frommont** v. Colchester met Maria de Geest v. Londen.
Oct.	1635	Hester	**Fromonentel** met Johannes Lukens.
Sep.	1603	Asuerus	**Frumenteel** j.g. v. Norwich met Maria de Bruijne j.d. v. Colchester. (v. Fromenteel).
Apl.	1609	Jacob	**Frutier** v. Antwerpen met Sara Obbelaer v. Londen.
Oct.	1699	Samuel	**Fuller** j.m. v. Norwich met Maria der Lee j.d. v. Londen.

6 Feb.	1662	Margriet	Gabriels met Joris Wesbrouck.
8 Mei	1593	Cijpriaen	Gabrij v. Antwerpen met Anna Malepart v. Ghendt.
10 Dec.	1584	Tanneken	Gaffels, we. Richard van Huijsen, met Hans Percheval.
21 Jan.	1630	Margareta	Gage met Cornelis Mouteken.
11 Jul.	1592	Pieter	le Gaij v. Armenturs met Cathorine de Bohout v. Antwerpen.
20 Jun.	1619	Abigail	Gallandt met Jan Pille.
13 Jan.	1572	Jan	Gallenarts van Engien met Tanneken s'Minners, ock van Engien.
5 Jun.	1593	Elisabeth	Gallioot, we. Christiaen Paradijs, met Gabriel de Viver.
.4 Nov.	1617	Abraham	van Galulen v. Norwich met Abigail Moenou v. Norwich.
21 Mei	1611	Janneken	de Gane met Franchoijs Walewijn.
2 Dec.	1628	Paulus	Ganne v. Leijden met Anna Regoot v. Haerlem, we. Baudewin Mattheus.
22 Jan.	1646	Samuel	de Gans j.d. v. Norwich met Martha Pietersen j.d. v. Londen.
8 Dec.	1577	Hans	Ganst v. Antwerpen met Catherijne van Doorne v. Antwerpen.
4 Feb.	1578	Cornelie	Garet met Heindrick de Walsche.
12 Sep.	1585	Pieter	,, v. Antwerpen met Abigail Bucerus v. Sandwytz.
22 Feb.	1575	Maijken	Garets, we. Jan van der Fonteijne, met Fransois Jacobs.
12 Feb.	1604	Elias	Garnoot v. Maidston met Elisabeth Panier, we. Laurens du Bois.
29 Dec.	1607	Enoch	,, v. Maidstone met Magdalena van Pe v. Maidstone.
5 Jul.	1614	Ester	,, met Samuel Alewijn.
.. Apl.	1626	Enoch	,, v. Maidston met Maijken Cox, we. Jacob Bens.
13 Apl.	1596	Daniel	Garnoots v. Maijdston met Magdaleene Meesens v. Antwerpen, we. Zacharias Ghysels.
12 Oct.	1630	Clara	Gaspoel met Willem Helden.
12 Jun.	1580	Gerardt	Gast v. Tiechol in Gulicker landt met Marijne Scholteten v. Dilsen in lande v. Luyck.
5 Aug.	1604	Maria	,, met Pieter Pietersen.
1 Aug.	1609	Elisabeth	,, met Aernont Cornelissz.
.. Mei	1616	Joris	Gatgen wt Surrey met Sara James v. Londen.
6 Oct.	1573	Laurynken	van Gavere met Hans Langhele.
15 Dec.	1697	Maria	Geelebaert met Teunis Jacobsen de Haen.
31 Jan.	1604	Susanna	Geeraerts met Maximilien Poictrin.
22 Mei	1610	Elizabeth	,, met Christofer Meijstner.
8 Nov.	1580	Cathrijne	Geerardt met M. Cautercel.
22 Jan.	1581	Marten	Geerardts v. Brugge met Cathoryne van Elspel, we. Michel Aalst.
14 Jul.	1584	Antonis	,, v. Juijchen bij 'sgraven met Catharine Lambrechts v. Londen.
17 Nov.	1607	Esther	Geerart, we. Jan Tijts, met Hendrick Archer.
9 Feb.	1889	Johannes Hendrikus	Geerkens j.m. oud 27 jaar met Wilhelmina Elizabeth Malefijt j.d. oud 29 jaar.
.. Jan.	1625	Maria	de Geest met Jacob Fronmont.
27 Apl.	1619	Dina	,, Geijter met Jan des Quiens.
5 Feb.	1612	Anna	,, Geijtere met Gillis van de Capelle.
2 Aug.	1579	Josyne	Geldolf met Jakes Muijshondt.
.. Feb.	1616	Margareta	Geleijns met Tobias Quatroos.
19 Jan.	1574	Lijneken	Gellekens met Hendrick Sweertsen.
9 Sep.	1571	Marcus	Geraerts v. Brugghe met Susanna de Crets v. Antwerpen.
19 Mei	1590	,,	,, v. Brugghe met Magdalena de Crits v. Antwerpen.
14 Apl.	1594	Cornelis	Geraets v. Vtrecht met Magdalena Huer v. Antwerpen.
22 Nov.	1703	Jacob	Gerart j.m. v. Delft met Pieternella Nuitsaert j.d. v. Delft.
7 Sep.	1630	Esther	Gerebardt met Jan Femeulen.
26 Mar.	1611	Anna	Gerrits met Arnouldt Meijer.
17 Jan.	1697	Willem	Gerritsen, wr. van Catharina Stockvelts, uijt het graefschap v. Meurs met Anna Pentilow, j.d. van Sudbury in Essex.
2 Sep.	1703	Catarina	Gerritsen met Adriaen de Ridder.
18 Oct.	1608	Jaques	Gerson v. Winseele met Judith Baes v. Norwich.
11 Dec.	1593	Catelyne	Getteels, we. Huybrecht Schaenaert, met Herman van Bolle.
1 Mei	1593	Pieter	Gheeldolf v. Meenen met Anne de Neve v. Brussel.
19 Mar.	1594	Jan	Gheeraerts v. Torlon met Lowijseken de Molijn v. Ghendt.
3 Feb.	1597	Hans	,, v. Bruijssel met Maeijken Verbeke v. Bolle.
24 Mei	1576	Ghijsbert	Gheeraertsson v. Vtrecht met Gheertruijd Heijndricksen v. Oldenkercke in Ghelderlant.
4 Jun.	1592	Hester	Gheerarts met Jan Trampzo.
9 Feb.	1602	Sara	,, met Isaac Olivier.
1 Mei	1576	Jan	Gheerartsen v. Valchenborch met Lijneken Denijs alias Ghyselars v. Zelandt.
24 Nov.	1577	Joos	Gheldolf v. Meeneue met Margriete Aelberts van Goch, we. Hans Drossaert.
30 Jul.	1591	Barbara	,, met Lambert Pieters.
21 Jan.	1582	Gielis	van Ghele met Helena Emondts v. Mascijck.
26 Sep.	1574	Jan	van Ghent v. s'Hertoghenbosch met Maijken Loocmans, de weduwe van Hans de Brun v. Hasselt.
31 Mei	1596	Janneken	Ghijsels met Anthony Reyniers.

2 Dec.	1595	Catelijne	van Ghijtele, we. Erasmus de Wilder, met Chrijstian Gorgu.
19 Jul.	1575	Albert	Ghijsbertssen v. Bernevelt met Antonyne Spitters, we. Mathys Anthonissen, v. Breussel.
13 Apl.	1596	Pieter	Ghijsbrecht v. Cuelen met Eva Iskens wt d'lant v. Gulick.
1 Mei.	1592	Zacharias	Ghijser v. Londen met Magdalena Moesens v. Antwerpen.
23 Sep.	1576	Matheus	Ghilbert v. Ghelykercke met Gheertruyt Escholt v. Minden.
8 Jun.	1592	Catheline	Ghilberts, we. Marten Boove, met Cornelis Eversen.
26 Jun.	1582	Elizabet	Ghiolen, we. Hendrick Feijten, met Pieter Coelbier.
3 Feb.	1594	Hans	de Ghuijt v. d'Euse met Catelijne van Wolden v. Meteren.
11 Jun.	1587	Martynken	Gieles, we. Mathijs Cokers, met Dierick Clopperijs.
27 Apl.	1596	Sara	Gijpsen met Jochim Mattheus.
14 Sep.	1602	Tanneken	Gijtel met Pieter van den Berge.
1 Nov.	1580	Trintgen	Gilberts met Marten Boves.
5 Aug.	1593	Catharine	„ , we. Cornelis Evaerts, met Abigail Roeter.
3 Dec.	1607	Elisabeth	Gilbo met Abraham Mets.
13 Jan.	1579	Jan	Gilbode v. Antwerpen met Maijcken Backer v. Arenduncke, we. Pieters Wellens
4 Jul.	1592	Yeken	Gillis met Phlips de Bauwlois.
5 Jun.	1604	Macijken	„ , we. Hans Buijs, met Jan Dawson.
24 Mei	1575	Anna	Giners met Cornelis Smulders.
26 Dec.	1587	Jan	Gipsen v. Maestricht met Elisabet Incermans v. Antwerpen.
3 Sep.	1605	Maieken	van Gisr . . . met Balthasar Lenerman.
10 Jan.	1604	Anna	„ Gistel, , we. Pieter van den Berghe, met Samuel Dries.
22 Jan.	1605	Pieter	„ „ v. Antwerpen met Debora van Steenput v. Antwerpen.
18 Jun.	1611	Tanneken	„ Gistele , we. Samuel Dries, met Guiljam Beijaert.
27 Mei	1574	Heindriexken	„ Goch met Lucas Hendriex.
21 Aug.	1593	Elizabeth	Goddens, we. Jan Davidts, met Cornelis de Neve.
10 Mar.	1573	Jan	Godschalck met Barbelken Anthonis, we. Jaspar van Dale.
23 Nov.	1602	Pieterken	Godschalck met Abraham Mets.
16 Apl.	1605	Maria	„ , we. Heyndrick Cuijl, met Nicolas Houblon.
12 Jul.	1608	Daniel	„ v. Nieukercke met Elizabeth Thijs, we. Hendrick Janssz.
4 Jul.	1609	Pieter	„ v. Tits met Christina Schonteken, we. Adam Hoorn.
6 Jan.	1572	Jois	Godtscalck v. Meessen met Josijne Ramans v. Houten bij Romen.
20 Mei	1600	Maria	Godtschalck met Hendrick Cuijl.
20 Jan.	1601	Elizabeth	„ met Daniel van Harinckoeck.
5 Jan.	1602	Janneken	„ met Jaeus de Rune.
22 Feb.	1603	Jacobus	„ v. Londen met Cathelijne van den Bemde v. Brussel.
21 Nov.	1626	Joanna	„ , we. Jaques Veriam, met Abraham van de Couter.
29 Aug.	1587	Susanna	Godtschalex met Heindrick Hoevenaer.
2 Dec.	1589	Sara	„ met Hans de Behout.
2 Jun.	1583	Nelleken	Goeswijns met Adriaan Walewijn.
25 Jan.	1573	Tanneken	Goethoens met Heijndrick Lodewijcks.
15 Mei	1638	David	Goetval j.g. v. Coninexberge met Catarina van Cotten j.d. wt t'landt van der Merck.
26 Jan.	1595	Macijken	de Goij met Jaspar Bouts.
28 Oct.	1606	Helena	„ Gols met Arnoldus Boot beijrman.
16 Aug.	1579	Jois	van Gomere v. Ghent met Esther Hermans van s'Hertogenbosch, we. Pieter Bourgoingne.
8 Nov.	1614	Hans	Gomertsz wt t'landt van der Merck met Lijdia Coppens v. Londen.
2 Aug.	1614	Catharina	Gommaerts, we. Hans Claessz, met Anthoni Cots.
5 Jun.	1604	Catharijne	Gommers, we. Hans Pannus, met Hans Claijssz.
3 Feb.	1602	Bastiaen	Gommersbagh, j.m. v. Wesel met Margarita Exalto D'Almeras, j.d. v. Leerdam. Met attestatie van St. James.
13 Feb.	1595	Cecilie	Gompfoets met Emanuel Vereijcke.
1 Jun.	1574	Maijken	Gooris, we. Jans Pollet, met Andrus Pot.
29 Mei	1637	Anna	Goose, we. Pieter Philips, met Lenaert Schaepheijsen.
5 Jan.	1595	Lenart	Goosens wt t'lant v. Gulick met Grietken Jansz wt d'lant v. Gulick, we. Salvador Hulet.
8 Jul.	1595	Anna	„ , we. Jan Achtschellinck, met Gillis Seghers.
13 Dec.	1596	Gillis	„ v. Ghendt met Maeijken Neijtens v. Audenaerde, we. Lieven van der Straeten.
1 Jan.	1582	Henrick	Gordtsen v. Swol met Nelleven Frantzen v. Sittardt.
28 Mei	1581	Christiaen	Gorgu v. Groostoek met Pierone Riekowaerts v. Meesene.
2 Dec.	1595	Chrijstiaen	„ v. Maestricht met Catelijne van Ghijtele v. Antwerpen, we. Erasmus de Wilder.
18 Oct.	1571	Maijcken	Goris met Jan Pollet.
7 Jan.	1680	Jan	Goslijn, wr. v. Londen, met Elisabeth Engels, we. v. Leyden.
20 Dec.	1703	Maria Sofia	Gout met Jan Pieter du Cros.
12 Mei	1703	Helena	Goutem met Steven Kemp.

8 Jan.	1857	Martina Marga-	s' Graeuwen met Henri Antoine van Overzee.
		retha Paulina	
2 Sep.	1571	Joos	de Graeve met Josine Sweme.
5 Aug.	1857	Johann Gonge	Graff , j.m., oud 27 jaar, met Anna Christina Margaretha Snock, j.d. oud 22 jaa
7 Oct.	1595	Maria	le Grand met Jacns de Maistres.
31 Jul.	1638	Sara	le Grant met Allaert de Lens.
23 Nov.	1582	Jan	de Grave v. Kassel met Mechtelde Puppings v. Minden int sticht v. Kolen.
17 Sep.	1583	Jan	,, ,, v. Kasselt, schumaker, met Jjtgen Janssens v. Ambsterdam.
12 Sep.	1587	Gielis	,, ,, v. Ghendt met Truijcken van Avesloot v. Brussel.
29 Jan.	1594	Aernout	,, ,, v. Eckelens met Magdaleene Andries v. Scherpenisse.
14 Dec.	1595	Jaens	,, ,, v. Ghendt met Martynken Vermeulen v. Brugge, we. Abraham Staelens.
6 Jan.	1596	Aaron	,, ,, v. Londen met Judith de Stiltere v. Haesebroeck.
28 Mei	1601	Goossen Gillis van der	,, met Magdaleenken Rijckaert v. Antwerpen.
22 Apl.	1623	Willem	de ,, v. bij Brussel met Susanna Adriaens, we. Jeffrey Rans.
17 Aug.	1637	Jan	Grevinckhof j.g. wt t'landt van der Marck met Catharina Salic j.d. v. Colchester.
14 Feb.	1587	Neelken	Grippens, we. Jan Rijers, met Hans Pieters.
19 Jan.	1595	Anna	van Groesbeck met Amos Schaep.
12 Mei	1680	Johanna	Grondeijs met Johannes van der Camer.
15 Oct.	1594	Josijnken	de Groone met Franchoijs Lampsens.
22 Mei	1578	Susanna	,, Groote met Gnilliaume Bogarde.
13 Dec.	1580	Raphael	,, ,, v. Antwerpen met Janneken Hagemans, we. Jans van Wijck, v. Heijnsberc
22 Jun.	1595	Pieter	,, ,, v. Antwerpen met Janneken Pieters v. Nieupoort.
8 Jul.	1617	Samuel	,, ,, v. Colchester met Elisabet Heuvenaer v. Londen.
25 Oct.	1812	Dirck Jansen	,, ,, , oud 30 jaren, met Janke Hiddes Kat, oud 22 jaren, beyde van der Eilan Ameland.
2 Jul.	1590	Janneken	s' Grooten , we. Philip Regier, met Joris Buwaert.
2 Sep.	1692	Jacob	Grootert j.m. v. Naerden met Catharina le Baiscur j.d. v. Leijden.
16 Feb.	1664	Anna	Grotens met Philippus Heulenberg.
9 Oct.	1586	Gillis	de Groune v. Gent met Cateline Fraussens v. Antwerpen.
23 Sep.	1599	Catheline	Gruters met Balthazar Stomfhousen.
.0 Nov.	1613	Clara	Guadia met Pieter van Dale.
1 Sep.	1575	Joos	van der Guchte v. Audenaerde met Gepken Reijns v. Embden.
3 Nov.	1573	Maijken	van Guiddeldonck met Jan Cnudde.
2 Apl.	1605	Jan	,, Gulick v. Emmerick met Margareta Coudron v. Brugghe.
4 Mar.	1691	Elizabeth	,, ,, , we. Cornelis Vernaels, met Lodewijck Zeekender.

15 Oct.	1594	Macijken	van Haecke, we. Hendrick Hermans, met Willem Pisteijns.
14 Feb.	1598	Gillis	van der Haeghen met Goemerijn Costens v. Antwerpen, we. Gulian Verhoeve.
10 Apl.	1575	Helena	Hael met Jan Beerman.
15 Dec.	1607	Teunis Jacobsen	de Haen j.m. v. Amsterdam met Maria Geelebaert j.d. v. London.
1 Jan.	1634	Pieter	Haertgens, wr. Maria Kelner, met Sara Wessel j.d. v. Londen.
16 Jun.	1592	Judith	Haentken met Jeremias Coudron.
12 Feb.	1594	Judith	,, , we. Jeremias Caudron, met Fransois Loosen.
15 Jul.	1599	Henrick	van Haes v. Dunswijck met Jacomynken Lloens v. Bruyssel.
7 Feb.	1576	Margriete	Haex , we. Cornelis Benen, met Jacob Janssen.
31 Jun.	1629	Jan	Hagedorne j.g. met Sara Lanotte j.d.
18 Oct.	1649	Jonatan	Hagedorn, wr. v. Colchester, met Janneken Degels j.d. v. Colchester.
13 Dec.	1580	Janneken	Hagemans, we. Jans van Wijck, met Raphael de Groote.
5 Feb.	1661	Pieter	van der Hagen j.m. v. Antwerpen met Dorethe Couinx, we. van Gerrit Engelaer.
10 Oct.	1594	Gillis	,, ,, v. Oudenaerde met Janneken Beeke v. Hassel, we. Jaspar van der Perchov
12 Feb.	1576	Janneken	Haghemans, we. Niclaes Ysebrants met Jan van Wijck.
1 Jun.	1595	Christine	van der Hagt met Cornelis Steenaert.
10 Sep.	1601	Catherine	Haiclsx, we. Mattheeus Heussem, met Fredrick Labberinck.
.. Jun.	1615	Catharina	Haije met Rombout Boxsteyns.
1 Sep.	1579	Jorijntgen	Haijwarden, we. Mattheus Stilte, met Lieven van der Stele.
16 Oct.	1689	Amarentia	van der Hair met Crijn Hendricx van der Bijl.
8 Jun.	1655	Mary	Hale met Hendrick Schenckel.
4 Jul.	1596	Hans .	van Halle v. Antwerpen met Catheline van Loo v. Bruijssel.
1 Sep.	1584	Lyntgen	Halffbunders, we. Jan van Tungerloo, met Antony Smidt.

19 Jan.	1689	Sara	Hall met Jan Hendrixen.
27 Nov.	1597	Christinen	Halters v. Nienkereke met Catelina de Hase v. Londen, we. Pieter de Meijer.
31 Mei	1680	Clara Jans	van Ham met Gisbert Verhaek.
15 Jul.	1595	Fredrick	van der Hamer v. Aernhem met Tanneken de Maer v. Antwerpen, we. Goijvaert de Zwerte.
1 Feb.	1579	Cathelijne	ver Hammen, we. Gillis de Lowijs, met Jasper Shuijssken.
6 Oct.	1601	Anna	Hammes, we. Christiaen de Hamer, met Jan Hendricx.
21 Apl.	1607	Jan	Hane v. Maestrick met Clos Leeuwerck v. Bruyssel.
1 Jan.	1627	Judith	de „ , we. met Jan Verraes.
9 Mei	1633	Jacob	„ „ j.g. v. Gent met Anna van den Broecke j.d. v. Londen.
19 Mei	1635	Elias	„ „ , wr., met Elisabeth Lauwercks. we. van Jan de Haene.
6 Nov.	1635	Franchoijs	van de „ j.g. v. Gendt met Johanna van den Broecke v. Londen.
5 Oct.	1574	Heindrick	Hansen v. Emblden met Maiken van der Biese, we. Hans Govaert, v. Diest.
21 Jan.	1588	Pieter	Hanthius v. Engien met Agneete Jacobs v. Antwerpen.
28 Jun.	1614	Abigail	Hanthuijs met Franchoijs Muller.
3 Sep.	1622	Joanna	van Haranghoeck met David Otgeer.
.. Feb.	1612	Hans	Hardewijn v. Sluijs met Catharine van Welden we. Hans Geest.
15 Jul.	1662	Anneken	Hardij met Cornelis Beerenbach.
8 Jan.	1686	Ds. Jacobus	Hardingh, wr, dienaer des Goddelycken woordts in de Nederduijtsche Gemeinte tot Colchester, met Julfru. Maria Cornelia Harley j.d. v. Dordrecht.
20 Jan	1601	Daniel	van Harinckoeck v. Sandwijts met Elisabeth Goltschalck v. Londen.
24 Apl.	1627	Elisabeth	Haringhcoeck met Hendric Hoevenaer.
8 Jan.	1696	Maria Cornelia	Harley met Ds. Jacobus Hardingh.
24 Jan.	1609	Catharina	van Harpe met Geerard Truije.
2 Aug.	1614	Jacob	Harruwijn v. Bremen met Maria van Soldt v. Londen.
29 Mar.	1703	Jan	Hartsbergen j.m. v. Cuijlembergh met Adriana van Riethroeck j.d. v. Wassenaer.
17 Feb.	1583	Lieven	de Hase v. Ghendt met Tanneken van Tungerin v. Antwerpen.
27 Nov.	1597	Catelina	„ „ , we. Pieter de Meijer, met Christinen Halters.
13 Dec.	1608	Josljutken	„ „ met Benjamin Everaerts.
17 Jul.	1597	Margriete	Hasen, we. Jan van den Bossche, met Jan de Fevre.
22 Aug.	1598	Judith	Haselaers, we. Pieter Verstraeten, met Abraham Veruloot.
12 Nov.	1594	Daniel	van Haseveldo v. Rouce met Tanneken Beeckmans v. Londen.
12 Mei	1576	Catherijne	van Hasevelt, we. Jans van Winghene met Adolf Verspelle.
3 Oct.	1612	Goijvaert	van Hasselt v. Cuelen met Elisabeth Opgingort.
11 Jul.	1585	Guilianne	Hatroen v. Meessene met Chrijstijnken Loijs v. Poperinghe.
5 Dec.	1581	Jois	Hauwe v. Kassel met Maijeken de Hemele v. Brugge.
17 Jan.	1587	Joos	„ „ v. Cassel met Margriete Pieters, we. Arent Arentsz.
14 Dec.	1602	Joos	„ v. Cassel met Anna de Beste v. Brugge.
3 Sep.	1603	Maeyken	„ met Christiaen Bonharinck.
23 Jan.	1607	Catharina	„ , we. Toussain Laps, met Hans Swart.
13 Sep.	1614	Catharina	„ , we. Hans Swart, met Joos Croppenbergh.
6 Mei	1673	Thomas	Hearne j.m. v. Londen met Aletta op de Beeck j.d., Getrout van Doct.: Mason in die Parochie genaemt Pieter de Pouvre.
18 Mar.	1578	Barbara	Heckaerts met Hans Peper.
14 Jan.	1597	Barbel	Heckaert, we. Jan Duijnmen, met Joos de Jonckheere.
21 Apl.	1579	„	Heckaren, we. Jan Peper, met Jan Duymen.
22 Jan.	1576	Betken	van Hecke met Jacques Palynck.
10 Oct.	1583	Lenyntgen	van „ , we. Sanders Engelgrave, met Jakes van Lowegen.
31 Mar.	1584	Janneken	de „ met Kaerle van der Warden.
17 Jan.	1591	Lijnken	van „ met Marten Jansen.
21 Jul.	1581	Sara	Heckelars met Jan Maas.
19 Aug.	1628	Jan	van der Hecken, wedr. van Maria Jes, v. Brussel met Sara van den Broecke, we. Melchior Martin, v. Londen.
12 Jan.	1599	Israel	Hecklaers v. Londen met Josynke Bricket v. Antwerpen.
11 Aug.	1594	Clara	van Heecke met Adriaen van Zevecote.
18 Aug.	1601	Janneken	van der Heed met Jonas Janssen.
23 Mei	1592	Catheline	d' Heer met Jaqnes Franssen.
9 Jan.	1607	Catharijna	d' Heere, we. Jaqnes Franssen, met Pieter Wijbo.
22 Oct.	1616	Pieter	Heeren v. Rouce met Catharina Bolle v. Sandwich.
20 Mei	1583	Willem	de Heese v. s'Hertogenbosche met Dorothea Koninke v. Dantzick, we. Thomas Diesslinck.
1 Jan.	1694	Hans Jurrigen	Heflee j.m. v. Augsburgh met Clementia Beseers van Thienen j.d. v. Leijden.
1 Aug.	1587	Eliaert	van der Heijde v. Bremen met Catelijne Cuijpers v. Antwerpen.
17 Jul.	1695	Trintje Antonissen	Heijde, van der, met Reynier Balthes Engelhof.
8 Jan.	1573	Elizabeth	van der Heijden met Anthonis van der Muelen.
27 Dec.	1596	Sara	„ „ , we. Hans van Hautloock, met Pieter de Busscher.
27 Dec.	1604	Beelken	„ „ Jan Evraerts, met Jan de Clerck.
12 Jun.	1582	Frants	Heijligers v. Baaswijler in lande v. Gulick met Maeyken Wieesen (?), we. Michiel Symons.

110   MARRIAGES

20 Jul.	1602	Boelken
1 Feb.	1573	Margriete
14 Jul.	1573	Helena
24 Mei	1576	Gheertruijd
30 Nov.	1572	Barbara
14 Sep.	1602	Laurens
9 Nov.	1572	Adriaen
17 Jan.	1604	Heylken
18 Dec.	1604	Rachel
.6 Apl.	1612	Erasmus
25 Feb.	1595	Jan

Heijlighers, we. Baltazar Poggen, met Jan Nuijwaert.
Heijndricks met Pieter Billen.
   ,,   met Olivier Alard.
Heijndricksen met Ghijsbert Gheernertssen.
   ,,   fa. Dierick met Jacob Hostens.
Heijndricx v. Gulick met Maeijken Verbeke v. Bc . . . , we. v. Hans Goerart.
Heijndrix met Katelijne de Hooghe.
   ,,   , we. Herman Couper, met Willem Alberts.
   ,,   , we. Herman Jordaen, met Marten Bigger.
   ,,   v. Flenslmrgh met Mcchlijnken Clant v. Gorcum.
Heijns v. Warnicke met Passchijnken van Aken v. Dessolghom, we. Guiliaei Ketele.

25 Feb.	1691	Fredrick

Heijsselaer j.m. v. Meulhuijsen met Dorothea Segwaert j.d. v. 'sGravenhaeg met attestatie van St. James.

13 Oct.	1646	Gerard
23 Feb.	1574	Rolof
7 Jun.	1586	Adriane
12 Jul.	1601	Anneken
13 Jan.	1572	Baudewijn
29 Sep.	1502	Raches
14 Jan.	1593	Dierick
12 Oct.	1630	Willem
11 Dec.	1582	Neelken
22 Oct.	1611	Tobias
30 Dec.	1628	Elisabet
5 Dec.	1581	Mayeken
10 Mei	1590	Marten Pauwels
27 Mei	1574	Lucas
6 Oct.	1601	Jan
5 Dec.	1609	Robert
14 Mei	1611	Elisabeth
. . Aug.	1613	Carel
20 Jul.	1619	Jan
27 Jul.	1623	Abel
31 Mei	1631	Herman
22 Jan.	1690	Cornelis

van Heythuisen j.g. v Wee . . met Anna Lodewijck j.d. v. Londen.
Heindrix v. Billen met Jacquemijne de Meij v. Mecssene.
   ,,   , we. Nicolas Fonteine, met Jan de Cucninck.
   ,,   met Thomas de Meijer.
de Heirde v. Gendt met Tannekcn Smartelaers.
Hckelaers met Isaac Theus.
Helden uit land v. Gulick met Sara Ootghoers v. Sandwitche.
   ,,   j.g. v. Londen met Clara Gaspoel j.d. v. Berck.
Hellewartz met Sijmon Klercks.
de Hem v. Norwich met Susanna Corselis v. London.
   ,,   ,, met Abraham Hudgebout.
   ,, Hemele met Jois Hauwe.
Hemskercke v. Haerlem met Sara Stenners v. Antwerpen.
Hendricx v. Dam in Groeninghorlant met Hendricxken van Goch v. s Hertogenbos
   ,,   v. Orson met Anna Hammes v. Ceulen, we. Christiaen de Hamer.
   ,,   v. t'laat v. Cleeff met Margareta Arnouts, we. Paulus Rutts.
   ,,   met Jan v. Steenberghe.
   ,,   v. Utrecht met Catharina Lie v. Altena bij Worcum.
   ,,   v. Andwerpen met Elisabet van den Steene, we. Jan Snoock.
   ,,   v. Embden met Maria Wademont v. Londen.
Hendricksen j.g. v. Amsterdam met Maria Vleijsaers j.d. v. Londen.
Hendricks j.m. v. Breskens in 't landt v. Cadsandt met Willemyntje Kressel v. Ter Tolen.

7 Mar.	1694	Jan
19 Jun.	1689	Jan

   ,,   j.m. v. Nieumegen met Jacomina Simonds j.d. v. Deventer.
Hendrixen, wr. v. Elsje Boeckman, met Sara Hall j.d. v. Dublin. Attestatie St. James.

. . Jun.	1620	Jacquos
16 Apl.	1592	Willem
29 Nov.	1597	Maijken
5 Oct.	1572	Sara
21 Apl.	1594	Pieter
12 Aug.	1595	Rachel
5 Jun.	1610	Herman
21 Dec.	1577	Claerken
9 Mei	1592	Anna
25 Aug.	1675	Sara
9 Oct.	1575	Heindrick
16 Aug.	1570	Esther
29 Jun.	1584	Dierijck
13 Jul.	1600	Heindrick
1 Dec.	1614	Maria
.6 Jan.	1621	Pieter
27 Dec.	1603	Jacob
24 Aug.	1581	Maijken
26 Aug.	1628	Maria
17 Mei	1631	Anna
6 Aug.	1579	Eva
27 Dec.	1593	Catherina
26 Jan.	1591	Catharine
19 Jun.	1610	Hendrick
11 Jul.	1587	Heindrick
9 Sep.	1604	Tannekon
2 Jun.	1594	Guiliame

Hendrixsz v. Andwerpen met Hermijne Vademondt, we. v. Willem Bosch.
Hennington v. Brugghe met Josijne Kokuts v. Beselaere.
Henricks, we. Sebastiaen Heuskens, met Simon Balaert.
Henricksen met Joris de Dobbelaer.
Henrix v. Aelst met Pieriuc van de Walle v. Meenene.
   ,,   met Herman Jordaens.
Herckers wt t'land v. Lujjck met Catherina van Holder, we. Abraham de Ryc
de Herde, we. Gabriel du Pourcau, met Lieven Temmerman.
l' Heremite met Franchois van der Peere.
van Hereveen met Wilhelm Colingcamp.
Hermans v. Turnhout met Neelken van Hoecke v. Turnhout.
   ,,   , we. Pieter Bourgoingne, met Jois van Gomere.
   ,,   van op Autens met Melken Adriaens v. Vianen.
   ,,   v. Londen met Susanna Hur v. Antwerpen.
   ,,   met Willem Theunissen.
   ,,   v. Bruijssel met Janneken Matthys, we. Francoijs Lambssens.
Hermanssz v. Louweerden met Lowijseken de Molijn, we. Jan Geeract.
Herremans met Cornelis de Mol.
Herrewijn met Timotheus van Vleteren.
   ,,   v. Harrewijn met Adam Boddens.
Herrisson met Jan de Springer.
van Hersaele, we. Jeronimus Custodes, met Jan Jams.
Hertblock met Johan Wigt.
Hertman wt Brunswijck met Hester de Vos v. London.
d' Hertoge met Elisabet Everaerts beyde v. Gendt.
   ,,   met Gillis de Wege.
d' Hertoghe v. Gent met Trijsken van Steenacker v. Ghendt.

13 Dec.	1603	Rogier	van **Herweghe** v. Brugge met Ester Beeckman v. Londen.
3 Nov.	1573	Janneken	**Herwijck,** we. Steven Herwijck, met Gillis Seghers.
20 Aug.	1584	Jan	**Hesterman** v. Vden int landt v. Kleve met Klaarken Voets v. Nieuwkercke.
16 Feb.	1664	Philippus	**Heulenberg** j.m. v. Mortlake met Anna Grotens j.d. v. Mortlake, getrout ablaet door D. Petrus Tessemorterus, Proponent.
25 Nov.	1606	Catharijna	van **Heur** met Jan Jasperssen.
3 Jul.	1586	Janneken	**Heuriblox** met Fransois van Belle.
26 Oct.	1591	Margriete	**Heurlinx** met Hans de Bick.
1 Jan.	1585	Hans	van den **Heuvel** v. Bruijssel met Maeijken Bourgeois, we. Pieter Provents v. Enge.
19 Jul.	1604	Abraham	van **Heuvel** v. Antwerpen met Maeyken Jacobs, we. Francoijs van Brakele.
5 Nov.	1691	Petronella	van den **Heuv.,** met Andries Hillebrandt.
13 Jul.	1589	Lambrecht	**Hilden v.** d'Iant v. Gulick met Levijne Itsen ock v. d'Iant v. Gulick.
21 Nov.	1587	Jacomyntken	**Hildernisse,** we. Joris van Daele, met Adam der Kinderen.
18 Feb.	1588	Tanneken	van **Hilegarde,** we. Jeronijmus Hermans, met Laurens de Boulougne.
8 Sep.	1577	Anthonyne	van **Hille** met Hans Pinaert.
5 Nov.	1691	Andries	**Hillebrandt** j.m. v. Terborgh met Petronilla van der Heuv..., j.d. v. Kakecken. Met attestatie v. 's Gravenhaegh.
2 Feb.	1591	Tanneken	van **Hillegaerde,** we. Laureins de Bouloigne, met Jacob Sweerts.
10 Sep.	1588	Neelken	**Hillegaert** met Baltazar Pigge.
15 Jul.	1576	Maijken	**Hillens** met Jan Janssen.
24 Jul.	1689	Hendrick	**Hilt** j.m. v. Oberenthorf bij Francfort met Maria Jans v. 's Gravenhaegh.
14 Feb.	1604	Jacques	**Hobbel** v. Kemmel met Josijntgen de Rijcke, we. Jan van de Riviere.
21 Feb.	1609	Anna	**Hobbels,** we. Adolf Staet, met Herman Sonbery.
26 Feb.	1639	Catherina	„ , we. Nicolaes Vereken, met Antonius de Bois.
20 Feb.	1582	Tanneken	**Hobels** met Adolf Staet.
17 Feb.	1583	Lijutge	van **Hoeck** met Pieter Kleijmans.
23 Apl.	1594	Jaques	do „ v. Ghent met Maeijken Pepermans v. Bruijssel, we. Cornelis Lampsen.
10 Oct.	1602	Jaques	„ „ v. Gent met Lijntken Kestloot v. Poperinghen.
14 Jan.	1617	Maijken	van „ met Hendriek van der Hoeve.
8 Nov.	1617	Jacob	do „ v. Londen met Thonijuken Brixe, we. Pieter Consenaer.
. . Feb.	1618	Hester	„ „ met Dierick Everts.
9 Oct.	1575	Neelken	van **Hoecke** met Heindriek Hermans.
3 Jul.	1575	Lijneken	de la **Hoer** met Arnout Cornelissen.
13 Sep.	1586	Sara	de **Hoeve** met Franchoijs Danian.
12 Sep.	1587	Cornelis	van der „ v. Brugge met Josynken van Baesbouck v. Oudenaerde, we. Bomaert van der Poorter.
14 Jan.	1617	Hendrick	„ „ „ v. Dordrecht met Maijken van Hoeck v. Turnhout.
29 Aug.	1587	Hendrick	**Hoevenaer** v. Ceulenborch met Susanna Goltschalcx v. Londen.
24 Apl.	1627	Hendric	„ met Elisabeth Haringhcoeck heijde v. Londen.
11 Jun.	1592	Isaac	**Hoffier** v. Edam met Anna van Cullenberghe v. Brussel.
10 Sep.	1553	Jan	**Hoffman** v. Bamberch met Lijsbeth Becke v. Maeseyck.
6 Oct.	1614	Judith	**Hofman** met Wessel Wessels.
10 Jan.	1585	Jacob	**Hofmans** v. Woert met Fransoise Lilaert v. Berg in Henegouwe.
2 Jul.	1635	Jan	**Hoijel** j.g. v. Amsterdam met Mary English j.d. v. Londen.
30 Nov.	1585	Jacus	de **Hoiju** met Catelyne de Moij, beijde v. Antwerpen.
21 Jan.	1593	Jacus	„ „ v. Antwerpen met Hesther Robson oock v. Antwerpen.
27 Dec.	1575	Gheeraert	de la **Hoir** v. Oudenarde met Betken van den Boische v. Oudenaerde.
25 Jul.	1571	Matthys	**Hoissts** v. Heijnsberch met Antonyne 's Beijrs, we. Pauwels de Beijr v. Mechlen.
27 Mei	1606	Catharine	van **Holder** met Abraham de Rijcke.
5 Jun.	1610	Catharina	van „ , we. Abraham de Rijcke, met Herman Herekers.
10 Jul.	1574	Janneken	**Holmans** met Joos Toebaeck.
4 Mar.	1691	Mary	**Holmwood** met Jan Terry.
6 Apl.	1629	Osens	**Holwet,** wr. van Anna Jansen, met Jenne de Nij, we. Jan Alman.
14 Feb.	1604	Elisabeth	des **Hommets** met David de Paus.
2 Sep.	1699	Hubertus	**Homoet** j.m. v. Loo in Gelderlandt met Johanna van Lom j.d. v. Deuter ht
11 Apl.	1587	Joos	de **Hondt** v. Waekene met Colette van der Keere v. Ghent.
19 Jan.	1585	Hans	**Honseer** v. Bruijssel met Catherine Els v. Turnhout.
14 Apl.	1628	Abigail	**Hooft** met Walter Brus.
9 Nov.	1572	Katelyne	de **Hooghe** met Adriaen Heijndrix.
10 Jul.	1593	Renier	„ „ v. Thielt met Susanna Felix v. Oostende.
29 Mei	1604	Romeijn	d' **Hooghe** v. Tielt met Judith Bisschop v. Londen.
3 Mar.	1584	Jakemyne	s' **Hoops,** we. Gillis Jacobs, met Marten van der Hovestadt.
12 Aug.	1593	Goos	**Hoornaert** v. Wernicke met Tanneken de Bruijne v. Brugge, we. Jan Daglets . . .
31 Mei	1597	Jacus	van **Hoorne** v. Antwerpen met Christijuken Wouters v. Turnho . . v. Anr . . . . . Jacobs.
6 Dec.	1590	Lijuken	„ **Hoplijden** met Rijckaert Marteus.
7 Feb.	1660	Maria	**Horn** met Dierick Blancke.
2 Jun.	1584	Koenrardt	**Horstgens** v. Nuijeen met Grietgen Luijekens v. Maescijck.

12 Aug.	1582	Pieter	**Hoste** v. Kortrijke met Baijken Aelmans v. Londen.
30 Sep.	1600	Susanna	„ met Samuel Dries.
12 Feb.	1601	Jossynken	„ met Matthys Lamberts.
18 Jun.	1605	Jacques	„ v. Londen met Sara Bronchorst mede v. Londen.
29 Jun.	1606	Abraham	„ v. Londen met Priscilla van de Velde mede v. Londen.
26 Apl.	1608	Daniel	„ v. Maidston met Anna Brunijnx v. Londen.
5 Nov.	1611	Sara	„ met Abraham Wessels.
.. Oct.	1613	Dierick	„ v. Middelborch met Joanna de Meter v. Londen.
.0 Oce.	1618	Janneken	„ met Abraham Laureijns.
30 Nov.	1572	Jacob	**Hostens** v. Audenarde met Barbara, fa. Dierick Heijndrickssen.
16 Apl.	1605	Nicolas	**Houblon** v. Ryssel met Maria Godschalck, we. Heijndrick Cuijl.
21 Feb.	1604	Daniel	**Houck** v. Londen met Tabitha Pauwels v. Londen.
28 Jan.	1578	Adrinen	**Hommes** van den Gouwe met Heijlken Isebrants vuten Haeghe.
2 Sep.	1571	Henrick	de **Hout** met Jakemijntghen Klayssens.
9 Feb.	1595	Joos	de „ v. Marke met Arijnken Mestlag v. Oudenaerde, we. Bernaert van de Putte.
18 Jun.	1631	Anna	van den **Houte** met Paulus de Knuijt.
8 Jul.	1617	Elisabet	**Houvenaer** met Samuel de Groote.
13 Apl.	1658	Hendrick	van **Houvnagen** j.m. v. Londen met Catalijne Bulst j.d. v. Buisingen.
.. Feb.	1615	Margareta	**Houwaer**, we. Pieter Houwaer, met Richard Stokes.
1 Jan.	1594	Catheline	**Houwe** met Toussain Lap.
2 Sep.	1571	Maeyken	van **Hove** met Henrick Oppennoke.
10 Apl.	1586	Janneken	op den „ met Fransois Polaert.
20 Jan.	1587	Janneken	van „ , we. Matheus Luls, met Lodwye Blommaert.
4 Mei	1591	Janneken	van den „ , we. Gillis Bastinck, met Jan Reijnont.
22 Aug.	1591	Sara	„ „ „ met Jacob Beelen.
3 Mar.	1584	Marten	van der **Hovestadt** oft Berntz v. Embden met Jakemijne s'Hoops v. Yperen, we. Gillis Jacobs.
9 Nov.	1600	Magdalena	**Hubers** met Gommaer van de Linden.
28 Oct.	1602	Willem	**Hubrechts** v. Andwerpen met Martynken Auerhout v. Waesten.
24 Feb.	1596	Charles	**Hudgebout** v. Ghendt met Maria le Bock v. Londen.
30 Dec.	1628	Abraham	„ j.g. v. Londen met Elisabet de Hem j.d. v. Colchester.
14 Apl.	1594	Magdalena	**Huer** met Cornelis Geraets.
10 Nov.	1646	Jan	van **Huevel** j.g. v. Harlem met Anna Schapelinck j.m. v. Brugge.
.5 Feb.	1612	Maijken	**Hugens**, we. Jaques de Causije, met Liborius Quant.
1 Feb.	1574	Laureins	**Hughers**, v. Valckenborch met Maijken Aemans v. Maseijck.
4 Feb.	1593	Catheliae	**Hugo** met Henrick Janssen.
29 Jan.	1605	Catharyne	„ , we. Heijndrick Janssen, met Jan de Vriese.
6 Sep.	1573	Lenard	**Hugues** uit Gelderlant met Eijlken Lenards v. s'Hertoghenbossche.
8 Jan.	1594	Laurens	**Huijgens** v. Venlo met Louwise de Neve v. Brussel, we. Arnout Meessens.
4 Mei	1595	Maeyken	**Huijghens**, we. Thomas Leewes, met Jaeus van der Consie.
12 Jan.	1580	Marguerite	**Huijga** met Gerard de Kobber.
.. Jun.	1573	Joos	**Huijsheere** v. Brugghe met Elizabeth Vroolick v. Ghendt.
8 Nov.	1571	Jacob	**Huijsman** v. Nairden met Geertruyt Claes v. Koedijek by Alemaer.
12 Jun.	1575	Jelijne	„ met Lowijs van Spiers.
14 Oct.	1595	Tanneken	**Huijsman**, we. Pieter Baufart, met Willem de Tepper.
11 Aug.	1584	Henrick	**Huijssman** van den Ham met Tanneken Wijckmans v. Audernarde.
12 Aug.	1578	Anltgen	**Huijsmans** met Henrick Beeckmans de jonge.
3 Oct.	1587	Gelijne	„ , we. Lowijs Verspiere, met Adriaen Meerschaert.
31 Mei	1597	Gelijnken	„ , we. Adriaen Mijrschaert, met Pieter de Keyser.
9 Apl.	1592	Salomon	**Hulet** v. Antwerpen met Margriete Janssen uit lant v. Gulick.
2 Sep.	1571	Martijntghen	van **Hulle** met Joris Orneck.
30 Dec.	1600	Lieven	**Hulst** v. Ghendt met Maria Ruytinck v. Noorwitz, we. Joannes Marquinus.
9 Aug.	1597	Pieter	„ v. Halle met Martha Baert v. Londen.
20 Apl.	1602	Jeremias	„ „ v. Colchester met Susanna Conniex v. Londen.
18 Jul.	1633	Catharina	van der „ met Geraert Verbeijt.
31 Mei	1585	Martijn	de **Hulster** v. Kolskam met Janneken de Lange v. Hosen.
25 Apl.	1614	Susanne	„ **Hulster** met Hans Wijnants.
26 Dec.	1625	Susanna	„ , we. Hans Winne, met Geraert Janssz.
12 Oct.	1585	Herman	van **Humbach** v. Aken met Janneken de Malynes v. Antwerpen.
.. Aug.	1613	Josijuken	**Hunnington**, we. Guliame Hunnington, met Lambert Jansz.
13 Jul.	1600	Susanna	**Hur** met Hendrick Hermans.
.. Feb.	1616	Peroontken	**Hureels** met Paul de Vos.
2 Mar.	1595	Maeijken	**Hurts** met Zeghel Jansz.
5 Jul.	1603	Charles	**Hutzebout** v. Gent met Paulijnken Anderlicht v. Breda.

3 Jun.	1571	Agnete	Jacobs met Gerardt Reire...rein.
22 Feb.	1575	Fransois	„ v. Turnhout met ... ij...en Carels, we. Jan van der Fonteyne, v. Rouse.
26 Dec.	1576	Lijneken	„ met Hans Lauw...t.
17 Jan.	1581	Willem	„ uth Gebberken ... ... Loui Dierickssen van der Gouwe, we. Geeradt Valck.
1 Apl.	1583	Heindricksken	„ , we. Lijd....... .... Cornelis P...on .
21 Jan.	1588	Agnete	„ met Pieter B... .
1 Mei	1594	Gheetgin	„ , we. Jan Poo....t... met Franchijs Franck.
31 Jun.	1601	Janneken	„ met Anthioy C...on.
23 Sep.	1602	Maeyken	„ , we. Th...us Louver... ... t Franchois van Brakel.
19 Jul.	1604	Maeyken	„ , we. Franedij v... Bral. 1 . met Abraham van Hovel.
18 Nov.	1604	Tryuken	„ met Lieven d... J...er.
. . Feb.	1612	Janneken	„ , we. Anthoni Cocom, met Wilebrord Spijs.
10 Dec.	1616	Maria	„ met Gillis van Brugh.
2 Apl.	1650	Anna	„ met Elias Peke.
23 Feb.	1587	Pieter	„ v. Antwerpen met Naeghen s'Martelaers v. Oudenaerde.
21 Apl.	1595	Pieter	„ v. Antwerpen met Sera ... as en v. Londen.
5 Dec.	1602	Willem	„ v. Eemblen met Anna M ...iquinus v. Londen.
6 Nov.	1604	Philips	„ v. Andwerpen met LB ...e S... v. Sol v. Londen.
2 Oct.	1606	Claijs	„ v. Leyden met Susanea Badermaker, we. Pieter Michiels.
. 1 Mei	1616	Nicolas	„ v. Berghen-op-Zoom met Marie van de Beke v. Londen.
. . Jun.	1640	Rombaet	Jacobson, wr. v. n Maria Libert. met Johanna Steen j.d. v. Londen.
10 Jun.	1606	Adriaen	Jacobson v. Amersfort met Susanna Beceman v. Londen.
22 Aug.	1585	Willem	Jacobssen van den Dam in Groeningerlant met Janneken Nutinx v. Provene.
3 Mei	1608	Catharina	Jacobsz met Geeraert von der Capelle.
24 Apl.	1620	Jacob	„ v. Middelborgh met Judith Des Meistres v. Londen.
15 Apl.	1604	Jaques	Jacobssz v. Berghen-op-Zoom met Jacabunynken Sarels, we. Jan Brumel.
22 Jul.	1571	Willem	„ v. Brugge met Catherijne van der Elst, we. Walramus Loslowijcksen.
26 Jul.	1601	Joos	Jacops v. Antwerpen met Janneken Verbrugge v. Londen.
23 Jan.	1582	Henrick	Jacopsen uwt Stiche v. Colen met Bertken Thyssens v. Aernem.
26 Jun.	1576	Jan	Jacquart v. Berghen in Henegouwen met Maijken Clerx v. St. Truyen.
28 Jan.	1578	Dierick	Jaeghers, we. Dierick van Eijcke, met Jacob van Bracht.
18 Nov.	1604	Lieven	do Jagor v. Gent met Trynken Jacobs v. Gelre.
28 Mei	1599	Lyntken	„ Jagers met Haeyman Jansz.
29 Mar.	1573	Mecholyne	Jaghers met Dierick van der Rijcke.
28 Oct.	1588	Sara	James met Jaeus Per-eval.
23 Jan.	1593	Catelina	„ , we. Hendrick Abrams, met Robert Range.
18 Jan.	1597	Neelken	„ met Leenard Lamer om.
25 Jul.	1598	Jan	„ de Jonge v. Londen met Sara van der Beke v. Antwerpen.
26 Apl.	1603	Isaac	„ v. Londen met Anna Manjet we v. Londen.
17 Apl.	1610	Tanneken	„ , we. Anthony Lodwijex, met Lieven Bandart.
. . Mei	1616	Sara	„ met Joris Gatgen.
28 Jan.	1578	Lyntken	Jannesen, we. Christiaen Crabbe, met Heindrick Achmans.
24 Aug.	1589	Cornelis	Jans met Catharina Lammens v. Ghendt.
7 Oct.	1619	Anna	„ met Anthoine le Quien.
21 Sep.	1681	Maria	„ met Ric Sicers.
24 Jul.	1689	Maria	„ met Hendrick Hilt.
11 Sep.	1580	Nelgen	Jansen met Adam Willems.
18 Feb.	1582	Pieter	„ v. Salinge met Margriete Sprinckhuysen v. Amsterdam.
17 Jan.	1591	Marten	„ v. Londen met Lynken van Hecke v. Antwerpen.
30 Dec.	1616	Geerard	„ v. Groeninghen met Anna de Jode v. Londen.
3 Jun.	1630	Anna	„ met A. de Cerf.
11 Mar.	1647	Engelken	„ met Gerart Muller.
7 Feb.	1705	Albert	„ v. Scharpensecl met Jennette Leslij. Met attestatie v. Westminster.
31 Jan.	1659	Annekon	Janson met Renert Carstens.
27 Nov.	1604	Clara	Janss met Nicasius Roussel.
30 Apl.	1594	Judith	„ met Cornelis Dregge.
19 Feb.	1573	Jacob	Janssen v. Valckenbergh met Margriete Wauters, we. Sebastiaen Pieterssen.
6 Oct.	1573	Elsken	„ met David Marien.
3 Aug.	1574	Wolter	„ v. Deventer met Soetken Brakelmans v. Ghent.
12 Jul.	1575	Stevon	„ v. Ghendt met Anna Quirintze vth den Hage.
12 Jul.	1575	Susanne	„ met Jan Klereksen.
4 Jan.	1575	Gheerart	„ v. Dorste met Lysken van Ash v. Mallssen.
2 Aug.	1575	Pieter	„ v. 'sHertogenbosch met Maijken Loo, we. Willem Jacobs v. Vendloo.
4 Dec.	1575	Rachel	„ , we. Abraham de Vriesse, met Cornelis Quirintssen.
3 Jan.	1576	Fimgaert	„ v. Sneken in West Vrieslant met Tanneken Bastiaens v. Emblen.
7 Feb.	1576	Jacob	„ v. Aernem met Margriete Haex, we. Cornelis Beuen, v. Lerinen in Oost Vriesland.
10 Mei	1576	Emmeken	„ met Nicolas Yselbrants

15 Jul.	1576	Jan	**Janssen** v. Delft met Mayken Hillens v. Maseijck.
9 Sep.	1576	Wolfaert	,, v. s'Hertogenbosche met Barbelken Elynck v. Rousse.
11 Apl.	1577	Maeyken	,, met Segher Cleymans.
9 Jun.	1577	Elisabeth	,, met Jacques de Kostere.
31 Oct.	1577	Marie	,, met Cornelis Crebboudtsen.
2 Dec.	1582	Janneken	,, met Cornelis Peper.
3 Sep.	1587	Trijnken	,, met Heindrick Bosman.
13 Feb.	1588	Christine	,, met Hubert de Page.
14 Apl.	1588	Lambrecht	,, v. bij Deventer met Eva Zeghers v. Engen.
6 Apl.	1589	Sara	,, , we. Thomas Spiere, met Jan Engelsfield.
17 Mei	1590	Eva	,, met Arnout Stalpaert.
24 Mei	1590	Henrick	,, wt lant v. Gulick met Goelken Stiers v. Antwerpen, we. Wynant Verhulst.
15 Nov.	1590	Dierick	,, v. Volthuijsen met Lijnken Soenbens v. Antwerpen.
17 Aug.	1591	Jacob	,, v. Antwerpen met Oijken Poppings v. Dokum, we. Pierson Bouchier.
9 Apl.	1592	Margriete	,, met Salomon Hulet.
26 Dec.	1592	Abraham	,, v. Antwerpen met Janneken Rademakers oock v. Antwerpen.
4 Feb.	1593	Henrick	,, v. bij Gulick met Catheline Hugo v. Antwerpen.
10 Feb.	1594	Maeyken	,, , we. Pauwel v. Eesberghe, met Hans Mol.
10 Dec.	1594	Jan	,, v. Medest (Midhurst) in Sussex met Magdalecne Spirincx v. Antwerpen, we. Joos de Waegenaere.
21 Apl.	1595	Sara	,, met Pieter Jacobs.
4 Jul.	1596	Hubert	,, v. Vtrecht met Claerken van den Boom v. Londen.
6 Dec.	1597	Hans	,, v. Antwerpen met Margen Trots v. Bruijssel, we. Gillis de Coster.
22 Nov.	1599	Heurick	,, wt t'lant v. Gulick met Janneken Overdaet v. Enghen, we. Philip Verburcht.
18 Aug.	1601	Jonas	,, v. Londen met Janneken van der Heed v. Roesselaere.
14 Nov.	1602	Pieter	,, v. St. Cruijs met Sara Bouters v. Gent, we. Lieven van Stoete.
1 Jul.	1604	Eva	,, , we. Arnouldt Stalpaert, met Jan Wittebroot.
12 Jan.	1607	Peryntgen	,, met Jan Schram.
25 Mei	1607	Herman	,, uyt Westphalen met Susanna Carnoit v. Maidston.
16 Jul.	1622	Cornelis	,, v. Londen met Elisabeth Beke v. Colchester.
13 Oct.	1579	Agnete	**Janssens**, we. Joris van Esse, met Rutger van Rumonde.
7 Jun.	1580	Judith	,, , we. Laurentz Thomassz, met Pieter van der Straten.
14 Sep.	1581	Geerardt	,, vth sticht v. Kolen met Jakemijne Jardewijns v. Antwerpen, we. Mattheewes Verhagen.
2 Dec.	1582	Henrick	,, v. Gijstkercke ondert Sticht v. Kolen met Maijeken Ijsebrande uit den Hage.
28 Mei	1583	Maijeken	,, , we. Henrick Willemsz, met Pauwels van Esbergen.
17 Sep.	1583	Ijtgen	,, met Jan de Grave.
2 Feb.	1584	Maycken	,, met Dierick van Voldthuijsen.
30 Jun.	1586	Digne	,, met Rogier Pieters.
17 Sep.	1587	Augustijn	,, v. Londen met Dina Creemers v. Antwerpen.
19 Oct.	1596	Jaspar	,, v. Antwerpen met Sara Ontheusden v. Dordrecht.
6 Dec.	1603	Grietken	**Janssz**, we. Leonart Goossen, met Craft Kessels.
21 Feb.	1604	Dirick	,, v. Wesel met Paschijnken van Aecken, we. Hans Heyns.
29 Mei	1604	Pieter	,, v. St. Cruijs met Anna Damforts v. Londen.
17 Mei	1608	Sara	,, met Henric Bincke.
26 Dec.	1625	Geeraert	,, v. Groeninghen met Susanna de Hulster, we. Hans Winne.
5 Jan.	1595	Grietken	**Jansz**, we. Salomon Hulet, met Lenart Goosens.
2 Mar.	1595	Zeghel	,, v. Delft met Maeyken Hurts v. Brussel.
2 Mei	1596	Margariete	,, met Denijs Bertholemeus.
8 Feb.	1597	Bernaert	,, v. Harderwijck met Susanna Poel v. Londen.
28 Mei	1599	Haeijman	,, v. Utrecht met Lijntken de Jagere v. Ghendt.
1 Jul.	1599	Elizabeth	,, met Maximiliaen de Bisson.
9 Apl.	1606	Augustijn	,, v. Londen met Abigail Letten v. Norwich.
1 Oct.	1611	Cornelis	,, van der Gouwe met Maijeken Somers, we. Jan Yde.
.. Aug.	1613	Lambert	,, wt t'landt v. Salandt met Josijnken, we. Guiliame Hunnington.
9 Jun.	1617	Geertruijt	,, met Richard Laurlijns.
27 Apl.	1619	Sara	,, met Pieter de Paus.
4 Dec.	1621	Susanna	,, met Jan Nicolas.
.. Apl.	1626	Maria	,, met Gabriel Doornaert.
16 Mei	1611	Marie	**Jarck** met Moses Mosen.
14 Sep.	1581	Jakemijne	**Jairdewijns**, we. Mattheewes Verhagen, met Geerardt Janssens.
25 Nov.	1606	Jan	**Jasperssen** v. Westphalen met Catharijne van Heur v. Londen.
.. Jan.	1619	Herman	**Jaspsz** v. Stemford (Stamford) met Ester Langeveld v. Middelborgh.
9 Mei	1594	Abigail	van Iesen, we. Wouter Casier, met Bartholomeus van Crombrugge.
27 Dec.	1593	Jan	**Jems** v. Antwerpen met Catherina van Hersaele v. Brussel, we. JeronimusCustodes.
26 Oct.	1574	Lyncken	**Jeems** met Christiaen Crabbe.

20 Oct. 1588 Tanneken — **Jens** met Anthony Lodewijckx.
14 Jun. 1597 Jan — **Jjde** v. Drongene met Maeyken de Somere v. Antwerpen, we. Lambrecht van Aken.
28 Aug. 1644 Catelijne — **Jjfler** met Cornelis Pels.
2 Dec. 1582 Maijeken — **Jjsebrande** met Henrick Janssens.
10 Mei 1576 Nicolas — **Jjsebrants** v. Leijden in Hollant met Emmeken Janssen v. Nieustad in Gheldor lant.
7 Nov. 1598 Jan — **Jjselaer** v. Oudekerek met Lijntken Deckers v. Antwerpen.
26 Dec. 1587 Elisabet — **Jneermans** met Jan Gipsen.
19 Mar. 1629 Martine — **Joachimi** met Joncker Muijs.
16 Jan. 1586 Jan — **Joachims** v. Winschoten met Maerken Meijs v. Oudenaerde.
21 Apl. 1594 Michil — de **Jode** v. Dendmonde met Tanneken Knijpers v. Antwerpen.
. . Nov. 1613 Tanneken — ,, ,, we. Michiel de Jode, met Jan de Febbre.
30 Dec. 1616 Anna — ,, ,, met Geerard Jansen.
4 Aug. 1573 Elizabeth, we. Gisbertus — **Johannis** met Lieven van den Pitte.
1 Jan. 1629 Elisabet — **Jonas**, we. Robert Franckx, met Abraham Elinck.
28 Apl. 1612 Janneken — **Joncheer** met Pieter de Veeker.
14 Jun. 1597 Joos — de **Jonckheere** v. Yseghem met Barbel Heckaert v. Antwerpen, we. Jan Huynnen.
10 Mei 1631 Jacob — ,, **Jonck-Hoer** j.g. v. Gendt met Janneken Raboy v. Weerdt in Brabant, we. Willem Meesen.
. . Feb. 1606 Wouter Aertsz — ,, **Jonge** met Anna Vercoijle.
. . Aug. 1728 M. A. — ,, **Jongh**, Leeraer deeser Gemeente met Maria van Linden j.d. v. Nijmegen.
17 Dec. 1588 Elizabeth — **Jonghe** met Anthonis Puijster.
1 Dec. 1594 Barbara — **Joossens**, we. Anthoni de Fosse, met Willem Smuijsers.
19 Jun. 1597 Susanna — ,, met Jan van Spiere.
14 Jul. 1588 Sara — **Jordaens** met Scipio Rademaeckers.
12 Aug. 1595 Herman — ,, v. Antwerpen met Rachel Henrix v. Londen.
. . Aug. 1752 Adolph — **Jorgens** j.m. met Johanna Maria Barbara Steenweg, j.d. wonagtig ten Gladbach.
. . Aug. 1620 Hans — **Jorigen** v. Prage met Elisabet Stigrits v. Londen.
28 Jul. 1579 Jois — de **Junckheer** v. Yseghem met Genofeve Kornes v. Ruwanen.
28 Jan. 1578 Heijklen — **Jsebrants** met Adriaen Honnes.
13 Apl. 1596 Eva — **Jskens** met Pieter Ghysbrecht.
13 Jul. 1589 Lenijne — **Jtsen** met Lambrecht Hilden.
26 Mei 1607 Abraham — van **Jxem** v. Norwich met Elisabeth van Crombrugge v. Geret.
. . Apl. 1618 Jan — ,, ,, v. Norwich met Susanna Beke v. Colchester.

20 Aug. 1644 Sibijlla — **Kalthoff** met Jochim Schets.
21 Dec. 1585 Catelyne — de **Kaluwe** met Lieven de Key.
8 Jan. 1635 Clara — van der **Kamme**, we. Nicolaus Mattheus, met Jan Daniel.
25 Oct. 1812 Janke Hiddes — **Kat** met Dirck Jansen de Groot.
27 Apl. 1596 Herman — **Kech** v. Emmerick met Ghertruijt Dongherin v. Londen, we. Herman Leck.
11 Apl. 1587 Colette — van der **Keere** met Joos de Hondt.
23 Mei 1586 Philips — de **Keerle**, (v. Kerle) v. Comene met Neelken Mansens v. Antwerpen, we. Jaques Gaffels.
21 Dec. 1585 Lieven — ,, **Key** met Catelyne de Kaluwe, beyde v. Ghendt.
13 Mei 1651 Stephen — ,, **Keijn** j.g. v. Diesburgh met Helena Erfurt j.d. v. Limerick.
9 Dec. 1593 Craft — **Kessels** v. Gulick met Chrijstijnken du Pont v. Antwerpen.
9 Feb. 1580 Herman — **Keijser** v. Walckneel in Gulickerlandt met Isebel Pauwels v. bij Dusseldorp int landt v. Kleve.
31 Mei 1597 Pieter — ,, ,, v. Vlissinghen met Jelijnken Huijsmans v. Rouee, we. Adriaen Mijrschaert.
17 Mei 1630 Maria — **Keysers** met Jan Molgeleam.
21 Nov. 1592 Pieter — op de **Kelder** v. Cleeff met Maerken Kaphels v. Duijsseldorp.
15 Apl. 1628 Willem — **Kels** met Barbara Veillars, beyde v. Londen.
20 Mei 1574 Wolter — **Kemens** v. Pete met Maijken van Ressolt v. Arenheuck.
12 Mei 1703 Steven — **Kemp** j.m. v. Montinaeh in Langnedoek met Helena Goutem, j.d. v. den Haegh.
27 Jul. 1572 Katherine — **Kempe**, we. Thoris Moijjenson, met Gillis Koster.
17 Oct. 1598 Magdalene — **Kempen** met Niclaes Trapper.
31 Aug. 1585 Jaquemynken — **Kempenaerts**, we. Heindrick de Drossaert, met Gillie Zeghers.
19 Feb. 1604 Janneken — van **Kerckhove**, we. Jan Roelants, met Pieter Baert.

18 Apl	1596	Neelken	Kerijns met Willem Faber.
18 Sep.	1606	Philips	de Kerle (v. Keerle) v. Comene met Prudentia Marquis v. Londen.
19 Mei	1640	Anna	Kersteleijn met Salomon Lamberts.
4 Apl.	1592	Margareta	Kes, we. Jeroninus Obrij, met Willem van Damme.
13 Jun.	1591	Kraft	Kessels wijt t'lant v. Gulick met Gelyne Plantsoens v. Rouce.
6 Dec.	1603	Craft	,, wt het lant v. Gulick met Crietken Janssz, we. Leonart Goossen.
13 Nov.	1610	Craft	,, wt landt v. Gulick met Trijnken Teunis mede wt landt v. Gulick.
10 Oct.	1602	Lyntken	Kestloot met Jaques de Hoeck.
10 Jun.	1595	Hans	Ketelbouter v. Brussel met Hester Soilot v. Brussel.
15 Nov.	1638	Willem	Keuckelhuijs, wr. van Maijken Pieters, int landt van der Marck met Hermintjen Wademont, we. Jacob Hendrix v. Gent.
23 Jul.	1594	Hans	van Kielwalts v. Acruham met Susanna Stell v. Londen.
6 Oct.	1584	Willem	de Kije v. Roussen met Soetgen Brakelmans v. Ghendt, we. Wouter Janssens.
27 Mei	1571	Adam	der Kinderen fs. Adams met Elijzabeth van Roken uit landt v. Gulick.
27 Mei	1571	Sara	,, ,, , fa Adam, met Jan Wessels.
8 Sep.	1573	Hans	,, ,, v. Londen met Pierijnken Basseliers v. Aelst.
14 Jun.	1586	Abraham	,, ,, v. Antwerpen met Lucretia van Meteren v. Londen.
21 Nov.	1587	Adam	,, ,, v. Londen met Jacomyntken Hildernisse v. Berghe op Zoom, we. Joris van Daele.
6 Aug.	1594	Sara	den ,, , we. Jan Weysels, met Batholomeus Pieters.
18 Nov.	1601	Mary	der ,, , we. Jan Claessens Dijckman, met Frans Berckers.
30 Nov.	1600	Eva	,, Kinders met Isbrandt van Meurs.
9 Mei	1626	Catharina	Kindt met Samuel Populaer.
1 Jun.	1572	Henrick	Klaassen v. Staphorst met Grietgen Ottgeers, fa. Caroli, v. Ghent.
2 Sep.	1571	Jakemyntghen	Klaijssens met Henrick de Hout.
29 Jun.	1579	Janneken	van der Kleijen met Jan Veemondt.
17 Feb.	1583	Pieter	Kleijmans met Lyntge van Hoeck, beyde v. Turnout.
24 Jul.	1581	Antonis	de Klerck v. Leijssel met Adriane Meeuwssen we. Martens van Dalem, v. Gorcum.
25 Jan.	1603	Sijmon	,, v. St. Truijen met Lijsken Robijns v. Mechelen, we. Dierick de Coster.
18 Apl.	1581	Agnete	Klercks, we. Christoffel Says, met Hans Scholands.
11 Dec.	1582	Sijmon	,, v. Sentruijen met Neelken Hellewartz v. Antwerpen.
21 Jul.	1584	Agnete	,, , we. Jan Scholle, met Pieter de Maijer.
12 Jul.	1575	Jan	Klercksen v. Her - - uyen (?) met Susanne Janssen v. Antwerpen.
14 Feb.	1604	David	Klijnckenborg v. Aecken met Catharijne de la Roche, we. Francoijs Cogge.
19 Aug.	1571	Catherine	de Klinckers met Christiaen Kuenen.
21 Oct.	1600	Maeyken	Knapparts met Pauwels van de Velde.
13 Sep.	1601	Michiel	,, Knuijt v. Volckmrekhouven met Maeyken de Smit v. Brugge.
25 Aug.	1629	Michel	,, , wr. v. Londen, met Catharina de Pont j.d. v. Sandwich.
18 Jan.	1631	Paulus	,, ,, j.g. v. Londen met Anna van den Houte j.d. v. Meulebeke bij Brussel.
12 Jan.	1580	Gerardt	,, Kobber v. Roussen met Marguerite Huijgs v. Londen.
21 Apl.	1579	Jan	Koekeel v. Ijperen met Lucijne Rotardtsz, we. Jakes Cornelissen.
22 Jun.	1585	Josijne	Koelpots, we. Pieter Stevens, met Antony Populaire.
2 Aug.	1603	Lysbeth	Koets met Jacob Barremeijer.
20 Apl.	1579	Frantz	Koipmans v. Diest met Jenne Brickée v. Valenceijn.
16 Apl.	1592	Josijne	Kokuts met Willem Henningten.
20 Mei	1583	Dorothea	Konike, we. Thomas Biesdinck, met Willem de Heese.
27 Jun.	1592	Clarken	Koninckx met Dierick Lupsen.
22 Jan.	1583	Rogier	van Koolge v. Kortricke met Tenneken van Asse, v. Londen, fa. Molssens.
21 Oct.	1571	Mayeken	Kools met Pauwels van de Velde.
6 Aug.	1577	Andries	Koppens v. Antwerpen met Grietgen Reniers, we. Michiels Vaijens, v. Antwerpen
21 Dec.	1588	Andries	,, v. Emden met Juliana van Oelant v. Volcheghem, we. Hendrick de Stonie.
16 Apl.	1582	Andries	Koppiers v. Antwerpen met Cathelyne Canipets v. Audenaerde, we. Steven Resboeck.
13 Apl.	1578	Hans	Korckeel v. Yperen met Jakemijntgen Strubbens v. Belle.
28 Jul.	1579	Genofeve	Kornes met Jois de Junckheer.
13 Mei	1572	Elizabeth	van den Korpet met Abraham van Dolden.
27 Jul.	1572	Gillis	Koster v. Brussel met Katherine Kempe, we. Thoris Moijenson.
17 Mei	1573	Gillis	de ,, v. Bruijssel met Josijnken Specckaerts v. Bruijssel.
9 Jun.	1577	Jacques	,, Kostere v. Brugghe met Elisabeth Janssen v. Schiedam.
30 Apl.	1588	Gillis	Kosters met Margriete Trots, beyde v. Brussel.
11 Sep.	1600	Gomerijne	s' Kosters, we. Gillis Verhaeghe, met Haus d'Oude.
24 Mei	1858	Johannes Jakobus	Kotzé j.m. oud 25 jaar van de Kaap de G. H. met Johanna Bernardina Immen Illom, j.d. oud 20 jaar v. Utrecht.
25 Dec.	1571	Christiaen	Krabbe (v. Crabbe) v. Ghendt met Adriaentgen Beck v. Brugge.
16 Oct.	1578	Kaarken	Kramers met Pieter Berntsen.
22 Jan.	1690	Willemijntje	Kressel met Cornelis Hendricks.

17 Jan.	1576	Maiken	de Krijts met Gheeraert Raessen.
8 Sep.	1584	Mayeken	„ , we. Gerraudt Raessen, met Jaspar Fredericks.
1 Mei	1606	Jan	Krom v. Nuijs met Jeeannintken Tops v. Niphoven.
4 Feb.	1584	Adriaan	de Kroock v. Ghent met Ke.. v. der Platzen v. Londen.
19 Aug.	1571	Cristiaen	Kuenen met Cathrina de Elsackers.
11 Mei	1626	Willem	Kuijckelhuijs mijt knecht v. Ge.. Raes.. Mertin, we. Pieter Pieter..en.
11 Mei	1572	Marten	Kuijper v. Thessel met Su.. tien, Ruckint v. Londen.
21 Apl.	1594	Tanneken	Kuijpers met Michiel de Jode.
6 Apl.	1703	Martijntjo	„ met Bernard Messgin.
29 Sep.	1590	Dierick	Kuster uit Sticht v. Coelen met Maeyken Dux v. Brugghe.

30 Aug.	1586	Maecken	Labus met Jan Solis.
30 Jul.	1622	Jaquelijne	Ladtbrugge me Joos Engels.
13 Aug.	1587	Catelijne	van Lacren met Jan Arents.
3 Jul.	1604	Joannes	de Laet v. Antwerpen met Jacobuxnfgen van Loor v. Londen.
28 Aug.	1700	Jan	Legestraet. wr van Geertruid Cleeson, met Mary Peters j.d. v. Delft.
29 Jan.	1600	Jaques	Lagniel v. Armentiers met Maeyken Plotevots v. Belle.
23 Oct.	1576	Margriete	du Laijs met Jan D nse.
17 Aug.	1623	Jan	Lake v. Londen met Esther Michielsz v. Leyden.
.. Apl.	1641	Susanna	Laken met Joh mnes Franquinot.
3 Feb.	1600	Jan	Lambert v. Derbischer met Fransynte van Weeyeghem v. Ghendt.
12 Feb.	1601	Matthys	Lamberts v. Londen met Josijpken Hoste v. Ghendt.
19 Mei	1640	Salomon	„ j.g. v. Amsterdam met Anna Kerstelcijn j.d. v. Colchester.
3 Jun.	1606	Catharina	Lambrecht met Abraham Weghe.
29 Jun.	1580	Cecilie	Lambrechts, we. Adrian Gouldtborn, met Jan Antuenis.
14 Jul.	1584	Catharine	„ met Antonis Geeraerdts.
6 Jan.	1595	Stijnken	„ we. Willem de Bill, met Gillis Tichman.
24 Aug.	1589	Catharina	Lammens met Cornelis Jans.
8 Jun.	1619	Sara	„ met Jan van Beersel.
18 Jan.	1597	Leenard	Lamertom v. Antwerpen met Neelken James, one v. Antwerpen.
28 Aug.	1571	Cathelyne	Lamoot met Godefridus Wingius.
21 Nov.	1592	Cathelijne	„ met Godefridus Wingij met Goosen Verbeke.
17 Sep.	1594	Franchoys	„ v. Reijuinghelts met Elizabeth van Auweghem v. Ghendt, we. Jaspar Baldens.
29 Nov.	1614	Catharyne	„ we. Goossens van Beke, met Pieter Tierenteijn.
15 Feb.	1603	Hester	Lamote met Jaques de Coninck.
.. Oct.	1618	Catharina	„ we. Pieter Tierentijn, met Daniel Robbert.
31 Jun.	1629	Sara	Lamotte met Jan Hagedoorne.
15 Oct.	1594	Franchoijs	Lampsens v. Brugge met Josynken de Groene v. Meyeghem.
25 Sep.	1597	Fransois	„ v. Brugge met Margriete de Coonen v. Ghendt.
10 Apl.	1610	Franchoys	Lamsen v. Brugge met Janneken Matthijssz, met Pieter David.
11 Sep.	1586	Cornelis	Lamsens, fs. Joos. v. Brugge met Maeyken Pepermans v. Brussel.
1 Dec.	1584	Janneken	de Lande met Henrick Berntz.
4 Oct.	1604	Jan Baptista	van Landen v. Arnhem met Hermken Tijssen, we. Jan Blomme.
31 Mei	1585	Janneken	de Lange met Martijn de Hulster.
8 Jan.	1572	David	Langeley v. Ruesen met Maijcken de Libans v. Antwerpen.
. Jan.	1619	Ester	Langeveld met Herman Jaspz.
9 Mar.	1698	Clara	Langevelt met Christiaen Besemaeeker.
7 Dec.	1619	Jan	de Langhe v. Gent met Abigaïl Frombout, we. Bernard la Fosse.
6 Oct.	1573	Hans	Langhele v. Meenen met Laueynken van Gavere v. Ghendt.
24 Mei	1586	Elisabeth	van den Langhevelde met Hans Mulderi.
11 Dec.	1593	Lowijse	de Lanou, we. Daniel Gijselinck, met Cornelis van Roosendiele.
1 Jan.	1594	Toussain	Lap v. Brugghe met Catheline Honwe v. Cassel.
10 Aug.	1580	Lambrecht	van der Lake v. Wesel met Maeyken Tsomers v. Antwerpen.
23 Oct.	1580	Lowys	van Lathem v. —inghen met Maria des Champs v. Norvels (Norwich).
26 Mei	1610	Adam	Laureijns v. Londen met Judith van den Brugghe v. Norwich.
6 Dec.	1610	Joannes	„ met Maria Stentelinx v. Middelborch.
2 Apl.	1611	Janneken	„ met Franchoijs Pennetier.
0 Oct.	1618	Abraham	„ v. Londen met Janneken Hoste v. Maidstone.

6 Jul.	1572	Lijntgen	**Laurens** met J. de la Choutiere.
5 Aug.	1572	Janneken	„ met Nicolaes Billeijn.
17 Nov.	1583	Loijschen	„ met Jois Marregaren.
9 Jun.	1617	Richard	**Laurlijns** v. Exeter met Geertruijt Jansz v. t'land v. Cleef.
26 Dec.	1576	Hans	**Lauwaert** v. Antwerpen met Lijneken Jacobs v. Antwerpen.
4 Feb.	1584	Bartholomeus	**Lauwardts** v. Geertsbergen met Josyne Stilters v. Hustbruck.
26 Jun.	1606	Maeyken	**Lauwens** met Peter Petrin.
19 Mei	1635	Elisabeth	**Lauwercks**, we. Jan de Haene, met Elias de Hane.
11 Oct.	1690	Maria	der **Lee** met Samuel Fuller.
9 Jun.	1588	Simon	**Leeman** v. Bruijssel met Pierinken Skieninx.
29 Mei	1689	Susauna	„ met Philip Philipsen.
22 Jun.	1590	Michiel	**Leemans** v. Bruissel met Maeijken Peperman ock v. Bruijssel.
9 Apl.	1577	Mechelijne	„ met Rogier van Peene.
21 Apl.	1617	Abraham	„ v. Londen met Maria le Sage v. Londen.
15 Apl.	1623	Samuel	„ v. Londen met Sara Brandsmede v. Londen.
. 9 Mar.	1624	Lucas	„ met Hester Clidlij, beyde v. Londen.
16 Apl.	1588	Daniel	van **Leemput** v. Turnhout met Sara van Baerle v. Antwerpen.
. . Apl.	1616	Jan	„ v. Embden met Sara Duffardt v. Norwich.
13 Nov.	1597	Gillis	**Leenaert** v. Comene met Tanneken de Letter v. Brugge, we. Roelant de Decker.
28 Apl.	1590	Joos	**Leenaerts** met Lijnken Colis beijde v. Antwerpen.
19 Aug.	1585	Rogier	van **Leerberghe** v. Ardoyn met Maerken Pent v. Kesselare.
20 Jan.	1692	Elias	de **Leeuw** j.m. v. Amsterdam met Elizabeth Coucke j.d. v. Amsterdam.
17 Aug.	1596	Hans	van **Leeuwerck** v. Turnhout met Elisabeth van Dalem v. Gent.
21 Apl.	1607	Clos	„ met Jan Hane.
9 Oct.	1586	Hans	**Legonce** v. Antwerpen met Quintinken Brakelmans v. Gent.
9 Dec.	1572	Margriete	**Lemmens**, fa. Gillis, met Robert Noortman.
23 Aug.	1579	Nelleken	„ met Bartholomeus in der Sittardt.
6 Sep.	1573	Eijlken	**Lenards** met Lenard Hugues.
. . Jun.	1616	Tanneken we. Gillis	„ met Pieter der Meersch.
28 Dec.	1625	Abigail	„ met Jan Coopland.
2 Mei	1626	Jacob	„ v. Vlissinghen met Grietken Stroomengels we. Cornelis van Ruijt.
21 Dec.	1600	Elizabeth	**Lenaertsz** met Pieter de Moor.
8 Mei	1610	Lysken	**Lenarts**, we. Pieter de Moor, met Albert Wtmans.
31 Jul.	1638	Allaert	de **Lens** j.g. v. Brussel met Sara le Grant j.d. v. Franedal.
10 Dec.	1611	Pieter	**Lepper** wt t'land v. Gulick met Judith Donck we. Nathanael Buls.
4 Oct.	1645	Cornelis	**Leraroson**, wr. v. Browershaven met Margeriete Beuns j.d. v. Harlem.
7 Feb.	1705	Jenneth	**Leslij** met Albert Jansen.
1 Jul.	1595	Nicolas	**Lestré** v. Doornicke met Jeremynken van der Splijck v. Antwerpen.
13 Aug.	1679	Frans	**Letoij**, wr v. Amsterdam, met Catarina Blancart j.d. v. Sandwich.
9 Apl.	1606	Abigail	**Letten** met Augustijn Jansz.
13 Nov.	1597	Tanneken	de **Letter**, we. Roelant de Deckere, met Gillis Leenaert.
1 Apl.	1700	Dirck	van **Leuwen** j.m. v. s'Gravenhage met Barbara Ba. . ge j.d. v. Leuwarden.
10 Jan.	1585	Fransoise	**Libaert** met Jacob Hofmans.
17 Apl.	1604	Tanneken	„ , we. Jacus Nachtegael, met Thomas Armedstede.
8 Jan.	1572	Maijeken	de **Libans** met David Langeley.
. . Aug.	1613	Catharina	**Lie** met Carel Hendricx.
24 Oct.	1609	Hans	**Liebaert** v. Sandwich met Maria Bollen mede v. Sandwich.
16 Jun.	1640	Carolus	„ v. Sandwich met Maria Beke, we. v. Colchester.
3 Jan.	1581	Jan	**Liebisch** v. Gulick met Tanneken Visschere v. Basmet in Gulickerlande.
18 Jun.	1627	Barbara	**Liesveldt** met Lion Beusken.
12 Sep.	1626	Sara	van „ met Abraham van den Broecke.
7 Mar.	1587	Jooris	**Lieven** v. Vueren met Margriete van der Clijte, we. Claeijs Siers.
29 Dec.	1574	Jan	**Lievens** v. Bijlvelde met Catherijne Cambiers v. Valenchijne.
3 Dec.	1592	Balthasar	van de **Lind** v. Antwerpen met Catheline Peters v. Nuijsse.
12 Oct.	1596	Goivaert	„ „ **Linde** v. Ballar bij Liere met Magdaleene Beti v. Bruissel, we. Phlips de Bryer.
25 Jul.	1575	Baltazar	„ „ **Linden** v. Antwerpen met Adriaenken Vencke, we. Pauwels de Maijere v. Gorcu
24 Jul.	1581	Balthasar	„ „ „ v. Antwerpen met Beelken Bossardt v. Yperen.
26 Mei	1584	Pieter	„ „ „ v. Oestende met Maijcken d'Engelsche v. Yperen, we. Jan Willems.
9 Nov.	1600	Gommaer	„ „ „ v. Ballaer met Magdalena Hubers v. Piroen.
. . Sep.	1613	Gommar	„ „ „ v. Ballaer bij Liere met Janneken van de Walle v. Witscharde wt Wr Vlaenderen.
. . Aug.	1738	Maria	van „ met M. A. de Jongh.
1 Jan.	1623	Margareta	**Linttenluff** met Jacob Lutkekeukelhouss.
30 Apl.	1594	Gillis	**Lioens** v. Brussel met Janneken Soens v. Colscamp.
15 Jul.	1599	Jacomijnken	„ met Henrick van Haes.
. 8 Jan.	1612	Gillis	**Lions** v. Brussel met Judith Bolle v. Middelborch.
9 Feb.	1613	Elizabeth	„ met Tobias Faillart.

23 Jul.	1577	Jacob	Lippart v. Antwerpen met Elisabeth Tutelaers v. Loven.
25 Jul.	1585	Hans	van Lippevelde v. Gent met Janneken de Prent v. Rousse.
25 Aug.	1591	Hans	Liscornet v. Brugge met Tonijuken van Peene v. Ypre.
27 Sep.	1642	Sara	de Lobeau, we. André Grande, met Gillis Wicks.
30 Aug.	1601	Jan Pieterson	Lobbestall j.m. v. Middelburgh met Maria Bellamelis j.d. v. Dordrecht.
8 Oct.	1592	Susanna	van Lochen met Hans van der Straten.
17 Aug.	1626	Maria	Lodewijck, we. Jan Galben, met Leonard van der Boom.
25 Jan.	1573	Heijndrick	Lodewijcks v. Billevelt met Tanneken Goethoens.
20 Oct.	1588	Anthony	Lodewijckx v. Antwerpen met Tanneken Jeus v. Antwerpen.
1 Feb.	1603	Tanneken	,, met Jan Storm.
13 Oct.	1646	Anna	Lodewijk met Gerard van Heijthuisen.
26 Feb.	1579	Mattgen	van der Lodwich met Thomas Engelsch.
2 Sep.	1575	Phlips	van Loenen v. Loenen met Janneken Auwers, we. Joos Nauwes v. Brussel.
28 Dec.	1585	Maurine	Loentgen met Willem Seijs.
22 Sep.	1607	Elisabeth	van Loer (v. van Loor) met Hans van den Benelen.
25 Jul.	1591	Pieter	t' Loers v. bij Maestricht met Cathelyne de Clerck v. Brussel.
28 Oct.	1588	Marie	Loij, we. Pieter Janssen, m. Gheeraert Coerdes.
27 Jun.	1592	Maria	Loijs, we. Gheeraert Coertes, met Hans van der Leke.
11 Jul.	1585	Chrystynken	,, met Guiliame Hatroen.
12 Nov.	1594	Macijken	,, met Hendrick Aelbertss.
20 Dec.	1625	Lodewyk	,, v. Bergen op Zoom met Sara de Visch, we. Steven Egberts.
2 Sep.	1899	Johanna	van Lom met Hubertus Homoet.
3 Mar.	1590	Dominick	Lommelle v. Londen met Janneken van Beaumont v. Antwerpen, we. Pieter van Asse.
3 Sep.	1605	Balthasar	Lonerman v. Crushurch met Maicken van Gisr . . . v. Antwerpen.
2 Aug.	1575	Maijken	Loo, we. Willem Jacobs, met Pieter Janssen.
4 Jul.	1596	Cathelino	van ,, met Hans van Halle.
4 Nov.	1600	Jan	,, ,, v. Rostock met Gheertruijdt Sterck v. Cripsware.
12 Jan.	1607	Jan	,, ,, v. Gent met Sara, we. Jan Vasseur v. Londen.
26 Sep.	1574	Mayken	Loocmans, we. Hans de Brune, met Jan van Ghent.
18 Jul.	1591	Bernaert Janssen	Loon, van, v. Swol met Lyntgen Aertsen v. Heynsburg.
12 Aug.	1578	Jenneken	Loopens, we. Jan Verkamer, met Adriaan Pelen.
3 Jul.	1604	Jacobmyntgen	van Loor (v. van Loer) met Johannes de Laet.
27 Sep.	1590	Francois	Loose v. Embden, met Celijuken Stelte v. Haesbroeck.
12 Feb.	1594	Fransois	Loosen v. Embden, met Judith Haentken v. Essex, we. Jeremias Caudron.
19 Dec.	1602	Jorijne	Loots, we. Jan de Pegghe, met Barthomeus Wademont.
.. Oct.	1618	Daniel	Looverbergh v. t'landt van Gulick met Mechtel Brocht v. Salinghen.
18 Oct.	1710	Elysabeth Margarita	Loperen, van, met Hugo Verboom.
8 Jan.	1590	Fredrick	de Lorreine v. Lens met Francynken Sanders v. Brugge, we. Gillis Lems.
10 Oct.	1583	Jakes	van Lowegen v. Brugge met Lenijntgen van Hecke v. Ghent, we. Sanders Engelgrave.
10 Sep.	1601	Fredrick	Lubberinck wt lant v. Gelder met Catherine Huickx v. Mascijck, we. Matheus Heussen.
14 Nov.	1609	Joannes	Luce v. Andwerpen met Anna Corselis v. Londen.
18 Aug.	1601	Susanna	van Luchen, we. Hans Verstraten, met Jan Niclaessen.
28 Feb.	1572	Nicolaus	van der Luffel v. Antwerpen met Kuerken van Aken, we. Jans Jansen.
25 Jan.	1592	Ester	van Luffele met Jans van der Buleke.
2 Jun.	1584	Greigen	Luijckens met Koenrardt Horstgens.
6 Feb.	1599	Geeraert	Luijten alias Graus v. Steeken met Macijken Dolfernes v. Brugge, we. Hendrick Lamberts.
24 Oct.	1857	Wilhelm Johann	Luis j.m. v. Hamburg met Elizabeth Sack j.d. v. Londen.
22 Oct.	1635	Johannes	Lukens j.g. v. Staden met Hester Frommentel j.d. v. Norwich. (v. Fromenteel.)
12 Jul.	1593	Arnont	Luls v. Antwerpen met Susanna de Beste v. Londen.
11 Dec.	1599	Arnout	,, v. Antwerpen met Margriete Raket v. Ypen, we. Abraham van Hawijck.
27 Jun.	1592	Dierick	Lupsen v. Mascijck met Clarken Koninckx v. Ghendt.
1 Jan.	1623	Jacob	Lutkekeukelhouss v. Brekerveldt tot t'landt v. Maret met Margareta Linttenlaff v. Norenburgh.

.3 Jul.	1582	Janneken	de Maars met Govart de Swerts.
6 Jan.	1572	Pauwels	Maas v. Rousse met Tanneken Brijeken, we. Klaes Happarts.

21 Jul.	1584	Jan	Maas v. Maaseijck met Sara Heckelars v. Londen.
12 Jan.	1591	Maeijken	Madou met Lucas Moreels.
15 Mei	1581	Janneken	Maecquies v. Steen Voort met Claeys Adryaentsen.
24 Feb.	1675	David	de Maegd, wr. van Francoisa Ophalvens, v. Mortlake met Esther Gilbert j.d. v. Colchester. (v. de Magth).
19 Mei	1607	Pieter	Maelbout v. Gent met Janneken Verbrugghe v. Londen.
15 Jul.	1593	Tanneken	de Maer, we. Goyvaert de Zwerte, met Fredrick van der Hamer.
29 Sep.	1590	Maertken	de Maere met Bernardt Petersen.
1 Jan.	1634	Abigail	Maertens, we. P. Weesel, met Laurens Wilkes.
9 Oct.	1586	Margriete	Maes met Herman Stappaert.
27 Dec.	1586	Lievijne	,, met Paschier Boddens.
. . Feb.	1614	Martha	,, met Nicolaus Melckelbeecke.
12 Mei	1700	Carel	Magdou-les j.m. v. Nieumgen met Jeronimina Adriana van Buren we. van Jan Hattem.
3 Apl.	1668	David	de Magth j.m. v. Mortlake met Francis Ophalven j.d. v. Mortlake.
21 Jul.	1584	Pieter	de Maijer v. Franssen met Agnete Klercks v. Antwerpen, we. Jan Scholle.
25 Jun.	1629	Josua	Maignet j.g. met Maria Penetier j.d. beijde v. Londen.
23 Mar.	1652	Elizabeth	de Maijerne met Pierre de Caumont.
17 Nov.	1614	Elizabeth	Maijnet met Denijs Noodstock.
7 Oct.	1595	Jacus	de Maistres v. Ceulen met Maria le Grand v. Antwerpen.
24 Apl.	1620	Judith	des ,, met Jacob Jacobsz.
9 Feb.	1859	Wilhelmina Elizabeth	Malefijt met Johannes Hendrikus Geerkens.
8 Mei	1593	Anna	Malepart met Cijpriaen Gabrij.
12 Oct.	1585	Janneken	de Malijnes met Herman van Humbach.
. . Mei	1606	Carel	de Man v. Scheurs met Sijken van der Waert v. Bruijssel.
10 Sep.	1629	Abraham	,, j.g. met Maria van de Cause j.d. beijde v. Londen.
10 Oct.	1633	Abraham	,, ,, , wr. van Maria Coucij, v. Londen met Sara de Bill, j.d. mede v. Londen.
3 Mei	1580	Gillis	Mangeon v. Brugge met Apollonie Peenartz v. Turnout.
1 Jan.	1617	Jacob	Manjat v. Londen met Susanna Terraij mede v. Londen.
20 Apl.	1596	Michiel	Maniet v. Antwerpen met Maeijken de Cousenaere v. Engien we. Tobias Bethurine.
26 Apl.	1603	Anna	Manjét met Isaac James.
23 Mei	1586	Neelken	Mansens, we. Jaques Gaffels, met Philip de Keerle.
20 Oct.	1573	Sara we. Christiaen	Maquereel met Marten de Visschere v. Antwerpen.
29 Mar.	1573	Hans	Marcelis v. Antwerpen met Tanneken Verstraten, we. Cornelis Boes.
11 Aug.	1590	Hester	Marchant met Josias Wijho,
8 Feb.	1597	Samuel	,, v. Londen met Paeschijnken Sibille v. bij Brussel.
8 Sep.	1579	Maijcken	Marckeys met Jan Wijlandtz.
7 Feb.	1585	Jan	Maren v. Marent int lant v. Luijck met Trijne Corijns v. Heijsberg int land v. Gulick.
21 Feb.	1637	Sara	de Marez, we. Pieter de Raedt, met Pieter Everard.
9 Sep.	1599	Willem	Mariate v. Derbyshier met Marie Backers wt Ghelderlant.
6 Oct.	1573	David	Marien v. Antwerpen met Elsken Janssen v. Londen.
25 Jan.	1579	Joos	Marisson oft Merseim v. Kassel met Passchijne van de Walle van Ypere.
6 Apl.	1643	Joanna	Marolois, we. Jacob de Backer, met Joannes de Conink.
13 Mar.	1655	Maria	,, met Francois Backet.
7 Nov.	1598	Joannes	Marquinus v. Londen met Marie Ruitinck v. Noortwitth (Norwich).
29 Sep.	1601	Cathelijne	,, met Joris Barnis.
5 Dec.	1602	Anna	,, met Willem Jacobs.
18 Sep.	1606	Prudentia	Marquis met Philip de Kerle.
17 Nov.	1583	Jois	Marregaren v. Ghendt met Loijschen Laurens v. Meenen.
2 Feb.	1584	Philips	,, v. Ghent met Tanneken Veuije v. Audenarde, we. Jans Verelst.
13 Jan.	1572	Tanneken	s' Martelaers met Baudewijn de Heirde.
28 Feb.	1587	Naenken	,, met Pieter Jacops.
9 Mei	1594	Maeijken	de Martelare met Wouter van Strijpe.
19 Jun.	1604	Maijken	,, , we. Wouter Verstrepen, met Jan Calandt.
3 Jan.	1585	Janneken	s' Martelaren met Cornelis Baert.
9 Aug.	1576	Naentken	Martens met Jan Boves.
18 Jan.	1586	Verroe	,, v. Bruijssel met Agatha van Strate v. Santen, we. Gillis Vershiele.
31 Mar.	1590	Jan	,, v. Nieuwegen met Catheline Bartholomeus, we. Willem Eylandt.
6 Dec.	1590	Ryckaert	,, v. Haerlughen met Lynken van Hoplijnen v. Antwerpen.
18 Jan.	1597	Willem	,, v. Herentals met Catheline Taverniers v. Meenene, we. Jan Angele.
27 Sep.	1576	Gottfridus van den	Mase v. Ganghelt met Sara de Peijster j.d. v. Londen.
28 Jan.	1630	Jan	Materlinck j.g. v. Emblen met Sara de Peijster j.d. v. Londen.
27 Apl.	1596	Jochim	Matthens v. bij Breda met Sara Gijpsen v. Londen.
2 Apl.	1605	Janneken	Matthijs met Pieter Davids.

. 6 Jan. 1621   Janneken   **Matthijs**, we. Francoijs Lambossens, met Pieter Hermans.
10 Apl. 1610   Janneken   **Matthyss**, we. Pieter David, met Franchoijs Lausen.
24 Aug. 1584   Mecheldt   **Mauritz**, we. Jan Martens, met Pieter Broeckstein.
5 Sep. 1586   Gheertruijt van **Mechelen**, we. Andries van Londen, met Nicolas van den Cornput.
4 Aug. 1584   Esther   ,, **Medegar**, we. Geeraldt Verstrijpe, met Lieven van den Putte.
9 Jun. 1588   Jan   ,, **Meenen** v. Dronckrocsbcke met Margriete Flinckenborg v. Antwerpen.
18 Oct. 1597   Thamar van der **Meersch**, we. Goyvaert Enghels, met Joos de Meij.
. . Jun. 1616   Pieter   der   ,, v. Gent met Tanneken, we. Gillis Lenards.
23 Nov.   . . . . (sic) van **Meerbeke** v. Enghen met Tanneken van der Poest, we. Anthonis van der Venne.
9 Feb. 1591   David   le **Meere** v. Antwerpen met Sara Trioen v. Londen.
. . Nov. 1617   Susanna   **Meersmans** met Jacob van der Biest.
3 Oct. 1587   Adriaen   **Meeschaert** v. Rousse met Gelyne Huysmans, we. Lowijs Ver piere onck v. Rouce.
29 Jun. 1590   Arnoudt   **Meesens** v. Antwerpen met Lucretia de Notre v. Brussel.
13 Apl. 1596   Magdaleene   ,,   , we. Zacharias Guijsel, met Daniel Garmoet.
20 Jan. 1583   . . . . de **Meessène** v. Yser in Artois met Maijcken Neijden van s'Hertogenbosch.
11 Apl. 1648   Jacob   ,, **Meester** j m. v. Sandwich met Maria van de Walle j.d. v. Hijde. (? Hytle near Sandwich.)

24 Jul. 1581   Adriane   **Meeuwssen**, we. Martens van Dalem, met Antonis de Kleerck.
19 Feb. 1572   Elias   de **Meij** v. Meessen met Tacneken Simons v. Middelborch.
23 Feb. 1574   Jacquemijne   ,, ,, met Rolof Heindrix.
6 Feb. 1592   Hans   ,, ,, v. Ghendt met Cathelyne Beijtins v. Poperinghe.
18 Oct. 1597   Jooris   ,, ,, v. Nieukerke met Thamar van der Meersch v. Brugge, we. Goijvaert Enghels.
22 Mei 1610   Pierynken   ,, ,, , we Joos Nachtegnel, met Pieter Tierenteijn.
2 Mar. 1579   Jenneken   s' **Meijs** met Abraham Vervludt.
16 Jan. 1586   Maerken   **Meijs** met Jan Joachims.
19 Sep. 1598   Jan   de **Meijer** v. Oudenaerde met Judith van der Plactse v. Londen.
29 Dec. 1586   Catelijne   ,, met Wouter Stappen.
4 Jun. 1594   Cateline   de ,, , we. Wouter Stappen, met Marten van Meurs.
12 Jul. 1601   Thomas   ,, ,, v. Bruijssel met Anneken Heindrix v. Emhelen.
1 Dec. 1607   Jan   ,, ,, v. Londen met Ester Somer v. Norwich.
26 Mar. 1611   Arnouldt   ,, ,, v. Cuelen met Anna Gerrits v. Nimwegen.
3 Jun. 1617   Andries   ,, ,, v, Wesel met Janneken Pieters, we. Mattheus van Ceulen.
13 Feb. 1631   Catharina   ,, ,, met Gerard Tilhorst.
15 Sep. 1573   Gheertruijdt we. Gooris   ,, **Meijere** met Jan Coene.

26 Aug. 1708   Johanna   **Meijers** met Johannes van Spawen.
16 Sep. 1623   Jan   **Meijm** v. Nieupoort met Anna de Beste, we. Daniel Godfroy.
6 Jul. 1600   Anthenius   **Meijss** van de Langcstraete met Geertruijt Costers v. Beke, we. Matheeus Scewes.
22 Mei 1610   Christofer   **Meijstner** wt den Slesen met Elizabeth Gheeraerts v. Londen.
. . Feb. 1614   Nicolaus   **Melckebeecke** v. Gendt met Martha Maes v. Londen.
25 Apl. 1603   Anna van **Melden** met Abraham de Puijt.
8 Sep. 1612   Cornelis   **Melsen** v. Goreum met Anna van Wortem v. Delft.
19 Oct. 1575   Dierick   **Melssen** v. Berghem op Soom met Luyschen van der Voorne, we. Lieven Slaken v. Ghendt.
. . Jul. 1615   Jacob   **Melsian** v. Norwich met Anna de Wale v. Colchester.
17 Dec. 1588   Carel   de **Man** v. Schorisse met Janneken Sagers v. Antwerpen.
24 Mar. 1573   Jaques   **Menet** v. Dans in Henegouwe met Tanneken Veijlens v. Maestricht.
13 Apl. 1690   Catharina van **Mengelinckhuijsen** met Johannes van Wijck.
2 Feb. 1595   Catholyne   **Mennise** met Lenaert Costerman.
7 Feb. 1604   Hendrick   **Mensvelt** v. Bruijssel met Jacobmijntken Forts, we. Laurens van Damme.
23 Sep. 1691   Cornelia   **Mente**, we. Joris Wintervoet, met David Andtiesen.
2 Feb. 1613   Judith   **Merregarin** met Sebastiaen Fille.
17 Jun. 1582   Thamar van der **Mersse** met Govardt Engelsch.
28 Nov. 1585   Bartholomeus   **Mertens** van den Bossche, beijde v. Antwerpen.
29 Sep. 1594   Rebecca   ,, met Peeter Michiels.
18 Jun. 1712   Christoffel   **Mes**, wr van Margaretha Breetvelt, met Pieternella Brouwsens, we. van James Gout.

7 Aug. 1590   Hans   **Mesmaker** v. Solingen met Metsken Canes onck v. Solingen.
. . Jan. 1621   Jan   **Messiaen** v. Norwich met Philippote Dammers, we. Richard Helsten.
6 Apl. 1703   Bernard   **Messingh** j.m. v. Sutphen met Martijntje Kuijpers j.d. v. Delft.
2 Apl. 1592   Aurijnken   **Mestdach** met Bernaert van den Putte.
9 Feb. 1593   Arijnken   **Mestdag**, we. Bernaert van den Putte, met Joos de Hout.
. . Oct. 1613   Joanna   de **Meter** met Dierick Hoste.
14 Jun. 1586   Lucretia van **Meteren** met Abraham der Kinderen.
6 Oct. 1601   Abigail   de ,, met David Stainerj.
4 Nov. 1590   Janneken van **Meters** met Ezechiel Stilter.
5 Feb. 1600   Ottilia   ,, **Metren** met Jan Alewijns.

                                                                        r.

1 Oct.	1633	Maria	**Mets** met Matthias Pietersen.
23 Nov.	1602	Abraham	„ v. Londen met Pieterken Godschalck v.[Dordrecht.
3 Dec.	1607	Abraham	„ v. Londen met Elisabeth Gilbo v. Londen. ⚓
29 Jul.	1578	Jan	**Metz** v. Louerich in Gulickerlandt met Nelleken Basen v. Steen bij Maastricht.
1 Mei	1582	Catherijne	van **Mets-hagen** met Jaques de Basijn.
10 Apl.	1597	Susanna	de **Metue** met Dominicus Bowens.
19 Mei	1590	Hans	„ **Meulemeester** v. Putthen met Josijnken de Rijcke v. Eeckeloo.
2 Apl.	1605	Jan	„ „ v. Puthem met Elisabeth Baten, we. Ampleunis van den[Berghe.
13 Jan.	1597	Elisabeth	**Meulemeesters** met Evaert Toeput.
8 Jan.	1573	Anthuenis	van der **Muelen** v. Oudenaerde met Elizabeth van der Heyden v. Loven.
16 Dec.	1589	Antheunis	„ „ „ v. Oudenaerde met Lynken van den Bossche v. Bruijssel.
7 Feb.	1604	Susanna	van „ , we. Jan Hartot, met Joris de Coninck.
25 Dec.	1751	Vincent	„ „ j.m. met Adriana van der Vinne, j.d.
15 Nov.	1590	Debora	s' **Meulenaers** met Ambrosius de Swerte.
15 Jun.	1585	Margriete	**Meuleners** met Rutgeer Stevens.
4 Jun.	1594	Marten	van **Meurs** v. Cuelen met Catheline de Meijer v. Meenene, we. Wouter Stappen.
30 Nov.	1600	Isbrandt	„ „ wt lant v. Gulick met Eva der Kinders v. Loven.
8 Jan.	1594	Lijnken	**Micharts**, we. Hendrick de Cantelo, met Davids.
27 Mar.	1592	Lijntgen	**Michiels** met Anthonis Valins.
1 Apl.	1594	Lijnken	„ , we. Anthony Vallijn, met Jan Poitou.
29 Sep.	1594	Peeter	**Michielss** v. Londen met Rebecca Mertens v. Londen.
12 Apl.	1604	Jan	**Michiels** wt lant van Luijck met Heijlken Benniers, we. Jan Pauwels.
16 Aug.	1608	Susanna	„ met David de Clerck.
20 Mei	1598	Pieter	**Michielssen** v. Londen met Susanneken Rademaeckers v. Antwerpen.
17 Aug.	1623	Ester	**Michielsz** met Jan Lake.
24 Jul.	1628	Sara	„ met Jan Worringem.
10 Mei	1668	Janneke	**Michils**, we. van der Briell, met Pieter Dollart.
12 Dec.	1609	Adriaen	**Middelaer** v. Engen met Neelken van der Elst, we. Joris Farcy.
21 Jul.	1594	Lynken	de **Mieckele** met Chrijstopherus de Peyster.
27 Aug.	1629	David	**Mienchol** j.g. v. Amsterdam met Maria de Clerck j.d. v. Colchester.
17 Apl.	1597	Lucijnken	van **Mierbeke** met Iscar de Clerck.
28 Oct.	1600	Abraham	„ „ v. Middelberch met Jacomyneken Davidts v. Ghendt.
.. Jul.	1613	Catharina	**Mijleman** met Matthys Aertsz.
17 Aug.	1626	David	**Mijlemans** v. London met Tanneken Nolle v. Gent.
3 Nov.	1601	Iken	**Mijsers**, we. Dierick Nuaert, met Hendrick Antheunis.
10 Jun.	1583	Apollonie	**Mijt** met Renier Neelsz.
2 Sep.	1628	Daniel	**Mijtens** v. Delft, wr. van Gratia Clijtsers, met Johanna Drossaert, we. Joos de N(
25 Feb.	1617	Susanna	de **Milan** met Jaques van Braken.
20 Apl.	1584	Dierick	**Mill** v. Zalinger int lande van den Berge met Maijcken van Walle v. Ijperen, Ferdinand Dollegins.
4 Aug.	1640	Margary	**Mills** met Picter Courts.
10 Dec.	1611	Ester	**Mils** v. Londen met Elko Abels.
25 Jun.	1588	Hans	**Mimaert** v. Bruissel met Janneken s'Visschers v. Berckchier.
2 Jul.	1707	Wiljam	**Minchang** j.m. v. Glocestershire met Clara Schouten j.d. v. den Haegh.
24 Mei	1603	Catharijne	s' **Minders** met Frederick van Domselaer.
29 Jul.	1604	Catharyne	„ „ , we. Frederick van Dompsvilaers, met Jeremias Damman.
22 Jun.	1591	Sigismundus	**Minghen** v. Noorimburg met Margriete de la Forterie v. Antwerpen.
28 Mei	1594	Janneken	**Minnaert** met „ van Damme.
4 Jun.	1611	Janneken	„ , we. Adriaen van Damme, met Thomas Dabbins.
24 Dec.	1588	Janneken	**Minnaerts** met Hans Staffeney.
13 Jan.	1572	Tanneken	s' **Minners** met Jan Gallenarts.
20 Jun.	1592	Lijnken	**Mocharts** met Bernaert Christiaenssen.
19 Sep.	1604	Lijntken	„ , we. Robert Davids, met Lambrecht Wiesen.
25 Sep.	1614	Catharina	**Mockaert**, we. Lambert Wils, met Zacharias Ruijtinc.
7 Aug.	1593	Catharina	**Mockaerts** met H. de Cautelen.
1 Sep.	1575	Barbara	**Moele**, we. Jacobs Vergoes, met Pieter Schulpen.
29 Apl.	1617	Judith	**Moenen** met Thomas Kuijs.
.4 Nov.	1617	Abigail	„ met Abraham van Galulen.
23 Oct.	1610	Joos	**Moerman** v. Brugge met Susanne Pont v. Colchester.
1 Mei	1592	Magdalena	**Moesens** met Zacharias Ghijser.
30 Nov.	1585	Catelyne	de **Moij** met Jacus de Hoijnu.
19 Feb.	1576	Lijneken	**Moijesoons** met Aelbrecht Fockes.
28 Oct.	1595	Elisabet	**Moijns** met Pieter van Dale.
24 Aug.	1581	Cornelis	de **Mol** v. Gent met Maijken Herremans v. Herlem.
10 Feb.	1594	Hans	**Mol** v. Antwerpen met Maeijken Janssen v. Bruyssel, we. Pauwels van Eesberg
14 Jun.	1627	Pieter	„ wt t'landt v. Cleve met Susanna de Pauw, we. Pieter van Nette.
14 Dec.	1578	Antonis	van der **Molen** uit Audenarde met Tanneken de Vriese met Antwerpen, we. Andriaan Lu

6 Mei	1645	D. Joannes	de **Molenaer** wr. met Susanna Beke, we William Shildrake.
17 Mei	1630	Jan	**Molgelcam** j.g. v. Wesel met Maria Keijsers j.d. v. Londen.
19 Mar.	1594	Lowijseken	de **Molijn** met Jan Gheeraerts.
23 Jun.	1594	Pieter	„ „ v. Ghendt met Lynken van den Bossche v. Brussel, we. Anthonis van der Meulen.
18 Mei	1602	Janneken	„ „ met Abraham de Backer.
27 Dec.	1603	Lowijseken	„ „ , we. Jan Geeract, met Jacob Hermanssz.
4 Jan.	1586	Betten	„ , we. Marc Schockaert, met Jan de Bick.
13 Dec.	1604	Elisabeth	„ , we. Jan de Bick, met Sibrand Arnol.
18 Jan.	1597	Catceline	**Molijns** met John Bick.
30 Oct.	1604	Janneken	„ met Marten Droeshout.
20 Dec.	1603	Nicolas	**Molkebeke** v. Gent met Maijken Verbrugge, we. Hendrick de Vaddere.
26 Jul.	1584	Maijken	**Momdiers** met Willem Schuijten.
20 Mei	1606	Jan	de **Moncij** v. Iperen met Margriete Courten, we. Matthijs Boudaen.
. 1 Apl.	1612	Susanna	„ „ met Andries van der Weijer.
17 Feb.	1579	Dionijs	„ **Mont** v. Weracken met Janneken van den Putte, we. Vincents van der Leijden.
3 Feb.	1573	Sophia	van **Montfort**, we. Anthonis de Witte, met Hans van Scheije.
21 Jan.	1630	Cornelis	**Monteken** j g. v. Norwich met Margareta Gage j.d. v. Middelburch.
18 Jul.	1688	Johannes	**Noone** wr. met Rachel Ferré j.d. beyde v. Amsterdam.
21 Dec.	1600	Pieter	de **Moor** wt d'lant v. Berge met Elizabeth Lenaertsz van den Grave.
9 Oct.	1604	Hans	der „ v. Franckfort met Susanna Schaep v. Londen.
27 Jun.	1615	Lynken	**Moornincx** met Anthony van Nups.
24 Feb.	1573	Tanneken	s' **Moors**, we. Jaspar van Houtte, met Guillame de Waghenare.
19 Mei	1584	Catherina	„ met Willem Ruchen.
24 Jun.	1612	Debora	**Morat** met Willem Ratlef.
12 Jan.	1591	Lucas	**Moreels** v. Bruyssel met Maeyken Madou v. Londen.
6 Jan.	1579	Margariete	**Moreijns**, we. Thomas de Klock, met Hans van Sevenkoten.
19 Sep.	1583	Margriete	„ , we. Jan van Sevenkoten, met Marten Bernts.
26 Feb.	1594	Thomas	**Morghen** v. Engleszee met Janneken van der Swaeleme v. Ghendt, we. Willem Joons.
9 Jul.	1594	Pieter	**Moriaen** v. Oodendaele met Susanna Calant v. Landeghem, we. Jacus van den Raede.
23 Aug.	1590	Truijcken	**Morlincx** met Eleasar Pont.
22 Oct.	1588	Jacus	**Morre** v. Brussel met Anthonette de Winalt v. Brussel.
16 Mei	1611	Moses	**Mosen** wt t'lant v. Gulick met Marie Jarck v. Northhamptonshere.
5 Nov.	1702	Aletta	**Moser** met Klaas van der Veer.
27 Apl.	1585	Elizabeth	**Mostlers** met Olievier Brassens alias Murkens.
14 Jul.	1601	Maria	la **Mote** met Franchoijs l'enetier.
22 Apl.	1604	David	van der „ v. Gent met Catharijne Verhulst v. Antwerpen.
2 Sep.	1662	Melchior	**Moulart** j.m. v. Mastricht met Anna van Castart j.d. v. Londen.
25 Oct.	1631	Janneken	**Mount** met Jan van Roose-beeke.
31 Mei	1632	Maria	de **Mouson** met D. Gerhard van der Port.
19 Apl.	1604	Susanna	**Muijart**, we. Peter Hendricx, met Pieter Buerman.
19 Mar.	1629	Joncker	**Muijs**, Jonckman, v. Dordrecht met Jonckvrouwe Martine Joachimi, j.g. van der Gooc.
2 Aug.	1579	Jakes	**Muijshoudt** v. Brussel met Josijne Geldolf v. Meenen.
24 Jan.	1585	Sara	**Mulan** met Simon Quirins.
24 Mei	1586	Hans	**Mulderi** met Elisabeth van den Langhevelde beijde v. Brussel.
18 Jun.	1594	Tanneken	van **Mulhem** met Jan van der Poest.
28 Jun.	1614	Franchoijs	**Muller** v. Dusseldorp met Abigail Hanthuijs v. Londen.
16 Mar.	1647	Gerart	„ j.g. v. Dordrecht met Engelken Jansen j.d. v. Lochum.
17 Mei	1576	Michiel	de **Munck** met Catherine Verschalen, we. Christiaen Servaes v. Eynthoven.
14 Apl.	1586	Tanneken	„ met Joos van den Broecke.
12 Dec.	1591	Tanneken	„ „ , we. Joos van den Broecke, met Jaques de Riddere.
2 Feb.	1630	Maria	**Munninckx**, we. Richard Pierson, met Joos Bollewijn.
			Murkens vide Brassens.
18 Jul.	1598	Tanneken	**Mus**, we. Joos van den Eijnde, met Sijbrecht Aernoult.
11 Jul.	1592	Pierijne	ver „ , we. Jacop de Vos, met Hieronimus Wales.

5 Mei	1594	Abraham	**Nabuer** v. Londen met Margriete de Bock v. Ypren.
21 Oct.	1578	Jan	**Nachtegaal** v. Audenarde met Pieryntge s'Rijken, we. Emanuels van Eijse v. Audenarde.
31 Mar.	1589	Jan	**Nachtegale** v. Oudenaerde met Lowijseken van Evenacker v. Ghendt.
15 Feb.	1603	Esaias	**Nachtegael** v. Londen met Anna Fenne v. Audwerpen.
19 Mei	1607	Jaques	**Nachtegael** v. bij Belle met Susanna Verbrugghe v. Londen.
1 Jan.	1594	Jan	**Nachtengale** v. Oudenarde met Helena Schellekens v. s'Hertogenbosche, we. Lienart Hughe.
. 0 Nov.	1613	Tanneken	**Nagelers**, we. Geerart Jansz, met Walraev de Pans.
30 Aug.	1575	Michiel	**Nauwe** v. s'Hertogenbosch met Isabella van Broecke, we. Pieter van Doorne v. Antwerpen.
28 Jan.	1598	Grietken	**Nauwins**, we. Jan le Neuven, met Jan Voets.
9 Feb.	1584	Laurent	de **Necker** v. Thielt met Janneken Visscher v. Londen.
5 Sep.	1591	Moses	,, **Neckere** v. Maidtston met Janneken van Beckhem v. Oudenaerde.
1 Mar.	1584	Pierijne	**Neckers** met Jan Rijssclinck.
28 Aug.	1599	Thomas	**Nederwaets** v. Joreschier (Yorkshire) met Susanna van Cauwenberge v. Deijnse.
10 Jun.	1583	Renier	**Neelsz** v. Heijnsberch met Apollonie Nijt v. Brugge.
28 Oct.	1583	Susanna	van **Neerhagen** met Karel Sohier.
13 Feb.	1706	Barbara Sophia	**Neernige** met Hendrick van Borchloon.
5 Jun.	1575	Janneken	**Neese**, we. Jooris Letwerk, met Gillis Snepgat.
23 Dec.	1578	Janneken	**Neesons**, we. Gillis Snepgatt, met Pieter Floerkin.
20 Jan.	1583	Maijeken	**Neijden** met . . . . de Maessene.
13 Dec.	1596	Maeijken	**Neijtens**, we. Lieven van der Straeten, met Gillis Goosens.
15 Aug.	1587	Janneken	van **Nelden** met Bernaert van den Putte.
13 Feb.	1610	Maijken	de **Nets** met Anthenuis de Conijnck.
8 Mar.	1575	Jaspar	,, **Neufville** v. Antwerpen met Jossijne Swinnen, we. Hans Spoliers.
1 Mei	1593	Anne	,, **Neve** met Pieter Gheeldolf.
21 Aug.	1593	Cornelis	,, ,, v. Ghistele met Elizabeth Goddens v. Maseick, we. Jan Davidts.
8 Jan.	1594	Louwise	,, ,, , we. Arnout Meeses, met Laurens Huijgens.
10 Apl.	1604	Joos	,, ,, v. Bruijssel met Susanna de Drossche v. Londen.
1 Aug.	1596	Jossijnken	,, , Janssens, met Willem van Schoonenvelde.
27 Jan.	1573	Johannes	**Nicasius** v. Oost Vriesland met Cecilia Fogghe v. Kortrijcke.
13 Aug.	1588	Hans	,, v. Antwerpen met Susanna Baetens v. Antwerpen.
2 Dec.	1606	Hans	,, v. Antwerpen met Sara Smith v. Liu (Lynn).
6 Aug.	1626	Anna	,, , we. Gregorius Wttespruijt, met Christiaen de Welcke.
31 Mei	1596	Jan	**Niclaesz** wt d'lant v. Gulick met Lievijne van der Stelt v. Ghendt.
18 Aug.	1601	Jan	**Niclaessen** wt t'lant v. Gulick met Susanna van Luchen v. Maidston, we. Hans Verstraten.
4 Dec.	1621	Jan	**Nicolas** v. Londen met Susanna Jansz v. Londen.
24 Mei	1597	Jan	**Nieuwiert** wt lant v. Cleven met Barbel Anthoni v. Londen.
20 Mei	1617	Joos	van **Niewenhuijse** v. Haselbroec met Janneken Piers, we. Paulus v. Mortele.
6 Apl.	1629	Jenne	de **Nij**, we. Jan Alman, met Oseus Holwet.
22 Dec.	1584	Calleken	van **Nimmeghen**, we. Comais Govertsen, met Phlips van der Strate.
25 Jul.	1619	Catharina	**Nison** met Noe Frombout.
17 Aug.	1626	Tanneken	**Nolle** met David Mijlemans.
17 Nov.	1614	Denijs	**Noodstock** v. Sittert met Elisabeth Maijnet v. Londen.
10 Oct.	1637	Janneken	,, met Lijon Busken.
9 Dec.	1572	Robert	**Noortman** v. Brugghe met Margriete, fa Gillis Lemmens v. Brugghe.
29 Jun.	1590	Lucretia	de **Notre** met Arnoudt Meesens.
11 Jun.	1594	Catherine	,, met Melchior van Pekom.
13 Dec.	1586	Sara	van **Nuffele**, we. Fransois Pieters, met Jan van Peene.
. . Jul.	1620	Pieter	**Nuffel** v. Brussel met Agneta Storcx v. Sittert wt t'landt van Gulick.
22 Nov.	1703	Pieternella	**Nuitsaert** met Jacob Gerart.
22 Aug.	1585	Janneken	**Nutinx** met Willem Jacobssen.
17 Mei	1608	Pieter	van **Nutte** v. bij Aecken met Susanne de Pauw v. Andwerpen.
20 Jul.	1602	Jan	**Nuijwaert** v. d'lant v. Cleve met Beelken Heijlighers v. Sittaert, we. Baltazar Poggen.
28 Nov.	1581	Dierick	**Nuwaerts** vt lant v. Cleve met Ikcn Sweers v. Aldekereke bij Gelderlant.

18 Apl.	1609	Sara	Obbelaer met Jacob Frutier.
3 Dec.	1611	Anna	Obrij met Geeraerd Valcke.
12 Apl.	1575	Maijken	Obrijs, we. Thomas Soen, met Melchior van Ashe.
21 Dec.	1588	Juliane	van Oelant, we. Hendrick de Stoute, met Andries Koppens.
3 Mei	1603	Pieter	Oevijn v. Armentiers met Catharijne van de Walle v. Torut van bij Brugge.
18 Mei	1595	Neelken	van Oije met Hans Daniels.
1 Jan.	1583	Judith	Oijevaers met Pauwels Toebast.
12 Feb.	1656	Pieter	d' Olijslager j.m. v. Middelburg met Elisabeth de Rijcke, j.d. v. Londen.
6 Jan.	1596	Mechelynken	Oijsteliouck, we. Bernaert de Swarte, met Minaert Sibbels.
6 Mei	1630	Johanna	Oils, we. Aernoudt Eeckhoudt, met Adriaen de Crook.
18 Dec.	1695	Geesken	Oldendijck, we. Jan Oldendijck, met Jan Reijnders.
26 Jul.	1586	Josijne	Oeghaerts, we. Willem de Meuleneester, met Cornelis Steenaert.
9 Feb.	1602	Isaac	Olivier v. Ronen met Sara Gheerarts v. Londen.
22 Sep.	1608	Jone	,, met Jan Rooseboom.
15 Dec.	1635	Philips	,, j.g. v. Norwich met Christina den Boven j.d. v. Meurs.
19 Oct.	1596	Sara	Ontheusden met Jaspar Janssens.
4 Oct.	1590	Maetken	Oons met Lieven Boudaert.
21 Feb.	1604	Joos	Ootger v. Gent met Maria van Strafeele, we. Jan Ryckwaert. (v. Otgeer.)
25 Oct.	1614	Janneken	,, met Pierre du Rieu.
14 Jan.	1583	Sara	Ootgheers met Dierick Helden.
13 Oct.	1612	Elisabeth	Opgingort met Goijvaert van Hasselt.
2 Sep.	1595	Ghijsbrecht	van Ophaeghe v. Deventer met Lydia de Reaumur v. Colchester.
3 Apl.	1668	Francis	Ophalven met David de Magth.
14 Jun.	1669	Jan	Ophalvens j.m. v. Mortlake met Anna Schouten j.d. wt den Hague.
2 Sep.	1571	Henrick	Oppenacke met Maeijken van Hove.
5 Dec.	1583	Abel	Oprun v. Antwerpen met Tanneken van Roomers v. Middelborch.
2 Sep.	1571	Joris	Orneck met Martijntghen van Hulle.
19 Jul.	1610	Hans	van Orsele v. Andwerpen met Judith du Bois v. Amsterdam.
28 Sep.	1585	Elisabet	van Oscelare, we. Joos van Wijnsberghe, met Jan Burdt.
27 Dec.	1574	Neelken	van Osse met Noel Bonnesen.
22 Sep.	1612	Elizabeth	Otgeer met Salomon van den Broeck.
3 Sep.	1622	David	,, met Joanna van Haranghoeck, beijde v. Londen.
17 Sep.	1633	David	,, , wr. van Joanna van Harinckoeock, v. Londen met Maria van Selt, we. Jacob Herrewijn v. Londen.
1 Jun.	1572	Grietgen	Ottgeers, van Ghent met Henrick Klaassen.
11 Sep.	1600	Hans	d' Oude v. Duijukerk met Gomerijne Skosters v. Antwerpen, we. Gillis Verhaeghe.
25 Nov.	1593	Hans	d' Ouwe v. Ghendt met Franchynken de Nenge v. Ghendt.
18 Dec.	1593	Janneken	Overdaet, van de Xe. met Philips van der Burcht.
22 Nov.	1599	Janneken	,, , we. Philip Verlarecht, met Hendrick Janssen.
8 Jan.	1857	Henri Antoine	van Overzee j.m. oud 27 jaar met Martina Margaretha Paulina 's Graeuwen, j.d. oud 24 jaar.

29 Mar.	1608	Susanna	van Paene met Thomas Santgen.
17 Apl.	1645	Pieter	Paff j.g. v. Bergen in Henegaw met Aletta Cowper j.d. v. Nimweghen.
18 Feb.	1588	Hubert	de Page v. Luyck met Christine Janssen v. den Gouwe.
7 Mei	1662	Robbert	Page j.m. v. den Hage met Maria Controix j.d. v. Eekelsheeck.
7 Dec.	1611	Willem	Paget wt t'landt v. Gulick met Maria Wittewrongel v. Londen.
22 Jan.	1576	Jacques	Palijnck v. Ghendt met Betken van Heecke v. Ghent.
12 Feb.	1604	Elisabeth	Panier, we. Laurens du Bois, met Elias Garnoot.
3 Feb.	1582	Colijntge	Pannekoecke met Hans van Berk.
17 Oct.	1594	Beetken	Parcklers, we. Gielis van der Sande, met Jans Schoutet.
11 Feb.	1584	Maijeken	Paret met Jan van der Bossche.
9 Dec.	1600	Lijnken	Partels, we. Pieter Ruijtinck, met Franchoijs van den Broecke.
14 Jun.	1603	Daniel	Passeman v. Emblem met Judith Eduwaerts v. Londen.
5 Oct.	1602	Hendrick	Patroon j.m. v. 's Gravenhaegh met Helena Exalto D'Almeras j.d. v. Leerdam.
1 Aug.	1613	Hendrick	Pauls v. Dalen met Magdalena de Beste v. Brugghe.
11 Nov.	1691	Salomon	Paulus j.m. v. 's Gravenhaegh met Anneke Symons v. Rotterdam.
14 Feb.	1604	David	de Paus v. Londen met Elisabeth des Hommets v. Middelburgh.
0 Nov.	1613	Walraev	de Paus v. Breussel met Tanneken Nagelers, we. van Geerart Jansz.
27 Apl.	1619	Pieter	,, ,, v. Londen met Sara Jansz mede v. Londen.

28 Oct.	1588	Jacus	**Perseval** v. Brugghe met Sara James v. Londen.
1 Sep.	1590	Hans	„ v. Brugghe met Elisabet van Brecht v. Antwerpen.
24 Feb.	1579	Pieter	**Persoons** v. Engien met Willehmijne van den Dorpe v. Audenarde, we. Antonis Nant.
1 Apl.	1585	Cornelis	„ v. St. Nielaes in Waes met Heindricksken Jacobs, we. Rijckaert Heth, van den Briel.
26 Feb.	1590	Tanneken	„ met Abraham Focket.
6 Jan.	1596	Pieter	**Peterins** v. Segelsen int land van Aelst met Lijdia de Bruijne v. Londen.
3 Dec.	1592	Catheline	**Peters** met Balthasar van de Lind.
28 Aug.	1700	Mary	„ met Jan Lagestraet.
8 Jan.	1594	Geertruijt	le **Petin** v. Brussel, we. Adam van Sinnick, met Baudewijn Achtscheelinck.
8 Mei	1596	Catheline	**Petit** met Lambert Pieters.
23 Nov.	1603	Catharine	„ , we. Lambrecht Pietersz, met Zibericht Arnold.
10 Apl.	1604	Geertruijt	le „ , we. Bauduwijn Achtschellinck, met Samuel Ashe.
26 Jun.	1606	Peter	**Petrin** met Maeijken Lauwens.
8 Aug.	1602	Pauwels	**Philips** v. Emblen met Maria Brabant v. Armentiers we. Willem Page.
13 Sep.	1691	Susannah	„ , we. Lodowijck Hermans, met Jacobus Peret.
28 Jul.	1594	Clerken	„ met Jan Timmers.
29 Mei	1689	Philip	**Philipsen** j.m. met Susanna Leeman j.d., beijde v. Amsterdam.
30 Nov.	1572	Neelken	van **Plebeke**, we. Mr. Matheus de Quester, met Robert Reynoudts.
24 Oct.	1585	Jossijnken	**Piers**, we. Gillis Valcke, met Marten de Vischere.
24 Dec.	1587	Jossinken	„ , we. Marten de Visscher, de Jonge, met Jacus Thijsman.
20 Mei	1617	Janneken	„ , we. Paulus van Mortele met Joos van Niewenhuyse.
24 Jan.	1572	Margriete	**Pieters** met Arnouldt Arnoudtz.
12 Feb.	1577	Dierexken	„ , we. Herman Thijssen, met Arent Cornelissz.
17 Mei	1579	Maijeken	„ , we. Jans Cornelissen, met Everd Steenvers.
22 Jun.	1585	Cornelis	„ v. Vtricht met Cathelyne Burchgrave, we. Jan van Dorne, v. Yseghem.
30 Jun.	1586	Rogier	„ v. Hamme met Digne Janssens v. Tielborch.
17 Jan.	1587	Margriete	„ , we. Arent Arentsz, met Joos Hauwe.
14 Feb.	1587	Hans	„ v. Antwerpen met Neelken Grippens, we. Jan Ryers v. Scralehier (Shropshire).
22 Aug.	1588	Segher	„ v. Erkelen met Jossijntken van den Batsele v. bij Oudenaerde, we. Christoffels Taelman.
9 Feb.	1591	Geraert	„ v. bij Berck met Jacomijne Ardewijns v. Antwerpen, we. Geraert Janssen.
27 Mei	1693	Sara	„ met Lenard Busch.
30 Jul.	1594	Lambert	„ wt t'lant v. Guylick met Barbara Gheldolf v. Meenene.
6 Aug.	1594	Bartholomeus	„ wt d'lant v. Gulick met Sara den Kinderen v. Londen, we. Jan Weijsels.
22 Jun.	1595	Janneken	„ met Pieter de Groote.
8 Mei	1596	Lambert	„ wt t'lant v. Gulick met Catheline Petit v. Ipsich (Ipswich).
6 Jan.	1600	Jan	„ wt sticht v. Ceulen met Colinken van den Berghe v. Mechelen.
22 Jan.	1604	Janneken	„ , we. Pieter de Groot, met Nicholas Woodcraft.
3 Jun.	1617	Janneken	„ , we. Mattheus van Ceulen, met Andries Meijer.
29 Sep.	1590	Bernardt	**Petersen** v. Wtrecht met Maertken de Maere v. Antwerpen.
1 Oct.	1633	Matthias	**Pietersen** j.g. v. Mazuck met Maria Mets j.d. v. Londen.
22 Jan.	1646	Martha	„ met Samuel de Gans.
17 Oct.	1677	Pieter	„ j.m. met Alemaer met Elizabeth Christianors j.d. v. Amsterdam.
19 Jun.	1582	Bartholomeus	**Pieterssen** v. Wassenbereh in landt v. Gulick met Elizabeth van Deke v. Ghendt, we. Jakns Palinck.
5 Aug.	1604	Pieter	„ v. Sullich met Maria Gast v. Londen.
11 Mei	1626	Maria we. Pieter	„ met Willem Kuijckelhuijs.
3 Aug.	1602	Martha	**Pieterssz** met Pieter Clinckaert.
12 Jun.	1610	Joachim	„ , we. Labeeck met Ann Sickraet v. Londen.
24 Nov.	1603	Maria	**Pietersz** met Richard Rong.
1 Mar.	1614	Tanneken	„ met Christofel Pin.
10 Jun.	1623	Leonard	„ v. der Gouwe met Oliva Peerle, we. Thomas Clerex.
5 Apl.	1597	Anna	**Pifferoen** met Joos van der Straeten.
11 Sep.	1604	Tanneken	**Pifron**, we. Joos van Steele, met Jan Soenen.
10 Sep.	1588	Baltazar	**Pigge** v. Rangelzoet met Neelken Hillegaert v. bij Tsittaert.
19 Oct.	1589	Dierick	**Pigghe** uit d'lant v. Gulick met Adriaenken van der Eijcke v. Bergen op Zoom.
8 Dec.	1607	Josijntken	**Pijcke**, we. Jacob de Coster, met Jan de Ruijck.
9 Jul.	1588	Apolonia	**Pijnaerts**, we. Gillis Meijncart, met Gillis Schoemaker.
13 Jul.	1630	Daniel	van **Pilcom** j.g. v. London met Catharina Bolle j.d. v. Amsterdam.
21 Apl.	1594	Susanna	**Pilkem** met Jaques Theeuws.
28 Nov.	1596	Willem	**Pill** v. Solinghen met Anna Dotignij v. Londen.
2 Feb.	1613	Sebastiaen	**Pille** v. Olphen met Judith Merregarin v. Colchester.
29 Jan.	1619	Jan	„ v. Nieckercke met Abigail Gallandt v. Sandwich.
1 Mar.	1614	Christofel	**Pin** v. t'landt v. Gulick met Tanneken Pietersz v. Helsenor.
3,8 (sic) Sep.	1577	Hans	**Pinaert** v. Turnhout met Anthonyne van Hille v. Antwerpen.

30 Jul.	1588	Janneken	**Pinceel**, we. Pieter le Mire, met Pieter de Vriese.
7 Sep.	1574	Hans	**Pinroen** v. Ghendt met Katheryue Noijsons v. Ghendt.
15 Oct.	1594	Willem	**Pisteijns** v. Antwerpen met Macijken vau Haecke v. Turnhout, we. Hendrick Hermans.
4 Aug.	1573	Lieven	van den **Pitte** v. Exarde met Elizabeth, we. Gisbertus Johannes v. Hasselt.
9 Mei	1591	Phlips	,, der **Plaetse** met Tanneken van der Biest, beide v. Enghien.
19 Sep.	1598	Judith	,, ,, ,, met Jan de Meijer.
4 Feb.	1584	Esther	,, ,, **Plaetsen** met Adriaen de Kroock.
. . Sep.	1618	Catharina	de **Plantere** met Timotheus Cruso.
25 Sep.	1586	Elisabet	**Plantsoen** met Hans Peperman.
13 Jun.	1591	Gelyne	**Plantsoens** met Kraft Kessels.
5 Jun.	1604	Philip	van der **Plassche** v. Engen met Auna de Bruyne, we. Zacharias van Horebeke.
15 Sep.	1607	Anna	**Plateboot**, we. Jan Broeders, met Isaac de Clerck.
29 Jan.	1600	Macijken	**Platevoets** met Jacques Lagnicl.
8 Feb.	1597	Susanna	**Poel** met Bernaert Jansz.
5 Feb.	1594	Janneken	van der **Poele** met Matheus Stilte.
18 Mei	1690	Christina	van **Poelenburgh** met Gerard Smith.
21 Jun.	1580	Grietgen	**Poels**, we. Jacob Vrolickhoven, met Jan Brugman.
29 Sep.	1573	Tanneken	van der **Poest** met Anthonis van der Vinne.
23 Nov.	1574	Tanneken	,, ,, ,, , we. Anthony van der Vinne, met . . . . . . van Meerbeke.
18 Jun.	1594	Jan	,, ,, ,, v. Oudenaarde met Tanneken van Mulhem v. Somerghem.
31 Jan.	1604	Maximilien	**Poictrin** v. Utrecht met Susanna Goemerts v. Antwerpen.
1 Apl.	1594	Jan	**Poitou** v. Antwerpen met Lijnken Michiels v. Oudenaarde, we. Anthonj Vallijn.
10 Apl.	1586	Fransois	**Polaert** v. Engen met Janneken op den Hove v. Houscoten.
14 Nov.	1598	FI'anchoijs	,, v. Engien met Auna de Coster v. Londen.
18 Oct.	1571	Jan	**Pollet** v. Alst met Maijeken Goris v. Walem.
19 Jul.	1584	Susanna	du **Pon** met Vijt Damen.
26 Nov.	1598	Eleazar	**Pondt** v. Honscote met Tanneken van der Donct v. Deijnse.
9 Apl.	1592	Susanna	de **Pont**, we. Vinceut Audrics, met Aruout Suit.
9 Dec.	1593	Chrystijnken	du ,, met Craft Keysels.
23 Aug.	1590	Eleasar	,, v. Hontschote met Truijcken Morlinex v. Antwerpen.
27 Nov.	1603	Eleasar	,, v. Hontscot met Maria van der Cappelle v. Londen.
23 Oct.	1610	Susanna	,, met Joos Moerman.
. . Oct.	1620	Maria	,, met Isaac van Arschot.
25 Aug.	1629	Catharina	de ,, met Michiel de Knuijt.
22 Apl.	1691	Hubrecht	**Poorsoo**, j.g. v. Leijden met Martyntje Vincente j.d. v. Arnhem, met Attestatie v. St. James.
11 Apl.	1591	Hans	van der **Poorten** v. Gent met Maeijken Snip v. Brugghe.
13 Apl.	1589	Nicolas	,, ,, ,, v. Engien met Janneken Noijvers v. Nieuwekercke, we. Jacus Mentyn.
6 Sep.	1590	Pieter	de **Poortere** v. Antwerpen met Barbelken van Dirkele v. bij Eecloo.
5 Jun.	1593	Pieter	,, ,, v. Antwerpen met Tanneken Bracts v. Zeghelisen bij Oudenaarde.
6 Jan.	1590	Lijntken	s' **Poorters**, we. Jau Elssen, met Pieter Rutinck.
16 Nov.	1600	Janneken	**Poorters** met Jaques Varen.
10 Oct.	1576	Oijken	**Poppings**, we. Mr. Jacob Soest, met Pieter Bouchier.
17 Aug.	1591	Oijken	,, we. Piersen Bouchier, met Jacob Janssen.
9 Mei	1626	Samuel	**Populaer** v. Londen met Catharina Kindt v. Andwerpen.
8 Jul.	1628	Samuel	,, wedr. v. Londen met Lea de Coninck j.d. v. Londen.
22 Jun.	1585	Anthony	**Populaire** v. Haussoby met Josyne Koelpots, we. Pieters Sterens v. Brugge.
31 Mei	1632	D. Gerhard	van de **Port**, wr. v. Zirxzee & leerar in ouse Gemente, met Jouffrou Maria de Mouson j.d. v. Amsterdam.
14 Jul.	1594	Gillis	de la **Porte** v. Nijvelle met Susanna Anthonisz v. Londen.
13 Dec.	1580	Catherine	s' **Portere** met Jacob Elssen.
13 Jun.	1596	Jan	**Post** v. Leyden met Elisabeth de Cock v. Lokeren, we. Adriaen Lammens.
22 Oct.	1598	Jan	,, v. Leyden met Sara de Coninck v. Londen.
1 Jun.	1574	Andrus	**Pot** v. Ectichove met Maijken Gooris, va. Jans Pollet.
26 Mar.	1592	Sara	van **Pottelsberghe** met Jaspar Fredrix.
8 Jul.	1623	Maijken	de **Potter** met Pieter van de Velde.
14 Mar.	1688	Johannes	van **Poucke** j.m. v. Aerdenburgh in Vlaenderen met Maria Derveau j.d. v. Amsterdam
26 Mar.	1611	Robert	**Prat** in Bockingomgshore (Buckinghamshire) met Jacobmijne Bossar, we. Jons de Cocq.
28 Jan.	1595	Janneken	des **Pren** met Jacus Verhule.
24 Sep.	1598	Thomas	**Prentis** v. Londen met Janneken Dayes v. Lyniste.
5 Feb.	1611	Arnould	,, v. Londen met Janneken Prija wt Shropheere.
. . Jun.	1620	Thomas	,, v. London met Maijken Sucht, we Jan Speeckart.
28 Jan.	1609	Carel	de **Pres** v. Gent met Sara Veureu v. Londen.
23 Feb.	1574	Anthuenis	,, **Preut** v. Rouse met Abigail de Vrient v. Moorden in Vrieslant.
25 Jul.	1585	Janneken	,, ,, (v. **Pruet**) met Hans van Lippevelde.

19 Nov.	1616	Abraham	de **Preut** v. Londen met Sara Damers v. Londen.
12 Sep.	1585	Gelijnken	**Preuts** met Arent Stalens.
8 Sep.	1612	Pieter	**Priem** v. bij Ypere met Margareta van den Bossche, we. Willem Bracklbinck.
2 Apl.	1646	Andries	„ j.d. v. Norwich met Elisabet Fromenteel j.d. v. Norwich.
2 Apl.	1579	Catherijne	**Priems**, we. Pieter Albrechts, met Adolps Staat.
5 Feb.	1611	Janneken	**Prijs** met Arnould Prents.
3 Jul.	1599	Pieter	de **Pril** v. Brussel met Maria Corselis v. Londen.
20 Apl.	1619	Maria	„ **Prill** met Isaac van Peene.
15 Jan.	1604	Meelken	**Prince** met Herman Stappaert.
28 Oct.	1595	Marie	**Proost**, met Tobias de Backer.
18 Dec.	1604	Maria	„ we. Tobias de Backer, met Sijmeon Ruijting.
3 Jan.	1604	Ester	„ , we. Symon Guijrin, met Samuel de Brussate.
22 Jan.	1690	Catharina	**Propis**, we. Jan Bosschaert, met Jan de Wit.
9 Dec.	1600	Auromijntken	**Provenger**, we. Michiel Verdonck, met Marten Verburck.
27 Feb.	1593	Lievine	de **Pruet** (v. **Preut**) met Pieter Fremant.
6 Mei	1581	Adriaen	„ **Prust** v. Rouse met Susanna Brakelers v. Rouse.
16 Jun.	1590	Jan	van **Pruijsschen** v. Berghen op Zoom met Janneken de Bruijne v. Nieukerke, we. Jan Verbrugghe.
25 Jul.	1602	Jan	„ **Puffleijn** v. Cleve met Catharyne de Deux-villes v. Antwerpen.
17 Dec.	1588	Anthonis	**Puyster** v. Oldenzeele met Elizabeth Jonghe v. Londen.
28 Jul.	1590	Jacus	de **Puijt** Ghendt met Carolije van Crombrugghen v. Ghendt.
25 Apl.	1603	Abraham	„ „ v. Debtfordt met Anna van Melden v. Brugghe.
. . Jul.	1613	Abigaijl	„ „ met Samuel Damert.
5 Mei	1579	Lois	„ **Puijth** v. Yperen met Pivone Vermote v. Belle.
25 Nov.	1582	Mechtelde	**Puppings** (v. **Poppings**) met Jan de Grave.
12 Apl.	1575	Pauwels	**Puts** v. Mechelen met Margriete Aernouts v. Danzwijck.
7 Sep.	1572	Maijeken	van de **Putte** met Hans de Smedt.
17 Feb.	1579	Janneken	van dem „ , we. Vincent van der Leijden, met Dionijs de Mont.
9 Jan.	1582	Raphael	van den „ v. Brugge met Pauline du Bois v. Antwerpen, we. Mr. Jan Rickpottes.
4 Aug.	1584	Lieven	„ „ „ v. Exarde met Esther van Medegar v. s'Hertogenbossche, we. Geeraerdt Verstrijpe.
15 Aug.	1587	Bernaert	„ „ „ v. Nuckercke met Janneken van Nelden v. Maeteren.
3 Dec.	1588	Margriet	van der „ met Hendrick Cos.
2 Apl.	1592	Bernaert	„ „ „ v. Nieukerke met Aurijuken Mestdaeh v. Oudenaerde.
10 Aug.	1596	Lucretia	van den „ , we. Niclaes Vincent, met Daniel Echler.
19 Jul.	1597	Magdalena	„ „ „ met Jan Sereijn.

20 Nov.	1571	Sybrecht	van den **Qoives** v. Emerick met Janneken van den Driessche.
5 Feb.	1612	Liborius	**Quant** v. Paterbory met Maijken Hagens, we. Jaques de Causije.
6 Sep.	1614	Maria	**Quatroos** met Christopher Eijgener.
. . Feb.	1616	Tobias	„ v. Middelborgh met Margareta Goleijns wt t'land van der Goes.
1 Sep.	1579	Cathlijne	de **Quesnoy** met Pieter Speelhoven.
7 Oct.	1619	Anthoine	le **Quien** de Valencien met Anna Jan v. Hoorn.
27 Apl.	1619	Jan	des **Quiens** v. Londen met Dina de Geijter mede v. Londen.
23 Oct.	1576	Rachel	le **Quienure** met Jan Soillot.
29 Mar.	1575	Sibille	**Quirins**, we. Matheus van der Goede, met Pieter de Sterke.
24 Jan.	1585	Simon	„ , Ranleraedt met Sara Mulau v. Londen.
4 Dec.	1575	Cornelis	**Quirintssen** v. Belken bij Leeuwarden met Rachel Janssen v. Marienhoven in Oost Vrieslant, we. Abraham de Vries alias Fockels.
12 Jul.	1675	Anna	**Quirintze** met Steven Janssen.
20 Mei	1571	Christiaen	**Quirintzen** uit de Hage met Adriaenken Adriaensz, we. Cornelis Jacobsz.
13 Mei	1593	Hans	**Quishout** v. Antwerpen met Maiken Scheers v. Honschote.

10 Mei	1631	Janneken	Raboij, we. Willem Meeson, met Jacob de Jonck-Heer.
5 Jun.	1610	Hendrick	Rademaecker v. Londen met Stijuken Wouters v. Amsterdam
14 Jul.	1588	Scipio	Rademaeckers v. Antwerpen met Sara Jordaens v. Antwerpen.
20 Mei	1598	Susanneken	„ met Pieter Michielssen.
13 Mei	1571	Jan	Rademaker v. Aken met Janneken Raketz v. Antwerpen.
2 Oct.	1606	Susanna	Rademaker, we. Pieter Michiels, met Claijs Jacobs.
14 Jul.	1607	Elisabet	Rademaker, we. Jasper Wauters, met Jasper van Enden.
26 Dec.	1592	Janneken	Rademakers met Abraham Janssen.
. . Feb.	1616	Simon	de Rae v. Brussel met Maria Rijewaert v. Londen.
13 Apl.	1572	Lijntghen	Raenens met Wouters van Sbinden.
17 Jan.	1576	Gheeraert	Raessen v. Lijgtevoorde met Maiken de Krijts v. Antwerpen.
4 Dec.	1576	Jan	de Raet v. Nieukerke met Barbara Vierendeels v. Steenvoorde.
26 Dec.	1603	Francoijs	„ „ v. Ypre met Oliva Perne, we. Pieter Verbouckel.
11 Dec.	1599	Margriete	Raket, we. Abraham van Hawijck, met Arnout Luls.
13 Mei	1571	Janneken	Raketz met Jan Rademaker.
21 Sep.	1591	Hester	Ram met Hendrick de Vos.
6 Jan.	1572	Josijne	Ramans met Jois Godtscalck.
16 Apl.	1582	Maeijken	Ramers met Hendrick Cane.
14 Feb.	1604	Magdaleene	Ramon, we. Louijs de d'Ethnier, met Hubrecht Franssen.
17 Jun.	1589	Rebecca	de Rane, we. Michiel de Hase, met Herman Schalker.
23 Jan.	1593	Robert	Range v. Chammerfoot met Catelina James v. Antwerpen, we. Hendrick Almans.
21 Nov.	1592	Martken	Raphels met Pieter op de Kelder.
24 Jun.	1612	Willem	Ratlef uijt Essex met Debora Mornt v. Londen.
2 Sep.	1595	Lijdia	de Reaumer met Ghijsbrecht van Ophaeghe.
10 Mei	1590	Willem	Rechaerts v. bij Sluijs met Celieken van de Walle v. Torhout.
3 Jan.	1574	Elizabeth	Redijnck met Jan Back.
17 Dec.	1605	Janneken	van Reckem, we. David Cambier, met Carol van Peene.
6 Aug.	1577	Margriete	Reeniers, we. Michiel Vaijens, met Andries Koppens.
16 Mei	1609	Ambrosius	van Regemorter v. Wesel met Johanna de Fray v. Antwerpen.
2 Dec.	1628	Anna	Regoot met Paulus Ganne.
17 Jul.	1576	Jan Willemssen	Reijbeke wt den Haoge met Perijnken van Schin v. Antwerpen.
1 Aug.	1588	Everaert	Reijers v. Vtricht met Maeijken van Tongheren v. Antwerpen, we. Hans Inischout.
15 Jul.	1593	Lijsken	„ met Thomas Peperman.
18 Dec.	1603	Jan	Reijnders j.m. Soldaet onder de Compe. van Capiteijn Massie - - met Geesken Oldendijck, we. v. Jan Oldendijck.
12 Oct.	1573	Lucas	Reijners v. Deventer met Claerken Faes v. Antwerpen.
31 Mei	1596	Anthony	Reijniers v. Brussel met Janneken Ghijsels v. Antwerpen.
9 Dec.	1609	Anthony	„ v. Brussel met Magdalena van Stelant v. Brugge, we. Jan Costerlinck.
. . Apl.	1612	Lydia	Reijnincx met Cornelis Sickract.
17 Mei	1608	Catharina d'huijsvrouwe Hubrecht	Reynols met Evert Claeijssz.
30 Nov.	1572	Robert	Reijnoudts, Enghelsman, met Neelken van Piebeke v. Brugghe, we. Mr. Matheus de Questor.
20 Mar.	1576	Conrad	Reijnouts v. Tienen met Tanneken v. Dalem v. Londen.
4 Mei	1591	Jan	Reijnout v. Ipren met Tanneken van der Hove v. Duijnkerke, we. Gielis Bastinck.
1 Sep.	1575	Gepken	Reijns met Joos van der Guchte.
11 Jun.	1576	Simon	Remons v. Lijre met Sophie van der Cruijce v. Antwerpen
21 Apl.	1680	Bartholmaus	de Rencl met Sara Rossel, hebbende hare geboden gehadt in Canvaije Eijlant volgens darune overgegevene, attestatie, van die selve Gemente.
23 Jan.	1575	Lijneken	van Rens met Pieter de Drossaert.
29 Mei	1590	Elisabeth	Rendtmeester met Nicolaijs Vaislin.
16 Feb.	1604	Elisabeth	Rentmeesters, we. Nicolas de Valens, met Goerart Cousijn.
. . Oct.	1621	Nicolaus	Resever v. Mombellair met Maria Dragon v. Loudon.
20 Mei	1574	Maijken	van Resselt met Wolter Kemens.
25 Dec.	1699	Johannes	Reap j.m. v. Leyden met Anna van Sprekens j d. v. s'Gravenhaegh.
19 Mar.	1587	Janneken	„ Reuterghem, we. Hendrick Winckens, met Jacob Speijts.
6 Sep.	1609	Johannes	„ Rhijn, wr. van Catharina Heuvels, met Johanna Smits, we. van Paulus Lowijs.
31 Mar.	1684	Anna	Richards met Thomas Thurston.
9 Sep.	1628	Cornelis	de Ricke v. Middelburch met Maria Roberts j.d. v. Sandwich.
28 Mei	1581	Pierone	Rickowaerts (. Rijckwaerts) met Christiaen Gorgu.
2 Sep.	1703	Adriaen	„ Ridder j.m. v. Bergen op Zoom met Catarina Gerritsen j.d. v. Bergen op Zoom.
12 Dec.	1591	Jaques	„ Riddere v. Antwerpen met Tanneken de Munck v. Ghendt, we. Joos van den Broecke.
13 Nov.	1571	Goeltghen	van Riemen met Giliaem Boogaerdt.
29 Mar.	1703	Adriana	„ Rietbroeck met Jan Hartsbergen.
25 Oct.	1614	Pierre	du Rieu v. Artois met Jannken Ootger v. Londen.
28 Mei	1601	Magdaleenken	Rijckaert met Goossen Gillis van de Grave.

5 Jun.	1626	Jacobmyne	Rijckaerts met Jeremias Coudron.
5 Oct.	1626	Catharyne	„ , wc. Anthony Farel, met Paulus van de Velde.
5 Mei	1574	Karolus	Rijckart, ghescit Theophilus, v. Nieukercke met Lowijseken Carbouiers v. Bevere.
9 Mar.	1573	Dierick	van der Rijcke v. Wassenberghe met Mechelijne Jaghers v. Haltem.
9 Mei	1590	Josijnken	de „ met Hans de Meulemeester.
4 Feb.	1604	Josijntgen	„ „ , wc. Jan van de Rivier, met Jacques Hobbel.
2 Feb.	1656	Elisabeth	„ „ met Pieter d'Olijslager.
7 Mei	1606	Abraham	„ „ , v. Oudenaerde met Catharine van Holder v. Engen.
8 Sep.	1578	Jan	„ Rijcker v. Kortrijke met Maijeken Backers v. Arendunck, wc. Jans Gilloole.
0 Sep.	1617	Susanna	Rijckwaerts met Salomon van der Broecke.
. Feb.	1616	Maria	Rijcwaert met Simon de Rae.
1 Jan.	1604	Jan	Rijcwaerts uyt d'landt v. Cleve met Elizabeth Cauwels v. Gloecestershere.
9 Jan.	1594	Abraham	de Rijke v. Oudenaerde met Ghijsbrechtken Willems v. Naerden, wc. Pieter Wijbo.
1 Oct.	1578	Pierijntge	s' Rijken, wc. Emanuel van Eijse, met Jan Nachtegaal.
1 Jan.	1575	Maijken	van Rijme met Jooris de Dobbelare.
1 Mar.	1584	Jan	Rijsselinck v. Roussen met Pierijne Neckers v. Thielt.
1 Jan.	1871	Talckien	Ringeling met Friedrich Oscar Beck.
3 Apl.	1576	Sibert	Rippen v. Emhden met Lyncken Faes v. Antwerpen.
7 Mei	1577	Saloman	van der Riviere v. Loven met Catherijne Blommaerts v. Antwerpen.
4 Mei	1596	Susanna	de „ met Samuel Dries.
8 Apl.	1612	Gulielmus	Rivius v. Londen met Susanna van der Strat, wc. Segers Schultijnck.
. Oct.	1618	Daniel	Robbert v. Steenwerck met Catharina Lamote, wc. Pieter Tierentijn.
9 Aug.	1626	Abigaijl	Robberts met Frederic de Clopper.
9 Sep.	1628	Maria	Roberts met Cornelis de Ricke.
5 Jan.	1603	Lysken	Robijns, wc. Dierick de Coster, met Symon Klerck.
1 Jan.	1593	Hesther	Robson met Jacus de Hoyon.
0 Jun.	1589	Guiliame	Robs v. Hoelaert bij Bruijssel met Lijsken Verhueghen v. Assche.
0 Aug.	1588	Catheline	de la Roche, wc. Arent Rijx, met Jan van Peene.
9 Apl.	1594	Catheline	„ „ , wc. Jan van Peene, met Fransois du Cogghe.
4 Feb.	1604	Catharijne	„ „ , wc. Franchoijs Cogge, met David Klijnckenberg.
5 Nov.	1593	Anna	Rockou met Pieter Doullay.
1 Mei	1573	Susanna	Roelant met Marten Kuijper.
4 Jul.	1588	Hans	„ v. Aelst met Janneken van den Kerckhoven v. Berghen bij Oudenaerde.
1 Jul.	1590	Margriete	Roelants, wc. Michiel Vots, met Jan Soillot.
5 Aug.	1593	Abigail	Roeter v. Sandtwyck met Catharina Gilberts wt d'lant v. Gulick, wc. Cornelis Evaerts.
1 Mei	1594	Cathelyne	Roevers met Nicholas van Buesecom de jonge.
6 Mei	1584	Martijntge	Rogiers met Cornelis de Boesijn.
9 Feb.	1696	Albertina	de Roij met Jan Symons.
2 Jan.	1581	Cornelis	Roisendaal v. Loven met Maijeken Backers v. Arendunck, wc. Jans de Rijker.
7 Mei	1571	Elijzabeth	van Roken met Adam der Kinderen.
6 Jan.	1658	Christian	Rolofsen, j.m. v. Holstein met Maria Dumbelle, j.d. v. Amsterdam.
8 Feb.	1586	Jacomynken	Rombouts met Lucas van Peene.
1 Jan.	1589	Pauwels	„ met Martinken Rosseau beyde v. Brussel.
4 Oct.	1584	Jan	Romeins v. s'Keijsersweirdt met Geertruijdt Thijssens van Gethkercke.
0 Nov.	1597	Abraham	van de Roo v. Londen met Elizabeth Eduwaerts v. London.
9 Sep.	1599	Sara	„ „ met Gillis Dierix.
5 Dec.	1583	Tanneken	van Roomers met Abel Oprun.
1 Aug.	1689	Barent	de Roos, j.m. v. Amersfort met Sara Barton, j.d. v. Amsterdam.
5 Oct.	1631	Jan	van Roose-becke, wr., met Janneken Mount.
2 Sep.	1608	Jan	Roose-boom wt t'land v. Gulick met Jone Olivier, Haertfordshecre (Hertfordshire)
1 Dec.	1593	Cornelis	van Roosendiele v. Loven met Lowijse de Lanou v. Rouce, wc. Daniel Gijschnck.
8 Jun.	1658	Hester	„ Rosebrech met Hendrick Veer.
5 Sep.	1577	Janneken	Rosseau met Cornelis van Essen.
1 Jan.	1589	Martinken	„ met Pauwels Rombouts.
1 Apl.	1590	Nicasius	Rossel v. Brugge met Jacomijnken Wils v. Meessene.
1 Apl.	1680	Sara	„ met Bartholmaus de Renci.
8 Dec.	1576	Lievyne	Rotars met Jacques Cornelissen.
1 Apl.	1579	Lucijne	Rotardtz, wc. Jakes Cornelissen, met Jan Koekerl.
4 Nov.	1603	Richard	Roug uijt landt van den Berge met Maria Pieterssz v. Londen.
7 Nov.	1634	Gerdtruij	Rousel met Jan der Driessche.
. Apl.	1616	Adriana	Rousseel met Passchier de Coninck.
7 Nov.	1604	Nicasius	Roussel v. Brugghe met Clara Jauss v. Antwerpen.
9 Mei	1584	Willem	Ruchen v. Epwijler in Gulicker landt met Catherina Moors van der Merssen.
7 Nov.	1603	Jacus	de Ruddere v. Antwerpen met Teysken van Steenacker, wc. Guillame de Hertoge.
2 Nov.	1672	Rebecca Elisabeth	Ruffler, van, met Ulrich Bergh.
8 Dec.	1607	Jan	de Ruijck v. Oudenaerde met Josyntken Pijcke, wc. Jacob de Coster.

29 Apl.	1617	Thomas	**Ruijs** v. Gorchnm met Judith Moenen v. Norwich.
9 Jun.	1617	Cornelis	van **Ruijt** v. Delft met Margareta Stroumelinck v. Gulick.
30 Jul.	1588	Hendricks	**Ruijters** v. d'lant v. Gulick met Willemijutken van de Velde.
25 Sep.	1614	Zacharias	**Ruijtinc** v. Norwich met Catharina Mochaert, we. Lambert Wilss.
5 Jan.	1589	Anna	**Ruijtincks** (v. **Rutinck**) met Josias Wijbo.
23 Jul.	1594	Elisabeth	**Ruijtinck** met Jacobus de Coninck.
19 Oct.	1602	Sijmeon	„ v. Noorwijts met Miriam Beijrens v. Londen.
14 Aug.	1604	Elisabeth	„ met Adrian van Damme.
30 Dec.	1600	Maria	„ , we. Joannes Marquinus, met Lieven van Hulse.
7 Nov.	1598	Marie	**Ruitinck** met Joannes Marquinus.
18 Dec.	1601	Symeon	**Rutijing** v. Norwich met Maria Proost, we. Tobias de Backer.
13 Oct.	1579	Rutger	van **Rumonde** met Agnete Janssens, we. Joris van Esse.
5 Apl.	1608	Abraham	**Russout** v. Gent met Catharine de Wale v. Engelmunster.
6 Jan.	1590	Pieter	**Rutinck** (v. **Ruijtinck**) v. Temscke met Lijntken s'Poorters, we. Jans Elssen.
3 Aug.	1602	Melchior	**Ruts** v. Autwerpen met Neeskeu Craene v. Dordrecht.
5 Jan.	1602	Jacus	de **Ruué** v. Londen met Janneken Godtschalck v. Londen.

27 Mei	1578	Marie	**Saals**, fa. Mr. Jacob, met Jan Severtsen.
24 Oct.	1857	Elisabeth	**Sack** met Wilhilm Johann Luis.
14 Oct.	1576	Anna	**Sael**, fa. Mr. Jacobs, met Jan Branwer.
7 Dec.	1602	Elisabeth	**Saers**, we. Eduaert Juhab, met Ananias Casier.
20 Apl.	1613	Susanna	le **Sage** met Abraham van den Bossche.
21 Apl.	1617	Maria	„ „ met Abraham Leemans.
17 Dec.	1588	Janneken	**Sagers** met Carel de Man.
5 Jun.	1604	Jan	**Sale** v. Rousel met Agncete Callaerts we. Geeraert van Basel.
1 Jun.	1619	Susanna	**Salé** met Abraham Bracht.
17 Aug.	1637	Catharina	**Salie** met Jan Grevinckhof.
8 Dec.	1590	Maeijken	**Samijn** met Nicolas de Deuxvilles.
7 Apl.	1608	Maria	„ , we Nicolaes de Deuxvilles, met Willem Adriaensz.
7 Nov.	1598	Jaques	„ v. Londen met Judith Artsen v. Londen.
26 Dec.	1586	Catelyne	van den **Sande**, we. Jan Janssen, met Adriaen van Damme.
15 Nov.	1593	Audricsijne	„ „ „ , we. Pieter de Ruijver, met Gulian de Waghenaer.
8 Jan.	1590	Francynken	**Sanders**, we. Gillis Lems, met Fredrick de Lorreine.
15 Jan.	1605	Thomas	**Santbens** v. Antwerpen met Catharijna Beelaerts v. Antwerpen.
29 Mar.	1608	Thomas	**Santgen** v. Antwerpen met Susanna van Paene v. Maldston.
27 Aug.	1605	Lijnken	**Santken**, we. Dierick Jansz, met Jeremias van der Elst.
15 Apl.	1604	Jacobmyntken	**Sarels**, we. Jan Bruuel, met Jacques Jacobsz.
28 Aug.	1571	Jacob	**Sargiant** v. Rouse met Barbel Scoort (?) v. Rouse.
.. Apl.	1615	Thomas	**Sarrel** v. Hamsbere (Hampshire) met Elisabeth van den Cornepnt wt den Haghe.
20 Sep.	1703	Anna Maria	**Sax** met Hendrick van Dijck.
13 Apl.	1572	Wouters	van **Sbinden** met Lijutghen Raenens.
5 Feb.	1583	Margnerite	**Sbockbriedt** met Hans Blummardt.
30 Sep.	1619	Arent	**Schaasberg** j.m. v. Deventer met Cornelia Catharina van Dijck, j.d. v. Utrecht, met attestatie van St.James.
11 Nov.	1571	Dirck	**Schaep** v. Donsborch met Tanneken Vermeer, we. Cornelis Reijnsen.
19 Jan.	1595	Amos	„ v. Londen met Anna van Groesbeck v. Antwerpen.
9 Oct.	1604	Susanna	„ met Hans der Moor.
.. Jan.	1619	Lenard	**Schaephuijsen** wt t'land v. Gulick met Anna Crijusen v. Londen.
29 Mei	1637	Lenaert	**Schaepheijsen** etc. met Anna Goose, we. Pieter Philips.
30 Apl.	1594	Willem	**Schaere** wt d'lant v. Gulick metMargariete Sweerts v. Houten, we. Henrick Jansa.
23 Aug.	1691	Jrnegard	**Schaff** met Hendrick Wapper.
17 Jun.	1589	Herman	**Schalker** v. Santen met Rebecca de Rane v. Antwerpen, we. Michiel de Hase.
20 Jan.	1572	Pieter	ver **Schagen** met Maijeken Schoerwijcksen beijde v. Antwerpen.
28 Mei	1590	Jan	**Schamparts** v. Liere met Lucretia Steenvaerts v. Oldenscele, we. Jans van den Berghe.
10 Nov.	1616	Anna	**Schapelinck** met Jan van Huevel.
.. Sep.	1620	Lenard	**Schaphusen** wt land v. Gulick met Trijnken Weerts mede wt t'land v. Gulick.
19 Jul.	1689	Pieter	**Scheffer** j.m. v. Weener in Oostenrijck met Engeltje Evers v. Delft.
21 Mei	1612	Cresken	**Scheel**, we. Pieter Suijders, met Hendrick Bosman.

13 Mei	1593	Maiken	**Scheers** met Hans Quishout.
3 Feb.	1573	Hans	van **Scheije** v. Antwerpen met Sophia van Montfort, we. Anthonis de Witte.
21 Aug.	1597	Sara	**Scheijrs** met Hans de Pauwe.
14 Sep.	1572	Wilhelmus	van der **Scheinhagen** met Marie van den Driessche v. Audenaerde.
1 Jan.	1594	Helena	**Schellekens**, we. Lienart Hughe, met Jan Nachtengale.
8 Jun.	1685	Hendrick	**Schenckel** j.m. v. Oudewater met Mary Hale j.d. v. Londen.
26 Jul.	1586	Joos	de **Schepp**, alias Mr. Kint v. Velst met Catheline Vierendael v. As, we. David Brents.
20 Aug.	1644	Jochim	**Schets** j.g. v. Meckelenburg met Sibijlla Kalthoff j.d. v. Solingen.
24 Oct.	1605	Jan	**Scheuninckx** v. Groeningh met Ester Schrenels v. Londen.
26 Mar.	1638	Samuel	**Schilt** j.g. v. Colchester met Sara Couper v. Sandwich.
17 Jul.	1576	Perijnken	van **Schin** met Jan Willenissen Reijbeke.
23 Mei	1587	Tanneken	**Schincks** met Jan de Vriese.
11 Nov.	1571	Tanneken	**Schippers**, we. Cornelis Hendries, met Gerardt Willemsz.
28 Apl.	1612	Matthias	**Schoaharen** v. Bruyssel met Susanna Vrolix v. Middelburgh.
19 Oct.	1598	Sara	**Schockaert** met David Toebast.
9 Jul.	1588	Gillis	**Schoemaker** v. Turnhout met Apolonia Pynaerts ооe v. Turnhout, we. Gillis Meynaert.
20 Jan.	1572	Maijeken	**Schoerwijcksen** met Pieter ver Schagen.
.. Jul.	1621	Martynken	**Schoesettes** met Passchier de Coninck.
18 Apl.	1581	Hans	**Scholands** v. Antwerpen met Agnete Klercks, we. Christoffel Says v. Antwerpen.
12 Jun.	1580	Maryne	**Scholteten** met Gerardt Gast.
.. Dec.	1712	Direck	**Scholte** j.m. v. Amsterdam met Agatha Peleil j.d. wonende in Westminster.
21 Apl.	1595	Maeijken	van **Schoonderhase** met Abraham de Bil.
1 Aug.	1596	Willem	„ **Schoouenvelde** v. Ruerne met Jossynken Neve Janssens v. Gendt.
6 Mei	1589	Maeyken	„ **Schouhuysen** met Guliam de Coninck.
3 Dec.	1587	Christijne	**Schouteden** met Adam Thoorn.
27 Sep.	1576	Lyneken	**Schouteyt** met Gottfridus van der Mase.
4 Jul.	1609	Christina	**Schouten**, we. Adam Hoorn, met Pieter Godschalck.
14 Jun.	1669	Anna	**Schouten** met Jan Ophalvens.
2 Jul.	1707	Clara	„ met Wiljam Min-bang.
17 Oct.	1594	Jans	**Schoutet** v. Ghendt met Beetken Parckhers v. Ghendt, we. Gillis van der Saude.
5 Feb.	1594	Lynken	**Schouteten**, we. Godfridus Masins, met Pieter van den Berghe.
12 Jan.	1607	Jan	**Schram** v. Aecken met Peryntgen Janssen v. Londen.
24 Oct.	1605	Ester	**Schrenels** met Jan Schouminex.
1 Aug.	1587	Pieter	van der **Schuere** v. Ninove met Janneken van den Berghe v. Cortryeke.
17 Jul.	1616	Susanna	**Schuijl** met Egbert Wybrands.
26 Jul.	1584	Willem	**Schuijten** v. Opeel met Mayken Mondiers v. Antwerpen.
6 Aug.	1588	Marie	**Schulder**, we. Willem Peters, met Mathys Darmans.
1 Sep.	1575	Pieter	**Schulpen** v. Zittert met Barbara Mocle, we. Jacobs Vergoes.
11 Dec.	1610	Zeger	**Schultijnck** v. Steenwijk met Susanna van der Straten v. Londen.
2 Mar.	1648	Georgius	**Schurstin** j.g. v. Coning met Mary Withal j.d. v. Blitchinglay in Surrcy.
10 Mei	1601	Joris	**Schut** v. Hamborch met Peroonken Corticls v. Londen.
28 Aug.	1571	Barbel	**Scoert** met Jacob Sargiant.
10 Jan.	1604	Jacobmyntken	**Secufs**, we. Richard de Merry, met Esechiel Wilckenhof.
1 Sep.	1573	Susanna	**Seghers** met Maurus Eeckholt
3 Nov.	1573	Gillis	„ v. Enghen met Janneken, we. Steven Herwijck.
11 Apl.	1571	Niclaes	„ v. Enghen met Jossyne van Auweghem v. Ghent.
8 Jul.	1595	Gielis	„ v. Engien met Anna Goosens v. Brussel, we. Jan Achtschellinck.
25 Feb.	1691	Dorothea	**Segwaert** met Frederick Heijsselaer.
6 Jan.	1596	Janneken	**Seijers** met Roelant Veltman.
28 Dec.	1585	Willem	**Seijs** v. Gent met Maurine Loentgen v. Hansbeke.
7 Sep.	1574	Katherijne	**Seijsens** met Hans Piiroen.
26 Aug.	1595	Lynken	„ , met Jan Pijfroen, met Jan Soillot.
17 Dec.	1601	Lynken	„ , we. Jan Serlot, met David van Vrijliehoven.
12 Dec.	1588	Jan	**Seis** v. Moldene met Lievine Skrox v. Ghent, we. Lieven Hempens.
29 Nov.	1590	Hans	**Sele** v. Rouee met Anna van Winterbeke v. Bruijsel.
13 Aug.	1611	Jacob	„ v. Andwerpen met Sara Wagenaer v. Londen.
3 Apl.	1599	Antonie	van **Seps** v. Antwerpen met Janneken Barotens wt Sticht v. Ceulen.
1 Jun.	1591	Catelyne	**Seraeckx**, we. Sijmon de Riddere, met Jacus van den Bossche.
19 Jul.	1597	Jan	**Sereijn** v. Diest met Magdalena van den Putte v. Antwerpen.
16 Oct.	1595	Huybrecht	**Sergeant** v. Rouee met Cathelyne van de Swalme v. Ghent, we. Pieter van de Linden.
15 Sep.	1578	Jacob	**Sergiant** v. Roussen met Maijeken s'Blauwers v. Roussen, we. Pieters Huygo.
6 Jan.	1579	Hans	van **Sevenkoten** v. Ghendt met Margariete Moreijns v. Audenarde, we. Thomas de Klock.
27 Mei	1578	Jan	**Seversen** v. Ambsterdam met Marie Saals v. Horne, fa. Mr. Jacob Saal.

15 Oct.	1605	Martynken	**Shonted**, we. Godefroy Gast, met Nicolyos Spalckman.
23 Nov.	1585	Jacomijnken	**Shouts** met Pieter van den Berghe.
6 Jan.	1596	Minaert	**Sibbels** v. Noorden met Mechelynken Oysteliouck v. Brugge, we. Bernaert de Swarte.
8 Feb.	1597	Paeschijnken .	**Sibille** met Samuel Marchant.
21 Sep.	1681	Rie	**Sicces** j.m. varentman v. Wouwsendo bij Snoeck met Maria Jans j.m. v. Delfshaven.
12 Jun.	1610	Anna	**Sickraet** met Joachim Pietersz.
.. Apl.	1612	Cornelia	„ v. Audwerpon met Lydia Reijninex v. Sandwich.
.. Feb.	1616	Cornelis	**Sickraed** v. Audwerpen met Elisabet, we. Thomas Cuyper v. Londen.
13 Sep.	1590	Jan	**Sijbrants** v. Amsterdam met Susanna Bultinx v. Londen.
11 Nov.	1691	Anneke	**Symons** met Salomon Paulus.
9 Feb.	1696	Jan	„ j.m. v. Bergen op Soom, soldaet onder de Compagnie van de overste Lieutenant Boham, met Albertina de Roy, j.d. v. s'Gravenhage.
11 Feb.	1623	Jacob	**Symonsz** v. Cleve met Elisabet Wils v. der Vere.
5 Nov.	1605	David	**Silverlinck** met Susanna de Flaudres.
7 Mar.	1694	Jacomina	**Simonds** met Jan Hendricks.
19 Feb.	1572	Tanneken	**Simons** met Elias de Mey.
27 Oct.	1590	Barbara	„ , we. Jacques van Navarre, met Ghyselbrecht Caerluijn.
31 Oct.	1592	Isaac	„ v. Antwerpen met Clarken Causemaker v. Steenweerte.
28 Nov.	1609	Jacobmyntge	**Sisaux** met Hans Franck.
23 Aug.	1579	Bartholomeus	in der **Sittardt** v. Dalen met Nelleken Lemmens v. Maastricht.
24 Jul.	1689	Jan Willem	**Sivel** j.m. v. Ziegen in't graefschap v. Nassau met Maria van der Steen v. s'Gravenhaegh.
21 Feb.	1600	Janneken	**Six** met Hartgeer Wouterssz.
12 Dec.	1588	Lievine	**Skrox**, we. Lieven Hempens, met Jan Seis.
.. Oct.	1621	Nathanael	**Slack** v. Suffolke met Sijken Tierentyn v. Enghen.
13 Mar.	1576	Marten	**Sleipen** v. Valkenborch met Janneken Volvoets v. Wacstene.
15 Oct.	1611	Martha	**Sleuwen**, we. Jan Lambert, met Michiel Droeshout.
21 Nov.	1594	Maeyken	**Slijnckenburg** met Pauwels Toelast.
1 Feb.	1579	Jaspar	**Sluijssken** v. Arnem met Cathlyne Verhammen v. Roist, we. Gillis de Lowijs.
7 Sep.	1572	Hans	de **Smedt** v. Antwerpen met Mayeken van de Putte.
20 Jul.	1581	Marie	„ met Godefroy Crijnts.
1 Sep.	1584	Anthony	**Smidt** met Lyntgen Halffbunders, we. Jans van Tungerlo, beyde v. Antwerpen.
3 Mei	1586	Hendrick	in de **Smit** v. Hemsberghe met Judith Berrenoet v. Londen.
13 Sep.	1601	Maeyken	de „ met Michiel de Knuijt.
9 Ap.	1592	Arnout	„ v. bij Maseijck met Susanna de Pont v. Antwerpen, we. Vincent Andries.
2 Dec.	1606	Sara	**Smith** met Hans Nicasius.
18 Mei	1690	Gerard	„ j.m. v. Zutphen met Christina van Poelenburgh j.d. v. Utrecht.
6 Sep.	1699	Johanna	**Smits**, we. Paulus Lowijs, met Johannes van Rhijn.
1 Dec.	1594	Willem	**Smuijsers** wt Sticht v. Toor met Barbara Joossens v. Aelst, we. Anthoni de Fosse.
6 Dec.	1597	Willem	„ v. Thoir, uit lant v. Luijck, met Trysken Scox v. Corten, we. Pieter Akeloot.
24 Mei	1575	Cornelis	**Smulders** v. Luenen met Anna Giners v. Addington.
9 Apl.	1594	Barbelken	**Sneckers**, we. Fransois de Clievere, met Picter van Belowys.
30 Mei	1626	Maijken	**Sneep**, we. Jan Busken, met Jan Vese. (v. Snicx).
27 Dec.	1624	Adriaenken	**Sneps** met Mattheus Denni.
5 Jun.	1575	Gillis	**Snepgat** v. Meeuene met Janneken Neese, we. Joris Letwerk, v. Borborch.
22 Jun.	1595	Maeijken	**Snicx**, we. Jan van den Poorten, met Hans Busken. (v. Snip, Sneep).
19 Feb.	1661	Pieter Janson	van **Snigelbergh** v. Tiel met Anna Dicricx v. Campen v. Sprang.
.. Mei	1621	Maeijken	**Snijders**, we. Eduward Simson, met Abraham de Biellards.
11 Apl.	1591	Maeijken	**Snip** met Hans van der Poorten. (v. Snicx).
8 Feb.	1615	Susanna	„ met Hendric van der Bancke.
5 Aug.	1857	Anna Christina Margaretha	**Snoek** met Johann Genge Graff.
.. Jun.	1640	Johanna	**Soen** met Rombaet Jacobsen.
10 Jun.	1622	Anna	„ met Martin Dierixsen.
15 Nov.	1590	Lijnken	**Soenbens** met Dierick Janssen.
11 Sep.	1604	Jan	**Soenen** v. Norwich met Tanneken Pifron, we. Jan van Steele.
3 Mei	1585	Marsijntgen	**Soens** met Everardt Steenverssen.
30 Apl.	1594	Janneken	„ met Gillis Lioens.
13 Apl.	1589	Janneken	**Soijvers**, we. Jacus Mentijn, met Nicolas van den Poorten.
23 Oct.	1576	Jan	**Soillot**, fs. Jans v. Breussel, met Rachel le Quienure v. Antwerpen.
21 Jul.	1590	Jan	„ v. Bruijssel met Margriete Roelants v. Doornick, we. Michiel Vots.
20 Nov.	1593	Jan	„ v. Bruijssel met Maeijken Valx v. Meenene.
26 Aug.	1595	Jan	„ v. Brussel met Lynken Scijsens v. Ghent, we. Jan Pyfroen.
10 Jun.	1595	Hester	**Soilot** met Haus Ketelbouter.

28 Oct.	1583	Karel	Sohier v. Ghendt met Susanna van Neerhagen v. Antwerpen.
6 Nov.	1604	Elisabeth	van Sold met Philips Jacobs.
2 Aug.	1614	Maria	„ Soldt met Jacob Harruwijn. (v. Solt.)
16 Mei	1609	Sijnken	Solens met Jacob Westerman.
30 Aug.	1586	Jan	Solis v. Bruijssel met Maecken Labus v. Labus.
30 Aug.	1586	Hans	van Solt v. Antwerpen met Janneken Wijgants v. Breda.
11 Nov.	1623	Abraham	„ „ v. Londen met Elisabeth Bonnecl v. Norwich.
17 Sep.	1633	Maria	„ „ , we. Jacob Herrewijn, met David Otgeer. (v. Soldt.)
1 Dec.	1607	Ester	Somer met Jan de Meyer.
29 Sep.	1631	Pieter	de „ , j.g. v. Yperen met Judith Caveele j.d. v. Colchester.
14 Jun.	1597	Maeyken	„ Somere, we. Lambrecht van Aken, met Jan Yde.
10 Aug.	1580	Maeyken	t' Somers met Lambrecht van der Lake.
1 Oct.	1611	Maijken	Somers, we. Jan Yde, met Cornelis Jansz.
21 Feb.	1609	Herman	Sonbery v. Cuelen met Anna Hobbels, we. Adolf Stact.
5 Nov.	1678	Janneken	Sondergelt met Pieter Derveau.
12 Jan.	1608	Jan	Sonnevil v. Neuleke met Paschyne van Aken, we. Dierlck Jansz.
12 Jan.	1637	Jacobus	Souburg j.m. v. Leyden met Emerentia van Velle j.d. v. Amersfort.
15 Oct.	1605	Nicolyes	Spalckman v. Anholt met Martynken Shoutal, (we.) van Godefroy Gast.
22 Aug.	1609	Catharina	Spaltman met Pieter Beeckman.
26 Aug.	1708	Johannes	van Spawen j.m. v. den Haegh met Jehanna Meijers j.d. v. Nimwegen.
14 Aug.	1586	Jan	Speeckaert v. Bruijssel met Maerken de Vriese v. Delft.
.. Mei	1613	Hans	„ , v. Brussel met Maijken Suijex, we. Thomas Peperman.
17 Mei	1573	Josynken	Speeckaerts met Gillis de Koster.
2 Feb.	1579	Josyne	Speeckardts, we. Gillis s'Kosters, met Arnoudt Buijs.
3 Mar.	1584	Josyntgen	Speeckarts, we. Arnoudt Buijs met Pieter Brache.
28 Sep.	1619	Jacob	Speckmeijer wt Westphalen met Susanne van der Weyer v. Londen.
1 Sep.	1579	Pieter	Speelhoven v. Luijth bij Maastricht met Cathlyne de Quesnoy v. Roussen.
19 Mar.	1588	Jacob	Speijts vut Sticht v. Cuelen met Janneken van Reuterghem v. Nevele we. Heindrick Winckens.
1 Jul.	1595	Jossinken	van der Spick met Charles Braems.
1 Jul.	1595	Catheline	„ „ met Hans Zeghers.
24 Jun.	1595	Pieter	„ „ Spiere v. Oijke by Oudenaerde met Maeijken de Winne v. Brussel, we. Hendrick Baetens.
19 Jun.	1597	Jan	van „ v. Oudenaerde met Susann Joossens v. Noorwith.
9 Apl.	1577	Magdalena	Spierijnx, we. Reynier Thyssens, met Joos de Waghenare.
12 Jun.	1575	Lowijs	van Spiera v. Mate bij Oudenaerde mes Jelyne Huijsman v. Rousse.
1 Jul.	1595	Jeremynken	van der Spijck met Nicolas Lestré.
. Feb.	1612	Wilebrord	Spijs v. t'landt v. Gulick met Janneken Jacobs, we. Anthoni Cotron.
. Apl.	1621	Wilbord	„ wt t'land v. Gulick met Maria de Deux-villes v. Londen.
23 Mar.	1573	Jan	Spillers v. Melden met Josyne Swinnen, we. Joos de Grave.
10 Dec.	1594	Magdaleene	Spirincx, we. Joos de Waegenaere, met Jan Janssen.
19 Jul.	1575	Antonyne	Spitters, we. Mathijs Anthonissen, met Albert Ghijsbertssen.
1 Mei	1597	Reynier	Spoormaecker v. Venlo met Anna Crimwaen v. Oxfortshier. (Oxfordshire.)
25 Dec.	1571	Magdalene	Sporincksen, we. Hans Brands, met Reynier Thyssen.
25 Dec.	1699	Anna	van Sprekens met Johannes Reup.
21 Oct.	1575	Peroneken	Sprents met Bartholomeus van Bossu.
18 Feb.	1582	Margriete	Sprinckhuysen met Pieter Jansen.
6 Aug.	1579	Jan	de Springer v. Brugge met Eva Herrisson, geboren te Londen.
23 Apl.	1633	Sara	Springers met Philippus van de Walle.
27 Apl.	1573	Allbrecht	Sprock v. Bremen met Margriete Appels v. Wulverghem.
26 Dec.	1586	Josijne	Sprooten met Bartholomeus van der Winckel.
2 Apl.	1579	Adolps	Staat v. Duijsseldorp met Catheryne Prents, we. Pieter Albrechts v. Meessene.
21 Sep.	1589	Anthony	Staelens v. Ghendt met Barken van Dacle v. Rouex.
20 Feb.	1582	Adolf	Staet v. Dusseldorp met Tanneken Hobels v. Wilverghem.
. Aug.	1620	Daniel	„ „ v. Londen met Elisabet Abeels v. Londen.
17 Jan.	1591	Lucas	Staffenay v. Bruyssel met Catherine Swynedons v. Belle.
24 Dec.	1588	Hans	Staffeney met Janneken Minnaerts, beijde v. Bruyssel.
6 Oct.	1601	David	Stainerj v. Ceulen met Abigail de Meteren v. Londen.
12 Sep.	1585	Arent	Stalens v. Ghent met Janneken Svisschers v. Aerslot bij West.
3 Sep.	1588	Hendrick	„ v. Ghent met Janneken Svisschers v. Aerslot bij West.
17 Mei	1590	Arnout	Stalpaert bij Brugghe met Eva Janssen v. Oxfort.
17 Nov.	1612	Franchoijs	Stampoen v. Lane met Tanneken de Brune, we. Bernard Bauwdwijn.
19 Oct.	1602	Maeyken	van Standonck met Pieter Cleymans.
15 Jan.	1604	Herman	Stappaert v. Callar met Neelken Prince v. Antwerpen.
9 Oct.	1586	Herman	„ v. Calekere in Cleve met Margriete Maes uit Westmerlant.
29 Dec.	1586	Wouter	Stappen v. bij Wynoxberghe met Cathelyne Meyer v. Meenen.
. Aug.	1613	Judith	van Stavele met Jacob Cole.

26 Jul.	1703	Maria	**Steckman** met Jan de Bruijer.
24 Jul.	1689	Maria	van der **Steen** met Jan Willem Sivel.
2 Jun.	1594	Trijsken	van **Steenacker** met Guiliame d'Hertoghe.
27 Nov.	1603	Teysken	„ „ , we. Guillame de Hertoge, met Jacus de Ruddere.
26 Jul.	1586	Cornelis	**Steenaert** v. Gendt met Jossyne Oleghaerts v. Petegem, we. Willem de Meule-meester.
1 Jun.	1595	Cornelis	„ v. Gent met Christine van der Haghen v. Ipren.
13 Mei	1585	Lucretia	**Steenberchs** met Jan van den Berge.
14 Mei	1611	Jan	van **Steenberghe** v. Deventer met Elisabeth Hendricx v. Londen.
20 Jul.	1619	Elisabet	van der **Steene**, we. Jan Snoeck, met Jan Hendricx.
22 Jan.	1605	Debora	van **Steenput** met Pieter van Gistel.
2 Jul.	1611	Debora	„ , we. Pieter van Gistel, met Passchier Thomaer.
28 Mei	1590	Lucretia	**Steenvaerts**, we. Jan van den Berghe, met Jan Schamparts.
17 Mei	1579	Everds	**Steen-vers** v. Oldenseel, van Twent ondert sticht v. Vtrecht, met Maijcken Pieters, we. Jans Cornelissen, v. s'Hertogenbosch.
31 Mei	1585	Everardt	**Steenverssen** v. Okleseele met Marsijntgen Soeus v. Yseghem.
.. Aug.	1752	Johanna Maria Barbara	**Steenweg** met Adolph Jorgens.
20 Aug.	1590	Lijnken	**Steffels** met G. int Choor.
5 Nov.	1696	Steven	**Stegman** j.m. v. Haerlem met Willemtje Balthes j.d. v. Amsterdam.
22 Jun.	1578	Everts	**Steijn-versen** v. Oldensteel ondert sticht v. Utrecht met Lyntgen Christiaens v. Londen geboren.
11 Aug.	1590	Abigail	**Stel** met Jan Clerck.
9 Dec.	1600	Magdalena	van **Stelant**, we. Jan Costerlinck, met Anthony Reijniers.
1 Sep.	1579	Lieven	van der **Stele** v. Ghendt met Joryntgen Haywarden, we. Matthens Stilte, v. Ghendt.
23 Jul.	1594	Susanna	**Stell** met Hans van Kielwalts.
7 Mei	1592	Lievon	van der **Stelt** met Sara Bouters, beyde v. Ghent.
31 Mei	1596	Lievijne	„ „ „ met Jan Niclaesz.
27 Sep.	1590	Celynken	**Stelte** met Francois Loose.
7 Mei	1611	Agnete	van der „ met Engel Annesen.
5 Apl.	1613	Sara	**Stelter** met Gedeon Faulcon.
.. Apl.	1612	Lucas	**Stendel** v. Staden met Maria Broynes v. Colchester.
10 Mei	1590	Sara	**Stenners** met Marten Pauwels Hemskercke.
6 Dec.	1610	Maria	**Stentelinx** met Joannes Lauroijns.
.. Feb.	1619	Judith	**Stepen** met Gerard Brand.
4 Nov.	1600	Gheertruijdt	**Sterck** met Jan van Loo.
12 Jul.	1590	Jossynken	de **Stercke** met Isaac Benij.
29 Mar.	1575	Pieter	„ „ v. Cortrijcke met Sibille Quirins, we. Matheus van der Goele, v. Zuytphen.
12 Aug.	1571	Rutger	**Stevens** v. s'Hertogenbosche met Janneken Deijnots v. Ghent.
15 Jun.	1585	Rutger	„ v. s'Hertogenbosche met Margriete Meuleners v. Putthem.
. 8 Jan.	1614	Susanna	„ met Lowys van Damme.
.. Jan.	1619	Jan	„ v. Radlinghen wt t'land van den Berge met Sara van den Broecke v. Colchester.
9 Apl.	1683	Maria	**Stevenson** met Maerten de Witt.
9 Jun.	1588	Pierinken	**Sticninx** met Sijmon Leeman.
24 Mei	1590	Goelken	**Stiers**, we. Wynant Verhulst, met Henrick Janssen.
27 Dec.	1593	Ghoolken	„ , we. Hendrick Janssen, met Dierick van Clopperys.
.. Aug.	1620	Elisabet	**Stigrits** met Hans Jorigen.
27 Oct.	1575	Jan	**Stilkens** v. Eijberghe met Maijken Taverniers v. Meenene.
5 Feb.	1594	Mathens	**Stilte** v. Vupkercke met Janneken van der Poele v. Douvre. (Dover).
4 Nov.	1599	Ezechiel	**Stilter** v. Doover met Janneken van Meters v. Ouseele.
6 Jun.	1596	Judith	de **Stiltere** met Aaron de Grave.
23 Oct.	1586	Philips	„ „ v. Haselbinert met Susanna Buens v. Londen.
4 Feb.	1584	Josijne	**Stilters** met Bartholomeus Lauwardts.
9 Jan.	1588	Hans	**Stockbrigs** v. Louden met Jacomynken van Peene v. Roesselare, we. Arthus van Campen.
.. Feb.	1615	Richard	**Stokes** wt Staffordshere met Margareta, we. Pieter Houwaer.
25 Sep.	1599	Balthazar	**Stomfhousen** v. Disternich wt lant v. Gulick met Catheline Gruters v. Maeijstricht.
.. Jul.	1620	Agnata	van **Storcx** met Pieter van Nuffel.
1 Feb.	1603	Jan	**Storm** v. d'lant v. Gulick met Tanneken Lodewijckx v. Antwerpen.
23 Dec.	1574	Arent	de **Stoute** v. Oudenaerde met Janneken van der Venne, we. Daniel van den Hove, v. Breussel.
23 Apl.	1592	Janneken	van der **Straete** met Marcus Willeboort.
27 Aug.	1588	Lisken	„ „ **Straeten** met Nicolaes Waghener.
5 Apl.	1597	Joos	„ „ „ v. Ghendt met Anna Pifferoen v. Londen.
21 Feb.	1604	Maria	van **Strafeele** met Joos Ootger.
28 Apl.	1612	Susanna	van der **Strat**, we. Segers Schultynck, met Gulielmus Rivins.

22 Dec.	1584	Phlips	van der **Strate** v. Mechelen met Calleken van Nimmeghen v. Poperinge, we. Conrrt Govertsen.
18 Jan.	1586	Agatha	van ,, , we. Gillis Vershiele, met Verroe Martens.
13 Feb.	1593	Lieven	van der ,, v. Gent met Maeijken Weijtens v. Oudenaerde, we. Gillis van Herweghen.
7 Jun.	1580	Pieter	,, ,, **Straten** v. Geertzbergen met Judith Janssens, v. Lorowoldt int laudt v. Benten, we. Laurentz Thomassz.
7 Jul.	1588	Lynken	,, ,, ,, met Jan Willemets.
8 Oct.	1592	Hans	,, ,, ,, v. Ghent met Su anna van Lochen v. Maidston.
11 Dec.	1610	Susanna	,, ,, ,, met Zeger Schultynck.
4 Aug.	1629	Margarita	**Strijck** met Jacob Swedersz.
14 Nov.	1591	Jacus	de **Strijgher** v. Camerick met Maeijken Vermeyren v. s'Hertogenbosch.
9 Mei	1594	Wouter	van **Strijpe** v. s'Hertogenbossche met Maeyken de Martelaere v. Ghendt.
2 Mei	1626	Grietgen	**Stroomengels**, we. Cornelis van Ruyt, met Jacob Lenarts.
9 Jun.	1617	Margareta	**Stroumelinck** met Cornelis van Ruijt.
13 Apl.	1578	Jakemyntgen	**Strubbens** met Hans Korckeel.
15 Feb.	1596	Elisabeth	**Stuijtelinx** met Lambrecht Wilsen.
. . Jun.	1620	Maijken	**Sucht**, we. Jan Speeckart, met Thomas Prentis
. . Mei	1643	Maijken	**Suijcx**, we. Thomas Pepermaen, met Hans Speeckaert.
27 Jun.	1615	Anthony	van **Sups** v. Antwerpen met Lynken Moerminex v. Amdwerpen.
10 Apl.	1586	Daniel	**Sutebeen** v. Emblen met Catheline van Pelt v. Ghele.
15 Jul.	1595	Macyken	**Sux**, we. Willem Adams, met Thomas Peperman.
26 Feb.	1594	Janneken	van der **Swaeleme**, we. Willem Joons, met Thomas Morghen.
16 Oct.	1595	Cathelyne	van de **Swalme**, we. Pieter van de Linden, met Huybrecht Sergeant.
23 Jun.	1607	Hans	**Swart** v. Lnbeeq met Catharina Hauwe, we. Toussain Laps.
4 Aug.	1629	Jacob	**Swedersz** j.g. v. Pater-borg met Margarita Strijck j.d. wi het laudt v. Gulick.
2 Sep.	1571	Josyne	**Sweme** met Joos de Grave. (**v. Swinnen**).
28 Nov.	1581	Iken	**Sweers** met Dierick Nuwaerts.
15 Nov.	1590	Ambrosius	de **Swerte** v. Hont-ooten met Debora S'Meulenaere v. Norwijts.
3 Jul.	1582	Govart	,, **Swerts** v. Vtrecht met Janneken de Maars v. Antwerpen.
2 Feb.	1591	Jacob	**Sweerts** v. bij Maseick met Tanneken van Hillegaerde v. Bruijssel we. Laureins de Boulogne.
19 Jan.	1574	Hendrick	**Sweertsen** v. Cranenburch met Lyneken Gellekens v. Antwerpen.
17 Jan.	1591	Catherine	**Swinedons** met Lucas Stallenay.
23 Mar.	1573	Josine	**Swinnen**, we. Joos de Grave, met Jan Spillers. (**v. Sweme**).
8 Mar.	1575	Jossijne	,, , we. Hans Speleers, met Jaspar de Neufville.
18 Jan.	1601	Tanneken	**Switsers** met Hans Donckel.
28 Mei	1524	Jan	**Swol** v. Emden met Marie v. Bocholt v. Hasselt.

26 Dec.	1593	Lijnken	van **Taeken** met Ghenaert Brans.
2 Oct.	1595	David	**Taelman** v. Maidston met Magdaleene van Dale v. Nuijsse.
7 Apl.	1620	Sara we. Josias	**Taelmans** met Abraham van den Broecke.
5 Jun.	1707	Helena	**Tammerus** met Arnoldus Emmori.
28 Jan.	1595	Fransois	**Tampoen** v. Lane met Lynken Thora v. Antwerpen.
11 Mar.	1572	. . . . . .	**Taneriers** (? **Taveniers**), we. Jans Weychmans, met Mattheus Tielen.
7 Oct.	1575	Maijken	**Taverniers** met Jan Stilkens.
8 Jan.	1597	Catheline	,, , we. Jan Angele, met Willem Martens.
1 Dec.	1577	Lieven	**Temmerman** (**v. Timmerman**) v. Ghent met Chaerken de Herde, we. Gabriel du Pourcau.
4 Oct.	1595	Willem	de **Tepper** v. Brussel met Tanneken Huijsman v. Rouee, we. Pieter Beaufart.
12 Feb.	1593	Jan	**Terayen** v. Emmerick met Susanna Felix v. Ghendt.
1 Nov.	1574	Gheerardt	**Terhille** v. Emmerick met Maijken Bouckelions, we. Jan Leeman, v. Veurne.
1 Jan.	1617	Susanna	**Terray** met Jacob Manjat.
4 Mar.	1591	Jan	**Terry** j.m. v. Amsterdam met Mary Holmwood j.d. v. Tendridge in Surrey.
3 Nov.	1610	Trijnken	**Teunis** met Craft Kessels.
1 Dec.	1614	Willem	**Theunissen** v. Haerlem met Maria Hermans v. Sandwich.
8 Sep.	1588	Catelijne	**Theeus** met Nicolas de Deuxvilles.
4 Jul.	1594	Maria	,, met Jacus Cool.
1 Apl.	1594	Jaques	**Theeuws** v. Antwerpen met Susanna van Pilkem v. Antwerpen.
9 Sep.	1602	Isaac	**Theus** v. Londen met Rachel Hekelaers ooc v. Londen.

T

12 Jul.	1608	Elisabeth	Thijs, we. Hendrick Janssz, met Daniel Godschalck.
24 Dec.	1587	Jacus	Thijsman v. Antwerpen met Jossinken Piers v. Oudenaerde, we. Marten d Visscher de Jonge.
25 Dec.	1571	Reynier	Thijssen uit Gulicker landt met Magdalone Sporincksen, we. Hans Branda.
10 Aug.	1602	Hermyntken	„ met Jan Bloeme.
4 Oct.	1614	Gillis	„ van der Veer met Anna de Coninck v. Londen.
25 Sep.	1649	Francois	„ j.m. v. Vlissingen met Dorothe Calant j.d. v. Londen.
23 Jan.	1582	Bertken	Thijsens met Henrick Jacopsen.
4 Oct.	1584	Geertruydt	„ met Jan Romeins.
2 Jul.	1611	Passchier	Thomaer v. Nieuwkercke met Debora van Steenput v. Antwerpen, we Pieter va Gistel.
.. Aug.	1621	Jan	Thomar v. Colchester met Catharina Fromenteen mede v. Colchester.
23 Dec.	1606	Sara	Thomare v. Leijden met Moses Calant.
9 Oct.	1610	Rachel	„ met Jan de Wijs.
3 Dec.	1587	Adam	Thoorn v. Eerpen met Christijne Schonteden v. Dilsen int lant v. Gulick.
28 Jan.	1595	Lijnken	Thora met Fransois Tampoen.
27 Feb.	1593	Abigail	Thoris met H. Christiaens.
4 Nov.	1673	Thomas	Thornberry j.m. v. Eckington in Worcestershire met Anna Catarina op de Beecl j.d. v. Loudon, getrout van Doct. Mason in die Parochie genaem Pieter de Pouvre.
31 Mar.	1584	Thomas	Thurston j.m. v. de Grave in Gelderlant met Anna Richards j.d. v. London.
11 Mar.	1572	Mattheus	Tielen met .... Taneriers, we. Jan Weijchmans.
6 Jan.	1595	Gillis	Tielman v. bij Loeven met Stijnken Lambrechts v. Eeckeloo, we. Willem de Bij
30 Oct.	1606	Jan	„ v. Turnhout met Neelken, we. Adriaen Vereycke.
20 Aug.	1583	Chistoffel	Tielmans v. Tour met Josijntgen van Boetsele, we. Pauwels Buijs, v. Audenard
22 Mei	1610	Pieter	Tierenteijn v. Eugene met Pierijnken de Meij, we. Joos Nachtegael.
29 Nov.	1614	Pieter	„ v. Eugene met Catharyne Lamoot, we. Goossens van Beke.
.. Oct.	1621	Sijken	Tierentijn met Nathanael Slack.
1 Sep.	1594	Cornelis	Tiers v. Ghendt met Maeijken de Dorpere v. Thelt, we. Dierick Rijenroij.
10 Sep.	1611	Jaspar	Tijan v. Londen met Anna Aelst, we. Joris Bolle.
4 Sep.	1610	Paulus	Tijpoots v. Diest met Ogken de Beijr, we. Fr. Michiels.
4 Oct.	1604	Hermken	Tijssen, we. Jan Blomme, met Jan Baptista v. Landen.
13 Feb.	1634	Gerard	Tilhorst j.g. v. Bronckhorst in Gelderlandt met Catharine de Meijer j.d. v. Cc chester.
26 Dec.	1638	Gerard	„ , wr. van Johanna Wessel, in Gelderlandt met Anna Bochiljoen j.d. Sandwich.
.8 Dec.	1611	Herman	Timmerman (v, Temmerman) v. Osenbrug met Alita Clant, we. van Jaques (Bije.
28 Jul.	1594	Jan	Timmers vut d'lant v. Gulick met Clerken Phlips v. bij Maseijck.
29 Apl.	1578	Sijmeon	Tirenteijns v. Aeynen met Magriete van Doornijck v. Ghelen.
10 Jul.	1574	Joos	Toeback v. Ghent met Janneken Holmans v. Antwerpen.
1 Jan.	1583	Pauwels	Toebast v. Ghent met Judith Oijevaers v. Londen.
21 Nov.	1594	Pauwels	„ v. Ghent met Maeijken Slijnckenburg v. Antwerpen.
19 Oct.	1598	David	„ v. Ghendt met Sara Schockaert v. Bruijssel.
13 Jan.	1597	Evaert	Toeput v. Hamborg met Elisabeth Meulemeesters v. Ghendt.
6 Feb.	1592	Dedier	de la Tombe v. Bruissel met Susanna Walschaert v. Antwerpen.
21 Apl.	1679	Maria	du Toij met Baltes Cassier.
8 Mei	1596	Maeijken	Tollens met Anthoni Woesthoff.
1 Aug.	1588	Maeijken	van Tongheren, we. Hans Inischout, met Everaert Reijers.
13 Dec.	1627	Thomas	Townsin j.g. v. Londen met Maria Willems j.d. v. Middelborgh.
4 Jun.	1592	Jan	Trampzo v. Rochester met Hester Gheerarts v. Brugghe.
5 Jul.	1638	Magdalena	Trappaert met Jan Wirne.
17 Oct.	1598	Niclaes	Trapper v. Antwerpen met Magdalena Kempen v. Antwerpen.
4 Dec.	1571	Cecilia	van Treinen met Pieter de Vosen.
20 Feb.	1603	Pieter	Tremont v. Harlinghen met Calleken van den Berghe v. Mechelen, we. J Pieters.
18 Jun.	1684	Pieter	Trenel j.m. met Jannexen Dailje j.d, beyde v. Amsterdam.
6 Nov.	1578	Geerardt	Trenijen v. Horebecke met Frantzijne Everarden v. Nieuw Aereken.
25 Feb.	1691	Hans Jacob	Trettenbach j.m. v. Berne in Switzerland met Cornelia Frissard, we. Will Stammelaer.
9 Feb.	1591	Sara	Trioen met David de Moere.
16 Oct.	1599	Abraham	„ v. Londen met Leonora Vierendaels v. Antwerpen.
3 Jun.	1600	Moses	„ v. Londen met Sara van der Peele v. Sandwits.
17 Jul.	1604	Esther	„ met Guillame Courten.
6 Dec.	1601	Jan	Troemans v. Turnhout met Clerken van der Fonteijne v. Andwerpen, we. Fr choijs Garret.
30 Apl.	1588	Margriete	Trots met Gillis Kosters.

16 Dec.	1599	Pieter
18 Oct.	1710	Hugo
26 Jul.	1601	Janneken
20 Dec.	1603	Maijken
14 Apl.	1628	Rachel
19 Mei	1607	Susanna
19 Mei	1607	Janneken
9 Dec.	1600	Marten
19 Jul.	1586	Janneken
6 Dec.	1601	Janneken
. . Feb.	1506	Anna
14 Oct.	1571	Janneke
13 Feb.	1575	Emanuel
30 Aug.	1606	Neelken we. Adriaen
. . Jan.	1626	Christopher
31 Mei	1680	Gisbert
9 Mei.	1602	Sara
13 Sep.	1584	Elardt
11 Aug.	1584	Tomtgen
24 Feb.	1575	Sophie
10 Jun.	1580	Lijsken
28 Jan.	1595	Jacus
22 Apl.	1604	Catharijne
8 Jan.	1605	Pieter
18 Apl.	1620	Thomas
11 Nov.	1571	Tanneken
14 Nov.	1591	Maeijken
14 Dec.	1595	Martijuken
20 Jan.	1603	Catelijne
1 Nov.	1631	Dina
31 Jan.	1576	Barbelken
5 Mei.	1579	Pirone
1 Jan.	1627	Jan
9 Jul.	1644	Lea
17 Mei	1576	Catherine
22 Mei	1585	Catheline
2 Mei	1756	Adolf
30 Oct.	1604	Jan
17 Feb.	1692	Gerrit Pauwels
29 Mar.	1573	Tanneken
. . Jan.	1618	Abraham
24 Jan.	1611	Susanna
22 Aug.	1598	Abraham
2 Mar.	1579	Abraham
11 Jul.	1592	Pierijne
22 Oct.	1592	Sara
30 Mei	1626	Jan
28 Jan.	1609	Sara
22 Aug.	1609	Elizabeth
11 Jul.	1633	Maijken
26 Jul.	1586	Catheline
16 Oct.	1599	Leonora
4 Dec.	1576	Barbara
14 Nov.	1605	Maijken
7 Jan.	1595	Susanna
11 Dec.	1586	Jossijuken
4 Nov.	1593	Rachel
4 Jan.	1594	Gelijne
22 Apl.	1595	Susanna
17 Apl.	1604	Jan
14 Nov.	1602	Elisabeth
8 Mei	1576	Anna
22 Apl.	1691	Martijntje

Verboeckel v. Belle met Olive Perne v. Ipren, we. Pieter de Mey.
Verboom j.m. v. Rotterdam met Elijsabeth Margarita v. Loperen mede v. Rotterdam.
Verbrugge met Joos Jacops.
   ,, , we. Hendrick de Vaddere, met Nicolas Molkebeke.
   ,, met Joos Breeders.
Verbrugghe met Jaqnes Nachtegael.
   ,, met Pieter Maelbout.
Verburck v. Hansbeke met Auromyntken Provenger v. Ipren, we. Michiel Verdonck.
Vercamer met Jan Wessels.
Verckmen, we. Jan Wessels, met Daniel de Bla.
Vercoijle met Wonter Aertsz de Jonge.
Verdoncke met Willem Bonte.
Vereijcke v. Cortrijcke met Cecilie Gompfaets v. Gatswiler.
   ,, met Jan Tielman.
Verhaeghen v. Londen met Anna de Cerf v. Londen.
Verhaek j.m. v. Rotterdam met Clara Jans van Ham, j.d. v. Delft.
Verhaghen met Jaqnes Duijs.
Verheijden v. Bremen, met Adriaantge s'Wachters v. Brugge.
Verhille, we. Jan Penartz, met Jacob Ederick.
Verhouve, we. Hans Verscheijen, met Gillis de Bode.
Verhueghen met Guiliame Robs.
Verhule v. Antwerpen met Janneken des Pren v. Ghendt.
Verhulst met David van der Mote.
   ,, v. Halle met Catharina Winterbeke v. Bruijssel.
Verloij v. Londen met Tonijne van Peene, we. Geeraert Beunt.
Vermeer, we. Cornelis Reijnsen met Dirck Schaep.
Vermeijren met Jacus de Strijgher.
Vermeulen, we. Abraham Staelens, met Jacus de Grave.
   ,, , we. Carel Fustaen, met Grysollis Cnappaert.
   ,, , we. Gillis de Bois, met Jan Leertens.
Vermote met Kaerle van Peene.
   ,, met Lois de Puijth.
Verraes met Judith de Hane, we. . . . .
Verras met Pieter Bell.
Verchalen, we. Christiaen Servaes, met Michiel de Munck.
Verscheijden, we. Michiel de Munckere met Fransois Coijo.
Verspelle v. Mechelen met Catheryne van Hasevelt, we. Jans van Winghene v. Rouse.
Verspire v. Oudenherde met Elisabeth Deynkens we. Willem Jong.
Versteegh, wr van Geertruijdt Gerrits, met Josina Dammas van der Borre, we. van Pieter Keldermans.
Verstraten met Hans Marcelis.
Verstripen v. Londen met Maria Bonneel v. Norwich.
Vervinck met Jacob Bellocher.
Vervloot v. Antwerpen met Judith Haselaers v. Aarnwelt, we. Pieter Verstraeten.
Versludt v. Antwerpen met Jenneken s'Meys v. Meessene.
Verwese, we. Jacob de Vos, met Hieroninnus Wales.
Verwilt met Pieter de Caluwe.
Vese v. Sandwich met Mayken Sneop, we. Jan Busken.
Veuren met Carel de Pres.
   ,, met Daniel de Vos.
Victors met Jan van de Valo.
Vierendael, we. David Brents, met Joos de Schepp.
Vierendaels met Abraham Trion.
Vierendeels met Jan de Raet.
de **Vijllarts** met Johannes van Ree.
Vijsschers met Hubrecht Francklijn.
van de **Vijvre** met Geeraert Truijwen.
   ,, ,, ,, met Dominicus van Wtwijck.
   ,, ,, ,, , we. Noel van Boutcheler met Gillis van Diepenrijck.
   ,, ,, ,, met Cornelis Cornet.
de **Villars** v. Piedmont met Dorcas Weetlant v. Londen.
Villers met Pieter de Waghe.
van **Villes** met Evart van Bres.
Vincente met Huijbrecht Poorsoo.

Vinck v. Oudenaerd met Maeijken Dirox v. Brugghe.
Vingius met Cathelyne Lamoots.
n der **Vinne** v. Bruyssel met Tanneken van der Post v. Oudenaerde.
, „ „ met Vincent van der Meulen.
Visais met Baltes Casier.
Visch met Steven Egberts.
de „ , we. Steven Egberts, met Lodewijk Loijs.
„ **Vischere**, fs. Martens, v. Antwerpen, met Jossynken Piers, we. Gillis Valcke, v. Oudenaerde.
Visscher met Laurent de Necker.
de „ v. Rouce met Leonora Arondeaux v. Antwerpen, we. Tilman Brevy.
„ „ v. Emden met Ester Clockaert, we. Jan Abeels.
„ „ , we. Walrave Lodewijck, met A. van Ceulen.
„ **Visschere** v. Antwerpen met Sara de we. van Christiaen Maquereel.
„ met Jan Liebisch.
Visschers met Tobias Bardt.
„ met Christoffel de Peijster.
s' „ , we. Christoffel de Peijster, met Sebastiaan Borman.
„ „ met Hans Mimaert.
„ „ met Hendrick Stalens.
de **Viver** v. Oudenarde met Elisabeth Gallioot, we. Christiaen Paradys v. Eeckloo.
Vlaminck met Michiel de Vos.
s' **Vleeshouwers** met Pieter de Drossaert.
Vleijsaers met Herman Hendricksen.
van **Vleteren** v. Sandwich met Maria Herrewyn v. Londen.
n der **Vliet** v. Antwerpen met Tanneken Anthonis v. Antwerpen.
de **Vo j.g.** v. Haerlem met Anna Widdouw j.d. v. Colchester.
Voets met Jan Hesterman.
„ v. Oudenaerde met Grietken Nauwin v. Wernicke, we. Jan le Neuven.
van **Voldthuijsen** v. Wesel met Maijken Janssens v. der Nersen in landt v. Gulick.
„ **Volthuijsen** v. Wesel met Claerken Cornelissen, we. Pieter Cornelissen v. Nieuwberghe.
Volvoets met Marten Sleipen.
Vonck met Bereniuk van der Beck.
n der **Voorne**, we. Lieven Shaken, met Dierick Melssen.
s' **Vos** met Adam Boute.
de „ v. Ghendt met Hester de Ram v. Antwerpen.
„ „ v. Londen met Elizabeth Veuren v. Londen.
„ „ met Hendrick Hertman.
„ „ v. Gent met Peroontken Hureels v. Nieukercke.
„ „ v. Dantzijck met Maria de Coster v. Cobham.
„ „ met Pieter Dentier.
„ „ wr. van Anna Widd.., v. Haerlem met Susanna Vlaminck j.d. v. Middelborgh.
„ **Vosen** v. Sneeck met Cecilia van Treinen uit het landt v. Guylick.
a **Voutier**, we. Jan Scott, met Philip la Fleur.
„ **Vraeije** v. Audenarde met Janneken Carpentier v. Mechelen.
„ **Vrancken** v. Rumunde met Susanna ver Eyeken v. Brugge.
Vriems met Jacob Beck.
„ **Vriendt** met Franchois Vauwe.
„ „ met Anthonnis de Preut.
Vrient met Gerart Cosijns.
„ „ , we. Franchois Nauwe met Jan van Breen.
Vrients met Dieric Wessels.
„ **Vriese** v. Bruijssel met Tanneken van den Berghe.
„ „ met Jan Speeckaert.
„ „ v. Brugge met Janneke Pinceel v. Brugge, we. Pieter le Mire.
„ „ v. Mechelen met Catharyne Hugo, we. Hendrick Janssen.
„ „ v. Mechelen met Catharijne de Waghe, we. Henrick Bredenbach.
„ „ , we. Andriaan Luffs, met Antonis van der Molen.
„ **Vrieste** v. Deventer met Tanneken Schincks v. Londen.
van **Vrijlichoven** v. d'lant v. Valekenberghe met Lijuken Seijsens v. Ghendt, we. Jan Serlot.
Vrolijcx, we. Carel de Borchtgraeve, met Wolfaert van Bijlet.
Vrolix met Kaerle de Burchgrave.
„ met Matthias Schoaharen.
Vrombouts met Bernard de la Fosse.

29 Jun.	1579	Jan	Vromondt v. Walutrigem met Janneken van der Kleijen v. Russelaar.
22 Dec.	1594	Hester	Vromont met Nicolaes Wageman.
.. Jun.	1573	Elizabeth	Vrootick met Joos Huijsheere.
2 Feb.	1590	Pierinken	de Vrul met Willem Fogghe.
5 Nov.	1689	Willem	Vuijst, wr. van Loijsa Ferguesson, v. Steenberge met Margaret ffield j.d. v Londen.

4 Dec.	1582	Jan	de Wachter v. Brugge met Janneken van Dalem v. Londen.
13 Sep.	1584	Adrinantge	s' Wachters met Elardt Verheijden.
19 Dec.	1602	Barthomeus	Wademont v. Gent met Jorijne Loots v. Ste . . . . , we. Jan de Pigghe.
27 Jul.	1623	Maria	„ met Abel Hendricx.
15 Nov.	1638	Hermintjen	„ , we. Jacob Hendrix. met Willem Keuchelhuijs.
9 Sep.	1645	Pieter	„ , wr. v. Brugge, met Abigail Drijver, we. v. Colchester.
25 Nov.	1593	Franchynken	de Waege met Hans d'Ouwe.
1 Mei	1595	Maeijken	Waeghenmaeckers, we. Anthony Tiets, met Jeronimus Walens.
18 Jan.	1592	Debora	Waelwijns, (v. Wallewijns) we. Fransois Beke met Willem Braem.
21 Dec.	1619	Pieter	Waemaes v. Antwerpen met Maria de Brul, we. Jonas van Eijckenschot.
.. Mei	1606	Sijken	van der Waert met Carel de Man.
25 Jul.	1590	Marinus	de Wage v. bij Hulst met Magdaleene van den Bossche, we. Michiel Loose.
9 Sep.	1604	Gillis	„ „ v. Gent met Tanneken d'Hertoge v. Londen.
25 Nov.	1604	Francijntgen	„ „ , we. Jan de Autre, met Nicolas de Pauw.
22 Dec.	1594	Nicolaes	Wageman v. Brussel met Hester Vromont v. Londen.
13 Aug.	1611	Sara	Wagenaer met Jacob Sele.
30 Dec.	1628	Sara	„ , we. Jacques Selam, met Michiel Droeshout.
3 Feb.	1590	Janneken	de Waghe met Michiel van Peene.
14 Nov.	1602	Pieter	de „ v. Gent met Elisabeth Villers v. Northamtonsheere.
28 Oct.	1606	Catharina	„ „ met Hendrick van Bredenbach.
24 Nov.	1607	Tanneken	„ „ met Severijn van Druf.
30 Mei	1620	Catharyne	„ „ , we. Henrick Bredenbach, met Jan de Vriese.
15 Nov.	1593	Gulian	„ Waghenaer v. Ghendt met Andriesijne van der Sande v. Ghendt, we. Pieter de Ruijver.
11 Sep.	1604	Jaques	„ v. Londen met Elisabeth Conincx v. Gent.
8 Jul.	1593	Guiliaeme	„ Waghenaere met Tanneken Deijnouts, beide v. Ghent.
24 Feb.	1573	Guliame	„ Waghenare v. Ghent met Tanneken Smoors, we. Jaspar van Houte.
9 Apl.	1577	Joos	„ „ v. Werdel int Sticht v. Ceulen met Magdalena Spierijnx, we. Reynier Thijssens.
27 Aug.	1588	Nicolaes	Waghener v. Brussel met Lisken van der Straeten v. Brussel.
25 Apl.	1581	Rutger	Wagonhorst v. Holte met Janneken van der Cruijce vt den Nordt Cost.
27 Dec.	1608	Clara	Walbrock, we. Pieter Willemsz, met Jan Clinckart.
5 Apl.	1608	Catherine	„ Wale met Abraham Russout.
.. Jul.	1615	Anna	„ „ met Jacob Melsian.
11 Jul.	1592	Hieronimus	Wales v. Haesbroeck met Pierijne Verwese v. Pitgam, we. Jacob de Vos,
1 Mei	1595	Jeronimus	Walens v. Haseboucke met Macijken Waeghenmackers v. Vleteren, we. Anthony Tiets.
2 Jun.	1583	Adriaan	Walewijn v. Yperen met Nelleken Goeswijns v. Ambsterdam.
21 Mei	1611	Franchoijs	„ v. Nieukercke met Janneken de Gane v. Antwerpen.
23 Mar.	1698	Hendrick	van der Wall, j.m. v. Rotterdam met Sarah Frijars j.d. v. Londen.
3 Jan.	1574	Maijken	van Walle met Ferdinandus Dotignij.
20 Apl.	1584	Maijken	„ „ , we. Ferdinand Dottegnis met Dierick Mill.
25 Jan.	1579	Passchijne	van den „ met Joos Marisson.
19 Mei	1590	Celieken	van de ., met Willem Reckaerts.
11 Apl.	1591	Macijken	„ „ „ met Pauwels Cornelissen.
21 Apl.	1594	Pierine	„ „ „ met Pieter Henrix.
3 Mei	1603	Catharijne	„ „ „ met Pieter Oevijn.
.. Sep.	1613	Janneken	„ „ „ met Gommar van de Linden.
27 Dec.	1632	Willem	„ „ „ j.g. v. Haerlem met Anna Velle j.d. v. Colchester.
23 Apl.	1633	Philippus	„ „ „ , wr. v. Sara . . . . , met Sara Springers j.d. v. Sandwich.
11 Apl.	1648	Maria	„ „ „ met Jacob de Meester.
3 Jan.	1585	Debora	Wallewijns (v. Waelwijns) met Fransois Beke.
6 Feb.	1592	Susanna	Walschaert met Dodier de la Tombe.

9 Feb.	1589	Janneken	**Walschaerts** met Nicolas Winterbeke.
4 Feb.	1578	Heindrick	de **Walsche** v. Bruessel met Cornelie Garet v. Antwerpen.
22 Jan.	1596	James	**Ward** wt Essex met Elisabeth Endraerts v. Ghendt, we. Heindrich d'Hertoge.
31 Mar.	1584	Kaerle	van der **Warden** v. Engien met Janneken de Hecke v. Valentzijn.
3 Feb.	1600	Francijne	van **Weeijseghen** met Jan Lambert.
4 Sep.	1628	Johanna	de **Weelde**, we. van Andries Boeve, met Johannes van Abeele.
15 Mar.	1699	Geertruijd	**Weerels**, we. Barent Koesvelt, met Leonard van Asten.
30 Apl.	1594	Margarieto	s' **Weerts**, we. Hendrick Janss met Willem Schaere.
. . Sep.	1620	Trynken	,, met Lenard Schaphusen.
9 Feb.	1591	Philips	,, v. Breda met Magdalena de Witte van Brugge.
17 Apl.	1604	Dorcas	**Weetlant** met Jan de Villars.
21 Sep.	1609	Abraham	**Wege** v. Zandwich met Elizabeth de Frenoij v. Londen.
3 Jun.	1606	Abraham	**Weghe** v. Santwich met Catharina Lambrecht v. Arques.
14 Apl.	1607	Heyndrick	van **Weijden** v. Antwerpen met Catharijna Wijtmans uijt t landt v. Gulick.
.1 Apl.	1612	Andries	van der **Weijer** v. Middelborgh met Susanna de Money v. Ypere.
28 Sep.	1619	Susanne	,, ,, ,, met Jacob Speeckmeijer.
13 Feb.	1593	Maeijken	**Weijtens**, we. Gillis van Herweghen met Lieven van der Strate.
21 Dec.	1602	Maijken	,, , we. Gillis Goossen met Tobias Baert.
6 Aug.	1626	Christiaen	de **Welcke** v. Dantzick met Anna Nicasius, we. Gregorius Wttespruljt.
. . Feb.	1612	Catharine	van **Welden**, we. Hans Geest met Hans Hardlewijn.
27 Mei	1571	Pieter	**Wellens** v. Antwerpen met Maijken Backers, we. Antonij Warein.
7 Apl.	1640	Adriaen	van der **Werf**, wr. v. Schoonhoven, met Anna de Clopper j.d. v. Sandwich.
30 Jul.	1588	Maria	**Werners** met Dierick Bierman.
11 Dec.	1599	Maijken	van **Werwijck**, we. Willem Pauwels, met Jan Braidense.
6 Feb.	1602	Joris	**Wesbrouck** j.m. v. Bergen op Zoom met Margriet Gabriels j.d. v. Bommel.
1 Jun.	1634	Sara	**Wessel** met Pieter Haertgens.
27 Mei	1571	Jan	**Wessels** v. Beveren in Kleve met Sara der Kinderen dochter Adams.
19 Jul.	1586	Jan	,, v. Swolle met Janneken Vercamer v. Hondscoten.
5 Nov.	1611	Abraham	,, v. Londen met Sara Hoste v. Haerlem.
15 Sep.	1612	Josias	,, v. Londen met met Cornelia de Buck v. Amsterdam.
20 Oct.	1612	Dirick	,, v. Swol met Alis Clarissz v. Gent.
6 Oct.	1614	Wessel	,, v. Swolle met Judith Hofman v. Londen.
. . Apl.	1616	Dierick	,, v. Swol met Maria Droeshoudt v. Londen.
.7 Jan.	1618	Dieric	,, v. Swol met Maria Vrients v. Norwich.
16 Mei	1609	Jacob	**Westerman** v. Leenwarden met Sijnken Solens v. Antwerpen.
6 Aug.	1594	Margriete	**Westhuijse**, we. Jan van Beveren met Jaens de Coster.
22 Apl.	1604	Anna	**Wevers** met Nathanaes Baes.
2 Mei	1626	Elisabet	**Wicke** met Dieric Evertsz.
27 Sep.	1642	Gilles	**Wicks** j.m. met Sara de Lobeau we. van André Grande.
9 Oct.	1627	Anna	**Widdouw** met Michiel de Vo.
12 Jun.	1582	Maeijken	**Wiessen** met Frants Heyligers.
21 Jan.	1606	Greleijn	van **Wiemes** v. Brughe met Cathleine van Loij, we. Hans van Halle.
17 Mar.	1631	Engel	**Wier** j.g. v. Overmobijck int landt v. Gulick met Sara de Calue j.d. v. Batteree. (Battersea.)
19 Sep.	1604	Lambrecht	**Wiesen** v. Londen met Lyntken Mocharts, we. Robert Davids.
22 Jan.	1604	Sara	de **Wiest** met Jan van Delft.
23 Sep.	1604	Michiel	**Wiestijnck** v. Brugge met Maria Frederick, we. Jan Luter.
. . Sep.	1613	. . . .	**Wigers** v. Andwerpen met Baijken Boeston, we. Aerts Solijns.
26 Jan.	1591	Johan	**Wigt** v. Beltfort (Bedford) met Catharina Hertblock v. Ghendt.
13 Oct.	1583	Pieter	**Wijbo** v. Thielt met Gijsbertgen Willems v. Narden.
5 Jan.	1589	Josias	,, met Anna Ruijtincks, beide v. Gent.
11 Aug.	1590	Josias	,, v. Ghendt met Hester Marchant v. Armeutiers.
20 Feb.	1593	Jacobus	,, v. Gent met Prudence Friscobaldi v. Antwerpen.
4 Dec.	1599	Sijnken	,, met Joos Calf.
9 Jun.	1607	Pieter	,, v. Putthem met Catharijna d'Heere, we. Jaques Franssen.
17 Jul.	1616	Egbert	**Wijbrands** v. Groeninghen met Susanna Schuyl v. Andwerpen.
11 Aug.	1584	Tanneken	**Wijchmans** met Henrick Huijsman.
6 Sep.	1573	Jan	van **Wijck** v. Horne met Beatrix Busse v. Sittert.
12 Feb.	1576	Jan	,, v. Remmide met Janneken Haghemans, we. Niclaes Ysebrants v. Heijnsburch.
13 Apl.	1690	Johannes	,, met Catharina van Mengelinckluijsen, Met attestatie v. St.James.
30 Aug.	1586	Janneken	**Wijgants** met Hans van Solt.
8 Sep.	1579	Jan	**Wijlandtz** v. Wijck bij Duren met Maijcken Marekeija v. Steenvordt.
25 Apl.	1614	Hans	**Wijnants** v. Antwerpen met Susanne de Hulster v. Londen.
22 Oct.	1574	Lieven	van **Wijnckele** v. Ghent met Katherine Beghuyt, we. Jan Pois v. Brugghe.
9 Oct.	1610	Jan	de **Wijs** v. Antwerpen met Rachel Thomasse v. Colchester.
24 Dec.	1588	Laureins	,, **Wijse** met Marie Vadon, beijde v. Antwerpen.

14 Apl.	1607	Catharijna	**Wijtmans** met Heyndrick van Weijden.
15 Dec.	1700	Juriaen	**Wil**, j.m. v. Franckfort, met Marijtje Engels j.d. v. Rotterdam.
10 Jan.	1604	Esechiel	**Wilckenhof** v. Andwerpen met Jacotmijntken Seeufs, we. Richard de Merry.
1 Jan.	1634	Laurens	**Wilkes** j.g. met Abigail Maertens, wo. van P. Wessel.
22 Apl.	1582	Grietken van der	**Wille** met Mahiou de Frenoij.
23 Apl.	1592	Marcus	**Willeboort** v. Brugge met Janneken van der Stracte.
7 Jul.	1588	Jan	**Willemets** v. Oudenaerde met Lijnken van der Straten v. Brussel.
14 Oct.	1571	Neeltgen	**Willems** met Jan Fait.
11 Sep.	1580	Adam	,, v. Valckenburch met Nelgen Jansen v. Scoverenburcht.
13 Oct.	1583	Gijsbertgen	,, met Pieter Wijbo.
29 Jan.	1594	Ghijsbrechtken	,, , we. Pieter Wijbo, met Abraham de Rijke.
4 Jul.	1609	Margareta	,, , we. Denijs Bartholomeus, met Abraham Coudron.
13 Dec.	1627	Maria	,, met Thomas Townsin.
.. Jun.	1621	Gomaer	**Willemsen** v. Bergen op Zoom met Anna Brijrens v. Londen.
1 Mei	1582	Lambrecht	**Willemssen** v. Vtrecht met Diericksken Berntz v. Vtrecht.
11 Nov.	1571	Gerardt	**Willemsz** alias **Dirckzen** v. Amsterdam met Tanneken Schippers, we. Corneli Hendricxs
8 Nov.	1576	Margriete	,, , we. Malachias van der Heijden met Gillis van Diepenrijck.
5 Jan.	1595	Margriete	,, , we. Willem Flud met Anthoni de Deuxvilles.
11 Feb.	1606	Jeronijmus	,, v. der Goes met Maeijken Carren v. Cortrycke.
2 Oct.	1606	Wendel	,, met Cornelis Valuwaert.
17 Sep.	1611	Humfrey	**Willis** v. Glocester met Maijken van den Berghe v. Londen.
21 Apl.	1590	Jacomynken	**Wils** met Nicasius Rossel.
11 Feb.	1623	Elisabeth	,, met Jacob Symousz.
15 Feb.	1596	Lambrecht	**Wilsen** v. Londen met Elisabeth Stuytelinx v. Antwerpen.
5 Jul.	1638	Jan	**Wims** j.g. v. Sandwich met Magdalena Trappaert j.d. v. Londen.
26 Dec.	1586	Bartholmeus van der	**Winckel** v. Ghent met Josijne Sprooten v. Nicukerke.
22 Oct.	1588	Anthonette de	**Windt** met Jacus Morre.
24 Jun.	1595	Maeijken	**Winne**, we. Hendrick Baetens met Pieter van der Spiere.
8 Jan.	1604	Maijken	,, ,, , we. Pieter Verspiere met Jan de Coster.
4 Aug.	1612	Hans	,, v. Londen met Lijdia van den Bossche v. Maidston.
15 Oct.	1616	Pieter	,, v. Londen met Maria Boke v. Colchester.
9 Feb.	1589	Nicolaes	**Winterbeke** v. Bruijssel met Janneken Walschaerts v. Antwerpen.
29 Nov.	1590	Anna van	,, met Hans Sele.
26 Oct.	1602	Anna	,, met Marten Droushout.
8 Jan.	1605	Catharina	,, met Pieter Verhulst.
22 Sep.	1605	Heyndrick	**Wiro** met Tanneken Doreijn v. Londen.
22 Jan.	1690	Jan	de **Wit** j.m. v. Tiel in Gelderlant met Catharina Propis, we. Jan Bosschaert v. Sluij in Vlaanderen.
2 Mar.	1648	Mary	**Withal** met Georgius Schurstin.
9 Apl.	1683	Maerten	de **Witte**, wr. van Sara Taylor v. Rotterdam, met Maria Stevenson, j.d. v. Enfield in Essex.
9 Feb.	1591	Magdalena	,, ,, met Philips Weerts.
1 Jul.	1604	Jan	**Wittebroot** v. Londen met Eva Janssen, we. Arnouldt Stalpaert.
. 7 Dec.	1611	Maria	**Wittewrongel** met Willem Paget.
3 Mei	1614	Jacques	,, v. Gent met Anna van Acker v. Antwerpen.
1 Jun.	1589	Jan	**Wittewronghel** v. Eeckeloo met Maeyken Beifkens v. Rouce.
8 Mei	1596	Anthoni	**Woesthoff** v. Nuijsse met Maeijken Tollens v. Eecloo.
3 Feb.	1594	Catelyne van	**Wolden** met Hans de Ghuijt.
6 Mar.	1700	Geertruijdt van der	**Wolf**, we. Joris Goudesael, met Hermannus Fabritius.
18 Jun.	1594	Jacob	**Wolfaert** v. Cuelen met Tanneken Clande v. Bruijssel, we. Pieter de Schepen.
18 Apl.	1581	Joris	**Wolff** v. Phiossen in Duijdstsland met Digne van der Clasen, we. Franchoi Cordier.
22 Jun.	1647	Ernst	**Wolft**, wr. v. Lubeck, met Sara Backlion j.d. v. Sandwich, tot Mortlake.
30 Mar.	1574	Christiaen	**Wolters** v. Stochen bij Zittert met Wendel Bees v. Zittert.
22 Jan.	1604	Nicolas	**Woodcraft** wt Hamsheere (Hampshire) met Janneken Pieters, we. Pieter de Groot.
14 Aug.	1604	Willem	**Wondec** v. Duijsburgh met Heijndrixken Feijt v. Utrecht.
18 Sep.	1610	Willem	**Wonder** v. bij Ceulen met Susanna van Coppenolle v. Sandwich.
.. Jul.	1621	Jan	**Worringen** v. Cuelen met Catharina de Drijver v. Colchester.
24 Jul.	1628	Jan	**Worringem** wedr. v. Ceulen met Sara Michielsz j.d. v. Middelburgh.
8 Sep.	1612	Anna van	**Wortem** met Cornelis Melsen.
19 Feb.	1573	Margriete	**Wouters**, we. Sebastiaen Pietorssen, met Jacob Janssen.
31 Mei	1597	Christynken	,, , we. Anthoui Jacobs, met Jacus van Hoorne.
5 Jun.	1610	Stijnken	,, met Hendrick Rademaecker.
21 Feb.	1609	Hartgeer	**Wouterssz** v. Deventer met Janneken Six v. Wesel.
28 Nov.	1585	Hugo	**Wtgheers** v. Ghent met Jaquemijnken Brakers, we. Reniers Sergeants v. Rouce.

8 Mei	1610	Albert	**Wtmans** v. Nieuwenhuijs met Lysken Lenarts, we. Pieter de Moor.
4 Nov.	1593	Dominicus	van **Wtwijck** v. s'Hertogenbossche met Rachel van der Vijvere v. London.
. . Apl.	1615	Rachel	„ „ met B. Champnes.
18 Mei	1626	Dominicus	„ „ v. s'Hertogenbossch met Margarita Baeck, we. Thomas Tobnam.
23 Aug.	1691	Hendrick	**Wupper** j.m. v. Solingen met Irmegard Schaff j.d. v. Feldt bij Solingen, met
„			attestatie v. Solingen.

13 Mar.	1595	Susanna	**Zaghers**, we. Walranous Corne. met Thomas Engelbender.
4 Mar.	1691	Lodowijck	**Zeckender,** wr. van Baldina van Dalen, met Elisabeth van Gulick, we. Cornelis
			Vermaes, met attestatie van St. James.
31 Aug.	1585	Gillis	**Zeghers** v. Rughen met Jaquemynken Kempenaerts v. Brüjssel, we. Hendrick
			de Drossaert.
14 Apl.	1588	Eva	„ met Lambrecht Janssen.
1 Jul.	1595	Hans	„ v. Antwerpen met Catheline van der Spick v. London.
11 Aug.	1594	Adriaen	van **Zevecote** v. Ghent met Clara van Heecke v. Turnhout.

30 Nov.	1569	Jaques	de la Schonkiere v. Antwerpen met Janneken Floris v. Uutrecht.
25 Dec.	1569	Dierick	Roest met Else Pieterssen.
24 Feb.	1570	Alexander	Bogaert v. Ghendt met Elijsabeth van Coppenhole v. Curtrijcke.
25 Feb.	1570	Joos	de Handschutter met Cornelie, we. v. Heindricks Claes.
9 Mar.	1570	Hans	Dorain v. Antwerpen met met Tanneken van Kelsbeke v. St. Truijen.
9 Mar.	1570	Christiaen	Clays v. Nijkercke met Jaentken van Nucours, we. v. Anthuonis Bernaerts, v. St. Pol.
16 Mar.	1570	Lieven	Verhulst v. Ghendt met Marie Caussije v. Poperinghe.
23 Mar.	1570	Willem	Trommel, Schotsman met ...... dr. van Gheraert Janssen, ende we. van Anthony Jonghe.
6 Apl.	1570	Jacob	Machen, wr., met Elysabeth Reyls, Inghelsche we.
22 Juu.	1570	Hans	Luuex met Gheertruijt Anthonissen.
22 Jun.	1570	Cornelis	Janssen met Arnolda Baudewijns, we. Henrick Karens.
13 Jul.	1570	Mattheux	Dijselaer met Agnes Gervais, Inghelsche.
6 Aug.	1570	Jeron	Galmaets met Barham Platevoets.
13 Aug.	1570	Gheeraert	de Hollander met Jehenne Blanchepain, we. Germyn Couvaert.
17 Aug.	1570	Christiaen	Claessen met Gheerdyne van Lancmes, we. Franchois Weersevelt.
3 Sep.	1570	Lieven	de Wolf met Catelijne Vermote, we. Jan Strobbe.
10 Sep.	1570	Erasmus	Sjaeghers, causmaekere v. Andtwerpen met Margriete, we. Jasper Bate.
21 Sep.	1570	Hans	Stel, wr., met Tanneken Teylers, j.d.
29 Sep.	1570	Michiel	Waterman v. Zwollen met Gheertruyt Gheerssen, j.d. v. Zwollen.
29 Sep.	1570	Lieven	de Weze, wr., met Lynken van den Kiele v, Andtwerpen.
19 Oct.	1570	Jan	Heindricx, wr. v. Mechelen met Martynken, we. Michiel de la Royere.
26 Oct.	1570	Hendrick	Haelman v. Mazeick met Mayken we. van Lodewyck Manteau.
5 Nov.	1570	Anthony	Kethele met .... , In an English Church.
5 Nov.	1590	.....	.... met ..... we. Herman, de schoemakere was in de Mynoris.
23 Nov.	1570	Coenraert	Janssens v. s'Hertogenbosch met Mayken Dignies, we. Pieter Jacobs, v. Bergher up den Zoom.
26 Nov.	1570	Mr. Cornelis van der	Maze met Elysabeth Hubertsen, Inghelsche.
7 Dec.	1570	Jan	Verpoest met Jacquemyne Verelst.
7 Dec.	1570	Franssiscus	Otsen j.m. out 31 jaren met Tanneken we. Jacob Janssen, mesmakere.
10 Dec.	1570	Hans	de Brune fs. Arendts met Maijken Lockmans v. Hasselt.
27 Dec.	1570	Gheeraert	Willemssen, wr. v. Venloo met Theunken Hermans, j.d.
30 Dec.	1570	Jacob	Janssen v. Maseick met Truijken Hubrechts.
1 Feb.	1571	Jjnghel	Marselis, wr. v. Bruessele, met Catherine, we. Joos van Hille.
2 Feb.	1571	Jan	de Weze, wr., van der Franscher Ghemeinte, met Janneken Overdaats v. Enghein.
15 Feb.	1571	Tobias	de Beij, wr., met Agnees van der Poest.
15 Feb.	1571	Nicolas	de Cueninck met Janneken Rombout, we. van Adriaen Vermote.
1 Mar.	1571	Willem	Proost v. Valckenborch met Maijken, we. van Pieter Verelst.
1 Mar.	1571	Adriaen	Verbeke, wr. v. Steenweick met Susanna Happaerts, we. Jan de Roze.
1 Mar.	1571	Laureins	Thomassen v. Venlo met Juyt, we. van Pieter Janssens.
18 Mar.	1571	Jacques	de Cocq met Margriete Smols, beyde v. Ghendt.
12 Apl.	1571	Marten	de Costere v. Mechelen met Barbele, we. Pieter van Amiens.
17 Apl.	1571	Pieter	de Kneselaere met Janneken Hedle, Ingelsche.
17 Apl.	1571	Jooris	de Dobbelaere met Margriete van Zevecote, beyde v. Ghendt.
19 Apl.	1571	Mr. Jan	de Radermakere, Auderlinck, met Janneken Raekets, dr. v. Jan ende Beatrix.
19 Apl.	1571	Baudewyn	de Keysere, v. Ghendt met Goelken van den Putte, suster van Raphel.
19 Apl.	1571	Pieter	de Kneselaere met ....
3 May	1571	Adolf	Visser v. Tolhus in Cleven met Martynken Janssen, we. Willem Schot.
3 May	1571	Pieter	Willems v. Audtwerpen met Maijken Backers, we. Anthony Warryn.
10 May	1571	Adam	der Kinderen met Elizabeth van Cockere vuyt landt v. Cleven.

10 May 1571 Gheeraert **Savegrein** met Agnees **Jacobs,** we. v. Jans Lackhuys.
10 May 1571 Willem **Jacobs** v. Brugghe met Cathelijne **Verelst,** we. van Walreve Loijex

Register van die Jene de welcke, volgens acte van den 26 April, 1657, In onsen Tempel sijn begraven worden, beneffens die Leeraar van dese Gemeente de welcke van tijdt tot tijdt sijn begraven worden : so sijn begraven worden als volgt.

22 Aug.	1757	Philip	van **Assendelft**, zoontje van de Heer Isaac.
25 Mar.	1776	Pieter	,, ,, , jongste zoon van Isaac van Assendelft in een familie graf, zie A 1757.
3 Mar.	1782	Isaac	,, ,, , ouderling in syn familie graf, zie A 1757.

4 Jun.	1825	Marie Susanne Louise	**Babut**, dochter van den Heer Eduard Francois Babut, overleden 31 Mei, oud ? maanden.
19 Feb.	1827	Marie Charlotte	,, , dochter van den Heer Eduard Francois Babut, overleden 13 Feb., oud (maanden.
16 Sep.	1810	DeHeer Gerard	**Backus**, ouderling, overleden den 7 Sep.
4 Jul.	1823	Frederick Albert	**Bagelmann**, o. 27 Jan., oud 11 jaren & gelegd in het familie graf van syn vader.
15 Feb.	1804	Harriot	,, , huisvrouw van Jacob Bagelmann.
25 Feb.	1825	Elizabeth Mary	,, , dochter van den Heer Jacob Bagelmann, o. 18 Feb., oud 18 jaren.
22 Dec.	1835	Jacob	,, , o. 23 Nov., in Eastcheap, Londen, oud 75 jaren. In het gemelzeld graf, No. 46.
25 Feb.	1804	Harriot	,, , huisvrouw van Jacob Bagelmann.
26 Nov.	1744	Nicholaus	**Bailij**.
26 Sep.	1740	Catharina	le **Baisseur**, we. der Grotert, bij haar man.
1 Nov.	1704	Collonel Bastian	**Bajer**.
12 Apl.	1740	Cornelius	**Bakker**.
17 Aug.	1745	Jan	,, in het keldertje van Mr. Cornelius Bakker.
18 Apl.	1704	Mr. Joas	**Bateman**.
5 Jan.	1712	Judith	
23 Oct.	1767	Henrietta	**Barbe**, dochtertje van James Barbe & Cornelia Ter Kinder.
25 Nov.	1768	Jan Hendrick	,, , zoontje van James Barbe & Cornelie Ter Kinder.
2 Aug.	1827	Lamke	**Bauerman**, huisvr. van den Heer J. B. Suwerkrop, Diaken; o. 28 Jullj, oud 4(jaren. In het familie graf, zie 21 Oct., 1816.
28 Jan.	1702	Mr. Jacob George	**Beek**.
. . Jan.	1675	Jacob op de	**Beeck**, fs. van onser broeder Mr. op de Beeck.
13 Jun.	1760	Maria Joanna van	**Beek**, we. van Henrik van Putter in den familie graf.
23 Jun.	1727	Helena	**Beirman**.
12 Mar.	1733	Mejuffer Cornelia	,, , dr. van Dr. Arnold Boot Beirman, in het graf waar haar moeder Eliza beth de Gols Ao. 1736 begraven is.
10 Apl.	1754	Dr. Arnold Boot	,, , ouderling.
7 Dec.	1756	Helena	,, , huisvr: van Do. Walker in het graf van haar E. Vader, zie 1754.
24 Nov.	1760	Maria Anna	,, , laast we. van Adam Millar, Pred: onder de Dissenters te Hamersmith in het graf van haar vader.
30 Nov.	1704	Mr Guilliame van den	**Berge**.
11 Apl.	1751	Caspar	**Bergman**.
13 Dec.	1729	Jacob	**Berkenhoudt**.
20 Dec.	1729	Anna Margarita	,, , bij haar broeder Jacob Berkenhout.

7 Mar.	1745	Benjamin	**Berkenhout.**
26 Jul.	1754	Isabella	,, bij haar man, zie 1745, Mar. 7.
28 Sep.	1777	Benjamin	**Berkenhoud,** in het familie graf, zie Dec., 1729.
18 Aug.	1785	Leonarda	,, , huisvrouw van Joseph Orme in het familie graf, zie 28 Sep. 1775.
18 Mei	1833	Benjamin	**Berthoud,** zoon van Francis Ami Guillaume & Louise Berthoud, geb. 3 Sep. 1832 & o. 12 Mei 1833.
28 Feb.	1837	Charles Louis	,, , zoon van Francis Ami Guillaume & Louise Berthoud, geb. 20 Jan. 1836, o. 20 Feb. 1837 in de Parish v. Clerkenwell.
21 Mar.	1687	Catharina	**Biscop,** dr. van onsen broeder Samuel Biscop.
19 Jun.	1700	Do. Samuel	,, .
18 Mar.	1725	Samuel	,, in sijn vaders graff.
27 Mei	1749	Sarah	,, , oudste dochter van D. Samuel Biscop, weleer Predik. alhier en we. van den Heere Willem Bucknalt, obiit 21 Meij 1749, oud 69.
2 Nov.	1758	Jan	**Blijdestein,** zoon van Jan Blijdestein, ouderling.
25 Apl.	1760	Marianne	,, , dr. van ,, ,, , ,, .
16 Jun.	1762	Abraham	,, , jongste zoontje van ,, ,, , ,, .
29 Aug.	1763	Mary	**Blijdesteijn,** ,, dr. ,, ,, ,, , ,, .
19 Feb.	1777	John	**Blydestein,** ouderling.
.. Apl.	1797	John	**Blydesteijn,** in het familie graf.
17 Feb.	1830	De Heer Isaac	,, , ouderling, o. den 7 Feb. In het f. graf.
21 Mei.	1838	Anna	,, , o. 13 Maart (oud 72 Jaren) in Westham & geleyd in het gemetseld familie graf No. 26, zie 17 Feb. 1836.
11 Mar.	1841	Judith	,, , we. van den Heer John Campbell, o. 4 Mar. te Westham, Essex. Oud 81 jaren. In het f. graf No. 26, zie 21 Mar. 1835.
. . . .	1675	Jouffrou	**Boddens,** die huisvrou van Mr. Jan Langeleij.
13 Jul.	1726	Daniel	**Bolten.**
3 Mar.	1737	Elizabeth	,, bij Daniel Bolten.
16 Sep.	1739	Do. Theodorus	,, , onsen Eerwaarden Leeraar, bij sijn vader.
8 Mei	1744	Sara	**Bolwerk.**
8 Aug.	1748	Matheus	,, , enige zoon van den Heer Gerard Bolwert, ouderling dezer Gemeente.
10 Apl.	1760	Gerard	,, , ouderling in een f. graf.
6 Feb.	1777	Isabella	,, , huisvrouw van de Heer Timotheus Nucella, in het familie graf.
25 Feb.	1778	Maria	,, , dr. van de Heer Gerard Bolwerk, int f. graf, zie 10 Apl. 1760.
9 Mei	1737	Doms. Fredk. Danl.	**Bongaar** - - - .
30 Nov.	1789	Adolf	**Boon,** ouderling, in het familie graf daar zyn eerste huisvrouw begraven is, zie 28 Dec. 1767.
9 Apl.	1774	Susanna	**Bosanquet,** we. van Charles van Notten, in haer f. graf, zie Ao. 1751.
22 Oct.	1692	Mr. Pieter	**Bourgeois,** en 6 maenden daernae zyn weduwe Constantia van Wachtendonck.
1 Mei	1735	Doms. Herman van	**Bracht,** naast Albert van Meurs.
17 Nov.	1740	Johannes Henricus	**Breijnius.**
6 Jan.	1810	De Heer James Ten	**Broecke,** overleden 1 Jan.
31 Dec.	1810	Anna Maria ,,	,, , dr. van Anthony Ten Broeke, ouderling. O. 25 Dec. 1810.
7 Oct.	1812	Anthony ,,	,, , ouderling, o. 30 Sep. 1812.
5 Feb.	1823	William Isaac ,,	,, , zoon van William Ten Broeke, o. 29 Jan & geplaastst in het graf van wylen Heer Anthony Ten Broeke, ouderling.
7 Mei	1824	John Smith ,,	,, , Diaken, o. 30 April.
15 Oct.	1853	Martha de	**Buck,** o. te Londen, St. Botolph, 7 Oct. oud 69 jaren, in het f. graf No. 51.*
21 Oct.	1726	Francois William	**Buirette,** Esq.
Apl.	1693	Conste.	**Burgoijce.**
7 Oct.	1714	Henry	**Bustijn.**

. . . .	1681	Juffr.	**Calant** j.d., suster van Juffr Tijssen.
7 Fep.	1785	Peter	**Callifies,** o. 30 Jan. 1785 aan zyn huis in Kingsland Road.
23 Mei	1739	Philip David	**Camp.**
26 Jul.	1773	Hermanuus	**Camperdijk,** in leven Coster onzer Kerke.
25 Mar.	1773	. . . . .	**Carteret,** Dogtertje van den Heer Capiteiu Carteret, in het graf van zyner Schoon-vader Doctor Silvester.
31 Dec.	1781	Govert	**Cassau,** Diacon.
3 Jun.	1687	Sarah	van **Castricum,** huisvrouw van Sir James Ward.

2 Oct.	1792	Benjamin	Catteau, Pensionaris van Vlissingen.
2 Mei	1718	Abraham	Ciprianus, in Sr. Mathew Delmé grav.
2 Jun.	1686	Arnoldina	van Citters, dochterken van sijn Excelltie. d'Heer Ambassadeur van Citters.
1 Apl.	1687	. . . .	„ „ , een doodt geboren kindt van ayn Exce. D'Heer Amb: van Citters.
25 Feb.	1698	Theodore	Cock, soon van Fr. Jan Cock.
23 Mei	1706	Mr. John	„ .
16 Apl.	1731	Hanna	„ , we. van John Cock.
22 Dec.	1706	Jacques	Cockon, v. Bordeaux.
15 Oct.	1768	Margaretha	Collier, huisvrouwe van Herman Meijer, ouderling.
5 Sep.	1727	Anna	Collignon, int graff van haar eerste man Mr Dupré.
23 Mei	1728	Paulus	„ V: D: int graff van Samuel Dupré.
31 Jul.	1772	Sara	Cope, huisvrouw van Hermannus Camperdijk, Koster onzer Kerke.
17 Mar.	1715	Mr. William Henrij	Cornelissen.
27 Aug.	1719	Elizabeth	„ .
29 Apl.	1692	Mevrouwe	Cornewall.
11 Apl.	1695	Juffru. Susannah	Corselis.
18 Oct.	1800	G . . .	Costerus van Surinam.
16 Jul.	1792	James	Des Cotes, ouderling.
29 Jan.	1732	Abraham	Craiesteijn.
18 Dec.	1754	Abraham	„ .
5 Oct.	1758	De Heer Franciscus	„ .
8 Mar.	1744	Rebecca	Craijestetijn, in het graff van Mr. Abraham Cracijestein.
. . . .	1676	Jouffrou Catharina	Cromling, we. van Mr. David Otger.
9 Dec.	1723	James	Crop.
28 Apl.	1727	Mrs. Abigail	„ .
24 Feb.	1744	Abraham	„ , in het graf van Mrs. Abigail Crop.
5 Jun.	1749	Mrs. Elisabeth	„ , we van den Heer Abraham Henckel, in leven Ouderling dezer Gemeente.
5 Mar.	1773	Jacobus	du Croz.
17 Oct.	1780	Alexander	„ „ , in het f. graf daar zyn vader ligt begraven den 5 Mar. 1773.
13 Nov.	1823	Ann	„ „ , we. van Alexander du Croz, voormalig Diaken deser Gemeente.
9 Oct.	1835	Samuel	„ „ , o. 2 Oct. in de Parish van St. Andrew, Brook St., Holborn. Oud 49 jaren. In het f. graf No. 45 * *, zie 13 Nov. 1823.

13 Dec.	1754	Sarah	Dade, we. van Cornelis de Keijzer.
9 Dec.	1750	Marianne	Daulnis, Huisvrouw van den Heer John van Neck.
1 Apl.	1772	Aletta Catharina Everardina	„ „ , „ „ Dr. John Silvester, onderling.
6 Mar.	1747	Johanna	Dellingham,
10 Apl.	1706	Mrs. Debora	Delme.
1 Feb.	1711	Mr. John	„ .
31 Jul.	178.	Jean Bernard	Descous.
19 Jul.	1770	Bernard	Diemel, in leven waardig Leeraar der Gemeente in de Hof Kapel te St. James, Westminster, in een graf alle naaste Zyn E. Schoonmoeder Sarah Dade, we. van Cornelis de Keijzer, zie 13 Dec. 1754.
2 Oct.	1786	Sarah Cornelia	„ , Huisvrouw van den Wel Eerw. Heere M. I. van Effen Bed. des Godd. woords.
6 Dec.	1794	Magdalena Christina	„ , we. van James Des Cotes.
19 Nov.	1736	Anna	Durant, Huisvrouw van Jan Frederick de Meije.
31 Dec.	1728	Sir Denis	Dutrij, Bart.
2 Apl.	1743	Dame	„ , we. van Neck, in het graf van Sir Denijs Dutrij.
5 Nov.	1800	Willem	van Duxra (?) van Demerary, gest. den 31 Oct. in Bloomsbury Square.

16 Mei	1778	Renira Christina van	**Effen,** oudste dogtertje van Dr. M. T. van Effen, in het graf van haar Grootvader Dr. Diemel, begraven is den 19 Jul. 1770.
30 Mei	1782	Justus Melchior ,,	,, , Zoontje van Do. M. T. van Effen.
23 Dec.	1785	Pieter Fredrik ,,	,, , ,, ,, ,, ,, ,, ,, ,, .
		Justus	
18 Dec.	1736	Hendrik Martin	**Elkinge.**
4 Apl.	1740	Henry	**Elking,** bij Martin Elking.
3 Oct.	1700	Mad: Anna	**Ellsworth** *alias* **Schapelinck.**
1 Mei	1795	Ann	**Emilie,** huisvrouw van Peter Stapel, o. 29 Apl. 1795.
26 Mei	1746	Jan van den	**Enden.**
10 Mar.	1757	Philip ,, ,,	,, , in zyn eigen graf, zie Ao. 1746.
9 Sep.	1765	Jan ,, ,,	,, , in het graf van zyn broeder Philip van den Enden, zie Ao. 1757.
16 Apl.	1772	Louis ,, ,,	,, , in het f. graf, zie Ao. 1765.
24 Feb.	1774	Lewis ,, ,,	,, , onderling in een f. graf, zie Ao. 1765.
23 Feb.	1718	Mr. John	**Esselbron.**
24 Mei	1733	Anna Maria	,, , int graff van John Esselbron.

27 Jul.	1825	Abraham	le **Fever,** 45 jaren, Koster dezer kerek, o. 20 Jul. oud 84 jaren.
15 Jul.	1831	Maria Magdalena ,,	,, , we. van Abraham Le fever, o. 10 Jul. oud 88 jaren.
27 Feb.	1738	Mary	**Field** bij Mary Jones & haar Grootvader. (v. Van de Velde.)
26 Mar.	1747	Laurence	,, in het graf van Mr. Laurens van de Velden.
28 Aug.	1750	Mrs. Mary	,, we. van de geweeze Koster Field & haar Zoon.
30 Oct.	1750	Laurens	,, , beide in het graf van Laurens van de Velden.
19 Mar.	1755	William	,, .
29 Jan.	1740	Gilbert	de **Flines.**
29 Mar.	1719	Geertruijd	du **Fort.**
25 Jul.	1763	Thomas Cooke	**Fremeaux,** zoon van de Heer Jacobus Fremeaux.
14 Jan.	1764	James	,, , jongste zoon van de Heer Jac. ,, .

15 Apl.	1842	Charles John	**Gehle,** zoon van den Eerw. Hy. Gehle, Th. Dr., o. 9 April in West Strand, oud 6 maanden.
13 Nov.	1758	Anna van	**Gelder,** Huisvrouw van William Isaak Kops, in een f. graf, zie 1727.
22 Jun.	1768	Philippina Susanna	**Giessenburgh,** van, Huisvrouw van den wel Ed. Heer Stephen Cottrel.
		Elizabeth d'Ablaing	
17 Jun.	1723	Francois van	**Gijssen,** Schoonsoen van Jacob Grotert.
26 Aug.	1723	Jacob	,, .
31 Aug.	1709	Maria	de **Gois.**
18 Mei	1712	Philip	,, **Golz, Jr.**
18 Mei	1714	Philip	,, **Gols, Sr.**
21 Apl.	1735	Maria Jacoba	,, , met Magdalena Pluijmert.
19 Feb.	1736	Willem	,, ,, .
10 Mar.	1737	Elizabeth	,, ,, , een nieuw graff in de breede plaats, naar dat de Lijken van Maria Jacoba de Gols & Willem de Gols eerst opgenomen & daarin zijn geleyt geweest.
24 Apl.	1754	Capt: John	**Gray,** Schoonzoon van wylen Dr. Arnold Boot Beirman.
2 Jan.	1750	Mejuffr. Catharina	**Groenen,** we. van Willem Standert, in leven onderling, by haar man.
3 Nov.	1697	Mr. Frederick	**Gronen.**
20 Dec.	1766	Albertus	**Groning,** I. W. D., geboortig van Bremen.
9 Nov.	1735	Jacob	de **Grootert.**
22 Apl.	1718	Jacob	**Grot.**
8 Oct.	1757	Ann	**Grote,** Huisvrouw van den Heer Andreas Grote, onderling.

13 Dec.	1788	Andreas	Grote, ouderling, in zijn f. graf daar zijn eerste huisvrouw begraven is den 8 Oct. 1757.
2 Jan.	1727	Maria	Grotert, in haar vaders graff.
6 Oct.	1768	Roelof	,, , in het graf van zijn zwager Nicolaas van Hoven, zie Ao. 1742.
21 Dec.	1772	Abraham	,, , in het graf van zyner vader.
17 Nov.	1779	Elizabeth	,, , we. laast van Nicolaas van den Hoven.
28 Dec.	1783	Katherina	,, , we...... Higgius, in haar f. graf daar haar broeder begraven is, zie 21 Dec. 1772.
4 Jan.	1800	Isaac	Guitard, kind van Arend Guitard.

6 Jun.	1765	Henricus	van Haemstede, in leven waardig Leeraar deser Gemeente.
24 Mar.	1722	Jacob	de Hane.
11 Aug.	1773	Didrich Jacob	,, .
27 Feb.	1741	Elizabeth	van Harthals.
31 Oct.	1753	Everd	,, , Diaken.
15 Sep.	1814	De Heer Edward	,, ,, , o. 8 Sep. & gelegd in het graf van zijnen vader.
17 Jan.	1721	Lydia	van Hattem.
11 Jun.	1770	Petronella	Heiliger, Huisvrouw van den Wel Ed. Heer Charles Pym Burt.
18 Sep.	1796	Anna	,, , we. van Samuel Thompson, o. 13 Sep. 1796 in het zelfde graf daar haar E. Zuster Mevr: Burt begraven is 11 Juny 1770.
3 Nov.	1721	Adriaan	van Helsdingen.
5 Jan.	1732	Pieter	,, .
19 Nov.	1719	Joachim	,, Hemert.
9 Mei	1734	Francois	,, ,, , bij sijn broeder.
24 Mei	1758	Jan	,, ,, , in het graf van zijn E. familie.
13 Jan.	1781	Elisabeth	,, ,, , we. van de Hr. Jan, in een f. graf, zie 24 Mei 1758.
22 Mar.	1786	Wolfert	,, ,, , in zijn f. graf daar den 13 Jan. 1781 Zijns Broers weduwe Elizabeth van Hemert begraven is.
13 Sep.	1739	Abraham	Henckell.
9 Jul.	1730	Isaac	Henkel.
....	1675	Mr. Jan	van Heijthuisen ende
,,	,,	Jouffrou Judith	van ,, .
17 Mar.	1693	Mr. Gerard	van ,, .
4 Dec.	1697	Johan	,, ,, , soon van Fr. Gerard van Heijthuisen.
27 Jun.	1701	Delmé	,, ,, .
29 Nov.	1720	Gerard	,, ,, , Jr.
31 Mar.	1722	Gerard	,, ,, .
29 Jul.	1722	Gerard	,, ,, , ouderling.
17 Nov.	1724	Robert	,, ,, .
20 Jun.	1733	Elizabeth	,, ,, .
16 Feb.	1769	Gerard	,, Heijthuizen, in het graf van John Delmé, zynde het zelfde graf waaarin ligt Elizabeth van Heythuizen, zie Jan. 1733.
13 Jan.	1777	Delmé	,, ,, in het f. graf, zie Ao. 1675.
2 Sep.	1790	Elizabeth	,, ,, , we. van Delmé van Heijthuizen, zie 13 Jan. 1777.
9 Sep.	1807	De Heer Pieter Hendrik	Hoogenbergh, o. 1 Sept.
17 Dec.	1761	Henrick	Hop, Hollandsche Envoijé, in zijn eigen graf. (v. Sweerts.)
25 Apl.	1780	Isabella Maria	,, , in haar f. graf, daar haar moeder, Ao. 1725, ende haar vader 1761 b begraven zyn.
22 Oct.	1742	Nicolaas	van der Hoven.
18 Jul.	1839	Gerrit Pieter	van Hulst, o. 12 July.

. . . .	1678	Mr. Herman	Jacobs.
20 Apl.	1759	Elizabeth	Jobut, Huisvr: van William Maas.
14 Jun.	1695	Mary	Jonas, uijt het Arm huijs.
23 Jun.	1745	Gerard	de Jongh, oud 14 Maanden.
4 Mar.	1748	Gerard	,, ,, , oud 1 jaar en 3 weeken.
21 Jun.	1802	Allegonda	Jongsma, we. Adolph Boon, in het graf, zie 25 Dec. 1767, & 30 Nov. 1789.

15 Jan.	1842	Lena	van der Kaaig, laast we. van der Eerw. Jan Werninek Th. Dr., oud 70 jaren, o. 7 Jan. In het graf No. 37, zie 6 Mei 1834.
10 Apl.	1711	Jannetje	van Kester.
23 Jul.	1694	Juffr. Sarah	Kersteman, we. van Mr. Gabriel de la Porte.
24 Aug.	1686	Pieter	,, , de soon van Fr. Pieter Kersteman.
7 Mar.	1704	Mrs. Sara	Kesterman.
5 Oct.	1710	William	,, .
12 Jun.	1712	Mrs. Hannah	,, , vrouw van Mr. James Kesterman.
8 Dec.	1715	Mr. Pieter	,, .
19 Apl.	1716	Mr. James	,, .
28 Jan.	1719	Otto	van ,, . (? Kesteren.)
29 Sep.	1749	Antony	Ter Kinder, oud 2 Jaren, zoontje van den Leraar H. Ter Kinder, Predikant in den Kapel.
21 Jul.	1763	Christina	,, ,, , 2de. dochter van Do. Ter Kinder, Predicant in St.James Chapel.
24 Aug.	1763	Gerrit Jan	,, ,, , zoon van Do. Ter Kinder, Predicant in St.James Chapel.
26 Aug.	1765	Esther	,, ,, , in het graf daar haar vader begraven is den 24 Aug. 1763.
21 Oct.	1772	Do. Joannes	,, ,, , Predicant in 't Konings Nederl. Capel te St.James, in het graf daar zijn E. Huisvrouw begraven is Ao. 1771.
22 Feb.	1778	Martin	Klencke.
11 Jun.	1735	Hannah	Kok.
24 Jan.	1781	Dr. John	Kooijstra, Diacon.
17 Jun.	1813	James Henry	Koppiers, zoon van Henry Koppiers, o. 13 Jun.
1 Nov.	1727	Jacob	Kops.
8 Jan.	1761	Anna	,, , dochter van de Heer William Isaak Kops.
12 Feb.	1774	William Isaak	,, , in een f. graf, daar zyn dogter Anna begraven is Ao. 1761 by't ander graf van deze familie.
31 Dec.	1781	Agnes	,, , (Coussemaker, geboren), in haar familie graf zie Feb. 1774.
26 Nov.	1735	Peter	Korten.
28 Oct.	1742	Johan Abraham	,, , ouderling, in het graf van Mr. Pieter Korten.
1 Jul.	1831	De Heer Simon	de Koster geboren te Middelburg en o. te Twickenham op den 22 Junij, oud 65 jaren
5 Nov.	1796	Frederick	Kothe.
8 Jul.	1736	Agnes	Koussemaaker, T. D. in het graf van haar Grootvader Isaac Kops, zie 1727.
23 Aug.	1749	Koenraad	Kraguelins.
13 Apl.	1687	Juffr. Magdalena	Kuffelaer, weduwe.

14 Mei	1740	Maria	Lanctilier, we. de Tudert, bij haar man.
. . Feb.	1733	Arnold	Lang, naast den Envoye van Vrijbergen. (v. Mee)
11 Apl.	1736	Benjamin	,, , in syn vaders graf.
7 Oct.	1736	Maria	,, .
12 Aug.	1740	Herman	,, .
2 Apl.	1745	Henry	,, .
30 Dec.	1769	Coenraad	,, .
31 Oct.	1800	Daniel	Levering, v. Demerara.

25 Jan.	1764	Harriot	**Lightfoot**, dogter van Samuel Lightfoot en Juffrouw Berkenhout.
2 Jul.	1794	Do. Gerard	**Lijdekker**, voorheen Predikant in Noord America. dog wegens de verandering in de regeering aldaar voorgevallen naar Engeland overgekomen en te Pentonville na bij London den 28 Juny 1794 overleden.
18 Jan.	1812	Maria	**Linden**, we. van de Heer Picter Hendrick Hoogenbergh. o. 13 Jan.
19 Sep.	1806	Andries Albert Jan Strick van	**Linschoten**, gestorven den 12 Sep. in Hackney Road, oud 8 maanden, Jongste kind van den Heer Francois Albert Leonard Strick van Linschoten.
8 Nov.	1815	Catharina Johanna Strick van	,, , o. den 31 Oct., gelegd in het f. graf.
8 Apl.	1816	Marius Catharinus Strick van	,, , oud 9 Maandeu, in het f. graf.
27 Dec.	1689	Mr. Ralph	**Lodowick.**
19 Feb.	1694	Juffr. Anna	,, , we. wijlen Fr. Gerard van Heijthuijsen.
24 Feb.	1723	Collonel Charles	**Lodwick.**
1 Apl.	1731	Margareta	,, , in haar mans graf.
2 Aug.	1709	Albert	**Loning**, van Bremen.

19 Mar.	1781	William	**Maas** in een graf waar zijn vrouw begraven is den 20 Apl. 1759.
11 Nov.	1776	Albert	**Mahlstede.**
10 Feb.	1716	Gerard	**Masakker.**
21 Jan.	1770	Elisabeth	**Mee**, we. van Arnold Lang in haar mans graf, zie 173?.
3 Mei	1784	Herman	**Meijer**, in zijn f. graf, dar zijn huisvrouw begraven is den 15 Oct. 1768.
1 Mei	1790	Christian Paul	,, , in het f. graf.
13 Jun.	1799	Christian	,, , ,, ,, ,, ,, .
7 Dec.	1799	Hannah	,, , we. van Christian Meijer.
10 Jun.	1807	JonkvrouwCatharine	,, , in het f. graf, zie 15 Oct. 1768, 3 Mei 1784, 1 Mei 1790, 13 Jun. 1799, en 7 Dec. 1799.
1 Jul.	1822	Louisa	,, , huisvrouw van Christian Paul Meyer in het f. graf, zie 10 Jun. 1807.
22 Feb.	1826	Den Wel Ed. Heer James	,, , o. 11 Feb. in de Parish van Enfield, oud 70 jaren, zie 1 Jul. 1822.
6 Jun.	1832	Christian Paul	,, , zoon van den Wel Ed. Heer Christian Paul Meijer, o. 25 Meij te Maxton bij Dover, oud 18 jaren.
29 Jun.	1832	De Wel Ed. Heer Herman	,, , o. 20 Junij in Forty Hall, Co. Middelsex, oud 75 jaren en gelegd in een nieuw graf naast het f. graf No. 39.
1 Aug.	1835	Christian Paul	,, , zoon van den Wel Edel. Heere Christian Paul Meyer. o. te Enfield 27 Jul. 1835, oud 11 maanden.
8 Mar.	1838	Anne Sophia	,, , o. 28 Feb., oud 20 jaren in Enfield, Co. Middlesex. In het graf No. 39, zie 1 Aug. 1835.
17 Feb.	1841	Ann	,, , o. te Chipping Ongar, Essex, 9 Feb., oud 75 jaren. In het graf No. 39, zie 8 Mar. 1838.
17 Jul.	1843	Louisa Joanna	,, , o. te Enfield den 9 Jul., oud 27 jaren. In het graf No. 39.
4 Jul.	1851	Anna Maria	,, , o. te Kemp Town, (Brighton) Sussex, 28 Jul., oud 58 jaren. In het f. graf, No. 39.
31 Aug.	1747	Christina	**Meijers**, we. van Antony Vos, Schoonmoeder van D. Ter Kinder. In het graf v. D. van Bracht.
27 Aug.	1703	Mrs. Agnieta van der	**Mersch.**
17 Sep.	1714	Mr. Picter ,, ,,	,, .
15 Jul.	1766	Mrs. Rebecca ,, ,,	,, , huisvrouwe van I. van der Mersch, in het graf van Picter van der Mersch, zie 1714.
25 Jun.	1773	Johannes ,, ,,	,, , Jr., in het graf van Picter van der Mersch, zie 1714.
29 Jun.	1774	John ,, ,,	**Meulen**, Diacon.
16 Dec.	1731	Albert van	**Meurs**, Jr.
.. ..	1675	D.	**Michaeli**, Predicant van die Fransche Gemeente.
23 Apl.	1757	Cornelia Kuijck van	**Mierop.**
7 Jul.	1774	Isaak ,, ,,	,, , in zijn eigen graf, zie Ao 1757.
29 Apl.	1799	Sarah Maria Kuijck ,,	,, , in het f. graf, daar haar vader en moeder begraven is.
3 Sep.	1724	Susanna van der	**Mijn.**
20 Dec.	1710	Abraham van	**Mildert** Jr.
4 Mei	1800	Catharine	**Miller**, huisvrouw van John Miller.

1 Feb.	1862	John	**Miller**, man van Catharine Miller.
8 Nov.	1747	Mr.	**Miré.**
28 Feb.	1696	Elizabeth	**Moller**, huijsvrouw van Mr. Jan Moller.
9 Mei	1772	Henry	**Mulman.**
16 Mar.	1795	Engelbert	**Mulhausen.**
28 Jun.	1726	William	**Muller**, int graff van Mr. Esselbron.

2 Jan.	1783	Diderick	**Nantes.**
29 Jan.	1814	De Heer Daniel	,, , onderling, o. 22 Jan. 1814.
24 Aug.	1750	De Heer Gerard van	**Neck,** ,, en Vooruaam Weldoender dezer Gemeente.
27 Oct.	1744	John	de **Neufville.**
27 Mar.	1788	Mary	**Nicolas**, huisvrouw van Lewis Nicolas.
20 Jun.	1804	Lewis	,, .
22 Jan.	1727	Cornelius	**Noerdwijck.**
4 Apl.	1717	Benjamin	**Noordwijck.**
6 Mei	1719	Maria	,, .
11 Jan.	1704	Daniel	**Noordtwijk.**
2 Aug.	1715	Lewis	,, .
11 Dec.	1716	Cornelis	,, .
22 Nov.	1714	Elisabeth	**Noortwijck.**
26 Feb.	1731	Anna Maria	,, .
2 Oct.	1707	John	**Noortwijk.**
1 Apl.	1719	Eleonora	,, .
12 Mar.	1751	Charles	van **Notten**, onderling.
8 Mei	1783	De Heer Pieter	,, ,, , (vide Pole) in een nieuw f. graf digt bij het f. graf van wijlen zijn broeder Charles van Notten. Zie 12 Mar. 1751. Gestorven den 1 Mei.
23 Mei	1762	Gerard Bolwerk	**Nucella**, derde zoontje van Timotheus Nucella, Diaken.
18 Sep.	1762	Isabella Maria	,, , dochtertje van Timotheus Nucella, Diaken.
26 Mei	1768	Elizabeth	,, , ,, ,, ,, ,, , ,, .
14 Aug.	1771	Sophia Ann	,, , dochter ,, ,, ,, ,, .
7 Nov.	1772	Gerard	,, , derde zoontje van de Heer Tim: Nucella.
13 Apl.	1781	Pieter	,, , zoon van Timotheus Nucella, Diakon.
14 Mei	1801	Timothy	,, , Diakon, in het f. graf.

10 Sep.	1701	Elizabeth	**Otger.**
12 Jan.	1704	Alice	,,
19 Aug.	1714	Abraham	,, .
21 Aug.	1686	Elizabeth	,, huijsvrouw van Fr. Justus Otgher.
20 Jul.	1711	Justus	**Otgher.**
4 Dec.	1727	Justus	,, in sijn vaders graff.
28 Oct.	1741	Jan	**Oudenaarden.**
4 Dec.	1716	Mr. Jan	**Oulrij.** (**Thomas**, ou Mon. Inscription.)
4 Nov.	1729	Sara	,, in haar mans graff.
28 Mar.	1731	Katherina	,, in haar vaders ,, .

1 Mar. 1806 Lambertus Henricus Paal, S. S. Theol. Doctr., in leeven Lerraar dezer Gemeente.
                Schippers
16 Jul. 1698 Mr. Ambrosius Paijne, v. Embden.
23 Jan. 1826 Vrouwe Marion Park, we. van den Wel. Eerw. Heer Thomas Peirson, o. 14 Janij, oud 82 jaren, zie
                20 Jul. 1820.
24 Dec. 1744 Cornelius Pater.
3 Jan. 1708 Catharina Paus.
20 Jul. 1820 Thomas Peirson, Th: Dr., voormaals Engelsch Predikant in Amsterdam, o. 12 Jul. in den
                ouderdom van 74 jaren.
9 Mei 1810 Mevrouw Mary Pepper, wede. van den Heer Jan Blijdesteijn, in het familie graf.
. . . . 1684 Mr. Jan van Pieren.
16 Aug. 1698 Jonas Pietersen, dienaer van Colonel Baijer.
20 Jul. 1820 Dirk Plokker, Diaken, o. 13 Jul. oud 44 jaren.
11 Mei 1733 Magdalena Pluymert, naast Daniel Bolten.
19 Aug. 1693 Het. van Mr. van der Poest.
22 Jun. 1698 Juffru. Mary „ „ „ ·
25 Dec. 1710 Adriaan „ „ „ ·
30 Jun. 1813 Sir Charles Pole, Bt., ouderling.
27 Nov. 1818 Millicent „ , wede. van den Heer Charles van Notten, naderhand genaamd Sir Charles
                Pole, Baronet, in leven Ouderling dezer Gemeente. In het graf van Pieter
                van Notten.
. . . . 1681 . . . . . van der Port, huisvrouwe van onser Leeraer Ds. van der Port, en haar Soon.
8 Jul. 1766 Clarissa Catharina Porter, huijsvr. van Sir James Porter, in het graf van den Heere James Fremeaux.
13 Aug. 1720 Samuel Du Pré.
2 Aug. 1716 Mr. Henry „ „ ·
25 Apl. 1696 Juffru. Maria de Puij, huijsvrouwe van Mr. Jan de Berdt.
9 Mar. 1797 Do. Hendrick Putman, in leven Predikant deser Gemeijnte.
30 Sep. 1744 Maria „ Putter.
8 Feb. 1760 Henrik „ „ , in een familie graf.

. . . . 1675 Mrs. de Raet.
12 Apl. 1705 Mrs. Cornelia „ Reaux.
31 Jan. 1706 Anna Rees, Morsatener.
12 Apl. 1738 Gerard Reesen, bij sijn grootmoeder.
28 Dec. 1767 Mary Bateia Rice, huisvrouwe van Adolph Boon, Diacon.
25 Aug. 1806 Cornelis Elias Roëll, van Berbice. Gestorven den 16 Aug. in Leicester Square.
1 Apl. 1817 HermanEverhar. van Rossum, zoon van den Heer Abraham Everhardus van Rossum, o. 27 Maart.
9 Oct. 1810 Louis Herman „ „ , zoon van Abraham van Rossum, o. 5 Oct.
31 Dec. 1823 Charles Thomas „ „ , zoon „ „ „ , oud 18 maanden.
12 Sep. 1760 Nicolaas Rotshouck, in een familie graf.
26 Nov. 1731 Jonas Rowlandson.
11 Aug. 1737 Elizabeth „ in haar vaders graff.
13 Feb. 1745 Elizabeth „ ·
1 Jan. 1749 Roeland „ , in het graf van Mr. Jonas Rowlandson.
15 Jan. 1756 Jonas „ „ , „ „ „ „ Roeland „ ·

19 Jan. 1845 John Sack, zoon van den Heer Frederick Sack, o. 13 Jan., in de Parish van Westhar
                in Essex, oud 10 jaren. In het f. graf, No. 105, zie 4 Jul. 1839.
13 Feb. 1690 Juffru. Josina Schapelinck. (vide Ellsworth).
1 Sep. 1758 Maria Scholefeild, dochter van James Scholefield en Elizabeth Lang. In het graf va:
                haar grootvader Coenraad Lang.

6 Mar.	1773	Elisabeth	**Scholefield**, huisvrouw van James Scholefield. In het graf van haar vader Coenraad Lang, zie Ao. 1769.
16 Jun.	1728	Jan	**Scholten.**
25 Feb.	1776	Caspar	**Schombart** in het f. graf, zie Ao 1709.
14 Mei	1789	Philip Anthony	**Schumacker**, ouderling.
10 Aug.	1728	Francois	**Seijdel.**
6 Jun.	1726	John	**Shomaker**, in't graff van Thomas Virool.
14 Apl.	1753	Mejuffr. Anna Maria	**Siebels**, we. van Jan Abraham Korten, bij haar man.
. . . .	1780	Johan Frederick	**Siffken**, zoon van de Heer Henrick Siffken, in het graf van der Heer Johan Siffken.
21 Jan.	1804	Elizabeth Harriet	,, , dochter van Henry Siffken.
23 Nov.	1821	Frederic	,, , tweede zoon van den Heer Henry Siffken, oud 20 jaren
18 Aug.	1836	Henry	,, , o. den 11 Aug., in de Parish van St.John, Hackney, oud 77 jaren. In het gemetseld graf, No. 48.
4 Mei	1840	John	,, , ouderling, o. 27 Apl. l. l., oud 78 jaren, en gelegd in het graf No. 95, zie 5 Jan, 1838.
8 Dec.	1845	Elizabeth	,, , weduwe van den Heer Henry Siffken, overleden te Hackney, 30 Nov., oud 77 jaren. In het graf No. 48, zie 18 Aug. 1836.
18 Nov.	1789	Sr. John	**Silvester**, Kt., M.D., ouderling, in het f. graf daar zyn E. huisvrouw begraven is, zie 1 Apl. 1772.
14 Dec.	1724	Raymondt	de **Smet.**
16 Jul.	1729	Herman Isaac	,, **Smeth**, int graff van sijn Broeder Raijmond de Smeth.
14 Mar.	1720	Pieter	**Smidt.**
11 Mei	1815	Jane	**Smith**, we. van den Heer A. Ten Broeke, o. 7 Mei.
13 Mei	1753	Mejuffer Catharina	**Snellen.**
25 Jan.	1742	Willem	**Standert**, ouderling.
27 Jan.	1754	Mejuffer Catharina	,,
16 Nov.	1801	Pieter	**Stapel**, in het f. graf, zie 7 Mei 1795.
6 Jun.	1782	Filida	van der **Steegh**, we. wijlen Jacobus du Croz, in haar f. graf. Zie Mar. 1773.
24 Apl.	1798	Johanna	van **Steenwijk.**
18 Sep.	1704	Mrs. Mary	**Stockton.**
7 Sep.	1671	Maria	van der **Straten**, de huisvrou van onsen broeder Philipp op de Beeck, Predicant van dese Gemente.
8 Nov.	1692	de Gravinne	van **Stijrum.**
. . Jan.	1815	Sarah Elizabeth	**Suwerkrop**, dochter van den Heer I. B. Suwerkrop.
21 Oct.	1816	Anna Elizabeth	,, , o. 14 Oct., en gelegd in het graf van den Heer I. B. Suwerkrop. Zie Jan. 1815.
4 Jul.	1839	John Bruhn	,, , ouderling. o. 28 Jun. l. l. In het f. graf, No. 105. Zie 4 Aug. 1827.
20 Apl.	1725	Vrouw Jacoba	**Sweerts**, vrouw van sijn Excel. d'Heer Envoij Hop.

7 Sep.	1776	Jan Hendrick	**Tatum.**
10 Nov.	1770	Frederick	**Teise**, N.B. Dit lijk is beloofd niet te zullen gevoerd worden gedurende de tijd van 20 jaaren hebbende de Heer Teise de suegens £30 aan onze Diaconie nagelaten.
19 Aug.	1742	Simon	**Theunmans.**
. . Feb.	1688	Ridley	**Tijssen.**
. . Apl.	1693	Eliza.	,, ,
23 Mar.	1699	Mr. Francois	,, , Senr.
22 Oct.	1739	Louis	de **Tudert.** (vide Lanctilier).

12 Feb.	1724	Laurence	van de **Velde.**
19 Nov.	1757	Albert	,, ,, ,, , Diaken.
2 Nov.	1781	De Heer Jan	**Verbruggen.** N.B. Een Looden kist, of mogelijk dit Lijk metter tijd na Holland zoude vervoert worden.
28 Feb.	1786	Pieter	,, , in het zelfde graf daar zyn vader begraven is 2 Nov. 1781.
5 Mei	1735	Johanna	**Verrijt.**
28 Nov.	1758	Josina Maria	,, , huisvrouwe van Gerard Bolwerk, ouderling in een f. graf.
14 Nov.	1754	Hanna	**Verveer.**
21 Jan.	1693	Elizabeth	**Vingerhoet,** huijsvrouw van Fr. Fredrick Gronen.
1 Dec.	1702	Mr Isaac	**Vink.**
25 Aug.	1735	Hester	van **Vliet.**
12 Feb.	1749	Maria	,, ,, , huijsvrouw van den Heer Jan Reessen, Diaken.
6 Aug.	1752	Fermijn	,, , onderling.
28 Jun.	1704	Mr. Thomas	**Viroot.**
5 Mar.	1767	Nathanael	**Voogd.**
3 Jan.	1784	Magda. Margareta	,, , huisvrouw van de Heer James Des Cotes, onderling, in haar f. graf, zie 5 Maart 1767.
22 Mei	1771	Margareta	**Vos,** huisvrouw van Do. Joannes Ter Kinder.
22 Aug.	1806	Petronella Francina	,, , jongste dochter van Hermannus Vos, o. den 17 Aug. l. L te Camberwell.
25 Sep.	1810	William Drummond	,, , zoon van Hermannus Vos. o. den 18 Sep., oud ses maanden.
8 Jul.	1711	De Heer Marinus van	**Vrijbergen,** Envoie, Etc.
27 Nov.	1815	Anna Bernardina	**Vromans,** huisvrouw van den Heer W. I. C. Rakle.

23 Feb.	1724	Gerard	de **Waal.**
25 Nov.	1699	M's Geertruid	,, **Wael.**
27 Sep.	1786	Christiaan	**Wagner.**
26 Nov.	1770	Dr. John	**Walker,** in zijn Wel Eerw. leven Predicant onder de Dissenters te Bethnall Green in een graf allernaast zijn gewezene huisvrouw, het zelfde graf daar de Hr. Noordwijk in begraven is Ao. 1727-28.
17 Jan.	1690	Sarah	**Ward,** huijsvrouw van onsen Broeder Samuel Biscop.
1 Mar.	1692	Sir James	,, ,
21 Jan.	1716	James	,, , Esqre.
10 Aug.	1808	Rebecca	**Waterhouse,** huisvrouw van James Ten Broeke, Diacon, o. 3 Aug.
6 Jun.	1685	Mr Willem	de **Werdt.**
6 Mei	1834	Jan	**Werninck,** Th. Dr. en Predicant deser Gemeente, o. 27 Apl. 1834 te Camberwell, oud 62 jaren.
2 Oct.	1710	John	**Westhuijs.**
14 Feb.	1743	Godfried	**Wichelhausen.**
6 Dec.	1712	Anna	**Willemse.**
11 Jan.	1688	Mr Jacob	**Willemsen.**
5 Jan.	1833	De Heer Diederick	**Willink,** ouderling, o. te Londen den 30 Dec. 1832, oud aren en gelegd in het graf, No. 95.
19 Mar.	1803	Mary Ann	**Wijnen,** huijsvrouw van Gerardus Wijnen.
23 Mar.	1803	Mary Ann	,, , dochtertje van Gerardus Wijnen, oud 5 dagen

North Aisle, East end.

No. 20

Hier onder rust, in hoope van een

zaelige opstandinge

D'Heer PIETER KORTEN, Coopman

hier in London gebooren tot Elverfeld

in 't Hertogdom Bergh den $\frac{11}{22}$ Iuly

Anno 1703 en overleeden den 19 Novbr. 1735.

Als mede D' Heer IOHN ABRAHAM

KORTEN, Koopman hier in London

en Ouderling van deese Gemeynte

gebooren tot Elverfeld $\frac{13}{23}$ October

Ao. 1690 en overleeden den 21 Oct.

O : S : Ao. 1742 oudt 52 jaaren.

En zyn e. huisvrouw

ANNA MARIA SIEBELS

geboren te Elberfeld Augustus

Ao. 1701, en overleden 4 April 1753.

——o——

No. 21.

Hier is begraaven de Heer

ARNOLD LANG, Diacon deeser

Gemeynte. Gebooren tot Bremen den 21

September 1686, overleeden tot London

den 24 Febravary 1734, out 47 jaaren 5 maenden.

Here also lieth the body of

BENJAMIN LANG, son of the abovesaid

ARNOLD LANG, who departed this life,

the 8th of April 1736, aged 11 years.

Here also lieth the body of MR. HENRY LANG,

second son of the above MR. ARNOLD LANG,

who died the 20th of March 1745,

in the 19th year of his age.

Also here lieth interr'd the remains of

MRS. ELIZABETH LANG, wife of the

above mention'd MR. ARNOLD LANG,

who died Janry. the 13th 1770, aged 69 years.

——o——

Hier leght begraven d' Heer

MARINUS VAN VRYBERGE

ordinaris gedeputeerde ter

Vergadering van haar Hoog: Moog:

D' Heeren Staten Generael

der Vereenigde Nederlanden

en der selver Extraordinaris

• Envoye aen t' Hof van Hare

Maiesteyt van Groot Brittanien,

overleden den 3en Iuly, 1711.

oudt 55 Iaaren.

Heer legt begraven

D' Heer[1] [RAYMONDT DE SMET]

gewees . .

geboo[ren]

den VII . . . . .

overle[eden . . . Dec. 1724.]

Als mede [syn broeder]

HERMAN [ISAAC DE SMETH]

coo[pman] . . . . . .

geboore[n] . . . .

overlee[den . . Julij 1729.]

(1) Vide Burial Register. The remainder of this
Inscription is covered by the Altar Steps.

Hier leght begraven

KATHERINA OTGHER

weduwe van DAUID OTGHER

overleden den 3 April

Ao. 1676.

En ELIZABETH OTGHER huys

vrouw van JUSTUS OTGHER

overleden 16 April

Ao. 1686.

En ELIZABETH OTGHER

overleden den 7 Sept. 1701

En ALICE OTGHER

overleden den 7 January 170⅟.

En JUSTUS OTGHER

Ouderling deser Gemeente

overleden den 23 July 1711

oudt 65 jaren.

ABRAHAM OTGHER

overleden 12 Augsti 1714.

En IUSTS. OTGER begrauen 4 Dec. 1727 oudt 43 jar.

Hier rust het lighaam

van JAN BLYDESTEYN

Zoon van JAN ende MARY

BLYDESTEYN;

gestorven 7 Septr., 1797

oud 31 Jaren.

Benevens het lyk

van ISAAC BLYDESTEYN,

Koopman binnen deze stad,

en Ouderling dezer Gemeente;

overleden den 7th Feb., 1830,

in den Ouderdam

van ruim 74 jaren.

ANNA BLYDESTEYN

overleden den 13 Maart 1838,

Oud 73 Jaren.

JUDITH BLYDESTEYN, weduwe

[van] JOHN CAMPBELL.

Overleden den 4 Maart, 1841.

oud 81 Jaren.

Chancel, Altar Rails.

No. 27

Hier legt begraven

IACOB BERCKENHOUT, Soon van

BENIAMIN en ISABELLA BERCKENHOUT,

overleden den 10 December 1729,

ovdt 13 weeken.

Ende ANNA MARGARETA BERCKENHOUT,

overleden den 18 December 1729,

ovdt 4 Iaren en 6 Maende.

—o—

No. 28

Hier rust het lichaam

van JAN BLYDESTEYN

zoon van

JAN ende MARY BLYDESTEYN

gestorven den 27 October

[1] [1758]

En van haar Dogter

MARIANNE BLYDESTEYN

gestorven den 21 April 1760.

Als mede

JAN BLYDESTEYN

Ouderling dezer Gemeente,

overleden den .. Februarij 1777,

oud 79 jaren.

En

MARY BLYDESTEYN

zyn Huysvrouw,

gestorven 30 April 1810,

oud 80 jaren en 4 maaenden.

(1) Vide Burial Register.

—o—

South Aisle, East End.

No. 33

Hier legt begraaven

NICOLAS van der HOVEN,

gestorven den 18 Octr.

1712, in syn 71ste jaar.

Als mede

ROELOF GROTERT,

overleeden den 29sten Sept.,

1768, in zyn 63sten Jaar

Gelijk ook

ELISABETH GROTERT,

laatst weduwe van NICOLAS

van der HOVEN, gestorven

den 10den November 177[9],[2]

in haar 85sten Jaar.

(2) Vide Burial Register.

—o—

North Aisle, East End.

No. 38.

Hier onder rust het lijk

van PIETRONELLA FRANCINA VOS,

gestorven den 17de Augustus, 1806.

Oud 14 Maanden

WILLIAM DRUMMOND VOS,

overleden 18 September 1810.

Oud zes maanden.

—o—

Hier ligt begraven

de Heer MATTHEUS BOLWERK

obiit 14 Aug. 1748, oud 24 jaaren.

Nevens zyn Ed. Moeder

Mevrouw JOSINA MARIA VERRYT,

Huisvrouw van den Heer GERARD BOLWERK

obiit 27 Dec. 1758, oud 66 jaaren.

Als mede de Heer GERARD BOLWERK,

Ouderling dezer Gemeente. Obiit 3 April

1760, oud 75 jaaren.

Gelijk ook hun Ed. Dogter Mejufrouw

MARIA BOLWERK, obiit 19 Febr. 1778. Oud 60 jaaren.

Gelyk ook hun Ed. Dogter Mevrouw ISABELLA

BOLWERK, Huisvrouw van den Heer

TIMOTHY NUCELLA, obiit 28den Jan. 1777, oud 49 jaaren.

Insgelyks de Heer TIMOTHY NUCELLA, Diaken

dezer Gemeente obiit 5den Mey 1801, oud 70 jaaren.

——o——

Hier rust het lichaam van

MARY LANG, huys vrouw van

CONRAD LANG, ouerleeden den

3 Octor., 1736. Oudt synde

33 jaaren, 4 maenden.

Mr. GERRIT PIETER van HULST

of Berbice.

Died 11th July, 1839.

——o——

Hier leght begraven

Mr. ABRAHAM HENCKEL,

Ouderling deser Gemeente,

ooverleeden den 7en September, 1739.

Oudt 71 Jaeren

ISAAC HENCKEL

[zyn Bro]eder : ooverleeden den 6 July,

[17]30. Oudt 48 Jaeren.

¹ ELIZABETH HENCKELL,

[Huysvr.] van Mr. ABRAHAM HENCKELL,

[overleden] den 30en May, 1749.

Oudt 70 Jaeren.

¹) Geboren Crop.

——o——

Hior light Begraven
² JAMES CROP

(²) The remaining portion of inscription covered by
raised floor of Chancel.

Hier legt begraeven

De Heer NATHANAEL VOOGD in syn leeven

Koopman deeser Stadt,

overleeden den 27 February, 1767.

Oudt 67 jaaren.

En

syne Suster,

Mevrouw

MAGDALENA MARGARETHA VOOGD,

huysvrouw van

den Heer JACOBUS DESCOTES,

Ouderling deezer Gemeente.

Obiit 20 December, 1783.

Oud 74 jaaren.

—o—

Here lieth the Body of Mrs. MARGARET
MEYER, who departed this life the 8th of
October, 1768, Aged 49 years.

Also the Body of Mr. HERMAN MEYER,
her late husband who departed this life
the 27th of April, 1784. Aged 69 years.

Also the body of CHRISTIAN PAUL
MEYER their Son, who departed this life
the 26th of April, 1790, Aged 32 years.

Also the Body of Mr. CHRISTIAN MEYER, who depart
this life the 7th June, 1799. Aged 74.

Likewise Mrs. HANNAH MEYER, widow of the above
Mr. CHRISTIAN MEYER, who died November 30th, 179
in the 75th year of her age.

Likewise the Body of CATHERINE MEYER,
Daughter of the above HERMAN and MARGAR ET MEYI
who died the 2nd of June, 1807,
in the 55th year of her age.

—o—

Hier legt begraven

De Heer JACOBUS DES COTES,

Ouderling deezer Gemeente,

overleeden den 6den July, 1792.

Oudt 66 Jaaren.

Als mede

Mevrouw

MAGDALENA CHRISTINA DIEMEL.

Weduwe van voorzeiden Heere

JACOBUS DES COTES, overleden 20

November, 1794, Oudt 50 Jaaren.

Hier legt begraven de Heer

FRANCIS CRAIESTEIJN, Koopman

van deese Stadt, gebooren tot London.

den 13 July, 1695. Overleeden

25 September, 1758.

—o—

North Aisle, East end.

No. 37

No. 40.

Hier onder rust het Lyk,

van den Hoog Eerwaerden

en Hooggeleerden Heere

LAMBERTUS HENRICUS

SCHIPPERS PAAL, S.S. TH. D.

gewezen Predikant alhier;

In den Heere ontslapen in London,

den 23ste February, A.D. 1806.

Oud 33 jaren.

Als mede

het Lijk van den Wel Eerwaarden

Zeer Geleerden Heer,

JAN WERNINCK, S.S. Theol. Doct.,

gedurende 31 jaren

Predikant dezer gemeente,

overleden den 27 April, 1834,

in den ouderdom van 62 jaren.

Hier rust het lighaam van

MARY BATHIA BOON,

Huysvrouw van ADOLPH BOON, (¹)

diacon van deezer gemeynte.

Overleeden den 21 December 1767.

Oud 42 jaaren.

Insgelyks het lighaam van Gemelden

ADOLPH BOON,

in leven laatst Ouderling deezer

gemeente. Overleeden

den 23 Nov., 1789. Oud 70 jaaren.

Alsmeede is hier begraven Vrouwe

ALLAGONDA BOON, geboore JONGSMA,

(tweede Huysvrouw van bovengenoemde

ADOLPH BOON.) Overleeden den 13 Juny.,

1802. Oud 70 jaaren.

(¹) Vide RICE.

——o——

——o——

North Aisle, East End.

No. 23.

Hier leght begraven IOHAN

Van HEYTHUYSEN, overleden

25 January 167¾, oudt 62

Iaaren.

Hier leght begraven GERARD

Van HEYTHUYSEN, Broeder van

IOHAN Van HEYTHUYSEN

overleden 11 Meert, 169⅝.

oudt 75 Iaeren.

Hier leght begraven ANNA

Van HEYTHVYSEN, Wedvwe van

GERARD Van HEYTHVYSEN, Senr.

overleden den 12 Febrvary

169⅓, oudt 70 Iaeren.

Hier leght begraven IOHAN

VAN HEYTHUYSEN, Soon van

GERARD en ELIZABETH en

Groot Soon van IOHAN Van

HEYTHUYSEN, over leden den

December 1697, oudt 15 Maenden,

ende DELME Van HEYTHUYSEN, Obiit

26 Junii 1701, æt: 17 Dagen.

——o——

Chancel, North End.

No. 24.

Here lyeth the body of Mrs.

DEBORAH DELMÉ, objit the 3d

of April 1706, æta : 59.

And of

Mr. JOHN DELMÉ, objit

25 Janvarij, 1711. Ætatis 79.

And

[1] RICHARD [Van HEYTHU]YSEN, Son

Van [GERARD HEYTH]UYSEN,

[2] [ende]   [ELIS]ABETH

[DELMÉ]   ndson

                                     obijt

                                     years

                             SARAH

                        rch 1722

        Nov.   [17]24

        n

        Mr.

        ecdo. elder

        y   173

Partly obscured by Altar Steps.

(1) Query Robert, vide Register
(2) Vide Register.

——o——

v

South Aisle, East End.

No. 36

JAMES MEYER, Son of

HERMAN and MARGARATTE MEYER,

Born 1755, died 11th Feb., 1826.

LOUISA MEYER, Daughter of

RAWSON HART BODDAM

Wife of CHRISTIAN PAUL MEYER, junr.

Born 23rd Octr., 1794.   Died 21st June, 1822.

CHRISTIAN PAUL MEYER, junr.

Son of CHRISTIAN PAUL and

LOUISA MEYER,

Born 28th March, 1814, died 25th May, 1832.

——o——

South Aisle, East End.

No. 39ª.

HERMAN MEYER, Son of
HERMAN and MARGARATTE MEYER.
Born July 20th, 1757.
Dyed June 20th, 1832.

CHRISTIAN PAUL MEYER, Son of
CHRISTIAN PAUL and ANNE MARIA MEYER.
Died July 27th, 1835,
Aged 11 Months.

ANNE SOPHIA MEYER, Daughter of
CHRISTIAN PAUL and LOUISA MEYER.
Born April 5th, 1818.
Died February 28th, 1838.

ANN, Widow of
CHRISTIAN PAUL MEYER,
and Daughter of
ISAAC and ELIZABETH SOLLY,
Born October 28th, 1765.
Died February 9th, 1841.

LOUISA JOANNA, Daughter of
CHRISTIAN PAUL and LOUISA MEYER.
Born September . . 1816.
Died July 9th, 1843.

Also
ANNA MARIA MEYER,
Wife of CHRISTIAN PAUL MEYER,
Died June 28th, 1851,
Aged 58.

——o——

Ile of North Aisle.

43.

Middle of North Aisle.

No. 52.

Hier legt begraven

De Heer ABRAHAM CRAIESTEYN,

Coopman van deeze Stadt, Gebooren

tot Haarlem den 31 May, 1666,

en overleeden den 22 January, 17⅜

En zijn Ed. Huijsvrouw, Juffrouw

REBECCA CRAIESTEYN,

in London

Gebooren den 7de December, 1658.

En Gestorven den 1te Maart, 17⅘: S : V :

Ende Haar Ed. Soon de Heer

ABRAHAM CRAIESTEYN,

Overleden den 7de Decembr, 1754.

Hier legt begraven

Vrouwe ANN STAPEL,

(geboren Emilie) Huisvrouw van

De Heer PETER STAPEL.

Zy is gestorven te Putney

in Surry den 29 April, 1795,

Oudt 88 Jaaren.

Als meede gezegde Heer

PETER STAPEL

geweezene voornaame

Koopman tot London

Overleeden te Putney,

den 10 November, 1801.

Oudt 92 Jaaren.

North Aisle, East End.

No. 41.

Hier onder rust het lyk,

van ALBERT ANDRIES

JAN STRICK VAN LINSCHOTEN,

Gestorven 12de Sepr., 1806.

Oud Agt Maanden.

Als mede

CATHERINA JOHANNA

STRICK VAN LINSCHOTEN,

Overleden 31 Octr., 1815.

Oud 14 Jaaren ende 2 Maanden.

Benevens

MARIUS CATHARINUS STRICK

van LINSCHOTTEN,

Gestorven den 29sten Maart, 1816.

Oud Agt Maanden

en Vyftien Dagen.

————o————

Middle of South Aisle.

No. 51.

[1] I ✠ K.

(1) Probably Dr. JOHN KOOIJSTRA, *vide* Register.

————o————

Middle of North Aisle.

No. 46.

Sacred

to the Memory of

Mrs. HARRIOTT BAGELMANN,

who died the 19th of Febry., 1804.

Aged 41 years, 6 months, and 3 days.

FREDERICK ALBERT BAGELMANN,

died the 27th June 1823. Aged 11 years.

ELIZABETH MARY BAGELMANN,

died the 18th Feb., 1825. Aged 18 years.

Son and Daughter of JACOB

and ELIZABETH BAGELMANN.

Also Mr. JACOB BAGELMANN,

died the 23rd November, 1835.

In his 75th year.

————o————

Hier onder rust het lyk

Van de HEER

PIETER HENDRICK HOOGENBERGH,

(gebooren tot Amsterdam)

overleeden te Londen

den 1sten Septr., 1807.

Oud 77 Jaaren.

Als mede

MARIA LINDEN,

Weduwe

Van de boven genoemde

PIETER HENDRICK HOOGENBERGH

¹ . . . .

den 13 January, 1812.

Oud 82 jaren.

(¹) This Stone is imperfect.

In memory of

Mr. ALEXANDER DU CROZ,

who died October 13th, 1789.

Aged 54 years.

Also

Mrs. ANN DU CROZ,

Widow of the above,

who died November 2nd, 1823.

Aged 79 years.

Also

Mr. SAMUEL DU CROZ,

last surviving Son of the above,

who died unmarried,

on the 2nd of October, 1835.

Aged 48 years.

Middle of North Aisle.

No. 45.

Hier rust het lyk van
REBECCA WATERHOUSE,
Huis vrouw van
JAMES TEN BROEKE,
Diacon deezer Gemeente,
Overleeden den 3de Augustus, 1808,
in den ouderdom van 33 Jaaren.

Als meede gemelde Heer
JAMES TEN BROEKE,
Diacon deezer Gemeente,
overleeden den 1 January, 1810,
Oud 38 Jaaren.

Alzoo het lijk van
ANNA MARIA TEN BROEKE,
Zuster van den booven genoemden.
Overleeden den 25ste December, 1810,
Oud 26 Jaaren.

Als meede de Heer
ANTHONY TEN BROEKE, Koopman
alhier, en Ouderling deezer Gemeente,
Vader van de boven gemelde gestorven,
den 30ste September 1812. Oud 78 jaaren.

Benevens JANE SMITH TEN BROEKE,
Wede. van laatst gemelden, overleden
den 7 Mey, 1815. Oud 68 Jaren.

En WILLIAM ISAAC TEN BROEKE, Zoon
van WILLIAM TEN BROEKE, overleden
den 29th Jan., 1823. Oud 8 Jaren en 4 Maanden.

———o———

Middle of North Aisle.

No. 48.

Sacred to the Memory of
ELIZABETH HARRIOTT SIFFKEN,
who died the 13: of January, 1804.
Aged 5 Months.

Also her Brother
FREDERICK SIFFKEN,
died the 16th Novr., 1821.
Aged 20 Years.

Also Mr. HENRY SIFFKEN,
died 11 August, 1836.
Aged 77 years.

Also of ELIZABETH,
Relict of the above
HENRY SIFFKEN.
Died November 30th, 1845
Aged 77 years.

———o———

Hier ligt begraven

[1] JAN PHILIP EILBRACHT.

geboren in Walworth

den 22 Mey, 1810

overleden in London,

den 20 Maart 181 . .

ANNA BERNARDINA VROMANS

Echtgenoot van W. J. C. RUKLE, [2]

geboren in Leyden den . . Juny, 1788.

Overleden te London den 22 Novr., 1815.

Also SIMON DE KOSTER, Esq.

Who died June 21st, 1831.

Aged 65 years.

NOTE—This Stone is very much broken.

(¹) This name does not appear to have been entered
Register.

(²) RAKLE in Register.

——0——

Hier legt begraven

het lyk van den Wel-Eerwaarden

HENRIK PUTMAN.

lid der Koninglyke Maatschappye

van Wetenschappen te London,

en oudste Predikant deezer Gemeente,

Gebooren te Amsterdam den 8sten April 1725,

Overleeden te London den 1sten Maart, 1797,

na dat hy aldaar ruim 46 Jaaren

het Leeraars ambt had waargenomen.

——6——

No. 53.

On a flat Stone the simple initials

[1] H. M.

(¹) HENRY MUILMAN, buried 9 May, 1772.
Vide Register.

——7.——

Middle of North Aisle.

No. 55.

To the Memory of

Mrs. CATHERINA ALLETTA EVERARDINA,

late wife of JOHN SILVESTER, M.D.

Daughter of COLLE. DAULNIS,

Born at Bois Le Duc, she departed

this life the 26th day of March, 1772.

aged 60.

As also

to the memory of

Sir JOHN SILVESTER, Knt., M.D.

who departed this life 8th November,

1789. Aged 75.

—o—

Middle of North Aisle.

No. 56.

Hier ligt begraven de Heer

PIETER Van NOTTEN,

geboren te Amsterdam, 18 Jan., 1710.

Gestorven te London, 1 May, 1783.

Voornaam Weldoener dezer Gemeente.

Hier legt begraven

Sir CHARLES POLE, Baronet,

voordeesen genaamt Van NOTTEN

Ouderling deeser Gemeynte. Gebooren

in London, 3 January, Anno 1735. O: S:

Overleeden 18 June, 1813.

Dame MILLECENT POLE,

Widow of Sir CHARLES POLE, Baronet.

Born 6th Feby. 1743, O: S:

Died 16th Novr. 1818, N. S.

—o—

Hier legt begraven

De Heer IAN de NEUFVILLE,

Oud 52 Iaeren, Gebooren tot Amsterdam,

En overleeden den 20 September, A. 1744.

D' Heer NICHOLAS ROTSHOUCK,

Æ'ta. 82, Ao. Do. 1760.

Een edelmoedige weldoender

aan dese Kerk.

Middle of North Aisle.

No. 54.

Hier rust in vrede

MARTHA,

de Hartelyk geliefde

[Ec]htgenoote

van

WYNAND JOH. DE BUCK.

Overleden den 7den Oct., 1853.

Begraven den 15den Oct., 1853,

in den ouderdom van

69 Iaren.

The family vault.

———o———

Middle of North Aisle.

No. 57.

Here lyeth the Body of

CHRISTIAN WAGNER, Esq., Merchant.

Born at Bremen.

Obiit 20th Septemr. 1786, Ætatis 65.

Hier rust het licham

Van de Heer PHILIP SCHUMACKER,

beroemd Koopman

en Ouderling van deeze Gemeente.

Gebooren te Bremen

en gestorven den 7den May, 1789.

Oud zynde 64 Jaaren.

———o———

Middle of South Aisle.

No. 58.

Here lie deposited the remains

of Mrs. CATHERINE MILLER

who departed this life

on the 28th day of April, 1800,

in the 62nd Year of her age.

Also JOHN

FREDERICK SIFFKEN,

Grandson of the above,

died 25th of August, 1800,

Aged . . Months, 23 Days.

Also Mr. JOHN MILLER,

Husband of the above

Mrs. CATHERINE MILLER,

who died 24th Jany., 1802.

Aged 72 Years.

———o———

West End of Nave.

No. 60.

Hier leght begraven Mr.

WILLIAM Van den BERGHE,

Geboren tot Cortryck, den

1en September, 1611, Overleden

tot London, den 25 November,

1704, Oudt 94 Jaren.

———o———

West End of Nave.

No. 65

Hier light begraven

JOSYNA SCHAPELINCK,

Oudt 76 Jaeren.

Gestorven en den 9 Feb.

16⅝⅝.

Ende

Haere Suster ANNA

SCHAPELINK, Wed. van

JOHN ELLSWORTHY,

overleden den 30 Sepr.,

1700.

Oudt 77 Jaren.

—o—

West End of Nave.

No. 94ª.

Hier legt begraven

ABRAHAM LEFEVER,

Koster dezer Kerk,

gedurende 45 Jaren,

overleden den 20 July, 1825,

in den ouderdom van 84 Jaren.

Als mede

MARIA MAGDALENA LEFEVER,

Weduwe van den boven gemelde,

overleden den 10de July, 1831,

in den ouderdom van 88 Iaren.

—o—

West End of Nave.

No. 70.

Begraef plaets

van

THEODORE COCK, Soon van

JOHN en HANNAH COCK. over

leden 21st Febr., 1697,[1] oudt 7 Jaeren.

Ende van

Mr. JOHN COCK, Ouderling deser

Gemeente. Overleden den 16 Mey,

1706, Oudt 47 Jaaren.

Hier leght ook begraven Mrs.

HANNAH COCK, Wede. van JOHN

COCK, ouerleden den 9 Aprill,

1731, Oudt 72 Jaaren.

(1) 1698. Vide Register and Stow's London, Bk. II, p. 116.

—o—

West End of Nave.

No. 70.

HENRY BUSTYN.

1714.

ADRIAEN Van HELSDINGEN,

Obijt 2en November, 1721.

Oudt 55 Iaaren

Ende

CAPTN. JOHN GRAY.

Obt. 17 Aprill, 1751.

— · —

Middle of South Aisle.

No. 61

Ter gedagtenis van den Wel Eerwaarde Heer

HENRIK Van HAEMSTEDE,

Lid der Koninglyke Societeit van London,

en Predikant laatst alhier.

Gebooren te Amsterdam den 8sten Septr., 1699.

Overleeden te Londen den 31sten May, 1765.

Hier rust 't gebeente van HAEMSTEE, d'eer der kerk

En liefde van God's Volk, die 't heylzaam Predikwerk

Verrigt heeft steeds getrouw, eerst meer dan zestien Jaar

Aan d'Amstel 't Ouwerkerk; daarna de Christen Schaar

Dees Tempels ook gestigt bykans het vierde deel,

Eens Eeuws: toen stierf verzwakt: dus is er in 't geheel

Op aarde niets, of 't sterft; dies leer hier uit o Mensch!

Den Hemel zoeken, wyl gy't doen meugt naar uw Wensch.

—o—

North Aisle.

No. 63.

Hier rust het lichaam

Van ANN GROTE,

Huisvrouw van

ANDREAS GROTE,

Ouderling van deze Gemeynte.

Overleeden den XXIX September,

MDCCLVII, Oudt zynde XXXVI Jaaren.

Als mede het lichaam van Gemelden

ANDREAS GROTE,

Beroemd Koopman en Bankier te London.

Overleeden te Blackheath, in Kent,

Den 8 Decr. 1788. Oudt zynde 78 Jaaren.

—o—

Beneath this Stone rest the remains
of the Rev. THOMAS PEIRSON, D.D.
formerly Senior Minister of the
Established English Church at
Amsterdam,
Died at Chelsea, 12 July, 1820,
Aged 74 Years.

Also
Mrs. MARION PIERSON, Widow of the above,
Daughter of ALEXANDER PARK, Esq.,
born at Amsterdam, 3 March, 1743,
died at Chelsea, 14 January, 1826.

Hier legt begraven
CORNELIA Van INGEN, Huysvrouw
van ISAAC KUYCK Van MIEROP.
Obiit 17 April, 1757, Ætatis 76 Jaaren.

Als mede
ISAAC KUYCK Van MIEROP.
Obiit 1 July, 1774, Ætatis 93 Jaaren.

Als ook
SARAH MARIA KUYCK Van MIEROP,
Dogter van bovenstaande
Overleden den 22ten April, 1799.
Oud 94 Jaaren.

North Aisle.

No. 62.

North Aisle.

No. 64.

Here lyes interred

CHARLES Van NOTTEN,

of London, Merchant, and one of the

Elders of this Church, Born in Amsterdam,

the 1st of November, 1702, N: S:

and dyed in London, 5 March, 1750-51, O:S:

And his Widow,

¹ SUSANNA Van NOTTEN,

Born in London the 13th January, 1704, O: S:

died at Low Layton, in Essex, 2 April, 1774, N: S:

(¹) Geboren Bosanquet.

Hier rust het Lichaam van

ALBERT MAHLSTEDE,

geboortig van Bremen,

in leeven Koopman te London,

Overleeden den 3den November, 1776.

Oudt LXI Jaaren.

——o——

——o——

Rust placts van ANNA REES,

Huysvrouw van GERARD MAES-ACKER.

Overleden den 26 January, 170?.

Oudt 74 Jaaren.

Ende van hare Dochter GETRUYD

Van DEURE, huysvrouw van NICOLAES

de WALE, overleden den 22 November,

1699. Oudt 30 Jaaren.

Ende van Mr. GERARD MAESACKER,

overleden den 6en Februari,

171?, Oudt 79 Jaeren en 9 Maenden.

(¹) Macsacker.

—o—

Hier legt begraven

DANIEL NOORTWYCK, Soon van

CORNELIS en ANNA MARIA

NOORTWYCK, overleden den

?den January, 170?, oudt 3 Jaaren.

Ende IEAN NOORTWYCK, overleden

30 Septr., 1707, Oudt 5 Jaaren.

En ELIZABET NOORTWYCK, overleden

17 November, 1711, Oudt 16 Jaren.

LOUIJS NOORTWYCK, overleden den 3 July, 1715,

Oudt 23 Weeken.

CORNS. CLDS. NOORTWYCK, overleden

4 December, 1716, Out 21 Jaeren.

ELEONORA NOORTWYCK, overleden

27 Meert, 1719, Oudt 8 Jaren.

MARIA NOORTWYCK, overleden

29 April, 1719, Oudt 25 Iaren.

HNIS.

—o—

West End of Nave.

No. 68.

Hier Leght begraven Mr. ISAAC VINCK,
Coopman, Geboren in de Stadt Norwich,
gewesen Ouderlingh deser Gemeynte,
is Geboren den . . Septembris, 1622,
en Overleden 27
Novembris, 1702.(¹)

Als mede
D'HEER GODFREY WICHELHAUSEN, van Erberfeld,
Ob. 14 Febr., 1702, Ætatis 31 Jaaren.

(¹) Aged about 80.   Vide Stow's London, Bk. II, p. 116.

West End of Nave.

No. 71.

Hier leght begraven

Mr. THOMAS VIROOT,

Ouderling deser Gemeente.

Overleden den 22 Junij, 1704.

Oudt 60 Jaaren.

Ende Mr. JOHN WESTHUYS, Diacon
deser Gemeente en Neef van Mr.
THOMAS VIROOT, overleden den
30 September, 1710, Oudt 32 Jaaren.

Ende Mr. JOHAN SCHOMAKER, Diacon
deser Gemeente, overleden den 30
Mey, 1726. Oudt 30 Jaren.

'est End of Nave.

o. 72.

Hier rust en wacht opde

Toekomste synes Verlossers

en Saligh Makers D'Heere

JESUS CHRISTUS

De Eersame Jongelinck Mr.

ALBERT LONING,

Geboren tot Bremen, en

Overleden binnen Londen,

den 29 July, 1709,

Oudt 19 Jaren.

Here also lyeth the body of

Mr. ALBERT VANDENVELDE,

Ob: 14th Nov. 1757, Ætatis 42 Years.

ALBERTUS GRONING, L.L.D., died

December 16, 1766. Aged 26 Years.

South Aisle, West End.

No. 73.

Here lieth the body of

Mrs. PETRONELLA BURT, late Wife of

CHARLES PYM BURT, Esquire,

and Daughter of the late

Governor JOHN HEYLIGER,

of the Island of St.Eustatius, in America,

who died at Hampton, in Middlesex,

the 8th day of June, 1770,

in the 29th Year of her age.

Haud ullam ingeniam[1] parem.

Also Mrs. ANNA THOMPSON,

Widow of the late Mr. SAM. THOMPSON,

and Daughter of the said

IAN HEYLIGER,

died Sept. 13th, 1795. Aged 45 Years.

(1) Sic.

AA

North Aisle.

No. 74.

Hier legt begraven

D'Heer JOHAN Van den ENDEN,

Soon van D'Heer PHILIP & Mejuff. WILHELMINA

Vanden ENDEN, Gebooren den 17 April, 1708,

en Overleeden den 21 May, 1746.

En D'Heer PHILIP Van den ENDEN,

Oud 73 Jaaren, A.D. 1757.

En D'Heer IAN Van den ENDEN,

Gebooren in Amsterdam, den

26 November, Ao. 1687, en overleeden

den 4 September, Ao. 1765.

En D'Heer LEWIS Van den ENDEN,

Gebooren den 31 January, 1690,

Overleeden den 10 April, 1772.

———o———

South Aisle, West End.

No. 87.

Mortalitatis . exvvias.

hic . deposvit.

JOANNES . HENRICUS . BREYNIUS.

JOANNIS . PHILIPPI . filivs.

JACOBI . nepos.

Jvris . vtriusqve . et . philosophiæ.

Candidatvs.

natvs . Ga'dani.

A . MDCCXV.

D . 1 . Octobris.

denatvs . Londini.

A . MDCCXL.

D . XXX . Octobris.

Longiori . vita.

Dignvs.

———o———

Hier legt begraven

den Eedelen Heer LOUIS De TUDERT,

Gebooren tot Geneve, ende Gestorven tot

Hoxton, den 16 October, 1739.

Oud 83 Jaeren.

Nog legt hier begraven

Vrouwe MARIA LANCTILIER, Weduwe

de TUDERT, Gebooren tot Manheim,

ende gestorven tot Hoxton, den 8 May, 1740,

Oud 77 Jaeren.

Hier legt begraven

Mejuffw. MARIA De PUTTER,

Dochter van

D'Heer HENRIK De PUTTER

en

Mevw. MARIA JOHANNA Van BEECK,

Geboren den 17 April, 1722,

en

Gestorven den 23 September, 1744.

En

D'Heer HENRIK De PUTTER,

Gestorven den 1ste February,

1760, Oudt 67 Jaaren.

En

Mevrouw MARIA JOHANNA De PUTTER,

Geboren Van BEECK. Gestorven den

9 Juny., Ao. 1760, Oudt 72 Jaeren.

Hier legt begraven
Mevrouwe MARIANNE Van NECK,
Gebooren DAUBUZ, Huysvrouw
De Heer JOSUA Van NECK,
Ouderling deeser Gemeente,
Obijt 1 December, Ao. 1750 Æt. 36.

Here lyeth interred the body of
Mrs. MARY PHILBERT MYRE,
Relict of Mr. ROBERT MYRE,
who dyed the 2d of November, 1745.
Aged 76 Years.

West End of Nave.
No. 80.

Nave, West End.
No. 81.

Hier legt begraven JACOB KOPS,

Zoon van WILLIAM ISAAC KOPS,

gebooren tot Amsterdam, den 18 Octobr.,

1713, N.S., & Gestorven tot London, den

27 October, 1727, O.S., Out 14 Jaaren.

Ende AGNES COUSSMAKER, Dogter

van BARNARD COUSSMAKER, gebooren

tot Westminster, den 7 February, 1737,

O. S., & gestorven den 30 May 1756, O. S.,

Out 19 Jaaren.

Ende

ANN KOPS, Huysvrouw van

WILLIAM ISAAC KOPS, gebooren tot

Amsterdam, den 4 April, 1685,

gestorven tot Hackney, den 5 November,

1758, Out . . Jaaren.

——o——

Hier legt begraven

HELENA De GOLS, Huysvrouw

van Dr. ARNOLD BOATE BEIRMAN

obiit Junii XVIII, Ao. MDCCXXVII,

Æt. XLIX.

Als mede

CORNELIA BEIRMAN,

ob. March 4, 1753.

En de Heer

Dr. ARNOLD BOOT BEIERMAN,

obiit 28 Maart, 1754, Æt. 80.

Gelyk ook

HELENA BEIERMAN,

Huisvrouw van den Wel Eerw.

Dr. WALKER, Pred. te

Bethnall Green, ob. 25

Nov. 1756, Æt. XLVIII.

——o——

Nave, West End.
No. 83.

Nave, West End.
No. 84.

Hier legd begraven

De Heer JOHAN ESSELBROUN,

Koopman,

Gestorven den 12 February 17$\frac{18}{19}$,

In het 72ste Jaar zyns Ouderdoms.

En De Heer WILLEM MVLLER,

Koopman, Gestoruen den 19 Juny,

1726, het 45ste Jaar zyn Ouderdom.

Hier legt ook begraven

ANNA MARIA ESSELBROUN, Gestorven

den 21 dag van Julius 1733, Oud 74 Jaren.

Hier leijt begraven

De Heer JOACHIM Van HEMERT,

Diacon deeser Gemeent, en Geboren tot

Amsterdam, den 30 September, 1688, ende

Overleeden in London, den 6 November,

1716, Ovd 31 Jaren.

Nog leijt hier begraven

De Heer FRANCIS Van HEMERT,

Geboren tot Amsterdam, den 3 Febrvary,

1692, ende Overleeden in London den

3d Maij, 1734, Ovd 42 Iaren.

Nog legt hier begraven

De Heer JOHN Van HEMERT,

Gebooren tot Amsterdam, den 16 August,

1694, en Overleeden in London,

den 16 May, 1758, Ovd 63 Iaaren.

—o—

—o—

h Aisle, West End.

86.

North Aisle.

No. 89.

Hier leght begraven

GILBERT de FLINES,

Gebooren in Amsterdam,

den 19 de Februarij, 1690, S:N:

en overleden in London,

den 14 de December, 1739, S:V:

Hier legt begraven

D' Heer NICOLAAS BAILLY,

Gebooren tot Hamburgh, 1681,

Gestorven in London, 1744.

West End, North Aisle.
No. 75.

Hier legt begraven

HESTER [1] GOCKELS, Huysvrouw

Van FERMYN VANVLIET, Coopman

tot London, gestorven den 18 Augustus 1735,

Oud zynde 45 Jaaren.

Hier legt mede begraven

GERRIT REESSEN, Soon van

JOHN REESSEN & MARIA VANVLIET,

Gestorven den 8 April, 1738,

Oud zynde 15 Maanden.

Hier legt mede begraven

MARIA Van VLIET, Huysvrouw

van de Heer JOHN REESSEN,

Diacon deeser Gemeente, gestorven

den 7 February, 1748-9, Oud 31 Jaaren.

Hier legt mede begraven

FERMYN Van VLIET, Ouderling

deeser Gemeente, gestorven

den 26 July, 1752, Oud synde

72 Jaaren.

(¹) *Query* GOEKELS. *Vide* Lidmaten Boek.

———o———

South Aisle, West End.
No. 85.

Hier legt begraven

D'Heer CORNELIS PATER,

Geboren tot Surinamen,

en

Gestorven tot London,

den 17 December, Ano. 1744,

Oud zynde 23 Jaeren.

En

SARAH DADE, Geboren te

Norwich, Weduwe van CORNELIS

De KEISER, Geboren

te Amsterdam,

Ob: den 9 den Decemb. 1754.

Æt. 67

———o———

Centre of Nave, West End.

No. 95.

Hier legt begraven het lyk

Van den Heer GERARD BACKUS,

Koopman in deze Stad, en Twintig

Jaren Ouderling dezer Gemeente,

Geboren te Maastricht, den 4 Sept. 1735,

en Overleden in London, den 7/Sept. 1810,

Oud 75 Jaren.

Als mede het lyk van den Heer DANIEL NANTES,

Koopman binnen deze Stad, en Een en Twintig Jaren

Ouderling dezer Gemeente, Geboren te Bremen, en

Overleden den 22 January, 1814, in den Ouderdem van 75

[Jaren.

Benevens

Het lyk van den Heer DIRK PLOKKER, Makelaar

binnen deze Stad, en ruim Acht Jaren Diaken

dezer Gemente. Geboren te Katwyk, en Overleden

op den 13 July, 1820, in den Ouderdom van 44 Jaren.

Als mede

Het lyk van den Heer JOHN TEN BROEKE,

Makelaar, 15 Jaren Diaken dezer Gemeente,

Geboren in deze Stad, en Overleden den 30 April, 1824.

Oud 44 Jaren.

Benevens

Het lyk van den Heer DIEDERICK WILLINK,

Koopman binnen deze Stad, en Onderling

dezer Gemeente, Geboren te Altona, en

Overleden den 30ste. December, 1832, in den

Ouderdom van 53 Iaren.

No. 95, continued.

Benevens

Het lyk van den Heer JOHANN SIFFKEN,

Koopman binnen deze Stad, en 32 Jaren Ouderling

dezer Gemeente, geboren to Bremen en overleden

den 27sten April (1840) in den Ouderdom van 76 Jaren

——o——

West End, North Aisle.

No. 100.

Hier legt begraven

Mr. THOMAS OULRY, Koopman in

Londen, en Ouderling deser

Gemeente, Geboren in Dordregt,

den 4 October, 1664, en Overleden

in Londen, den 27 Novembr.

1716.

Hier legt ook begraven

SARAH OULRY, Wede. van

THOMAS OULRY, Overleden

den 1 Novr., 1729, ovdt 67 Jaaren.

Hier legt ook begraven

CATHERINA OULRY, Dogter

van THOMAS en SARAH

OULRY, Overleeden den 24

Mairt, 1732, Ovdt 31 Jaaren

——o——

West End, North Aisle.
No. 90.

Memoriae Sempiternae

FRANCISCI GUILELMI,

ex antiqua et nobilissima

Bvirettiorvm Gente,

Patre

JOHANNE GVILELMO de BVIRETTE,

ab Oehlefeld Domino in Wilhelmsdorf,

Potentifs. Borvss. Regis Consiliario et

Presidente

Norinbergae

A. C. MDCCVI, XXV Febr. prognati, VIII Mart. ast.

in pulcherrimo aetatis vernantis flore

cum spem de se longe maximam

(sic) pra tantia indolis formae dignitate

morum elegantia

fecissit.

Magnaeque Britanniae regnum,

in quo

Avorum ejus facta praeclara

No. 90, continued.

quondam extiterunt

Vox ingressus esset,

Londini, ex morbo, fatorum inclementia

d. XV Octobr: A.C. MDCCXXVI

abrepti

Monumentum hoc poni curavit

Mater moestissima

ELIZABETHA, Vidua BVIRETTIA,

Nata Campognia.

———o———

Nave, West End.
No. 106.

Hier onder rust het lyk

van de Heer CORNELIS ELIAS ROELL

Gebooren te Amsterdam,

Gverleeden in Londen den 19de Augt,

1806,

Oud 37 Jaaren.

Als mede

de Heer WM. Van DURA, M.A.

Gebooren te Veere in Zeeland,

Overleeden in Londen den 31te Octr.,

1806,

Oud 44 Jaaren

———o———

West End, North Aisle.
No. 92.

West End.
No. 93.

Hier legt begraven

Sir DENIS DUTRY, Baronet,

en

Mylady DUTRY, Geboren RENEU

Douariere van gemelde Heer,

en

in tweede huwelyk

Huysvrovw van

D'Heer GERARD Van NECK,

Ouderling deeser Gemeynte.

Als mede gemelden Heer

GERARD Van NECK,

Ouderling en Voornaam

Weldoender dezer Gemeente.

Obiit 17 August, 1750, Æts. 58.

ANN KOPS, jongste Dochter van

WILLIAM ISAAC KOPS, Geboren tot

Amsterdam, den 27 July, 1716, Gestorven tot

Hackney, den 28 December, 1761.

Out 41 Jaaren.

Als Mede

De Heer WILLIAM ISAAC KOPS, Koopman,

Geboren te Amsterdam, den 20 September, 1687,

Overleeden te Hackney, den 4 February,

1774. Ætatis 86.

Als mede

AGNES COUSSMAKER, Weduwe van

BARNARD COUSSMAKER, & Dogter van

WILLIAM ISAAC KOPS, geboren tot

Amsterdam, 20th January, 1710, & gestorven

tot Hackney, 21sten December, 1781.

Oudt 71 Jaaren.

West End.

No. 94.

Centre of Nave, West End.

No. 96.

Hier legt begraven MARIA

JACOBA De GOLS, ob: 14 April,

Ao. 1735, Æt. 52.

Als mede

WILLEM De GOLS, ob: 13 February,

Ao. 1735, Æt. 47.

Als mede

ELIZABETH De GOLS, ob: 3 Maart,

Ao. 1736, Æt. 55.

Hier legt begraaven

ELIZABETH Van HEMERT,

Weduwe van JAN Van HEMERT,

Overleeden den 6 January, 1781,

Oud 65 Jaaren.

Als mede legt hier

WOLFERT Van HEMERT,

Gebooren te Amsterdam,

den 30sten July, 1703.

Overleeden te Londen.

den 15den Maart, 1786.

—o—

—o—

West End, North Aisle.

No. 91.

North Aisle.

No. 103.

Hier leght begraven de Welgeboren Vrouw

IACOBA SWEERTS,

Huysvrouw van de Heer HENRIK

HOP, Extraords. Envoye, van Haer

Hoog Mogen. de Heeren Staten

Generael der vereenigde Nederlande,

aen het Hoff van syn M. van

Groot Brittannien, Gestorven den

26 April } 1725.
. . Mey }

Out 35 Iaren. Insgelyks

Gemelde Heer HENRIK HOP, overleeden

. . Decemb. 1761, Oud 75 Jaaren. Als mede

syn Wel Ed. dogter ISABELLA MARIA HOP,

overleeden 18 April, 1789, Oud 71 Jaaren.

Hier legt begraaven de Heer

CORNELIUS BACKER, Koopman

Deezer Steede, Gebooren in

Amsterdam den 24e January, 1693,

N: S: en Gestorven den 7e April, 1740.

O: S:

Als mede

legt hier begraven den Heer

JOHN BACKER, Koopman

Deezer Steede, Geboren in

Amsterdam, 22 November, 1694, N. S

en Gestorven 11 Augustus, 1745, O: S:

South Aisle, West End.
No. 97.

South Aisle, West End.
No. 98.

Ter gedagtenisse van Mr. HERMAN Van BRACHT,
Geweeze Leeraer deezer Gemeente,
Gebooren te Dortrecht, den 11en December, 1691.
S:N:, Overleeden den 16en April, 1735.

Heir rust het overschot, de lykasch van Van BRACHT,
vorst CHRISTUS bybeltolk ; die door zyn pen, de Kragt
van't Ongodistendom groothartig dorst verbreeken
en nu gereed was het de hartaer af te steeken
wanneer de naare dood hem maakte tot een lyk
nu is hy anderaniet dan enkel stof en slyk.
Dit laat hy egter na, dit blyft van hem in't leeven,
een roem die eeuwig is, een ziel aan God gegeeven.
Gy egter wandelaar, Bedrieg, u zelve niet,
ik weet gy waand, dat gy's mans graf hier voor u ziet
om dat dees blauwe zark de lykbus dekt, ende aerdt
waarin zyn koud gebeent met droef geween na waerd,
wierd ingedolven. Neen, want zyn door luchtig Graf
is in het dankbaar hert, dat hem zyn kudde gaf.
maar de eere, en Glory (na zyn dood is't onbedwongen)
blyft niet bepaald in't hert, maar zweefd op alle tongen.

————o————

Mr. AALBERT Van MEURS, Iunr., gebooren te Rotterdam,
gestorven den 10 December, 1731, Out 17 Jaaren,
was een Iongerling van zeergroote hoop.
Schrander van Geest,
Vriendelyk in Omgang,
Opregt van Wandel.
Syn God & Salighmaker vreesende
Waarom hy was onuyt Sprekelyk bemint, by
Ouders & Susters hartelyk gelieft van
syn Bloedverwanten, Seer geaght van syn
Bekenden Dog de Doot, Sneed deeze Schoone
Bloem in zyn eerste lenteyeught aff, en
Voerde hem in de gemeenschap synes,
Salighmakers laatende zyne naaste
Bloedverwanten in de diepste droeffenisse,
zyn Bekenden in rouwe, & zyn Sterffelyk deel
in dit Graff in verwagting van een vrolyke
en Salige Op Standing ten Iongsten Dage.

————o————

t End, North Aisle.
107.

West End of Nave.
No. 108.

Hier leght begraven

HENRY DUPRE, Geboren

tot Haerlem den 10 April, 1685,

Overleden tot London, den

28 Juli, 1716, Oudt 31 Jaren.

JOHN DUPRE, Ouderling deezer

Gemeente, Gebooren te Haarlem,

Overleeden te London, den 24 Feb.,

1739.

Oudt 55 Jaren.

Hier leght begraven

SAMUEL DUPRE, Geboren

tot Haerlem den 30 November,

1681 & Overleeden in London

den 6 Augustus, 1729,

Oudt 46 Jaaren.

Als mede ANNA,

in haer leven Huysvrouw van

De Voorgenoemde, maer den

Overleden Vrouw van

D. PAVLUS COLLIGNON,

Iegen woordig Leeraer deezer

Gemeente. Gestaven den

29 Aug., MDCCXXVII. Ætat

Welke Eerw. Heer overleden den 17 May

Ætat 77, en ook hier rust hebbende naer

zyn diener bekleedt 9 Jaaren, 8 maenden.

Hier leght begraven het Lichaem

van IANNETIE Van KESTEREN, Huysvrou

van OTTO Van KESTEREN, Geboren in Delft,

en Overleden in Londen, den 7en Aprill,

1711, Oudt 51 Iaeren.

Ende van OTTO Van KESTEREN,

Geboren tot Kesteren, 1659, en

Overleden in Londen, den 23

Ianuary, 1719-20, Oudt 60 Iaren.

Als mede

Mr. IONAS ROWLANDSON,

Gestorven den 21 November, 1731,

Oudt 51 Iaaren.

MRS. ELIZABETH ROWLANDSON,

Huysurouw van

MR. IONAS ROWLANDSON,

Gestorven den 28 Iuly, 1737,

Oudt 53 Iaeren.

— o —

Hier legd begraven

SARAH ELIZABETH SUWERKROP,

Geboren 17 April, 1812.

Gestorven 9 January, 1815.

Als mede

ANNA ELIZABETH SUWERKROP,

Overleden den 14 Oct., 1816,

in den Ouderdom van 29 Jaren.

Als mede

LAMKE SUWERKROP,

Overleden den 26 July, 1827,

in den Ouderdom van 49 Jaren.

Als mede

JOHN BRUHN SUWERKROP,

Ouderling dezer Gemeente,

Overleden den 28 Junij, 1839,

in den Ouderdom van 73 Jaren.

— o —

West End.

o. 99.

Hier legt begraven

Collonel CHARLES LODWIK,

In syn leven Ouderling deser

Gemeente, gebooren in Londen,

Overleden den 16 Feb. 172¼,

Out 66 Jaaren,

En MARGERITA LODWIK, zyn Huisvrouw,

Geboren tot Utritch, 1664, ende

Overleden tot Londen, den 26 Maert,

1731.

Hier legt het lyk van

LAWREN[CE VAN DEN]

VELDE . . . . o

Koster . . dezer Kerke

•   •

Ouerleeden [Feb.]

172 , Oud . . .

• • • • • •

M[ARY FIELD]

Overleeden [. Feb.]

173¼. . . •

The following Inscriptions, from STOW'S London, Book II, p. 116, Ed. 1720, are probably covered by the Vestries or raised Chancel.

ELIZABET PHILIPPINE, Widow of wylen ALBERT GEORGE, Graaf tot BRONCHORST and [1]LAMBURG STIRUM; borne Baronesse of BOETZLAER; Dyed Oct., 1692.

([1]) Limburg.

——o——

JACOB GEORGE BECK. Merchant, Born in Frankford at Mayne: Dyed in London, 22 Jan., 1702-3.

——o——

JOAS BATEMAN, 13 Apr., 1704.

——o——

KATHERINE BISCOP, Daughter of SAM. and SARAH BISCOP; Dyed 1686-7, five years old. SARAH BISCOP, Wife of the said SAMUEL, 1689-90. And SAMUEL BISCOP, who very commendably served in the office of Preacher in this church 32 years; Dyed Jun. 11, 1700 Aged 58.

——o——

AGNETA Van der MERCH, Born at Harlem; Dyed Aug. 21, 1703.

North Wall, on a Marble Monument.

LOUISA

MEYER,

ob.

MDCCCXXII,

In a vault beneath

are deposited the remains of

LOUISA MEYER,

wife of CHRISTIAN PAUL MEYER,

and daughter of the late

RAWSON HART BODDAM,

she died June XXI, MDCCCXXII,

Aged XXVII, leaving

three Sons and three Daughters.

JAMES MEYER,

of Leadenhall St., and Forty Hall, Enfield,

Born Sept. 3, 1755, Died 11 Feb., 1826.

ıth Wall, on a white Marble Tablet.

In

gratefull remembrance

of

HERMAN MEYER,

of Forty Hall, Enfield, Middlx.

He was a kind friend,

a truly honest man,

and died in peace

20th June, 1832,

Aged 74.

——o——

a tablet beneath the above.

In memory of

ANN, Widow of CHRISTIAN PAUL MEYER,

and Daughter of

ISAAC and ELIZABETH SOLLY ;

Born October 28, 1765, died February 9, 1841.

——o——

th Aisle, East End, partly obscured by Vestry.

Hier leght begraven ARNOLDINA,

Dochter van d'Heer ARNOLD Van CITTERS,

Ordinair Ambassadeur van haer

H. M. D'Heeren staten generael [1]

. . . .

. . . .

Stow's London, Book II, p. 116: to his Majesty of
eat Britain. She dyed Jun. 5, 1686. Aged 5 Years.

——o——

North Aisle, East End, partially obscured by Vestry.

Hier ligt begraven de Heer

EVERD Van HARTHALS,

Koopman en Diaken deezer

Gemeente, Oud 49 Jaaren, Obiit

Oct. 1753. Als mede zyn E. Dochter.

[ELIZABETH Van HARTHALS] [1]

. . . .

(1) Vide Register.

——<——

At entrance of South Vestry, in the door-way, a square
brass, at the top a coffin and hour-glass on it, at the bottom
a skull and cross-bones and small armories, D'azur à trois
chev. d'or.

Hier liet

Begraven

Dom. JOHANNES Van ROOYEN,

Oud 44 Jaren,

Gestorven den 10 Maert,

Anno 168⅗.

——o——

By one of the Pillars North-west of Nave, on a stone
without number.

[2] P. B.

1692.

(2) Mr. Pieter Bourgeois, vide Register.

——o——

North Wall, on a Marble Tablet.

Hier legt Begraven
D'Heer DENIS DUTRY,

Baronet, voornaem Koopman en Banquier in London.
Bewindthebr. van de Oostind : Comp. en de Bank.
Geboren tot Amsterdam in Hollandt, den 2 Novemb.,
1663, hij wierdt verheeven tot Baronet in't tweede
Jaar, van de Regeeringh van Koningh GEORGE
D'Eerste, hij was getrouwt den 26 Maart, 1695, met
MARIA RENEW, eenige Dogter en universele
Erfgenaam van D'Heer HILLAIRE RENEW,
welke in de tyde van de Frause vervolgingh uyt
liefde tot de gereformeerde Godsdienst, syn
geboorte plaats Bordeaux in Vrankryk heeft
verlaten en medebrengende een aensienlyk
Capitaal sigbinnem London heeft gevestight.
S. DENIS reysde van hier met syn gemelde
huysvrouw om haar geboorte plaats, Bordeaux
te sien, maar is aldaar na eeniger dagen siekte,
den 26 Oct., O.S., 1728, overleeden en syn Lighaam
volgens syn Bergeerte hier overgebraght en
begraven den 31 Decemb., 1728, synde altydt
geweest een Edelmoedige Weldoender voor
KERCH en ARMEN.

———o———

North Aisle, East End, partially obscured by Vestry.

Vide Stow's London, Book II, p. 116.

ELIZABETH GRONEN, Wife of FREDERICK GRONEN,
Merchant, Jun. 18, 1693. And FREDERICK GRONEN,
beforenamed, Oct. 28, 1697.

———o———

North Aisle, East End, partially obscured by Vestry.

———o———

Nae by dese plaets leght het
lichaam van Vrouw MARGARITA
LAURENTIA, Dochter en erfgenaem
(by syn huysvrouw CLARA
VELTERS) van LAURENTIUS HUYSSEN,
Heer Van WEELDE, in Zeelandt
die't kindts kindt was van JOHAN
de KNUYT (eerste Edele van
die Provincie) by syn Dochter
MARGARITA.

Vrouw MARGARITA LAURENTIA
was getrouwt met den Edelen
Colonel HENRY CORNEWALL van
Bredwardine, in Herefordshire,
op den XI van October, MDCLXXXIII, by
welcken sy twee Sconen gehadt
heeft, HENRY noch levende,
geboren den XII January, MDCLXXXV,
en WILLIAM HENRY, geboren den
IV January MDCLXXXVII, en gestorven in
April volgende.
Sy leyde dit Sterflyck leven af
op den XXVI April, MDCXCII.

———)———

South Aisle, East End, rest obscured by Vestry.

South Aisle, East End, partly obscured by Vestry.

—c—

—o—

South Aisle, East End. rest obscured by Vestry.

West End, North Aisle.

No. 101.

Hier legt begraven

CATHARINA PAUS, Wede. van

DIRCK DECKER, geboren tot

Dordregt, den 23 Augusti, 1643,

Overleden tot Londen, den 28

December, 1703, Oudt 63 Jaren.

—o—

—o—

PRETER KREURSS KMEARNS TO ENIMAARNA GEND.
ÆTATIS DYED BYIT 8 30 AUGUST.I
1686
SARAH KERSTEMAN VIDVA

Vide Register, PIETER KERSTEMAN, 24 Aug., 1686.

Vide Stow's London, Book II, p. 116:

SARAH KERSTEMAN, Widow of GABRIEL DE LA PORTE, July 15, 1694.

FINIS.

No.	Year	Name	Surname	Born	Died
1.	1550	Johannes	A Lasco,	born in Poland,	died at Cracow in Poland,
2.	,,	Martinus	Micronius,	,, ,, Flanders,	,, ,, Norway,
3.	,,	Walterus	Delænus,	,, ,, Brabant,	,, ,, London,
4.	1559	Adrianus	Hamstedius,	,, ,, Zeeland,	,, in Friesland,
5.	1560	Petrus	Delænus,	,, at Alkmaar,	,, at London,
6.	1562	Nicolaus	Carinæus,	,, ,, Edam,	
7.	1563	Godefridus	Wingius,	,, ,, Liege,	
8.	1568	Bartholdus	Guilhelmi,	,, in Holland,	
9.	1570	Georgius	Wybotius,	,, ,, Putten,	
0.	1573	Johannes	Cubus,	,, ,, Antwerp.	
1.	,,	Jacobus	Regius,[1]	,, at Courtrai,	,, ,, London,
2.	1580	Johannes	Soilot,	,, ,, Brussels,	
3.	,,	Johannes	van Roo,		
4.	1581	Assuerus	Regemorterus,	,, ,, Antwerp,	
5.	1586	Lucas	van Peene,	,, ,, Rouselare,	
6.	1592	Jacobus	Wybotius,	,, ,, Ghent,	
7.	1597	Johannes	Marquinus,	,, ,, London,	
8.	1601	Johannes	Regius,		
9.	,,	Symeon	Ruytinck,	,, ,, Norwich,	
0.	1604	Leonardus	Moyart,	,, ,, Heerentals,	
1.	1608	Ambrosius	Regemorterus,	,, ,, Wesel,	
2.	1624	Guilhelmus	Thilenus,	,, ,, Middelburg,	,, ,, Middelburg,
3.	1628	Timotheus	van Vleteren,	,, ,, Sandwich,	,, ,, London,
4.	1632	Jeremias	Larenus,	,, ,, Arnemuiden,	
5.	1639	Cæsar	Calandrinus,	,, ,, Staden,	
6.	1640	Phillipus	op den Beke,	,, ,, Wesel,	
7.	1644	Jonas	Proostius,	,, ,, Colchester,	
8.	1668	Samuel	Biscop,	,, ,, Flushing,	
9.	1680	Gerard	van de Port,	,, ,, Zierickzee,	
0.	1686	Johannes	van Royen,	,, ,, Middelburg,	
1.	1688	Adrianus	van Oostrum,	,, ,, Wateringe,	
2.	1692	Æmilius	van Cuijlemborg,	,, ,, Wageningen,	
3.	1701	Willem	Biscop,	,, ,, Middelburgsche Polder in Zeeland,	
4.	1711	Theodorus	Bolten,	,, ,, Leiden,	
5.	1714	Ludolphus	de With,	,, ,, Rotterdam,	
6.	1718	Paulus	Collignon,	,, ,, Hesse Cassel,	
7.	1728	Herman	van Bracht,	,, ,, Dordrecht,	
8.	1735	Frederik Daniel	Bougardt,	,, ,, Sluys,	
9.	1736	Marten Adriaan	de Jongh,	,, ,, Bommel,	
0.	1740	Henricus	van Haemstede,	,, ,, Amsterdam,	
1.	1751	Henrick	Putman,		
2.	1765	Melchior Justus	van Effen,	,, ,, Hague,	
3.	1784	Conradus	Schwiers, SS. Th. D.,	,, ,, Bremen,	
4.	1801	Lambertus Henricus Schippers	Paal, SS. Th. D.,	,, ,, Amsterdam,	
5.	1802	Jan	Werninck, SS. Th. D.,	,, ,, ,,	
6.	1815	Rutgerus Seyen	ten Harmsen,	,, ,, ,,	
7.	1830	Hendrik	Gehle, Th. D.,	,, ,, Haarlem,	
8.	1874	Abraham Adama Van Dirk	Scheltema,	,, ,, Borsele.	

(1) Couinck.

1550	Johannes	Utenhovius.
	Jacob	Saal.
	Willem	Roux.
	Joannes	Engelram.
	Louijs	Thiery.
	Claude	Doligny.
	Jan	Lamote.
	Philips	Garey.
	Anthonius	Assche.
	Franciscus	Martinus.
	Jan	Danelu.
	Pieter	de Bert.
	Pieter	Carpen.
	Pieter	Carpenter.
	Francoys	Clerck.
	Jan	van der Beke.
	Gysbertus	Johannes.
1571	Guilliam	Rogaert.
	Johannes	Ramaecker.
	Jan	de Coninck.
	Hercules	Fremont.
	Thomas	Soenen.
	Lieven	de Herde.
	Lucas	van Peene.
	Jacob	Heyns.
	Lucas	de Heere.
	Hubrecht	Elinck.
	Johannes	Woudanus.
	Jan	Beaugrand.
1573	Johannes	Soilot.
	Louys	Wingene.
	Christian	de Rycke.
	Geleyn	de Beste.
1578	Adriaen	Gyselinck.
	Mattheus	Luls.
	Hans	Gast.
1580	Jan	van Beke.
	Jan	de Clerck.
	Willem	Bruninck.
	Sebastien	Heukins.
	Albrecht	Sproek.
	Adriaen	de Poorter.
1582	Denys	de Mont.
	Jan	Beele.
1583	Hendrik	Guyle.
	Abraham	Delden.
	Christiaen	Strasele.
1585	Geraert	Platteel.
	Lodewijk	Theus.
1586	Guilliam	Courten.
	Michiel	Corselis.
	Guillam	van Liebeeck.
1587	Jan	van Peene.
	Rogier	van Peene.
	Jan	Molyn.
1588	Jacques	Hoste.
1591	Willem	Proost.
	Jan	Edwart.
1591	Jan	Ruytinck.
1593	Jan	de Backer.
	Pieter	de Drossate.
1594	Engelbert	Kampen.
	Hans	de Solt.
1595	Carel	van Peene.
	Jan	van Solt.
	Jeronimus	Pottelberg.
1599	Paulus	Typoots.
	Pieter	de Pril.
1601	Seger	Corselis.
	Pieter	Jacobs.
1604	Augustyn	Jansen.
	David	Clinckenberg.
	Cornelis	Spierinck.
	Jan	Abeels.
1609	Pieter	van Loor.
	Jacques	Wittewrongel.
1600	Samuel	de Visscher.
1611	Cornelis	Godfroy.
	Mattheus	Stelte.
1612	Godfroy	Rutgers.
	Daniel	Haringhoeck.
	Geraert	Cousyns.
1614	Joos	van Bossche.
1616	Jan	Luce.
1617	Carolus	Liebaert.
	Joos	Godschalck.
1621	Jean	de Monchy.
	Adam	Boddens.
1624	Jacques	Cole.
	Abraham	Beek.
1626	Gillis	van der Putte.
	David	Bonneel.
	Lucas	Corselis.
	Joan	Lamote.
	Jacob	Herrewyn.
1628	Dierick	Hoste.
	Christopher	Loots.
	Pieter	Verhulst.
1630	Jan	van den Abeele.
	Gillis	van Brugh.
1632	Adam	Laureyns.
	Hendrick	Pauwels.
1636	Guillam	van der Cruyssen.
	Abraham	Dolens.
	Thomas	Ruys.
1638	Jan	Stevens.
1639	David	Otgher.
	Willem	de Visscher.
1641	Jan	Rushout.
1643	Walrave	Lodewyk.
1647	Jan	van den Abeele.
	Nicolas	Corselis.
1651	Willem	Boeve.
1653	Abraham	van Ceulen.
	Pieter	van de Put.
1654	Abraham	Clerck.

1655	Pieter	Hoet.
1657	David	Bonneel.
1658	Arnout	van der Beke.
1660	Jan	Adriaen.
	Willem	Rushout.
1662	Geeraert	van Heythuysen.
	Nicolas	van Acker.
1665	Nathaniel	Letten.
	Abraham	Otgher.
1665	Pieter	Matheus.
	Christ. Paulus	van Zanten.
1668	James	Burkin.
	Francoys	Tyssen.
	Jacob	Willemsen.
1670	Abraham	Dolens.
	Pieter	Kersteman.
	Joas	Eversen.
1673	Pieter	Haringhoek.
	Isaac	Vinck.
1678	Daniel	Demetrius.
	Joas	Bateman.
	Nathaniel	Bonnel.
1680	John	Langley.
1683	John	Loveroo.
	Chrisostomus	Hamilton.
1688	Jan	de Berdt.
	Jean	de la Chambre.
	Justus	Otgher.
	Adryaen	Beyer.
1692	Daniel	de Mildert.
	Francoys	Tierens.
1695	Pieter	van der Mersch.
1699	Francoys	Tyssen.
	Jasper	van den Bussche.
1703	Thomas	Viroot.
	Willem Henry	Cornelissen.
	James	Crop.
1704	John	Cock.
	John	van Hattem.
1707	William	Kersteman.
	Gerard	van Heythuysen.
1710	Walter	Cock.
1711	Cornelis	Noortwyck.
	Isaiah	de Walpergen.
	Thomas	Oulry.
1713	Sir Justus	Beck.
	William	Standert.
	Charles	Lodwick.
1715	Abraham	Henckel.
	James	Kersteman.
	Jacob	Henckel.
	Abraham	Crop.
1717	Abraham	Demetrius.
	Philip	van den Enden.

1717	Gerard	Bolwerck.
1718	Johan Leonard	d' Orville.
	Daniel	Burn.
1723	Dr. Arnold	Boot Bierman.
	Nicolas	Bailly.
	Fermyn	van Vliet.
1727	John	Dupree.
	Gerard	van Neck.
	Philip David	Camp.
1739	John Abraham	Korten.
	Joshua	van Neck.
	Jan	van Rixtel.
1742	Herman	Jacobs.
	Charles	van Notten.
1743	Jan	Blydesteyn.
1744	Benjamin	Berckenhout.
1748	Couradt	Lang.
	Isaac	van Assendelft.
	Abraham	Henckel, Jr.
1750	John	Reesen.
	Willem	Kersteman.
1756	Dr. Joan	Silvester.
	Andreas	Grote.
1761	Jacob	van Wylick.
	Herman	Meyer.
	Jan	van Rixtel.
1772	Louis	van den Enden.
1774	Jacobus	des Cotes.
	Charles	van Notten.
1785	Adolph	Boon.
1786	Phil. Ant.	Schumacker.
1787	Gerard	Backus.
1789	Daniel	Meilan.
	Sebastian	Fridag.
1792	Daniel	Nantes.
1803	Isaac	Blydestein.
	Anthony	ten Brocke.
	Abraham	Visscher.
1808	Johann	Siffken.
	Thomas	Simpson.
1813	Arend Jacob	Guitard.
	Thomas Gregory	Smith.
1815	Jan Hendrik	Ohrly.
1832	John Bruhn	Sawerkrop.
	Diederick	Willink.
1839	Paulus Alex.	van Boomart.
1840	Jacob Bernelot	Moens.
1846	Fred. Wilhelm	Sack.
1850	Wilem Jean	Bauerman.
	Pieter	van den Ende.
1858	Adrien	Pompe.
	Gerard	Wynen.
1880	Hermanus	Krickbeck, Jr.
	Adriaen	van der Hoeven.

1550	Francoys	Clerck.
	Willem	Fogge.
	Jan	Daneln.
	Geleyn	de Beste.
	Guilham	Bogaert.
	Johannes	Cubus.
	Gillis	Huereblœk.
	Mattheus	Verhoeve.
	Pieter	Bauters.
	Melchior	van Assen.
	Gillis	Versiele.
	Lupaert	Herruxs.
	Cornelis	Joost.
	Reynier	Pastor.
1572	Francoys	Guissen.
	Jan	Soelot.
	Marten	van Peene.
	Louys	van Wingene.
	Christiaen	de Rycke.
	Pieter	Carpentier.
1573	Lodewyck	Theus.
	Joris	de Dobbelaere.
	Jacob	Beck.
	Jan	Denwart.
	Anthony	Walens.
	Philips	Hendrix.
1574	Cornelis	de Neve.
	Andreas	Nauwe.
	Guillam	Courten.
	Jacques	Hoste.
	Willem	Jacobs.
1575	Jean	van de Cruce.
	Jacob	Janssens.
	Dennis	de Mont.
	Michiel	Corselis.
1578	Guillam	Bruininck.
	Rogier	van Peene.
1580	Abraham	Delden.
	Willem	Proost.
	Michiel	Maynet.
	Pieter	Tryon.
	Jean	van de Peele.
1581	Cornelis	Bossin.
	Hendrick	Voets.
	Elias	de Meyere.
1583	Jan	Angele.
	Engelbert	Kempen.
	Hendrick	Beckman.
	Richaert	Stevens.
1585	Carel	Burgrave.
	Simon	Tyrentein.
1586	Pieter	Drossaert.
	Carel	van Peene.
	Jan	van Soldt.
1587	Jacob	Coussenaere.
	David	Frilichoven.
1589	Gilles	Aels.
	Marten	Bonne.

1589	Jacob	Bursken.
	Hans	van Soldt.
1591	Nicolas	de Witte.
	Michiel	Maynet.
	Herman	van Hembach.
	Marten	Gerards.
1593	Baudewyn	Denweke.
	Marten	Boneval.
	Jacob	de Pau.
	Hans	van Prussen.
1594	Louys	van Ludicken.
	Tobias	Baert.
	David	Clinckenberg.
	Segers	Corselis.
	Nicolas	Deuxvilles.
1595	Pieter	de Pril.
	Pieter	Jacobs.
	Philips	van der Burch.
	Joos	Otgher.
	Dominus	Vaerheyl.
1596	Jean	van der Vinck.
	Geraert	Ryckaert.
	Augustyn	Jansen.
1599	Daniel	van Hazevelt.
	Abraham	der Kinderen.
	Joos	van de Eossche.
1601	Geraert	Cousyns.
	Samuel	Dries.
	Simon	Querm.
	Gilles	Diepenryck.
1603	Mattheus	Stelte.
	Lieven	de Haese.
	Charls	Hugebout.
	Rogier	van Herweghe.
	Andries	Boeve.
1609	Rogier	Huerlout.
	Samuel	Visscher.
1610	Daniel	Harinckhoeck.
	Hans	Jansen.
	Cornelis	Godfroy.
	Godfroy	Rutgers.
1611	Hendrick	Jansen.
	Anthony	Tierens.
	Joos	Godtschalck.
	Jeronymus	Willems.
1612	Jean	Moussy.
	Jan	Luce.
	Jacques	de Beste.
1614	Joos	de Neve.
	Adam	Boddens.
1616	David	Bonneel.
	Jan	van den Abeele.
1617	Philips	Jacobs.
	Lucas	Corselis.
	Jacob	Herrewyn.
1621	Leinardt	de Vette.
	Jacques	Wagenaer.
1624	Hendrick	Pauwels.

Year	Name	Surname
1624	Gillis	van Brugh.
	Jacques	Kint.
1626	Jan	Stevens.
	Isaac	van Peenen.
	Guilliam	van der Cruyssen.
	Abraham	Dolens.
1628	Adam	Laurens.
	Andries	Meulemeester.
	Walrave	Lodewyck.
1630	Jacques	Hoste.
	Thomas	Ruys.
	Timotheus	Cruso.
	Salomon	van der Broeck.
1632	Willem	de Visscher.
	Jan	Rushout.
	David	Otgher.
	Nicolas	Corselis.
1636	Jonas	de Peyster.
	Jean	Casier.
	Paulus	Ganne.
	Francoys	Laeyon.
	Jan	Nicolas.
	Mattheus	Beuns.
1638	Willem	Boeve.
	Jacques	Butler.
1639	Abraham	de Deuxvilles.
	Pieter	Hoet.
	Jan	de Groote.
	Abraham	Baert.
1640	Jean	Becx.
	Abraham	Otgher.
1643	Dr. Assuerus	Regemortel.
	Abraham	Clerck.
	Aernout	van der Beeke.
	Heyndrik	Hoevenaer.
1648	Pieter	Hoet.
	David	Bonneel.
	Willem	Rushout.
	Nicolas	Abeels.
	Francoys	Lodewyck.
	Dr. Johannes	de Koninck.
1649	Pieter	Marelois.
	Hearlock	Momma.
	Jan	Dolens.
1651	Christn. Paulus	van Zanten.
	Pieter	Mattheus.
1652	Pieter	Lupaert.
	Andries	Droogboter.
	Geeraert	van Heythuysen.
	Nicolas	van Acker.
	Abraham	van Hecke.
1654	Pieter	Lombaert.
1655	Jacob	Burkin.
	Willem	van de Walle.
1657	Christiaen	Eylers.
8165	Nathanael	Letten.
	Francoys	Tyssen.
	Francoys	Elison.
	Sinnon	Delbo.
1661	Pieter	Kersteman.
	Joos	Eversen.
	Daniel	Demetrius.
	Theodoro	Cock.
	Pieter	Haringhoeck.
	Abraham	Loefs.
1662	Abraham	Delins.
1662	Isaac	Vinck.
	Simon	van Sangelandt.
1664	Jacob	Willemsen.
	Gerardt	Weymans.
	Gillis	van Brugh.
1666	Joos	Bateman.
	Guilliam	van den Berge.
1668	Adriaen	Beyer.
	John	Langley.
1670	Chrisostos.	Hamilton.
	Johannes	Dorville.
	Francoys	Beyer.
1672	Johannes	Riches.
	Johannes	de la Chambre.
	Johannes	Cranenburgh
	Johannes	Lo croo
1675	Samuel	Beecke.
	William	de Werth.
	Jan	de Berdt.
	Justus	Otgher.
1678	Christiaen	de Breda.
	Johannes	Hoet.
	Daniel	van Midert.
	Elias	Adriaen.
	Gabriel	de la Porte.
	Francoys	Tiereus.
1681	Jasper	van den Bussche.
	Frederick	Gronen.
	Samuel	Shepheard.
	Johannes	Loyd.
	David	de Barry.
1683	Abraham	Otgher.
	Adam	Cronen.
	Pieter	Hacker.
1688	Frederick	Harlah.
	Thomas	Viroot.
	Willm. H.	Cornelisen
1690	Simon	Lodwik.
	John	Cock.
	William	Kersteman.
1692	Geradt	van Heythuysen.
	James	Crop.
1695	Cornelis	Noortwyck.
	Thomas	Oulry.
	Raymond	de Smith.
1699	Denis	Dutry.
	Isaiah	de Walpergen.
1703	Willem	Staudert.
	Henry	van Berchem.
	Charles	Lodwik.
	Abraham	Len Kell.
1705	Jacob	Len Kell.
1707	James	Kersteman
	Abraham	Crop.
	Philip	de Werth.
	Abraham	Lem trius
1709	Abraham	van der Elson
	John	We Buys
1711	Abraham	van Midert.
	Philip	van den Euden
	Martin	Arnouts
	Nicolas	Barry.
1713	Frederick	St dert.
	Gerardt	B werck.
	Jan Leonard	Dr Orville.
1715	Christopher	Teigken.

1715	Joachim	van Backus.
	Fermyn	van Croz.
	John	Bemert.
	Louis	van den Fliet.
	Samuel	Dubourg.
1717	Abraham	Enden.
	John	Dupre.
	Phenix	Berckenhout.
	John	Dupre.
1718	Christr.	Hurgronie.
	Geradt	van Muller.
1720	Philip David	Gildemeester.
	Cornelis	Neck.
	Hendrick	de Camp.
1722	Arnold	Backer.
	Petrus	Putter.
	John Abraham	Lang.
	John	Lucas.
1723	Henry	Korten.
	John	van Schomaker.
1726	James	Muilman.
	Joshua	van Hemert.
	Jan	van Henckell.
1727	Herman	Neck.
	Charles	van Rixtel.
	Jan	Jacobs.
	Benjamin	Notten.
1731	Conrad	Blydesteyn.
1734	Isaac	van Berckenhout.
	Herman	Lang.
	Abraham	Assendelft.
1739	Evert	van Broyet.
	John	Henckell, jr.
	Frederick	Harthals.
	Jan Lodk.	Reesen.
1742	Abraham	Standert.
	William	Kraeguelius.
1743	Johan	Blydesteyn.
1744	Andrew	Kersteman.
1745	Barthw.	Silvester. M.D.
	Jacob	van Grote.
1750	Albert	van den Nedderman.
	Louis	van den Wylick.
	Herman	Velde.
	Engelbert	Enden, jr.
	John	van Meyer.
1753	Jan	van der Hake.
	Jan Jacob	Rixtel, jr.
1755	Jacobus	des Meulen.
1756	Timothy	Zornlim.
	Charles	van Cotes.
1761	Adolph	Nucella.
	James	van Notten.
1766	Govert	Boon.
	Johan	Rixtel.
	Philip Aertsen	Cassau.
1769	Gerardt	Spittah.
	Alex.	du Shumacker.

1772	Christiaen	Woosthoven.
	Daniel	Meilan.
1774	John	Kooystra.
	Nicolaas	Hane.
1785	Daniel	Nantes.
	Isaak	Blydesteyn.
1786	Sebastian	Fridag.
	Gysbert	van Voorst.
	John Lewis	van den Enden.
	Hendk. Willm.	Nantes.
1789	Antony	ten Broeke.
	Abram.	Visscher.
1792	Willem	Bosma.
1798	Johan	Siffken.
	Thomas	Simpson.
1799	Arend Jacob	Guitard.
	Thos. Gregory	Smith.
1803	Jan Hendrik	O'hrly.
	Edward Buckley	Fox.
1808	James	ten Broeke.
	John Bruhn	Suwerkrop.
	Gerard Arnd.	Herklots.
	Diederich	Willink.
1809	Johan Philip	Eilbracht.
	Christian Fredk.	Kahle.
	John	ten Broeke.
	Dirk	Plokker.
1813	Anty. Hendrik	Buchler.
	Adn. H. Bikker	Caarten.
1815	Abraham	Bordier.
1822	Paul. Alexr.	van den Boogaart.
	Jacob Bernelot	Moens.
1826	Friedk. Wilhelm	Sack.
	John	Vink.
1830	John Price	Simpson.
	Hille. Jean	Bauerman.
1832	Ludolf Balthazar	Schroeder.
	Henry Hope	Wernink.
1836	Pieter	van den Ende.
1839	Nics Theods.	Schermers.
1846	Gerrit Jan Dl.	van Houten.
1848	Chas. Fredk.	Guitard.
	Jan Van Enshot	Hollertt.
1851	Jens Christn.	Bergendahl.
	Math. F. M.	van Swyndregt.
1856	A.	Pompe.
	H. A.	van Overzee.
	J. W. K.	Baerselman.
	J. F.	van Oppen.
1858	Simon	van der Willigen.
1875	Diederik B.	Jordaan.
	Hendrik F.	Lingeman.
1877	Hermanus	Koekkoek, jr.
1879	Adriaan	van der Hoeven.
1880	Cornelius Joh.	Westenenk.
	Francois W. C.	Vogel.
	Jean T. C.	van Dulken.

Pedigrees of the following families are recorded in the Visitation of London of 1633-1635.[1]

Abeels of Ronselaere.
Beck of Aucon in Germanie.
Blome of Amsterdam.
Brandt of Hamburgh.
Buckett, born in the dominions under the Emperor nigh Hedleborow.
Bulteel of Tournay.
Burlimachi.
Coteel of Antwerp (whose evidences were burnt at the sacking thereof about Ao. 1567).
Courten of Flanders.
Cruso of ,, .
De Best of Bruges.
De la Barr of Mans in Henault.
De Quester of Bruges.
Des Maistres of Holland.
De Visscher of Flanders.
Du Boys of Lisle in Flanders.
Emans.
Forterie of Flanders.
Fortrye of Lisle.
Frese, from Saxony.
Godschalk of Newchurch in Flanders.
Hamee (or Hamius).

Heldt of Ditmarsh in Holsten and of Hamburg
Henrix of Antwerp.
Hoste of Audenarde.
Jacobson of Antwerp.
Keermer of Rouremont in Gelderland
Kipp of Cullud in Germany.
La Mott of Ipres.
La Tombe of Turcoigne near Tournay.
Lennarts of Gulick.
Le Thieullier of Valenciennes.
Mathews of Heluen in Brabant.
Mico al's Micault of Lisle de France.
Oyles or Oells of Brussels.
Otgher of Ghent.
Paggen of Gulick.
Rychaut of Brabant.
Speede.
Taverner.
Van de Put of Antwerp.
Van Wijckersloot of Utrecht.
Vermuyden of St.Martinsdyke in Zeeland.
Vyolet of Antwerp.
De Water of ,, .

Mr. Cooper gives the following names of families whose pedigrees are recorded in the Visitation London, 1664 and 1687.

Corsellis of Ruselaere.
Duthais of St.Martins in the Isle of Rec.
Hovener.
De Lilliers.
Lucie of Antwerp.
Beake of Flanders.

Lordell of Flanders.
Parravicini of Valtelin, near Milan (who came to England from Antwerp).
Tyssen of Vlissingen.
Waldo.
Hughessen of Dunkirk.

The entries of these families give some three or four generations, and also numerous alliances with other belgic families.

(¹) Harleian Pub. 1880 and 1883. Mr. Cooper gives most of these in the Camden Soc. Pub. 1862.

Several of the more important Strangers and their descendants were Knighted, and the following were made Baronets.

Samuel Tryon of Layer Marney, Co. Essex, 28 March, 1620.
Peter Courtene of Addington, Co. Worcester, 18 May, 1622.
Peter van Lore of Tylehurst, Co. Berks, 2 November, 1628.
William Boreel of Amsterdam, 21 March, 1644.
Matthew Valckenburgh of Middleing, Co. York, 20 July, 1642.
Joseph van Coulster of Amsterdam, 28 February, 1644-5.
Gualter de Raedt of the Hague, Holland, 30 May, 1660.
James Rushout of Milnst Maylards, Co. Essex, 17 July, 1661.
Cornelius Martin Van Tromp, Admiral of Holland and West Friesland, 25 March, 1673-4.
Richard Tulpe of Amsterdam, 23 April, 1675.
Gelebrand Sas van Bosch, Secretary of the Admiralty at Rotterdam, 22 October, 1680.
Cornelius Speelman of Holland, 9 September, 1686.
John Pieter van der Brande, Heer of Cleverskerke and Burgomaster of Middelburg, 9 June, 1699.
Nicholas van Acker of London (whose nephew took the name Sambrook), 31 January, 1700-1.
William des Bouverie of London (whose grandson was created Lord Radnor), 19 February, 1713-14.
Theodore Janssen of Wimbledon, Surrey, 11 March, 1714-15.
Denis Dutry of London, 19 June, 1716.
Mathew Decker of London, 29 July, 1716.
Peter van de Put of Twickenham, Co. Middlesex, 7 November, 1723.
Francis Baring of London and Stratton, Hants, M.P., 29 May, 1793.
Joshua Van Neck of Heveningham Hall, Suffolk, and of Putney, Surrey, 14 December, 1751.
William Hoste, K.C.B., K.M.T., Captain, R.N., 21 September, 1814.
John Silvester, Recorder of London, of Yardley House, Essex, 20 May, 1815.

The following were raised to the Peerage, viz :—

Schomberg.	Baron of Teyes, Earl of Brentford, Marquis of Harwich, and Duke of Schomberg, 1689.
	Baron of Mullingar, Earl of Bangor, and Duke of Leinster, 1691.
Keppel.	Earl of Albemarle, Viscount Bury, and Baron Ashford, 10 February, 1695-6.
	Viscount Keppel of Elvedon, Co. Suffolk, 22 April, 1782.
	Lineage—Arnold Joost van Keppel, Heer van Voorst, 1692, page of honour to Prince of Orange, 1688, descended from Walter van Keppel, Heer van Keppel, 1179 and 1231.
Baring.	Baron Ashburton, 1835.
	Lineage—John Baring of Larkbeer, Co. Devon, son of Franz Baring, Minister of the Lutheran Church at Bremen.
Baring.	Earl of Northbrook, 10 June, 1876.
Vereker.	Viscount Gort, 1816, Ireland, and Baron Kiltarton, 1810, Ireland.
	Lineage—Connel Vereker of Roxborough, Co. Limerick, son of Henry Vereker of Grange, Co. Cork, and Mary, dau. and heiress of Rd. Connell, Esq., of Limerick, and grandson of John Vereker of Grange, Co. Cork, a native of Brabant.
Hope.	Earl of Hopetown, Viscount Aithrie, and Baron Hope, 1703, Scotland.
	Baron Hopetown, 1809, U. K. Baron Niddry, 1814, U. K.
	Lineage—Sir Thomas Hope, elder son of Henry Hope, a Dutch merchant at Amsterdam, of Scotch descent.
Van Neck.	Baron Huntingfield, 1796, Ireland.
	Lineage—Sir Joshua van Neck of Heveningham Hall, Suffolk, and of Putney, Surrey, and London, merchant, son of Cornelius van Neck, paymaster of the land forces of the United Provinces. Baronet, 14 December, 1781.
Rushout.	Baron Northwick, 1797, G.B. Baronet, 1661, E.
	Lineage—Sir James Rushout of Milnst Maylards, Essex, (son of John Rushout, who came over to England).
Bentinck.	Duke of Portland and Marquis of Tichfield, 1716, G.B., Earl of Portland, Viscount Woodstock, and Baron Cirencester, 1689, E.
	Lineage —William Bentinck (3rd and youngest son of Henry Bentinck, Heer van Diepenheim in Overyssel), page of honour to William, Prince of Orange.
Bouverie.	Earl of Radnor, 1765, G.B., Viscount Folkstone and Baron of Longford, 1747, G.B., Baron Pleydell-Bouverie, 1765, G.B.
	Lineage—Sir Edward des Bouverie, Kt., son of Laurence des Bouverie of Sainghen, near Lille, who settled at Canterbury, circa 1568.

Labouchere. Baron Taunton, 15 Aug., 1859.
Lineage—Rt. Hon. Henry Labouchere, son of Pierre Cæsar Labouchere. Partner of the firm of Messrs. Hope and Co., of Amsterdam.
Van Sittart. Baron Bexley, 1 March, 1823.
Lineage—Peter van Sittart of Dantzic.
Kirckhoven. Baron Wotton of Wotton, Co. Kent, 31 Aug., 1650, and Earl of Bellomont, in Ireland.
Lineage.—Charles Henry, son of John Polliander Kirckhoven, Heer van Heindest, Holland.
De Nassau. Earl of Rochford, 10 May, 1695.
Lineage.—William Henry de Zuleistein, son of Frederick de Nassau, who was n. son of Henry Frelerick de Nassau, Prince of Orange.
De Nassau. Earl of Grantham, 24 Dec., 1689.
Lineage.—Henry de Auverquerque, son of Henry de Nassau, Heer van Auverquerque, who came to England in 1670 in the train of the Prince of Orange.

The following Artists from the Low Country were resident in England.

PAINTERS :—

John de Baan, b. 1633, d. 1702. Invited to London by King Charles II, returned to the Hague.
Jacob de Baan, son of John, b. at Hague 1673, d. 1700. Came to England when 20 years of age, left England for Italy.
Dirk van den Bergen, b. at Haerlem, d. 1689.
Abraham Biderman, member of the Dutch Church, London, 1686, with attestation from Altena.
Jan Boekhorst, ,, ,, ,, ,, ,, 1686, ,, ,, ,, Cleve.
Simon du Bois, b. at Antwerp, d. 1708.
Cornelis Bol, with his wife, member of the Dutch Church, London, 1636, with attestation from Paris.
Daniel Boon, b. in Holland, d. 1698. Settled in England in the reign of Charles II.
Assuerus Borgart, member of Dutch Church, 1671.
Jan van Breda, son of Alexander, b. at Antwerp 1683, d. 1750. Came to London with Rysbrack the sculptor, returned to Antwerp in 1746.
Joas van Cleeve, b. at Antwerp, d. 1536.
Francis Cleyne or Klein, b. at Rostock, d. 1658, designer at the Tapestry factory at Mortlake.
N. Closterman, b. in Hanover 1656, d. 1713. Came to London 1681.
James Corsellis, b. in Antwerp, had been 30 years in England before 1635.
Hieronymus Custodes, of Antwerp, member of Dutch Church, 1592.
Adrian van Diest, b. in the Hague 1655, d. 1704.
Jeronimus van Diest, with his wife Dina Leemans, member of Dutch Church, 1684.
Simon van der Does, b. Amsterdam 1653, d. 1717. Was one year in England ; returned to the Hague.
Sir Anthony van Dyck, Kt., b. at Antwerp 1599, d. in London 1641. Was invited to London by King Charles I, w knighted him as said in 1630. The return of Strangers in 1635 records that he came from Linmeer and that he had been two years in England, and that he lived in Blackfriars with six servants. His will was proved at the P.C.C. [Evelyn 151].
Willem Egberts, member of Dutch Church, 1621, a painter on glass.
Paulus Fossier, ,, ,, ,,
Dirk Freres, b. at Enkhuysen, d. 1693.
Sir Balthazer Gerbier, b. at Antwerp, d. 1661. Was knighted by Charles I.
Mark Gerards, b. at Bruges 1561, d. 1635. Came to England about 1580 and was appointed Court painter by Queen Elizabeth.
Johannes Gool, member of Dutch Church, London, 1707.
Benjamin van der Gucht, drowned in the river Thames, buried at Mortlake 25 September, 1794.
Jan Hanneman, b. at the Hague 1611, d. 1680. Was in England 16 years.
Adrian ,, , b. ,, ,, ,, . Had been 9 years in England in 1635.
Egbert Hemskerck, b. at Haerlem 1645, d. 1704. Was long in England.
Jan van der Heyden, b. at Gorcum 1637, d. 1712.
Isaac Hondius, member of Dutch Church, London, 1684.
Jacob Huysman, b. at Antwerp 1656, d. 1696.
Jacob van Huysum, b. at Amsterdam 1680, d. in London 1740.
Cornelius Janssens, b. ,, ,, ,, , died 1665. Patronised by James I.
Bernard Jansen, (qy. of Harderwyck), residing in London 1626. Designed the triumphal arch for mem   the Dutch Church at the accession of Charles I.
..... Jansen van Keulen, b. in London, d. 1655. Born of Dutch parents, employed by Charles I. Qy. very same as preceding.]
Sir Godfrey Kneller, Kt., b. at Lubeck 1648, d. 1726. Came to London after studying in Italy. He was knighted at Kensington 1691.
Sir Peter Lely or van der Faes, b. at Soest 1617. Studied at Haerlem, came to England in 1641, and was painter to King Charles II ; d. 30 November, 1680. He lived at Kew, co. Surrey. He was knighted at Whitehall 1679, and was also a Kt. of the Holy Roman Empire. Was buried in Covent Garden Church.

Balhazar van Lemens, b. at Antwerp 1637, d. 1704.   Came to London after the Restoration.
Bernard Lens, d. at Knightsbridge 1741.   Was painter and enameller to the King.
Jan Lievens, b. at Leyden 1607.   Was three years in London ; he returned to Antwerp.
Jean Baptiste van Loo, son of Lewis and grandson of Jacques, b. at Aix 1684, d. 1745.   Being recommended to Si
    Rt. Walpole he came to London.   He returned to Aix in 1742.
Jan de Mabuse or Mabeuge, b. at Maubeuge in Hainault, d. 1562.
Johannes Mars, was member of the Dutch Church, London, with attestation from Franeker.
Giovanni Battista Medina, chevalier, born at Brussels 1660, d. 1711.   Came to England 1686 and painted many por
    traits in Scotland.
Jan Baptist Monnoyer, b. at Lille 1635, d. 1699.   Came to England from Antwerp.
Antonio More, chevalier, b. at Utrecht 1519, d. 1575.   Came from Portugal to England, whence he went to Spain.
Kerman van der Myn, b. at Amsterdam 1684, d. 1741.   Painted portraits at London.
N. Mytens.   Was principal painter to King Charles I before Vandyck came to England, when he returned to hi
    native country.
Pauwel van Overbeke.   Living in London 1605.
Isaac Paling.   Came to England with his wife Susanna from the Hague, member of the Dutch Church in 1682.
Cornelius Poelemburg, b. at Utrecht 1516, d. 1660.   Invited to the Court at London by King Charles I, but did no
    remain long in England.
Sir Peter Paul Rubens, Kt., b. 1577, d. 1640.   Came to England as Envoy of the King of Spain.   He had apartment
    at Whitehall, where he was knighted by King Charles I.
Godfrey Schalcken or Scalken, b. at Dort 1643, d. 1706.   Painted at London, patronized by King William III.
Jan van Son or van Zoon, the young, son of Joris, b. at Antwerp 1661, d. 1702.   Settled in London.
Jan Skoost, member of the Dutch Church, London, 1635.
Paul van Someren or van Somer, b. in Antwerp 1576, d. 1621.   Portrait painter in England.
N. Sorewe, member of the Dutch Church, London, 1635, having resided 4 years with his wife and two children i
    St. Sepulchre's parish.
Palamedes Palamedesz Staevarts or Stevers, b. in London 1607, d. 1638.   His father was a Fleming and a worker i
    agates and precious stones, who had been invited to London by Kin
    James I, but he returned to Delft with his son, who became a painter.
N. van der Straeten, b. in Holland 1680.   Came to London and painted there.
Johannes Tielius.   Came to London with attestation from Hilvarenbeeck.   Member of Dutch Church 1694.
Simon Verelst, b. at Antwerp 1664, d. 1710.   Came to England and was patronised by the Duke of Buckingham.
Herman Verelst, elder brother of Simon, d. 1700.   Settled in England.
Daniel de Vos.   Living in London 1605.
Jan Vosterman, b. at Brussels 1643, d. 1693.   Was employed by King Charles II at Windsor.   He died during
    voyage to Constantinople, being in the train of Sir William Soames, the English Ambassador.
Gerard Wigmara, b. at Worckum in Friesland 1673, d. 1741.   He visited London.
Willem Wissing, b. at the Hague 1656, d. 1687.   He came to England and worked with Sir Peter Lely.   Afterward
    painter to King James II.
Jan Wycke, the young, a son of Thomas, and b. at Haerlem, d. 1702.   Resided many years in London and the suburb
Gerard Pietersz van Zyl, b. at Amsterdam 1607, d. 1667.   Lived in London with Vandyck and after the death of th
    latter he returned to Amsterdam.

The Baptisms, Marriages, and Burials being arranged in alphabetical order, the principal names are included in this index.

ERRATA ET ADDENDA.

Page XII.   5th   line from bottom, for in read or.
  „ XXVI.   28th   „   „   top, for Duke read Earl.
  „ XXXVII,   16th   „   „   bottom, for 1842 read 1642.
  „   3   28th   „   „   top, for 1917 read 1617 second column
  „   95   19th   „   „   bottom, for Steckman. we. Thomas Laurens read Charles van Andweryen.
  „ 103   13th   „   „   bottom, for we. read wedr.
  „ 151   15th   „   „   top, for 1718 read 1718-19.
  „ 154   14th   „   „   top, for 1723 read 1723-4.
  „   „   19th   „   „   top, for 1716 read 1716-17.
  „ 155   16th   „   „   top, for 1704 read 1704-5.
  „ 156   6th   „   „   top, for 1708 read 1708-9.
  „   „   18th   „   „   bottom, for 1706 read 1706-7.
  „   „   „   „   bottom, for Morsatener read Maesacker.
  „ 157   8th   „   „   bottom, for .. Feb. read 3 Feb.
  „   „   7th   „   „   bottom, for .. Apl. read 7 Apl.
  „   „   after 4th „   „   bottom, add 1 Dec. 1699, Dorothea Tyssen. Int. Graff No. 1
  „ 215   „ 21st „   „   top, add Charles (van Notten Pole, of Wolverton, Hants, 28 July,
  „ 150   17th   „   „   bottom for Daubrin read Daubuz & for John read Josua